Decline and Fall of the Habsburg Empire, 1815–1918. His other books include *The Survival of the Habsburg Empire: Radetzky, the Imperial Army and the Class War, 1848* and *Britain's Decline: Problems and Perspectives.* His books have been translated into German, Italian, Chinese and Japanese. He himself has translated a book from Hungarian. At present he is writing a history of Europe in the nineteenth century and the *Penguin History of Post-War Europe.* He is preparing studies of the 1848 revolutions and Metternich, and is also interested in the history of the USA. He is a Fellow of the Royal Historical Society.

Chris Cook was educated at St Catharine's College, Cambridge, and Nuffield College, Oxford. He is currently Head of the Modern Archives Unit at the London School of Economics. He has previously been Lecturer in Politics at Magdalen College, Oxford, and Head of History at the former Polytechnic of North London. His many previous publications include the six-volume *Sources in British Political History, 1900–51* and (with John Stevenson) the Longman Handbooks of Modern British, European and World History. A Fellow of the Royal Historical Society, he is currently compiling the forthcoming *Longman Guide to Sources in Contemporary British History.*

PENGUIN BOOKS

POST-WAR BRITAIN

Alan Sked was educated at the University of Glasgow and Merton College, Oxford. He is currently Senior Lecturer in International History at the London School of Economics, where during the 1980s he was also Convener of European Studies. He is editor (with Chris Cook) of Crisis and Controversy: Essays in Honour of A. J. P. Taylor, editor of Europe's Balance of Power, 1815–1848, and author of The Survival of the Habsburg Empire ...

ALAN SKED AND CHRIS COOK

POST-WAR BRITAIN

A Political History

FOURTH EDITION

PENGUIN BOOKS

PENGUIN BOOKS

Published by the Penguin Group
Penguin Books Ltd, 27 Wrights Lane, London W8 5TZ, England
Penguin Books USA Inc., 375 Hudson Street, New York, New York 10014, USA
Penguin Books Australia Ltd, Ringwood, Victoria, Australia
Penguin Books Canada Ltd, 10 Alcorn Avenue, Toronto, Ontario, Canada M4V 3B2
Penguin Books (NZ) Ltd, 182–190 Wairau Road, Auckland 10, New Zealand

Penguin Books Ltd, Registered Offices: Harmondsworth, Middlesex, England

First published 1979
Second edition 1984
Third edition 1990
Fourth edition 1993
10 9 8 7 6 5 4 3 2 1

Printed in England by Clays Ltd, St Ives plc
Filmset in Monophoto Ehrhardt

For Helen and Donald McNab

CONTENTS

INTRODUCTION AND
ACKNOWLEDGEMENTS

In writing this book we have sought simply to give the reader an intelligible account of Britain's political past since 1945. Our objective has been to explain the changing fortunes of the British political parties and to show how Britain's role in the world has altered since the Second World War. We have not attempted to compose a work of political sociology, nor have we written a social and economic history. Rather, we have limited ourselves to ordering the political life of the country within a chronological framework and to demonstrating the significance of major figures and events. Given, of course, that we have had to work from largely secondary sources, our judgements and conclusions must necessarily be tentative.

One temptation which we have striven to resist has been that of turning the book into an analysis of 'Britain's decline'. Superficially, this may strike the critic as a mistake, but to have done so would have involved us in writing a political tract, not political history. In any case, for most of the period we cover Britain has simply not been in decline (i.e., her GNP and standard of living have gone up each year until very recently) and it is far too soon to see the most recent years in any kind of historical perspective. Clearly the oil crisis of the mid-seventies arrested Britain's economic development, but likewise the discovery of oil in the North Sea made the setback a relatively temporary one. On the other hand, it cannot be denied that in comparison with other countries Britain has suffered a *relative* decline. But the causes of this decline, it seems to us, are not mysterious in any way. The sacrifices which Britain made in the cause of freedom during the Second World War had long-term consequences for the British economy, as had Britain's post-war role as Europe's leading military power and international policeman. For although it is now fashionable to sneer at Britain's imperial past, it should be remembered just how long Britain maintained her role as a world power (if not a super-power). None of her trading rivals, for sound historical reasons, could occupy such a role or had to worry about defence and overseas expenditure on a similar (or anything like a similar) scale; they were able to invest their resources in domestic development and growth. Moreover, they had psychological incentives to spur them on in a way which Britain did not. For Britain, after years of war and austerity and of shouldering imperial responsibilities, indulged in a mood of national relaxation at the very time when her former enemies (Germany and Japan) were restoring their prestige through economic drive and enterprise. But this is not the place to investigate comparative social psychology. We would merely make the point that all sorts of complex and contradictory attitudinal differences between Britain and other powers in the period after 1945 will have to be examined before a convincing history of Britain's relative decline can be written. This is only one reason why we have deliberately limited our objectives in writing this book.

The difference in outlook between Great Britain and her Continental neighbours was particularly marked, it seems to us, in the period up until about 1963. Thereafter, although under such prime ministers as Sir Alec Douglas-Home and Harold Wilson (both remarkably conservative national leaders), attempts were made to carry on as in the past, the reality of Britain's altered station in the world impressed itself ever more clearly on the British national consciousness. Still, the change did not even begin to come about until de Gaulle's veto of 1963, the collapse of British nuclear independence and the cost of her military presence east of Suez challenged Britain's self-assurance. Domestic events, too, facilitated a mood of critical reappraisal: the economic difficulties of the early sixties and the scandals of the Macmillan government undermined the faith of the British public in the so-called British 'establishment'. Thus the period 1962–4 seems to us to mark a watershed in British history. Up until then Britain could regard herself as a prosperous world power which could afford to take things easy after the hardships of the war and its aftermath. She had a stable two-party system, a stable social system and political institutions and even the transformation of her Empire into Commonwealth had been achieved with commendable continuity. But after 1964 things were never quite the same again. Her economic stability began to disappear as economic crisis followed economic crisis and budget followed budget; her two-party political system came under ever-increasing attack, and since then faith in nearly all her institutions (the monarchy, ironically, excepted) has been steadily undermined. Today even the unity of the United Kingdom can no longer be taken for granted. In fact since 1964 political life in Britain has become almost, it seems, disoriented.

It is here, however, that historians can perhaps offer a word of comfort. In spite of all the strains, the country has remained exceptionally calm. There has been practically no political violence in mainland Britain, and this, in an age of escalating inflation (over 30 per cent not very long ago), is perhaps a cause for national self-congratulation. Political liberties have survived intact and political extremism – save in the special case of Northern Ireland – has (at least as yet) not taken root. Thus if the country has recently become a poorer place to live in, it has not as yet become an uncivilized one to inhabit. Indeed, in many unexpected ways it is now more civilized than ever before. Should an economic revival or recovery take place in the near future, as a result of the discovery of North Sea oil, there are therefore reasons to expect that Britain's political balance will be regained.

Our view of contemporary British history – a stable period lasting till about 1963, a much more unstable and rather disoriented one following from 1964 to the present – has determined the way in which this book has been written. More space has been devoted to the earlier part and our judgements on it are firmer. In the period since 1964 we have been more inclined to let events speak for themselves, although special attention has been paid to Mrs Thatcher's controversial first government.

We would like to express our indebtedness to the work of others in enabling us to produce a work of synthesis such as this. In particular we have been aided by the pioneer work in social history of Arthur Marwick, by the foreign policy analysis of Elizabeth Barker, not to mention the debt we owe to David Butler and others whose manifold studies of general elections have served as reference works. Our debt to them and to others, whose books are listed in the bibliography, it is only proper to record. We must also record our debt to friends like Bill Bishop and Paul Wilce, who were kind enough to look over our manuscript, although our greatest thanks must be reserved for Dr John Ramsden of Queen Mary College, London, whose critical comments proved invaluable. Any errors which remain are entirely our own. Finally, we owe a debt to the secretaries of the Department of International History at the London School of Economics for their help with typing the manuscript and to Peter Carson at Allen Lane for his valued support and advice in seeing this project to completion.

ALAN SKED

CHRIS COOK

1 | THE GENERAL ELECTION OF 1945

For the greater part of the Second World War Great Britain was led by a national government headed by Winston Churchill. The latter had succeeded Neville Chamberlain as premier in 1940 and had come to power with Liberal and Labour as well as Conservative support as Hitler's most dedicated political enemy. Thereafter he had presided over a coalition of Conservative, Labour and Liberal ministers until after five years of magnificent national leadership he could witness Hitler's defeat and the downfall of Nazi tyranny. But with the defeat of Adolf Hitler there no longer seemed to be a need for coalition government in Britain, with the result that on 23 May 1945 the wartime government came to an end. The Prime Minister duly officiated over its obsequies in the House of Commons and stated that in forty-two years of parliamentary life there had never been a government to which he could give 'more loyal, confident and consistent support'. He was – as he later described it – 'deeply distressed at the prospect of sinking from a national to a party leader'. However, a general election was in the offing and, in Churchill's words, the old comrades-in-arms had become 'rivals for power'.

There had been an atmosphere of impending dissolution in the House since October 1944, when Churchill himself had moved the second reading of the annual Prolongation Bill – usually the task of the Home Secretary. His language on that occasion had made it clear that the 1944 Act would be the last of its kind and that the cooperation of the political parties which had enabled the 1935 parliament to survive so long – normally it would have expired in November 1940 – could not be expected to outlast the war. This view was echoed at the Labour and Liberal party conferences at the turn of the year, and with Herbert Morrison's appointment in January 1945 to chair a Labour Party campaign committee the stage was set for 'politics as usual'.

The war in Europe reached its close on 7 May, and on the following day the Western Allies celebrated VE Day. Churchill found himself on the horns of a dilemma: he personally wanted the coalition government to continue until the end of the Pacific War; the Labour Party, on the other hand, was spoiling to fight an election. When it became clear that Labour's leaders would not agree to a further prolongation of Parliament, Churchill, who was determined to go to the country in the guise of national leader, promptly fixed the election for a date much earlier than Labour desired. Polling day was to be 5 July and the results would be declared three weeks later, once the forces had cast their votes. At this point Labour withdrew from the coalition government (which Churchill re-formed without them) and awaited the outcome of the general election.

Most observers appeared to assume that the Conservative Party would win. This was the view of most British politicians and journalists, and even Stalin believed it. He told Churchill at Potsdam that according to Russian and Communist sources the Tories would have a majority of eighty – a figure to which by the end of the campaign Conservative Central Office itself was looking expectantly. Labour Party stalwarts viewed the poll with apprehension and Labour Party leaders were even accused of seeking their own defeat. Thus Arthur Greenwood, then Chairman of the Parliamentary Labour Party, was forced to declare in January 1945: 'I am not a defeatist. The idea that we are not going out to win is absolutely untrue. Every ounce of our strength, every pound of our treasure will go into the fight.' But not everybody was convinced. The loyalty of many Labour leaders to the coalition government was widely known; so too, was their reluctance to break with it. The result was that, as one Labour journalist put it, 'the rank and file of Labour MPs suspect[ed] another 1931 trap'. However, at the beginning of April Ernest Bevin was persuaded to make a partisan attack on Churchill, declaring that 'this has not been a one-man government'. He hesitated a long time before he made the statement, but having been asked by 'a large trade union' whether he intended to become 'another Ramsay MacDonald' he felt compelled to assert the Labour Party's independence. Once he had done so, he recalled, 'my stock went right up'.

When the election results were declared, the pundits were confounded. Labour had won and, as Churchill later recorded, 'the verdict of the electorate had been overwhelmingly expressed'. Its absolute majority –

Labour's first in British history – stood at no less than 146, and if this did not represent an absolute majority of the popular vote and was less than some previous government majorities, the swing recorded – about 12 per cent – was on the scale of 1832 and 1906; only after these elections had the Conservatives' position been worse. In the course of victory Labour had taken 210 seats from the Tory camp and recorded seventy-nine wins in seats which never before had returned a Labour member. The Labour vote compared with 1935 had increased from 8,325,000 to just 12 million, while the Conservative vote had fallen from 11,792,000 to 10 million. The Liberals had gained 2,248,226 votes but as a result of the first-past-the-post electoral system secured only twelve parliamentary seats. The electoral system as well as the maldistribution of seats had favoured Labour. It took 30,000 votes to elect a Labour member, 47,000 to elect a Conservative and no less than 187,000 to elect a Liberal. The results, in tabular form, were as follows:

Party	Votes gained	Percentage of vote	Average vote per MP	Number of MPs
Conservative	9,988,306	39·8	46,892	213
Labour	11,995,152	47·8	30,522	393
Liberal	2,248,226	9·0	187,352	12
Communist	102,780	0·4	51,390	2
Common Wealth	110,634	0·4	110,634	1
Others	640,880	2·0		19
	25,085,978	100·0		640

Source: Derived from D. Butler and A. Sloman, *British Political Facts, 1900–75*.

No less remarkable than the extent of Labour's victory was the geography of Labour's success. In 1935 there had been no Labour candidate in Northern Ireland. In 1945 there were six, and an Independent Labour candidate even managed to get elected. In Scotland Labour consolidated its strength by winning another fifteen seats; in Wales it gained six seats, among them the three in Cardiff. It was, however, in England that the great landslide had taken place. The English boroughs, excluding London, returned 173 Labour MPs compared with only fifty-three beforehand. In London itself, Labour representation increased from twenty-seven to forty-nine MPs. Yet the chief sensation was the results from the English counties. These had traditionally been the strongholds of Conservatism, but they now returned 110 Labour members as opposed to 112 Tories. Moreover, in terms of the popular vote, Labour had actually come out on top in these areas with 4,606,000 votes compared with 4,412,000 for the Conservatives. The latter had to be content with wresting the West Country and parts of Wales – including Lloyd George's old seat of Carnarvon Boroughs – from the Liberals, who had suffered a great defeat and were reduced to a rump of twelve MPs. At long last, therefore, it seemed that the Labour Party had been awarded a mandate to legislate socialism, something which practically nobody at the time had expected to happen.

It is more difficult in retrospect to explain the surprise than the results of the 1945 election. There had, in fact, been a number of indications that Labour was heading for a famous victory. By-elections held during the war, for example, had certainly not favoured the Conservatives. However, since these had been held under abnormal conditions – evacuation, conscription, blackout, outdated registers, petrol rationing, enforced mobility of labour and the truce between the major parties, to mention only the most obvious – their results were generally held to be devoid of political significance. Even when the Conservatives lost both Chelmsford and Motherwell in April 1945 it struck the leader-writer of *The Times* that 'there was nothing very remarkable about the result'. An examination of opinion polls, on the other hand, should have stimulated a more critical analysis of voting trends. These had been registering a leftward swing since 1943 at least, when the British Institute of Public Opinion had found the following results among committed voters:

	June		*August*	
Conservative	25 per cent		23 per cent	
Labour	38 ,, ,,		39 ,, ,,	
Liberal	9 ,, ,,		9 ,, ,,	
Communist	3 ,, ,,		3 ,, ,,	
Common Wealth	2 ,, ,,		1 ,, ,,	

More meaningful, perhaps, were the findings of the research organization known as Mass Observation. These indicated a general belief that some form of socialism was inevitable, and showed a desire, especially on the part of the young, to return to party politics. Moreover, more people described themselves as 'anti-Conservative' than as 'anti-Labour', and by 1943 25 per cent of interviewees had declared that their views had shifted to the left. A majority believed that Labour would win when an election was called. Most ominous of all from the Conservative point of view were the polls taken on the popularity of national leaders. For although these showed that as a war leader Churchill was enormously popular – he always got about nine points out of ten for doing a good job – they demonstrated also that he was not at all attractive to the nation as a future peacetime leader. When people were asked to indicate their choice of post-war leader only about two in every ten nominated Churchill.

By 1945 the nation's mood had not much altered. A Gallup Poll published in the *News Chronicle* on 11 July gave Labour 47 per cent of the vote, the Tories 41 per cent and the Liberals 10 per cent – a forecast which proved accurate to within 1 per cent. The Tory Party Chairman, Ralph Assheton, after polling his regional officers, also warned Churchill of possible defeat. 'Informed opinion,' however, took little notice of indications such as these, and all Assheton achieved was the elimination of Central Office from any major influence on the election campaign. People were simply not yet accustomed to weighing up election results in the light of psephological data. Moreover, once the war had been won and Churchill was finally established as a national hero, it appeared that nothing at all could beat him; the Tories even won the only by-election to be held after VE day. Thus, compared to the tangible evidence of the premier's popularity, such new-fangled techniques of electoral analysis as opinion polls and the dissection of series of by-election results – not to mention the more exotic analogies which could be drawn from contemporary Commonwealth voting behaviour – appeared a trifle 'academic'.

Foreigners in particular were surprised by Britain's election result. One American commentator later wrote: 'The voters not only had short memories; many of them seemed to have political amnesia.' Yet the truth was altogether different. Churchill had lost the election because the voters refused to forget. They refused to forget the years after the First World War when Lloyd George's promises went unredeemed; they refused to forget the depression years, the unemployment and the General Strike; and they refused to forget the failure of Chamberlain's appeasement policies which Churchill himself had taught them had led to the Second World War. In short, the voters refused to forget the failures of the inter-war period when political life in Britain had been dominated almost exclusively by the Tory Party. As Lord Hailsham later confessed: 'The result of the election was not intended as a vote against Mr Churchill . . . The decision can only be explained as the consequence of a long, pent-up and deep-seated revulsion against the principles, practice and membership of the Conservative Party.'

In truth, even Churchill could not be totally divorced in people's minds from the Conservative Party record. It was true that he had come into office in 1940 over the heads of Conservative MPs and that his elevation to the premiership 'had caused pain to many honourable men'. On the other hand, he was regarded by nearly everybody as the quintessential Tory and by working people as their most intransigent political enemy. It was he who had *supposedly* suppressed the Tonypandy miners, and it was certainly he who had taken the lead in publicly opposing the General Strike. Moreover, there was another aspect to Churchill's past which now ironically served him badly. His natural belligerence and martial spirit – all those virtues, in fact, which he had displayed in Africa, Cuba and in two world wars – had given him the reputation of a 'man of war'. The nation, having won the war, was seeking an enduring peace.

The nation had also, in a sense, changed. The British people, in the words of one historian, had 'come of age' in resisting Hitler. People of widely differing social backgrounds had found it possible to live and work together when faced with common tasks and common dangers. They had accepted the need for controls and restrictions and had been impressed by the results of their common effort. They assumed quite naturally that after the war they would share in common rewards, that is, in better housing and better social services. And if these entailed continuing government planning and interference, they were more than ready to put up with it. They knew that these benefits were more likely to be provided by Labour than the Tories. In the forces, too, such thoughts had taken root. The Army Bureau of Current Affairs, which had been established in 1941, had organized platoon-level discussions of contemporary social and political problems so that soldiers as well as civilians had given thought to what the war was all about and what sort of society should emerge from it. Some people, indeed, believed that the Bureau had won the forces' votes for Labour, and Churchill himself after 1945 asserted that the army had 'had a big say' in his defeat. Yet it would be wrong to conclude that the country's natural leaders had in some way been betrayed by left-wing intellectuals operating within the forces or for that matter on radio or in the newspapers. The truth is rather that the leaders of the Conservative Party – and Churchill in particular – totally misjudged the national desire for social change and the leftward current of opinion in the country. This was to be seen in many different ways, from popular regard for the Soviet Union to rising membership figures for the Communist Party. But these and many other indicators were ignored by those at the top. The Government's handling of the Beveridge Report was one indication of this; Churchill's management of the 1945 election campaign was yet another.

The Beveridge Report had been published in December 1942. Expected to be rather a technical report on social insurance, it turned out instead to be a 'new declaration of human rights brought up to date for an industrial society and dealing in plain and vigorous language with some of the most controversial issues in British politics'. So great was its impact that it succeeded in removing most of these issues from the field of controversy entirely by establishing a national consensus on the future development of the social services. That this was so was really not surprising. The Report had been published shortly after the victory of El Alamein, and to believe in Beveridge was to have faith in a successful outcome to the war; more than that, it meant believing in a democratic distribution of the spoils of victory, since Beveridge had recommended the establishment of a comprehensive system of social insurance and the foundation of a national health service. The Government, however, despite accepting the Report in principle, succeeded in gaining no credit whatever from its publication. Churchill was advised by his Conservative Chancellor that the country could probably not afford the Beveridge proposals, so that when they were debated in the House of Commons in February 1943 the Government maintained a very stony reserve. Everyone, they argued, agreed that the aims of the Report were admirable, but would a post-war administration be in any position to implement them? They would therefore go no further than accepting the Report in principle, and in June they repeated this position in a pamphlet to the army.

Such a response occasioned bitter opposition. Inside the House, Greenwood, the minister who had been responsible for Beveridge's appointment but who had been relegated to the back-benches after a cabinet reshuffle, led a back-bench attack on the Government. 'The people of this country', he said, 'have made up their minds to see the plan in its broad outlines carried into effect and nothing will shift them.' When the vote was taken the Government faced the greatest parliamentary challenge to its wartime authority. They survived the division by 339 votes to 119, but all but two of the Labour members outside the Government voted against them, supported by the Liberals and the Tory Reformers. Beveridge later wrote:

I doubt whether, after this affair, Mr Churchill could have avoided defeat whenever a general election came. The troops from this action got it firmly into their heads that for social reform they must look elsewhere than to him. But Churchill could have avoided the decision at the end of the debate of February 16–18, 1943, which marked the Labour Party as the one hope of a better world after the war.

During the election campaign of 1945 the Labour Party pressed home this advantage. Its manifesto, entitled *Let Us Face the Future*, promised, in addition to the nationalization of many parts of the economy, both a comprehensive social security system and a national health service. Churchill's *Declaration of Policy to the Electors*, struck a somewhat different note, although he also offered most of the social benefits that Labour promised. He emphasized, however – and the emphasis was all-important – the need to 'guard the people of this country against those who, under the guise of war necessity, would like to impose upon Britain for their own purposes a permanent system of bureaucratic control, reeking of totalitarianism'.

The words 'control' and 'totalitarianism' proved to be straws in the wind. In the forthcoming election Churchill spoke less about social security than of the totalitarian menace which lurked behind the Labour Party's plans. Thus in the very first broadcast of the election campaign he accused his former colleagues in the National Government of harbouring some very sinister intentions indeed:

My friends, I must tell you that a socialist policy is abhorrent to British ideas of freedom ... there can be no doubt that socialism is inseparably interwoven with totalitarianism and the abject worship of the state ... No socialist government conducting the entire life and industry of the country could afford to allow free, sharp or violently worded expressions of discontent . . . they would have to fall back on some form of Gestapo . . .

And so the tone was set for the campaign. Tory speakers stressed the danger of bureaucracy under Labour and the threat this would pose to democratic institutions. One of them, echoing the note struck by Churchill, went so far as to say: 'The Socialist State of Cripps is to be the same as the Fascist State of the Blackshirts.' Churchill's dominance, therefore, was not an unmitigated blessing for the Tory Party. His tactics displayed a grave lack of judgement and the tone of his speeches was out of touch with the sentiments of the nation as a whole. Most Conservatives, nevertheless, were content to follow his lead. Their election slogan was 'Vote National – Help him finish the job', and their whole conception of the campaign was a triumphal progress by Churchill. Unhappily, their only other major touring speaker was Lord Beaverbrook, and his views on electioneering were even more eccentric than Churchill's own. The latter's themes, meanwhile, were adequately described as 'reach-me-downs from the tub-thumping twenties', one of which was his faith in what he pleased to call the British 'genius for invention'. He himself clearly shared this genius for he spent a large amount of time in a rather silly attempt to convince the electorate that the Chairman of the Labour Party National Executive Committee, Professor Harold Laski, constituted a threat to parliamentary democracy in Britain. The upshot of all this was that many older voters of Conservative sympathies abstained from voting, while those who were voting for the first time – and there had been no general election since 1935 – gave their votes by and large to the Labour Party.

The Labour Party campaign, in contrast to the Conservative Party's, seemed well-prepared and efficiently organized. Their best speakers toured important marginal constituencies and concentrated their remarks on the need for social reform; if their manifesto stated that Labour was 'a socialist party and proud of it', this was not greatly emphasized. In any case, life was made easier for the Labour Party by Churchill's curious rhetorical forays, and Attlee was able to use the Gestapo jibe to ridicule the Prime Minister. Replying to Churchill's broadcast, he said:

He wanted the electors to understand how great was the difference between Winston Churchill the great leader in war of a united nation and Mr Churchill, the party leader of the Conservatives. He feared lest those who had accepted his leadership in war might be tempted out of gratitude to follow him further. I thank him for having disillusioned them so thoroughly.

The Conservative record was also an easy target to attack. Taking up the theme of 'the guilty men' – the title of a book published by the Left Book Club – Labour blamed the Conservative leadership for Britain's ills before the war – and much effort was expended on contrasting Lloyd George's promises after the First World War with what had actually come about.

Thus Churchill lost the election. The man who had led Britain through her 'finest hour' no longer piloted the ship of state. Yet if he had lost a general election, as leader of the Conservative Party his position in British politics had never before been so secure in peacetime. He would live to rule another day, although this was by no means clear at the time. When Mrs Churchill consoled him with the thought that his defeat might be a blessing in disguise, the great man replied: 'At the moment it seems quite effectively disguised.'

2 | THE LABOUR GOVERNMENT, 1945-50

The majority won by Labour in 1945 meant that Clement Attlee came to power with an authority never before possessed by a socialist prime minister. Both previous governments which Labour had formed – those of Ramsay MacDonald in 1924 and 1929–31 – had been in a minority in the House of Commons and could only execute policies which commanded either general consent or Liberal support. With a majority of 146 Labour was now in a very different position. It could push through its legislation without much regard for opposition views, and ministers could confidently plan their legislative programmes on the basis of four parliamentary sessions. Moreover, in contrast to the past, Attlee's ministers – his senior ones, at least – were all men of great experience. Churchill had been exceedingly generous to Labour while leading the wartime National Government. Although the House of Commons at that time had been an overwhelmingly Conservative assembly, he had given Labour almost equal representation in his war cabinet and had allowed them to secure a disproportionate share of coalition power (if not of government appointments). By the end of the war, therefore, it seemed as if the entire home front was being run by Labour ministers. Attlee was Lord President and Deputy Premier; Bevin was at the Ministry of Labour; Morrison was Home Secretary and Minister of Home Security; Dalton was President of the Board of Trade; and Tom Johnston was Scottish Secretary. The complaint of one right-winger in 1945 appeared to be fully justified: 'We've had a Labour government for five years ... Winston hardly touched the home front and that's why he's out'. The shared experience of coalition also meant that after 1945 the opposition was not as factious as it might otherwise have been. There had been a genuine desire amongst the party leaders towards the end of the war for the parties to cooperate in peacetime, too, if that were possible. Some would have liked to have seen the establishment of a peacetime national government and although this had proved impossible to attain, constructive attitudes had nevertheless survived. Thus Churchill, for example, had declared in his first speech as Leader of the Opposition:

... it is evident that not only are we two parties in the House agreed on the main essentials of foreign policy and in our moral outlook on world affairs but we also have an immense programme, prepared by our joint exertions during the Coalition, which requires to be brought into law and made an inherent part of the life of the people. Here and there, there may be differences of emphasis and view but, in the main, no Parliament has ever assembled with such a mass of agreed legislation as lies before us this afternoon.

As a result, Labour could put through a legislative programme involving about twice the annual parliamentary output of the 1930s.

The new Prime Minister, Clement Attlee, had been leader of the Labour Party since 1935. No 'horny-handed son of toil', he had been born into a comfortable, middle-class home, had had a public school education and was a graduate of University College, Oxford. As a child he had received most of his early teaching from his mother, a well-educated woman, and a little from his sisters' successive governesses, one of whom had previously been employed in Lord Randolph Churchill's household looking after the young Winston. His career after university, however, had been a model of Socialist propriety. Abandoning all hope of becoming a successful barrister, he had devoted himself to social work in London's East End and to lecturing at the London School of Economics. He was also a prominent member of the London I L P. After the First World War – in the course of which he rose to the rank of major – he resumed his political activities, and in 1922 was elected Labour MP for Limehouse. Thereafter he rose to prominence within the Parliamentary Labour Party: he was appointed Under-Secretary for War under the first Labour government; between 1927 and 1930 he served on the Indian Statutory Committee; he succeeded Mosley as Chancellor of the Duchy of Lancaster in 1930; and, having survived the 1931 débâcle, he was elected deputy leader of his party. In 1935 he succeeded Lansbury as Labour leader and led the party into coalition with Churchill in 1940. He was made Deputy Prime Minister in 1943 and expended most of his energy supervising schemes for post-war reconstruction, although occasionally he chaired the War Cabinet. He was therefore clearly in a strong position to lead the post-war Labour government.

Yet his leadership was not by any means unchallenged. Attlee's had never been a dominating personality, and many suspected that he had risen to the top merely through want of competition. In their opinion he had reached the first position in the Labour Party only because potential rivals had lost their seats in 1931. The Editor of *The Times* summed up a not uncommon view of the future premier when he wrote in 1942: 'He is worthy but limited. Incredible that he should be where he is. Impossible to discuss any matter of policy with him. He would be too unsure of himself, too doubtful about being given away.' But if he was outshone by larger, more dominating personalities within the Labour movement, he nonetheless possessed undeniable qualities of leadership, and behind the laconic and impassive visage there was a tough and tenacious politician who had a particular talent for managing his colleagues. Thus he had no difficulty, for example, in weathering the occasional attempt to remove him from the leadership and was never the 'sheep in sheep's clothing' which Churchill described him as. Even his supposed defects had their corresponding compensations. If he appeared inoffensive, he had no real enemies; his dullness meant that he was more likely to pursue the party's programme than to invent one for himself.

In short, Attlee was the perfect leader of a team, and he chose a good one. Bevin went to the Foreign Office; Dalton to the Exchequer; Morrison became Lord President and Leader of the Commons; Aneurin Bevan was put in charge of housing, health and local government; and Cripps was made President of the Board of Trade. They faced a tremendous challenge, for they were embarking upon a programme of legislation more ambitious than that of any previous government. But, in Dalton's words, Labour wanted 'to go off with a big rush and win public confidence while the Tories were still stunned'. The King's Speech on 16 August, therefore, foreshadowed the nationalization of the Bank of England, the coal industry and civil aviation; the establishment of a national health service and increased social security; the repeal of the Trades Disputes Act of 1927; government drives to produce more houses and more food; and there were, of course, financial provisions to meet the cost of all these programmes. It was a very large undertaking for men who had already spent five hectic years at the top. By 1947 Morrison was ill; Attlee was in hospital early in 1951; and by 1952 both Bevin and Cripps were dead. By then, however, much had been accomplished and Labour, although no longer in office, could look back upon a record of substantial achievement.

LABOUR'S ECONOMIC POLICY

The new government entered office on an optimistic note. 'There was exhilaration among us,' wrote Dalton. 'We felt exalted, dedicated . . .' It was as if they were 'walking with destiny'. Almost immediately, however, they were faced with the problem of the country's desperate economic situation. During the war Britain had lost approximately one quarter of her national wealth – some £7,000 million.* As a deliberate act of policy she had sacrificed approximately two thirds of her export trade; her economy had been distorted from top to bottom to produce the maximum war effort; and even in 1945 the number of people serving in the armed forces, civil defence and war industries amounted to 9 million – four and a half times the pre-war figure. Her total merchant shipping had been reduced by 28 per cent, and with the end of the war the terms of trade had turned against her. Clearly, therefore, it would take some years to re-establish her international trading position and to reconvert her industries to peacetime production. Meanwhile her internal economy also gave cause for concern. Wartime inflation – the cost of Britain's war effort for four years had exceeded her national income by 50 per cent – meant that as note circulation increased the value of the pound declined. In fact its purchasing power over the whole range of consumer goods and services, taking 1914 as 100, declined from 65 in 1937–8 to 43 in 1944–5. The national debt meanwhile had tripled, while the country's standard of living had fallen heavily. Although it is true to say that thanks to its policy of 'fair shares for all' the coalition government had enabled large sections of the population to enjoy a better standard of life

* The sale or repatriation of overseas investments accounted for over £1,000 million alone. The rest of the figure is made up as follows:

Increase in loans and sterling balances	£3,000 million
Depletion of dollar and gold reserves	152 ,,
Destruction and damage to property	1,500 ,,
Shipping losses	700 ,,
Depreciation and obsolescence of stock	900 ,,

than they had ever experienced in peacetime, British expenditure *per capita* on consumer goods and services had declined by 16 per cent between 1938 and 1944 compared with an equivalent increase over pre-war figures in Canada and the USA.

It was Britain's international trading position, however, which constituted the most pressing problem for the new Labour government. The country, having sacrificed its export trade and not yet being able to pay its way in the world, was absolutely dependent upon American aid. Yet on 21 August 1945 President Truman abruptly cancelled lend-lease, the system of American wartime aid to Europe, since the 'economic royalists' – as they were stigmatized – within his administration could not see the wisdom of quickly restoring a worldwide trading equilibrium. Instead, they were much more concerned to consolidate the economic advantages which had accrued to America as a result of the war. They seriously underestimated Britain's recent economic sacrifices and already regarded her as a potential trading rival. Little wonder, therefore, that in the House of Commons on 24 August Attlee spoke of Britain's 'very serious financial position' and that no less a figure than Keynes himself was dispatched to Washington to negotiate with the Americans. His instructions were to secure a grant-in-aid of $6,000 million to cover Britain's 'dollar gap' until such time as Britain increased the volume of her exports to 75 per cent above the pre-war figure. The US negotiators, however, rejected this scheme and even a request for an interest-free loan was turned down. The best terms that Keynes could extract from America's atavistic Secretary to the Treasury, Vinson, provided for a loan of $3,750 million at 2 per cent interest, with repayments to start in 1951 and to be spread over fifty years. Moreover, Britain had to promise to abide by the terms of the Bretton Woods agreement to which the loan was linked. This meant that within a year of the loan becoming operational, sterling was to be made freely convertible for purposes of current trading; that imperial preferences should be abandoned; and that Britain should settle with her sterling creditors before 1951. This would then enable them to buy freely in the dollar market.

Since America herself refused to promise to reduce her own high tariffs or to envisage any reduction in her enormous export surplus, it is not surprising that there was considerable resistance inside Britain to Parliament accepting such terms. They appeared to many people to be beneath the nation's dignity, and the *Economist* summed up the national attitude when it declared: 'Our present needs are the direct consequences of the fact that we fought earliest, that we fought longest and that we fought hardest. In moral terms we are creditors; and for that we shall pay $140 million a year for the rest of the twentieth century. It may be unavoidable; but it is not right.' Parliament accepted the loan with reluctance. The agreement was signed in December 1945 and the loan itself became available in July 1946. A Canadian loan of $1,250 million was also negotiated so that $5,000 million were available to cover Britain's dollar gap.

It was hoped that recovery could be achieved by 1951. In fact by July 1947 the loan was almost entirely exhausted. Thus when convertibility was restored there was an immediate run on the pound and a 'convertibility crisis' which led once more to suspension. By then, for various reasons, only $400 million of the loan remained: some $234 million had been spent on the British occupation zone in Germany; income from invisibles had been very disappointing; and, more important, the terms of trade had deteriorated and a fuel crisis had hit the country in 1947. As far as the terms of trade were concerned, American prices in particular had shown a marked rise upwards. They had increased by approximately 45 per cent between December 1945 and July 1947 and this had caused a further drain on the American loan. As for the fuel crisis, the winter of 1946-7 had been particularly severe – the worst, in fact, since 1880-81 – with the result that the coal industry had been unable to meet the extra demand for power. There had consequently been massive cuts in supply which had led to enormous temporary unemployment. The situation was aggravated by bad industrial relations, and eventually some £200 million of export orders – or so it is estimated – were lost.

Thus by September 1947 the Labour government had practically run out of dollars and had no convertible currency. Since exports had – in spite of the 'exports drive' – climbed only 17 per cent above the pre-war level, they also presided over a balance-of-payments deficit of £438 million. It looked, therefore, as if the Government's economic policy had failed, and there was widespread demand for 'leadership' and 'planning'. This led not only to a cabinet crisis in July 1947, when Cripps and Dalton sought to replace Attlee with Bevin as Prime Minister – a move which failed in large part due to Bevin's own reluctance to challenge Attlee – but also to the appointment at the end of September 1947 of Sir Stafford Cripps as Minister of Economic Affairs. Labour, it seemed, had now embarked upon a new, more strategic course, an impression which was reinforced the following month when Cripps replaced Dalton at the Treasury. The latter had confessed to leaking a budget secret and had therefore resigned. To his austere successor was entrusted the daunting task of planning the nation's economic recovery.

It was not entirely a new beginning, however. Labour's experiments with planning had really begun with the advent of the post-war government. The King's Speech had, after all, referred to a large number of nationalization proposals, and these were measures which had not been designed simply to appease the more radical members of the party. Rather, it was still a firm belief among Labour supporters that the nationalization of the 'commanding heights' of the British economy would enable a socialist government to pursue a policy of indicative planning within a mixed economy. Yet the Labour Party, as it turned out, despite a long history of socialist rhetoric, had simply made no plans for implementing a large-scale nationalization programme. The archives at Transport House were ransacked for the products of Labour thinking over the years but all they revealed were 'two copies of a paper written by Jim Griffiths, one of them a translation into Welsh'. The Minister of Fuel and Power, while speaking on the subject of the nationalization of coal, confessed to an audience of Co-operative Society members in 1948: 'We thought that we knew all about it; but the matter of fact was that we did not.' Since much the same was true of the rest of the nationalization programme, the Government had to proceed with caution. The industries and services nationalized by Labour thus all shared certain characteristics. All had been the subject of public discussion and often of public reports. All were already subject to some measure of public control, if only in some cases as a result of wartime requirements, and several of them were already partly publicly owned. Thus, in the words of the leading authority on nationalization, Sir Norman Chester, 'none could claim at the time to be pure and unadulterated examples of private enterprise'. Nevertheless, the mines, the railways, canals, road haulage and the iron and steel industry were owned by commercial companies and depended for their survival on their profitability even if their long-term survival on such a basis looked less than likely.

But what was to be done with them? Given the lack of party planning, Herbert Morrison, who, as Lord President, chaired the Committee on the Socialization of Industries, adopted the familiar expedient of the 'public corporation'. This had already been used with regard to the Central Electricity Board in 1926, the BBC in 1927 and BOAC in 1939. There were also local government equivalents in the Port of London Authority and the Metropolitan Water Board. The model of the public corporation therefore provided the government with some sort of practical basis for its socialist plans. Eventually a pattern of government action emerged whereby national boards were appointed to manage each concern; after this the legislative details were worked out; and, finally, a 'vesting date' was fixed on which each board assumed control.

The Bank of England was nationalized first, its vesting date being set for 1 March 1946. Civil aviation came next on 1 August of the same year; coal, cables and wireless followed in 1947; transport and electricity were given vesting dates in 1948; gas in 1949; while political considerations delayed the vesting date for iron and steel until 15 February 1951. Afraid that the Conservative Party would employ its majority in the House of Lords to reject the Iron and Steel Bill, the Government postponed the introduction of this legislation until the parliamentary session of 1948–9. Meanwhile, during the 1947–8 session a Parliament Act was passed which reduced the delaying powers of the House of Lords from three successive sessions over a period of not less than two years to two sessions and one year. It was only after the 1950 election, therefore, that the vesting order for iron and steel was given parliamentary approval. Still, by the end of 1949, Labour could boast that legislation had been introduced providing for the nationalization of all the industries and services included in its 1945 manifesto.

Despite the obvious zeal with which the Government had pursued their programme, their nationalization measures were not accorded great respect by British socialists. It would have been unrealistic to have expected Conservatives to approve of what had happened, but even the traditional supporters of nationalization withheld their praise for what the Government had done. They were, in fact, astonished and disappointed at its timidity and naïveté. For, as time went on the defects of the programme became ever more apparent. To start with, it seemed that many of the previous owners had been compensated overgenerously; £164,600,000 was paid out, for example, to the mine owners, leaving miners to think that the fruit of their labour was destined even yet – and for some time to come – to find its way into familiar pockets. Moreover, since these former owners were now able to invest this money in much more profitable enterprises, it seemed as if the Government had really rewarded capital instead of labour.

Thus nationalization signified no new beginning for labour. No transformation of its relationship with capital occurred. In practice all that happened was that the state bought out the former owners and allowed the former management to remain. Labour was accorded no greater say in industrial decision-making, and since it shared in no profits it gained no economic benefit either. The Labour government had approached the question with no imagination whatsoever. Clearly there had been no intention on their part other than to execute an administrative manoeuvre, and this was all too obvious to the workers. Cripps said: 'I think it would be almost impossible to have worker-controlled industry in Britain, even if it were on the whole desirable.' Little wonder, therefore, that the miners were not inspired by government spokesmen to increase their output during the fuel crisis. The Government, in fact, despite their efforts, had succeeded neither in 'controlling' nor even in capturing the commanding heights. Control had been surrendered to the public corporations so that the Bank of England, for example, far from being subjected to the 'streamlined socialist statute' which Dalton believed he had drafted, was now made *less* dependent on the Government.* In other ways, too, Labour had made government control impossible. Coordination of fuel policy was hardly promoted through the establishment of separate Gas and Electricity Boards, while the separate boards administering rail and road transport did nothing to encourage the development of an integrated transport system. Finally, there was the criticism of Labour's policy (from the socialist point of view) that in spite of all the fuss the commanding heights had never really been attacked. The 20 per cent of the economy taken over by the government was to a large extent the unprofitable part, while the profitable sector remained firmly in the hands of private enterprise. Socialist planning of this type was acceptable even to Conservatives.

Other aspects of government planning also left much to be desired. For example, with the return of peace the Ministry of Production was dismantled and the Government decided that there should henceforth

---

* Incidentally, there was a nice piece of irony involved here. The increased independence of the Governor of the Bank of England resulted from Clause 4 of the relevant Act.

be no restrictions on production. They therefore rejected any idea of establishing a peacetime 'Economic General Staff' such as Keynes had proposed. Instead, they merely retained at their disposal the services of the Central Statistical Office and of the Economic Section of the Cabinet. Supervision of government policy was left to a network of cabinet committees (the most important of which was the Lord President's) and any difficulty, it was assumed, could be ironed out by the normal workings of inter-departmental machinery. The results were disappointing. According to one junior minister, senior ministers had such 'a deep dislike' for working with their colleagues that when the fuel crisis broke there was considerable lack of government cohesion. The Treasury, too, reverted to its usual, secretive behaviour. In 1946 Dalton had set up a consultative National Investment Council. But according to one of its members: 'It was a waste of time. The Council was denied by the Treasury all power, all information, all staff and all dignity. We used to meet in the Chancellor's room for tea and a pleasant chat ... The thing was a farce and everyone knew it. No planning of national investment was ever discussed.' One suspects that members of the other advisory bodies which proliferated around the Treasury – such as the National Joint Advisory Council or the National Production Advisory Council on Industry – lived out their official lives in a similar atmosphere of futility.

Dalton himself placed what faith he had in the Government's ability to control the economy in a 'cheap money policy', and in his first budget speech in October 1945 he announced a reduction of ½ per cent in the rates on Treasury Bills and Treasury Deposit Receipts. Shortly afterwards he took steps to reduce the rate on long-term securities. Motivating these actions was his determination that capital reconstruction should not be prejudiced by the need to pay more than the minimum rates possible. Yet the Chancellor's policy was a controversial one. City critics maintained that it was feeding inflation and were not impressed by the Government's defence that lower rates of interest could not be inflationary 'at a time of strict Government control over the level of capital investment'. They pointed to the failure of the Capital Issues Committee (another example of planning under Labour), the aim of which was to control the level of new investment. This body was powerless to deal with issues of less than £50,000 and had no authority to interfere with bank advances either. The Government's defence, as a result, was not as tight as it appeared. Dalton's real achievement, however, was that although inflation continued, full employment was maintained. Thus the greatest fear which had haunted Labour had been successfully allayed. Moreover, in the budget he had presented on the eve of his resignation, Dalton had at last attempted to come to grips with inflationary pressures. His proposals of 12 November 1947 were designed to take some £200 million out of the economy. But having made these proposals, he had, as we have seen, to resign.

His successor at the Treasury, Sir Stafford Cripps, was a grim, unsmiling moralist whose name is forever associated with the word 'austerity'. The novelist Evelyn Waugh was later to look back upon his Chancellorship as a period when 'the kingdom seemed to be under enemy occupation'. Cripps had fallen foul of the official Labour Party leadership when in the period prior to the war he had led the campaign for a Popular Front. Nobody, however, doubted his moral and political integrity. Thus during the war Churchill had assigned him to a number of important positions, and with the formation of the Labour government he had been made President of the Board of Trade. Having held that office with distinction – and having substituted for Morrison when the latter fell ill in 1947 – there was much logic in his appointment later that year as Minister of Economic Affairs. The decision to create such a ministry, on the other hand, was not necessarily a cause for rejoicing. While it had been assigned a new Central Planning Staff under the direction of the new Government Chief Planner, Sir Edwin Plowden, and while the Lord President's Committee had been abolished, the continued separation of planning from finance portended a possible split within the Cabinet. With Dalton's resignation, however, this danger was averted. Cripps brought with him to the Treasury his former departmental staff, so that henceforward the Exchequer alone presided over the nation's economic destiny. It remained to be seen what the new Chancellor would make of this position.

By the end of 1947 the Labour government had reached a watershed in their career. The nationalization of iron and steel apart, most of their major legislative proposals had already become law with the result that in 1948 Morrison called for a period of 'consolidation'. Addressing delegates to the Labour Party conference, he stated: 'You must expect the new programme to be of a somewhat different character and a somewhat different tempo from the last . . .' It was very sensible advice. Ministers were visibly running out of steam and ideas. Above all else, they had been shaken by the way in which the economy had apparently collapsed beneath their feet in 1947. Cripps's task, therefore, was to revive the economy and to restore the Government. He had to give it time, at least, to regain its composure, and for a while it seemed as if he had succeeded.

A number of factors contributed to the upturn in the economy during the first year of his Chancellorship. Planning somehow seemed to become more effective. The system of inter-departmental cooperation was tightened up; general supervision was assigned to the Economic Policy Committee under the chairmanship of the Prime Minister; Cripps presided over a sub-committee on production; and a network of committees and sub-committees connected these to the Central Economic Staff, the Import Programme, the Investment Programme and all the other bodies – Regional Boards and Development Councils, etc – which cooperated both in drawing up and attempting to achieve the 'targets' set out annually in the 'Economic Survey'. Cripps's immense personal authority no doubt contributed to this apparently improved position. Yet it is exceedingly difficult to judge how genuine the improvement was. Interest groups were consulted and the public informed and exhorted regarding government aims; but the achievement of export and production targets was really as much a matter of luck as of policy and a lot depended on the state of public morale. And since the real control in the planning system was the control over imports and the system of rationing food and clothes which had been maintained since the war, morale was a tricky problem.

Even before Cripps's appointment, however, morale had received a considerable boost. The US Secretary of State, General George Marshall, had convinced himself of the need to extend further aid to Europe – this even before the July convertibility crisis – and had offered to finance a European Recovery Programme if only the Europeans would jointly assume the responsibility of organizing it. A grateful Britain took the lead in accepting the American offer – by the end of 1947 her trade deficit with America had risen to £655 million – and in 1948 agreements were signed concerning 'Marshall Aid'. In accordance with the figures arrived at in September of that year Britain was to receive $1,263 million out of a total $4,875 million available and, after France, became the second-largest recipient of aid. In turn she undertook to grant $312 million to other European countries, although she benefited by a grant of $30 million dollars from Belgium. The results of these arrangements were generously acknowledged by the British public, which accepted the Government's assessment that without Marshall Aid the country would have suffered both severe unemployment and a considerably reduced – probably depressed – standard of living. On the other hand, the partial recovery made by Britain's economy during 1948 was due to other factors also: import restrictions plus the export drive were at last producing results, so that output over pre-war figures was 36 per cent up in 1948 and 50 per cent up in 1949. By 1950 the Government could finally boast that exports had risen 75 per cent over the 1938 level.

The cost of these achievements had to be borne, of course, by the British people, and it said much for their national pride that having gone through the war they were equally determined in their fight for national recovery. For they had much to endure. Their food supplies had been rationed in 1940 and the system had survived the war with wider application. Nor did Cripps have much to offer them by way of relief, in spite of America's belated decision to come to Europe's aid. His priorities as he outlined them were as follows: 'First are exports . . . second is capital investment in industry; and last are the needs, comforts and amenities of the family.' He wanted people to 'submerge all thought of personal gain and personal ambition' in their desire for future happiness. For in his own particular way he, too, had only blood, toil, sweat and tears to offer. His economic policy was one of 'disinflation'. But Cripps was no advocate of monetary deflation and his budget of April 1948 – in spite of its 'capital levy' – was an inflationary one when taken as a whole. His real objective, rather, was to regulate the economy by means of wage restraint.

The Labour Party had agreed to a policy of wage restraint in the Coalition White Paper of 1944. In the period 1945–51, with an appalling shortage of goods, it would have been difficult to avoid one. A White Paper of January 1947 had shown the total amount of income available after tax in 1946 to be well over £7,000 million; the value of goods and services available, on the other hand, was only about £6,000 million. The implication was clear: any rise in wages adding to excess demand would merely serve to create more bottlenecks in the production process and so reduce supply. Stocks of all materials were so low as it was that factories already had occasionally to close down for a period to let them build up.

Thus in February 1948 another White Paper declared: 'It is essential that there should be no further general increase in the level of personal incomes without at least a corresponding increase in the volume of production.' The Government, in short, desired a 'pay pause', and the unions, thanks in part to Cripps's personal authority, agreed to cooperate so long as the claims of those 'below a reasonable standard of subsistence' were met and 'essential differentials' maintained. Despite the fact that many claims slipped through this hole in the net, wage rates in real terms were lower in 1948 than in 1947. Not surprisingly, therefore, Cripps's policy came under attack at the TUC conference of June 1949. He responded with this typically Crippsian reply: 'It is not more money which we want ... it is more goods ... Our party has always insisted upon the supremacy of moral values.' Thereafter, wage costs rose more quickly than the Chancellor wanted, although less fast than workers desired. The unions, however, displayed remarkable responsibility and exercised considerable restraint. From 1948 till August 1950 wage rates rose by only 5 per cent while retail prices rose by 8 per cent. Indeed between 1945 and 1951 average weekly wages rose in real terms by only 6 per cent, in other words, 'under six years of socialism the workers had to work a great deal of overtime to improve their standard of living by a tiny 1 per cent a year'. It was not until 1950 that the TUC resolved to oppose restraint, by which time Cripps had destroyed whatever credit he had managed to accumulate by mismanaging a serious sterling crisis.

The 'Economic Survey' for 1949 described 1948 as 'a year of great and steady progress'. Production had risen rapidly; exports had risen even more spectacularly, and the balance of payments appeared at last to be swinging into surplus. The budget in 1949 therefore constituted what journalists describe as a 'no-change' budget. Yet there were clouds obscuring the horizon. British gold reserves were relatively small and a run on sterling or a drop in overseas demand could well set off a call for a devaluation of the pound. A storm was not far off. By the summer of 1949 the trading position of the sterling area had weakened owing – in part at least – to a recession in the United States. There was also worldwide speculative pressure against the pound as a result of an American campaign within the IMF, so that a feeling rose in the money markets that a devaluation was inevitable. There had in fact been a growing consensus in favour of such a course among economists for other reasons: the temporary character of Marshall Aid, the inclination of industrialists to invest abroad and the knowledge that the balance of payments was still not as strong as it might be.

By June 1949, according to the *Banker*, the City was taking it for granted that a devaluation was on the way. Cripps, however, refused to contemplate a change in the exchange rate and nothing was done, even when it became known that in the second quarter of 1949 the dollar deficit had worsened and Britain had lost £160 million of gold. Instead, the Chancellor fell ill and retired to Switzerland to recuperate. Temporary direction of economic policy was then assumed by the President of the Board of Trade, Hugh Gaitskell, who, alarmed by the mounting pressure on sterling, prepared contingency plans for a devaluation. Most of his colleagues were persuaded of the wisdom of such a course and it appears that Cripps himself fell into line before resuming his duties in mid-August. Concerned to put a final stop to worldwide speculation against the pound, the Chancellor proceeded to administer in overdose the medicine he had for so long resisted prescribing. Sterling was devalued from $4.03, not to the $3 level which Gaitskell had apparently been contemplating, but to $2.80. This was seen as a panic measure and as such brought reassurance to no one.

The extent of the devaluation – 30·8 per cent – caused considerable concern. Could a mini-recession on the other side of the Atlantic really justify such a change in the exchange rate? Should not the Government have resorted to deflationary measures first? Deflation, instead, came afterwards with the announcement by Attlee on 24 October of cuts in the 'capital expenditure of the fuel and power industries, the expanding education programme, new housing, and the larger field of miscellaneous investment'. There was also to be a charge of one shilling for prescriptions under the National Health Service.

Still, Labour's confidence was not broken. Austerity had, after all, become a way of life, and it might even be argued that the underlying trends in the economy gave room for optimism. Inflation was under control, full employment was being maintained, and exports were rising slowly but surely despite some recent setbacks. Moreover, if there was still a plethora of controls and if wage increases hardly kept up with the rise in prices, the standard of living had definitely improved since 1945. Labour's social reforms had seen to that.

LABOUR AND THE WELFARE STATE

It is simply not correct to argue, as some historians have done, that the 'Welfare State' – perhaps Britain's greatest post-war achievement – was thought up by Beveridge and imposed on the Labour Party. While Labour's tactics in the 1930s had been defensive in character – aiming, that is, to conserve what had already been achieved rather than looking forward to a new stage of policy-making – the fact remains that Labour had even before the publication of the Beveridge Report put firmly on record its whole-hearted commitment to a comprehensive programme of social security. The Labour Party conference in 1942, having accepted a motion moved by James Griffiths, had called for (a) one comprehensive scheme of social security; (b) adequate cash payments to provide security whatever the contingency; (c) the provision of cash payments from national funds for all children through a scheme of family allowances; and (d) the right to all forms of medical attention and treatment through a National Health Service. Labour back-benchers had revolted at the coalition government's attitude towards the Beveridge proposals and in 1944 the Labour Party had criticized the government's White Paper for not going far enough with respect to benefits. Before as well as after the general election of 1945, Labour was committed to a far-reaching programme of social reform. The Conservative Party had also accepted the Beveridge Report – in principle, at least – and had embraced it once again in the shape of the White Paper. Its embrace, however, appeared to lack the passion of conviction just as in 1946 the stated grounds for Conservative opposition to the National Health Service Act – the costs and administrative arrangements involved – did not appear to tell the whole story. Thus although one can be certain that had a Conservative administration emerged from the 1945 election some sort of advance would have been made in the field of social security, one is nevertheless unsure as to how far it would have extended.

Labour's own route was marked by two great milestones in the history of social reform: the National Insurance Act of 1946 and the National Health Service Act of the same year. In its approach to both these measures the Government displayed a spirit of true egalitarianism by espousing the principle of 'universality'. This ensured that their legislation bore a distinctive left-wing stamp; it also ensured that everyone in future would have equal rights to social welfare. Conservative opponents of the Government argued that on this account the needs of the poor were being sacrificed to left-wing ideology. According to their point of view, it would have made much greater sense to have selected the really poor from the mass of the people and to have given them greater benefits. However, this would have involved a 'means test' and no Labour government could have been expected – at least not then – to have imposed the well-known indignities of such a test upon their working-class supporters. Besides, there was a 'canny realism' behind the Government's intentions as far as the poor were concerned. They would, or so it was argued, only get the best available if resources were shared with the rich. Finally, by arranging things the way they did, the Government left open the possibility of the future integration of the social services on the basis of a common core of principle, so that their case was altogether an attractive one.

As it was, the Labour plan was hardly an ultra-radical proposal. People were to be entitled to draw sickness and unemployment benefits and to receive free medical attention if and when this was necessary; however, they would only be so entitled if they had paid their share of national insurance contributions and even then could claim their benefits for a limited period only. The social security programme was established on a sound actuarial basis. Benefits were not in any way tied to the cost of living and the individual was free to take out additional cover from private companies if he or she believed that this was needed. The result was that Beveridge's scheme for a 'national minimum' was not in fact established.

According to its preamble, the 1946 National Insurance Act was designed 'to establish an extended system of national insurance providing pecuniary benefits by way of unemployment benefit, retirement pension, widows' benefit, guardians' allowance and death grant'. With the exception of school-children and pensioners, married women and the self-employed earning less than £104 per annum, everyone henceforward was to become insured under the Act under one of three categories: employed persons who were eligible for all benefits; the self-employed who were eligible for all save unemployment benefits; and non-employed persons who were ineligible for sickness and unemployment benefits. By Clause 12 of the Act the basic condition was spelled out that claimants must have paid both a minimum number of contributions and a specified number during the year before, if benefits were to be awarded. The left wing of the Labour Party attacked this clause, Sydney Silverman, Barbara Castle and others asserting that the unemployed had an absolute right to maintenance. However, the amendment which Silverman tabled in the House of Commons and which enshrined this point of view was defeated by 246 votes to forty-four, so that the left was forced to look for concessions elsewhere. Greater success awaited them with regard to Clause 62. This provided for 'extended unemployment benefit' to be paid in particular cases which. were to be investigated by local insurance tribunals and immediately raised the spectre of a means test being applied surreptitiously. Silverman and friends were able to amend the wording of the clause in order to remove any such implication, although the exact meaning of the amended version was far from clear as a result. Finally, one other provision of the Government's Bill was amended, this time as a result of Conservative as much as of left-wing pressure. The Government had proposed that the self-employed should wait for twenty-four days before becoming eligible for benefits, a proposal which was eventually eliminated altogether. Conservatives claimed that it displayed a bias against the self-employed, although, to be fair, the Government had reduced the waiting period to twenty-four days from the thirteen weeks proposed by Beveridge. In a similar fashion, they had gone beyond Beveridge's recommendation in providing for old age pensions to be paid at the full rate of 26s. and 42s. right from the start despite the extra costs involved. On the other hand, Beveridge's important suggestion that national assistance – the money paid to those in need who failed to qualify for national insurance benefits or whose benefits were insufficient to meet their needs – should be administered by a Ministry of Social Security responsible for all social security benefits was not adopted by the Government. Instead, the 1948 National Assistance Act established a National Assistance Board whose regional area officers administered a personal means test for those who applied for relief. Nonetheless, the social security structure erected by the Government was welcomed by everyone as a great advance on previous legislation and the Opposition declined to oppose either the second or third readings of the National Insurance Bill.

The debate over the establishment of a National Health Service was conducted much more vigorously. The Opposition affected to support the scheme in principle but opposed the second reading of the National Health Service Bill in February 1946 on the grounds that it prejudiced the patient's right to an individual family doctor, retarded the development of the hospital services by destroying local ownership, menaced all charitable foundations and weakened the responsibility of local authorities. Quite clearly the Conservative Party was caught on the horns of a dilemma: on the one hand, it knew how popular the idea of a national health service was in the country at large; on the other, it quite naturally wanted to exploit the hostility of the medical profession to the Government's proposals. Nor can there be any doubt that the fact that these proposals were being introduced by the Government's *enfant terrible* produced a spirited political reaction.

The minister responsible, Aneurin Bevan, was a noted Labour left-winger of decidedly socialist convictions and of working-class background and upbringing. He had been expelled from the Labour Party in 1939 and there had again been talk of his possible expulsion in 1944. Yet in the following year he had been one of the Labour Party's foremost standard-bearers at the polls and had been rewarded for his efforts with the Ministry of Health. This was not as surprising as it seemed. His contributions to debates within the party had always been informed and his skill as a speaker was already renowned, so that the party leadership appreciated that he had both the energy and the understanding to deal competently and boldly with the problems he would confront as a minister. The Conservatives – not to mention the doctors – underestimated the man who was to create the National Health Service. 'We expected to see a vulgar agitator,' one of the BMA spokesmen later confessed, '. . . [but] were quite surprised to discover he talked English.' In fact, the doctors' leaders came to have a reluctant respect for their chastiser. According to Dr Guy Dain, then Chairman of the BMA Council: 'He knew his subject in a very short time. He was extremely efficient. All that really mattered we settled with him. He knew what he wanted and so did we.'

The aims of the National Health Service were set out in the opening sentences of the National Health Service Act of 1946:

(1) It shall be the duty of the Minister of Health to promote the establishment in England and Wales of a comprehensive health service designed to secure improvement in the physical and mental health of the people of England and Wales and the prevention, diagnosis and treatment of illness and for that purpose

to provide or secure the effective provision of services in accordance with the following provisions of this Act.

(2) The services so provided shall be free of charge except where any provision of this Act expressly provides for the making and recovery of charges.

The new health service was not designed to be fully comprehensive – the health of factory workers continued to fall within the scope of the Factory Acts, and the responsibility for children's health services continued to be assumed by the Ministry of Education – yet it constituted an almost revolutionary social innovation since it improved the quality of life of most of the British people. Labour reaped a rich political harvest on this account and Bevan deserved much of the credit. It was he who made the fundamental decisions which established the character of what was soon to become the social institution of which the British would feel most proud.

Bevan was particularly concerned as a former Welsh miner to ensure that all areas of Britain would receive the same standard of care under the health service. Otherwise it would hardly deserve the description 'national'. He was only too well aware that as things stood few areas of the country could boast as many doctors or such up-to-date equipment as the South-East of England. But how was he to rectify this situation? Labour Party thinking had traditionally stressed the role of local government with regard to health programmes and many Labour-controlled local authorities looked forward to playing a part in the administration of any future health service. Yet Bevan himself was well aware of the shortcomings of local administration and foresaw the difficulties involved in maintaining uniform standards throughout a highly decentralized health service. Ineluctably, therefore, he was driven to a more radical solution of the problems involved, as the following conversation, recorded by the then President of the Royal College of Physicians, suggests:

BEVAN: I find the efficiency of the hospitals varies enormously. How can that be put right?

MORAN: You will only get one standard of excellence when every hospital has a first-rate consultant staff. At present the consultants are all crowded together in the large centres of population. You've got to decentralize them.

BEVAN: That's all very well but how are you going to get a man to leave his teaching hospital and go into the periphery? (He grinned.) You wouldn't like it if I began to direct labour.

MORAN: Oh, they'll go if they get an interesting job and if their financial future is secured by a proper salary.

BEVAN (after a pause): Only the state could pay those salaries. This would mean the nationalization of hospitals.

Bevan consequently proposed to do what – as the Conservative Party complained – nobody had ever suggested before, and nationalize the country's hospitals in order to establish the National Health Service on a rational basis. Since local government had not been reformed, Bevan envisaged creating a new administrative structure to run the hospitals: fourteen regional hospital boards, each centred on the medical faculty of a university and appointed by the Minister of Health were to be set up. These, in turn, were to appoint the management committees of 388 hospitals within the system, although in the case of thirty-six teaching hospitals the boards of governors were to be appointed by the Minister himself. In Scotland the situation was slightly different. The National Health Service (Scotland) Bill proposed five regional boards (four based on the ancient universities, the fifth based on Inverness) and eighty-four hospital boards of management. In Scotland teaching hospitals were not to be separately administered except insofar as medical education committees, appointed partly by the Secretary of State for Scotland, partly by the regional boards and partly by the universities, were to be set up to advise the regional boards on matters concerning teaching and research.

In Britain as a whole a new administrative structure was to be established respecting the general practitioner, primarily, it may be said, as a result of pressure from within the medical profession itself. Thus the supervision of general practice was to be assigned to 138 executive councils in England and Wales (twenty-five in Scotland) on which local professional interests were strongly represented (twelve members out of twenty-five). These councils were to employ general practitioners, Bevan having rejected the idea that doctors should be in direct contact either with the Ministry of Health or the local authorities. In similar fashion, Bevan had also rejected the idea of a full-time salaried service. He could not see how under such a system the doctor's right to refuse a patient or the patient's right to choose a doctor could be adequately upheld. Moreover this had been the issue over which the doctors had been complaining most. He therefore proposed as a method of payment the combination of a small basic salary plus capitation fees according to the numbers on the doctors' lists. Private practice, therefore, could continue as before and the medical profession was requested in return to cooperate in correcting the maldistribution of general practitioners by accepting a twofold system of controls. A Medical Practices Committee was to be established to prevent doctors setting up practices in areas in which they were not really needed, while the buying and selling of practices was to be stopped within the service. Bevan believed that as a result of these proposals he could create a health service which would not only be national in character, but which would protect the professional interests of doctors. Its final structure was to be completed by leaving a number of 'local health services' – maternity and child welfare, domiciliary midwifery, health visiting, ambulance transport, home nursing and vaccination – to the larger local authorities. The net cost of these services was to be shared equally by the authorities and the central government. It was the latter, however, which was to bear the main cost of the service as a whole. Only one twentieth of the National Health Service was to come directly out of national insurance contributions. The rest would come from taxation. Dalton, the Chancellor, agreed with Bevan's more grandiose conception of what the Health Service was all about as well as with the need to support it financially from central government funds. The Minister of Health therefore had an indispensable ally during the preparatory stages of his work and Dalton, after Bevan, according to Michael Foot, was 'the chief architect of the National Health Service'. The formulation of these proposals, however, was only the first stage of the battle to establish the National Health Service. It still remained to be seen whether Parliament and the doctors would accept them.

Bevan had the inestimable advantage of knowing that his case was almost irrefutable. The Opposition might oppose on detail, therefore, but could not oppose on principle. His case was also a popular one: people knew that money counted in matters of health and they knew that this was wrong. Justice and common decency demanded that the situation be corrected. Given this basic assumption, the rest of Bevan's case was logical. A National Health Service demanded a truly rational basis; maldistribution of services would have to be eliminated; general practice had to be supported by specialist services; and the needs of the community with regard to mental health, spectacles, teeth and deafness simply had to be met. Thus the Conservative Opposition contented itself with objecting to nationalization of the hospitals, to the powers of local executive committees and to the proposed decentralization of general practice. Otherwise it was content to let the doctors make the running, seeking to secure its position by sheltering behind a shield of respectable professional protest. Bevan's greatest battle, therefore, was fought not so much with the Opposition as with the British Medical Association.

He refused to 'negotiate' with this body directly – ostensibly on the grounds that he was responsible only to Parliament and that parliamentary sovereignty must not be infringed – but met regularly with its representatives in order to take account of their views. The views which they put forward to him were consistently hostile, and as the date of the inauguration of the service approached – it was 5 July 1948 – opinion amongst practitioners hardened determinedly against the scheme. The Royal Colleges, it is true, adopted a much more conciliatory attitude towards the minister's proposals – on account no doubt of the more solicitous fashion in which their own interests were being met – but in February 1948 a BMA plebiscite demonstrated that about 90 per cent of members were hostile to Bevan's plans. Only when Bevan explicitly declared that there would be no salaried service and gave the doctors assurances that after three years every doctor could choose to be paid either by salary plus fees or by fees alone, did opposition begin to crumble. Bevan hoped that his announcement would 'finally free doctors from any fears that they [were] to be turned in some way into "salaried civil servants"', and it succeeded in doing just that. Another BMA plebiscite in April 1948 showed that intransigent opposition had dropped to 64 per cent of members and when the scheme came into operation on 5 July more than 20,000 general practitioners – some 90 per cent of the total – participated from the start. By September 93 per cent of the population had enrolled as patients and the scheme won lasting national approval. Both doctors and patients benefited from it and Bevan's National Health Service came to be regarded as an intrinsic part of Britain's way of life.

Moreover, it proved to be less expensive than its critics had predicted. The Guillebaud Committee, set up in 1953 to investigate its costs, reported that 'The widespread popular belief that there has been an increase of vast proportions in both money cost and the real cost of the National Health Service is not borne out by the figures.' The 'cost *per head* at constant prices was almost exactly the same in 1953–4 as in 1949–50'. Thus the Committee concluded: '[The] Service works much better in practice than it looks on paper . . . We are strongly of the opinion that it would be altogether premature at the present time to propose any fundamental change . . .'

Those alone who had genuine cause to be disappointed were perhaps the members of the Socialist Medical Association, who had pioneered the idea of a national health service in the 1920s but who had always envisaged a fully salaried service, controlled by popularly elected local assemblies and working through local health centres. In their opinion, Bevan's proposals simply did not go far enough. However, it is difficult to believe that, initially at any rate, much more could have been accomplished. Bevan simply had to work with the materials at hand and, given differences in Cabinet, professional opposition and eternal excuses for backsliding, his achievement was a prodigious one. When he died in 1960, the editor of the *British Medical Journal* paid tribute to the 'the most brilliant Minister of Health this country ever had', while a study of the NHS produced a few years later concluded: 'In the light of past accomplishments and future goals, the Health Service cannot very well be excluded from any list of notable achievements of the twentieth century.'

In the field of housing, Bevan, who was the minister responsible here also, did not achieve such notable success. Partly this was because he was preoccupied with other matters, partly also because the problems he faced were immense and susceptible to no quick or easy solution, despite Labour's rhetoric during the 1945 election campaign. Then Bevin had promised 'five million homes in quick time' and Cripps, allegedly, had claimed that 'housing [could] be dealt with in a fortnight'. Yet the problem was a very serious one. The population as a result of the war was crowded into 700,000 fewer houses than in 1939 and no one knew how large had been the unsatisfied pre-war demand for homes. Nor was it foreseen that in the first three years after the war there would be 11 per cent more marriages and 33 per cent more births than in the last three years before the war, or that full employment and changing social patterns would increase the demand for separate houses to an unprecedented degree. It was in many ways a pity, therefore, that the Labour government failed to implement its election pledge to create a separate Ministry for Housing.

Yet Bevan's record with respect to housing is often underestimated.

True, it was not until Harold Macmillan became Housing Minister in the early fifties that more than 300,000 houses were built in one year, but Bevan's record should not necessarily be judged in comparison with Macmillan's, which was achieved under slightly different circumstances. In any case, even if a comparison is made, the Labour minister comes off much better than is normally appreciated. For if one looks at the figures, the number of new houses completed was 55,400 in 1946, 139,690 in 1947 and 227,616 in 1948. Other forms of building brought the 1948 total up to 284,230. Thus despite serious shortages of building materials, only three years after the war the Government were constructing not far short of Macmillan's magic figure. Bevan suffered, however, from his preference for quality over quantity, for 'while we shall be judged for a year or two by the number of houses we build,' he told a conference, 'we shall be judged in ten years time by the type of houses we build'. Thus local authorities were instructed to build houses of an average 1,000 sq. ft (as against the previous average of 800), houses which were also to be provided with the most up-to-date amenities. He declared: 'We don't want a country of East Ends and West Ends.' Macmillan, in contrast, was to achieve his figures by putting quantity before quality, and if Bevan had done the same and had adopted the same building specifications as his successor, he would have built 300,000 houses in 1948. He might well have reached the magic figure in any case in 1949, but since the housing programme was cut in the wake of the financial crisis of 1947, the number of houses built under Labour after 1948 declined. The figures for 1949, 1950 and 1951 were 217,240, 210,253 and 204,117 respectively. The Conservatives could not reasonably complain about these totals. Churchill's caretaker government in March 1945 had predicted that 750,000 new houses would be needed after the war 'to afford a separate dwelling for every family desiring to have one'. This figure had been reached by 1948 and by the time Labour left office twice that many additional units of accommodation had been provided. The trouble was that the 1945 prediction had seriously underestimated the dimensions of the post-war housing shortage, a situation which by 1950 was clearly visible to all.

Bevan's task was not simply to build more houses. As the minister in charge of housing he was also responsible for a series of measures which, although in no way radically improving housing problems, nevertheless left their mark. His Housing Acts of 1946 and 1949 removed an important limitation under which local authorities laboured, namely that they should build only for the 'working class'. His Rent Control Acts of 1946 and 1949 protected the interests of private landlords' tenants by retaining rent tribunals and rent control. Meanwhile he pursued a policy of building temporary prefabricated housing which both helped to boost his figures and to alleviate demand. Between 1945 and 1950 some 157,000 such 'prefabs' were constructed.

In keeping with Bevan's concern for the quality of life, however, his efforts with respect to the environment were perhaps his most important innovatory contribution as minister.* Thus the Town and Country Planning Act of 1947 removed planning functions from the smaller local authorities, increased the duties and obligations of the larger ones, extended powers of compulsory purchase and promised aid to planning authorities from central government. Planning authorities were also to have powers to control advertisements and to preserve historic buildings, while the Government undertook to levy a development charge on any increase in land values brought about by development or projected development. Another piece of important legislation was the New Towns Act of 1946. This set up a number of development corporations which were entrusted with the building of new towns in various parts of the country, a programme which was ultimately to achieve considerable success. Less important was the National Park and Access to the Countryside Act, the aims of which were embodied in its title.

One final point has to be raised in any attempt to form an overall judgement of Bevan's ministerial career. Nearly all his legislation brought about important changes affecting local authorities. Yet he never succeeded in getting around to reforming local government. Apparently he had worked out a number of proposals but lacked either the time or the energy to promote their acceptance by the Cabinet. Had he succeeded in pushing through a programme of local government reform, his work would have constituted a more symmetrical monument to his talents. As it was, that monument was imposing enough as it stood. Bevan was the chief architect of Britain's welfare state, a minister whose power of decision-making and imagination were highlighted by the fact that in a

* The main legislative responsibilities for these were in fact borne by Lewis Silkin, Minister of Town and Country Planning.

comparable field – education – little advance was made on Butler's Education Act of 1944 * by ministers of a less determined or speculative cast of mind, who saw their main task as implementing Butler's aims in peacetime.

LABOUR'S OVERSEAS AND DEFENCE POLICY

Hugh Dalton, it had been generally assumed, would become Labour's Foreign Secretary when the party emerged victorious from the 1945 election. Instead Attlee assigned the Foreign Office to Ernest Bevin. His choice was an unexpected one but turned out to be inspired: Bevin proved an able, energetic and far-sighted holder of the office. Superficially, however, his qualifications for the job seemed slight; his career to date had been that of Britain's leading trade unionist, the organizer of the Transport and General Workers' Union and Minister of Labour in Churchill's coalition government. But that was not the full measure of the man. For during the thirties Bevin had played an important part in reconciling the Labour movement to the task of rearmament and, during the war, as a member of the war cabinet, had taken a special interest in foreign affairs. He had established extremely good personal relations with Churchill and Eden and was well-equipped to assume responsibility for foreign policy on behalf of the post-war government. Moreover, his trade union background proved in no way to be disadvantageous. He entered office as a skilled and tough negotiator and prided himself in knowing how to handle Communists. Molotov, he once said, was just like a Communist member of a local Labour party: 'If you treated him badly he made the most of his grievance and if you treated him well, he only put up his price and abused you next day.' Thus his dealings with the Russians assumed the same earthy flavour as those of Harry Truman.

Yet there was also an intellectual side to Bevin. If he had his prejudices – which he undoubtedly had and which were directed against the middle classes, Communists and Zionists – he also had a grasp of ideas. As a member of the 1929 Macmillan Committee he had been one of the few prepared to argue with Keynes on equal terms, and his policies as a rule were well thought out. The trouble was that he always expected others to

---

* It provided for secondary education for all up to the age of fifteen.

agree with him and tended to characterize criticism of any sort as a 'stab in the back'. The middle-class intellectuals of the 'Keep Left' group in Parliament were in this respect the particular object of his contempt. One of his supporters told them in language which he himself might have used that 'they would learn more if they spent more time in working-class pubs than in attending gatherings of Bloomsbury Bolsheviks'. Criticism of this type, however, was not anti-intellectual; rather it represented the frustration of men who thought of themselves as realists with the woolly thinking of critics who had failed to come to terms with the realities of the post-war world.

There was, in fact, a great deal of muddled thinking on the part of the theorists. Michael Foot, for instance, could proclaim at the beginning of the 1945 Parliament that Great Britain stood at the summit of her power and glory because she had 'something unique to offer' – a middle way between Communism and Capitalism. If only she would combine the 'economic democracy' of Russia with the 'political democracy' of the West, according to Foot, she could have the moral leadership of the world. Britain, in short, together with the Commonwealth, could form a 'third force' which would transform the world by its example. Richard Crossman in March 1946 tried to give more substance to such grandiose ideas when he set out his schemes for a 'Western Union'. This, he argued, should be composed of the states of Western Europe and the British Commonwealth, united in support of a declaration that they would not be party to a third world war between the super-powers. Crossman affected a spurious realism when outlining his plans by dis-missing contemporary notions of an Atlantic Alliance or a Federal Europe. His scheme, however, was hardly a convincing one. Bevin, backed from the Opposition front bench by Churchill and Eden, viewed the world through less rose-coloured spectacles.

With the end of the Second World War a power-vacuum had been created in Europe and a 'Big Three' leadership had been established in international affairs. The 'Big Three' powers, however, were in fact the big two – the USA and the USSR – plus Great Britain. Britain had been exhausted by the war and had neither the military might nor the economic resources to compete with American or Soviet influence. Since there was nothing to be gained from playing off these powers against each other – the policy, in fact, of Bevin's critics – the obvious policy for Great Britain was to ally with the United States in the hope of influencing her decisions. In particular, it would be Britain's task to persuade the United States to maintain a worldwide balance of power. This had traditionally been Britain's role, but the traditionalists were now prepared to surrender it, if America would adopt their point of view. Wartime experience had prepared them for the role of second fiddle and it was only the left-wing idealists who still cherished hopes of conducting an orchestra. Bevin, whose outlook was that of the traditionalists, was concerned most of all to maintain a balance of power in Europe and his number one priority became to tie American troops to the Continent – a far from easy task in the first two years after the war. For if Stalin had clear ideas about Soviet post-war aims and interests the same could not be said of the USA. American thinking about the post-war world varied from the fuzzy to the non-existent, and revisionist historians of this period who claim to perceive in American policy a devious, self-seeking strategy of Machiavellian cunning have been influenced less by the facts than by the theology and demonology of Vietnam. Not till 1946 or perhaps even 1947 did America have a true appreciation of what the balance of power implied and thereafter even this was obscured by the rhetoric of 'cold war' ideology.

Stalin, on the other hand, had given considerable thought to the problem of post-war frontiers and problem areas. Even in December 1941, with the Germans only five or six miles from the gates of Moscow, he had insisted on discussing the Polish frontier with the British Foreign Secretary. His aims were those of a traditional Russian imperialist*: control of the Balkans, Poland and as much of Central Asia as he could possibly secure. Given also that German power had been destroyed – and at a cost in Russian lives of perhaps 20 million people – Stalin was also concerned to exercise hegemony in Central Europe. Thus he planned to create around the borders of Russia a system of client states and wanted to help determine the fate of Germany. The wartime conferences at Teheran, Yalta and Potsdam were intended to secure agreement on these objectives and in his dealings with the Western powers the Soviet dictator proved remarkably successful. Even before Soviet troops had reached the vital areas of Central and Eastern Europe Stalin had had drawn up the boundaries of the occupation zones in Germany and the

* At a banquet held in September 1945 Stalin alluded to the Russo-Japanese War of 1904–5 in his remarks concerning the end of the war against Japan. The old generation of Russians, he said, had long awaited this final reckoning with the Japanese.

spheres of influence of the Allied powers. There is little evidence to suggest, however, that he was intent upon the conquest of the world or even the Sovietization of the whole of Europe. He pursued a remarkably passive policy on Greece and was surprised by American weakness over Central Europe. In China he was probably much more interested in creating a client state in Manchuria than in hastening the birth of the People's Republic. Finally, the Communist Parties were not encouraged to make a bid for power in France or Italy. Nor was this 'moderation' the consequence of American nuclear blackmail. The territories controlled in Eastern Europe had been taken over when Russia lacked the atom bomb and while the Russian army was being reduced from 11 million to 3 million men. Rather, Stalin knew exactly what he wanted and got most of it. In contrast, his allies, to their eternal shame, were even prepared to hand over to him millions of refugees whom they knew to be facing death or slavery in concentration camps.

Roosevelt presented a picture of perfect aimlessness. He had little interest in Eastern Europe and thought that the political problems of the wartime world could be solved by free elections after victory. He objected to Churchill's old-fashioned 'power politics' and relied on his fellow republican and anti-imperialist, Stalin, to help him create a 'world of democracy and peace', since the Russians, he believed, had 'no crazy ideas of conquest'. Roosevelt's views were not as unrealistic as they have sometimes been portrayed, but they were certainly remarkably complacent. Only one hour before he died he wrote to Churchill: 'I would minimize the Soviet problem as much as possible because these problems in one form or another seem to arise every day and most of them straighten out.' He did add, it is true, the rider, 'We must be firm, however,' but evidence of firmness is not easily adduced. Thus British proposals to capture Vienna, Prague or Berlin before the Russians arrived were overruled by the Americans, and despite the fact that Western troops at the time of the German surrender were more than 100 miles beyond the limit agreed on with the Russians, no attempt was made by the Western Allies to exploit this unexpected advantage. Instead, Eisenhower and Truman chose to surrender an area of some 400 miles long and 120 miles wide to Soviet occupation forces, against Churchill's advice. Such territory could perhaps not have served in any decisive way as a bargaining counter with the Russians but the fact remained that it was just about all the Western Allies had with which to negotiate with

Stalin over the fate of Eastern and Central Europe. Otherwise they were forced to rely upon Russian good faith in order to secure the full implementation of the Yalta agreements. Until 1947, however, America was still prepared to believe in that good faith and Stalin, it was thought, would allow the establishment in his client states of democratic governments and institutions which were anathema in Russia itself. The British Foreign Office took a much less sanguine view of events.

Britain suffered at this time not merely from American naïveté with regard to Soviet Russia. She also had to endure American hostility towards her Commonwealth and Empire, as within the American administration 'economic royalists' and anti-imperialists alike combined to undermine Great Britain's world position. The immediate post-war period therefore witnessed considerable Anglo-American friction, and the problems which proved the most divisive were above all economic. Even during the war itself the Foreign Economic Administration – part of the Lend-Lease Administration – had given a foretaste of what was to come. In October 1943 it had declared that a number of important capital goods – machine tools and petroleum equipment amongst them – would no longer be eligible for lend-lease. This list was later extended despite the fact that 'reverse lend-lease' from Britain and the Commonwealth was proportionately higher than American aid. The Americans were determined to keep Britain's dollar balances down, and an upper limit of $1,000 million was imposed on lend-lease by President Roosevelt, who subjected Churchill to constant pressure to limit British demands. No notice was taken of Churchill's protest that Britain had 'incurred for the common cause liabilities of at least ten billions', that the dollar balances in fact now constituted Britain's 'total reserves' or that British exports had fallen to a minimum as production had been geared to the war effort. As soon as the war in Europe was over, lend-lease was abruptly cancelled altogether. Some measure of agreement over international monetary problems, it is true, had been reached at Bretton Woods at the conference of 1944, when the distinguished British economist, Lord Keynes, had played an important part in securing the establishment of the International Monetary Fund and the Bank for Reconstruction. Yet even there, there had been important Anglo-American differences, differences which were to emerge more sharply and give rise to much more friction both in the negotiations which preceded the American Loan Agreement of

1946* and those which led to the General Agreement on Tariffs and Trade (GATT) signed in 1947.

The Americans adopted what in retrospect appears to be a curious double standard over questions of international trade. They violently objected to the British system of imperial preferences and to the sterling balances accumulated by Britain during the war; yet they felt entirely free to defend their own high tariff barriers at a time when they had no possible economic rivals. Britain was treated by them not as a junior partner who had impoverished herself in the struggle against the tyrant but as a powerful potential trading rival who was exaggerating her economic difficulties. Thus the *New York Times* could run the incredulous headline, 'British quote statistics to show they contributed far more relatively than we did', while Keynes's exposition of the facts to the populist US Secretary to the Treasury, Vinson, was answered with the response, 'Mebbe so Lawd Keynes, mebbe so, but down where I come from folks don't look at things that way.' Vinson's point of view, like that of the powerful vested interests which he represented, was that Britain should dismantle her empire and its tariff structure and accept a worldwide 'open door' and US competition. Given America's wartime profits, her lack of trading rivals and her highly protected home market, this was nothing less than a sure-fire remedy for control of the world economy. It is not surprising, therefore, that it should have met with vigorous British resistance. Besides, in purely economic terms the Americans were demonstrating a surprising lack of sophistication. For only when Europe could afford to buy American goods would the world economy grow. It was entirely in America's own interest to aim for a relatively smaller share of by far a larger market. But in the immediate post-war period such thinking was still unfashionable and American economic policy was still designed to dislodge Great Britain's hold on her traditional markets. Thus Britain was excluded from the treaty signed in November 1946 between the United States and Nationalist China; American exporters were encouraged to look to huge gains in Asia when Britain pulled out of India; nothing was done to ease Britain's position in the Middle East; and little sympathy was accorded to British policy in the Eastern Mediterranean. Britain was still regarded as an imperialist power with imperialist designs as dangerous as those of

* See above, pp. 27–8.

Russia. Only the United States themselves were in the comfortable position of knowing that their material interests and political idealism coincided.

Having been the first of Britain's colonial possessions to wrest their independence, the United States were not unnaturally hostile to the idea of the British Empire. This hostility had been displayed, for example, by Roosevelt when he had inserted in the Atlantic Charter 'the right of all people to choose the form of government under which they will live'. Moreover, during the course of the war itself he had kept open a wary eye for any manifestation of British imperialism. He had also prompted Britain to move with greater speed regarding the independence of India and had even raised the matter with Stalin during the conference at Teheran. However, it was Palestine rather than India which was to give rise to the greatest friction between the two countries as far as colonial matters were concerned, and between 1944 and 1947 the question of British policy in Palestine threatened to split the common front with the USA.

Britain found herself faced with an almost insoluble problem in the Holy Land. In 1917 the carefully worded Balfour Declaration had promised to facilitate the 'establishment in Palestine of a National Home for the Jewish people', 'it being clearly understood' that nothing would be done to 'prejudice the civil and religious rights of existing non-Jewish communities' there. Zionists immediately interpreted the Declaration as a promise to establish a Jewish state, while Arabs not unnaturally regarded it as a betrayal by Britain of their national rights. The problem seemed to fade in the 1920s, but with the rise of anti-semitism in Europe in the 1930s, and the advent of Hitler in Germany in particular, there was a flood of refugees to Palestine which in turn gave rise to an Arab revolt which the British had to suppress. This they did between 1936 and 1939, but when war broke out in September 1939 the British government felt they could not put their sympathy towards the Jews before the friendship of the Arabs and the security of the Middle East. By this time, in any case, a White Paper had already limited the number of Jews who might enter Palestine to 75,000 by the end of March 1944 and had promised thereafter to place the matter of immigration in the hands of the Arabs themselves. The same White Paper of May 1939 also restricted the right of Jews to buy land and promised eventual independence to Palestine under Arab majority rule. In short, it seemed as if the

Zionist dream was no longer attainable, although the Arabs themselves still doubted the worth of Britain's promises. They had in fact every reason to do so, since as the war dragged on the British government came under increasingly heavy pressure to relax its anti-Zionist policy.

Most of this pressure came from the United States, although as news leaked out of Nazi extermination programmes many involved in the formulation of British policy became aware of the agonizing moral dilemma. Yet to give in to Zionist demands, it was feared, might cause the revolt of the Arab world, perhaps with ultimately even more ominous consequences for the Jews themselves. The Zionists approached the problem from a totally different perspective. It was difficult for them to imagine what more could happen to the Jews, and the experience of the Second World War made the need to establish a Jewish homeland one of the utmost urgency. Having lost all faith in Britain fulfilling the terms of the Balfour Declaration – at least as they interpreted them – they adopted in 1942 in America what soon became known as the 'Biltmore programme'. This aimed at placing the responsibility for immigration into Palestine in the hands of the Jewish Agency and the establishment there 'as soon as possible' of a Jewish state once a Jewish majority had been created. Little regard was paid to the rights of the existing Arab majority but, given the generally good press which the Zionists had in both Great Britain and the USA, not to mention the sympathy which was to be felt for a people who had suffered so terribly at Hitler's hands, by the time the war was over the Zionists had won substantial and influential support. Roosevelt, who was sensitive to Jewish pressure with the approach of the 1944 presidential election, promised that justice would be done 'to those who seek a Jewish National Home'. Both American political parties inserted pro-Zionist planks in their election platforms and in October 1944 Roosevelt pledged, if re-elected, to help establish a Jewish Commonwealth in Palestine. The election safely over, however, the President neglected Zionist demands and fell under the unlikely influence of King Ibn Saud of Saudi Arabia. As a result his successor, Harry Truman, came under determined Zionist pressure.

In Britain, too, the Zionists appeared to have been making considerable political headway. Indeed, the Labour Party conference which was held in December 1944 adopted a resolution which today seems almost racialist in tone. It ran: 'But there is surely neither hope nor meaning in a "Jewish National Home" unless we are prepared to let Jews, if they wish, enter this tiny land in such numbers as to become a majority ... Let the Arabs be encouraged to move out as the Jews move in.' The wording of the resolution had been drawn up by Dalton, whose notes on the conference motion included the following revealing sentence: 'We should lean much more than hitherto towards the dynamic Jew, less towards the static Arab.' But Bevin at the Foreign Office was not to be persuaded by such blatant racialist nonsense. He strove instead for an honourable compromise and was concerned to uphold British influence in the Middle East as a whole. In short, he simply had no intention of adopting his party's programme of 'Zionism plus'.

The wartime coalition government had come to the conclusion that the only possible solution to the problem of Palestine would be a partition between Arab and Jews. The rub was that such a settlement would have to be imposed by force, whereas the Labour government instead preferred to seek solution by means of negotiation. Bevin subsequently consulted Arab and Jewish leaders but found to his bitter disappointment that no compromise was acceptable. Consultations continued throughout 1945 and 1946. Meanwhile Britain attempted to secure American aid in her search for a possible settlement. An Anglo-American committee of inquiry was set up in November 1945 and reported at the end of April 1946. Truman publicly endorsed its recommendation to issue an extra 100,000 visas to Jews who wished to enter Palestine but to the great frustration of the British government refused to commit himself to the accompanying conditions and qualifications. American policy on the issue of the Holy Land was therefore revealed as totally unhelpful. Truman acted as if only America had sympathy for Jewish refugees while at the same time he refused to help enforce a solution in Palestine or even allow more Jews to enter the United States. Moreover, he also rejected the 'Morrison Plan' of July 1946, which in retrospect came nearest to a possible resolution of differences. This was a scheme to organize Palestine as a federation under a British High Commissioner. The latter was to control defence, foreign affairs, customs and immigration, but policy on immigration was to be formulated by autonomous Arab and Jewish provinces. With American rejection of the Morrison proposals the problem was referred in February 1947 to the United Nations. It was not yet Britain's intention to surrender the Palestine mandate but in September 1947 the decision to quit was announced. The mandate would come to an end on midnight 14–15 May 1948.

The British decision to withdraw was motivated by a number of important factors. British public opinion, for a start, had been outraged by systematic Jewish terrorism, and the destruction of the King David Hotel in Jerusalem with 150 casualties, as well as the public hanging of two young British sergeants, served to undermine the public's consent that the Government should continue to treat with such adversaries. The cost of operations was another important influence. No less than £100 million had been spent between 1945 and 1947 on keeping the peace in Palestine but with the economic crisis of 1947 the Government no longer felt justified in spending such enormous amounts of money for so little visible return. Finally, there were wider considerations of policy which had to be taken into account: the desire to let America come to grips with political reality; the recent partition and independence of the Indian sub-continent; additionally, after 1947 it became clear that the port of Haifa would not be needed as the principal British military supply base for operations in the Middle East. Until then the British government had looked to Haifa to serve in that capacity in the event of a third world war.

Nothing was sadder, however, than the manner in which the British departed. In November 1947 the United Nations voted in favour of partitioning Palestine, but the British government, which had always resisted such a solution, refused to be party to the plan. It lacked the means to impose such a policy on the area and, since the United Nations did not intend to furnish it with any, it saw no reason to make its bad position worse. Moreover, Bevin was still concerned to treat Arab and Jew alike and was still determined to preserve what influence he could with other Arab states. To Zionist supporters he posed the essential question: why should Arabs become a minority in a Jewish state when Jews refused to be a minority in an Arab one? There were as a result of the war prodigious emotional and human factors involved, but there remained considerations of policy and logic which Bevin simply could not afford to ignore. He has been accused of being an Arabist, but the charge is easy to refute. No doubt he expected the Arabs to win the civil war which everyone knew was imminent, but his main consideration was that the British should not become involved. Thus if he refused to accept the Zionist case, he also refused to accept the case of any particular Arab leader. He had done his best, in his opinion, to sort the situation out, and if his efforts had ended in failure the fault was certainly not his or his alone. The only policy left to Britain was to get out before getting caught in the consequences of failure. British rule in Palestine therefore ended amidst growing anarchy and chaos. The world waited for the war which would finally, it was thought, resolve the issue and falsely and often hypocritically attributed the tragedy of the situation to British imperialism and misrule. The truth was that the situation had arisen thanks to an inappropriate sense of fair play on the part of a decolonizing government.

Britain was in a sense in a distinctly unenviable position regarding her imperial possessions. As long as she held on to them she was a wicked, imperialist power; but as soon as she offered to relinquish them she was thought to be demonstrating her decline. If the transfer of power was not smooth, she was held to have mismanaged her colonial rule. All these factors worked against the British mandate in the Holy Land, but it was more of a surprise to the British government that they coloured the granting of independence to India. For this was seen by many foreigners as a reluctant acceptance of the inevitable, whereas as far as the British government was concerned it was part of an enlightened programme of deliberate decolonization. In actual fact, there was much to be said for both viewpoints.

Bevin had written in 1942 that 'empires as we have known them must become a thing of the past'. In December of that year, with Cripps, he had drawn up a 'Social and Economic Policy for India' which had proposed a development programme to the Cabinet which would cost between £400,000 and £500,000 per year. By the end of the war it was clear that such plans were no longer feasible. Britain could simply not afford them at a time when all her resources were needed to finance her own post-war development. The Cabinet therefore decided to speed up the granting of independence to India. They had really no honourable alternative: the coalition government's policy of 'wait till the end of the war' had entitled Indians to view any proposed delay in constitutional progress with justifiable suspicion. There was in any case no reason for holding on: India had its own political parties which had widespread local support; the British obviously lacked that support; moreover, their administrative machine was running down; finally, and most important, since Britain could not afford to improve the lot of Indians she had lost the moral right to govern. The Labour government understood this and prepared to transfer power to native leaders. The problem which remained was how to do this and how to do so in such a way as to keep India within the Commonwealth. Attlee took the view that it would be for the best to let the Indians solve this problem as much as possible by themselves.

As in Palestine, however, it proved impossible for the local populations to agree to live together. The Indian Congress Party under Nehru and the Muslim League under Jinnah could not resolve the differences which divided Hindu and Muslim from each other. Britain attempted to mediate between the two sides but her efforts were to no avail. Negotiations went on during the course of 1946 and 1947, but Britain withdrew from the sub-continent in August 1947, leaving it partitioned between two sovereign dominions, India and Pakistan. 'Divide and quit' – as Jinnah labelled British policy – led to over 200,000 deaths in the Punjab and the accusation from Conservative leaders that Britain had 'betrayed' India as well as her own traditions there. Attlee replied that the 'difficulties in India [were] not due to any fault of this country but to the failure of Indians to agree among themselves'. There had been, he added, 'no weakness and no betrayal . . . but [rather] limitations to our powers'. The British people in 1947 were only too well aware of these limitations and were grateful that Attlee had recognized them. The Government's grant of independence was therefore greeted as a sensible, far-sighted and courageous act, and the decision of both new states to remain within the Commonwealth appeared to symbolize the Government's success.

More critical observers, on the other hand, and historians of Indian independence since, have questioned this traditional interpretation of the emergence of Britain's 'new Commonwealth'. In particular, it has been asserted that British policy was reluctantly determined by the threat of mutiny within the Royal Indian Navy, and that Britain had a deliberate plan of partition in order to keep the successor states dependent and weak. On a more general level, the proposition is often asserted that the real stimulus to independence were the wartime victories of Japan. Yet the answer to all these criticisms and assertions is that they simply lack a basis in fact. The Cabinet had already decided on independence before the naval mutiny took place. Moreover, it can be easily demonstrated that government policy with regard to partition was not determined by an imperialist spirit. True, no effort was made to enforce unity by threatening to repudiate the sterling balances and no threat was made to deduct from them the costs of maintaining law and order. But, equally, no use was made, despite the wishes of some Muslim leaders, of white legislators within the Bengali assembly in support of partition. The truth is that the Government were determined not to impose a settlement of any kind upon the native population but to allow the latter to work out their own solution. Thus, for example, despite the fact that imperial defence plans postulated a militarily united India, the Cabinet were not prepared to exert on the Muslim League pressure of a sort which might backfire. The Muslim League had popular support and could not simply be wished away. Rather, Britain gave full negotiating powers to the Viceroy and announced a terminal date for the Raj. This was startling proof that Britain was in fact willing to accept whatever settlement was arrived at.

The argument concerning Japan can only be discussed in a wider context. It is certainly true that the Japanese had seriously undermined the prestige of the European empires and that Dutch rule in the East Indies ended because post-war Holland lacked the power to crush the Indonesian nationalists under Sukarno. Similarly, it cannot be denied that the recognition by Japan in 1943 of Burmese independence was a powerful factor in promoting the rise of Burmese nationalism. Henry Pelling has argued, on the other hand, that 'the Dutch East Indies became independent more because Holland was occupied by Germany than because the Indies were occupied by Japan' and that the countries of the British Empire which secured independence, including dominion status, in the immediate post-war years were 'those in which the development of self-government had advanced the furthest in the 1930s'. He points out that in fact only one of these countries (Burma) had been conquered by the Japanese whereas other countries which had spent years under Japanese occupation – Malaya, Singapore, Sarawak and North Borneo, for example – 'were restored to British rule for a long period, some of them right up to the present day'. Two other points are made in support of this way of looking at the emergence of the new Commonwealth: firstly, that, by bringing Churchill to power, the Second World War might conceivably have delayed the granting of independence to India; and secondly, that the effect of Japanese victories was more immediately felt in Australasia. Both Australia and New Zealand took stock of their defence and foreign policies after the fall of Singapore. The result in 1951 was the signing of the ANZUS defence agreement with America from which Britain was entirely excluded.

Britain herself, on the other hand, undertook no reappraisal of her commitments East of Suez as a result of constitutional changes there. Burma and Ceylon followed India and Pakistan in acquiring independence in 1948, yet no defence review was undertaken. Instead, there was much support for the view of Auchinleck that Britain was 'still morally bound to aid India and Pakistan against an aggressor' and if the loss of the Indian Army amounted to the loss of 'the keystone of the arch of our Commonwealth defence' (in the words of Field-Marshal Lord Alanbrooke), Ceylon had been good enough to acquiesce in a defence agreement which provided for the maintenance of British naval and air bases on the island. Thus the need for a reappraisal did not yet seem urgent.

There remained a multitude of overseas commitments, however, which simply could not be ignored. For example, it was taken for granted that an attack on either Australia or New Zealand would be tantamount to an attack on Great Britain herself. Again, the ink was scarcely dry on the Indian Independence Act when Communist violence in Malaya forced Britain to embark upon a twelve-year campaign of counter-insurgency there. Britain still had a constitutional responsibility for the defence of her remaining colonies in Africa and Asia, while she was also a signatory to numerous defence treaties with the sheikhdoms and emirates of Arabia and the Persian Gulf. Thus there were solid grounds for believing that 'the route to India' would have to be protected as in the past. Attlee, it is true, tried to force a change in British Middle Eastern strategy in 1945, but he was defeated by a combination of Bevin and the Chiefs of Staff. In the light of unrest in Palestine and Egypt – where Egyptian nationalists were demanding the annexation of the Sudan to Egypt and where Britain's military presence had been reduced to a base on the Canal Zone – the premier had proposed that Britain should withdraw from the Middle East to a line further south in Africa stretching from Lagos to Kenya, with the latter keeping most of the troops. Bevin, however, who at the time was alarmed by Russian ambitions in the Middle East, supported the Chiefs of Staff, who had opposed the plan to the point of threatening resignation. Dalton supported Attlee but the military won the day, although the idea of using Kenya as a supply base lingered on in Whitehall until 1949.

Altogether, therefore, the granting of independence to India made little impression on defence planners. They agreed with the Foreign Secretary, who declared in a House of Commons debate:

So far as foreign policy is concerned we have not altered our commitments in the slightest ... His Majesty's Government do not accept the view ... that we have ceased to be a great power, or the contention that we have ceased to play that role. We regard ourselves as one of the Powers most vital to the peace of the world, and we still have our historic part to play.

The independence of India, Pakistan, Burma and Ceylon did, however, signify the emergence of a new Commonwealth and of a new Commonwealth policy and spirit. For if Burma chose to sever her links with Britain completely, India, Pakistan and Ceylon accepted the formula of the Commonwealth Premiers' Conference of 1949 whereby the king became 'the symbol of the free association of its independent member nations and as such Head of the Commonwealth', and they were therefore able in future to play a full and distinguished part in its affairs. This formula came just a little too late to retain the allegiance of the Republic of Ireland – independent in fact since 1936 – but another formula, 'external association', was employed to maintain special links here too, with the result that the Labour government were able to lay the foundations for a worldwide free association of independent states. Henceforth the British Labour and Liberal Parties could therefore view the Commonwealth with affection and admiration.

The 'new era' in the development of the Commonwealth was also signified by more material progress, Great Britain having resolved at the end of the war to tackle her colonial responsibilities with renewed vigour. The autonomy of colonial governors, for example, was brought to an end and, domestic problems notwithstanding, a determined effort was made to assist the colonies socially and economically in a way simply never attempted before the war. The staff of the Colonial Office trebled between 1938 and 1950 but, more important, the Labour government, building on the Colonial Development and Welfare Act of 1940 – which had provided some £10 million for the colonies – set aside another £120 million for the years 1945–55 and in 1950 increased this figure to £140 million. An Act of 1948 meanwhile established two public corporations – the Colonial Development Corporation and the Overseas Food Corporation – to improve living standards in the colonies, and there was also a considerable expansion of colonial education, including higher education, a measure which helped provide Africa with a new generation of leaders.

On the other hand, despite the emergence of the new Commonwealth as a worldwide organization transcending the boundaries of race, colour and creed, no attempt was made by the Labour government to develop it institutionally. Even Labour Party activists showed no particular enthusiasm to move in this direction and only once, in May 1947, was it ever suggested that British and colonial Labour Parties should meet together – a proposal which, by the way, was never discussed. In the context of Europe, too, the Commonwealth ideal did not figure prominently as an alternative to federalist thinking. Labour opposition to the idea of a united Europe was by 1950 most often being articulated in terms of political and economic sovereignty. For despite Bevin's insistence that Britain was still a world power, there was considerable evidence of 'little England-ness' around.

Britain's main focus of attention during these years was Europe, and Bevin's most important task with regard to Europe was to take appropriate measures in defence of Western interests there. He had, in particular, to decide what to do *vis-à-vis* Germany and to define Britain's relationship with America and the Continent in the context of the Soviet challenge. In terms of his own assessment of the situation he was to prove remarkably effective. His main objective came to be to tie America irrevocably to Europe, and as a result of the Truman Doctrine, the Marshall Plan and the establishment of NATO that is exactly what came about.

Western suspicions in regard to Stalin's intentions were first aroused by Soviet policy in the Eastern Mediterranean and the Middle East. Greece, Turkey and Iran were the first states beyond the immediate grasp of the Red Army to feel the pressure of the Soviet Union, and it was as a result of that pressure that America began to reassess her policy. The Soviet Union began to exercise her power in Iran in early 1946. Russian troops had been there since 1941, when both Russia and Britain had invaded the country to put an end to pro-Nazi developments as well as to use it as a corridor through which to channel Western aid to Russia. At the end of the war Britain had withdrawn her troops but Russia, seeking to establish a permanent influence, had not. Pressure had also been exerted on Turkey. The latter had been requested to agree to a revision of the Montreux Convention on the Dardanelles, to cede several border areas to the Soviet Union, to conclude a special treaty with her and to lease her land and naval bases on the Straits. If Turkey had agreed to these requests, she would undoubtedly have taken the first step to becoming a satellite of the Soviet Union. In Greece, meanwhile, a civil war was going on which eventually was only won by the anti-Communists thanks to British support and intervention. This civil war had in fact been in progress even during the period of the German occupation. Then when the Germans withdrew and the British landed, the Communists had attempted to take over Athens; they were prevented from doing so only after several weeks of bloody street fighting by the landing of British reinforcements. A truce was signed in January 1945 and in March 1946 a general election was held in which the right-wing won a majority. But the crisis did not end there. Greece was economically and physically exhausted by the German occupation; her traditional markets had been lost; and it proved well-nigh impossible for the new régime to restore any measure of prosperity. Moreover, much of the country's resources had to pay for the large army required to protect her from her Communist neighbours, for not only had the Red Army taken over Bulgaria, but the Communist partisans who had liberated Albania and Yugoslavia had established themselves in power in these countries, with the result that Greece was surrounded by enemies on all sides. If Britain had not financed, equipped and trained her army, she would most probably have also succumbed to the partisans.

Developments in the Eastern Mediterranean, therefore, were not calculated to improve East–West relations. Britain and America were compelled to act and in the summer of 1946 a tougher attitude was displayed in dealings with the Soviet Union. Strongly worded notes were delivered to Russia concerning her actions in Iran, while in the case of Turkey not only did both Britain and the United States reject the Soviet demands but in August 1946 the United States sent a naval task-force into the Mediterranean. This policy of strength succeeded: Russian troops were withdrawn from Iran, and Turkey was able to resist Soviet diplomatic pressure. America, however, in spite of these developments, was not converted to any systematic policy of resistance, and Churchill's famous speech delivered in the spring of 1946 at Fulton, Missouri, in which he warned that 'an iron curtain (had) descended across Europe', was not greeted with great enthusiasm by Americans. They did not like his reproof that 'our difficulties and dangers will not be removed by mere waiting to see what happens; nor will they be relieved by a policy of appeasement'. It was to take shock tactics on Bevin's part before America finally moved.

The crunch came over Greece. Guerilla warfare had been resumed there in the autumn of 1946, with Communist forces receiving supplies from their northern neighbours, and by the spring of 1947 it looked as if the Greeks were on the point of going under. If this happened, it was assumed not only that Turkey and Iran would fall to the Communists but that Italy and even France would be affected. Italy, in particular, seemed threatened by events: there was a large, well-organized Communist party in Italy; Yugoslavia was disputing her right to Trieste; moreover, Russia was demanding a trusteeship over her former North African colonies, so that the collapse of a non-Communist state in the Eastern Mediterranean, it was believed, could not but have serious implications for her. Indeed, the possible ramifications of a Communist victory in Greece amounted to no less than a 'domino theory' of Mediterranean calamities, which only British action in Greece itself – or so it was thought – was preventing from becoming a reality. America had not viewed events in quite this perspective in 1945 when – unlike Russia – she had objected to British policy in Athens, but in 1947 Bevin was able to concentrate her thinking on the matter. On the afternoon of 21 February 1947 the British Embassy in Washington abruptly informed the State Department that in the light of her economic difficulties Britain would no longer be able to meet her obligations with respect to Greece and Turkey, and that if these two countries were to be saved from Communism, America would have to assume the responsibility of doing so herself.

As it happened, official American thinking had been slowly changing with regard to Russia. Harriman and Kennan had since early 1946 been submitting pessimistic reports from Moscow, and in February 1947 Kennan had been appointed chief of the newly created Policy Planning Staff at the State Department. Bevin's bombshell, therefore, was exceptionally well timed and drew a positive response from Truman. On 12 March the President, addressing a joint session of Congress, gave voice to what has since become known as the Truman Doctrine. He said: 'I believe it must be the policy of the United States to support free peoples who are resisting attempted subjugations by armed minorities or by outside pressure.'

He asked for – and secured – $400 million worth of aid for Greece and Turkey as well as the authorization of the dispatch of US civilian and military personnel to both countries. More important was the fact that the doctrine clearly had wider applications: the foreign policy of the United States had in fact reached a revolutionary turning point. Henceforth isolationism was rejected in favour of Kennan's policy of containment, and the implications, especially for Europe, were immense and reassuring. The price which had to be paid for this was the excesses of cold-war rhetoric and ideology, but in retrospect these pale beside the security which was obtained. Truman's speech therefore signified the start of a new era in the foreign policy of the United States, but for Britain too it was to foreshadow new developments.

In Cleveland, Mississippi, in May 1947, the American Under-Secretary of State, Dean Acheson, speaking in the spirit of the Truman doctrine, declared that the United States was ready to provide long-term help 'to aid free peoples to preserve their independence'. The following month, in a speech at Harvard University, the Secretary of State, George Marshall, went a great deal further. Asserting that it was only 'logical' for America 'to assist in the return of normal economic health in the world without which there can be no political stability or assured peace', he invited the European nations to meet to detail their needs and promised that America would respond to them. 'The initiative,' he stressed, however, 'must come from Europe. The role of this country should consist in friendly aid in drafting a European programme and of later support of such a programme, so far as it may be practical to do so. The programme should be a joint one, agreed by a number, if not by all European nations.' At a press conference a few days later, Marshall explained that he also counted Russia as a European nation.

This, then, was the birth of the 'Marshall Plan', the aims of which were fairly straightforward: to restore stability and prosperity to Europe by putting an end to its 'dollar gap'; and in this way to save Europe from Communism, thereby safeguarding the security of the United States. The offer to include Russia was a skilful piece of diplomacy. An acceptance on the part of that power would almost certainly have sunk the scheme; however, the insistence on European cooperation made the prospect of Russian cooperation unlikely.

In Britain the response to Marshall was swift. Bevin greeted the proposals as a 'lifeline to a sinking man', quickly consulted Attlee and instructed the Embassy in Washington to inform the Secretary of State of immediate consultations with the French. The latter were in the middle of a government crisis, but talks got under way and on 27 June –

only three weeks after Marshall's speech – the Foreign Ministers of Britain, France and the Soviet Union met in Paris for preliminary discussions. Bevin had invited Molotov to try to breach the gap with the Soviet Union, hoping, as he said, that 'perhaps they *will* play after all'. But it was not to be: Stalin had no intention of instituting economic cooperation with the West; he had, as he told Marshall, no interest in the quick recovery of Western Europe; and he wanted, if he participated, to secure most of the available aid for Russia. Molotov therefore denounced the American proposals and forbade the Eastern European governments from participating in the plan. Stalin had in fact committed an egregious diplomatic blunder – the US Senate would never have approved massive US aid to Russia – and had presented the West with the opportunity to act.

In early July 1947 Bevin, along with Bidault, the Foreign Minister of France, invited all the European states (with the exception of Spain, which was still considered fascist) to join in framing a reply to Marshall's proposal. The Soviet block refused, but fourteen other states attended a conference in Paris on 12 July at which it was agreed that a sixteen-nation Committee of Economic Cooperation should be established. Before the end of September this Committee succeeded in presenting Marshall with a four-year plan for European economic reconstruction. Four objectives were agreed upon: increased production, particularly of agricultural products, fuel and modernized equipment; internal financial stability; economic cooperation amongst the participating states; and the elimination of the dollar gap with the United States as a result of increasing exports. This plan was duly accepted, and the sixteen nations established permanent liaison through the Organization for European Economic Cooperation set up in Paris on 18 April 1948.

This body turned out to be a great success. Using $12 billion of the $17 billion assigned to America's Economic Cooperation Administration under the Foreign Assistance Act of 8 April 1948, it accomplished nearly all the aims set out in the original report to Marshall. European production was increased; trade barriers (mainly import quotas) were lowered; bilateral bartering agreements between Western European nations were replaced by a European Payments Union, which settled accounts collectively; and by the end of the four-year period dependence on America had been virtually eliminated. Even by 1950 the success of the Marshall Plan was plain: Europe was already exceeding its pre-war production level by 25 per cent; and by then the dollar gap had been also reduced from $12 billion to $2 billion. British exports were doing well, West German production had reached Germany's 1936 level, and French inflation was being brought under control. America had also benefited from the plan, since at the cost of only a tiny fraction of her national income she had achieved a brilliant diplomatic success and engineered a domestic economic boom.

The Marshall Plan raised two other closely related problems. Should Europe cooperate in other ways? In particular, should the countries of Europe seek to unite themselves economically? Moreover, should they coordinate their defence arrangements? The experience and success of the Marshall Plan gave rise to the first of these problems; Russian hostility to the Marshall Plan as well as developments in Germany precipitated the second.

The idea of a more closely integrated Western Europe, that is of a federal Europe or even of a 'United States of Europe', was fairly widely debated during the lifetime of the post-war Labour government. Many impulses had given rise to it: the desire to assert the interests of Europe in face of the domination of the super-powers; the need to heal the wounds inflicted by the Second World War; the tendency among American statesmen and politicians to interpret the European experience in the light of their own past; and, last but not least, the political influence of men such as the French economic planner, Jean Monnet, who even before the war had been actively propagating this idea. The idea had also won many adherents among Europe's underground resistance movements during the war. It was powerfully reinforced when Churchill spoke at Zurich in September 1946 of the need to create 'a kind of United States of Europe' based on Franco-German reconciliation. He also urged the setting up of a 'Council of Europe', but it appeared that Britain was to be a 'friend and sponsor' rather than a member of it. Then in January 1947 the formation was announced in London of a United Europe Committee with Churchill as its Chairman. The aim of this body was the creation of a 'unified Europe' and Britain, it was declared, in spite of special obligations to the Commonwealth, was to play her full part in it. Speaking in the Albert Hall on 14 May, Churchill reasserted this objective, whereupon the movement grew rapidly. In July the same year a French committee was formed, and in December British, French, Belgian and Dutch members set up an

International Committee for a United Europe, chaired by Churchill's son-in-law, Duncan Sandys.

The scene was set, therefore, for a 'Congress of Europe', and this duly took place at the Hague in May 1948. Prominent Conservatives such as Eden and Macmillan attended along with other Conservative MPs. So too did a few Labour members, as well as such luminaries as Bertrand Russell and Lord Beveridge. Delegations were present from other European countries – including, significantly, Germany – and there were representatives-in-exile from the Eastern European states. The main speaker at the Congress was Churchill, who delivered a very moving speech which brought not a few tears to the eyes of delegates, although the substance of what he said was vague and difficult to interpret. He foresaw three regional councils dominating international affairs: one based on the Soviet Union; the Council of Europe, 'including Great Britain joined with her Empire and Commonwealth'; and one in the Western Hemisphere with which Britain would be linked through Canada and 'other sacred ties'. What exactly this amounted to was anybody's guess, but more precise was the resolution of the Congress to create a European economic and political union and its call for a European Assembly to be chosen from the parliaments of the member states. Overall, Churchill and his Conservative colleagues had succeeded in giving the impression that their party stood for a united Europe whereas the Labour Party did not.

In Britain the Labour government adopted a thoroughly sceptical attitude towards the question of a federal Europe. As far as they were concerned, Britain was still a world power and her links with the Commonwealth and America meant more than any ties she might have with the Continent. The people of Britain, they held, felt closer to their cousins in Australia and New Zealand than they did to former continental enemies. Moreover, it was all too easily asserted that the ideal of a United Europe was for those who had suffered defeat in war. Their 'national pride' had been broken whereas that of Great Britain had not. The Labour government, therefore, did not encourage their members to visit the Hague, and Bevin replied to the Hague Conference resolutions in tones of (albeit sympathetic) disagreement. He said: 'I feel that the intricacies of Western Europe are such that we had better proceed ... on the same principle of the association of nations that we have in the Commonwealth.' The 'right way to approach this Western Union prob-

lem', therefore, was by 'adopting the principle of an unwritten constitution, and the process of constant association, step by step, by treaty and
agreement, and by taking on certain things collectively instead of by
ourselves'. Like Churchill's contribution, this amounted in practice to
nothing, but by its evident lack of rhetoric it was meant to be understood
to do so. Labour's leaders, in fact, desired to have nothing to do with
European integration and made this crystal clear, particularly in their
dealings with the French over the sixteen-nation committee. Thus the
suggestion by the latter to establish a European Customs Union was
quietly put aside and the powers demanded by the French for the
Secretariat of the OEEC were significantly scaled down by the British.
In much the same spirit, Bevin in 1949 informed Alphand, the principal
French official who dealt with economic matters and who had proposed
the drawing up of a five-year plan for Anglo-French economic cooperation: 'We don't do things like that in our country; we don't have plans;
we work things out practically.' Labour, it seems, did not even trust
European Social Democrats, for in the foreword to a history of the
Labour Party published by Transport House in 1948 Attlee could write:
'The Labour Party is a characteristically British production differing
widely from Continental Socialist Parties. It is a product of its environment and of the national habit of mind.' The workers of the world, it
seemed, would take a long time to unite if the British Labour government
had anything to do with the process.

More generously, perhaps, it can be argued that the issue turned not
so much on matters of national pride and prejudice as on the question of
priorities. Bevin was prepared to give some thought to the long-term
possibility of a more integrated Europe, but in the short term his first
priority was to secure adequate defence arrangements. And since that, as
far as he was concerned, meant involving the United States in some
commitment to defend the Continent, he was much more interested in
strengthening Europe's links with America than in fostering European
cooperation for the sake of cooperation. Besides, when it came to matters
of European defence his map was necessarily a small one: neither Germany nor Italy had armies and that of France was still untried. His
determination regarding the link with America was, therefore, not un-
natural.

Bevin knew, on the other hand, that American cooperation was much
more likely to be forthcoming if Britain and France were seen to be

cooperating first. Thus when the French Prime Minister, M. Gouin, had proposed in March 1946 the signing of an Anglo-French alliance, he had responded in an enthusiastic manner, and an Anglo-French Treaty, which was to last for fifty years, was signed at Dunkirk in the following year. The choice of Dunkirk was a political ploy to emphasize the treaty's ostensible anti-German character, but it is far from clear, to say the least, whether the governments of Britain and France had been genuinely exercised by the threat of a resurgent Germany. The Germans, in any case, were in no position to complain, and there could be little doubt of the fact that hostility to Germany still formed the strongest common bond between Britain and France. Moreover, the treaty's anti-German character undermined the effectiveness of the protests which it provoked on the part of the Soviet Union, for it was very similar in style to the Franco-Soviet Treaty of December 1944.

The true emphasis of Bevin's diplomacy became clearer, however, one year later when the Benelux countries – Belgium, Holland and Luxemburg – were brought into a system of European defence through the Brussels Treaty of March 1948. The Brussels Treaty, unlike the Dunkirk one, was not specifically directed against German aggression. Article 4 enjoined its signatories to afford all possible military or other aid to any party to the treaty which had merely become 'the subject of armed attack in Europe'. Moscow reached the obvious conclusion that the treaty was directed against them; two weeks later the Soviet authorities inaugurated the Berlin blockade. This was not in fact primarily the result of the signing of the treaty – rather, the disputes between the Allied powers over Germany had reached a crisis point – but it served to reinforce Bevin's determination to make the treaty as effective as possible. To this end, therefore, he encouraged the development of a common military infrastructure, and in September 1948 the Defence Ministers of the Western Union (as the Brussels Treaty was known) met in Paris to establish a permanent organization under their own authority with headquarters at Fontainebleau as well as a Chiefs of Staff Committee under the leadership of Field-Marshal Montgomery. The French General Lattre de Tassigny was appointed Commander-in-Chief, Land Forces Western Europe, while a British Air Marshal was put in command of air forces and a French Vice-Admiral in command of ships. Joint planning and exercises soon got under way although, inevitably, there were disagreements between the British and the French. The British were less disposed than they might have been to accept the French on equal terms, and after one particular dispute with the French Attlee again gave lyrical expression to his 'national habit of mind'. 'What the hell right', he asked, 'have they got to criticize us? Tell them to go and clear up their own bloody stable. They haven't got any decent generals. They haven't had a decent general since Prince Eugene and he served their enemies.' European integration, even on matters of defence, would, it seemed, be beset by the usual disagreements over integration on the Continent.

Nonetheless, the more federalist-inclined European politicians who had had a hand in the creation of Western Union were determined as much as possible to make the result live up to the name. The French in particular were keen that more than just a common military structure should be the final result of the treaty and, spurred on by the currents of opinion which had manifested themselves at the Hague Congress that year, they persuaded the Ministerial Council of the Western Union to set up a committee on European Union under the chairmanship of Herriot, then President of the French National Assembly. This was duly established, but its efforts were soon deadlocked by British opposition to the proposed creation of a European Assembly. A compromise was reached in 1949 (by which time five more states had signed the Brussels Treaty), according to which a Council of Europe was to be created consisting of the Ministerial Council and a 'Consultative Assembly' of parliamentarians. Its aims, as might have been expected, were left deliciously vague: 'to achieve a greater unity between its members for the purpose of safeguarding and realizing the ideals and principles which are their common heritage and facilitating their economic and social progress'. Great Britain had thus succeeded in rendering the Council of Europe fairly harmless, and if further proof was needed that this body had been emasculated at birth it was to be found in the regulations governing the functioning of the Ministerial Council. A complex voting system had been established which laid down that in 'important matters' decisions could be taken only by a unanimous vote.

The creation of the Western Union had come about partly as a result of developments in Germany. For if Soviet policy towards Eastern Europe had disappointed the West – and 'alarmed' would be a better word to use in connection with the Communist *coup* in Czechoslovakia in February 1948 – their behaviour in Germany seemed uncooperative to the point of being threatening. The Western powers were as a result forced to pursue a new course towards their former enemy, the consequence of which was the *de facto* division of Germany which persists to the present day. This had in no way been intended when the war in Europe had come to an end, but as the cold war lowered the political temperature it had become the unavoidable consequence of ideological hostility and economic disputes. As the Russians cut off grain supplies to the Western zones and stripped their own of industrial plant, Bevin was determined not to allow them 'to loot Germany at our expense'. In other words, Britain and the United States were not going to be forced to pay for German recovery, and if no agreement could be reached with the Soviet Union (and none was) the Western zones would be allowed to unite and develop as a new and separate state, a process which was well under way by 1948.

Inevitably, this invited Soviet counter-measures. Thus two weeks after the signing of the Brussels Treaty the Soviet Union restricted Western land access to Berlin, and nine days after the announcement of recommendations on Germany's political future she quit the four-power military command in Berlin. Thereafter an attempt was made by the Soviets to extend a currency reform to East Berlin, a move which forced the Western powers to extend their own new currency reform to West Berlin and which in turn led the Russians to restrict all access by land to the city from the west. The Soviet objective seems to have been to starve West Berlin into political submission, but it was not to be. The United States, with considerable aid from Great Britain, organized the famous Berlin Air Lift, which supplied the beleaguered city by air for 324 days. The point was reached at one stage where Western supply aircraft were landing at three-minute intervals. In May 1949 the Russians admitted defeat and the blockade was lifted. The Soviet gamble had failed. Meanwhile the day when a West German state was established was brought much closer. This eventually came about once a West German constitution had been drawn up which could be approved by the Western powers and by the West German political parties. Elections were then held – in August 1949 – and as a result Konrad Adenauer was elected by the Bundestag as the first West German Federal Chancellor. The state over which he ruled was not yet sovereign but at least it was democratic. The foreign policy of Ernest Bevin had helped bring about this satisfactory state of affairs.

The events of the spring of 1948, however, had brought the world to the brink of a third world war. Had the West attempted to lift the Berlin blockade by land or had the Soviets attempted to interfere with the supply of West Berlin by air, it is perfectly possible that another world war would have been the outcome. Feelings in Europe were running high at the time and General Clay, the American commander in Berlin, reflected these emotions. After the Communist *coup* in Prague and the blockade of West Berlin – events which merged together in people's minds as evidence of the preliminary stages of Soviet aggression – he warned his superiors in Washington: 'A new tenseness in every Soviet individual with whom we have official relations ... gives me a feeling that war may come with dramatic suddenness.' Despite the relaxation of tension caused by the end of the blockade, therefore, a new appreciation was felt by leading Americans that more would have to be done for the security of Europe. Concern, in fact, had already been shown as early as June 1948, when an epoch-making resolution had been passed by the US Senate. Introduced by Senator Vandenberg, this had urged that the United States should associate itself 'by constitutional process, with such regional and other collective arrangements as are based on continuous and effective self-help and mutual aid and as affect its national security'. Passed by sixty-four votes to four, this resolution clearly opened the way for the United States to adhere to the Brussels Pact. Exploratory talks were therefore held with the Western Union states and Canada in July 1948, and more detailed negotiations were conducted between December 1948 and April 1949. President Truman was able to declare in his inaugural address in January 1949 that America was working out with a number of countries 'a joint agreement designed to strengthen the security of the North Atlantic', and on 12 April 1949 he submitted a North Atlantic Treaty for the advice and consent of the Senate. Some alterations were made to accommodate those who feared for the rights of Congress, but on 21 July approval was overwhelmingly expressed when the Senate voted to accept the treaty by eighty-three votes to thirteen. The document provided for a twenty-year defensive and military alliance with Western Europe which was to continue automatically unless two years' notice of termination was given. In respect of America's traditional relations with Europe, therefore, it was clearly revolutionary. By the tortuous wording of Article 5, the parties agreed in future that an armed attack against one or more of them in Europe or North America shall be considered an attack against all of them and consequently agree that, if such an armed attack occurs, each of them, in exercise of his right of individual or collective self-defence ... will assist the party or parties so attacked by taking forthwith, individually and in concert with other parties, such action as it deems necessary, including the use of armed force, to restore and maintain the security of the North Atlantic area.

Moreover, the Atlantic Pact of 4 April 1949 did not really apply merely to the North Atlantic for, besides Canada, the United States and the Brussels powers, not only were Norway, Portugal, Italy and Iceland signatories but soon too were Greece and Turkey. Bevin's insistence, which dated back to 1945, that the Mediterranean should also be protected, had therefore been taken into account. Some critics complained at the time that the tortuous wording of Article 5 meant that the treaty in fact lacked teeth, but they were almost certainly wrong. For even before it had been finally ratified by the US Senate it had already won a significant victory. The lifting of the Berlin blockade meant that Stalin had admitted that once again he had committed a diplomatic blunder, and the nations of the Western world could regard the treaty with reassurance and satisfaction. Bevin, indeed, looked upon it as the crowning work of his career, the commitment which at last tied America to Europe. Its significance was everywhere accepted. The French Foreign Minister noted: 'Today we obtain what we sought between the two wars', while Truman declared: 'If [this document] had existed in 1914 and 1939, supported by the nations who are represented today, I believe it would have prevented the acts of aggression which led to two world wars.' With the signing of the North Atlantic Treaty, therefore, it seemed that a decisive step had been taken to prevent the outbreak of the Third World War. The feeling was widespread that the United States had at last come to terms with its destiny and that the balance of power would be preserved. Ernest Bevin could take pride that his diplomacy had in no small measure contributed to America's new position.

PARTY POLITICS, 1945–50

The election débâcle of 1945 was a bitter blow to Churchill and the Conservative Party, but it was a blow from which they would recover. Churchill, predictably, got over his defeat in his own fashion and left the Conservatives to be reorganized by others. However, the former wartime premier did not assume the mantle of Opposition leader very easily. Despite – perhaps because of – his behaviour during the election campaign, he now conducted himself as a world statesman who could not be expected to spend his time indulging in the posturing partisanship of Tory Party opposition. He limited himself, therefore, to making statements of international significance on topics of defence and foreign policy – statements which were designed not merely to define the position of the Conservative Party but also to influence national and international opinion. His speeches at Fulton, Zurich and the Hague were all a piece in this respect and the effect which they produced was a measure of the success of his strategy. Nor could the Conservative Party reasonably complain about the wisdom of such tactics – Churchill was always in the news and what he said resounded with the *gravitas* of statesmanship.

Yet it was all too apparent from the party point of view that Churchill's contribution to party policy, particularly on home affairs, was somewhat less than positive. He did make speeches on internal matters, but they were delivered without the conviction – and failed to produce the impact – of his speeches on foreign affairs. Not one of them was destined to be remembered. In his handling of the Shadow Cabinet Churchill also failed to give a lead. Gatherings were social rather than businesslike in character, with the result that sometimes the agenda was not even discussed. Moreover, in his fear of giving hostages to fortune in the shape of party promises, Churchill tended to force the party to stick to principles rather than to details. Speakers were not encouraged to concentrate on any particular field of policy and in debates in the House of Commons a member of the Shadow Cabinet might be put up to speak on anything. No doubt this made for broad perspectives and encouraged a sense of intellectual cohesion, but it led Harold Macmillan to complain of Churchill's outdated sense of the grandiose and Lord Woolton to warn against the danger of sounding vague. If Conservatives were really changing, they complained, it would be harmful to leave the nation with the impression that its philosophy still dated from the thirties.

One must be careful, on the other hand, not to exaggerate the negative aspects of Churchill's leadership, for, despite his individualist approach, his presence was arguably a factor which encouraged party change. A case can be made out that his ideals of 'Tory democracy', that is, of a paternalist but magnanimous state that would intervene to protect the underprivileged members of society, constituted a very effective screen behind which the necessary party re-thinking could proceed. From this point of view it was useful in the final analysis for Tory reformers in their struggle against the party reactionaries to have at the helm of the party a pilot whose faith in traditional institutions was known to be as robust as his love of country. In this way, changes could take place in party policy without endangering party unity. They might not be the products of Churchillian initiative but Churchill made no attempt to block them.

Changes were thus made with regard to both party policy and organization. As far as organization was concerned, there was a general recognition that something badly needed to be done. The election defeat in 1945 had been aided by the deficient state of the party machine and as a result of that defeat the morale of party workers had in no way been improved. Moreover, since Conservative organization had traditionally been better than the Labour Party's at election times, there was clearly an urgent need to restore the previous position if the verdict of the electors was to be reversed. The man entrusted with the job of achieving this was the wartime Minister of Food, Lord Woolton. He had been a well-known and popular figure during the war years – when he had acquired the nickname 'Uncle Fred' – although, curiously enough, he had only joined the Conservative Party in 1945. Churchill, however, had been impressed by Woolton's skill as an administrator and in 1946 he appointed him Conservative Party Chairman. His first impulse in that capacity was to scrap the Tory party machinery altogether, but on second thoughts he decided to concentrate on increasing party membership and funds. Both objectives were achieved and it was even possible to introduce in 1948 a rule forbidding candidates to donate more than £25 per annum to constituency funds. This was designed not merely to show that wealth was not a necessary prerequisite to advancement within the party; it was also meant to stimulate fund-raising and other activities within the constituencies. The Maxwell-Fyfe Committee, which had just reported on the state of the party machinery, had noticed that 'the organization of the party was weakest in those places where a wealthy candidate had made it unnecessary for the members to trouble to collect small subscriptions'. Steps were therefore taken to ensure that such disincentives were removed and the party was encouraged to open its doors to wider membership and talent. The result of Woolton's work (as well as of the Maxwell-Fyfe Committee's report) was the emergence almost everywhere of better-organized and larger constituency parties, so that by 1950 there were no less than 527 full-time local agents in England and Wales alone. The Labour Party employed approximately half that number in Great Britain as a whole. There can be little doubt that this radical improvement in organization paid dividends. In the general election of 1950 it has been estimated that through the determined soliciting of postal votes the party was able to win at least ten extra seats, and henceforward at election times the old Conservative advantage of superior organization was once again maintained.

The reforms within the party had more than merely a mechanical significance. Not only did they give some meaning to Tory faith in individualism and participation, they also fitted in quite smoothly with attempts to educate the party more politically. Thus through the organization of Conservative Political Centres it was possible to sound out the views of local organizations on party policy so that the rate of change in political thinking could proceed at a pace acceptable to all. Internal party communication was thereby much improved and it is not without significance that there was a relative lack of dissent when major policy statements came up for endorsement.

New thinking on party policy had begun as early as 1941 with the establishment under the guidance of Butler and Maxwell-Fyfe of the Post-war Problems Committee. In 1945 this body was transformed into the Advisory Committee on Policy and Political Education. By the end of the war, however, not a great deal had been achieved. Conservative ministers had been restrained by the demands placed upon them by their own departments, and the work of the party committee had necessarily been overshadowed by the Government's Reconstruction Committee headed by Lord Woolton. Finally, the frigid atmosphere of Churchill's wartime coalition had not encouraged party-political policy initiatives so that pressure on the party had tended to be exerted from the backbenches through groups of parliamentarians such as the Tory Reform Group led by Quintin Hogg and Lord Hinchingbrooke. The latter had had some success in pressing the acceptance of the Beveridge Report on Conservative ministers, and it had exerted pressure on a number of other issues also. At the very least it could claim that it had encouraged Tories to question their assumptions, and with the party's defeat in 1945 this process inevitably continued.

Just as Lord Woolton had been the chief architect of the Conservative Party's internal reforms, the chief architect of its policy changes was R. A. Butler. Already famous for his 1944 Education Act, Butler was now presented with the opportunity of further influencing social and economic policy after his appointment in November 1945 as Chairman of the Conservative Research Department. He was assisted in his work by some of the brightest Conservative hopefuls, including future ministers such as Maudling, Powell and Macleod. Other figures within the party also offered powerful political and intellectual support. Oliver Lyttleton and David Maxwell-Fyfe were two, but also important was the wartime Minister-Resident in North Africa and pre-war figure of the Conservative left, Harold Macmillan, the author of the book *The Middle Way*, and someone who, like other Tory reformers, saw his task as one of bringing up to date the principles of Burke, Peel and especially Disraeli. Anthony Eden, it is important to add, also lent his support to reformist trends within the party.

Two years were to pass before any substantial results emerged from Conservative re-thinking. Then in 1947 the party's 'Industrial Charter' was produced by an Industrial Policy Committee. This was, in effect, a declaration by the party that it now accepted a welfare state and a managed economy. As Butler was later to put it: 'The Charter was . . . an assurance that, in the interests of efficiency, full employment and social security, modern Conservatism would maintain strong central guidance over the operation of the economy.' There was a lurking fear, however, in the minds of some of its authors, that despite its deliberately boring style, the document might be rejected either by Churchill or by the rank and file. In 1947, therefore, Eden was given the job of presenting the report to the annual conference, a ploy which succeeded admirably. Eden declared that the party was not a 'party of unbridled, brutal capitalism' and, reminding delegates of their tradition of social reform, succeeded in getting the report accepted. In fact, there was comparatively little opposition to overcome within the party. Everyone was only too concerned to lay the foundations of a future electoral victory, so that the 'Industrial Charter' could be followed up by statements on agriculture, the Empire, Scotland and Wales. The party committed itself to extending social services as well as to reducing taxation. Its policy of encouraging private enterprise, it was hoped, would enable it to do both. It would be a mistake, however, to believe that reforms in party policy and organization themselves revitalized the Tory Party by 1950. It is true that they played their part, but Conservative self-confidence was only really restored after 1951 (perhaps even 1953). In the meantime the mistakes and failings of the Labour government were at least as important in restoring opposition morale as any remedial efforts of their own. However, these years in opposition were very important ones for Conservatives.

THE GENERAL ELECTION OF 1950

With the approach of 1949 the political parties began to prepare themselves for the next general election, which had to be held by July 1950 at the latest. The Labour government were anxious most of all to see an upturn in the economy and to rid themselves, if possible, of rationing and controls. But since the fate of the economy depended on external as well as internal factors, their hands were inevitably tied. Nonetheless, the young President of the Board of Trade, Harold Wilson, did all in his power to demonstrate to the public exactly what the Government's intentions were, so that bit by bit, from 1948 onwards, controls were dismantled as fast as prudence allowed. Potato rationing was ended in the spring of 1948, bread rationing in July and jam rationing in December. Clothes rationing was eased, footwear ceased to be rationed altogether and on 4 November 1948 Wilson proudly declared that the need for no less than 20,000 licences and permits had been removed since February. In March 1949 the Board of Trade announced the removal of yet another 900,000 licences – a 'bonfire of controls', in Wilson's words, which heralded the end of all clothes and textile rationing later in the month and the doubling of the petrol ration for the summer. Meat still remained in short supply, but there could be little doubt in which direction the Government was moving.

1949, however, was not the Government's best year economically. Cripps was forced to devalue the pound and even the Government's ability to plan the economy of underdeveloped colonies came under heavy attack with the collapse of the East African groundnuts scheme. This had been launched in 1946 under the Government's new Commonwealth legislation in an attempt to reduce the UK deficit of oils and fats as much as to increase African employment and had been described by John Strachey, the Minister of Food, as 'one of the most courageous, imaginative and well-judged acts of this Government for the sake of the world that has been taken in the life of this Parliament'. By 1949 the scheme had come to nought, at a cost to the taxpayer of £36,500,000, having provided neither groundnuts nor margarine for Britain nor employment for the Africans. The groundnuts could have been used to increase the margarine ration in Britain; but even had they materialized no provision had been made for the transport needed to bring them here.

In 1949, too, the passage of the Parliament Act as well as the introduction of the Government's proposals on iron and steel had revived the debate on nationalization, something about which the Government were none too happy. The Cabinet had lost their enthusiasm for nationalization and were worried about the opposition the measure would arouse in the country. They therefore agreed, in return for the House of Lords' withdrawal of certain amendments to the Bill, not to make any appointments to the Iron and Steel Corporation until 1 October 1950, nor to transfer properties to the Corporation until 1 January 1951. In other words, they would not proceed with the nationalization of iron and steel until the country had had an opportunity to vote on the issue.

Politically speaking, this was a bad decision, for it gave the go-ahead to private enterprise to launch a campaign against the Government's proposals. The steelmakers in particular were keen to persuade the public of the danger and stupidity involved in any nationalization measures, and they were afforded massive assistance by other private companies which suspected the Government of harbouring hostile intentions towards their own interests. Thus agents were mobilized by insurance companies – which set up 400 anti-nationalization committees up and down the country – and used as doorstep canvassers against the Government's programme. The most spirited campaign in favour of private enterprise was waged by Tate and Lyle, the sugar refiners. All the techniques of modern advertising were employed, and the result, to quote A. A. Rogow's study of *The Labour Government and British Industry, 1945–51*, was:

Mr Cube, a cartoon-style figure sugar lump proclaiming anti-nationalization slogans, appeared each day on more than two million sugar packages, on 100,000 ration book holders distributed to housewives by Tate and Lyle and on all Tate and Lyle delivery trucks. Propaganda was inserted into material on the sugar refining industry sent out to 4,500 schools. Six mobile vans toured the entire United Kingdom and more than 3,000 speeches and lectures were delivered to factory and working-men's clubs, youth and university organizations, women's clubs, schools and even groups of soldiers in His Majesty's Forces. Stories or news items concerned with sugar and sponsored by Aims [i.e., Aims of Industry, the public-relations firm founded to promote business interests and employed by Tate and Lyle] filled 15,000 column inches in 400 newspapers, approximately £200,000 worth of space.

All this, of course, was grist to the Conservative mill, but Lord Woolton was careful to dissociate his party from these campaigns. The issue, he proclaimed, should be debated thoroughly as soon as an election was called, at which time the industrial campaigns should stop.

Churchill had meanwhile laid down the guidelines for the Conservative assault. 'Socialism,' he said, 'with its vast network of regulations and restrictions and its incompetent planning and purchasing by Whitehall officials, [was] proving itself every day to be a dangerous and costly fallacy.' He continued: 'Every major industry which the Socialists have nationalized, without exception, has passed from the profitable or self-supporting side of the balance sheet to the loss-making, debit side . . .' In short, the Tories would attack the Government's economic record and their programme of nationalization. The Welfare State, on the other hand, was not an issue. The Conservative Party had reconciled itself to that, and indeed it was an error in Labour's strategy not to seize upon this fact and to exploit it. In fact the Tories were able to capitalize upon their acceptance of the Welfare State by making themselves appear as men of moderation in contradistinction to Labour's class warriors. For Labour spokesmen had given many a hostage to fortune in this respect, with Bevan declaiming that the Tories were 'lower than vermin', Shinwell announcing that he 'didn't give a tinker's cuss' except for organized labour, and Mrs Bessie Braddock proclaiming: 'I don't care two hoots at any time if the other side is not alright; I don't care if they starve to death.' Such statements did not easily match up to Labour's claim to be constructing a new and more humane society.

All these statements had been made before 1950. When the election came in February that year, it turned out to be a 'demure' affair after all. This was Churchill's own description of it, and there were few who would have quarrelled with him, for when the battalions came to fight it out they did so over a remarkably narrow battle-ground. The reason was fairly obvious: the Welfare State had already been accepted and, despite suggestions by the Tories that it was proving unnecessarily expensive, there was no proposal to dismantle it. Nationalization was, of course, an issue, but not one on which the Labour government was anxious to launch a new crusade. Their policy document for 1949 entitled *Labour Believes in Britain*, had marked down a rather curious list of priorities for public ownership, and its 1950 manifesto, *Let Us Win Through Together*, had not pursued the matter with any forthrightness. It was, in fact, an open secret that leading Labour politicians had had their fill of nationalization. On matters of foreign policy and defence there was likewise little debate. Churchill was to claim in 1952 that 'the whole substance and purpose of what [he had been saying had been] adopted and enforced by the Socialist Government', and he praised the 'foresight and wise courage' of the by then deceased Ernest Bevin. Eden, in turn, was later to recall how often he and Bevin had discussed foreign affairs in private, adding, 'I would publicly have agreed with him more, if I had not been anxious to embarrass him less.' The real critics of Bevin's foreign policy had been found within the Labour Party, although even there the debate was not as forthright as it might have been. The old 'Keep Left' group of 1946 had by 1950 published a second pamphlet, *Keeping Left*, which had, however reluctantly, accepted the American alliance, and for those who were not prepared to do this the room for manoeuvre was extremely small. Five MPs between 1945 and 1950 were expelled from the Parliamentary Labour Party for 'fellow-travelling', and in the cold-war atmosphere of the time this meant the effective end of their political careers. There was, however, one foreign policy exchange in the course of the election campaign itself which came when Churchill, to everyone's surprise, proposed 'another talk with Soviet Russia upon the highest level' in a 'supreme effort' to end the 'hatred and manoeuvres of the cold war'. Labour leaders immediately dismissed the suggestion as an election stunt but no doubt they wished that it had been they who had made it in the first place. All they could do by way of reply was to recount the difficulties involved in negotiating with the Russians while Churchill persisted in his view that issues of life and death were proper subjects for electoral debate.

What the voters thought about all this was to be known very shortly. They were voting under slightly different circumstances this time, since Labour's Representation of the People Act of 1949 had abolished university representation, the business premises' vote and the representation of the City of London as a separate constituency. It had also created seventeen additional constituencies. For all that, it would be fairly easy to compare the voting results with those of 1945, and the verdict of the polls was as follows:

Party	Votes gained	Percentage of vote	Average vote per MP	Number of MPs
Conservative	12,502,567	43·5	41,955	298
Labour	13,266,592	46·1	42,116	315
Liberal	2,621,548	9·1	291,283	9
Communist	91,746	0·3	—	—
Others	290,218	1·0		3
	28,772,671	100·0		625

Source: Derived from D. Butler and A. Sloman, *British Political Facts, 1900–75.*

The electorate had proved to be extremely interested: the poll was 10½ per cent up on that of 1945 and at 84 per cent the heaviest recorded in British history. This meant that nearly 4 million more voters than last time had turned out on polling day. The results of the election were somewhat paradoxical: Labour had received more votes than at any other time in its history, but it had also seen its overall majority reduced to only five. The Liberal and Communist parties had lost further ground, despite increased numbers of candidates. Finally, the Conservative Party had failed to win the election although it had gained an extra 2 million votes. There had been a swing to the Tories of 3·3 per cent, a swing which was most marked in the suburbs of the south. Labour had frightened the middle classes in the suburbs of the home counties and the north as well, although it survived this loss of popularity because it could count on enthusiastic working-class support. Both parties, in fact, could see in the election results some form of moral victory: the Conservatives on account of their impressive gain in seats, Labour on account of its unprecedented number of votes. It was the Labour Party, however, which had won the victory which mattered. For the Liberal and Communist Parties there was simply no consolation. 319 out of 475 Liberal candidates lost their deposits, while their parliamentary representation was cut from eleven to nine. Ninety-seven out of 100 Communist candidates lost their deposits and not a single one this time was elected.

Needless to say, the electoral system once more held back the Liberals. It took only 42,000 votes to elect a Labour or Conservative MP, while to elect a Liberal member, on the other hand, required almost 300,000 votes.

| # THE LABOUR GOVERNMENT, 1950–51

The election over, the Labour government returned to office, albeit physically and ideologically exhausted. Hugh Gaitskell later confessed: 'Most of us who were in the 1945–50 Parliament knew that we just about had as much as we could conceivably digest in those five years.' The new government did not present parliament with much in the way of a legislative programme, and the King's Speech in March 1950 was a very dull affair. Practically the only controversial measure to which the Government committed themselves was the nationalization of iron and steel, a legacy from the previous parliament. The vesting date for this had been set for February 1951 and, some truculence on the part of the Iron and Steel Federation notwithstanding – a sort of managerial boycott had been threatened – the Government were able to push their legislation through. This apart, the Cabinet were hoping for a quiet life: they had, after all, only a small working majority which made parliamentary life very difficult. Sick MPs were having to be brought into the Commons on stretchers, and, in the words of Herbert Morrison, 'the Inner Lobby was not a pleasing sight'. Moreover, the party leaders were old and ailing: Cripps and Bevin would retire from office before the next election, and Dalton, Morrison and Attlee seemed destined to end their political careers quite shortly. Under these circumstances, not much was to be expected from the Government and, indeed, not very much was achieved.

To begin with, all went well. Cripps produced a cautious, 'no-change' budget, limiting food subsidies to £140 million, reducing income tax for the less well-off, while raising the level of tax on petrol and commercial vehicles. In similar fashion, the Economic Survey for 1950 outlined a very modest series of objectives which led the *Economist* to describe it as a 'humble document, weak almost to the point of being meaningless'.

The Government's good fortune, however, did not last. On 25 June 1950 North Korean forces invaded South Korea and any hopes that the Government had of avoiding the political limelight quickly disappeared when the United Nations, taking advantage of the temporary absence of the Soviet delegation, condemned North Korea's act of aggression.

Foreign affairs in general did not go well for the second post-war Labour Government. Problems arose in the Middle East and in Europe which proved difficult to solve, while the Korean War turned out to be an unmitigated disaster.

As far as the Middle East was concerned, problems arose in Iran and Egypt. In Iran the Prime Minister, Dr Mussadegh, attempted an act of socialism much bolder than anything ever contemplated by Britain's Labour leaders by taking over the Anglo-Iranian Oil Company, which controlled the Iranian oil-fields. The premier, not unnaturally, desired to run this monopoly in the interests of Iran. His approach to the problem demonstrated, on the other hand, an arguable lack of sophistication. Instead of extorting higher payments from, and greater representation on, the board of the company concerned, he persuaded the Majlis (Parliament) to nationalize the oil-fields. This, in fact, did not begin to solve his problem since Iran lacked both a tanker fleet and marketing organization with which to sell the oil produced, so that eventually some sort of compromise had to be worked out.

Mussadegh's dramatic gesture created an irritable and unenviable problem for Britain's Labour government and in particular for Herbert Morrison, who had succeeded Bevin as Foreign Secretary. Morrison had little experience of foreign affairs – it was said of him that whereas Bevin could not pronounce the names of foreign places, he did not know where they were – yet he possessed instinctive Palmerstonian reactions in a crisis. Over Persia, therefore, he was in favour of 'sharp and forceful action' but found that he was simply in no position to carry any out. Thus he contented himself with organizing naval demonstrations in the Persian Gulf and explaining to his colleagues why tougher action would probably fail. The Americans were afraid of an anti-imperialist backlash in the area as well as of the possibility of Soviet intervention, and without US approval the Government were in no position to undertake a major military operation. Thus, thanks to American diplomatic sagacity and British unpreparedness, the Labour government were saved from an imperial war with Persia. Events in Iran, however, served to exacerbate Britain's mounting difficulties with Egypt.

Egypt, whose treaty with Great Britain was due to expire in 1956, had been of crucial strategic importance to Britain in the course of the Second World War. With the end of the war it was still of tremendous importance on account of the Suez Canal. Yet clearly a new relationship would have to be established between Great Britain and the Egyptians. The granting of independence to the Indian sub-continent as well as the cost of bases in the Suez Canal Zone was causing Britain to reconsider her position. The rise of Asian nationalism as well as the example of Mussadegh weakened Egypt's desire to cooperate with London. Negotiations therefore took place to establish a compromise agreement between competing imperial and national claims. The issues at stake were control of the Suez Canal and the presence of British troops. These negotiations started in 1946 but largely on account of Egypt's claim to the Sudan, a claim which Britain refused to recognize, they never reached a successful conclusion and were still proceeding when Morrison succeeded Bevin at the Foreign Office. In October 1951, a fateful stage was reached. Egypt abrogated the 1936 Treaty and proclaimed her monarch, Faruq, King of Sudan. Morrison was once again placed in a difficult and frustrating position, and this time his performance appeared more pitiful than usual since British military and civilian personnel in the Canal Zone were made the objects of a violent nationalist campaign. Morrison did what he could to protect them, but his response, inevitably, seemed weak and undignified and the impression was reinforced that he simply was not up to the job. Two other issues had undermined his position in this respect. The escape of the Foreign Office spies, Burgess and Maclean, to Moscow in May 1951 had badly damaged the prestige of his department, while the signing of the ANZUS pact in September delivered a more substantial blow to British policy. To many it seemed good fortune that with regard to Europe and the Far East the guidelines of British policy had already been laid down by Bevin.

The problem arising in Europe concerned the future of Western Germany. The invasion of South Korea had caused a panic in Western Europe, where Stalin was feared to be preparing to launch an attack against the West. This, of course, was nonsense. Stalin had turned his attention to Korea because he had been rebuffed in Western Europe and was under the mistaken belief – derived from a misreading of important

American policy speeches – that the United States would not involve itself in a land war in Asia. At the time, however, it was difficult to divine the dictator's intentions and the Germans in particular were alarmed by the parlous state of their defence arrangements. Four weak British and American divisions alone protected them from twenty-two of the Soviet Union's, which were backed by the military potential of the East German 'People's Police'. Moreover, the early Communist victories which were being reported from Korea did nothing to bolster faith in the credibility of the Western Alliance.

Something clearly had to be done to restore the morale of West German public opinion. Adenauer proposed the creation of a West German Federal Police Force consisting of 150,000 men while simultaneously demanding a demonstration of military strength on the part of the Western Allies. He also gave his approval to a speech made at this time by Winston Churchill who suggested the creation of a European army. Churchill had made this speech without consulting Bevin; in the army which he proposed he foresaw the inclusion of German troops. Bevin did not like the plan, nor did the French and German Socialists, but when the foreign ministers of Britain, France and the USA met in New York in September 1950 to discuss the German question all sorts of possible solutions were discussed throughout the course of very tough and exacting negotiations. Bevin backed the Adenauer plan; the French put forward a complicated scheme for the political and economic integration of NATO; the Americans refused to contemplate a larger military role in Europe unless provision were made to incorporate West German military units within a reformed alliance. To make matters more complicated, there were also divisions within these camps. Shinwell, the British Defence Minister, backed by his chiefs of staff, favoured West German rearmament, while the French planner, Jean Monnet, was known to be working on a separate scheme for a European army. In the end, a compromise was reached which temporarily shelved the question of West German military participation. The defence of Western Europe would be provided for by an integrated NATO army operating under a centralized command structure with an American supreme commander. Eisenhower was given this job in January 1951 and America committed more troops to the defence of Western Europe. The result was yet another success for Bevin despite the scrapping of the Adenauer plan: German rearmament had not yet come about; and, despite its supra-national elements, NATO represented a pragmatic Atlanticist advance rather than a concession to European federalism.

The federalists in Europe, however, were on the verge of a major victory. Thwarted by Britain over the issue of the constitution of the Council of Europe, they resolved that British nationalism should not in future sabotage their plans. The issue on which they chose to demonstrate their new determination was the proposed creation in May 1950 of a European Coal and Steel Community. The idea had originated, not surprisingly, in the fertile mind of Jean Monnet and was promoted politically and diplomatically by the French Foreign Minister, Robert Schuman. Both Frenchmen wanted to find a solution to the German problem; both were committed to the ideal of a federalist Europe. Since it was clear that Germany would in the long term recover from her defeat, they now sought to marry idealism with realism and to absorb a potentially powerful Germany within a supra-national framework. Thus in May 1950 came the announcement of the 'Schuman Plan'. France and Germany, the French Foreign Minister declared, should place the control of their coal and steel production under the aegis of a single High Authority; other countries could adhere to the scheme too, if they so desired, and in this way a very important step could be taken in the direction of European integration. The plan was evidently designed to obviate any future aggressive German rearmament but was presented in its other, genuinely idealistic, federalist guise.

The manner of its announcement had not been calculated to win British sympathy or support. Great Britain had not been consulted beforehand and the Labour government were bound to disapprove of the supra-nationalist implications of the scheme. Moreover, since British iron and steel were in the process of being nationalized, the project threatened to reopen a debate which seemed to be almost over. For what was the point of nationalization if control of the industries which had just been nationalized would pass immediately into foreign hands? British socialists had not conquered the commanding heights only to surrender them to German capitalists. It was little wonder, therefore, that the latest federalist proposals were received without enthusiasm in London. Finally, the fact that the American Secretary of State, Dean Acheson, had privately been warned of the scheme in advance and later accorded it his warm and wholehearted support led Bevin to believe that he was being made the victim of a diplomatic plot. Thus Attlee informed the House of Commons that the scheme would require detailed study and consideration. He sympathized with attempts to resolve Franco-German differences but could not commit his government to support the scheme immediately.

The French, however, were determined to retain the diplomatic initiative. Within a month of the announcement of the 'Schuman Plan' they invited Britain, Italy and the Benelux countries to enter into negotiations on the plan and placed upon these discussions the condition that the principle of supra-nationality should be accepted in advance. Britain, of course, could not accept this arrangement and argued that the details should be thrashed out first. Her objections were overruled and the discussions were held without her. Their outcome was the treaty signed in April 1951 which set up the European Coal and Steel Community. Recognizing what had happened, Great Britain now adopted a conciliatory attitude towards the newly established body and at the end of November 1951 appointed a permanent delegation to the High Authority.

Overshadowing all of these events was the outbreak of the Korean War. This not only committed British troops to action but involved the risk of a third world war. Since America's finger was on the atomic trigger, it also sharpened Anglo-American differences. Britain had to try to influence American military strategy from a position of relative military weakness and with a different political assessment of some of the problems involved.

Anglo-American differences over the threat posed by Communism in the Far East have often been exaggerated, however. British units were sent without demur to join United Nations' forces in South Korea and if the British government became concerned about the attitudes of the American commander, General MacArthur, so too did the American President, who dismissed him. The truth is that Great Britain, as much as America, was anxious to effect the containment of Communist China. She was spending £50 million per annum and employing more than 100,000 troops to combat Chinese influence in Malaya; moreover, as Churchill mischievously revealed in February 1952, in May and September of the previous year Morrison had acquiesced in portentous American contingency plans regarding Chinese action in Korea. Speaking in the House of Commons, Churchill stated:

... in May of last year, before the truce negotiations began ... the late Foreign Secretary replied to an inquiry [by the United States] that His Majesty's Government had decided that in the event of heavy air attacks from bases in China upon United Nations Forces in Korea, they would associate themselves with action not confined to Korea ... [Furthermore] in September last year the Americans proposed that in the event of a breakdown of the armistice talks and the resumption of large-scale fighting in Korea, certain action should be taken of a more limited character ... Whereas in May the right of prior consultation had been required by the late Government in the specific instance, before our consent could be assumed, in the more limited proposals of September the Socialist Government did not insist upon this right.

These revelations came as a considerable shock to those who had assumed that it was British policy to prevent a full-scale war breaking out between the United States and China. They were even more of a shock to those who were terrified by the prospect of the atomic bomb being used. For when the possibility of employing the bomb had been alluded to in a press conference by President Truman in the autumn of 1950, Attlee had, with uncharacteristic drama, found it necessary to fly to Washington for reassurances. His visit had turned out to be something of an embarrassment: Truman constitutionally could not give Attlee the guarantees which he demanded; he had no intention of using the atom bomb in any case; and Attlee somehow or other managed to give Acheson the impression that he wanted an American defeat in Korea. However, a form of words was agreed between the President and the Prime Minister which satisfied both men.

Despite this apparent agreement, British policy on the war as a whole was far from clear. Only on the issue of recognizing Communist China does it seem that a definite position was adopted – at least in the first instance. The Chinese civil war ended with Communist victory in 1949 and by 1950 the régime of Mao Tse-tung had firmly established its hold on power. In accordance with traditional British diplomatic practice, therefore, the British government wished to extend it diplomatic recognition. The United States opposed the move. The American government still recognized Chiang Kai-shek as leader of the Republic of China despite the fact that his forces had had to retreat from the Chinese mainland to Taiwan; Britain's policy on recognition, however illogically, was regarded as being 'soft on Communism'. In an attempt to keep the Americans happy, therefore, a compromise was reached. Britain recognized not only the new Communist régime in China but also the Chinese régime in Taiwan which, under American patronage, occupied the Chinese seat on the Security Council of the United Nations. The Labour government were, as usual, much softer on America than they had ever been on Communism.

By 1951 Britain had almost reached the stage of producing her own atomic bomb. The decision to manufacture one had been taken as early as 1946, even before the passage of the US McMahon Act which that year ended Anglo-American nuclear cooperation. Work on the bomb had continued steadily although progress was screened from both Parliament and from the Cabinet. Macmillan was to record that Attlee had 'succeeded in the important and invaluable task of making the atomic bomb for Britain without even informing Parliament by hiding away by some manipulation of the estimates the necessary £100 million'. The Defence White Papers between 1945 and 1951 contained scarcely a single reference to the development of atomic energy and as late as December 1949 the Ministry of Defence could inform the public that it was not in its interest to reveal whether Great Britain possessed the bomb or not – despite the fact that possession of such a weapon made Great Britain a primary Soviet target in the event of a third world war.

The Conservative Opposition connived in the Government's stand, so that what resistance there was to Government policy was expressed from the Labour back-benches. Emrys Hughes, for instance, protesting at the difficulties he encountered in obtaining information about Britain's bomb, declared: 'When we ask questions in this House about it, one would think that an atomic bomb had been dropped. When an Hon. Member asks the Prime Minister about the atomic bomb, he looks at him as if he had asked something indecent.' The bomb was successfully tested in 1952, with results that are difficult for the contemporary historian to gauge. What difference it made strategically perhaps only Soviet military strategists can tell. Diplomatically, it seemed to put (or help keep) Great Britain on the same level as the USA and the USSR. At any rate, it enabled Britain to enter future negotiations with the super-powers on how to get rid of what had been created. Whether this enhanced the prestige of British diplomacy much more than the Duke of York had enhanced the prestige of the British army 150 years before, it is also hard to tell. There is certainly a case to be made out to the effect that building up the British economy would in the long run have done more for Britain's position in the world than did the bomb. However, it was not until the later 1950s that the force of arguments over 'guns versus butter' began to be apparent. Meanwhile, British diplomatic influence was better served by the size of her conventional forces, now boosted by conscription.

Conscription had never been a popular cause within the Labour Party, but in March 1947 a National Service Bill was introduced by the Labour government which provided for a call-up period of eighteen months. Seventy-two Labour MPs defied the whip on the issue and the Government contemplated reducing the length of the call-up period to twelve months as a result. A threatened revolt on the part of the army chiefs of staff led by Montgomery, however, ensured that the original terms of the Bill survived. The Act came into operation on 1 January 1949 and Montgomery confessed that 'when all is said and done one must pay tribute to the courage of the Labour Government'.

Given the need to tie America to Europe, not to mention the lack of a German army and the inexperience of the French one, Britain at this time could only maintain a large standing army. She was the leading European power and had an obligation to defend the gains of the Second World War. America apart, no other nation was capable of defending Western Europe, and her crucial role was demonstrated both by the Berlin Crisis of 1948 and by the organization of NATO after 1950. For if the former signified the restoration of the Anglo-American alliance, the latter virtually enshrined it. Thus NATO's standing body was little more than the revival of the Second World War Chiefs of Staff Committee save for the addition of France, and SHAPE (its headquarters) was to all intents and purposes the reincarnation of SHAEF (Allied headquarters in Europe during the war). Appointments, too, reflected the importance of Anglo-American power. General Eisenhower was NATO's first Supreme Commander; Lord Ismay, its first Secretary-General. Thus the so-called 'special relationship' was based on military realities as well as on sentiment and diplomatic expediency. For this reason Britain was able to resist American economic and diplomatic pressures, which might otherwise have been compelling. For instance, Britain could have come under overwhelming US pressure to abandon traditional Commonwealth ties in order to form part of a more integrated Western European trading block. As it was, Senator McCarren, Chairman of the Senate Foreign Aid Committee, was forced to confess by

1950: 'The fact is that in spite of the many policies which the United States has in common with the United Kingdom, despite the great good will which the two nations have for each other, the British objectives with respect to European integration are fundamentally opposed to those of the United States.' So long as Britain made a special contribution to Europe's, and indeed the world's, defence, she could not be treated like just another European nation. The time would come when the cost of Britain's defence bill would undermine her ability to make that special contribution and thus would limit her diplomatic freedom in a way in which as yet it had not been restricted. The Korean War gave a hint that fundamental choices, a re-ordering of priorities, might soon become necessary, but the time for really big decisions had not yet finally arrived.

The Korean War was nonetheless in many ways decisive. It brought about the integration of the Western Alliance, it heralded the rearmament of Western Germany, and it consolidated America's change of heart about the world and her place within it. In all these respects – quite apart from the failure of the North Koreans to subjugate their 'comrades' in the South – it represented a colossal diplomatic failure on the part of Stalin. On a less exalted level, the Korean War had yet another consequence: it gave rise to a quarrel inside the Labour Party which helped defeat the Labour Party at the general election of October 1951.

The quarrel concerned the means of paying for the enormous rearmament programme which the Government, under pressure from both Churchill and the Americans, announced in September 1950. This was to cost no less than £3,600 million over a period of three years (the figure was revised upwards to £4,700 million in January 1951) and was aimed at establishing six to ten regular army divisions. An extra £830 millions had to be found for the year 1951–2 and the man who had to find it was Cripps's successor as Chancellor, Hugh Gaitskell. On 10 April he introduced his budget, and put guns before butter: income tax was increased by 6d. in the pound; purchase tax on motor cars, radios and domestic appliances was doubled; and the tax on distributed profits was raised from 30 to 50 per cent, despite the abolition of initial allowances. Most important politically was the Chancellor's decision to charge adult patients of the National Health Service half the cost of their spectacles and dentures in future. This led to the resignations from the Government of Aneurin Bevan, Harold Wilson and John Freeman. It also led the *Daily Express* to describe the budget as a truly 'Tory' measure. Bevan and Wilson spelled out their disagreements with the Chancellor in their resignation speeches. They did not believe that the Government's programme was a 'physically practicable' one, given the resources available; moreover, the decision to levy charges on National Health Service patients, they maintained, could be justified neither by necessity nor by principle. Taking £13 million out of a budget total of £4,000 million, at a time when Treasury estimates were usually hundreds of millions of pounds out, was condemned by Bevan as 'the arithmetic of Bedlam'. Wilson said: 'It is a minor cut, I agree, but I cannot believe it to be necessary.' Gaitskell had proved remarkably insensitive politically in drawing up his balance-sheets, and in retrospect it is hard to avoid the conclusion that the ministers who resigned were right. Their resignations, on the other hand, did nothing to help a government which had only recently lost the services of both Bevin and Cripps. It was now clearly divided and saddled with a failure at the Foreign Office, a politically unsure Chancellor and an ageing Prime Minister. It was also about to face an economic crisis which it unnecessarily bungled.

A balance-of-payments crisis arose in the summer of 1951 which was simply not anticipated. 1950 had seen exports reach the staggering total of £2,254 million compared with £920 million in 1946, and the Government had been so pleased at what they took to be the firm re-establishment of the export trade that they had been rash enough to dispense with a possible further year's quota of Marshall Aid as well as to remove the extra import restrictions which had been imposed at the time of Cripps's devaluation. The outbreak of the Korean War should have tempered this optimism: imports rose in 1951 from £2,390 to £3,501 million due to stocking up for rearmament and to the expansion of domestic trade, and the sharp rise in world commodity prices following closely on devaluation meant that the general rise in the price of imports amounted to 50 per cent. Meanwhile a large round of wage increases as well as the ministerial resignations served to undermine international confidence in the pound.

Speculative pressure against sterling was answered with little style or resolution. The restrictions which had been removed in 1950 were simply reimposed and no thought was lent to levying import quotas or even to the possibility of organizing stand-by credits. Least of all was any consideration given to a cutting-back of the rearmament programme, and the Government appeared to lack the political will to do anything but rely on the orthodox advice of their civil servants. It was Douglas Jay, after all, who had proclaimed that the 'man in Whitehall' 'knew best' and so, in the words of Richard Crossman, 'in 1951 the Attlee government quietly expired in the arms of the Whitehall Establishment'. Parliament was dissolved on 5 October when the Government, most likely from sheer exhaustion, let the voters take control.

THE GENERAL ELECTION OF OCTOBER 1951

If the 1950 general election had been demure, the 1951 campaign was scarcely more exciting. Labour's manifesto avoided any specific pledge on nationalization and – if cynics can be believed – on practically anything else for that matter. The Conservative Party promised, if elected, to build 300,000 houses per year, a promise which, like Churchill's offer during the previous election campaign to hold talks with the Russians, was dismissed by Labour as rank electioneering. However, since the country was at war, the topic most debated was the relative ability of the parties to lead the nation at such a time, and since Churchill obviously had claims to some experience in this regard, a large part of the Labour Party's efforts was devoted to rebuffing them. Labour went out of its way to represent Churchill and his colleagues as war-mongers. The *Daily Mirror*'s headline on election day – 'Whose Finger On The Trigger' – gave rise to a famous libel suit. Actually, by election day the theme was hardly a new one. Labour speakers everywhere had denounced the Tory threat to peace. Herbert Morrison suggested that the Conservatives would have started a war with Persia. James Callaghan condemned them as a 'menace to peace'. Shinwell asserted that Churchill could not 'be trusted to keep the peace', while the Labour candidate for Bridgwater listed the 'hazards of Toryism' as 'War against India . . . Against Argentina . . . Against Russia . . . Against Persia . . . Against Egypt . . .' In Michael Foot's opinion the threat of world war under Tory rule was the 'main issue' of the election campaign and the proposition 'Churchill + MacArthur = Atomic War' was bandied about irresponsibly by many Labour candidates. It is amusing to contemplate in retrospect how safe these people felt in the hands of Herbert Morrison. War-mongering apart, the Labour Party had yet another scare with which to frighten the electorate. This was the Tory Party's pre-war unemployment record, and it was used for all it was worth. Alfred Robens, a former Minister of Labour, declared: 'You can't possibly guarantee full employment unless you have a planned economy and the Tory Party just does not believe in a planned economy'. Michael Foot warned against 'the mass unemployment which we always have under the Tories', and Harold Wilson averred that 'mass unemployment which would most surely follow a return of the Tories to power would lay the country open to the evils of Communism'. When they were not frightening the voters with the perils of the Conservative Party, the Labour Party leaders defended their record in government since 1945.

The Tory Party naturally attacked the record which Labour defended. Socialism, it charged, inevitably brought about a weak economy and a neglect of the nation's interests. Churchill frightened his listeners with 'Abadan [Persia], Sudan and Bevan'. The record of the Attlee governments apart, the Tories based their hopes on promises of more houses and fewer taxes as well as on their ability to exploit Churchill's reputation for statesmanship. Their morale was encouraged by the findings of opinion polls in which they led throughout the election campaign although their lead was cut to 2·5 per cent by polling day, a sign perhaps that Labour's tactics were succeeding in frightening the voters. Yet when the results were finally declared, Churchill discovered that he had won a general election at last. The figures were as follows:

Party	Votes gained	Percentage of vote	Average vote per MP	Number of MPs
Conservative	13,717,538	48·0	42,731	321
Labour	13,948,605	48·8	47,283	295
Liberal	730,556	2·5	121,759	6
Communist	21,640	0·1	—	—
Others	177,329	0·6		3
	28,595,668	100·0		625

Source: Derived from D. Butler and A. Sloman, *British Political Facts, 1900–75*.

Once again the election had attracted enormous interest, an interest which was demonstrated by a poll of 82 per cent. Despite Labour's slight lead in votes, there had been a swing against it in the country which gave the Conservative Party a majority in the House of Commons. Two factors were instrumental in producing this. In the first place, Labour tended to accumulate its votes in large majorities in safe constituencies. Secondly, the comparative lack of Liberal candidates undoubtedly helped the Conservatives. 475 Liberal candidates in 1950 had secured more than 2·5 million votes and over 9 per cent of the poll. In 1951 only 109 Liberal candidates presented themselves and took less than 3 per cent of the poll with less than three quarters of a million votes. The majority of former Liberal voters, it was estimated, therefore, had this time voted for the Conservative Party.

For the Liberals themselves, the election was an unmitigated disaster: their representation in Parliament was reduced from nine MPs to six; their plight was surpassed only by that of the Communist Party which received a derisory 0·07 per cent of the poll. Once again, the results could be claimed as a moral victory for both the major parties. The Conservatives had won a majority of parliamentary seats contested; the Labour Party, though defeated, had won more votes than ever before and for the third time since the war had secured more votes in an election than the Conservative Party.

THE LABOUR PARTY IN POWER:
SOME REFLECTIONS ON THE PERIOD 1945–51

The advent of the Labour government in 1945 gave rise to many hopes and fears: hopes of a new and better age in which values would be transformed; fears that a bureaucratic socialism would slow the beat of the nation's pulse. In fact, life continued much as before for the society which had experienced the war: the nation's leaders were familiar and its social and political structures remained essentially, if not entirely, unaltered. Both optimists and pessimists were proved right in their predictions, although the former more profoundly so than the latter. For despite the rationing and the controls, society's values were transmuted for the better. The Labour governments refused to put the clock back and pursued a programme designed to consolidate and strengthen the social cohesion engendered by the war. And so successful were they in their aims that they even converted the Conservative Party. By 1951 there could simply be no return to the society of the 1930s: the Welfare State had been accepted; full employment had become a common objective; and the social morality of the means test had given way to the doctrine of universality. The Labour Party itself had changed by becoming a respectable and natural party of government. The Conservatives in this respect could claim it as a convert and did so by pointing to its tough and realistic policy on foreign affairs. The idea that 'Left could speak unto Left' had little basis in fact by 1951. The foreign policy of the Labour Party now resembled very closely that of the Conservative Party. The truth was that the parties had come together in their vision of the post-war world. If there were still important differences between them, their similarities outweighed these differences.

Still, despite the successes of Attlee's governments, there remained a great deal to be done. The economy still had to be stabilized and a system of economic priorities worked out. In fact, the decade of the 1950s would be an absolutely crucial one for Britain's long-term economic prospects. In foreign policy, also, there was perhaps the need for some re-assessment. Britain's hopes of an American alliance had been signally fulfilled and it was already time perhaps to take stock and to consider new priorities. France had already outmanoeuvred Britain diplomatically for the first time since the war and the implications of the Schuman Plan were due for critical and careful evaluation. It was not at this time true to say of Britain that she had 'lost an empire and . . . not yet found a role' but, with the independence of the Indian sub-continent and the emergence of the super-powers, her role in the post-war world could no longer be taken for granted. In foreign policy as in economic matters the decade of the 1950s would therefore be critical.

4 | THE CHURCHILL GOVERNMENT, 1951-5

Winston Churchill was seventy-seven when he formed his only peacetime administration. He had already suffered two strokes and was to suffer two more in the course of his premiership. According to his doctor, his 'old capacity for work had gone and with it much of his self-confidence'; nonetheless, this same physician urged him to remain in public life and to assume the responsibilities of office lest retirement should undermine his physical and mental health completely. Churchill's ministerial team was also rather elderly and reflected very much the premier's personal attitudes to government. The average cabinet minister was sixty years old and the most important ones were of the aristocratic semi-independent type by whom Churchill liked to feel surrounded. Many were relics from the Second World War – Lord Woolton (Lord President), Lord Ismay (Commonwealth Relations) and Lord Cherwell (Postmaster-General), for example – and if old cronies such as Beaverbrook and Bracken were not appointed cabinet ministers, they nonetheless retained considerable political influence.

Churchill's cabinet therefore almost inevitably came to resemble his wartime one, and there is no doubt that the old man would have liked to run his peacetime administration along familiar lines. His 'overlords' experiment, for example, was only one indication of this. Between 1951 and 1953, in an attempt to reduce the cabinet's size, the Prime Minister grouped several ministries under a number of super-ministers or 'overlords'. Thus Lord Cherwell as Paymaster-General was supposed to coordinate scientific research and development; Lord Woolton as Lord President of the Council was made responsible for food and agriculture while Lord Leathers, yet another wartime colleague, was meant to coordinate Transport, Fuel and Power. As a result, the Ministers of Agriculture and Fisheries, Food, Transport and Civil Aviation and Fuel and

Power could all be excluded from the Cabinet. In itself the system had a lot to recommend it. The trouble was that the 'overlords' all sat in the House of Lords and this made parliamentary procedure difficult.

Another reminder of the good old days was Anthony Eden's appointment as Foreign Secretary and *de facto* Deputy Prime Minister. Eden would have liked a change from foreign affairs but Churchill would hear none of it. He had grown to rely on Eden's acknowledged expertise in this area and depended on being able to do so in the future. Indeed, the only other person he seems to have considered qualified for the job was himself, so that when Eden fell ill in April 1953 Churchill suffered another stroke as a result of assuming personal command of his deputy's department. Foreign affairs apparently constituted an area over which only those groomed for the top could preside, and Eden – nobody doubted this – was Churchill's chosen successor. As long as he occupied the Foreign Office, he was accorded the greatest possible deference and no mere cabinet colleague dared to question his authority in foreign affairs.

Two other appointments were also of great significance. R. A. Butler's selection as Chancellor of the Exchequer and Harold Macmillan's appointment as Minister of Housing showed that Churchill was aware of recent Conservative thinking on domestic policy. In other words, there would be no attempt to put the clock back to the 1930s. Butler was acknowledged to be the leading 'progressive' Conservative (and not merely on account of his 1944 Education Bill) while Macmillan – although he was not yet seen as a 'major' figure – was known to have been out of sympathy with pre-war Conservative policies. Both men had of course occupied important posts during the war, but given the 1945 general election result the Prime Minister had little new blood to infuse into his government. Some bright young men – Iain Macleod, Enoch Powell and Edward Heath, for example – were nevertheless appointed to their first government posts in Churchill's peacetime administration.

On the whole the prospects seemed bright. The nation acquired early in 1952 a new monarch as well as a new government. The popular and dutiful King George VI died on 6 February and was succeeded by his daughter, the equally popular and dutiful Princess Elizabeth. Her coronation did not take place till 1953 but already people looked forward to a second Elizabethan age, and Churchill's towering presence as premier served to enhance their hopes of national recovery and glory. There were of course problems to be solved before any of this could come about and the number one problem facing the new Conservative government was the state of the British economy.

The Korean War had imposed a number of strains on an already overburdened economy. The rise in world commodity prices would have led to balance-of-payments difficulties anyway, but the fact that many of the countries which were exporters of raw materials were also members of the sterling area brought peculiar problems for Britain. Because of their increased wealth these countries began in 1951 to buy from outside the sterling area, running down their sterling balances in London. This gave rise to speculation against the pound so that the surplus on current account recorded in 1950 – some £300 million – became a £400 million deficit in 1951. As has been mentioned before, the resignations of Bevan, Wilson and Freeman, together with a large round of wage increases, did nothing to stem the tide; but the most decisive blow of all was the worsening of the terms of trade by 12 per cent compared to the year before. When the Conservatives came into power, therefore, they found a deficit on the balance of payments of nearly £700 million.

The new government took action immediately to deal with this un-happy situation: measures were announced to reduce imports; credit was restricted; food subsidies were cut; travel allowances were slashed; and there was even a reduction in strategic stockpiling. Churchill maliciously confessed that Bevan had been right on his predictions after all: the Government could not carry out their rearmament programme nor even spend the money which had been appropriated. Too many bottlenecks had developed in supply. As a result of the Government's measures the balance of payments improved.

The improvement was in fact so spectacular – by the end of 1952 there was again a surplus of £300 million – that it was clear that other factors had also been contributing. Conservatives who pondered this problem accredited the success to Butler's monetary measures. The Chancellor had raised bank rate in Britain for the first time since 1932, initially from 2 to 2½ per cent and then soon afterwards to 4 per cent. His objective was to reduce demand and hence relieve the strain on the economy, but in fact by the time he had announced these measures there was no 'excess demand' in the economy and if anything some slack was beginning to appear. Industrial investment was therefore needlessly cut back and Butler in-augurated the first 'stop' of Tory 'stop-goes' in the fifties. 'Go' came with his budget of 1953 when income tax was reduced, the excess profits levy removed, initial allowances restored and building licences liberalized.

The fact that the economy was all the time recovering obscured the inappropriateness of Butler's monetary measures. The real cause of Britain's balance-of-payments improvement was the dramatic improvement in the terms of trade which took place in 1952. These moved decisively in Britain's favour by 6 per cent between 1951 and 1952 and by a further 6 per cent between 1952 and 1953, causing the balance-of-payments deficit to disappear in spite of falling exports (Butler's real contribution). This, however, was only dimly understood at the time, and Tory Chancellors in the 1950s and 1960s developed confused and inaccurate ideas regarding the way in which the economy worked. For example, it seems that they believed they could effect an improvement in the balance of trade by the use of monetary restraint at a time of full employment without either reducing home investment or consumption.

Butler can be judged as the first of the Tory Chancellors who, in Samuel Brittan's words, were not merely 'innocent of economic complexities, but ... did not even have the practical financial flair that one might reasonably expect from a party with business links'. His record between 1951 and 1955 gives ample proof of this. Thanks to the continued improvement in the terms of trade as well as to the benefits accruing from the 1949 devaluation (delayed by the Korean War), there were no balance-of-payments problems between 1952 and 1955. Instead, the danger was that once the economy got back on an even keel, an investment boom might lead to unnecessary ('demand-pull') inflation. At first, of course, there was every reason to encourage investment; the bank rate was cut in 1952 and 1953 and the 1954 budget (otherwise neutral) introduced investment allowances. Vacancies registered therefore grew well in excess of numbers unemployed and a boom got under way. Bank rate accordingly was raised from 3 to 3½ per cent in January and to 4½ per cent in February 1955. But instead of applying a 'stop' in his budget in April 1955, Butler, with an eye to the forthcoming general election, took 6d. off the income tax and gave out higher personal allowances. It was only after the 1955 election had been won and a special autumn budget introduced that Butler confessed that he had been mistaken in his judgement and raised both purchase and distributed profits tax. Not surprisingly, perhaps, he was replaced as Chancellor before the year was out.

Meanwhile, comforted and protected by the good fortune of steadily falling prices in the world markets, the Conservative régime was able to convince the voters that the improvement in Britain's economic prospects was due to the fact that 'Conservative freedom worked'. This was really to mistake cause for effect – that is, the dismantling of all sorts of controls was rendered possible only on account of improved trading conditions – but it was not a difficult task to convince an electorate which had just endured a war and socialist austerity that freedom must have benefits. It did, of course, but they were not necessarily the ones which the Tories extolled. Be that as it may, with the return of confidence in sterling, the Conservative government were able to bring about a return to free market conditions. Thus food was de-rationed in part in 1953 and totally in 1954. In 1953 also, iron and steel as well as road haulage were de-nationalized, while the Ministry of Materials and the Raw Cotton Commission were abolished in 1954. The same year saw the international commodity markets reopened, hire purchase trading eased and a number of wartime building restrictions removed. Since the economy was improving all the time it was easy to argue that these measures were causing the improvement and that the businessman should lead the way. And not unnaturally in the absence of a capital gains tax, the Stock Exchange witnessed a spectacular boom in equity shares. Their price more than doubled between June 1952 and July 1955, while the Financial Times Index of Industrial Ordinary Shares rose from 103 to 224. If at the same time there was a moderate rise in prices and the cost of living, it was proportionate to the rise in wages and to the increase in production in the factories (4–5 per cent) during 1953 and 1954. Conservative freedom and Conservative measures therefore, it was argued, had brought about the return of economic prosperity. The Conservative cabinet in time perhaps suspected that this was not the whole truth. Certainly, it never seems to have had much faith in its grasp of economic problems. Thus when in 1952 Butler proposed a controversial plan to his colleagues involving the floating of the pound they lacked confidence either in his understanding of the plan or in the mechanics he proposed for carrying it out. 'Operation Robot', as it was called, was never implemented.*

Butler's willingness to toy with new ideas, sensible or otherwise, marked him off from many of his colleagues. One of them, Harold Macmillan, was interested in one idea only at this time. The Tory Party

* Eden apparently was decisive in defeating it.

conference in 1951 had demanded the building of 300,000 houses per year and Churchill had entrusted Macmillan with the job. Churchill had asked him to 'build the houses for the people', telling him that his record at the Housing Ministry (at that time still called the Ministry of Local Government and Planning) would 'make or mar' his political career. The Prime Minister had added, 'but every humble home will bless your name if you succeed' – and Harold Macmillan was determined to succeed. In 1953, 327,000 houses were built and in 1954, 354,000. It was a remarkable achievement and did much to mark out Macmillan as a future Prime Minister.

Macmillan had achieved his objectives for a number of reasons. First of all, he had selected an able team with which to work – Dame Evelyn Sharp, Ernest Marples, Sir Percy Mills and Freddie Bishop. Again, he himself strove with great ingenuity to coordinate the work of his own department with that of others (through the building committee of the Cabinet, for example), something which undoubtedly paid dividends. Throughout his struggles to reach the magic figure of completions he had the support of key cabinet colleagues – Churchill, Swinton and Stuart, in particular – and was able consistently to surmount the hurdles thrown up in his path by the Treasury. Macmillan, indeed, seems to have had little patience for Butler. 'Rab', he once said, 'is one of those men who cannot cook without meat! I can cook with bread and water.' There was a lot in this.

Macmillan's housing policy was a radical one. Whereas Labour ministers had relied almost exclusively on the public sector to produce the goods, Macmillan was determined to extract much more from private enterprise. This is not to say that he held the public sector back. Housing subsidies were raised from £22 to £35 per standard home in 1952, and if the standards were changed – to make slightly smaller houses – everything was done to increase the efficiency of allocation of supplies. Still, the major innovations concerned incentives to private builders. Thus from 1 January 1952 local authorities were empowered to issue licences to private contractors to build houses up to the same number as they themselves were building (previously the ratio had been 4 : 1 in favour of the public sector), and in 1953 they were permitted to issue licences for all smaller houses and for large ones on their merits. Macmillan also encouraged local authorities to extend their power to issue mortgages, so that by the end of 1954 almost 30 per cent of housing completions were being constructed by the private sector. Other measures likewise served to encourage private enterprise: local councils, for example, were encouraged to seek loans on the open market rather than from the Treasury, and Town and Country Planning Acts abolished the development charge on land. New town developments also proceeded apace, the towns in question being encouraged to house the overspill populations of large cities. But although much progress was recorded here, no new 'new towns' were actually designated by the Conservatives. Macmillan already had enough to do in giving reality to Labour's paper plans without attempting to enlarge a programme which itself had not yet properly got under way.

The only real criticism which could be made of the Housing Minister was that he was trying to do too much. Might it not be better to allocate some of the resources he was using to industrial development? Was he not risking inflation in the housing market? These were legitimate questions, but the Minister, in turn, had legitimate answers. Badly housed workers, he maintained, were unproductive workers; and as for the risk of inflation, it was one which simply had to be run if inroads were to be made on the housing problem. In retrospect, it seems that Macmillan's reception at the Tory Party conference at Scarborough in 1954 was thoroughly justified. There he proclaimed that he had made housing a 'national crusade' and was greeted like Richard the Lionheart.

His achievement was all the more outstanding for the scarcity of other developments on the home front. The Government received three important official studies on the working of various aspects of the Welfare State – national insurance, old age pensions and the National Health Service – yet, despite the fact that Conservative pronouncements had sometimes been critical of the way in which money was supposedly squandered in administering these services, the Government's only action, having considered the reports, was to increase the scale of benefits with respect to pensions and national assistance. Significantly, nothing was done to alter the machinery of the National Health Service. Gaitskell's changes were retained and a prescription of two shillings was introduced, but the NHS was already something of a sacred cow and the Guillebaud Committee's report to the Government had presented excellent grounds for continued official reverence. By 1955, therefore, there was no reason to fear that Conservatism regarded the Welfare State with hostility. Indeed, the *Economist* had by this time coined the word 'Butskellism' to describe the political consensus on the home front, and Edward Hyams in 1953 wrote a novel, entitled *Gentian Violet*, in which the hero managed to get elected to Parliament as both Conservative and Socialist without being discovered.

In foreign affairs, too, a bipartisan approach was continued and it must have been very difficult for a foreigner to discern any departures from the general direction of British post-war foreign policy as it had been laid down by Bevin. In the words of one ditty:

> The Bevin or the Churchill touch
> Seem both alike to Danes or Dutch;
> If Socialist or Tory speaks
> It's all the same to French and Greeks.

There was, of course, *one* important difference. Eden conducted foreign policy in a manner very different from Morrison. The latter's tenure had been an unhappy interlude in the history of the Foreign Office, but with the return of Eden Great Britain was once again represented with style and assurance abroad. Moreover, in contrast to Morrison, as Foreign Secretary Eden was undoubtedly a great success.

Of all the problems he had to face when he once again took charge of the Foreign Office, the most intractable was the German question. This had been temporarily solved in September 1950 but diplomats were under no illusions that a more permanent solution could not be long delayed. And so a number of proposals were put forward. The Soviet Union, for example, which had an obvious interest in defeating any move to arm West Germany, suggested late in 1950 that an all-German constituent council should be created on which both Germanies would be equally represented. Since East Germany had only one third the population of West Germany and since there was clearly nothing representative about the government which managed it – the 1953 uprising of the workers in East Berlin would soon give striking, if tragic, proof of that – this proposal was rejected by both the West Germans and the Western Allies. Preliminary talks nonetheless took place in Paris the following year concerning the possibility of holding a 'four-power conference' on Germany. Since the West insisted, however, on free elections as a *sine qua non* for substantive discussions, these preliminary talks proved futile. Then on 10 March 1952 the Soviet Union seemed to move much closer to the Western position. A note to the Western powers proposed the signing of a German treaty which not only allowed for withdrawal of all foreign troops: the reunited Germany which was fore-seen was also to be permitted to have its own armed forces and to produce its own military equipment although it was to promise not to enter into any military alliance directed against any power which had been part of the anti-Axis coalition during the Second World War. That is to say, it would not be able to enter NATO. The Allies, foolishly perhaps, did not take this note very seriously and allowed the Soviet proposals to fall through when the Soviet Union refused to allow a UN commission into East Germany to investigate political conditions there.

It is not very likely in retrospect that the Soviet note constituted much more than a tactical manoeuvre on the part of Russia to delay West German rearmament, but certain Germans have since argued that on this occasion both Adenauer and the Western Allies missed the only genuine opportunity after 1945 to negotiate the reunification of Ger-many. The Austrian State Treaty of 1955, which created a neutral free Austria, is sometimes held out as an example of what might have been negotiated for Germany in 1952. But, as we shall see, the diplomatic climate had much altered by 1955, and the East Berlin uprising of July 1953 seemed to indicate to the Allies exactly why the UN commission had been refused entry into East Germany and why they were right to have treated the note of 10 March 1952 with such suspicion. After all, in 1954 the Soviet Union was to offer to join NATO to solve the German problem and nobody was to consider that proposal seriously. A four-power conference eventually did convene in Berlin in January 1954 in an attempt to settle East–West differences over Germany. Here unfortun-ately no agreement could be reached over the holding of free elections and the Russians (not unreasonably) objected to the proposal that a reunified Germany should have the right to enter into any alliance it chose. The conference therefore achieved nothing so far as Germany was concerned; its only positive result was an agreement among the powers to hold a conference that April in Geneva on Indo-China.

The background to the Soviet Union's feverish diplomatic activity in these years was formed by yet another bid by Europe's federalists to promote the integration of Western Europe. This time their proposals involved the rearmament of West Germany, for it looked as if a European Defence Community would be created. The idea had once again originated with Jean Monnet and had been communicated to the world by the French premier René Pleven. It was an ingenious – perhaps ingenuous – attempt to 'rearm the Germans without rearming Germany' and was very complicated in its details. Still, the main outlines were fairly straightforward. There was to be a European Defence Community paid for by European taxes, controlled by a council of European ministers and run by a European commissariat. The analogies with the European Iron and Steel Community and the later European Economic Community are too obvious to need outlining. The European army (the real core of the Defence Community) was to be an integrated one, consisting of national units of 12,000–13,000 men, but no army corps was to contain two divisions of the same nationality except for tactical or organizational needs. West Germany was to provide 500,000 men, in twelve divisions of ground forces, a tactical air force and a coastal defence. Significantly, however, West Germany and Italy (which was also to be rearmed) would only possess armed forces insofar as they were part of this European army; other states, but notably France, would be allowed to keep separate armed forces to defend colonial territories and serve in other capacities overseas. This, then, was the main outline of the plan as it was finally thrashed out by France, Germany, Italy and the Benelux countries in 1952.

For a variety of reasons it was never actually implemented. Europe – least of all the Germans themselves, the majority of whom wanted nothing to do with the scheme – was simply not ready for German rearmament, which was only grudgingly contemplated as a cold war necessity. It was therefore very difficult for the authors of the plan to raise a great deal of positive enthusiasm for it. Moreover, as it was first presented in 1950 it seemed a little half-baked from the point of view of organization. German fighting units were envisaged as consisting only of 800–1,200 men, whereas the Americans considered units of 6,000 men to be barely adequate for combat service. The US point of view was important since no matter what the Europeans worked out, the European army still had to be integrated into NATO and the legal position of West German military forces still had to be negotiated with the Allies. Acheson viewed the original scheme with 'consternation and dismay', as did both Marshall and Truman, although in public, for obvious diplomatic reasons, the plan was given a welcome. The Labour government adopted the same attitude as they had adopted towards the Schuman Plan. They were sympathetic and interested but could not undertake to participate. They therefore only sent observers to the negotiations conducted between 1950 and 1952 at which the 132 clauses of the EDC treaty were eventually thrashed out. With the advent of the Churchill government in the autumn of 1951, however, European federalists looked forward to a change in British policy.

But it was not to be. Despite his earlier speeches on the theme of European unity – and in particular his call for the creation of a European army – Churchill had never thought in terms of Britain herself forming part of a united Europe. Moreover, he had found the original details of the Pleven Plan quite comical and had described them to Harold Macmillan as a 'sludgy amalgam'. Probably he did not understand them since, according to both Acheson and Eden, he kept conjuring up a picture of 'a bewildered French drill sergeant sweating over a platoon made up of a few Greeks, Italians, Germans, Turks and Dutchmen, all in utter confusion over the simplest orders'. Yet even if he had understood them, there can be little doubt that Churchill would never have been willing to surrender British sovereignty. Eden certainly was not prepared to do so. He still thought in terms of three big allied powers and looked on the European states from the perspective of *de haut en bas*. At a press conference in Rome on 28 November 1951 he made it perfectly clear that the new Conservative government had no more intention of joining the EDC than had their predecessor. This came as a shock for Europe's federalists and a 'humiliation' – in his own word – for Sir David Maxwell-Fyfe, who had only a few hours earlier informed the Council of Europe at Strasbourg of the British government's intention to give the Pleven proposals a 'thorough examination'. On the other hand, between that date and 1954 Eden worked with the French, Americans and Germans – but particularly with the French – to demonstrate that although the British could not join the EDC, they would in practice come near to doing so. Thus in 1952, together with America, Great Britain pledged that she would regard any threat to the integrity or unity of the EDC as a threat to her own security. Eden even signed a treaty with the EDC in 1952 extending to it as a whole the military aid which Britain had pledged in the Brussels Treaty. Finally, in 1954 a whole series of unilateral undertakings were given by Great Britain: she would not withdraw from the mainland of Europe so long as there was a threat to the EDC; she would consult with the EDC on matters of mutual concern, including the number of troops which would serve with

NATO; British armoured and air force units would be included in EDC formations and vice versa within the NATO framework; and Britain would regard her 1952 treaty with the EDC as being of 'indefinite duration'. Eden also made it clear that a British minister would attend meetings of the EDC Council of Ministers and that a permanent British representative would be in constant contact with the EDC Board of Commissioners. Short of joining the Defence Community itself – which British pride, prejudice and public opinion would not have permitted – there was little more that he could offer.

Still, this was not enough. Six governments (France, Germany, Italy, Belgium, the Netherlands and Luxemburg) had signed the Treaty in 1952. Five of these had ratified it by 1954. The French parliament still had to give its approval, without which the Community clearly had no future. Britain's refusal to join the EDC, however, was now decisive in preventing the French from according it their final assent. With Britain outside, and French armies deployed in the colonies, the EDC, it was argued, would be dominated by Germans and Americans. French interests would therefore be neglected and France would be reduced to a minor power. In August 1954 the National Assembly refused to ratify the Pleven Plan and any idea of a European Defence Community was destroyed. In fact the French were still unsure about their sentiments towards the Germans and about German rearmament in particular. Their decision respecting the EDC meant that the whole question was reopened once again. The Americans were not unnaturally furious. Eisenhower and Dulles had become wholehearted converts to the idea of the EDC, and Dulles had already in December 1953 promised an 'agonizing reappraisal' of America's commitment to European defence unless the French proceeded to ratify the treaty. Now they had rejected it there was the threat that this reappraisal might indeed be carried out.

It was at this juncture that Eden succeeded in pulling off his most celebrated diplomatic *coup*. Given the American threat to reappraise and Western Europe's sense of guilt at having finally failed to solve the problem of West German rearmament, the Foreign Secretary was able to negotiate a comprehensive resolution of outstanding differences. He did this by a lightning tour of European capitals, and by skilfully managing a diplomatic conference in London at the end of September 1954. As a result a nine-power agreement was signed at Lancaster House on 3 October by representatives of the Six, Great Britain, the USA and

Canada. It was a highly important document. Not only did it establish the permanent basis of Western defence but signally restored inter-Allied faith after a very difficult period of European diplomacy. The agreements brought an end to the occupation of West Germany by the Western Allies; provided for German and Italian membership of NATO (Germany was to provide for Europe's defence to the same extent as she would have done under the EDC treaty); reaffirmed the commitment of US and Canadian troops to Europe's defence; and brought a permanent British military presence to the Continent. It was really this last commitment on the part of Eden which enabled him to save the day. Great Britain promised to maintain four divisions and a tactical air force on the Continent with much stronger guarantees against withdrawal than those which she had offered to the EDC. The French and the Lancaster House agreements were ratified by the French parliament at the end of 1954. The new arrangements, known thereafter as the Paris Agreements, came into force in May 1955.

Moscow denounced them, of course. Not only that, but the Soviet Union set up its own version of them – the Warsaw Pact – in retaliation. Given Russian domination of Eastern Europe, this was hardly a diplomatic blow. In fact, it may have indirectly been to the advantage of the West since, reacting to the development of two armed camps in Europe, Moscow next attempted a reconciliation. Thus in the same month that the Paris Agreements came into effect the Russians signed the State Treaty which gave freedom to Austria,* and in June 1955 they declared their desire to establish diplomatic relations with West Germany and invited Konrad Adenauer to visit Moscow. All this was part, perhaps, of a strategy of showing the Germans how stupid they had been to rely on the West; but it was also probably part of the preliminaries to the summit conference of 1955, which was held in Geneva after the British general election of that year.

The German problem, of course, had not been the only one to confront the Conservative government when they came to power in 1951. The Korean War was still in progress and the problem of Persia still awaited a solution. Britain also had to reach an agreement with Egypt over the future of the Suez Canal, and in all these matters it was expedient to

---

* As a result of the establishment of the Warsaw Pact the USSR had a new excuse for keeping troops in Hungary and Romania; until then their excuse had been that they were needed for lines of communication with Austria.

seek American cooperation. This was especially the case with regard to Korea. British leaders were perpetually anxious lest America should use the atomic bomb to rid the north of that country of the Chinese 'volunteers' who had poured into it after America had bombed Chinese installations on the Yalu river. America was clearly losing patience with the war and under the influence of Senator McCarthy and others a powerful wave of anti-Communist hysteria was building up on Capitol Hill. The effect of this on American policy did nothing to bolster British faith in US statesmanship, and British efforts were therefore geared to promoting the peace negotiations which began at Kaesong in 1952. These were later transferred to Panmunjon, where fortunately an armistice was signed on 22 July 1953. Korea was divided along the 38th parallel and South Korea signed a defence treaty with the United States of America.

In 1953 and 1954 things also began to sort themselves out in the Middle East – or so it seemed. In Persia a *coup d'état* in August 1953 restored the authority of the Shah, and Dr Mussadegh, whose nationalist policies had by now nearly bankrupted his country, fell from power. The Persian oil industry was reorganized in 1954 when an international consortium, in which Britain held 40 per cent of the shares – she sold the rest to the Americans and others for £214 million – was set up and the oil began to flow again. The settlement could hardly have been to the liking of Persian patriots but undoubtedly represented a victory for the British Foreign Office, whose delaying tactics were finally vindicated. In Egypt also progress appeared to be being made, despite the twists and turns in Egyptian politics and in Anglo-Egyptian negotiations. King Faruq had been overthrown in July 1952 and on 12 February 1953 an agreement was reached with the new Egyptian ruler, Colonel Neguib, on the future of the Sudan. This was to become self-governing after the departure of British and Egyptian forces in three years' time and was to be governed in the meantime by a Governor General and a commission on which the Sudan, Britain, Egypt and Pakistan were represented. The only bone of contention remaining between Great Britain and Egypt therefore appeared to be the future of the Suez Canal Zone. The problem had been eased in part by the decision of the British government in December 1952 to remove the British Army's headquarters in the Middle East from Suez to Cyprus, but there were still a number of issues outstanding between the British and Egyptian governments, chiefly the future of the Suez base once the British had withdrawn. Nonetheless, in

October 1954 agreement was reached on these issues also. British troops were to be withdrawn within twenty months; meanwhile certain key installations were to be jointly maintained by British and Egyptian civilian personnel; the base was to be reactivated in the event of an armed attack on Egypt or any other member of the Arab League or Turkey; and the agreement providing for all this would last for seven years. It seemed a very sensible arrangement – in particular since Egypt also agreed to respect the Constantinople Convention of 1888 regarding freedom of navigation through the Suez Canal – but, inevitably perhaps, it aroused dissatisfaction amongst extremists on both sides of the argument. The so-called 'Suez Group' of Conservatives went so far as to vote against the Government when the matter was debated in the House of Commons; while in Egypt the new arrangements provided further ammunition for the opponents of Colonel Neguib. One of these, Colonel Nasser, took over the reins of power in November 1954.

Eden's tenure of the Foreign Office appeared, therefore, to be justifying the reputation which he had built up of an able and distinguished diplomat. This was enhanced in 1954 by yet another success in negotiations. However, the price he paid for this success – the alienation of the new American Secretary of State, John Foster Dulles – was later to cost him dear.

The American presidential election of 1952 had resulted in the victory of Dwight D. Eisenhower, the former Allied commander of the Second World War. Politically he was something of an unknown quantity, but less unknown were the views of his Secretary of State, John Foster Dulles. The latter had long experience in foreign affairs and was known to take a strong line against Communism. He did not go so far as some leading American Republicans, who at that time professed to believe that even the USA itself was being directed by a coterie of Communist agents, but his strong language and vivid phrases – 'agonizing reappraisal', 'massive retaliation', etc. – not to mention his expressed hopes of 'rolling back the Communist world empire' and 'liberating the captive peoples' of Eastern Europe, adumbrated usually in tones of moral self-righteousness, undoubtedly served to sustain McCarthyist hopes of a radical change in US foreign policy. This was not to pass. Eisenhower, under British pressure but led also by his own conservative instincts, concluded a moderate peace in Korea and at one point even seemed prepared to contemplate the entry of Communist China into the United

Nations.* All this came as a shock to right-wing American Republicans and, together with Dulles's inability to help the East Berlin workers in 1953, it could be interpreted – and was interpreted by right-wing Americans – as proof that the US was failing in its duty to protect the free world from Communism. Eisenhower and Dulles, therefore, were very sensitive to charges in 1954 that they were committing similar errors in their policy towards Indo-China.

The Indo-China problem was the product of the decline of French imperialism. France had ruled the area for almost a century; at the end of the Second World War she had established three independent states in the area – Laos, Cambodia and Vietnam – as part of the French Union. In 1946 Vietnam saw the proclamation of a counter-state, the 'Democratic Republic of Vietnam', in the north by the Viet Minh nationalists under the leadership of Ho Chi Minh. The latter had been forced underground with the re-establishment of French rule, but by 1954, with help from the Communist Chinese, their struggle against the French was about to reach a climax. Much of North Vietnam had already fallen to them and the French government was by this time dependent on America as far as financing the war was concerned (80 per cent of French military expenditure in Indo-China was now underwritten by Washington). With the siege of Dien Bien Phu in March 1954 it became clear that more than money was needed if the French war effort was to be sustained. Vice-President Nixon told newspaper editors that 'we may have to put American boys in', and the Secretary of State began to sound out America's allies on the prospect of intervention. The US plan was to threaten air and naval action by the US, France and Britain (and any other interested power) against the Chinese coast together with the threat of active intervention in Indo-China itself. Britain's response would be critical so far as implementing the scheme was concerned.

Fortunately, the plan was rejected. Churchill and Eden took the view that only a general war could now reverse the French defeat in Vietnam and that British public opinion would refuse to aquiesce in the launching of such a war. Moreover, Britain's Commonwealth partners (particularly the Asians) would firmly repudiate such a venture, which might easily

---

* Later on – in 1955–8 – he was prepared to defend Formosa, Quemoy and Matsu with the US Seventh Fleet against Communist Chinese bombardment, but he forced the Nationalists to withdraw from certain offshore Chinese islands and was not prepared to underwrite the forward policies of Chiang Kai-shek and the China Lobby.

also involve the intervention of the Soviets. On these grounds and others – the fate of Hong Kong was one material factor – the British advised the Americans to seek a peaceful solution to events in Indo-China. This in fact meant negotiations to partition Vietnam, and at the Geneva Conference of May 1954 – already arranged at the futile Berlin Conference earlier that year – that is precisely what came about. The final agreement provided for the partition of Vietnam along the 17th parallel, with free elections to be held later to determine the future relationship of north and south. Separate treaties established the neutrality and independence of Laos and Cambodia, but America refused to put her signature to the accords. Dulles had left the conference only a week after it had begun, leaving the diplomatic initiative to Eden, who had steered the conference to a successful conclusion. The US Secretary of State, however, regarded the result as yet another victory for Mao Tse-tung and laid the blame largely at Eden's door. Relations between the two men deteriorated thereafter and Eden was later to write, 'My difficulty in working with Mr Dulles was to determine what he really meant and in consequence the significance to be attached to his words and actions.' As Churchill rightly at the time suspected, the tension which existed between them boded ill for Anglo-American relations.

Eden's success at Geneva heightened his awareness of the dangers confronting the world as a result of the division between the superpowers. It also heightened his awareness of the deterrent power of nuclear weapons. 'I was sharply conscious', he was to write 'of the deterrent power of the hydrogen bomb', and added, 'I do not believe that we should have got through the Geneva Conference and avoided a major war without it.' A Defence White Paper of March 1955 therefore announced the decision to manufacture a British hydrogen bomb. Churchill and Eden believed that this would make war less likely and at the same time increase Britain's diplomatic standing with the Americans. The decision to manufacture had been taken in fact as early as 1952, but having admired the way in which Attlee had tricked Parliament over the A-bomb, the Conservatives were happy to trick it once more over the H-bomb. Or not quite. It can be said in their defence that they hid their intention for only three years, whereas Labour had been devious all along the line. Still, it is significant that the announcement of the decision to manufacture the H-bomb came early in 1955. The diplomacy of 1954 had obviously convinced Churchill and Eden that Britain's presence at the top was necessary for the peace of the world.

Equally clear, however, was the fact that the manufacture of the bomb would take several years. In the meantime, therefore, Eden pursued a policy of preserving peace and security in the world through the creation or support of a number of alliances.

The formation of the first of these was almost announced before the end of the Geneva Conference, by which time America had organized Great Britain, France, Australia, New Zealand, Pakistan, the Philippines and Thailand as her allies in the South-East Asia Treaty Organization (SEATO). As a military alliance this was hardly the equivalent of NATO: member states were bound to view an attack on any one of them merely as endangering their 'own peace and safety'; no automatic response was called for and no standing army or joint command was created. The inherent weaknesses of SEATO, in fact, were fairly obvious from the start and were underlined by the separate protocol which was attached to it which extended its scope to cover Laos, Cambodia and Vietnam, although these states could not themselves enter into alliances.* But it was the best the Eisenhower administration could do – apart from sending equipment and 'advisers' to South Vietnam – to bolster the security of South-East Asia in the aftermath of Dien Bien Phu. Despite these factors, however, Dulles was glad to have patched something up and wanted to announce the result of his efforts as soon as possible. He called a meeting of the proposed non-Asian members of SEATO while Eden was still at Geneva and a conference of non-aligned nations was taking place at Bangkok. Eden was furious. He rightly feared that his efforts at Geneva, efforts which were designed after all to prevent a general war in Asia, could be wrecked by any premature *démarche* and sent the following telegram to his US counterpart: 'Americans may think the time past when they need consider the feelings or difficulties of their Allies. It is our conviction that this tendency becomes more pronounced every week [and] that it is creating mounting difficulties for anyone in this country who wants to maintain close Anglo-American relations.' The meeting was postponed.

The second multilateral defensive structure to be formed at this time was the Central Treaty Organization (CENTO), which grew out of

---

* This later became one of America's legal grounds for intervention in Vietnam.

the Baghdad Pact signed between Turkey and Iraq in February 1955. The Pact was open to other states with a defence interest in the area to join, and Great Britain, which had been giving much thought to an alternative defence strategy in the Middle East since her withdrawal from the Suez Canal base, saw in it the beginning of a 'northern tier' strategy. Thus Britain joined the Pact in April 1955, to be followed later in the year by Pakistan and Persia. Since Turkey and Great Britain were also members of NATO and Pakistan and Great Britain members of SEATO, it seemed as if a bridge could be provided by CENTO to link the other two treaty organizations in a worldwide defence network against Communism. The keystone to such a bridge, however, would have to be America, but America refused to join. The United States could never make up its mind in the Middle East which it objected to more – the possible spread of Russian influence or the continued presence of the British. Since Russia had by and large kept out of Middle Eastern affairs since 1946 and since Egypt and Syria were hostile to the new alliance structure, the United States therefore saw no reason to identify itself with British interests. But if Dulles could then pay back old scores, it was at the price of undermining his own objectives. Eden later commented: 'An ounce of membership would have been worth all the hovering and saved a ton of trouble later on.'

In spite of this setback Eden could point to a very distinguished record as Foreign Secretary overall. Since the economy had also been faring well – despite rather than on account of Butler's management – the Conservative government were clearly well placed to win a general election. One problem only remained – the question of Churchill's retirement. The leader of the Conservative Party was now over eighty years old and no longer in complete possession of his faculties. He had already suffered four strokes and their toll on his mental and physical health could no longer be concealed from the public. In Cabinet he rambled on at great length about his previous career and exasperated many of his busy colleagues. He was aware that several of them believed he should go, but he still clung to the hope of meeting the Soviet leaders at a summit and he therefore remained in office. He had high hopes of being able to secure the peace of the world and regarded himself as uniquely qualified to negotiate with the Russians. But the Russians – their leadership in some confusion since the death of Stalin – would not negotiate, so that by April 1955, under pressure from Macmillan, the old man agreed to retire. Macmillan confessed: 'Now that he has really decided to go, we are all miserable.' Yet under the new prime minister, Sir Anthony Eden, the party was poised to win the forthcoming election.

The Opposition, on the other hand, presented a very different picture. The Labour Party had since 1951 been rent by strife over a number of issues and between a number of powerful and articulate personalities. In particular, the group of left-wing M Ps around Aneurin Bevan – the 'Bevanites', as they came to be known – had sought to change the party's policies and had proved to be a thorn in the flesh of the Labour leadership. The two wings of the party seemed unable to agree on anything and only the de-nationalization of iron and steel and road haulage – a godsend from the Tories – provided them with some common ground from which to conduct an effective opposition. Both right and left wings had at first believed that Tory failures would unite the Labour Party, that unemployment or world war would lead to a second era of Labour government. Thus when instead the economy proved stable and Eden's diplomacy recorded successes, the traditional leadership of the party was left with very little to oppose. The vacuum of opposition was therefore filled by left-wing noise.

The first signs of discontent were registered soon after the start of Conservative rule. At the end of the debate on the Government's re-armament programme in March 1952 – a programme, of course, which had been largely inherited from Labour – no less than fifty-seven Bevanites voted against the party line. The official line was that while Labour supported the rearmament programme it had no confidence in the Government's ability to carry it out. Labour M Ps had therefore been advised to abstain at the end of the debate and a letter to this effect had been sent to each of them by Attlee. The rebellion of the Bevanites was greeted with great alarm, and as a result of their behaviour the Standing Orders of the Parliamentary Labour Party, suspended since 1945, were reimposed. These enabled the Parliamentary Labour Party to withdraw the whip or to expel a member if he or she refused to vote as the party wished. Nevertheless, the revolt against the leadership's inaction continued at party conferences in the fifties, where the Bevanites were able not only to present their point of view but to elect their leaders to the Party's National Executive Committee. This they first achieved at Morecambe in 1952 when Bevan, Driberg, Wilson, Mikardo, Crossman and Castle swept Dalton, Morrison, Shinwell, Callaghan and Gaitskell from various positions on the National Executive. Thus for the first time in its history the NEC had a majority among its MPs who did not support the official party leadership and who within the Parliamentary Party were organized as a highly effective political faction

It was very much more difficult, though, for the Bevanites to carry policy motions at conferences. Here the block trade union votes were crucial and the trade union leadership was close to the official party leadership. Bevan's death was sorely felt, of course, but trade unionists like Arthur Deakin were vociferous in their denunciation of the Bevanites. Deakin himself at the 1952 conference condemned 'those within the party who set up a caucus' and demanded that they 'realise that the ordinary rank and file party member or trade unionist has no time for their disregard of those principles and loyalties to which our movement has held so strongly through the whole course of its existence'. In many ways Deakin was unfair in his criticisms. The Bevanites had strong support within constituency parties and trade union branches and they were stronger perhaps in their adherence to traditional party policies than the party leadership itself could claim to be. The latter was now hiding, for example, behind the smokescreen of 'consolidation' as far as the nationalization of further industries was concerned. The Bevanites, on the other hand, made little secret of their desire to nationalize more industries and to do so quickly.

It was clear, however, that they would achieve very little unless they converted the party leadership, a task which Bevan undertook. But such a task was beyond him and, realizing this, he resigned in 1954 from the Shadow Cabinet. He had already been defeated (by Morrison) in the election for the deputy leadership of the party in 1952 and in 1954 he was again defeated (by Gaitskell) in the election for the party treasurer-ship. In the spring of 1955 he had the whip withdrawn from him and was very nearly expelled from the Labour Party altogether, having abstained, along with another sixty-two Labour MPs at the end of the defence debate in March. Bevan had been a persistent critic of NATO, CENTO and SEATO (which he regarded as an instrument of neo-colonialism in Asia) and when he heard that Britain was embarking upon constructing an H-bomb he was appalled at what membership of these alliance structures might mean. He was therefore determined to seek guarantees about the use of the bomb and in the course of the defence debate not only poured scorn on Churchill and Eden but attacked Attlee's leadership as well: 'We want from my Rt. Hon. Friends the leaders of the Opposition an assurance that the language of their amendment, moved on our behalf, does not align the Labour movement behind [the policy of the Tory government].' He closed ominously with the threat: 'because if we cannot have the lead from *them*, let us give the lead ourselves'.

The Labour Party, it appeared, was thus irreparably split on the leading question of the day on the eve of a general election. A round of strikes involving printers, miners, dockers and footplatemen at the end of April did nothing to improve its prospects, and even the Liberals seemed to be benefiting from Labour's internal divisions. Their party membership had doubled in 1954 and at the end of that year they actually secured second place in a by-election at Inverness. They now began to think of themselves as a non-socialist alternative to the Conservatives although with only six MPs in Parliament they clearly had a long way to go.

Having been appointed Prime Minister on Churchill's resignation, Eden decided to call a general election, and polling day was set for 25 May. There was every reason for him to call one. He was a new prime minister; his party had a record in government which could be easily defended; the Opposition was hopelessly divided; and by-elections had indicated popular support for his party. Not a single one had been lost by the Government since 1951, and South Sunderland had been gained from Labour in 1953. The 1955 municipal elections had produced good results for the Government and the opinion polls showed a majority in favour of continuing Conservative rule. Moreover, Butler's blatantly electoral budget, with sixpence off the income tax and other political inducements, suggested that only an unexpected national calamity could prevent the Government from renewing their mandate. In the event, they had been able to arrange a summit conference with the Russians, and Eden, they modestly suggested, was the obvious candidate to represent Great Britain. Everything therefore appeared to be going their way. Prosperity had returned; statesmanship was at a premium; Everest had been conquered; and even the Ashes had been regained. The new Elizabethan age, it was argued, had already become a reality. Why then should the Labour Party take over the reins of government?

Labour itself did not really know the answer. Its manifesto was entitled *Forward with Labour*. But where to was anyone's guess. It promised that a Labour government would 'start new public enterprises' ... 'where necessary' and would not approach defence or foreign policy in a 'party spirit'. Clearly it was so split from top to bottom that it could give no hostages to fortune; in any case, its prophecies at the last election had proved so utterly misguided that there was little need to repeat them during the present campaign.

The election was therefore in every sense a quiet one. Eden quietly impressed the electorate and Labour quietly suppressed its divisions. The result was a foregone conclusion in a way in which few British general elections have been. The turnout figures reflected this, dropping from 82·5 to 76·7 per cent. The votes recorded for the three main parties were:

Party	Votes gained	Percentage of vote	Average vote per MP	Number of MPs
Conservative	13,286,569	49·7	38,624	344
Labour	12,404,970	46·4	44,783	277
Liberal	722,405	2·7	120,401	6
Others	346,554	1·2		3
	26,760,498	100·0		630

Source: Derived from D. Butler and A. Sloman, *British Political Facts, 1900–75.*

The Conservatives thus emerged with an overall majority of no less than sixty seats and were the first party in a century to increase their majority in Parliament as a result of a general election. The Tory vote, it is true, had dropped by almost half a million, but the Labour Party vote had fallen by more than a million and a half. The marginal voter, it seemed, was happy to let the Conservatives carry on. For the Liberal Party the election once again offered little comfort. No seats were lost, it is true, but the party had been looking forward to an increase rather than a fall in its vote and if its share of the poll had increased, the increase – from 2·5 to 2·7 per cent of the poll – was totally insignificant. Much the same could be said in general about the party's role in British politics.

Few British prime ministers can have entered office assured of such general support as Sir Anthony Eden. Regarded more as an international statesman than a mere British politician, and possessing the charm and manners of the quintessential British gentleman (to say nothing of the looks of a cinema matinée idol), he appeared a fitting successor indeed to Winston Churchill. The *Daily Telegraph* commented: 'Training, knowledge and courage are in high degree the unquestionable assets of our new Prime Minister.' In home affairs as well as in foreign policy Eden seemed to embody the new Conservatism. Since 1945 he had been speaking of the Tory Party's new attitudes to social questions and he liked to use the phrase 'a property-owning democracy' with regard to his vision of Great Britain in the new Elizabethan age.

It was in foreign affairs, however, that he was acknowledged as an expert, and soon after the election the public were given another demonstration of their prime minister's international standing.* Eden participated in the summit conference with the Russians at Geneva which Churchill had in vain been seeking to arrange for years. Little came of this meeting, save perhaps a vague feeling of assurance on the part of the Soviets that the West harboured no aggressive designs against them. Nonetheless, Eden could be seen to have striven to secure world peace. One small result of the summit was his invitation to the Soviet leaders to visit Britain the following year, so that in April 1956 the public had the uncanny experience of playing host to Bulganin and Khrushchev. The most interesting aspect of this, as it turned out, was the clash which took place between the Soviet leaders and some leading Labour politicians, as

* The signing of the Austrian State Treaty during the election campaign – on 15 May 1955 – had been another reminder of Eden's statesmanship.

a result of which the Russian guests informed incredulous journalists that if they were British citizens they would undoubtedly vote Conservative.

Eden's honeymoon with the British electorate, however, was not destined to last very long. Perhaps they had expected too much of him or perhaps the knowledge that they expected so much gnawed away at the nerves of the Conservative leader. At any rate, within a relatively short space of time Eden's reputation had been radically revised. It was argued that he had had to act as Deputy Prime Minister for too long, or that he was really not interested in being Prime Minister. Great stress in particular was laid on his poor health, and it became a widely held opinion that his ministerial apprenticeship had been too narrow for the premiership. In fact, all these opinions were rationalizations of his rather poor show at 10 Downing St. For having installed himself there, Eden simply failed to demonstrate the leadership which so many had expected of him.

Almost from the start, he mishandled a number of issues. Thus, although he was determined to retain personal charge of foreign affairs, he appointed Harold Macmillan, a man of very strong character, to replace him at the Foreign Office. In other areas, Selwyn Lloyd became Minister of Defence and Lord Home Secretary of State for Commonwealth Relations, but the thorough Cabinet reshuffle which many commentators believed was necessary did not take place until December 1955. Even then it did not bring in much new blood and Macmillan's replacement as Foreign Secretary by Lloyd seemed to confirm earlier fears that Eden could not cope with a strong personality at the Foreign Office. The press came to believe that the Prime Minister was not in control of his government.

Developments in economic policy had served to strengthen this impression. Butler had had a fairly easy ride at the Treasury up until 1955, but in the later months of the year he seemed to lose what grip he had. His budget had created problems by expanding an economy which was clearly already over-heated and he simply lacked the ability to solve these problems gracefully. Instead, rumours of deflation and speculative pressure on sterling forced him to state explicitly at a meeting of the IMF in Istanbul in July 1955 that the pound would not be devalued. Hire purchase restrictions came into force about the same time and in October a supplementary budget was introduced in the Commons which had the effect of taking back from the electorate the extra spending power which it had been given as recently as April. This was done by raising purchase tax, amongst other things, and Gaitskell savagely condemned the Chancellor's 'pots and pans' budget. In the December reshuffle, therefore, Butler was replaced by Macmillan, who in February and April 1956 took steps to raise bank rate (to $5\frac{1}{2}$ per cent), restrict the purchase credit, cut public investment and suspend investment allowances. The new Chancellor had less faith in *laissez-faire* than his predecessor and a greater flair for public relations. The measures he took were therefore not only more directed towards dampening down the economy, they were also accompanied by measures designed as political sops to the trade unions. The tax on distributed profits was raised to $27\frac{1}{2}$ per cent and that on undistributed profits to 3 per cent.

By this time, however, Eden's reputation had fallen so far that in January 1956 he was forced to issue a statement denying rumours of his forthcoming resignation. Speculation had been stimulated by a campaign in the press – including the conservative press – against him, and a celebrated article in the *Daily Telegraph* had called for the 'smack of firm government'. Eden's response hardly demonstrated that, and so his popularity fell further. Gallup polls revealed that in the spring of 1956 only 40 per cent of the electorate approved of him as premier compared with 70 per cent the previous winter, while the Tonbridge by-election in the summer saw the Tory majority drop from 10,196 to 1,602. Indeed, all by-elections save one during Eden's premiership recorded a swing against the Government.

The effect of all this was merely to increase the pressure on Eden's nerves. Butler later wrote of 'those innumerable telephone calls on every day of the week and every hour of the day, which characterized his conscientious but highly strung supervision of our affairs'. Yet despite the Prime Minister's constant interference in the departmental affairs of his colleagues – perhaps indeed on that account – the Government seemed unable to give a lead on various matters.

For example, there was a vigorous debate proceeding at this time on the question of capital punishment. A number of murder trials had stimulated interest in the matter and the chairman of the Royal Commission on Capital Punishment had been converted to abolition. Public opinion began to swing in the same direction and in 1955 a Labour MP, Sydney Silverman, introduced a Bill to end hanging. This proved unsuccessful but in July 1956 the Commons in a free vote gave him their support, thereby putting the Government in a difficult position. For up until then they had been opposing the abolitionists and had only allowed their MPs to vote freely on the assumption that the abolitionists would fail to carry the day. Given their success, more positive action was called for. The result was that after the Bill's defeat in the Lords a new Government Bill was drafted which retained hanging as expected but conceded ground to the abolitionists. Neither side viewed it as a satisfactory piece of legislation.

Even in his chosen area, Eden's grasp began to falter. In March 1956, for example, he made a poor speech in the Commons on the dismissal of General Glubb (the commander of the Arab Legion and the British *éminence grise* behind the Jordanian throne), while his handling of the strange affair of Commander Crabb – a frogman who disappeared simultaneously with the discovery of an unidentified decapitated body in Portsmouth Harbour at the time of Khrushchev's and Bulganin's visit – was curiously unimpressive. But most inexplicable of all was the fact that for a month before the Suez expedition, the Washington Embassy was left unfilled. Moreover, both the Minister of Defence and the First Lord of the Admiralty were replaced shortly before the expedition sailed.

The Suez affair itself provided the tragic climax to Eden's career. It has been variously interpreted since 1956 but no interpretation has managed to flatter the part which Eden played. By any plausible yardstick, the affair turned into a fiasco. Eden, it is true, did not resign on account of it, but the strain it imposed on his health led directly to his leaving office – an event which seemed to many to be required by justice also.

His difficulties began with Nasser's assumption of power in Egypt. The new Egyptian leader saw himself as a second Mehemet Ali and attempted like that nineteenth-century pasha to play the great powers off against one another in order to further Egyptian ambitions. There was, he believed, in the Arab world 'a role wandering in search of a hero', and he was determined to fill it through public relations and by soliciting aid from East and West. He was also particularly active in non-aligned diplomacy and became a spokesman for the neutralist countries of Africa and Asia. He expected to benefit from 'imperialist' rivalries and ultimately perhaps to be able to find a solution to the problem of

Israel. Certainly he sought to make Egypt's voice respected once again in the Middle East. Thus he signed a friendship treaty with India, attended the conference of non-aligned nations at Bandung in April 1955, visited Moscow in August 1955 and concluded an arms deal with Czechoslovakia which lessened his dependence on the West.

Nonetheless he succeeded in persuading the Western powers to support his schemes to build a High Dam at Aswan on the Nile. This was a complicated and expensive construction project which, it was reckoned, would cost at least $1,300 million to build. However, the US promised to contribute $56 million, Britain $14 million, the World Bank $200 million, so long as $900 million came from Egypt herself. The Egyptians, therefore, were not being 'given' a monster dam by the West, for the vital Western contributions would only be meaningful if Egypt herself could manage her economy. This became less likely when Nasser mortgaged her cotton crop to pay for the Czechoslovak arms. True, he talked about his hopes of gaining a Soviet loan, but this in no way impressed John Foster Dulles, who feared lest America be saddled with the total cost of the dam. Since the US Senate was equally alarmed by Nasser's brand of international politics, the State Department on 19 July 1956 withdrew the offer of the loan. This meant that both Britain and the World Bank were forced to follow suit, which meant in turn that if the dam was ever to be built a further source of revenue would have to be discovered. Nasser therefore nationalized the Suez Canal Company and declared that its revenue would henceforth finance the construction of the dam.

The British reaction to the Egyptian takeover was hysterical and violently emotional. Nasser was considered to have undermined the very foundations of international law and order and to have threatened the security of the Western world. He was likened immediately to Adolf Hitler and every shade of British opinion demanded that Eden should stand no nonsense from this Arab guttersnipe. Churchill as usual summed up the national mood when he told his doctor: 'We can't have this malicious swine sitting across our communications.' The reaction was articulated by left as much as by right. Gaitskell said in Parliament that Nasser was just another Hitler or Mussolini and Bevan confided to Julian Amery, a leader of the 1954 'Suez Group', 'This proves that you were right.' Nobody thought to consider how British opinion would feel if Egyptians were running the cross-channel ferries. The only question was how Nasser could be forced to relinquish his ill-gotten gains. Even the Labour Party was all along prepared to contemplate the use of force. It differed from the Conservative Party only in that they held that such force would first of all have to be sanctioned by the United Nations. This was a curious theological requirement, since clearly the United Nations would never sanction the use of force against a country such as Egypt. However, it saved the Labour leaders from coming to grips with political logic.

Eden, on the other hand, had to come up with a realistic answer to this tricky diplomatic problem. He had none (as it turned out) but he was offered a number of solutions by dubious diplomatic friends, solutions which ranged from conciliation to retribution. Dulles and Eisenhower from the American side persistently counselled caution; the French government on the other hand advised unleashing the dogs of war. Eden, instinctively a man of peace, was prepared to go along with the Americans first, but at the same time, since he was caught up in an atmosphere of rabid, jingoistic imperialism, made contingency plans with the French. He no doubt hoped to achieve a peaceful diplomatic settlement but was simply not prepared to 'appease' Colonel Nasser to achieve one. Losing control of the canal to Egypt represented for him the end of British influence in Africa and Asia, so that like his colleague Harold Macmillan he was prepared to see Britain 'go down against Egypt with all flags flying rather than submit to the Suez despoliation'.

Dulles at first appeared to Eden to be holding out some measure of real support. During a discussion which obviously keenly impressed the Premier, he said: 'A way has to be found to make Nasser disgorge what he is attempting to swallow.' He then hinted that if Nasser would not cooperate with the United Nations or with other states then military force might indeed prove necessary after all. However, Eden should have known not to put much weight on such utterances. Eisenhower was up for re-election in November 1956 and was running on a peace platform. He was hardly likely, therefore, to want to become involved in any military adventures which might prejudice his chance of a second term in office. The situation might well have been different had Eden delayed military action until after the election. But, of course, he did not.

Dulles's first attempt at a solution was his proposal for a Suez Canal Board which would supervise the international operation of the canal. This was supported by eighteen states and put to Nasser by Robert

Menzies, the Prime Minister of Australia. Nasser rejected the scheme, and Dulles did nothing to save it. Instead, he proposed the creation of a Suez Canal Users' Club which might control the canal in conjunction with the Egyptians. Nasser again refused to have anything to do with his proposal and so the matter was referred to the United Nations. A series of general principles emerged – they included free and open transit of the canal, recognition of Egypt's sovereignty, agreement on tolls and the arbitration of disputes – but there was no way of forcing them on Egypt. When Britain and France made moves in this direction in New York, these were vetoed by the Soviet Union. The whole question therefore reduced itself to one of effectiveness, and in this respect American cooperation and advice were of no avail. Eden believed that he had been strung along by Dulles. Dulles, on the other hand, insisted that the talk of a betrayal was unfair: 'There is talk of teeth being pulled out of the plan, but I know of no teeth: there were no teeth in it.' This was precisely the problem, for, to twist the *mot* of one French diplomat concerned with negotiations at the time, it was necessary either to '*canaliser le colonel ou coloniser le canal*'. Since the colonel would not repent, the alternative was adopted.

The French government had no reason to like Nasser. French oil supplies also came through the Suez Canal, and, more importantly, France was at this time engaged in a war with Algerian rebels whose main support was the Egyptian dictator. The French therefore believed that if Nasser could be deposed their difficulties with respect to Algeria would suddenly disappear. Throughout the course of 1955 France had aligned herself with Israel.* The French Prime Minister, the socialist Guy Mollet, was an ardent supporter of Israeli independence and had been happy to equip the Israeli armed forces to withstand an Arab attack. Indeed by 1956 military cooperation between France and Israel had reached such an unprecedented state of intimacy that it seemed only natural in response to the Suez crisis that both countries should coordinate their reactions.

Mollet and others now succeeded in bringing Eden into their schemes. On 14 October General Challe outlined at Chequers a plan involving Anglo–French intervention and mediation in the case of an Israeli-

---

* Israel was under constant Egyptian pressures at this time. Eilat was blockaded, incursions into Israeli territory were being undertaken by the Fedayeen, and the Egyptian army was spoiling for revenge for 1948.

Egyptian war. To his surprise the response of the British Prime Minister was simply to murmur, 'Good idea'. Two days later Eden and Selwyn Lloyd met the French Prime Minister and Foreign Secretary in Paris, where they agreed to underwrite the scheme which Challe had proposed. Further talks took place between the British, French and Israelis, and by 26 October the undertaking had been agreed in writing and incorporated into the so-called Treaty of Sèvres. Israel, responding to Egyptian provocation, would launch an attack on Egyptian positions in Sinai. This would spark off a full-scale Arab-Israeli war in which an Anglo-French force would intervene to preserve the security of the Suez Canal. Thereafter some new arrangement could be worked out concerning the future of the international waterway.

Israeli action began on 29 October. On the 30th the British and French demanded that both sides withdraw ten miles each side of the canal. A day later the Anglo-French ultimatum expired and the day after that Egyptian air fields were bombed. On 5 November Anglo-French paratroopers landed at Port Said, which was captured within twenty-four hours. At midnight the following night, however, a ceasefire was arranged as a result of American pressure. With only a week to go before the American elections, Eisenhower felt betrayed by his allies and had their action condemned at the United Nations. The General Assembly voted in favour of a ceasefire and for a UN force to occupy the Canal Zone in place of Britain and France. Britain agreed on 6 November – the original combatants were no longer engaged; there were hints of Soviet intervention; Eden was exhausted; and there was a run on the pound which could only be stopped by American support for a loan from the IMF – and forced France to agree to withdraw also. The whole Canal Zone, it was reckoned, would have been captured within another few days but military considerations were no longer primary. The last British troops left Egypt shortly before Christmas 1956.

The affair appears in retrospect to have been a blunder of huge proportions. Why was there such a pressing need to control the canal? After all, Eden himself had only two years earlier negotiated Britain's evacuation of the Canal Zone, and the Cyprus base was supposed to provide the necessary mobility to safeguard British interests in the Middle East. Moreover, the Egyptians were perfectly capable of running the canal – as we had implicitly accepted in 1954 – and since nobody supposed that they would deny us our oil supplies in the aftermath of nationalization (they needed the revenues from tolls) the Suez expedition would appear to have been unnecessary in the first place. Several questions therefore have to be answered regarding the aims of the expedition. What did Eden expect to do with the canal if he secured it as a result of the expedition? Did he really expect that Nasser would be overthrown and replaced by some tame Egyptian anglophile? Probably he half expected this, but this represented a step back for Eden rather than a step forward. It merely meant that he would have to negotiate the 1954 agreements again at some point in the future. The kindest explanation is that he believed that a new government in Egypt would have agreed to international control of the canal. His very own policy, on the other hand, not to mention the response it occasioned in Egypt, made such a solution impossible. Eden's tortured mind had never got round to working out the possible consequences of his actions. He had not really even decided whether the whole of Egypt was to be held down by force if necessary or not. The French for their part had definitely assumed that this would be the case, whereas Eden and the British army laboured under the assumption that Cairo could be left unoccupied. The result was that, although the investing of Port Said was conducted with admirable military efficiency, the organization of the expedition was marked by substantial Anglo-French differences over important logistical and strategic considerations.

Should Eden have defied the UN and allowed the expedition to capture the whole Canal Zone? Churchill is reported to have said, 'I am not sure I should have dared to start, but I am sure I should not have dared to stop.' Dulles remarked to a British delegate at the UN: 'Why on earth didn't you go through with it?' It was very unlikely in the view of some commentators that another few days would have made much difference. However, the same respect for international law and order which had prompted Eden's initial reactions to Nasser's action compelled him to respect the wishes of the UN. There was perhaps a paradox at work here. The truth was that Eden simply didn't have a moral case with which to challenge the UN. Practically everybody had seen through the excuse of separating Israeli and Egyptian armies, and collusion was assumed by all. Eden and Selwyn Lloyd would later deliberately mislead the House of Commons over the facts of the Treaty of Sèvres, but internationally they already stood condemned. Ironically, had Eden moved against the Egyptian dictator without waiting to invent an excuse, he could most likely have presented the world with a *fait accompli*, just as Nasser succeeded in doing. Of course, the British forces were in no position to do so at the time – another valid criticism of Eden.

These criticisms were made of Eden at the time. Most of the press was hostile to him, although the *Express* and the *Sketch* supported his policy. City opinion was sceptical and middle-class opinion was cool. The BBC maintained an independent stand – much to Eden's and the Government's consternation – and the right of reply it afforded to Gaitskell after a broadcast by the Prime Minister sparked off a debate on the role of the media. On the other hand, there was probably substantial popular support for Eden's strong line. According to one opinion poll, support for Eden increased from 48½ per cent on 30 October to 60½ per cent on 21 November; another had it rising from 40 to 53 per cent in the fortnight ending 14 November; and in a by-election at Chester on 15 November the Conservative poll fell by only 5 per cent. Finally, Bevan on 4 November in a famous anti-Eden philippic in Trafalgar Square was careful to state his position with circumspection for fear of alienating pro-Eden working-class opinion: 'I am not saying – and let us get this right – that because Eden is wrong, Nasser is right. I am not saying for a single moment that the Israelis did not have the utmost provocation. What we are saying is that it is not possible to create peace in the Middle East by jeopardizing the peace of the world.'

Among Members of Parliament the debate over Suez was violent. The Tory Party contained those who were dissatisfied with Eden's retreat as well as those who were shocked by British intervention in the first place. Two government ministers (neither of them in the Cabinet) – Anthony Nutting and Sir Edward Boyle – resigned; eight anti-Suez rebels abstained from supporting the Government on 8 November; but the majority of those at odds with Eden (probably between twenty-five and forty) refrained from challenging the Government. In similar fashion after British troops withdrew in December the 'Suez Group' confined their protests to speeches and a few abstentions. On the Labour side, one MP (Mr Stanley Evans) resigned both his seat and his membership of the Labour Party on account of his support for government policy. Some Labour elder statesmen, too, made sympathetic noises, but by the beginning of October the strength of Labour's opposition was clear. Gaitskell's broadcast on 3 November included an appeal to Eden's supporters to overthrow him and in the Commons between 6 and 8

November there were scenes of unusual bitterness and barrack-room behaviour. The Suez expedition clearly aroused deep political emotions.

The diplomatic consequences of the affair were serious for Britain despite attempts on the part of certain Conservative commentators to argue otherwise. Eden's own apologia included the sentence, 'Our intervention at least closed the chapter of complacency about the situation in the Middle East.' Maybe, but if so it had done this only at great cost to Britain's prestige and standing in the area. Likewise no great weight can be attached to the claim that the authority of the United Nations was inadvertently enhanced by Suez. Conservative and Labour apologists afterwards affected to take pride in this 'achievement', but the claim is hypocritical nonsense. The United Nations proved totally incapable of keeping peace in the Middle East and in 1967 its observers were withdrawn from the frontier between Egypt and Israel at the request of the Egyptian president. Only those who fooled themselves into thinking that a new 'world policeman' had at last emerged could argue that Suez had strengthened the UN. The fact that two major powers had submitted to the will of that organization was a consequence of the policy of the United States and had nothing to do with the consensus of world opinion.

For other reasons also, Suez should be treated as a diplomatic disaster. Firstly, although Israel's position had been strengthened,* Nasser's wayward and ambitious presence in the Middle East had also been reinforced, his military defeat obscured by a spurious diplomatic victory over the imperial power whose influence in Arab affairs had until so recently been all-pervasive. Secondly, the breach which had been made in the Anglo-American alliance threatened to undermine the foundations of post-war international relations – the solidarity of the West in face of Soviet diplomatic manoeuvring. And thirdly, world attention was diverted from events in Eastern Europe, where the Soviet Union was crushing the Hungarian uprising at the same time as British paratroopers were landing at Port Said. It may be that even if there had been no Suez expedition the West would not have intervened to establish the independence of Hungary. However, the Suez affair robbed the West of its moral advantage over the Communists at a time when it was becoming important to be able to influence the countries of the emerging 'third

---

* Eilat was no longer blockaded and there were fewer attacks by the Fedayeen.

world'. As far as they were concerned, there seemed as a result of Suez to be little difference between 'Western imperialism' of either the Communist or capitalist variety. Both resorted to force to secure their political objectives.

The Suez affair was also unhelpful insofar as it served to underline Great Britain's dependence on America. Britain had in fact served notice to the world that she was no longer a great power. This should perhaps have been apparent beforehand, but it was still fairly easily overlooked and until 1956 Britain was still able to live off much of the political credit she had accumulated during the war. After 1956, however, this was simply no longer possible. Sir Pierson Dixon, Britain's representative at the UN, wrote in his diary in 1957:

> ... at the time I remember feeling very strongly that we had by our action reduced ourselves from a first-class to a third-class power. We revealed our weakness by stopping; and we threw away the moral position on which our world status largely depended. We were greater than our actual strength so long as people knew that we went to war in defence of principle – which is what we did in 1914 and 1939 ...

The French in particular were conscious of what had happened. The franc had not come under pressure as had the pound in the course of the Suez affair – British gold reserves fell by £100 million in the week after 6 November – and the French had as a consequence been less willing to submit to United States reproofs than had the (to them perfidious) British. In the light of Britain's withdrawal, therefore, the recently revived *entente* between Britain and France collapsed. This was to have far-reaching and serious consequences for future relations between these two countries.

On another level, too, Britain's prestige had also suffered. The British people now began to question the nature of their country's world role. Perhaps Britain had not really been acting from the highest motives. Perhaps British troops had been employed merely to protect commercial interests and client states. As a result of dwelling on such thoughts, the British were perhaps better prepared for the decolonization of the sixties than they might otherwise have been. Disillusion with empire and with the burdens of empire had already begun to set in. If so, this was one of the few positive results of Suez.

Finally, there was the resignation of Eden as Prime Minister on medical advice.* Suez had thoroughly exhausted him and his physicians ordered his retirement. The Tory Party had made no such demand but it was probably glad to see him go. Speculation was intense as to whom the Queen would appoint his successor. The choice was clearly between Butler and Macmillan, and on 10 January 1957 Macmillan accepted office. Eden meanwhile retired as premier convinced that his actions had been right. He had been cheered on 17 November when at a Young Conservative rally in London he had declared: 'We make no apology and shall make no apology for the action that we and our French allies took together.' And he never did.

* This at least was the official version. Eden's latest biographer, however, has suggested that Eisenhower demanded the Prime Minister's resignation and that Macmillan, Butler and Churchill dutifully helped to engineer it.

6

THE START OF
THE MACMILLAN ERA, 1957–9

Harold Macmillan was a fascinating personality, publicly self-confident
but privately introspective, a strange mixture of the hard-headed professional politician and the amateurish, country-gentleman sort of public
servant. He indulged a somewhat theatrical, Edwardian style of political
presentation but at the same time trailed with him a reputation for social
awareness that made him a contemporary political thinker. He was often
referred to as an example of 'ambiguity' and appealed to people as a
sympathetic curiosity, a sort of updated Disraeli who, despite his affected
manner and aristocratic tastes, nonetheless could peddle a histrionic sort
of patriotism which struck a responsive chord among the British people
in the aftermath of Suez. Again like Disraeli, he cared about the 'politics
of sewage' – the material condition of the nation – although in the end
he was to be accused of caring too much, in the wrong way and for the
wrong reasons. For all that, his spell was hard to resist and contemporary
historians have found it unusually hard to shake off. He mesmerized the
public with his lugubrious wit and epigrammatic phrase and by 1959 his
political ascendency seemed all but complete. In contrast to Eden he
thoroughly enjoyed the exercise of power – his predecessor had the in-
feriority complex of a natural deputy in office – and quickly established
his authority over his cabinet colleagues. He had clearly always felt a
need to be in command. This had been noted of him as a back-bench
rebel in the 1930s and by Herbert Morrison under whom he had served
(briefly) during the Second World War. It perhaps accounted for his
uncanny ability to create a political base, an ability which he had brilliantly demonstrated after 1942 when Churchill appointed him British
Minister-Resident first in North Africa, then in the Mediterranean Area
and finally in Italy.

Another aspect of Macmillan's undisguised ambition was his appetite for work. His record as Minister of Housing in Churchill's peacetime government was outstanding in this respect, and as Chancellor under Eden he once again asserted himself after the unhappy experience of attempting to run the Foreign Office while Eden was still at No. 10. By the time of the Suez crisis, therefore, Macmillan was the strong man of the Cabinet. His attitude to this problem was, however, inconsistent: from an enthusiastic backer of the use of force over Suez, Macmillan turned almost overnight into an exponent of withdrawal when, as Chancellor, he was confronted with the realities of sterling's external weaknesses. His turnabout can be interpreted either as political realism or as lack of nerve, but it cannot be denied that it was executed with such dexterity that his political career in no way suffered from it. Butler, rather, was the one who suffered, by making little secret in private of his doubts about government policy and of his irritation with Eden, whom he had once described in a telling phrase as 'the best prime minister we have'. Macmillan, on the other hand, never failed to support his leader or to assert that, whatever its consequences, the decision to use force had been right in principle in the first place. He was therefore the overwhelming choice of the Conservative Party for the post of Premier in 1957 – the information conveyed by Churchill and Salisbury to the Queen. As Prime Minister he entered office with great enthusiasm and exuberance, resolved to revive the flagging fortunes of his party. The outlook was glum. Labour led in the opinion polls by thirteen points and he jokingly remarked that his government would only last six weeks. In fact he was to govern Britain for the next six years.

His first task, as he saw it, was to patch things up with America. Yet he would not apologize for Suez. In his first broadcast as Premier he declared, 'True partnership is based upon respect. We don't intend to part from the Americans and we don't intend to be satellites,' adding, 'I am sure that they don't want us to be so.' He told Eisenhower at Bermuda: 'You need us for ourselves; for the Commonwealth; and as leaders of Europe. But chiefly because without a common front and true partnership between us I doubt whether the principles we believe in can win.' There was almost something of de Gaulle about Macmillan – the exaggerated use of the national manner, the reliance on the nation's pride in past achievements to obscure its uneasy transition to a less exalted status as well as the desire to mediate between East and West. However, in contrast to de Gaulle, Macmillan never conceived of the notion of independence from America. He believed it was unrealistic and, priding himself on his ability to 'handle Americans' – he was half-American himself – he preferred to work in partnership with the USA.

In point of fact, the damage done by Suez to the transatlantic relationship was not nearly so great as had been feared. The presidential election over, Eisenhower was prepared to get tough with the Arab left. On 5 January 1957 he appeared before a joint session of Congress and introduced the 'Eisenhower Doctrine'; henceforth if nations of the Middle East were threatened 'by alien forces hostile to freedom' they could request American military aid and assistance to resist 'armed attack from any country controlled by international Communism'. A fund of $200 million was set up to provide such aid as would be necessary, and soon indeed some was. King Hussein of Jordan was forced to appeal (in April 1957) to America to help him resist a Nasserite revolt and in May the following year American marines were landed in Beirut to protect the government of Lebanon. By this time Syria and Egypt had joined together to form the United Arab Republic, and a pro-Nasserite *coup* had been staged in Iraq. Hussein once again felt threatened and in July British paratroopers had to be dropped into Amman. This was done, of course, with American approval and caused many a wry smile inside the British Foreign Office. It was not a case of 'come back Eden, all is forgiven', but the ironies of the situation were certainly much remarked upon.

The Anglo-American alliance had been well patched up. Eisenhower and Dulles had met Macmillan and Selwyn Lloyd on British soil at Bermuda late in March 1957 (where they had reaffirmed the Security Council's resolution of October 1956 about the freedom of the canal) and in October 1957 the Queen and Prince Philip visited the USA after an official visit to Canada. The final seal was set on restored partnership and amicability when Macmillan and Eisenhower, following up the success of the Queen's visit, signed a Declaration of Common Purpose that same month.

The presence of Selwyn Lloyd at Bermuda as Foreign Secretary was a symbol of Macmillan's determination not to apologize for Suez. It was also an indication that Macmillan intended to direct foreign affairs himself and to assert his role as Premier. He therefore kept Butler on at the Home Office and gave him the Leadership of the House of Commons. But, foreseeing difficulties with Antony Head, he replaced him as

Defence Minister with Duncan Sandys before giving him a peerage and packing him off to govern Nigeria. Lord Hailsham, a strong personality, was persuaded to stay on at the Ministry of Education, but a number of other ministers were allowed to retire, enabling the Prime Minister to bring in new blood. Thus only four of Macmillan's ministers (after March 1957) had served in the 1951–5 cabinet, and most of his team was composed of younger men who had entered Parliament since 1950. Macmillan could therefore set his personal stamp on the Government.

Duncan Sandys's appointment as Minister of Defence – with a new directive from the premier arming him with greater powers to control the service ministries – anticipated policy changes of a major order. Since 1952, following a review by the Chiefs of Staff, British strategy had come increasingly under scrutiny. The development of the British hydrogen bomb – successfully tested in 1957 – not to mention the considerable cost of National Service, now suggested that a major re-thinking of defence policy was necessary if not overdue. Several factors underlined this – Britain's NATO commitment under the Paris agreements of 1954 (which boosted defence spending overseas by £50 million per year); the traumas of the Suez crisis; and the vulnerability of sterling – with the result that a White Paper on Defence was published on 5 April 1957. It was not in itself the revolutionary document which many affected to see it as – rather it drew together the various threads in British thinking which had been emerging in recent years – but it certainly constituted a landmark in the history of Britain's defence policies.

Britain's dilemma was fairly obvious. At a time when her economic resources were pushed to the limits and when there seemed no hope of limiting her commitments, she could no longer cope as before with a bill for defence which already amounted to 8 per cent of the GNP and which was expected to rise by over 6 per cent a year. (Between the wars it had only been necessary to spend 3 per cent of the GNP on defence and then there had been no more than 300,000 men in uniform compared with 700,000 in 1957.) Clearly something would have to be done. Moreover France was spending only 6 per cent of her GNP on defence and Germany only 4 per cent – half the British contribution – at a time when Continental exports were beginning to challenge Britain's export trade. British industry could not effectively respond so long as 24 per cent of its shipbuilding and 14 per cent of its engineering output was committed to defence and so long as the requirements of government defence spending prevented industry from finding the money to invest in modernization. The Government's answer, therefore, was to stake the credibility of British defence on the development of an independent nuclear deterrent. This would enable Great Britain to lay claim to super-power status internationally; to do away with National Service; to limit the defence budget; and to assert its independence of the USA. In short, it seemed the answer to the Government's prayers. No longer would a huge conventional army be required to look after Britain's commitments. Instead a better-equipped, smaller, but highly mobile force could attend to local difficulties. The main burden of British defence would now rest on a nuclear force which even by itself could threaten the Soviet Union with 'massive retaliation' in case of attack. This force was to consist in part of a fleet of Vulcan bombers which could deliver British H-bombs, but the Government also committed themselves to developing the Blue Streak missile. The 1957 White Paper therefore promised to end conscription by 1960 and to reduce the size of the army to 165,000 professionals by 1962. The armed forces by that time would altogether account for only 400,000 men and defence expenditure would be held at 7 per cent of the GNP.

It was a bold stroke and at first all seemed to augur well. Delivery of hydrogen weapons to the bomber force began in 1958 and in the same year America amended the McMahon Act to allow disclosures about atomic weapons to countries which had already substantially developed their own nuclear technology. Criticisms were levied by Britain's European allies against what in fact amounted to a unilateral change in NATO strategy (13,000 troops were to be withdrawn from West Germany within one year), but at home the Government's policy met with fairly mild resistance. Those within the Labour Party who had doubts about the reductions in the strength of British troops were unable to make much of their criticisms on account of Labour's commitment to abolish National Service. In like fashion there could be little attack from principle in view of Gaitskell's support for nuclear weapons. 'Our party', he had said only a few days before the publication of the White Paper, 'decided to support the manufacture of the hydrogen bomb . . . because we do not think it is right that this country should be so dependent . . . upon the USA.' His statement highlighted the sense of reassurance which the White Paper would give to those who were worried by Britain's decline as a world power. For them the Government's new policy appeared to provide the means to reclaim world status on the cheap. Randolph Churchill, Winston's son, declared in 1958: 'Britain can knock down twelve cities in the region of Stalingrad and Moscow from bases in Britain and another dozen in the Crimea from bases in Cyprus. We did not have that power at the time of Suez. We are a major power again.' And so it seemed.

Only the Liberal Party – on so many issues at this time the most advanced in its political analyses – officially opposed the independent British deterrent. It advised the Government to make a better contribution to conventional defence and pointed out that future challenges would come in the shape of local, not nuclear, wars. Like the *Manchester Guardian*, it doubted whether defence expenditure could be effectively reduced without a corresponding cut in defence commitments, and like *The Times* – for once unblinkered – it branded the new deterrent an object of 'prestige rather than military necessity'. The Liberal Party, however, attracted only very small support electorally, so that real opposition to nuclear policy had to be mobilized by the Campaign for Nuclear Disarmament after 1957. This set out to convert (with moral arguments) a Labour Party which was bitterly and sharply divided on the issue. However, it was not the moral issues involved in nuclear armament which were gradually to undermine the foundations of the Government's new policies. Rather it was the escalating cost of nuclear research and development, the failure to construct a suitable missile, the persistent need to station substantial forces abroad and the unavoidable and continual dependence on America which did that. But by 1959 the flaws in the Government's case were not yet generally apparent. Their policy was still on trial and since most people still took it for granted that Britain should remain a world power the jury was a fairly sympathetic one.

Britain's obsession with world status was naturally bound up with her position at the centre of the British Empire and Commonwealth. By the mid-1950s strains were beginning to appear in the imperial edifice and British governments faced the challenge of preparing new nations for independence. The hope was that if this were achieved successfully then Empire might be peacefully and appreciatively transferred into Commonwealth. But there were many problems to overcome. In Kenya and Cyprus in particular there was violent opposition to British rule, and in other parts of the world British policy was meeting with resistance.

Different peoples reacted to British overlordship in different ways, and the smooth transition which British leaders would like to have seen from dependency to independence was not always possible. On the whole, however, Britain succeeded in divesting herself of her empire with remarkable dignity and skill. She was known to have decided not to hang on to her colonies for ever – it had long been realized that such a policy was both impracticable and undesirable – so that nationalist leaders understood that their real quarrel with Great Britain was over the timing of independence rather than over independence itself.

This being the case, most quarrels concerned Great Britain's estimate of how ready native peoples were to assume the mantle of self-government. British ministers wanted to hand over power only when a sufficiently numerous educated class was ready and able to administer their country, and until they were convinced that one existed they felt they would betray their responsibility to native populations should they relinquish their authority prematurely. Native leaders, on the other hand, and particularly those in Africa, pointed out with considerable justice that since Britain had only begun to educate her imperial subjects after the war, it was bound to take generations before such people could be properly trained. Britain should therefore increase her efforts to prepare them for independence, give proof of her good intentions by bringing natives into the government process and in general act in such a manner as to win the cooperation of local leaders. In Africa, unfortunately, such a course was not always straightforward. In East Africa in particular there were large numbers of white settlers of British descent who were eager to safeguard their vested interests, while almost everywhere the Africans themselves were divided by tribal rivalries. British policy therefore had to cope with many divergent and conflicting interests.

That this was so can be seen for example with regard to British policy in Kenya, which in the 1950s ran into serious trouble. African political consciousness in Kenya first manifested itself in the 1920s with the emergence of several organizations there which centred around the Kikuyu tribe. The latter lived near the colonial capital of Nairobi, were most affected by land alienation, low wages and racial discrimination, and could more readily perceive the general political suppression of the Africans. In 1924 the Kikuyu Central Association was formed and in 1928 Jomo Kenyatta became its secretary-general. By the 1930s its influence had spread to other tribes in Kenya; in 1940 it was banned. After

1944, however, British policy became more enlightened. One African was appointed to the Kenya legislative council in 1944 and another in 1947. In 1952 an African was even appointed to the Governor's Executive Council, but the European settlers were determined to resist further native advance. Consequently Africans in Nairobi and Mombasa lent increasing support to the Kenyan African Union which had been founded in 1944. The KAU protested against rising prices and low wages, unemployment, unused land in the White Highlands (Africans were often evicted and sent to overcrowded reserves) and racial discrimination. It also exerted pressure for greater African representation on the legislative and executive councils and for the holding of direct elections. When protests failed to secure the redress of various grievances, the KAU solidified its strength by the traditional African practice of oath-taking and protest soon degenerated into violence. Between 1952 and 1956 the so-called Mau Mau rebellion took place, claiming the lives of ninety-five Europeans and some 13,000 blacks. Mau Mau adherents employed particularly savage means of terror so that from 1952 till 1959 emergency regulations were introduced and Kenyatta and other Kikuyu leaders were placed in detention camps, although they denied they were responsible for the rebellion. There was a scandal in 1959 when it was found that eleven prisoners had died from beatings administered by African wardens in one such camp, but by then the Government had taken steps to redress African grievances. The Mau Mau rebellion had if anything encouraged the Government to speed up the process of Africanization. In April 1954 the Colonial Secretary announced a new constitution which had a multi-racial dimension. 1956 saw the introduction of some land reform and of an African franchise. Meanwhile Mau Mau had affected British policy in other parts of Africa too.

The foundation in 1953 of the Central African Federation of Southern Rhodesia, Northern Rhodesia and Nyasaland was likewise a major event in the growth of African nationalism. The Federation had come into being despite the wishes of the Africans, who had boycotted the congress which founded it from fear of being sacrificed to the white settlers of Southern Rhodesia. These fears were well founded. The 1953 Constitution ensured that only one third of the Federal Assembly should be filled by Africans but allowed the Federal Constitution to be amended by a majority of two thirds. True, there was provision for an African Affairs Board, but since this had no powers Africans placed little faith in British promises of gradual self-rule. What faith they had was further undermined in 1957 when, by the London Agreement of that year, more concessions were made to the white Federal Government of Sir Roy Welensky; it was rumoured that the Federation would be granted dominion status by 1960. The Constitutional Amendment Act of 1957 was an even greater blow to African aspirations – Britain now promised not to amend or repeal any Federal Acts – and the Electoral Act of 1958 seemed to be the very last straw, confirming as it did the political supremacy of the white minority. Not surprisingly, disturbances broke out (Dr Hastings Banda, who had returned to Nyasaland in 1958, had in any case raised the political temperature); the settler population took fright and security precautions taken by the authorities to counter Banda's activities led to the establishment of something like a police state. Lord Devlin was appointed as a result to conduct an official inquiry into the matter and his criticisms of official behaviour, as well as his view that most Africans opposed the Federation, led the Government to set up the Monckton Commission in July 1959 with instructions to review the Federal Constitution. The end of the Federation, therefore, was clearly in sight. However, Mau Mau atrocities had meantime helped foster official British sympathy for the settler point of view.

Elsewhere they produced a different result, speeding up the movement for self-government in West Africa, for example. There Africanization had begun as early as the 1920s. Direct election to the legislative council had come in Nigeria in 1922, in Sierra Leone in 1924 and in the Gold Coast in 1925. The franchise was limited and Africans, it is true, had little political power, but the movement towards independence had already got under way. After the Second World War it proceeded more rapidly. New constitutions were promulgated for these three territories in 1946 and 1947 and political parties were formed or re-formed as a result. In the Gold Coast in particular Kwame Nkrumah built up a strong nationalist movement as head of the Convention People's Party and demanded early self-government. Imprisoned after the Accra riots of 1950, he became a nationalist martyr and popular hero and in the elections of 1951 led his party to victory. He subsequently became Prime Minister and in 1957 the Gold Coast was granted independence as Ghana. With Ghanaian independence, the independence of Nigeria and Sierra Leone could not be long delayed. Elsewhere in British Africa progress was also being made. Julius Nyerere had established a national following in Tanganyika and an international reputation for moderation after visits to the United Nations in 1956 and 1957.

Africa was on the verge of liberation from British rule and the British were trying to make the best of it. By the end of the 1950s this was perhaps the only possible response. The Second World War, Suez, the independence of the Indian sub-continent, the Mau Mau rebellion and Ghanaian independence meant that Britain's remaining African subjects expected independence too. It only remained for Britain to establish a timetable for withdrawal, and Macmillan was probably aware of this. At the end of his 1958 Commonwealth tour (which, however, had not included Africa) he voiced his admiration for the modern development of the Commonwealth, and there is little reason to believe that he saw much point in hanging on in Africa or elsewhere.

Most Britons would have agreed with him. They had been sickened by EOKA violence in Cyprus – where Colonel Grivas and Archbishop Makarios were striving for union with Greece – as much as by the Mau Mau rebellion in Kenya and were happy to see Cyprus gain its independence in February 1957 (when Malaysia had also been granted independence). Finally in 1958 the West Indies had been accorded independence as the West Indies Federation, so that by 1959 a definite pattern had emerged. Besides, the white man's burden no longer seemed worth bearing, with the result that there seemed no particular reason why the Empire should continue. The will to imperial power had slackened considerably by 1959; the job of government was now to persuade the newly independent colonies to join the Commonwealth and remain on good terms with Great Britain. It said something for British rule, perhaps, that in this the Macmillan government proved consistently successful.

Britain's concern with her Commonwealth and Empire, with trans-atlantic relations and with her independent nuclear deterrent meant that the British public had even less regard for what was happening in Europe than it usually had. This was a great pity, because developments there in the late 1950s were taking a decisive and fateful turn. The French had taken little pride in their rejection of the EDC. It had after all been originally a French creation and had been accepted by Germany, Italy and the Benelux countries. For France to kill it off, therefore, had seemed a peculiarly shameful act. The result was that the French were all the more determined to ensure the success of the next proposal which

Europe's federalists put forward. This was nothing less than the suggestion of a European Common Market,* presented in a memorandum of the Benelux governments to the governments of France, Germany and Italy on 20 May 1955. On 2 June the Foreign Ministers of the Six met at Messina in Italy to consider the proposal. There they set up an intergovernmental committee under Paul-Henri Spaak, the Belgian Foreign Minister, to prepare a detailed plan. In the following spring it submitted a report. The drafting of the treaties which established the European Economic Community and Euratom then followed. These were signed in Rome in March 1957 and ratified by the Six in the following months. They took effect from 1 January 1958. France, on this occasion, was well satisfied; the Common Market was to cover not merely industrial goods but also agricultural produce.

Not unnaturally, the speed with which these events occurred took Britain by surprise. Ever since the fiasco of the EDC Great Britain, rather smugly, had poured scorn on the European federalist movement and did not expect another initiative to come so soon. Instead, the federalists, determined to make up for their defeat over the EDC, had moved forward on a new front very quickly. Britain was caught off guard. Yet there had been no attempt, as in the case of the Schuman Plan, to exclude Britain from the start by insisting on a supra-nationalist commitment in advance, and at the Messina conference Britain was invited to participate in the work of drafting the initial treaties. However, Harold Macmillan, then Foreign Secretary, had responded very coldly and only an under-secretary from the Board of Trade was sent to represent Britain on the Spaak committee.

Moreover, the differences between Britain and the Six became clear very quickly. In particular they held different views regarding the proposed external tariff. The Six supported the view that they should establish a single tariff structure with regard to the rest of the world, thus strengthening their hand in tariff negotiations. Britain, on the other hand, would not accept the idea. She had her system of Commonwealth preferences to protect; she wanted to retain the OEEC as the European organization responsible for conducting tariff negotiations; and she disliked the supra-national implications of a Common Market external tariff. The British representative was therefore withdrawn from the

* They also proposed a common system for transport and atomic energy but the idea of a Common Market was the important thing.

Spaak committee and Eden, who was absorbed with problems in the Middle East and with relations with the Soviet Union, probably placed little significance on what was happening. It was not until the beginning of 1956 that Britain, under US pressure, gave some thought to Western Europe and came up with the idea of a European free trade area which would include the Six, Great Britain and the other OEEC countries. A free trade area differed from a common market in that its members would cooperate through their respective governments and in that there would be no common external tariff. The British themselves had no real enthusiasm for this idea – Commonwealth trade was still considered by them to be of much greater importance than European trade – but it had been pushed by other OEEC members and Britain, in search of some solution, had reluctantly taken it up. A special study of it was made by the OEEC, and in October 1956 Eden presented a British plan for a free trade area in all goods except foodstuffs. This plan, in fact, represented a considerable step forward in British thinking and attracted some support in Europe: Ludwig Erhardt in Germany and Pierre Mendès-France in France were both impressed by it. Not only did it offer the prospect of an enlarged trading market for industrialists, but it tied Britain more securely to Europe.

In retrospect a good case can be made out to the effect that Europe made a mistake in rejecting this proposal. But rejected it was, and there were a number of sound economic reasons. The French, for example, were clearly scared at the prospect of being subjected to both British and German industrial competition while securing no advantage for their farm products. Furthermore, if there were no common external tariff on agricultural imports a country like Britain which had access to cheap food from her Commonwealth might well be able to cut costs on her wage bill and hence be able to undercut her European industrial competitors. Britain never paid enough attention to these objections. Instead, she assumed too readily that Europe would do anything to entice her in and totally underestimated the force of pro-Common Market sentiment. The Rome Treaties, therefore, were signed without her.

Macmillan remained determined to secure a free trade area. But the outlook was glum. In particular General de Gaulle had returned to power in France in 1958 and Macmillan, whose knowledge of de Gaulle went back to the Second World War, was aware of his distrust of the 'Anglo-Saxons'. The prospects grew even dimmer when America and

Great Britain rejected a proposal from the General dated September 1958 that a directorate of France, Great Britain and the USA should run the Western Alliance. Moreover, America had by this time already offended de Gaulle by making it clear to him that France, unlike Great Britain, would not be made party to its nuclear secrets under the terms of the McMahon Act. Nevertheless, Macmillan tried to convince de Gaulle that Europe should not be further divided. He tried, too, to enlist the support of Adenauer, although his efforts were to no avail. De Gaulle was determined to assert Europe's independence of America by limiting British influence, and with the outbreak of the second Berlin crisis Adenauer's freedom of manoeuvre *vis-à-vis* de Gaulle was strictly limited. The General could therefore bid successfully for the leadership of Europe, and the negotiations which Reginald Maudling was conducting with the Six on Britain's behalf were broken off after the French Minister of Information curtly announced on 14 November 1958 that it was 'not possible' to form a free trade area without a common external tariff.

Britain now took up the only diplomatic option remaining open to her. Together with the Scandinavian countries, Switzerland, Austria and Portugal she formed a European Free Trade Association (EFTA), which came to be known as the 'outer seven'. This was established by the Stockholm Convention of 4 January 1960 which, unlike the Common Market Treaty, contained no supra-national element. Nor did the free trade area apply to agricultural products. The Convention was therefore a fairly simple document and it allowed each EFTA member to withdraw from the association so long as twelve months' notice was given of the intention to do so. For a while hope lingered that EFTA and the EEC might one day merge into one, but by 1960 it was clear that Western Europe was economically divided and the OEEC, whose role was now redundant, became the OECD (Organization for Economic Cooperation and Development), which included America and Japan. No longer a European body, it became a club of rich industrial nations designed to monitor one another's trading and financial policies.

Few people in Britain at the time took much notice of these developments. Britain was still regarded by the British as the leading power in Europe and there was little expectation even in official circles that the Common Market would amount to very much. The Liberal Party argued for British entry but its voice carried little political weight. Most people were more impressed by the independent deterrent, the Commonwealth and the 'special relationship' with America which Macmillan had so successfully restored. Indeed, Macmillan seemed to be cutting a rather fine figure internationally, for his setback over Europe had been obscured by yet another diplomatic exchange with the Soviet Union.

In the course of 1957 the Prime Minister had been very cool towards the Russians. He had rejected proposals for a summit meeting and had resisted pressure to take up the idea of a nuclear-free zone in Central Europe which had been put forward by the Polish Foreign Minister, Rapacki. However, developments soon convinced Macmillan that a more active diplomacy was needed. In November 1958 Khrushchev demanded that the Allies leave Berlin. He gave them six months to withdraw their troops and advised them to come to an agreement with East Germany regarding access routes to West Berlin. His objective, clearly, was to force the Allies to recognize the East German government and to begin the process of incorporating West Berlin within East Germany. The Allies rejected the Soviet demand and Dulles declared that West Berlin would be defended 'if need be by military force'. Once again, therefore, it seemed possible that war might break out over Germany.

Macmillan now decided to visit Moscow. He had already turned down Soviet invitations to top-level talks but now he felt that a visit might do some good. He might discover just what the Russians were up to, or he might just be able to relax East–West tension a little. At the very least he would show that Britain could still act independently of America, and this would, no doubt, be an asset for him in what was generally expected to become an election year. His allies – West Germany especially – were not at all happy to see him go (Adenauer was reminded of Chamberlain's flight to Munich and had no idea what might be agreed behind his back). In the end nothing was settled and all that Macmillan gained was the publicity. Likewise, a conference of foreign ministers that summer at Geneva failed to solve the Berlin crisis, as did a visit of Khrushchev in September to America. However, the six-month ultimatum had by this time expired with no dire consequences, so that by the time the British general election came in October it seemed plausible that Macmillan's efforts had contributed something to the cause of peace. The Prime Minister, indeed, could enter the election campaign with an apparently respectable record in foreign affairs. He had restored the 'special relationship' with America; he had refashioned British defence policy in such a way as to preserve the country's great-power status; he had handled difficult problems in Commonwealth affairs with patience and not without success; he was retrieving Britain's position in Western Europe by negotiating a European Free Trade Area; and he had shown Britain's desire for peace in the world by negotiating with the Russians. How fragile some of these claims really were would only be clear after 1959.

In home affairs, also, matters were in a state which might be described as superficially successful by October 1959. As far as economic policy was concerned, this had not at first seemed likely. The 'stop' which had been inaugurated late in 1955 had had to be prolonged in 1956 on account of the run on sterling which had developed during the Suez crisis. The Government had been obliged to seek an IMF loan – the first time in British history that this had been necessary – in order to replenish the reserves, and the 'stop' was to last two years. Demand fell until in 1958 the annual increase in GNP dropped below 1 per cent and the country experienced its first lengthy period of Conservative stagnation. Things were made worse by the fact that Macmillan's new Chancellor, Peter Thorneycroft, was an out-and-out monetarist in economic affairs. Thus although he introduced a fairly liberal budget in April 1957 – cutting purchase tax and giving higher earned income relief – by the autumn of that year he was convinced that he had made a mistake: a run of £200 million on Britain's reserves during the summer had underlined the need for further deflation. Contrary to Thorneycroft's belief, foreign confidence in the pound was probably not suffering on account of Britain's domestic performance. The country was enjoying a satisfactory surplus in the balance of payments and all the economic indicators were pointing to the early stages of cyclical decline. It is, in fact, much more likely that foreign money markets were speculating on a likely revaluation of the Deutschmark. However, the Chancellor was convinced that wage increases were at the root of the problem and that the economy was suffering from over-heating. He therefore resorted to monetary remedies and in September 1957 raised bank rate to 7 per cent and introduced restrictions on investment. He announced his determination to maintain the parity of the pound even at the cost of higher unemployment, and before the year was out he was talking about holding government expenditure at 'the level attained this year'. One result of his policies was that he had no influence with the TUC. In July 1957 he had set up a three-man Council on Prices, Productivity and Incomes headed by the monetarist Sir Denis Robertson. The TUC at first co-operated reluctantly with this body, but when it approved the Chancellor's measures in its very first report it was not surprisingly boycotted.

By February 1958 the Chancellor's hard-line policy had led to further developments. In January, having insisted on continuing deflation, he was sacked by Harold Macmillan. His whole Treasury team resigned, but Macmillan, who as MP for Stockton during the depression had seen the results of hard-line monetary measures, was simply not prepared to put up with Thorneycroft's intransigent monetarist policy. The Treasury resignations he dismissed to journalists as 'little local difficulties' and with characteristic unflappability set off for his Commonwealth tour. Thorneycroft was replaced at the Treasury by Heathcoat-Amory, a mild-mannered, little-known businessman who at first continued the 'stop' but who managed to restore business confidence in April by establishing a single rate (10 per cent) for profits tax. Bank rate was reduced in November and credit restrictions were also lifted, so that by 1960 Britain was enjoying a Tory boom. Heathcoat-Amory, of course, should have anticipated this in 1959 but, like Butler in 1955, he was under strong political pressures and once again, therefore, just before an election, proper economic considerations were disregarded. Income tax was cut; purchase tax went down; beer was reduced in price; post-war credits were released; and investment allowances were restored. If this was no prescription for the country's economic condition, it nevertheless enabled Mr Macmillan to persuade the electorate that good times were here at last.

Only one piece of legislation cast a shadow over the Tory record in home affairs, namely the controversial Rent Act of 1957 This was a logical development of Macmillan's own policies as Housing Minister and was savagely attacked by Labour as a 'landlords' charter' to exploit poor tenants. The Act removed 810,000 houses from rent control and allowed rent increases for 4.3 million still controlled. The Housing Minister, the unloved Henry Brooke, argued that unless rents went up landlords could simply not afford to repair their properties or to bring new houses on to the market. The Opposition argued, on the other hand, that there was no obligation on the landlord to repair, that rents would simply rise and that landlords would pocket the extra money. In retrospect, it would appear that both sides of the argument were wrong: rents did not rise spectacularly and few houses came on to the market. The passion aroused by the Act was therefore curiously unrelated to reality. By 1959, however, this passion was largely spent. The Government were able to look forward to an election with every hope of defeating the Opposition.

Once again the Labour Party presented a fairly uninspiring picture. It had had issues enough over which to launch an attack on the Conservative government, but as Enoch Powell has written: 'At no stage were the Opposition benches able to establish a decisive ascendancy over the Government in morale and in debate, even when all the cards which a Government's opponents could possibly want had been thrust into their hands.' This was even more surprising on at least two counts. Firstly, there had been a change of leadership with the retirement of Clement Attlee; secondly, the Bevanites had also lost their leader when Bevan himself, having accepted the post of Shadow Foreign Secretary, had opposed the left-wing campaign for unilateral nuclear disarmament. It would not be right, he said, to send a Labour Foreign Secretary 'naked into the conference chamber', and on this rather feeble excuse appeared to abandon his opposition in principle to nuclear weapons. The traditional Labour leadership therefore now seemed to have the chance to re-establish unity within the party. That this did not happen was due in no small measure to the personality of the new party leader, Hugh Gaitskell, a courageous and honest man but one who lacked the necessary guile to lead a major party in Opposition.

Gaitskell had secured 157 votes in the leadership election of December 1955, compared with Bevan's seventy and Morrison's forty. Morrison, who took the result rather bitterly – in fact he was too old for the leadership and should have realized this – more or less withdrew from the political arena. He resigned the deputy leadership and let Gaitskell get on with managing the party without him. This was quite a job in the years 1955–9, for Gaitskell had lost the services of both Dalton and Attlee. Nor did he have the assured support of the leading trade unions. These had moved to the left in the mid-fifties under the influence of men like Frank Cousins (head of the TGWU) and were growing increasingly critical of official party policy. Gaitskell himself was experienced enough – he had entered Parliament in 1945 and had held top ministerial appointments – but on the other hand his abrasive personality did not endear him to the left. Instead, once he had made up his mind on any issue he tended to propagate his views both forcefully and eloquently, leaving his opponents within the party to come to terms with his stand unilaterally. All this was a matter of principle with him but it did tend to emphasize just how divided the party was, often over the most important issues.

The greatest division was evident over defence and nuclear policy. Gaitskell was a firm supporter of Britain's need to have nuclear weapons. Others in the party were opposed to this, although they were content to remain part of NATO (Wigg and Crossman, for example). Others still, on the far left of the party, were by 1959 adopting a roundly pacifist stance. These people – and they included Frank Cousins, whose union in June 1959 voted for unilateral British disarmament – were against any form of nuclear defence, independent or collective. They were members of both the Labour Party and of CND and wanted to convert the former to the aims of the latter. It was their belief that Britain's renunciation of the bomb would win her 'the moral leadership of the world' – a form of ethical imperialism to which Labour was very much addicted. Gaitskell, on the other hand, refused to pay much attention to them, although he was forced to do so later on.

On home affairs – or rather on the philosophical basis which underlay Labour's domestic policies – the party was also split three ways. The traditionalist left supported an all-out campaign to commit the party to further measures of nationalization along the lines mapped out in 1918 and consecrated in Clause IV of the party's constitution. The traditional right affected to believe in nationalization in principle but were opposed to it in practice – or too much of it in practice – on the grounds that much research was necessary before new industries could come under state control. No matter how sincere they were they never produced convincing evidence that they were undertaking this research. Finally, there were the revisionists, men like Healey, Crosland and Jenkins, who simply saw nationalization as irrelevant to the nation's problems. Crosland in particular was not afraid to say so and in his book, *The Future of Socialism*, published in 1956, he argued that socialism was about equality rather than public ownership. Like Gaitskell, Crosland saw nationalization as a means rather than an end in itself and in the era of the 1950s not even a very efficient one to achieve the equality which socialists desired. He argued that the great advances made by post-war Labour governments had been made through the Welfare State and that the nationalization legislation of 1945–51 had hardly affected the national good. Thus the place of nationalization in the revisionists' scheme of things was restricted to those industries which were obviously 'failing the nation'. In other words, the economic model used by the revisionists was one of a mixed economy with public ownership applying only to specific industries which failed to make a profit.

It was Gaitskell's job to reconcile all these differences within the party, and assuredly his task was not an easy one. Some progress was made, however, before the 1959 election. In 1957 a document entitled *Industry and Society* was adopted by the Labour Party conference despite its obvious concessions to revisionist thought. Another, entitled *Disarmament and Nuclear War*, was published in 1958 and, together with a paper entitled *Disengagement in Europe*, put forward compromise proposals on nuclear defence. Briefly, Labour wanted the suspension of nuclear tests, British control of US missile bases in Britain,* and a nuclear-free zone in Central Europe. Finally, in 1959 the party proposed the creation of a 'non-nuclear club' in the hope that an agreement could be reached with most countries – with the exception of the Soviet Union and the USA – not to test, manufacture or possess nuclear weapons. By all these means it was thought that Labour could present itself to the electorate as a credible alternative party of government.

Yet there were doubts as to Labour's ability to do this. Suez in no way proved an electoral windfall for the party, and by-elections began to show a trend towards the Liberals. That Labour would not necessarily benefit from Conservative discomfiture was first revealed at the Tonbridge by-election. For although the Conservative vote fell dramatically there the Labour vote simply failed to rise. Instead, it was the Liberals who began to attract new votes. Thus at Edinburgh South in May 1957 and at Gloucester in September their intervention caused the Conservatives to lose when the Liberal candidates took more than 20 per cent of the poll. Once again there was no marked change in the Labour vote. Then in February 1958, at Rochdale, the Liberals won what amounted to a moral victory. Their candidate, the broadcaster and journalist Ludovic Kennedy, failed to win the seat but he secured second place with nearly 18,000 votes, so that the scene was set for the first Liberal by-

---

* Until Blue Streak was constructed, America had agreed to give Britain US Thor missiles.

election win in post-war British history. This came at Torrington in March 1958 when Mark Bonham-Carter, Asquith's grandson and brother-in-law of the new Liberal leader Jo Grimond, defeated the 'National Liberal and Conservative' candidate. The Labour vote (as in Rochdale) fell below the figure recorded at the 1955 election. Thereafter the Liberals did less well and the Conservative Party better. But there was little comfort in the by-election results for Labour. Grimond, it appeared, was a fresher and more exciting leader than Gaitskell.

When the general election date was announced – 8 October 1959 – the Labour Party was perhaps the least prepared for it. The Conservatives, under the skilful guidance of Lord Hailsham, had already spent nearly half a million pounds on a public relations campaign between June 1957 and September 1959, while business interests had spent three times that much campaigning against Labour Party nationalization proposals. Once the election campaign got under way more money went into extolling the virtues of 'Super-Mac' and the Conservatives formulated a strategy based on Britain's new prosperity and affluence. 'Life is better with the Conservatives,' they proclaimed, and added, 'Don't let Labour ruin it.' They looked forward in their manifesto to 'The Next Five Years' and hoped to double the standard of living of the British people within a generation. The Labour Party, on the other hand, was not sure how to respond to these claims and was at a loss as to how to fight back. The Conservative record was not unnaturally assailed, but Labour discovered that it was felt to be unpatriotic to bring up the Suez affair and that recent budgeting favours had done much as far as the public was concerned to vindicate Conservative rule. Curiously enough, the splits within the Labour Party did not seem to damage it as much as might have been expected. Nationalization was in any case played down, but even before the election campaign took place the pollsters discovered that almost 40 per cent of the voters believed that it made no difference which party was in power. There was just no positive reason to turn to the Labour Party to form a government.

Gaitskell perhaps felt that he could capitalize on Tory blunders in the course of the campaign, but if this was in fact his aim his strategy backfired. He instead was the one who blundered, and his party paid the price. For having promised a 10-shilling rise in pensions as well as more hospitals and the municipalization of rented accommodation, the Labour leader still felt able to promise not to raise the level of income tax. That was on 28 September. He compounded his error on 1 October by promising to remove purchase tax from a range of essential goods. Macmillan described these promises as 'the biggest budget leak in history', while Butler commented 'a bribe a day keeps the Tories away'. Given that the Tories had been guilty of such blatant budget electioneering in April, it took great skill on the part of Gaitskell to allow their pot to call his kettle black. Gaitskell, however, simply lacked the political gifts of the unflappable and theatrical Macmillan. Moreover, since television now came into its own as an election medium this disparity was made more obvious. The opposition leader who really discovered how to make use of the medium was Jo Grimond.

When the election results came in, therefore, there was a shock awaiting Labour. The Conservative Party had won another decisive victory and had increased its overall majority to 100 seats. Labour's vote had fallen by 189,000, while the Tory vote had increased by no less than 463,000. The Liberal share of the poll had doubled from 2·7 to 5·9 per cent. But although it had gained nearly an extra million votes it had secured no net increase in seats, despite the fact that it had forwarded 106 more candidates than last time. The final figures were:

Party	Votes gained	Percentage of vote	Average vote per MP	Number of MPs
Conservative	13,749,830	49·4	37,671	365
Labour	12,215,538	43·8	47,347	258
Liberal	1,638,571	5·9	270,095	6
Others	125,096	0·9		1
	27,729,035	100·0		630

Source: Derived from D. Butler and A. Sloman, *British Political Facts, 1900–75.*

The election result represented a personal triumph for Harold Macmillan. He had come to power in the aftermath of Suez expecting to have to relinquish office fairly soon. Instead, he had revitalized his party and led it to its greatest post-war electoral victory. It was a truly remarkable achievement and one which seemed to be full of great political significance. Was affluence undermining the whole pattern of British voting? Would the Labour Party ever again be called upon to govern Britain? It seemed as if the Conservative Party, having won three elections in a row, each time with an increased majority, had discovered the secret of eternal power. If booms could be engineered before election dates by employing Keynesian economic methods and if the Prime Minister alone was responsible for choosing the election date, why could not an intelligent prime minister – and Macmillan was certainly that – cling on to power for ever? All these questions were posed time and time again as social scientists now turned to investigate the society which had grown up in Britain since the war.

| # THE CONSERVATIVE ANTI-CLIMAX, 1959–64

The years after 1959 – or so it seemed in the wake of the general election of that year – would mark the zenith of Conservative rule. The party had in Harold Macmillan a leader whose enormous political talents had already earned him the nickname 'Super-Mac', while the policies of his government seemed poised to secure prosperity at home and respect abroad. Britain, it seemed, could attain 'world status without tears'. But it was not to be, and well before the next election – by which time Macmillan was no longer Prime Minister – the failure of his policies had become apparent. The economy was in serious trouble, while in the realm of foreign affairs and defence the tone of the debate was set by Dean Acheson's judgement that Great Britain had lost her Empire but had not yet found a role. Even in the arena of party politics, the Conservative Party found itself hard-pressed by a revival of the Liberal Party under Grimond, so that by 1964, under the unlikely leadership of Sir Alec Douglas-Home, it no longer exuded the confidence of Britain's 'natural governing party'. By then, too, the superstar of British politics was no longer the leader of the Conservative Party but the new Labour Leader of the Opposition, Harold Wilson. The period 1959–64, therefore, can be seen to mark the anti-climax of Conservative rule in Britain.

Things began to go wrong for the Conservatives – not surprisingly, in the light of Heathcoat-Amory's budget of 1959 – with regard to the economy. The pre-election spending spree had made sense only in the crudest political terms, so that once the election had been won the economic situation still had to be addressed. This meant that a 'stop' had to be applied to the serious hire-purchase boom which had got under way. Profit taxes were raised to 12·5 per cent in the budget of 1960, and only a few weeks later severe credit restrictions and dearer money had to be imposed. Bank rate, which had already been raised to 5 per cent in

January, was up to 6 per cent by June. The Cabinet lost faith in the Chancellor of the Exchequer, of whom the Lord Chancellor was to write: 'it was evident that he had lost his grasp over economic matters'. It could hardly have been a great relief, on the other hand, to see him replaced in 1961 by Selwyn Lloyd.

The new Chancellor had little experience of economic affairs and little greater notion of economic management than his predecessor. Moreover, he had already acquired the reputation of lacking independent political judgement and was – predictably – too easily impressed by his Treasury advisers. The result was that he was often willing to adopt their proposals without first having analysed the likely political effects of their recommendations. Thus, although he attempted to introduce new policies – policies which might, if sensibly applied, have made some contribution to economic recovery – his total lack of political flair served to undermine their effectiveness. This unfortunate want of political skill was demonstrated even in his very first budget. Having introduced a number of counter-inflationary measures, including the new device of 'regulators' (i.e., the power to raise certain taxes immediately), the Chancellor still felt able to raise the threshold for surtax payers from £2,000 to £4,000.

The full measure of Selwyn Lloyd's political ineptitude was revealed later in the summer. Treasury predictions had gone awry and Britain had run up a deficit of £258 million on her balance of payments; the Chancellor found himself forced to deal with a sterling crisis. This was, for the most part, met in the usual way – bank rate was raised to 7 per cent and heavy loans were negotiated from the IMF and central banks – but the Chancellor now also determined to tackle the problem of wage inflation, which he believed had contributed to the crisis. Thus in addition to the usual measures he announced the introduction of a 'pay pause', designed to block thirty-five wage claims which would, in the opinion of his advisers, add £500 million to the country's wage bill in a year when it was also estimated that wages would rise by about 50 per cent faster than output. His idea was that wages should simply be frozen until productivity increased. However, if there was something to be said for having a more rational approach to collective bargaining, there was even more to be said for preparing the political groundwork before launching an attack of this kind on the traditional system of wage nego-tiations. But this never occurred to the Chancellor, who, instead, succeeded in undermining the Government's position by denying pay increases to nurses, teachers and hospital workers – people whose plight evoked widespread public sympathy – while industrial workers who were better organized were able to negotiate terms much more to their liking. The truth was that, since the Government had control of only a minor sector of the economy, they could not introduce a proper wage policy without having first secured a wider measure of agreement from trade unionists and employers. And Selwyn Lloyd's failure to achieve this damaged any future prospects of agreement.

The result was that, although the run on the pound had been stopped by the autumn of 1961, the Government now found themselves in serious difficulties with the unions. The latter had, it is true, reluctantly decided to cooperate with the Government by serving on the new National Economic and Development Council, set up by Macmillan to appease them (it had the task of charting the growth of various sectors of the economy and of finding ways in which this growth might be planned), but they were suspicious of the Chancellor's high-handedness and were unimpressed by his schemes to buy their support with proposals such as a temporary capital gains tax rather than through, for example, dividend restraint. Thus, he was unable to secure union agreement to a 2·5 per cent guideline for wages in 1962 and had to endure strikes that year by railwaymen, postmen and nurses when he tried to apply his policy in any case. Nor was he helped by the fact that private industry was still awarding greater increases. The Government therefore decided to set up a National Incomes Commission with the task of examining wage increases in the light of the public interest. But even although this body lacked the power to set aside increases to which it objected, the trade unions would not cooperate with it. The 1962 budget therefore continued the policy of deflation. It did include a levy on speculative gains – in other words, a tax on stocks and shares which had been held for less than six months – but this obvious sop to union opinions still failed to change their attitude. Macmillan decided to make a fresh start politically and economically by removing Selwyn Lloyd and others from his cabinet.

Lloyd's successor as Chancellor of the Exchequer was Reginald Maudling, whose tenure of office lasted through the change of party leadership until the general election of 1964. Originally a Conservative backroom boy, he had been given office by Churchill and Macmillan and had acquired considerable experience of economic affairs. According to one observer, he gave the impression in 1962 of being 'young, bouncing and clever'. He certainly exuded confidence and had a happy command of economic vocabulary which differentiated him from his predecessors, with the result that not long after he had assumed the Chancellorship he was being mentioned as a possible successor to Macmillan as premier. However, his promise outran his performance, and if he offered the chance of a new beginning, his policies, too, failed in the end.

The effect of Selwyn Lloyd's deflationary policy, not to mention the very bad winter of 1962–3, had been to push up unemployment until it reached the 800,000 mark. This had contributed to the Government's growing unpopularity and even the theatrical appointment of Lord Hailsham as minister with special responsibility for the North East in 1963 and the later appointment that year of Edward Heath as Minister for Industry, Trade and Regional Development had done little to increase the public's faith that the Government were really in command of their economic strategy. Moreover, there was a general feeling among the public that, since the balance-of-payments deficit still remained, deflation was no longer necessarily the answer to Britain's problems. Thus the discovery that Maudling was ready to alter government economic policy must surely have come as a tonic to their morale. A change in policy, of course, had always been possible – the government might at some stage have decided to limit its overseas military commitments – but the curious, although at that time attractive, quality of the strategy advanced by Maudling was that it enabled the Government to inflate the economy without reappraising military spending. The Chancellor, in fact, presented himself as the apostle of economic growth and planned to engineer a boom which, he held, would generate an increase in productivity; this would lead to a rise in exports, which in turn would solve Britain's balance-of-payments difficulties. Furthermore, the Chancellor predicted that such a process could be made self-generating, since once business confidence and investment had revived, the cycle of stop and go could at last be broken. This new approach, however, was fraught with dangers, the main one being that steps to stimulate the economy would merely worsen the balance-of-payments deficit by encouraging the import of supplies of raw materials. In fact, if a boom of any sort was to be engineered, this danger was really inescapable. The Chancellor had an answer for his critics, which he gave in his budget speech of 1963. He said: 'In so far as there is a stocking-up movement related to expansion, it is perfectly reasonable and sensible to finance such a movement out of our reserves or out of our borrowing facilities in the IMF and elsewhere.' But this was unconvincing, for if an economy had reached the point where it could not be fully stretched without incurring a massive deficit on current account it was already out of equilibrium. In other words, Maudling's plans would only make sense if he were first to devalue or else wait for a surplus on the balance of payments which would cover the expected initial deficit. To expect to finance that deficit by borrowing, in the hope that some unproved growth mechanism would solve all the problems in the end, was to defy the simplest laws of economics. Nevertheless, this was the course pursued by the Chancellor for about a year, until by the summer of 1964 it was clear that his plans had collapsed. Wilson was later to make great play indeed of Maudling's yawning trade gap, which he set at £800 million.

DEFENCE AND FOREIGN POLICY

As in economic affairs, so too in defence and foreign affairs the Government's position began to crumble almost as soon as it had won re-election. Thus the grand design of nuclear independence, which had been inaugurated with the Defence White Paper of 1957, ended in 1962 with complete dependence on the Americans, while the hope of reducing defence expenditure by relying on nuclear weapons turned out to be a pipe-dream. Finally, just when Harold Macmillan appeared to have saved the day by pulling off the Nassau Agreement with President Kennedy in December 1962, this very agreement was seized upon by General de Gaulle to destroy the Government's hopes of entering the European Common Market. This was a blow from which the Conservatives never really recovered, although at the time this was perhaps not understood.

In matters of defence, the realization that the Government's nuclear strategy might not after all be such a panacea had been dawning upon them even in 1958. Information received from the Americans under the new arrangements which had been worked out that year had demonstrated just how out of date British nuclear technology really was, while the emergency in Jordan – also in 1958 – had highlighted the continued need to station British troops abroad. (There were more than 100,000 British troops stationed in the Middle and Far East at this time.) Matters deteriorated thereafter. In 1961, for example, Britain was forced not only to retain the services of her last conscripted troops but to call up reserves when a coincidence of crises over Kuwait and Berlin found the army over-committed and under-manned. The 1963 confrontation between Malaysia and Indonesia once again pinned down British forces in the Far East, so that hopes of reducing the defence budget were never realized. Indeed, the defence estimates for 1963 were some £150 million higher than those for 1962. The idea that nuclear defence would mean cheaper defence was, therefore, proving unrealistic.

This was becoming clearer in any case thanks to the escalating costs of nuclear research and development. By 1960 British plans for producing Blue Streak had been scrapped and Britain admitted that she would have to rely on America to supply her with a viable nuclear missile. The British independent nuclear deterrent would therefore no longer be British after all. But would it be independent? The Government asserted that it would. They had negotiated the supply of America's Skybolt missile in return for leasing the Americans a nuclear submarine base (near Glasgow) and Skybolt, the Government maintained, could be delivered by British Vulcan bombers operating under British control. Moreover, Skybolt represented a great strategical advance on Blue Streak since Skybolt, being an air-to-ground missile, would not be dependent on vulnerable, fixed ground-silos. In 1962, however, the Americans announced that they were scrapping Skybolt, thus leaving the Government without a defence policy. As Macmillan quickly realized, his national and indeed his international credibility depended on the Americans selling him Polaris missiles.

Polaris was America's latest sea-to-air missile, which could be fired from nuclear submarines. Since Britain did not yet possess any of the latter she had not been interested in procuring the missile in 1960. However, with the cancellation of Skybolt by the Americans her choice was now more restricted. In fact the choice was really not hers at all, for the question was, rather, would the Americans agree to sell Polaris? The man who would answer that question was no longer President Eisenhower (who had agreed to the Skybolt deal) but his successor, President Kennedy, who had recently warned Western Europe on television that it ought to do more to strengthen its conventional forces. He added: 'We don't want six or seven powers in Europe diverting their funds into nuclear power, when the United States has got this tremendous arsenal.' Moreover, Kennedy's Under-Secretary of State for Western European affairs was George Ball, a believer in the European Idea who favoured a policy of refusing Britain nuclear technology in the hope of encouraging her to behave more like an ordinary Western European power. She could, he believed, play a more constructive role as part of a united Europe which, in turn, could form a 'second pillar' within the Atlantic Alliance.

Kennedy's own ideas on the subject of Europe were not yet really very clear. The Cuban Missile Crisis earlier in the year – which had arisen when America had discovered that the Russians were installing nuclear missiles in Cuba and which had led to an American blockade of the island – had encouraged him to believe that in times of crisis there should only be one centre of 'crisis management'. He had therefore informed his allies of his diplomacy with the Russians afterwards rather than beforehand and by so doing had made it clear to them that he did not want to have to deal with them as nuclear partners. On the other hand, in the words of Ball, 'President Kennedy was fond of Prime Minister Macmillan and ... had a relationship of extraordinary confidence and intimacy with the able British Ambassador, David Ormsby-Gore,' so that when he met Harold Macmillan at Nassau in December 1962 his attitude was that 'They were nice people and we should try, if we could, to help them out.'

Macmillan was able as a result to secure American agreement to sell the Polaris missile on the following terms. The missile was to be fitted with British nuclear warheads into British nuclear submarines which were to be part of a NATO multilateral nuclear force (something which, in fact, never came into being). They were to be chiefly used for purposes of Western defence, but in deference to the Prime Minister a clause was negotiated (without which the agreement would have been of little political use) which ran, 'except where the British Government may decide that supreme national interests are at stake'. Macmillan could therefore claim that British nuclear independence had been maintained. Indeed, he even gave the assurance that he had affirmed 'the moral commitment which we and the United States already have, that is, not to use nuclear weapons in the world without prior consultation with each other, if circumstances permit'. Just exactly what this meant was not clear, although if it meant what it seemed to mean then Kennedy had given Macmillan the assurances which Truman had refused to give Attlee on American constitutional grounds in 1950. Probably what it meant was that Britain had promised not to use her nuclear weapons without American consent, rather than vice versa. The Prime Minister also stressed that, although it would take two years for Britain to set up her Polaris fleet, the missile represented an advance even on Skybolt. It could be fired from submarines operating anywhere at sea and might therefore not occasion a direct retaliatory attack upon Great Britain. Moreover, unlike Skybolt, it was 'a weapon which should last for a generation', so that the Nassau Agreement was represented by him as a major diplomatic victory for Britain.

Others, predictably, were more critical of the Premier's achievement. Harold Wilson, speaking for the Opposition in the House of Commons, derided the Nassau Agreement as a 'sop thrown by the Americans to a Prime Minister who knew in his heart that what he was asking had no defence relevance, but who knew that he dare not return and face some of his more atavistic supporters without it'. Later on, in a famous jibe, he maintained that the 'independent British deterrent' was neither independent nor British nor even a deterrent. He also pledged on behalf of the Labour Party that a Labour government would renegotiate the Nassau Agreement and would follow a policy of strengthening the conventional forces of NATO. This, of course, served admirably to paper over the cracks in Labour's own defence policy, but when Labour eventually did return to office nothing was done to alter Britain's nuclear role. The really important critic of Britain's defence policy, as it turned out, was not Harold Wilson but General de Gaulle, who disapproved of the Anglo-American 'special relationship' in all its aspects and saw in it a potential threat to European independence.

De Gaulle had also been offered Polaris missiles, but as he was to put it at a famous press conference, 'It would be truly useless for us to buy [them] when we have neither the submarines to launch them nor the thermonuclear warheads to arm them.' The Nassau Agreement had only served, as far as he was concerned, to highlight France's nuclear weakness. Indeed, the whole display of Anglo-American friendship in the early sixties – from Macmillan's supporting role at the futile 1960 Paris summit conference (when the shooting down of an American spy-plane by the Russians put a quick end to Macmillan's efforts to try to negotiate an end to the cold war), to Britain's signature on the Test Ban Treaty of 1963 (a treaty to which Britain had given strong support and which banned nuclear explosions in the atmosphere, in outer space and under water) – served merely to demonstrate France's and Europe's lack of political weight. No doubt there was an element of jealousy involved and no doubt, too, de Gaulle's wartime memories jarred at the thought of the restoration of the Anglo-American alliance, but de Gaulle was genuinely afraid lest Britain's concern to influence America would blind her to factors which one day might lead to fundamental differences between Europe and the United States. For if America controlled Britain's nuclear capacity, Europe's ability to defend her own interests might one day be endangered. De Gaulle's genuine Europeanism therefore led him to oppose Britain's special relationship with the USA and, in particular, to denounce the Nassau Agreement, which in his eyes had merely put an end to British and perhaps European sovereignty. His policy become one of building up an independent French nuclear deterrent which could be used if necessary to defend European interests as a whole. Arguably, this was a policy which lacked political realism, but none the less, in view of Britain's application to join the Common Market, it was a policy which mattered, since France would play a key role in determining whether Britain's application would be accepted or rejected.

The decision to apply to 'enter Europe' had been taken slowly and, in fact, dishonestly as far as Britain was concerned, for the motives behind the application had not been those of European federalism and Macmillan had no intention of making Britain a 'European power'. The real reason behind the British application was the need to find a theatre in which Britain could act the leading role and thereby increase her reputation on the international stage. Once inside the Common Market, Macmillan planned to organize it into a sort of 'second pillar' of Western defence and lead it, in cooperation with America, as part of an extended Atlantic partnership. The Prime Minister had therefore taken pains to secure United States approval for his plans, approval which Kennedy had eagerly bestowed. He, too, regretted Western Europe's division into two camps (EEC and EFTA) and looked to European trading and economic union to lay the foundations for a really strong NATO.

Britain's decision to apply for membership of the Common Market therefore hardly constituted a new departure by the British, but should be seen rather as a means of restoring Britain to her old position at the intersection of the three circles – Europe, America and the Commonwealth. However, in order to avoid offending both European opinion across the Channel as well as more traditional opinion at home, Macmillan could not put forward his case in these terms, with the result that a policy emerged of application by stealth. Ministers were sent to tour the Commonwealth to discover the reactions of our Commonwealth partners, while approaches were made to Europe stage by stage. Macmillan himself underplayed the whole affair and encouraged his ministers to do the same. Thus Selwyn Lloyd, in a Commons debate in 1960, stressed the need 'to be careful' when talking about the possibility of joining Europe, and even when announcing Britain's decision to join the Common Market in July 1961 Macmillan stated bluntly that a disruption of 'longstanding and historic ties' with the Commonwealth would mean that the 'loss would be greater than the gain'. The political implications were entirely discounted and the Prime Minister spoke of the application as a 'purely economic and trading negotiation' – a piece of rank dishonesty in view of the government's all but total ignorance of the likely economic consequences of a successful approach.

The fact was that the probable economic results of success and failure were not at all clear. Thus there was no great fear that if the application failed British industry would be crippled by Common Market tariffs, while, equally, there was a general expectation that if Britain did succeed in entering the Common Market the national economy would benefit. Indeed, it was even held that it would be no bad thing if inefficient British industrialists were forced to brace themselves for the 'cold shower' of European competition; the realization had not yet dawned that many would be destined to catch pneumonia. Thus economic considerations were not of primary importance in determining Britain's first attempt to enter Europe. True, they were used by the Government to camouflage their real political motives, but that was really their whole significance.

Political reaction to Britain's application was rather muted, since little was known in the country about the Common Market and its works. Learning about it was rather like learning Esperanto – a new and rather artificial vocabulary was involved in studying both – with the result that few people had bothered to take the trouble. Macmillan's rather matter-of-fact announcement in the Commons was greeted, therefore, with a certain indifference by MPs. Parliament was not as yet aware of any threat to its much-vaunted sovereignty, and since the Prime Minister was not speaking the language of European federalism the honourable members could afford to sit back and await developments. What reaction there was from the Labour front bench, however, demonstrated that if Macmillan should change his tune the Opposition was ready to trundle into action. Gaitskell maintained that public opinion should not neglect her Commonwealth ties. It was only gradually that the Labour Party united in opposition to entering Europe.

The odds had always been that the Labour Party would move against rather than in favour of a British application. The Shadow Cabinet was strongly against entry, as was also a majority of the Parliamentary Party. Thus although such leading figures as George Brown and Ray Gunter were prepared to lend the application their support, they were unable to make their views prevail against the doubts of colleagues such as Barbara Castle, Richard Crossman, Denis Healey and James Callaghan. The party's spokesman on foreign affairs, Harold Wilson, was also un-enthusiastic about the Market and – characteristically as it was to turn out – was content to follow on this matter rather than to lead. Thus his pronouncements on the subject at this time were hostile to British entry. In 1961 he wrote: 'We are not entitled to sell our friends and kinsmen down the river for a problematical and marginal advantage in selling washing machines in Düsseldorf.' The following year, he claimed: '. . . a dying government does not possess the right, constitutionally or morally, to take a divided nation into the Common Market'. However, a rather non-committal statement was drawn up for the 1962 party conference, emphasizing the conditions which would have to be fulfilled before Britain could enter Europe, but leaving the decision in principle still open. It was the clearly and passionately enunciated opposition of Gait-skell himself in his speech to the party conference which finally swung the party into an expressly hostile position. To the cheers of party delegates Gaitskell declared, in ringing tones of assertive leadership, that entry into the Common Market would mean 'the end of a thousand years of British history'. After this speech there could be little doubt that the Labour Party was opposed to Macmillan's initiative.

Opposition, both inside the country as a whole and inside the Labour Party in particular, had been building up as a result of the difficulties experienced by the Government in securing Commonwealth support for the British application.

The leaders of the Commonwealth Labour Parties, for example, had declared in September 1962 that the Government did not appear to be adequately safeguarding Commonwealth interests and that unless they altered their approach 'great damage would inevitably be done to many countries in the Commonwealth and thereby to the unity of the Commonwealth itself'. But by this time, too, it was clear that the Commonwealth premiers were also unhappy with the way negotiations were going. Britain was experiencing difficulties protecting the agricultural exports of the older Commonwealth countries (Canada, Australia and New Zealand), while the new Commonwealth states of Africa and Asia were also concerned about their exports and unhappy about becoming 'associate members' of the EEC. Macmillan put the best possible face on things at the Commonwealth Premiers' Conference of September 1962 – explaining that as Britain got richer, the importance of the Commonwealth would increase – but his Commonwealth colleagues gave voice to many anxieties. It was only their recognition that responsibility for entry rested in the final analysis with the British government that left an impression of some agreement. Further pressure, therefore, was exerted on the British negotiating team, led by Edward Heath, to do more to safeguard Commonwealth interests.

Heath, a late convert to the cause of Europe, was one of the so-called 'Europeans' given office by Macmillan (others included Duncan Sandys and Christopher Soames). Appointed Lord Privy Seal with special responsibility for European affairs, it was only logical that he was put in charge of the negotiations in Brussels. His opening statement to the Commission (made in Paris in October 1961) seemed to get things off to a good start. He declared that Britain desired 'to become a full, wholehearted and active member of the European Community in the widest sense' and that she wished to participate 'in the building of a new Europe'. On the other hand, since his task was one of safeguarding the interests of Great Britain and the Commonwealth – not to mention her EFTA partners – he could expect to meet with stiff resistance once negotiations got under way in earnest. However, negotiations could not get seriously under way until the Six had first of all settled important problems of their own.

The main difficulty was the mechanics involved in the adoption of a Common Agricultural Policy. This was to consist of a system of levies on agricultural imports, a system of supports for European agriculture (maintained through a Common Agricultural Fund) and a system of subsidies for European agricultural exports. Not unnaturally, negotiations between the Six on this subject took a long time to complete. Eventually agreement was reached in January 1962 on a policy which was intended both to boost and modernize European agriculture. The main beneficiary of the new system was France, who had made it clear that she would only countenance industrial competition from Germany and Britain if her agricultural base was protected first. The natural corollary, however, was that she was in no mood to make concessions of any sort to Britain over agricultural imports from the Commonwealth when negotiations at last got under way in the spring of 1962. Nevertheless, despite difficulties over this point, some progress was made on other Commonwealth problems before negotiations were adjourned on 5 August, and according to some observers the outline of a possible deal was just about becoming visible. More progress was made after negotiations were resumed in October but then, once the problem of British agriculture itself came up, more difficulties were encountered. Britain's request for a long transition period in order to change over from her traditional system of farming subsidies, low food prices and cheap Commonwealth food to the Common Agricultural Policy of high prices and levies on imported food was not acceptable to the Commission, which demanded that Britain should apply the Common Policy as soon as she entered the Market. Deadlock seemed inevitable because although the British negotiators quite understood the political pressures which French and German farmers were exerting on their governments, they equally understood that Parliament – not to mention British public opinion – would never agree to such impossible demands. Would it, therefore, prove impossible to reach some sort of economic understanding with the Six?

Macmillan, meanwhile, had been trying to win over the French in another way. Realizing that French demands were not entirely motivated by economic pressures, he attempted to demonstrate to General de Gaulle that Britain and France could cooperate in Europe on certain political issues. Indeed, as it became ever more impossible to split the French and Germans over trade his attempts to reach a political understanding with de Gaulle became increasingly important. The ground chosen for a *rapprochement* were the schemes being mooted at that time by the General for some sort of European political union. But although Macmillan went out of his way to let it be known that he agreed with de Gaulle, that

Europe should be organized on the basis of a '*Europe des états*' or a '*Europe des nations*' rather than through supra-national political institutions, his plans to effect some sort of an understanding with the French President were destined to ultimate failure. For by 1962 de Gaulle was talking in terms of some sort of European political cooperation which implied a breach with NATO, and since neither Great Britain nor France's partners in the Six were sympathetic to such a breach, Britain's request to participate in the ongoing discussions in Europe was seen by the General as an attempt to manoeuvre these partners against him. Thus Macmillan's efforts to begin a political dialogue with France at the expense of her more genuinely European-minded partners reached an ironic conclusion when de Gaulle suspected agreement was being sought at his expense.

Macmillan's other political initiatives had also failed. He had tried to encourage the Americans to allow him to pass on nuclear knowledge to France and tried as well to persuade Chancellor Adenauer to give him the special support of West Germany. In the first case the Americans would not agree, while in the second Adenauer, who had never got over the Allies' refusal to demolish the Berlin Wall (erected in 1961) and who did not trust Macmillan in any case (he considered the Prime Minister too ready to deal with the Russians), would not endanger his special relationship with France to help the British out. Thus it proved impossible to resolve the economic divisions between Britain and France by recourse to the obvious expedients of diplomatic practice and on 14 January 1963, at a time when Heath was set to propose a package deal to the Commission, the British application was vetoed by de Gaulle.

The motives behind the General's veto were fairly straightforward. Basically, he did not trust the British to put the interests of Europe, as he saw them, before those of the Atlantic alliance. He also believed that Great Britain's entry would upset the balance of power between the member states of the EEC itself. Finally, he could not really believe that agreement was possible over the question of Commonwealth imports, for as he put it: 'You who eat the cheap wheat of Canada, the lamb of New Zealand, the beef and potatoes of Ireland, the butter, fruit and vegetables of Australia, the sugar of Jamaica – would you consent to feed on continental – especially French – agricultural produce, which would inevitably cost more?' He could not convince himself, therefore, that even if the great issues of principle which divided Britain from the

Continent did not exist, it would be possible to reach agreement over practicalities. Thus Britain was excluded from the Common Market. She wisely made no attempt to organize a revolt within the Six and left the negotiating table more in sorrow than in anger, refusing, incidentally, to withdraw the British application. Heath declared: 'We in Britain are not going to turn our backs on the mainland of Europe or on the countries of the Community . . . We shall continue to work with all our friends in Europe for the true strength and unity of the continent.' He was later awarded the Charlemagne Prize for his services to Europe, services, which as it was to turn out, were not yet at an end.

As a result of de Gaulle's veto, Macmillan's foreign policy was more or less destroyed. Britain, no longer an independent nuclear power, had not been allowed to restore her prestige by capturing – however belatedly – the leadership of Europe. She could no longer, therefore, present herself as a world partner – even a junior one – of the United States of America. De Gaulle had seen through Macmillan's diplomacy and had taken the first step to establish a European voice which would speak independently of the United States. On the other hand, since anti-Americanism was not yet a European disease, de Gaulle was claiming to speak for a Europe which as yet did not exist. As far as British and much Continental European opinion was concerned, therefore, his veto was seen as an irrational and selfish act. The British, in particular, refused to see it as a national defeat or humiliation and far from causing the Government political trouble it saved them perhaps from political difficulties. For if they had been forced to accept unpalatable formulae in order to reach agreement with Europe over agriculture, there is little doubt that public opinion inside Britain would have turned even more sharply against the Conservatives. As it was, the experience of negotiating with the Common Market had so disillusioned even the British who had taken an interest in it that the final blow of the General's veto had been accepted with a sigh of relief. It constituted, in the words of Elizabeth Barker, little more than 'a nine days' wonder'. People simply wondered why there had been all the fuss in the first place and the blow which had been received by the Government was therefore only dimly understood. Since the Common Market was not yet regarded as a panacea for British ills, there was simply no sense of loss and the matter, insofar as it was discussed by the public, was interpreted in the light of the General's notorious idiosyncracy. Besides, for many people, the Common Market had only been of interest when it had some bearing on Commonwealth affairs. These were matters of which they had some experience, whereas the Common Market, like the peace of God, was something which passed all understanding.

In Commonwealth affairs the process of decolonization proceeded apace. But in this sphere, too, Conservative policies were meeting with less success. The Government had taken to organizing colonies into federations but, once established, these federations had to withstand severe and often overwhelming strains imposed by the forces of local secessionist sentiment. Even those states which gained their independence as unitary bodies with federal constitutions did so in face of tremendous internal difficulties, so that the policies of the Colonial Office – the quick papering over of colonial cracks by lumping territories together in federal relationships – did not succeed in combining unity and diversity in quite the manner which had been desired. Thus the Central African Federation, the West Indies Federation, Malaysia, the South Arabian Federation, Cyprus, Nigeria and Uganda all encountered serious centrifugal strains. Eventually all the federations broke up – the Central African in 1963, Malaysia in 1965, South Arabia in 1968 and the West Indies in 1962 – while Nigeria, Uganda and Cyprus secured their independence under the shadow of probable future strife. With respect to many of these cases, Britain was in an almost impossible position. Her rule over many years had created an artificial sense of unity which would depart with the British flag, which in turn meant that with her departure the outlook in many regions would be pretty grim. Yet since continued British rule was neither practicable nor desirable, the process of decolonization would simply have to go ahead. Thus in 1960 independence was granted to Nigeria; in 1961 to Cyprus, Sierra Leone and Tanganyika; in 1962 to Jamaica, Trinidad and Uganda; and in 1963–4 to Kenya, Zambia, Zanzibar, Malawi and Malta. All these countries joined the Commonwealth (only three of them choosing to do so as republics), which meant that by the end of the Conservative period of government the whole character of the Commonwealth had radically changed. No longer a white man's club, it had to adjust to the problems which its new multiracial character presented.

The first of these problems concerned the racial policies of South Africa, where the Afrikaaner nationalists had been in power since 1948 and where they had proceeded, despite their profession of Christian principles, to establish what Mr Gladstone might well have referred to as 'the negation of God erected into a system of government'. Dr Malan, their leader, had pursued a policy of releasing pro-Nazi criminals and had imposed upon the majority of the inhabitants of the country a cruel system of racial segregation which was known by the name of apartheid. At first the rest of the world ignored these developments, but with the rise of African nationalism and the emergence of new African states in the early 1960s, the true nature of the South African state became apparent to the outside world. The result was that another form of apartheid developed, namely a gulf between the defenders of Afrikaaner tyranny and those who upheld the values of Western and Christian thought. Macmillan himself, while touring the African continent in 1960, warned the South African government that the tide of world opinion had turned against them. Speaking in Cape Town to the South African Parliament on 3 February at the end of his tour, he said:

The most striking of all impressions I have formed since I left London a month ago is of the strength of this African national consciousness. In different places it may take different forms, but is happening everywhere. The wind of change is blowing through the continent. Whether we like it or not this growth of national consciousness is a political fact ... our national policies must take account of it.

He also made it clear that the British government could not support apartheid since to do so would be to be 'false to our own deep convictions about the political destinies of free men'.

In Britain this speech by the Prime Minister aroused considerable public interest, and soon afterwards a campaign was organized by Labour and Liberal Party supporters to boycott South African goods. The Government, naturally, dissociated themselves from such political manoeuvrings – there was after all a long list of politically despicable régimes around the world to which boycotts were not being applied – preferring, instead, to exercise more subtle pressures on the South African government. But with the Sharpeville massacre of March 1960 – when nearly seventy Africans were shot during clashes with South African policemen in a campaign designed to get rid of South Africa's oppressive pass laws – the South African issue became one of major public importance and Macmillan came under pressure to condemn the South African régime at the forthcoming Commonwealth Conference – this despite the fact that there was a general rule at conferences of this type for British governments never to interfere in the domestic affairs of Commonwealth member states. So great was public feeling on this issue that the rule was put aside and the South African premier was given to understand that the policies which his government were pursuing were not designed to win Commonwealth approval.

The following year the South African issue re-emerged in an even more acute form, for having, as a result of a referendum held in 1961, become a republic, South Africa had to decide whether to remain in the Commonwealth or not. The South African Prime Minister, like Macmillan himself, supported continued membership. The British leader could see no way in which the lot of the black South African could be improved as a result of South Africa's expulsion from the Commonwealth and so, when the 1961 Commonwealth Conference convened, he made his views known to his colleagues on this important and now pressing matter. For between March 1960 and March 1961, South Africa had become the main problem facing the Commonwealth premiers for decision. The matter, as it turned out, was quickly settled: having sounded out the views of the premiers, Dr Verwoerd, the South African leader, discovered that more than half of his colleagues were hostile. Moreover, since Canada, in particular, appeared to object to the anomaly of the South African position, he could not write off the opposition he had encountered as merely that of the new African and Asian states. He therefore withdrew the South African application and much to the regret of the British government, which still cherished hopes of being able to influence South African developments for the better, led his country out of the Commonwealth. On the other hand, agreement was reached between the governments of Britain and South Africa that the two countries should cooperate 'in all possible ways', despite the Commonwealth decision. Thus South Africa, although no longer a member of the British Commonwealth, was allowed to retain her Commonwealth trade preferences.

The second problem which arose at this time as a result of the changing nature of the Commonwealth was the issue of immigration, which became a bone of political contention in Great Britain as a result of the Commonwealth Immigration Act of 1962. It was now the British rather than the South African government that stood accused of condoning racial prejudice, an accusation which in the light of the fuss made over South Africa was one which greatly embarrassed them.

Commonwealth immigration into Britain increased dramatically after the war. It was easier to travel; Britain was enjoying affluence; and as the centre of a democratic Commonwealth, she constituted a natural focus for people in the colonies who had been brought up to admire the British way of life and institutions and who aspired to a British standard of living. The trouble as far as Britain was concerned was that as a result of her imperial past no less than a quarter of the world's population (Butler's figures) were legally entitled to enter the country. The question arose, therefore, whether there should be a limit to those who wished to enter, if Britain – already more densely populated than most other countries in the world – was not to experience serious social problems in the future. A number of factors were already attracting people's attention in this respect.

One was the sharp increase in the number of immigrants who had arrived in Britain in the 1950s. West Indians, for example, who as a result of the McCarren–Walter Immigration Act of 1952 were no longer eligible to settle in the USA, were beginning to settle in England. So, too, were increasing numbers of Indians and Pakistanis. The result was that by 1959 some 20,000 were entering the country each year. In 1960 the number rose to 58,100, and in 1961 it reached 115,150. This spectacular rise was due in part at least to rumours of restrictive legislation but there could be little doubt that, whether this was a main cause or not, a new burst of immigration was highly likely in the 1960s. The question was, could Britain cope with such immigration? Insofar as the immigrants had certain skills, there is no doubt that they were welcome. Enoch Powell, for example, at the Ministry of Health, was anxious to secure as many overseas nurses and doctors as possible to support an expansion of the health service and, together with other ministers, he appreciated the value of immigrants who kept the British transport and postal services going. However, concern was aroused by the tendency – a perfectly natural one psychologically – for immigrants to congregate in certain cities and within certain areas of certain cities, since the cities concerned – London and parts of the Midlands, in particular – began to feel a strain on their social services.

The Government therefore began to give some thought to the situation. They had after all to plan their future needs as far as housing, health and education were concerned and if they could not calculate how many newcomers were entering the country their planning might prove disastrously wrong. Besides, they had also to take into consideration to what extent the British economy could absorb large numbers of unskilled immigrants and whether the British people would tolerate a dramatic shift in the demographic balance. These were proper matters for government concern and were all too often overlooked by those who shouted 'racialism' first and thought about the matter, if at all, only afterwards. Moreover, racial disturbances in Nottingham and in London's Notting Hill in 1958 had already given rise to widespread public concern about the future of race relations in Britain. These disturbances had fortunately not escalated into full-scale racial riots, but the fact that they had taken place at all indicated a new and unattractive aspect of British social life. What, if anything, did the Government intend to do?

The Government reacted in 1962 by bringing in the Commonwealth Immigration Bill, which became law that July. Its provisions were to last for a trial period of five years and laid down that Commonwealth citizens – apart from those who could support themselves from private means – could apply for Ministry of Labour vouchers only if they met one of three conditions. Either they must have a job to come to, or they must possess skills or educational qualifications likely to be useful in the United Kingdom, or, finally, they might enter as part of a quota of immigrants, the size of which was decided at any given time by the Government. The Bill immediately gave rise to great political controversy.

The reactions were politically rather curious. The Government themselves were divided between those who recognized a continuing obligation to Commonwealth citizens and those who were troubled by the prospect of unlimited immigration. The Labour Opposition as well as the Liberal Party condemned the Bill as a nasty, racialist piece of legislation which introduced a 'colour bar' since the number of white Commonwealth immigrants was hardly likely to be affected by it. (Incidentally, this was not a difficult case to present since the Bill did nothing to regulate the inflow of unskilled labour from the Republic of Ireland.) On the wider issues concerned, however, their case was far from clear, for it seemed that both opposition parties were content to tolerate unlimited immigration. Moreover, to the embarrassment of the Labour Party, it was demonstrated by opinion polls as well as by speeches at party conferences that working-class opinion approved the Government's measures. Thus even after the Labour Party returned to office, no move was made to repeal this so-called racialist legislation.

The Commonwealth Immigration Act constituted the only major piece of domestic legislation passed under Macmillan's second government. Towards the end of the Conservatives' period in office, it is true, a number of reports were submitted to the Government but, although some of these were accepted, the Tories were not in office long enough to build upon them. The only other slightly controversial, although in the long-run ineffectual, piece of legislation enacted at this time was the Bill, sponsored by Edward Heath, to abolish Resale Price Maintenance. This was a system whereby retailers agreed not to sell goods below a minimum price which was fixed by wholesalers, and therefore constituted a restrictive practice. Heath – quite courageously in view of the opposition he had to face within his own party from those who feared for the future of Britain's small shopkeepers – set out to end this practice and succeeded in doing so in 1964. When the final vote was taken on the Bill, however, it was discovered that twenty-one Conservatives had voted against, twelve had abstained and twenty-three had absented themselves.

PARTY POLITICS 1959–64

It did not take long before the public realized that the promise of Macmillan's rule had failed to become reality. Sterling crises, the pay pause, rising prices, difficulties abroad, a tottering defence policy and lack of initiatives on the home front meant that the Tory voter began to protest, with the result that in the period 1962–3 a tendency arose for normally Conservative sympathizers to give their votes to Liberal candidates at by-elections. Grimond was still exerting a strong personal magnetism as Liberal leader and his incisive, radical brand of opposition suggested that there might indeed be a case for voting Liberal after all. Under his leadership the Liberal Party seemed to be asking serious questions not only about British society but about Britain's place in the world, so that there was a certain disposition among Tory voters to show their disenchantment with the government by lending temporary support to the Liberal cause. Boredom, too, was a factor: the Conservatives had now been in power for a decade and the slogan, 'it's time for a change', was not unpersuasive.

The first indication that a real revival of Liberal fortunes was on the way came in 1961 in the Paisley by-election when the Scottish patriot John Bannerman, fighting on a Liberal ticket, came within 2,000 votes of victory in a Labour seat. This proved an untypical result, given that the Liberals failed dismally to make any inroads into Labour territory in the course of the revival, but it certainly marked the beginning of a change in British voting patterns over the next two years. For in the space of the following ten months the Liberals managed to secure second place in eight by-elections in which the party had been third in 1959. Similarly in municipal elections, the party improved its base in May 1960 (130 Liberals elected) and in May 1961 (196 Liberals elected), so that by 1962 a strong Liberal tide was flowing in the country. The climax of the revival came in March 1962. On 14 March a Liberal candidate came within 973 votes of victory in the rock-solid Conservative seaside resort of Blackpool North, while on the following day, when the votes were counted in the Kent commuter suburb of Orpington, it was discovered that the Conservative majority of 14,760 had been turned into a Liberal one of 7,855. The Conservative share of the poll had fallen by no less than 22 per cent to give Eric Lubbock a resounding Liberal victory – indeed, one which seemed to herald the dawn of the promised land. It was shortly after this (28 March 1962) that the *Daily Mail*'s National Opinion Poll discovered that the Liberals were the most popular party in the country. The figures were: Liberals 30 per cent, Labour 29·9 per cent, Conservatives 29·2 per cent. Meanwhile, on the same day as Orpington, the Liberals had forced the Tories into third place at Middlesbrough East. The revival continued for the rest of 1962. In April the party took 27 per cent of the poll at Stockton-on-Tees and 25 per cent at Derby North; they then managed to retain the Welsh seat of Montgomeryshire on the death of their former leader Clement Davies; while in the by-election at West Derbyshire the party missed victory by a mere 1,220 votes. An excellent Liberal showing at the North-East Leicester by-election of 12 July had an unexpectedly dramatic result. Macmillan, determined to do something to restore the waning popularity of his government, took the unprecedented step of sacking one third of the cabinet. The Liberal MP Jeremy Thorpe remarked: 'Greater love hath no man than this, that he lays down his friends for his life.'

The cabinet ministers sacked by Macmillan – and in many cases they were given only a few hours' notice – included (most spectacularly) Selwyn Lloyd, the Chancellor of the Exchequer, the Ministers of Defence, Housing and Education, the Secretary of State for Scotland, the Minister without Portfolio and the Lord Chancellor. Three days later nine ministers outside the Cabinet were also sacked by the premier. This piece of political butchery became known as the 'Night of the Long Knives', but although it was dramatic there is little evidence that it did the Conservative cause much good. For when another round of by-elections was held in late November 1962 the swing against the Government, although reduced, was still on a scale large enough, if repeated at a general election, to give a 100-seat majority to Labour.

The reasons for this were as follows. First, the winter was a bad one, with unemployment climbing steadily upwards; secondly, the newcomers to Macmillan's cabinet, although often enjoying the virtue of youth (Maudling, the new Chancellor, was forty-five years old; Sir Keith Joseph, the new Minister of Housing, was forty-four; the new Minister of Education, Sir Edward Boyle, was only thirty-eight), were scarcely charismatic (a fair comment, surely, on such figures as Henry Brooke, Michael Noble, Peter Thorneycroft and Lord Dilhorne); and by the end of 1962 the Government were enmeshed in scandal. All of these factors made it difficult for the Conservatives to regain their popularity.

Scandal was suspected in October 1962 after an Admiralty clerk, William Vassall, was imprisoned for eighteen years for spying for the Russians. Vassall, as it turned out, had been blackmailed on account of his homosexuality and rumours were rife in Fleet Street that before his arrest he had enjoyed the protection of government ministers. Two ministers in particular were under suspicion – Mr Thomas Galbraith, a former Civil Lord of the Admiralty who now occupied another government post, and Lord Carrington, still First Lord of the Admiralty – and it was not until April 1963 that they were cleared by a judicial inquiry headed by Lord Radcliffe. By then, however, Galbraith had been driven to resign as the breath of scandal polluted the political atmosphere. Then, not long after the Vassall affair died down, a new scandal erupted. This was politically a more disastrous one for the Government since, on account of an unhappy coincidence, it enabled the new Leader of the Opposition to challenge Macmillan's handling of security problems. Moreover, Wilson did this with such skill that he revived the morale of his back-benchers quite spectacularly. After years of sterile opposition the sight of the Government on the defensive proved as water to a dying man for them. In fact, a thorough transformation was effected.

Three years before, in the aftermath of its third general election defeat (the second under Gaitskell), the Labour Party had presented a very different picture. Gaitskell had reacted to the 1959 result by demanding a controversial change in the party's constitution, a demand which had given rise to a furious debate amongst the faithful and which had come close to tearing the party apart. Shortly afterwards Gaitskell had also been defeated over the issue of unilateral disarmament, with the result that for the most part of his premiership Harold Macmillan had not had to fend off any serious parliamentary challenge from the Opposition. Indeed, until Harold Wilson replaced Gaitskell as Labour Party leader in 1963 the Opposition had not really been a united force.

The attack on the party's constitution – or more precisely on Clause Four of the constitution (the clause which committed the party to the common ownership of the means of production, distribution and exchange) – was launched by Gaitskell immediately after the 1959 election as a means to reassure the electorate that Labour had accepted the modern age. Clause IV, according to the party leader, implied that 'the only precise object' of Labour's programme was 'nationalization' and gave people the impression that 'we propose to nationalize everything', while the truth was that 'we have ... long ago come to accept ... a mixed economy'. The party constitution would therefore have to be altered to exclude the offending clause. But when he put forward this proposal to a special conference summoned in November 1959 to examine the election result, he found that his views were opposed by many of the party faithful, who accused him of 'betraying socialism'. Speakers such as Barbara Castle and Richard Crossman argued passionately for the retention of the 1918 constitution and although Anthony Crosland and others berated them for their 'conservatism' in this regard, the truth was that they were in the majority. For not only did they have the traditional left behind them; they also enjoyed the support of the pragmatic right. This consisted of people like Harold Wilson who saw the dispute in practical rather than in ideological terms. As he put it later: 'We were being asked to take Genesis out of the Bible. You don't have to be a fundamentalist to say that Genesis is a part of the Bible.' That is to say, Gaitskell had disrupted the party unnecessarily, by introducing a divisive issue into the forefront of party debate. In Wilson's view there were simply more subtle ways of leading the party and of outmanoeuvring the left. Eventually Gaitskell had to admit defeat. In July 1960 the National Executive decided 'not to proceed with any amendment or addition to Clause IV of the Constitution'. Gaitskell confessed: 'in view of the reaction, not only of people who would ordinarily be regarded as left-wing ... but of many other people in the movement ... we decided to drop the idea.' Meanwhile he had to fight another battle over the issue of unilateral disarmament.

Many of the defenders of the 1918 constitution were also supporters of the Campaign for Nuclear Disarmament. They in turn were supported by many in the Labour movement whose views approached but did not coincide with those of that campaign. The result was that support for unilateral nuclear disarmament ran very strong inside the Labour Party, and with the conversion of the Transport and General Workers' Union and other unions the unilateralists were in a position to challenge the party leadership over defence policy. This was done at the conference of 1960 when Frank Cousins, the transport workers' leader, introduced an appropriate resolution which, to the consternation of Gaitskell and the Shadow Cabinet, succeeded in obtaining a majority. Despite the fact that a majority of Labour MPs and constituency parties supported the leader, there was nothing he could do save denounce the 'pacifists, unilateralists and fellow-travellers' who had supported the motion and to promise to 'fight, fight and fight again to bring back sanity and honesty' to the party he loved. The following year, therefore, saw a battle within the party over this issue. The right wing mobilized itself through the Campaign for Democratic Socialism, while left-wing MPs refused to follow the official line in Parliament – seventy-two abstained in one debate – on the ground that conference had adopted a different defence policy.

The issue was not settled until 1961, when conference accepted British possession of nuclear weapons and membership of NATO, although opposition was still expressed to training German soldiers on British soil and to the establishment of American Polaris bases in Britain. Nonetheless, Gaitskell had succeeded in restoring his position and he consolidated his leadership thereafter by uniting the party against British entry into the Common Market. By 1963 he seemed finally to be on the brink of establishing the effectiveness of the Opposition, but he died suddenly in January of that year at the age of fifty-six as a result of complications following an attack of pleurisy. His successor as leader of the Labour Party was Harold Wilson.

Wilson was a former Oxford don and civil servant of middle-class background who had retained his Yorkshire accent. He had entered Parliament in 1945 and at the age of thirty-one had become the youngest cabinet minister since the Younger Pitt when Attlee made him President of the Board of Trade. He was extremely ambitious and if not considered very trustworthy nonetheless possessed a mastery of parliamentary debate and oratorical skills which marked him off as leadership material. He also had an extraordinary ability to project a working-class and anti-establishment image which gave him credibility with Labour voters, as well as a skill for political manoeuvring which a seventeenth-century cardinal might well have envied. His politics were those of pragmatism rather than principle, but in view of the party strife of the 1950s this was hardly a liability. Indeed, the robust frankness of his opponent for the leadership, George Brown, had merely served to highlight the need for a more subtle approach to party unity. Thus although Gaitskell had defeated Wilson in 1960 when the latter had challenged his leadership of the parliamentary party – the first time in the history of the party that an incumbent leader had been challenged – and although Brown had been elected deputy leader in the same year despite left-wing opposition, when it came to choosing Gaitskell's successor it was Wilson, not Brown, who was elected. His careful presentation of Labour's position on the Common Market had shown how party unity could be preserved. The voting figures on the first ballot for the Labour leadership were: Wilson, 115; Brown, 88; Callaghan, 41. On the second ballot, they were: Wilson, 144; Brown, 103. The parliamentary skills of the new leader were soon put to masterly use, for almost as soon as he became Leader of the Opposition, Macmillan's government became immersed in a new scandal.

The particular scandal which broke in June 1963, like that concerning Vassall the previous year, centred around a salacious mixture of sex and security. This time the details were rather more interesting since the Minister for War, John Profumo, had been sleeping with a Miss Christine Keeler, who had also been a bed-partner of a Russian diplomat named Captain Ivanov. Rumours to this effect had been rife in London for months but no one, it seems, had bothered to transmit them to the Prime Minister, the man responsible for national security. The matter became a cause for public concern when on 22 March 1963, in response to a question in the House of Commons, Profumo denied that any improper relationship with Miss Keeler existed. The Lord Chancellor then conducted an inquiry into the matter at the Prime Minister's request – Macmillan had come under pressure from Wilson to order one –

during the course of which Profumo admitted that he had lied. A report by Lord Denning which was published in September cleared him of any breach of security, but by this time he had resigned from Parliament in disgrace and Macmillan had been forced to take the consequences.

On 17 June Wilson electrified the Commons with a speech attacking the Prime Minister. Why had Macmillan himself not interrogated Profumo? What were the implications for national security of Profumo's link with Keeler? Was the Prime Minister properly fulfilling his responsibilities as head of national security? Macmillan simply defended himself by revealing his intense distaste for matters involving personal affairs. It was an attitude which attracted sympathy, but proved less able to attract support. Twenty-seven Tory backbenchers abstained from voting against the Opposition censure motion, with the result that the Government sustained something of a moral defeat.

The impact of the Profumo Affair was further reinforced by several factors. The press and television inveighed with unctuous hypocrisy against the lack of morality in public life and reached unheard of heights of santimoniousness by hounding to death a Dr Stephen Ward, who had rented Christine Keeler a flat. (He committed suicide after having been arrested for living off immoral earnings.) In fact, in the interests of sheer sensationalism, the lives of many people were made unpleasant in the extreme and it took Lord Hailsham to blurt out on television his view that adultery was not restricted to the Tory Party or even to the rich. But in the mood of 1963 his voice was destined not to be heard. *The Times* lamented the decline in public standards while every weekend the BBC allowed the party leaders to be mercilessly lampooned by bright young things from Oxbridge whose cutting sense of humour was not noticeably restrained by any sense of social responsibility. Rather, they were content to exploit the satirical potential of the BBC against the establishment in order to become establishment figures themselves. The very fact that they could ridicule the Government each weekend on a non-commercial channel, however, perhaps attested more eloquently than they to the fundamentally healthy state of public life.

Meanwhile, Wilson was able to make great play with another issue which had attracted attention as a result of the Profumo scandal, the exploitation of private tenants by slum landlords in London and elsewhere, which was known by the label of 'Rachmanism'. The name derived from the practices of Peter Rachman, a slum landlord whose name had come to light in some of the investigations surrounding the Keeler case. Wilson held that he was a natural product of the 1957 Rent Act and committed the Labour Party to repealing it when they eventually came into power. The Housing Minister, Sir Keith Joseph, denied that Rachman's operations were typical and set up the Milner–Holland Committee to investigate. But the damage had already been done. As a result of the Profumo affair and its aftermath, it seemed as if the top of British society was wallowing in decadence while the poor were left to the mercy of assorted bullies and thugs. In reality, therefore, it was only a privileged few who had 'never had it so good'.

In spite of this sort of image, Macmillan was still determined to lead the Conservative Party into the next general election. There was a year to go and the Prime Minister was as aware as the new Leader of the Opposition that 'a week is a long time in politics'. If he no longer seemed the 'Super-Mac' of 1959, there was still no doubting his extraordinary skills as a politician and he was confident in his own mind that he could still lead the party to victory. However, the events of the past year had taken their toll of the Prime Minister's health, and at the beginning of October 1963 he was rushed to hospital for an operation to his prostate gland. Since he expected to be incapacitated for several weeks he resigned the leadership after all and Lord Home, the Foreign Secretary, was instructed to inform the party of this decision. Meanwhile Macmillan himself, from his hospital bed, arranged for the processes to be undertaken whereby a new Prime Minister would emerge.

The prospect of acquiring a new leader would at any time have caused excitement in the Tory Party, but Macmillan's decision, as it happened, had been taken on the very eve of the party conference. There the news of his resignation created a huge political stir and the Blackpool assembly changed almost immediately from the normal kind of super-rally into something which in exuberance and vulgarity resembled a nominating convention of the American type. However, if factions were formed to prosecute the claims of individual candidates, the conference could not become a convention in the proper sense of the word. The leader would not be elected but would 'emerge' instead. In other words, the 'time-honoured processes' would be instituted whereby the Queen would take the advice of leading Conservative statesmen and invite the prospective premier to form a government. Her chief adviser on this occasion was, of course, to be Harold Macmillan himself. The bed-ridden premier had already arranged for 'soundings' to be taken within the party. The Lord Chancellor was to report the view of the Cabinet, the Chief Whip in the Commons the view of MPs, the Chief Whip in the Lords the view of the peers, while the view of the constituency parties was to be reported by Lord Poole, the Party Chairman. The job of all these people was not just to discover how many individuals supported this or that candidate; they were also to take into account the intensity of support and opposition aroused by all contenders. The Cabinet approved these arrangements on 15 October and by the 18th a new Prime Minister had emerged.

The candidates for the premiership included R. A. Butler, Lord Hailsham and Reginald Maudling. The first of these was undoubtedly the most experienced contender in the race. He had been Chancellor of the Exchequer under Churchill and Deputy Prime Minister to Macmillan. Renowned for his 'progressive conservatism', he was much admired in the country for his unassuming style of statesmanship. However, among constituency workers he was widely regarded as rather dull. 'Competent but uninspiring' was their verdict, and it seems to be one which Macmillan fully shared. He, like the constituency faithful, supported the claims of the highly individual, rather wayward but nevertheless brilliant Lord Hailsham, whose magnificent powers of rhetoric could be relied upon to inspire even the most dejected Conservative supporter. Hailsham had never held really high government office – he was after all a peer – but as chairman of the party in the 1950s he had won the affection of all sections of Conservative opinion. He threw away what chances he had of success, however, by too obviously playing to the Blackpool crowd. For soon after the news of Macmillan's decision had become known he had announced that he would renounce his peerage – a sure sign that his hat was in the ring. This was simply 'not the done thing', and his candidacy suffered accordingly. The other candidate in the field was Reginald Maudling, tipped by some as 'the dark horse', by others as the 'candidate of youth'. Maudling, in fact, was much duller than Butler and had as yet to establish any real claim to lead the party. Only his position as Chancellor had pushed him into the limelight and it would soon enough push him out again.

Party opinion therefore began to swing in favour of the Foreign Secretary, Lord Home, whom practically no one had considered to be in the running and who himself had informed the Cabinet that he should not be considered a candidate. Everybody's second choice, Home benefited from the rule about intensity of feeling governing the taking of soundings within the party. He also secured the support of Harold Macmillan, who seems to have thrown his weight behind him when it became clear that Hailsham had destroyed his own chances. Home, in fact, had inadvertently pursued the strategy which Hailsham himself might well have adopted – that is to say, that of the retiring but dutiful party servant, a strategy which according to the reports which Macmillan received made him the choice of the Conservative Party as their leader. Macmillan, therefore, when visited in hospital on 18 October by Her Majesty the Queen, reported that she should summon Lord Home to the Palace. This she did that afternoon, and on the following day Butler, Hailsham and Maudling all agreed to serve under him as premier. On 23 October he renounced his peerage; shortly afterwards he fought a by-election which had been conveniently arranged for him in a safe Scottish seat; and in early November he entered the Commons as Sir Alec Douglas-Home. It was an astonishing turn of the political wheel and one which no one had anticipated.

Sir Alec was obviously a nice man, a decent chap, a reliable fellow, etc. But politically he was something of an anachronism. His grouse-moor image stood out rather awkwardly against the background of modern Britain and his aristocratic origins and education – Eton, Christ Church, the fourteenth earldom of Home – served to emphasize his almost total lack of experience in British domestic politics. If the British people knew little about him, he knew little more about them. His choice as premier was therefore resented by many who asked why it was that the Tory Party could not provide a leader from the House of Commons? Was Sir Alec, for all his decent qualities, really the kind of person who should be leading the party in 1963? Two of his former colleagues did not think so. Both Iain Macleod and Enoch Powell – perhaps the brightest of the younger members of Macmillan's cabinet – refused to accept office under the new Prime Minister. Indeed Macleod, who as Minister for Commonwealth Relations had clashed with Home as Foreign Secretary over the speed of decolonization in Africa, condemned Sir Alec's selection as a victory for the 'magic circle' politics of the Tory establishment in a famous article in the *Spectator*. He had been a Butler supporter in the leadership contest and believed that Butler – the choice of the majority of the Cabinet – should have been given the party leadership. It was Macleod's view that only Macmillan's personal antipathy to Butler had led to Home's selection. Sir Alec, however, believed that he had won the leadership fairly and squarely and having done so deserved the support of his former colleagues. He regarded the refusal of Powell and Macleod to serve under him as an unnecessary blow to party unity (and one which would prove decisive later on). In his opinion, he had as much a claim to lead as anyone else in Macmillan's cabinet and it was hypocrisy for anyone to deny that claim in the name of democracy or social equality. If he was the fourteenth Earl of Home, then Mr Wilson, as he later put it, was the fourteenth Mr Wilson.

This did not, of course, prevent the Leader of the Opposition or the television satirists from depicting the new Prime Minister as a political troglodyte. He himself had confessed to having no training in economics and had joked that he always counted with matchsticks. Harold Wilson was therefore able to represent him as someone who was completely out of touch with the modern world. This might not have mattered very much, but Wilson at this time was presenting the Labour Party as the party of technological change, the party of science and of scientific attitudes, and the selection of Sir Alec as Tory Party leader helped enormously to emphasize the contrast which the Labour leader was seeking to present between the Government and the Opposition. Labour, led by an economist, stood for the 'white heat of the technological revolution'; the Conservative Party, led by a former earl, stood for muddling through with matchsticks.

This was an astute move on the part of Wilson and his advisers and it was pushed for all it was worth. Thus a document produced by the National Executive of the Labour Party in 1963, entitled *Labour and the Scientific Revolution*, offered 'a new deal for the scientist and technologist in higher education, a new status for scientists in government, and a new role for government-sponsored science in industrial development'. All this was necessary, it stated, to revive the economy and to get Britain moving again. Wilson had provided the Labour Party with exactly the right means to revive itself. For science not only offered the movement an image of modernity which it had recently lacked; it also provided a vocabulary with which Labour's traditional divisions could be obscured. Middle-class technocrats were prone to understand by it that the Labour Party was now committed to support modern, private industry, whereas the old war-horses of the left understood by it that the state would now nationalize the most up-to-date of private industries in the name of government-sponsored technological advance. Little wonder, therefore, that the party closed ranks behind its leader at the party conference of 1963. Left-winger Mrs Judith Hart declared that 'socialists and scientists together can make their dreams a reality', and right-winger Dr Bray asserted with equal conviction that Labour would form a partnership with science which would 'amplify the freedom of ordinary people'. In short, a new idea had been born which could reconcile all sections of the Labour movement. And this was important, for the next general election was only a year off at the most.

The year before the general election of October 1964 saw a polarization of public opinion as Wilson united the Labour Party and as Conservatives closed ranks behind Sir Alec Douglas-Home. The Liberal revival, which had been the great phenomenon of 1962, now began to disappear. This had been clear from the autumn of that year, when Liberal support as recorded by opinion polls was already down to 20 per cent. Throughout the course of 1963 it fell steadily and uninterruptedly, until by June 1964 it was down to 9 per cent. The local election results of May 1963 slightly disguised the extent of the Liberal decline, but a lost deposit at the Luton by-election of November 1963 and a decreased share of the poll at Sudbury and Woodbridge in December 1963 indicated all too clearly the trend among the voters. The results of the last round of by-elections held before the general election (in May 1964) served merely to confirm this trend. The truth was that the Liberal vote was really a function of the unpopularity of the other two parties, especially the Conservatives. It did attract some positive support, but what support it had was too thinly spread and too unorganized for the Liberals to build upon it in order to challenge the two-party system successfully. As the general election drew nearer the voters returned in increasing numbers to their traditional voting allegiances.

In the run-up to the election, Wilson concentrated on bolstering the unity of his party and in attacking the feudal image of the new Conservative premier. He particularly enjoyed tackling him at question time in the House of Commons – of which Sir Alec had little experience – and did what he could to turn this particular constitutional practice into the socialist equivalent of a blood-sport. Again, his acknowledged television technique was put to consummate use. Sir Alec concentrated on the subjects with which he was most familiar, and in Tory propaganda an increasing emphasis was put on defence and foreign affairs, subjects on which the Prime Minister, although really only a very average Foreign Secretary in his time, was held to be an authority. Great stress was laid, in particular, on the threat that Labour would dismantle the British independent deterrent, although the evidence suggested that the public at large were not interested in defence or foreign affairs.

Nonetheless, the lead in the opinion polls which Labour had built up since 1961 was slowly worn down during the course of 1964 (Maudling's 'run for growth' brought similar dividends as had accrued from Butler and Heathcoat-Amory's pre-election budgets), until by the summer they were only a few points ahead. In June, therefore, the Prime Minister was kind enough to let it be known that he would not hold an election until the autumn. By that time, with any luck, a pleasant summer and more experience of Wilsonian blandiloquence, he reckoned, might put the voters in a rather less radical mood. Moreover, Labour's lead still seemed to be melting steadily, so that there was every reason to hang on until October. Polling day was finally fixed for the 15th. The Government were tempted to continue in office even longer, but the fear that a sterling crisis was looming on the horizon persuaded Sir Alec to meet his fate in mid-month. At last the suspense was over and the electorate could decide whether it was time for a change or not.

The Conservative manifesto was entitled *Prosperity with a Purpose* and stressed, like many of their television broadcasts, the need for an independent nuclear deterrent. It also promised that a Conservative government would review the role of trade unions, tackle monopolies and mergers, take action on rating reform, and construct 400,000 houses per year. Sir Alec did his best to sell this document to the people and undertook a much-heckled tour of constituencies to put his points across. The tour did not show him at his best. He had little experience as a soap-box orator and unlike Wilson had difficulties in coping with cat-calls and general abuse. His speaking manner was rather prim and he had considerable difficulties in communicating to a non-party audience. He was helped out to a considerable degree by that natural orator Quintin Hogg (the former Lord Hailsham who had also renounced his title, as promised to the Blackpool crowd) and speakers of the quality of Edward Heath and Edward Boyle, but the presidential flavour, particularly of the television campaign, meant that the spotlight was firmly fixed on him. And when it came to television broadcasts the premier was something of a flop. For unlike Wilson or Grimond, both of whom were consummate performers in the television studio, Sir Alec was obviously ill at ease and his cadaverous appearance and peculiar accent did nothing to render his image in any way sympathetic to voters. That, at least, was the view which was taken by those interested in political cosmetics. On the other hand, it is possible that the Premier's obvious contempt for media methods acquired a certain sympathy for him among traditional voters.

The Labour Party was skilfully led by Wilson, who conducted a brilliant campaign of personal promotion. George Brown as deputy leader was also an asset as stump-orator, but it was Wilson's personal appearance at set-piece party rallies which gave direction to the whole campaign. His cutting phrase, his zest for political argument, his virtuoso platform and television performances completely revived the Labour Party, so that it fought the whole election enthused by the scent of victory. Wilson looked and sounded a Prime Minister throughout the electoral battle, and every Labour Party worker expected him to win.

The Labour manifesto was entitled *The New Britain* and concentrated on internal rather than on foreign affairs. Growth and scientific change were given special prominence and in accordance with the line which Labour had been pursuing the party promised to establish a new ministry devoted to technology. Also promised was a Ministry for Economic Affairs which would plan the long-term economic future and leave the Treasury to deal with day-to-day affairs. In this way, it was supposed, the gains derived from technological change could be harnessed for the national good. The party also promised to establish a Parliamentary Commissioner or Ombudsman to deal with complaints against government departments, and they pledged themselves to set up regional planning boards. Thus the return of a Labour government presaged a shake-up of the government machine. In other fields, Labour promised to repeal the 1957 Rent Act, to set up new ministries for Wales and Overseas Development, to reorganize education along comprehensive lines and to stimulate the economy through tax reforms. The manifesto was therefore in many ways an attractive one: it stressed planning rather than nationalization, ignored the party divisions on foreign affairs and, in spite of promising more activity in Whitehall, included measures designed to appeal to those more interested in regional affairs.

The regionally minded had also been made the special object of attention by the Liberal Party, which was campaigning on the theme of a federal Britain in a federal Europe. The Liberals were in fact campaigning very seriously; for the first time since 1950 they were fielding candidates in more than half of Britain's constituencies. And under Grimond's ever-inspiring leadership they seemed to be making some impact. One commentator described the Liberal leader as possessing 'probably the best television image in the country'. Thus, with the Conservatives defending hard, the Liberals fighting to secure a breakthrough and Labour sensing victory, the stage was set for an exciting finish to the election. The result was one of the closest in modern British election history and marked a political watershed.

Party	Votes gained	Percentage of vote	Average vote per MP	Number of MPs
Conservative	12,001,396	43·4	39,479	304
Labour	12,205,814	44·1	38,504	317
Liberal	3,092,878	11·2	343,653	9
Others	347,905	1·3		—
	27,637,993	100·0		630

Source: Derived from D. Butler and A. Sloman, *British Political Facts, 1900–75.*

On a 77·1 per cent poll there had been a swing to Labour of 3·5 per cent, producing a working majority of four for a Labour government – the smallest since 1847. Labour had not increased its overall vote, but quite clearly, as a result of Wilson's leadership, the party faithful had turned out to see it safely home. The Labour Party's victory, therefore, was almost certainly due to the restoration of Labour's morale. The Conservative vote, on the other hand, had slumped by between 1 and 2 millions as Sir Alec's demonstrable lack of charisma had driven many normal Conservative supporters either to stay at home or to vote for the Liberals.

To some extent he had also been unlucky. Just one day after polling day, news came that Khrushchev had fallen from power in Russia and that the Communist Chinese had succeeded in exploding their first atomic bomb. Had the news of these events been received a couple of weeks earlier, perhaps his emphasis on foreign affairs and defence would not have sounded so misplaced. He was also let down in the course of the campaign by his Chancellor, Reginald Maudling. The latter had described Labour's election proposals as a 'menu without prices' but had taken so long to have them costed by the Treasury that when he finally came up with a figure of £1,000 million it was already too late to influence the course of the campaign. Wilson, meanwhile, had seized the initiative and was waging an onslaught on 'stop-go', 'thirteen wasted years' and a looming deficit of £800 million which the figures released by the Treasury for the second quarter of the year allowed him to hang around Maudling's neck with devastating political skill.

The swing to Labour was uneven. The capital swung to the left, but in the South-East and in the Midlands the Tories held their ground. Indeed, in certain Midland seats there was even a swing to the Conservatives, and in one at least – Smethwick – it was held that this was the result of a racialist campaign against local immigrant communities which had been run by the Conservative candidate, Peter Griffiths. There was some controversy over the exact nature of Griffiths's appeal, but when he entered the House of Commons after his election there was no doubt of the intensity of Labour's indignation at his election. Wilson condemned him as a 'parliamentary leper' and hoped that all members would treat him as one. Elsewhere in the country the swing was in favour of Labour, although the Liberals did particularly well in the Scottish Highlands. They also retained Orpington against all the predictions of the pundits and managed to win a seat from the Tories in the West Country. Their sense of political achievement, however, was marred by the fact that not only had they lost two seats, but their overall performance had been frustrated by the electoral system. For having doubled their vote in the second election in a row – this time to 3 million votes – they were still rewarded with fewer than ten seats. The voting system was undoubtedly a democratic one, but it could not be described as fair. Still, a new, radical premier – or so it was thought – had been elected, and Grimond appeared to find some solace in that.

THIRTEEN WASTED YEARS? SOME REFLECTIONS ON CONSERVATIVE RULE IN BRITAIN DURING THE PERIOD 1951–64

Superficially, the thirteen years of Conservative rule between 1951 and 1964 appear to have been fairly successful ones. Great Britain still behaved as a world power internationally while at home people experienced 'the affluent society' and were told that they had 'never had it so good'. After years of austerity they could afford to relax, and if they spent their money on bingo or beer, who could blame them? Had they not already risen to the most supreme of challenges in the World War and had they not, therefore, earned the right to take things easy for a while and to take advantage of the opportunities which Macmillan's hire-purchase society offered them? After so many years of rationing, why should they not have washing-machines, refrigerators, vacuum cleaners and televisions and all the other consumer goods which technology could now provide? Americans already enjoyed these gadgets and from all accounts life in the United States had much to recommend it. Everyone from the middle-aged mum with her domestic appliances to teenagers with their transistor radios agreed on that; besides, was there necessarily anything wrong with adopting the lifestyle of the television set or movie screen? The public evidently thought not.

Life at last seemed less of a struggle for many people. Thanks to the Welfare State, there were few worries regarding health, and since 1944 children had a better chance of staying on at school and going to university. People lived longer, enjoyed a rising standard of living and were not troubled about unemployment. They married younger, had children earlier and therefore had more children. Britain came, in fact, to have an unusually young population which was better-fed, better-clothed and educated to a higher level than ever before.

There were, of course, criticisms of the affluent society. Complaints were made about materialistic values, striptease clubs, drink, gambling and the alarming increase in juvenile delinquency, prostitution and illegitimacy. The Profumo and Vassall affairs were held up as examples of a decline in sexual morality and concern was expressed about the waning influence of established religion. But was the Britain of this time really a decadent society in any meaningful sense? Surely not. Young people were certainly more sceptical about traditional values, but that was their traditional right. Moreover, there is ample evidence to suggest that they cared about cultural values. The paperback revolution in printing made them generally more aware of all sorts of currents of thought, and sensible television programmes extended their range of interests. Moreover, there was great creativity at this time in many fields. In ballet, opera and architecture, for example, much was happening, and in scientific research and development there were many great accomplishments. Technologically the country had produced the jet engine, the hovercraft, the nuclear power station and much of value in electronics. It was therefore no surprise that British scientists were awarded so many Nobel Prizes. Even in the field of theology, Britain experienced creative debate and the intense interest aroused in 1963 by the publication of the Bishop of Woolwich's *Honest to God* demonstrated a concern for spiritual values. Britain was in fact in a healthy moral and spiritual state, a judgement supported by data as varied as enrolment for Voluntary Service Overseas and the greater public tolerance towards homosexuals which was recommended by the Wolfenden Report. In this context it is useful to remember the advice of David Thomson:

... in no society have moralists found it difficult to discover vice and omens of decadence, especially among a generation younger than their own; it is always easy to confuse the silly with the sinful, the merely trivial with the vicious. A generation which had known extermination camps like Auschwitz, the devastation of Hiroshima, the highest scientific intellects devoted to destruction, could hardly avoid some nihilism. Dilemmas so absolute did not evoke orthodox reactions. The young supporters of the Campaign for Nuclear Disarmament who marched from Aldermaston at Easter or the pacifists [led by the aged Earl Russell] who sat down in Trafalgar Square, were heirs of the Peace Pledge Union of the thirties. Their actions, however strange, suggested no spirit of indifference to the deepest spiritual problems of the age.

No, the Britain of the affluent society was not a decadent one.

The problem remains, however, whether the Conservative governments of the period can be given much credit for this generally healthy state of affairs. For in many ways it would seem that Britain was prospering for reasons which had very little to do with them. In fact, it might well be argued that they were undermining rather than advancing this prosperity.

The point has already been made that as far as fiscal and economic policy was concerned the Tories did very little in their years of power. Cushioned by the turn in the terms of trade they abolished rationing, reduced taxes and manipulated budgets but gave very little impression of knowing how the economy really worked. Little attention was paid to Britain's sluggish economic growth or the long-term challenge posed by Germany and Japan. Industrial relations were treated with a 'we/they' attitude and no thought was given until late on in the day to the problems created by Britain's prosperity. Instead, the Government sat back and did nothing in the belief that there was nothing to do, and for most of the time their energy was devoted to maintaining Britain as a world power whatever the cost to the economy. One result, in the words of the sociologist T. R. Fyvel, was

the evident belief of the Government that the country could not *afford* to build a single new hospital – or prison: none were built during the decade [of the 1950s]. There was the lag in subsidized housing; the inadequate provision for old-age pensioners; the relative slowness in replacing antiquated school buildings, in providing youth clubs and playing fields . . . There was the persistent shortage of nurses (what would have happened but for girls from overseas?), of teachers in state schools, of policemen, penal officers, midwives, youth workers (or for that matter of clergymen).

The Government refused to pay for them; they preferred instead to maintain their world role. However, the justice of these criticisms began to be realized by the early sixties. In 1961, for example, the Government founded four new universities, and two years later they accepted the Robbins Report and promised to found six more. They accepted in principle that there should be a huge expansion of higher education. Likewise in 1962 the Minister of Health, Enoch Powell, announced that ninety new hospitals would be built in the next ten years at a cost of £500 million and set a final target of 200 new hospitals and the replacement of half the existing ones. But it was a belated recognition of a major social problem and the Tories were out of power before they could do anything about it.

Moreover, Tory economic complacency ensured that the necessary economic growth would never be generated. Not enough money was channelled into key industries; stop-go policies undermined the confidence of industry to invest in the long term; too much money was allowed to be exported abroad; and too much money was spent on defence. Moreover, bad industrial relations bedevilled attempts to put things right, for the workers began to see that the real beneficiaries of the affluent society were those who had money to invest. Affluence among the working class was the result of hire-purchase arrangements rather than greater wealth. As Nicholas Davenport has pointed out, their rewards under the Conservative régime were not particularly striking ... A gain in their real standard of living of only 50 per cent in about thirteen years does not stand up against the rise of 183 per cent (in real terms) in the value of equity shares (225 per cent with net dividends added) which the owners of capital enjoyed. With the purchasing power of the 1951 £ down to 13s. 6d. by 1964 the workers must have felt that they had fought a losing battle. And they never managed to win a larger slice of the national income. Their share remained at a little over 42 per cent throughout the Conservative regime.

Well-known figures who knew how the system worked were active at this time, it is true, in promoting unit trust companies. But these were schemes for the middle class, not the working class, who had no surplus capital to invest. With the economic crises of the early 1960s – crises which hit them hardest and for which they were often unjustly blamed – it began to be apparent that Tory affluence would soon come to an end. The scandals of the Macmillan era merely served to reinforce the impression that a watershed had been reached in the country's history, and foreign affairs appeared to teach a similar lesson. For with the decline of empire, the burden on the economy imposed by Britain's East of Suez commitments, the veto on entry into the Common Market and the collapse of British aspirations to produce an independent nuclear deterrent, it seemed indeed that Britain had lost an empire but had not yet found a role.

The tragedy was to be that, having expelled the Tories from office under Sir Alec Douglas-Home, the country acquired a new Prime Minister with equally conservative instincts. For Harold Wilson also believed that Britain was a 'world power' whose frontiers 'lay on the Himalayas'. He too was determined to uphold the sterling system and the value of the pound, with the result that all the mistakes of the 1950s were repeated in the 1960s. After 1963-4, then, things were never the same again. But in another sense they were never really different.

The year 1964 witnessed a clear break in British political history. The long years of Tory rule had come to an end. Harold Wilson now prepared to govern Britain with a tiny parliamentary majority. Politics suddenly seemed much more unpredictable, and economic crises, sensational by-election results and mini-budgets soon reinforced this impression. Still, Wilson was determined to start off on the right foot. In his first television broadcast as Prime Minister he declared that his small majority would not affect his ability to govern. He insisted that the electorate had given Labour a mandate, and that mandate would be carried out. In the event, Labour succeeded in governing for no less than seventeen months, with a majority over the Conservatives and Liberals that fluctuated between five and only one, before an election was called.

Wilson's decision to form a Labour government was a very natural one. The alternative – a formal coalition, which would have involved him in days or even weeks of difficult negotiations and seriously limited his freedom of manoeuvre – was an unattractive proposition to a party with memories of 1931. A short-term arrangement with the Liberals was totally unnecessary, since no one doubted that Labour could carry on by itself for a limited period. A long-term arrangement with the Liberals would have created dangerous strains within his own party ranks. Wilson, in characteristic form, was embarking on an experiment. If the experiment failed, he could quite easily go back to the country and ask for a proper working majority, with no damage to the party whose unity he had striven to forge.

The cabinet appointments announced by Wilson reflected his desire to build the strongest team around him: James Callaghan was given charge of the Exchequer; George Brown went to the Department of Economic Affairs (DEA), the first of the newly created ministries and reminiscent of the old Attlee policy on the economy; Frank Cousins headed the new Ministry of Technology with special responsibilities for modernizing industry. Another innovation in the government machine was the appointment of the first Minister of Land and Natural Resources, Fred Willey. A further ministerial post with no direct counterpart in Sir Alec Douglas-Home's administration was filled by Lord Caradon who, as a Minister of State at the Foreign Office, was made Permanent British Representative at the United Nations. Lord Chalfont, formerly defence correspondent of *The Times*, was appointed a Minister of State with special reponsibility for disarmament. The former Department of Technical Cooperation was replaced by a new Ministry of Overseas Development, headed by left-winger Barbara Castle.

The new Labour administration contained 101 ministers, eleven more than the Conservative government. No less than eighty-seven of these were in the Commons. The Cabinet numbered twenty-three, the same size as the outgoing Douglas-Home cabinet.

The apportioning of posts had also been allocated with a shrewd eye to keeping the potentially rebellious left wing in check. Three leading left-wingers were given ministerial posts: Frank Cousins as Minister of Technology; Barbara Castle as Minister for Overseas Development and Anthony Greenwood as Colonial Secretary. Wilson had thus built up his cabinet with a careful balance from both the left and the right of the party.

It is difficult to exaggerate the degree to which the new Labour government was dominated by Harold Wilson. During the election campaign he had shown himself to be a politician of the first rank. He was extremely good on television and a brilliant performer in the House of Commons. With his familiar pipe, he soon became a father-figure, somewhat akin to Stanley Baldwin in the inter-war period. Wilson's policies also seemed peculiarly suited to the mood of the country. He was offering a 'New Deal' that was not *too* new, but seemed to mark a distinct break from the apparent decline and disappointments of the previous years.

With so slender a majority, Labour's period in office was always conditioned by its assessment of its own opinion poll and popularity ratings. In terms of the Government's standing in the country, their popularity rating in the opinion polls fell into four clearly marked phases. The first lasted from polling day in 1964 until the end of January; it was terminated by the disastrous Leyton by-election. The second lasted until May 1965 and saw a decline in Labour's lead in the polls. In the third phase, from May to early September 1965, the Conservatives gained ground in municipal elections, in two by-elections and in the opinion polls. The fourth phase, extending into the 1966 election campaign, brought a sharp increase in the standing of both the Prime Minister and the Government.

The 1964–6 Parliament was always overshadowed by the prospect of a second election. In many ways, the tone of the administration – and its economic mistakes – have to be judged against this electoral backcloth.

THE ECONOMY

The whole period of the Labour government from 1964 to 1966 was dominated by the problem of the economy. Though their domestic reforms were important, though equally important events were occurring on the diplomatic front, and though important changes in party politics were taking place, it was Labour's management of the economy that overshadowed the period. Indeed, the very outset of Wilson's 'hundred days' (the period of galvanized political activity with which Wilson had promised to open his administration) was largely dominated by a major sterling crisis. The arguments over the background to this crisis were debated bitterly at the time. Not unnaturally, the Conservatives asserted that the situation was well under control until Labour's rashness caused foreign holders of sterling to lose confidence. Labour, equally naturally, argued that their party had inherited a balance-of-payments deficit so large that a crisis of confidence was inevitable once the facts became known. It is difficult to deny that part at least of Labour's economic difficulties were of Wilson's own creation. During the 1964 election campaign Wilson had made a positive decision to ram home the question of the balance-of-payments deficit and to blame it on the Tories. This had the effect of putting an albatross around the necks of his Chancellor and Government. His constant references to 'Labour's tarnished inheritance' and 'the Tory mess' created the scenario Wilson wanted – a scenario in which a Labour government, tough, determined, purposeful, would be contrasted with a fractious, irresponsible Opposition who had just bequeathed to Labour one of the largest balance-of-payments deficits in Britain's peacetime history. In the short term, Wilson's tactics were successful. The Conservatives were thrust on to the defensive and kept there. The Prime Minister asserted his claim to national leadership by portraying the Conservative leaders as unworthy and even unpatriotic. This was the political front which hid the unpalatable truths.

The Prime Minister and his senior colleagues were informed of the full dimensions of the balance-of-payments problem on 16 October. Within three days, and almost without serious discussion (if Crossman is to be believed), devaluation was ruled out by Wilson, Callaghan and Brown. Instead, the Government opted for a 15 per cent surcharge on imports, imposed on 26 October in an attempt to remedy the deficit. At the same time the Government announced that they were inquiring into ways of cutting expenditure.

The economic problem was exacerbated by the fact that Labour was pledged to increase old age pensions and to abolish prescription charges. For humane as well as political reasons it was important to take prompt action on these promises. The Chancellor was equally convinced that an autumn budget which set out the increased taxation by which these measures would be financed would display the Government as a pillar of financial rectitude. Taken together with the advance notice of the introduction of capital gains and corporation tax, the budget, in Callaghan's view, must help George Brown at the Department of Economic Affairs in his efforts at longer-term planning of the economy. Hence on 11 November the Chancellor introduced a special budget.

Its total effect was meant, if anything, to be mildly deflationary. On the one hand, the budget honoured election pledges. The earnings rule for widows was abolished. Old age pensions, sickness and unemployment benefits were to be increased from March 1965. The prescription charge under the National Health Service was to be abolished as from 1 February 1965. On the other hand, national insurance contributions were raised and the duty on petrol increased. In addition, the Chancellor announced that the standard rate of income tax would go up in spring 1965 and confirmed that he would then also introduce a capital gains tax and replace the existing income and profits taxes on companies with a corporation tax. It was a budget designed to redeem Labour's election pledges on pensions and prescription charges; it was also designed as a gesture to the trade unions, to encourage them to cooperate in working out an effective incomes policy.

Callaghan's autumn budget in fact proved a disastrous step. To both the city and foreign observers, it seemed to mean that the Labour government were giving their social policies priority over the strength of sterling. Hence the heat was turned on the pound. The first sterling crisis of the Wilson era had begun.

In the two days after the budget there were heavy sales of sterling from Europe and North America. On Thursday 19 November, however, the Government took the decision not to raise bank rate. By the weekend the run on sterling had reached such a point that action could no longer be avoided. But the decision to raise bank rate on Monday* by 2 per cent was taken to be a step born of desperation. Sales of sterling accelerated. The answer, Wilson concluded, was to make sterling strong. After a lengthy meeting with the Governor of the Bank of England, it was decided to raise a massive overseas credit. By the evening of 25 November Lord Cromer (the Governor of the Bank of England) had mounted a $3,000 million rescue credit which for the moment made sterling safe. The immediate crisis was over.

The budget represented only one part of the Government's determination to restore Britain's balance of payments. The prices and incomes policy was Wilson's new weapon. The Government recognized that a successful incomes policy required the support of both sides of industry and on 9 November 1964 George Brown told trade union leaders that he wanted an agreement relating wage increases to increased productivity by Christmas. A Declaration of Intent on Productivity, Prices and Incomes was signed at Lancaster House on 16 December. The Government undertook to set up machinery to review the movement of prices and incomes. Management and the unions undertook to try to remove obstacles standing in the way of greater efficiency, and to assist the workings of the new prices and incomes machinery.

To make specific recommendations on the basis of this policy, the Government set up a National Board for Prices and Incomes. It consisted of an independent chairman, a number of independent experts, a businessman and a trade unionist. The Prices Review Division of the Board could investigate the price of any goods in the economy, and the Incomes Review Division had power to investigate all claims and settlements relating to wages, salaries and other incomes. In less than five years of operation the Board produced over 150 reports on

* Not the normal day for such announcements.

prices and earnings. There was no statutory authority to enforce the recommendations of the Board; reliance was placed on voluntary methods and the power of persuasion and public opinion. However, in late 1965 the Government introduced a compulsory 'Early Warning' system, whereby the board was notified in advance of any intended increase in incomes or in certain prices. As a result, the Government and the board had time to consider increases before they were put into effect.

Prior to Callaghan's second budget two other important economic events took place. In February 1965, as part of a major review of government expenditure, Wilson announced defence cuts involving the cancellation of the P 1154 fighter and the HS 681 jet transport. Further cuts followed. In March the fifth Polaris nuclear submarine order was cancelled, while in April the TSR-2 aircraft was likewise axed. In March 1965 a White Paper was published on prices and incomes. This argued that average annual increases in money incomes should not exceed a maximum of 3½ per cent. In the event it was largely ignored, and wage rates during 1965 rose by an average of 9 per cent.

It was against this background that Callaghan's second budget was introduced on 6 April 1965. Intended to be mildly deflationary, it raised an extra £323 million in tax. Corporation tax, capital gains tax, and 6d. on income tax were there as promised, but the Chancellor delighted the Labour left by drastically curtailing businessmen's entertainment allowances. This budget was vigorously opposed by the Conservatives. Indeed, Heath's reputation was greatly enhanced by his clearly demonstrated debating skills. The Finance Bill was not finally passed without three government defeats (on 6/7 July) and the introduction of no less than 243 amendments by Callaghan himself to take account of points raised.

The rough passage received by the Finance Bill, however, was the least of the Government's economic worries. It was becoming clear that George Brown's efforts to achieve restraint on prices and incomes were coming unstuck. Both prices and incomes were rising too fast. The Retail Price Index, which had been fairly steady during the last half of 1964, rose by 2½ per cent in the first four months of 1965 (increased taxes accounting for a large proportion of the rise). George Brown brought increasing pressure to bear on firms to hold prices back, and from May onwards he regularly referred increases to the Prices and

Incomes Board. Partly as a result, the rate of inflation slowed markedly; the rise in the last eight months of 1965 was only 2 per cent. Wage rates and earnings, however, continued to rise.

Against these economic indicators, the need to reassure foreign holders of sterling and so keep devaluation at bay led to yet another budget in July 1965 – the third within the Government's first year. The July budget was again deflationary, cutting public investment as well as the defence programme and tightening restrictions on hire purchase.

Not surprisingly, critics of the Labour government were quick to point to the seemingly different approaches in economic matters of George Brown (who remained at the DEA throughout the first Wilson government), James Callaghan at the Exchequer, and a third centre of power in the shape of Professor Balogh, the Prime Minister's personal economic adviser. It seemed obvious that the Treasury was bent on always dampening economic initiatives, while the DEA was equally busy producing new ones. George Brown himself was later to admit that during this period 'There were too many of us, advising and counter-advising one another.' Rarely for a statement from George Brown, no one disagreed with this verdict. There were parallels in this situation with the divided management of the economy that Attlee's government had instigated.

Although the Government had managed to weather the sterling crisis, difficulties were rapidly arising in other areas. One such area was the aircraft industry, where the Government were determined to cut back on a number of 'prestige' projects, including the supersonic Anglo-French 'Concorde' and the TSR-2. In the face of stiff French resistance, the Concorde project eventually went ahead, but the aircraft industry remained in a state of unrest.

Economic confidence was not helped, either, by an early and sensational by-election defeat for the Government. On 21 January 1965 Labour's Foreign Secretary, Patrick Gordon Walker, failed by 205 votes to return to Westminster from Leyton, supposedly a safe Labour seat. The swing against Labour was 8·7 per cent. At Nuneaton the same day Frank Cousins, the Minister of Technology, held the seat for Labour, but with a much reduced majority. The results seemed to signal an abrupt decline in Labour support. The Government in fact absorbed the Leyton defeat surprisingly rapidly and, apart from a brief moment in February, Labour continued to lead in both major opinion polls. Swings to Labour were recorded in two by-elections during 1965.

LABOUR'S REFORM PROGRAMME

Despite Labour's problems with the sterling crisis and with prices and incomes, and despite the limitations imposed by their precarious majority, an important series of measures nonetheless began slowly to appear before Parliament. The delay was partly due to preoccupation with foreign policy and the creation of new administrative departments, but the main reason was undoubtedly that most of Labour's proposals, as with housing and land, existed only in outlines. Ministers and civil servants needed time to work the proposals out in detail.

The introduction of the Rent Bill in March 1965 marked the beginning of one important measure. The Rent Bill was intended to reverse the 'landlords' charter', the Rent Act, which had long been a target of Labour hostility. The 1965 Act was designed to fix fair rents for private tenants and to provide greater security of tenure. In fact, the only lasting solution to the housing problem would have been a massive house-building programme, but Crossman had neither the resources nor money for this.

Two important measures reached the statute book in the field of Employment and Industrial Relations. The 1965 Trade Disputes Act gave union leaders full legal protection from actions which arose because there had been a threat to break the contract of employment. Secondly, the Redundancy Payments Act provided for compensation for workers made redundant through no fault of their own. Payments were calculated according to length of service and were to be paid for by employers and the government. In the same area, the Government also established the Donovan Royal Commission in 1965 to investigate the trade unions.

An important item of Labour's social reform legislation was the 1965 Race Relations Act. The aim of the Act was to deal with racial discrimination in public places and with the problem of incitement to racial hatred. The original intention of the Bill was to make incitement to racial hatred a criminal offence. In deference to criticism from both sides of the House, the Government on 25 May tabled amendments under which racial discrimination was no longer subject to penal sanctions. A Race Relations Board, with Mark Bonham Carter as chairman, was set up with a network of local conciliation committees to try to iron out disputes without recourse to the courts, which would be invoked only after all conciliation procedures had failed. The Opposition supported the Bill as amended and it became law on 8 November 1965.

The item of legislation which provoked the most political controversy during Wilson's first administration – and which finished up as a fiasco – was the proposal to re-nationalize the steel industry. Ever since the war the steel industry had been caught in a game of political shuttle-cock. It had originally been nationalized by Labour in 1951 and subsequently de-nationalized by the Conservatives on their return to power. The re-nationalization of steel had been pledged in Labour's 1964 manifesto, and Labour candidates had particularly campaigned on this issue in Yorkshire, the North East and South Wales. Though public opinion was still lukewarm on further nationalization, to Wilson it was an issue that would help keep the Left happy.

Hence on 30 April 1965 a Government White Paper was published proposing the nationalization of the fourteen largest steel companies. The measure was partly portrayed as a rationalizing reform which would improve efficiency. Nonetheless, the Liberals as well as Conservatives made it clear they would oppose the measure.

Trouble also came from Labour's own right-wing back-benchers. Late on 6 May it seemed possible that Labour votes against the White Paper would lead to a Government defeat. Two Labour rebels, Desmond Donnelly and Woodrow Wyatt, had made clear their opposition to nationalization. However, a few conciliatory remarks from George Brown at the end of the debate pacified them. The Government got a majority of four (310 votes to 306), but at the cost of outraging the Labour left. It was perfectly clear to most observers that this measure would not reach the statute book and had done nothing to improve Labour's electoral standing. Indeed, the steel fiasco, followed by a heavy burst of sterling sales and an attack of nervousness on the Stock Market following a £109 million May trade deficit, all made it imperative for Wilson to reassert that the Government would go on governing and that there would be no snap election. This Wilson achieved in a speech at Glasgow on 26 June, in which he pledged there would be no election that year.

The precarious position of Labour's majority was again highlighted during the summer recess with the death of the Speaker, Sir Harry Hylton-Foster. His successor was a Labour MP, Dr Horace King, the Deputy Speaker. Wilson, however, was able to preserve the Government's majority at three by persuading the Liberal MP, Roderic Bowen, to serve in the non-voting office of Deputy Chairman of Ways and Means.

.The narrowness of Labour's majority and the danger of by-election losses rather obscured the degree of restlessness which existed within Labour's own ranks. From its earliest days internal back-bench discontent was marked, most particularly from the left wing. Although discontent from its back-benches had occasionally erupted under the Conservatives, the persistence, scale and regularity of Labour revolts – especially after 1966 – marked something of a new departure in British political life. The first such rumblings were audible as early as November 1964 in protest at the Government's refusal to speed up the payment of increased old age pensions which had been announced in the autumn budget. In February 1965 the Government's announcement of the establishment of a Royal Commission on the Trade Unions (under Lord Donovan) also met with left-wing dissatisfaction.

By far the most vocal left-wing opposition, however, was centred round foreign policy, in particular Britain's support for America's growing involvement in Vietnam. On 4 March 1965 forty-nine MPs put down a motion calling for the Government to declare their inability to support US policy. In June 1965 fifty Labour MPs wrote a private letter to Wilson warning of the growing dangers of escalation of the Vietnam conflict. At the Blackpool Party Conference in September 1965 the Government's support for American policy in Vietnam came in for bitter criticism from left-wingers, and in February 1966 almost 100 Labour MPs cabled Senator Fulbright to protest against the American resumption of bombing in North Vietnam. There were other issues, too: the large number of troops making up the Rhine Army in Germany was one such target. There was also considerable protest at American intervention in the Dominican Republic in April 1965. On the domestic front, the Government's immigration White Paper in August, and the absence of steel nationalization from the Queen's Speech in November, also provoked left-wing anger.

Although, in general, these left-wing revolts met with little success (partly because such natural leaders of the left as Crossman and Castle were in the Government), they were a portent of the great revolts that were to occur between 1966 and 1970. They were significant also in bringing many younger MPs, not traditionally associated with the old left-wing issues of Clause IV and CND, into the left-wing camp on such issues as immigration and Britain's role East of Suez.

FOREIGN POLICY

It was perhaps not surprising that left-wing anger tended to be concentrated on foreign affairs, for the new Labour government showed an essential continuity with the previous Conservative administration on the key questions of British foreign policy. At the centre of this policy was the Anglo-American alliance – an alliance which, during the whole period, had to stand the strains imposed by the American involvement in the Vietnam War.

By 1965 the United States was becoming more committed than ever to the survival of South Vietnam; the State Department in Washington was convinced that if America withdrew and left South Vietnam to the Vietcong and to North Vietnam, Chinese expansionist ambitions would be encouraged. According to the domino theory, this would leave other South-East Asian allies such as Thailand and Malaysia as the next victims. The United States therefore decided to give South Vietnam even more direct support.

The 'Americanization' of the war by President Johnson took place in successive stages between August 1964 and June 1965. On 2 August 1964 the destroyer USS *Maddox* of the Seventh Fleet was attacked by three North Vietnamese patrol-torpedo boats in the Gulf of Tonkin. In retaliation American planes flew sixty-four sorties over North Vietnam on 5 August, attacking naval bases and oil installations. On 7 August the United States Congress approved the Gulf of Tonkin Resolution, allowing the President to 'take all necessary measures to repel any armed attack against the forces of the United States and to prevent further aggression'. President Johnson in effect now held a blanket authorization to expand the American military commitment in South-East Asia. On 8 March 1965 the first American combat unit landed at Danang. This was followed by a rapid build-up. At the end of 1964 there had been 23,000 American servicemen in South Vietnam; by November 1965 there were 165,700.

America was now at war in South-East Asia. Back in 1954 Lyndon Johnson had been one of the leading senators who opposed American intervention to save the French at Dien Bien Phu. Ten years later he was determined not to go down in history as the President who 'lost' South Vietnam. And the war was spreading. Contingents of troops to fight on the American side were sent by Australia, New Zealand and South

Korea. In March 1965 Russia threatened to send 'volunteers' to North Vietnam, and China warned the world at large that she would not stand idly by if there were further American attacks on North Vietnam.

The Labour government were thus faced with a difficult dilemma. The Anglo-American alliance made it vital to give at least moral support to US policy; but Labour's left wing, as has been seen, was bitterly critical. Wilson, in fact, made strenuous efforts to achieve a Vietnam peace. In June 1965, at the Commonwealth Prime Ministers' Conference, he proposed a Commonwealth Peace Mission to Vietnam. But this came to nothing and Chou En-lai pronounced the whole idea a hoax. On 8 July Wilson sent Harold Davies, Joint Parliamentary Secretary to the Ministry of Pensions, to Hanoi, but very little of substance emerged from this visit either.

If the Anglo-American alliance was one cornerstone of British diplomatic policy, the other was Britain's position as the focal point of the Commonwealth. Nowhere was the change in Britain's role in the world more dramatic than in relation to the countries of the Commonwealth. Between 1964 and 1966 a variety of important changes took place. On coming to power, Labour had created a new Ministry of Overseas Development, headed by a minister of cabinet rank, to direct economic aid to the most needy parts of the Commonwealth. Another development, in 1965, was the setting up of the Commonwealth Secretariat.

Britain's Commonwealth relations during this period centred around three different problems: the granting of independence to former colonies; friction between members of the Commonwealth (notably India and Pakistan); and the special problem of Rhodesia.

Among the Commonwealth countries to be granted independence in 1964 were the central African states of Zambia and Malawi, as well as Malta. In 1965 the Gambia and Singapore also became independent. In 1966 they were joined by Barbados, Botswana, Guyana and Lesotho. In some ways, the granting of independence to the Gambia in February 1965 marked the start of the era of new, economically unviable ministates, independent but heavily subsidized by Britain. At the opposite end of the scale, Britain was bitterly attacked by both Spain and the United Nations for refusing to end the dependent status of Gibraltar – although the inhabitants of Gibraltar steadfastly made it clear they wanted to remain linked to Great Britain.

A different kind of strain within the Commonwealth came to a head when war broke out in September 1965 between India and Pakistan over the bitterly disputed question of Kashmir. It was a significant reflection of the changing world diplomatic scene and the decline in British power that it was Russia, rather than Britain or other Commonwealth members, who succeeded in bringing the warring parties to the conference table at Tashkent in January 1966.

As the Indo-Pakistan war raged, Britain was confronted also with her most vexed problem stemming from decolonization: the UDI by white Rhodesia in November 1965. Rhodesia was first buffeted by the 'winds of change' blowing through Africa in 1953. The threat to the strongly entrenched 270,000 white population from black nationalist political parties emerged from the ill-fated federation imposed by Whitehall on Northern Rhodesia (Zambia), Nyasaland (Malawi) and Southern Rhodesia. The Zimbabwe African People's Union (ZAPU) was officially formed in December 1962, the Zimbabwe African National Union (ZANU) a few months later. Both were banned by the right-wing Rhodesian Front government in 1964 and their leadership put in detention.

It was against this background that the attitude of white Rhodesians hardened considerably. As early as 1963 there were rumours of a Unilateral Declaration of Independence. Labour continued the talks started earlier in 1964 by the Conservative government. In January 1965 Ian Smith had a meeting in London with Harold Wilson and the Lord Chancellor, and in February the Lord Chancellor and the then Commonwealth Secretary, Arthur Bottomley, visited Rhodesia. These visits achieved little. In April 1965 a Rhodesian government White Paper argued a strong case for independence. Elections in May 1965 gave Ian Smith's Rhodesian Front a landslide victory. The European settlers were clearly behind Smith, and in November he took the plunge and declared independence.

Wilson was confronted with perhaps the severest test of his political skill since he had come to office. Although the left wing and the African states called for the use of force, this option had already been ruled out by Wilson. He had now to satisfy the African clamour for immediate action yet keep the problem in British hands, and carry with him the British people. In the Commons he outlined his plan to impose economic sanctions gradually, holding out at every stage the chance of negotiations, provided only that Rhodesia returned to the path of constitutional development. Despite the opposition of a group of back-benchers led by Julian Amery, the Conservatives supported the Government in applying immediate economic sanctions against the Smith régime. However, on the later order imposing an oil embargo, Conservative divisions were glaringly exposed in a back-bench rebellion. On 17 October 1965, over the issue of the oil embargo and a blockade of the Mozambique port of Beira, fifty Conservative back-benchers defied the whips by voting against the Government, while thirty-one voted for them.

In the House of Commons, Wilson had handled a difficult crisis with skill. But he had given hostages to fortune by declaring that it would be only a matter of a few weeks before the illegal régime was brought down. Sanctions were to prove all too easy to avoid.

PARTY POLITICS

The Rhodesian issue, though it presented Wilson with a grave and complex crisis, also presented problems for the Conservatives. Indeed, all was not well with the Opposition, which was finding it very difficult to take advantage of Labour's political and economic difficulties. The Tories, it seemed, were held responsible for the crisis for, according to National Opinion Polls, only one third even of Conservative supporters were prepared to blame the Labour government. A Liberal win in the Roxburgh by-election thus gave new impetus to Tory discontent with Sir Alec's leadership – a discontent which the party whips had failed to still with their announcement in mid-January that Home would not be resigning. The chance of an early election had precluded immediate change, but the idea had already spread that the time for Sir Alec to go would be just before the summer recess. Wilson's categoric pledge on 26 June that there would be no general election during 1965 thus immediately served to raise the Conservative leadership question. It was discussed at the 1922 Committee Executive and on 5 July the Executive split into two halves, with Heath's supporters in the forefront of the revolt. Heath's strong performance in the debates on the Government's Finance Bill undoubtedly came at an opportune moment, while in the constituencies there was a clear waning of support for Sir Alec.

On Tuesday 13 July *The Times* revealed the proceedings of the 1922 Committee. This was followed two days later by an NOP poll reporting an increase in Labour's lead. Finally, on 18 July a long article by William Rees-Mogg in the *Sunday Times* was headed 'The Right Moment to Change'. Sir Alec began to be visibly affected. A poor performance in the foreign affairs debate on 20 July turned out to be decisive. Sir Alec decided to resign the leadership. The election which followed (in February, the party had decided on a new procedure for electing its leader and Sir Alec insisted that his successor should be chosen under it) proceeded smoothly and uneventfully. Maudling and Heath were nominated at once. After some hesitation, Enoch Powell made it a three-way contest. Inside the Parliamentary Party the campaign for Heath was strongly organized by Peter Walker; Maudling's campaign, which was organized by Lord Lambton, seemed amateur in comparison. On the first ballot, Heath polled 150 votes to Maudling's 133 and Powell's 15. Both rivals promptly stood down, and Heath became leader of the Conservative Party.

Born in July 1916, Edward Heath could hardly have presented a more marked contrast with his predecessor. After education at Chatham House School, Ramsgate and Balliol College, Oxford, he had seen war service in Europe. He had entered the Commons in 1950 (the same year as Powell, Maudling and Macleod) as MP for the Kent suburban seat of Bexley. After a long stint in the Whips' office, Heath served as Chief Whip from 1955 to 1959. A 'Macmillan man' since pre-war days at Oxford, Heath rose swiftly in the Macmillan era – Minister of Labour during 1959–60 and then Lord Privy Seal – effectively to become 'Mr Europe' and second to Lord Home at the Foreign Office. When out of office after 1964, Heath served as Home's policy planner and economic spokesman. He had a reputation as a doer, a leader and a man with vision and purpose. They were qualities urgently needed if the party was to reform its ranks for an early election.

The task facing the new leader was clear. The unity of the party had to be re-established. For although the party had rallied behind Sir Alec, the wounds and bitterness created by his selection as leader had never really healed. On 5 August Heath announced his Shadow Cabinet. Reginald Maudling became Deputy Leader, while Sir Alec Douglas Home remained in the Cabinet in charge of foreign affairs. One of the most crucial appointments was that of Iain Macleod to take charge of economic and financial affairs.

The return of both Iain Macleod and Enoch Powell to the Shadow

Cabinet (both of whom had refused to serve under Sir Alec) was an obvious and visible sign of the healing of these old divisions. Yet, despite this strengthening and coming together of the Tory ranks, the party's standing in the country remained a cause for concern. Although, in the wake of the steel débâcle, there had been a temporary swing to the Conservatives, after the summer things went Labour's way again. Heath's own rating in the opinion polls started slipping alarmingly, and Conservative organizers became worried at the cold and aloof image he seemed to project.

The first major publication of Conservative philosophy under Heath came in October 1965 in a document entitled *Putting Britain Right Ahead*. The most notable features – a strong commitment to entry into Europe, reform of the trade unions and industrial relations and a major reduction in direct taxation – were all essentially policies on which the party had fought in 1964. But there were important organizational changes within the party, rather reminiscent of 1945. Central Office was streamlined under the guidance of Edward du Cann. In the constituencies, urgent efforts were made to modernize the party image as the prospect of an election during 1966 became more likely.

The problems facing the Conservative Opposition were to some extent shared by the Liberals. In the tightrope parliamentary situation between the general elections of 1964 and 1966 the Liberals found that few things went in their favour. Almost the only exception was the victory of David Steel in the Conservative-held seat of Roxburgh in the by-election of March 1965. Even this victory in a seat with a fairly strong Liberal tradition, though giving a boost in morale to committed Liberals, had little wider impact.

The narrow Labour victory in 1964 had made much more difficult the cherished Liberal hope of replacing Labour as the alternative to the Conservatives. The Liberal Party, after 1964, seemed to have lost something of the sense of purpose and direction that had characterized the Orpington years. Their dilemma took an unexpected twist when Grimond gave an interview to the *Guardian* in which he quite clearly indicated that he would be prepared to contemplate coming to terms with Labour if the parties could agree on long-term policies and aims. Whatever Grimond intended to produce by these remarks, he must have been considerably pained by the instant hostility aroused in the Liberal Party. The idea was shelved, but the future role the party should play in a 'hung' parliament remained somewhat undecided. Such divisions within the Liberal hierarchy did nothing to improve the image of the party, while the longer the parliament continued, the worse showing the party achieved in by-elections – nearly all of them in unpromising territory.

These Liberal difficulties, and the Conservative preoccupation with electing a new leader, all gave advantages to Labour. By the end of 1965 Wilson was considering the timing of his general election appeal. The Cabinet re-shuffle of December 1965, which brought Roy Jenkins to the Home Office and switched Barbara Castle to the Ministry of Transport, had strengthened Wilson's team as well as bringing in new faces.

Should Wilson risk an appeal to the country? The Prime Minister remained unconvinced that the electorate wanted an election. But there were other factors. Troubles threatened on the industrial front. At Westminster the Government had survived a debate on the future of the Territorial Army by a mere one vote, a reminder of their vulnerability. The Labour back-benches were increasingly restive over Vietnam. With Iain Macleod as Shadow Chancellor, the Finance Bill would face a very rough ride.

In the event, it was the Hull North by-election which decided Wilson. The Conservative Opposition had convinced themselves that they could win there on 27 January 1966. Labour in fact held the seat with a 5,000 majority, on a swing of 4·5 per cent to the Government. In an age accustomed to by-election reverses, this was a remarkably good omen for Labour. After Hull North an atmosphere of electioneering pervaded Parliament. Despite all his difficulties, Wilson rode a wave of confidence. Labour began dressing the window for the election. By the time Wilson left for an official visit to the Soviet Union on 21 February it was quite clear that the campaign was about to begin. On 28 February Wilson ended speculation concerning the date of the election and polling day was fixed for 31 March.

All the portents favoured Wilson. The Gallup Poll survey of 4 March showed Labour with an eleven-point lead over the Conservatives. Labour had carefully published a series of proposals and promises – the Land Commission; leasehold reform; an option scheme for home loans, at a rate of interest $2\frac{1}{2}$ per cent below the prevailing interest rate, for people with low incomes; rating proposals to relieve domestic ratepayers of about half the annual increase in rates; a Parliamentary Commissioner, or Ombudsman, to investigate complaints against the administration; new aid for the arts; the amalgamation of pensions and national assistance payments; an Industrial Reorganization Corporation with £150 million to back mergers and amalgamations and to finance 'new projects or expansions of special importance to the economy'; and disclosure by companies of political contributions. The Labour manifesto, *Time for Decision*, was launched by Wilson himself. Having stressed Labour's achievements over the previous eighteen months, the manifesto centred on one theme – planning. There would be selective investment to concentrate capital where it was needed; regional planning was stressed; a national transport plan would reorganize road and rail transport; a housing target of 500,000 houses a year was set; and major expansion of education and medical services was promised. With the exception of the promise to re-nationalize steel, socialism was conspicuously absent.

The Conservative manifesto, *Action not Words*, presented a programme of 131 points of action by the 'party of the pacemakers'. The major pledges included reform of the trade unions, a check on rising prices, remodelling of the Welfare State and restoration of respect for Britain. For the Liberals, the prospect of a second election within two years was not an enviable one. Not only was the party relatively short of candidates, it entered the election generally unable to present itself as the 'alternative' party and internally divided over Grimond's future as leader of the party. Putting a brave face on it, their manifesto, *For All the People*, emphasized the moderating role played by the party and committed the Liberals to major defence cuts, entry into Europe and a new approach to industrial relations.

The nature of the election campaign reflected the significance of the 1964-6 period. For Labour the 1966 election was the second phase of the 1964 campaign. This time, however, Labour had the distinct advantage of being the party in office – not, as in 1964, a party that had been in opposition for thirteen years. It made effective use of its slogan 'You *Know* Labour Government Works', and also emphasized the need for a 'mandate' to complete the work already begun. For the Conservatives, not only was there the unaccustomed experience of fighting as the Opposition, they were also fighting with a new leader whose electoral popularity was in doubt. Thus the 1966 election was for the Conservatives a new contest – not the second round of a bout begun in 1964. Yet many of them were privately doubtful even at the outset of the campaign whether they could win. And from the start Labour dominated: despite the Conservative claim to be 'the party of the pacemakers', there was no doubt that the pace of the election campaign was set by Harold Wilson.

The first results left no doubt that Labour had won a decisive victory. The results were:

Party	Votes gained	Percentage of vote	Average vote per MP	Number of MPs
Conservative	11,418,433	41·9	45,133	253
Labour	13,064,951	48·0	35,937	363
Liberal	2,327,533	8·5	193,961	12
Plaid Cymru	61,071	0·2	—	—
SNP	128,474	0·5	—	—
Others	263,144	0·9		2
	27,263,626	100·0		630

Source: Derived from D. Butler and A. Sloman, *British Political Facts, 1900–75*.

For the first time in history, an outgoing Labour government had been returned with an increased majority. It was an election triumph for Wilson and a hard blow for Heath, even though Heath had privately resigned himself to the likelihood of defeat as the campaign wore on. Labour gained forty-eight seats while the Conservatives had a net loss of fifty-one. Over the country as a whole the swing to Labour was 2·7 per cent. It was highest in England (2·9 per cent), lower in Scotland and Wales. In general, however, the results demonstrated an unusually high degree of uniformity of swing.

For the Liberals, the results provided both disappointment and some cause for rejoicing. Although, with a reduced field of candidates, the Liberal vote had fallen by more than 750,000, the party had emerged with its representation increased to twelve. On the 'Celtic fringe' the party had lost two seats but gained North Cornwall and West Aberdeen-shire, with other encouraging gains in Cheadle and Colne Valley. On the other hand, the election which produced the largest Liberal contingent for over twenty years also seemed to mark the end of the 'Orpington-style' Liberal revival. This was particularly true of the seats in which the

Liberals had been the major challengers in 1964. Then, the party had finished second in fifty-five constituencies. By 1966, this total had fallen to twenty-nine. Even these twenty-nine seats (largely confined to safe Conservative suburbs or remote agricultural seats and equally safe Labour-held industrial backwaters) were hardly promising territory. In only eight constituencies throughout Britain were the Liberals within 5,000 votes of victory. The 1966 election marked the end of the road for them in another sense also. For it was followed, not very long afterwards, by the resignation of Jo Grimond as leader of the party and his replacement by Jeremy Thorpe.

It was perhaps only natural that the election campaign waged by Labour had painted a picture of the 1964 government which was more distinguished by its gloss than by its accuracy. For whilst there had been some record of social achievement – increased old age pensions, the 1965 Housing Act and so on – the crushing success of the 1966 election victory concealed much that had gone wrong and still more that had been shelved. The deficit on the balance of payments in 1965 amounted to £265 million, and although exports stood at 9 per cent above their level for the first few months of 1965 the dangers of inflation had been emphasized over and over again during the election campaign. On 1 April 1966, therefore, as Wilson returned to Downing Street in the euphoria of victory, there were serious economic problems on the horizon, and within two years of his resuming office the economic crisis had shaken the Labour Government to its foundations.

THE ECONOMIC CRISIS

The new administration started with few surprises. The speech from the throne on 21 April proposed a major, if predictable, programme of legislation. There were to be Bills providing for steel nationalization and the establishment of a Land Commission and an Industrial Reorganization Corporation. Comprehensive education was to be developed, a Ministry of Social Security created and public control over the docks extended. Most significant of all, however, was perhaps the announcement that the Government were ready to negotiate terms to enter the European Economic Community.

Even a month after the election, Labour's euphoria still persisted. In the Gallup Poll there was a lead for Labour almost as large as in the days of Profumo in 1962, whilst the proportion of the electorate who believed Wilson was doing a good job reached record size. The Prime Minister himself knew only too well that the economy needed urgent attention. Still, he believed that with an incomes policy he had not only the alternative to orthodox deflation but a cause to which he could commit the party and the unions.

Less than a week later, on 16 May 1966, Wilson's economic strategy lay dangerously exposed by one of the very unions that was to be part of the new economic deal. The occasion was a strike by the National Union of Seamen. Its impact on the economy was immediate: exports fell sharply; the London docks were slowly paralysed; foreign bankers feared the unions were getting out of control (a view strengthened by the London Labour Party's decision to back the strikers); the pound began to slip on the foreign exchange. Wilson's attempts to persuade the strikers to return to work were rejected. The unions were adamant, and Wilson, infuriated, blamed the strike on Communist agitators.

The Premier's anger in part succeeded: the NUS Executive voted for a return to work, though Wilson's image with his own left wing had taken a severe mauling. It was a significant episode – foreshadowing the battles with the unions which were to come and marking the end of Labour's honeymoon. It was rapidly followed by another blow from the left. The introduction of the promised Bill to provide advance warning of wage and price increases, and to empower the Prices and Incomes Board to defer them while they were investigated, precipitated a Cabinet resignation. Frank Cousins, the Minister of Technology and former Secretary of the Transport and General Workers' Union, refused to accept this restriction on free collective bargaining. On 3 July he resigned.

Against a worsening economic background, it was becoming clearer day by day that the Government must take tough measures. The choice was equally clear – deflation or devaluation. The Cabinet was deeply divided. George Brown (intent on seeing through the National Plan*) was prepared to accept devaluation; he had the support of such ministers as Roy Jenkins and Anthony Crosland.

Callaghan, at the Exchequer, became increasingly concerned at the loss of confidence in sterling by overseas holders. Unless a Treasury

* A document produced by the DEA which had set out a number of aims for the British economy.

package was implemented at once, he warned that he might have to join the devaluers. Meanwhile on 5 July sterling fell to $2·78\frac{11}{16}$, its lowest point for twenty months, while on the Stock Exchange War Loan stock slumped. Harold Wilson returned from a visit to Moscow on 19 July to find himself confronted with a major economic crisis. The publication of the Prices and Incomes Bill on 4 July had not reassured foreign banking opinion, while the by-election loss of Carmarthen to a Welsh Nationalist (see page 239) did not enhance political stability.

On Wilson's return the Cabinet met for a series of crucial meetings, but although George Brown had been rallying support for a devaluation, any incipient revolt faded out. Only six members of the Cabinet argued against the final package and only George Brown offered his resignation – an offer that he subsequently withdrew. Wilson survived with his Cabinet intact, but at the price of reversing many of the policy pronouncements of the past decade. The Cabinet had decided on a massive dose of deflation.

The £500 million package announced by Wilson left the Labour back-benches in dismay and disbelief. The measures included stiffer terms for hire-purchase repayments, a ceiling of £50 a year per person for overseas holidays, as well as a 10 per cent increase on purchase tax, wine, spirit and tobacco duties. Of all the measures, the most bitter controversy was aroused by the wage freeze. Wilson told the Commons there was to be a legally binding freeze on wages and prices for six months, to be followed by a period of severe wage restraint. It was hastily incorporated into the prices and incomes legislation, and was given short shrift by the Tories. When the Bill came before Parliament on 4 August the Government's majority dropped from ninety-five to fifty-two. George Brown, who fought the Bill through in committee with immense skill, said that the Government did not expect that they would have to activate these powers; to do so would require an Order in Council confirmed by a Commons vote; and in any case, he promised they would last no more than a year.

The July package was followed shortly afterwards (on 10 August) by a Cabinet reshuffle. George Brown left the Department of Economic Affairs to become Foreign Secretary in place of Michael Stewart, who duly filled the vacant chair at the DEA. Herbert Bowden replaced Arthur Bottomley at the Commonwealth Relations Office. Richard Crossman became Lord President of the Council and Leader of the

House. Anthony Greenwood moved to the Housing Ministry, Callaghan remained at the Treasury.

The economic package and the Cabinet shuffle seemed to have saved Wilson, and the Prime Minister retired to the Scilly Isles on 11 August far more satisfied than he should have been. The possible threat to his position from a Brown–Callaghan axis had been eliminated. The pound was safe again. His dominance over his colleagues seemed largely un-impaired. But his position was less secure than it appeared. The possi-bility of devaluation, having once been discussed, might raise its head again. And although the CBI had reluctantly accepted the freeze, the TUC had only knuckled under after a bitterly fought vote.

Six months later, in February 1967, the wage freeze duly gave way to the 'period of severe restraint'. The Government's optimism mounted. There had been a welcome balance-of-payments surplus during the last quarter of 1966. On 26 January bank rate was reduced to 6 per cent. On 2 March a conference of trade union delegates in London voted to support the TUC General Council in operating a voluntary wages policy after the period of severe restraint. The removal of the import surcharge back in November 1966, plus a variety of fortuitous factors in world trade, had also encouraged an optimistic (though false) assessment of the health of the economy. When the year-long 'freeze' ended on 1 July 1967 the Government decided to retain a reserve power to delay wage increases for a further year from 12 August 1967. In the division on the order, on 17 July, twenty-two Labour MPs abstained, reducing the Government's majority to fifty-six.

This debate coincided with the beginning of serious economic doubts. As the summer of 1967 continued there was growing concern over the effectiveness of the measures announced in July 1966. On 4 July it was revealed that the country's gold and dollar reserves had fallen by £36 million. The June trade figures revealed a trade gap of £39 million. Unemployment in mid-July, at 496,000, was the highest for that month since 1940. Faced at the end of July with an Opposition motion of 'no confidence' in the Government's economic policies, James Callaghan declared: 'Those who advocate devaluation are calling for a reduction in the wage levels and the real wage standards of every member of the working class of this country ... Devaluation is not the way out of Britain's difficulties.'

Despite Callaghan's brave words, the economy was not growing as predicted. Wilson attempted to blame the growing sterling crisis on the Arab–Israeli 'Six-Day War' (although the pound began its slide three weeks before the conflict started). In fact, the Government's announcement of their intention to enter the EEC was much more a factor – since it was no secret in government and financial circles that the existing sterling parity and Common Market entry were incompatible. Thus a variety of factors – domestic and worldwide – combined to force the government to take action.

Faced with a deterioration in the economy, on 28 August Wilson took direct command of the economy and personal charge of the DEA. The next day – against Treasury advice – he relaxed hire-purchase controls to help stimulate a consumer boom. He exuded optimism. At Newport on 8 September he reiterated that at long last the Government had reached a 'turning point' and he also found the courage to address the annual TUC conference which began on 4 September. The following month, on the eve of the Labour Party conference at Brighton the Government was forced, as a result of a legal action undertaken by the white-collar union ASSET, to invoke the compulsory powers section of the Prices and Incomes Act. Wilson managed to live that problem down as well.

But things went from bad to worse. At home Labour's by-election losses mounted. In Europe the prospects for British entry were looking gloomy. At home, too, a major dock strike in Liverpool and London was the prelude to another poor set of trade figures. The effect of these and other issues on foreign confidence in the pound was soon felt. On 19 October bank rate was raised to 6 per cent. This did nothing to stop the outflow of funds, and on 4 November Callaghan warned Wilson that the drain on the reserves was intensifying. As well as informing Wilson that the Common Market finance ministers were already making contingency plans for a British devaluation, Callaghan advised Wilson that the situation could not be held.

This time Wilson decided that, despite growing criticism from within Labour's ranks, devaluation would have to come. On 8 November the Cabinet Committee on Economic Policy was informed of the proposal; on the 9th bank rate was raised to 6¼ per cent. The trade deficit for October reached a massive £162 million, partly as the result of the prolonged unofficial dock strike. During the weekend any hopes of a massive foreign loan were dashed. On 13 November, after a speech by the Prime Minister at the Guildhall, a small ministerial group was brought into the preparations, though the Cabinet was not told until the 16th. On Saturday night, 18 November, the Treasury announced a 14·3 per cent devaluation of sterling from $2·80 to $2·40 to the pound. The Prime Minister broadcast to the nation the next day, explaining that 'this does not mean that the pound in your pocket . . . had been devalued'. In reply Edward Heath declared that three years of Labour government 'had reduced Britain from a prosperous nation to an international pauper'.

Devaluation had been widely anticipated by the speculators, and on the day before there was a run on the pound said to be greater than any previously experienced. The devaluation had unfortunately been delayed by the need to achieve international cooperation so as to prevent a flurry of competitive devaluations. As it was, only a few minor currencies were devalued with sterling. It was also agreed among central bankers that Britain should be given credits of up to $3 billion, including $1·4 billion stand-by credit from the IMF. This credit protected the reserves against speculation, but it would have to be paid back out of balance-of-payments surpluses over the next few years.

The defeat of the Government's economic policy immediately provoked conjecture about the future of the Chancellor of the Exchequer. The Conservatives, not unnaturally, were howling for Callaghan's blood and Callaghan, although defending devaluation with dignity, agreed that he should resign. Wilson finally persuaded him to exchange offices with Jenkins. On 29 November Jenkins became Chancellor and Callaghan switched to the Home Office.

Jenkins opened his period as Chancellor with an unfortunate slip. He told the House that the IMF had not attached conditions to the loan and that no deflationary policies were involved, yet when the IMF letter was published the following day, the promise to cut home consumption by £750 million was there for all to see. In an emergency debate on 5 December, therefore, the Chancellor went through a baptism of fire. Some eighteen Labour MPs voted against the Government and perhaps the same number abstained.

The devaluation crisis had naturally produced speculation that Wilson would not be able to remain at No. 10 after such a complete volte-face. There were press reports that a *coup* against Wilson would be attempted, and in the background the opinion polls showed a Conservative lead that had shot up from 7½ per cent before devaluation to 17½ per cent afterwards. Wilson's own position, however, was secure. He was safeguarded by private assurances from the left wing of his party – his old allies in Opposition days – against any attempt to remove him. Nonetheless, dissatisfaction in the Cabinet reached new heights, held back only by the absence of any agreed successor and an uncomfortable realization that only Wilson had the nerve and the political resilience to rescue the party from catastrophe.

The consequences of devaluation dominated the political scene. In its wake came further cutbacks in public spending. Curiously, however, the very controversy of the November devaluation eased the major expenditure cuts which were announced on 16 January. All British forces in the Far East (except for Hong Kong) and the Persian Gulf were to be withdrawn by the end of 1971, aircraft carriers were to be phased out of service in the Royal Navy after 1971, and the order for fifty American F-111 strike aircraft was cancelled. On the home front, the Prime Minister announced a charge for prescriptions issued under the National Health Service, subject to certain exemptions. The charge for dental treatment rose and free milk for pupils in secondary schools was withdrawn. The raising of the school-leaving age was deferred from 1971 to 1973 and the housing programme was reduced by 16,500 houses per year. These were draconian measures for a Labour government. The humiliation for Harold Wilson, who had himself resigned from the Attlee government over the decision to impose prescription charges, was very great. In fact, despite deep Cabinet divisions, only one minister resigned – the Earl of Longford, Leader of the House of Lords and Lord Privy Seal.

Two months elapsed after these January measures before Jenkins's budget of 19 March. By then the Chancellor had not only to contend with the British economy but with worldwide danger signals – namely the increasing flight from the dollar into gold and silver. For on 8 March the United States Treasury revealed that, in the previous three months, the US's gold reserves had fallen by $1,000 million, and as efforts to halt the flight failed, the British government received an urgent request to close the London Gold Market. At midnight on 14 March, therefore, the Queen held a meeting of the Privy Council to proclaim 15 March a Bank Holiday, and on 17 March, the Governors of the Central Banks, meeting in Washington, hastily conducted a holding operation. The bankers reaffirmed their determination to maintain the official price of gold at $35 an ounce. The British government agreed to keep the London

Gold Market closed until 1 April. Stand-by credits to the sum of $4,000 million were made available to safeguard sterling against speculators.

It was against this background of crisis that Roy Jenkins presented his budget to the House. There was no pretence over its severity. The Chancellor promised a stiff budget followed by two years' hard slog. 'Stiff' proved an understatement: the increase in taxation amounted to £923 million, nearly all raised by indirect taxation on cigarettes, alcohol and petrol. Most unpopular of all was the increase to £25 in the motor-car road licence fee. Jenkins's determination to achieve substantial expenditure cuts was unshakeable. The result was a ruthless massacre of prejudices and election promises which fanned the growing discontent of the Labour Party to the point where regular back-bench revolts occurred. When the House of Commons voted on prescription charges in May no less than forty-seven Labour members voted against.

The monetary crisis of spring 1968 provided the occasion for the final departure of George Brown. An abortive attempt by Brown at a Cabinet revolt was quelled by Wilson. All the Cabinet critics except Brown stayed on. But this time Brown's resignation was final. Michael Stewart took his place as Foreign Secretary. However good Brown's reasons for criticizing the handling of events by Wilson, his own timing and explanation of his motives were poor. His accusations that Wilson governed in quasi-presidential style were a little hard to take from one who a few days before had urged the Prime Minister to defer less to his Cabinet.

To some extent, after the traumatic devaluation of November 1967 and the international monetary crisis of March 1968, the summer of 1968 was peaceful on the economic front. Yet, despite devaluation, there was no real sign of recovery in the balance of payments. In his Letter of Intent to the IMF immediately after devaluation, the Chancellor stated that the Government's aim was to improve the balance of payments by at least £500 million a year. However, progress after devaluation was disappointing and fell obstinately short of official expectations. The current account showed a deficit for 1968 of £274 million, only a slight improvement on the deficit for 1967 of £300 million. Moreover, this improvement came on the invisible account: the trade gap actually widened considerably.

The balance of payments also suffered from a series of strikes which were helping to undermine the incomes policy. Nor did the annual

TUC Congress improve the climate. Congress voted 7·7 million to 1 million against the Government's wages policy. The TUC's own voluntary incomes policy scraped through by a bare 34,000 votes. A similar vote of nearly five to one against an incomes policy was registered at the Labour conference.

It was in this context that, as winter approached, the economy once again dominated the final months of 1968. Sterling was seriously affected by pressure on the French franc and the parallel strength of the German mark. On 18 November the French government announced their determination to defend the franc, and the pound sagged disastrously on the foreign exchanges. On 22 November, therefore, on returning from a meeting of Western finance ministers at Bonn, the Chancellor announced yet another series of emergency measures to the Commons. The taxes on petrol and alcohol were once again increased, as was purchase tax. An import deposit scheme was introduced in an attempt to curb imports. Still, on 25 November, an Opposition motion of 'no confidence' was defeated by 328 to 251. The Labour back-benchers had duly rallied to the defence of the Government, if only because the alternative was too awful to contemplate.

The gravity of the financial crisis was seen on 3 December, when the gold and dollar reserves for November showed a fall of £82 million. Three days later, on 6 December, extraordinary rumours spread through the City that Harold Wilson was to resign and a coalition was to be formed. They proved a mixture of wishful thinking and sheer malicious invention.

After this last financial crisis of November 1968, it did at last seem that the worst was over. The panic outflow of funds from London had calmed itself and, gradually, some sort of stability returned. When on 27 February bank rate was raised again to 8 per cent, there were signs of a gathering demand for sterling. Jenkins sensibly refused to be deceived by this short-term monetary inflow, so that his budget of 15 April 1969 was calculatedly low-key. It was carefully designed not only to buy time to allow the benefits of devaluation to work but also to wait for the outcome of the forthcoming German elections in September 1969 – with whatever outcome these might have vis-à-vis the revaluation of the mark. The budget, although increasing taxation by £340 million, largely through an increase in Selective Employment Tax, was favourably received by the public – thankful, no doubt, that the rise in taxation was relatively small.

INDUSTRIAL RELATIONS

However, just as the economic crisis that had dominated the Labour government seemed at last to be behind them, they embarked on the stormiest piece of legislation of the 1966–70 period. The issue centred around their resolve to tackle the issue of strikes, which, they believed, had done so much damage to the economy.

Both Harold Wilson and Barbara Castle, the Employment Secretary, were convinced that trade union reform must be undertaken. Worries about strikes organized by unrepresentative, militant, left-wing shop stewards, as well as the massive lay-offs caused by strikes in such industries as the Midlands motor trade, had persuaded them that reform was long overdue. They were also well aware that public opinion was on their side.

Labour had begun by setting up a Royal Commission under Lord Donovan. Its report, published in 1968, disappointed those who had hoped for quick, clean solutions. The Commission refused to accept the view that legal curbs on unofficial strikes would achieve what was wanted, and concentrated on detailed procedures for improving industrial relations. Its most important single recommendation was the setting up of an Industrial Relations Commission to examine situations in which the system appeared to have broken down. Harold Wilson and Barbara Castle thought Donovan's remedies inadequate. During November Mrs Castle became convinced that penal sanctions should be part of the White Paper that would precede legislation. It was here that the Government made a major tactical blunder on an issue which raised the most fundamental emotions in the Labour movement.

The draft White Paper, *In Place of Strife*, was to go to Cabinet early in January. Because it was known that Callaghan would be opposed to the measure, the Cabinet Committee on industrial relations, to which he belonged, was by-passed, and the document was shown to the TUC on 30 December, before the Cabinet had seen it. The Cabinet meeting on 3 January was not altogether happy, and Wilson arranged further meetings with his colleagues. The Cabinet, however, was in an impossible position. The White Paper went beyond Donovan, chiefly in recommending that a twenty-eight day conciliation period should be ordered in certain cases and a ballot of members imposed when a strike was threatened. There would be legal sanctions to ensure that unions could in the last resort be forced to comply with the law's provisions.

Such proposals were bound to divide the Cabinet deeply. The strongest opponents of the White Paper were Callaghan (who, as Party Treasurer, knew only too well the party's dependence on the unions) and Marsh, but they had vociferous support from both Crossman and Crosland. To some extent all four ministers were worried on party grounds – both about the effect on party unity in the run-up to an election and about the flow of trade union money into Transport House. On the Labour back-benches, such proposals from Barbara Castle were greeted with incredulity; the left simply could not believe in rumours of compulsory ballots and cooling-off periods. With the publication of the White Paper, therefore, there was an outcry from the unions and the Labour back-benchers and when, on 3 March, the White Paper was debated in the House, there was a major back-bench revolt.

On the Conservative side, Robert Carr welcomed the White Paper as a step in the right direction, although he maintained that many of the proposals were inadequate or indeed wrong. On the Labour side opposition mounted. On 26 March the NEC voted to inform Barbara Castle that they could not agree to support legislation on the suggestions in the White Paper. Callaghan himself voted for the final NEC motion, which had been carried by a majority of more than three to one. He did not resign from the Cabinet, although Wilson let it be known that he had reprimanded him during a Cabinet meeting. On 10 April Wilson himself saw the TUC to hear their objections. The meeting changed nothing. Meanwhile, the opponents of the Bill had begun to organize against it. Eric Moonman had called a meeting of the 113 Labour MPs who had either abstained or voted against the White Paper, and seventy of them attended and elected a committee which sounded out back-bench opinion. By the middle of May they possessed the names of sixty-one Labour MPs who would oppose the projected legislation.

On 12 May the General Council of the TUC published their own *Programme for Action*, which was to be put before a special TUC Congress at Croydon on 5 June. It was attacked by Barbara Castle as a 'pious hope' and Wilson himself stated that the TUC proposals did not go far enough on unofficial strikes. Further talks between Wilson and TUC leaders such as Vic Feather, Jack Jones and Hugh Scanlon made no progress. The Croydon conference gave overwhelming approval to the

TUC's own proposals as well as confirming the movement's determined opposition to compulsory legislation and statutory financial penalties.

Despite further meetings between Wilson, Castle and the TUC General Council, progress was slow. The Government had now come to the point where decisions had to be taken. On 12 June Wilson formally confirmed that they were prepared to drop those parts of the legislation which the TUC found controversial if only the latter would agree to a fundamental change in union rules. Then, on the evening of 16 June, Wilson received a letter from the party's liaison committee which warned that there was no chance of the Government carrying in the Commons a strike-curb Bill containing any penal clauses. At the Cabinet meeting on 17 June, therefore, the Prime Minister's proposals reached the end of the road. A succession of ministers followed the Chief Whip in warning that the Bill would not get through.

Faced with this news, Wilson and Castle had no option but to capitulate. On 18 June 1969 a face-saving formula was announced in which the TUC General Council gave a 'solemn and binding undertaking' that member unions would observe the TUC's own guidelines on regulating unofficial strikes. Since the General Council had no powers to compel anyone, the undertaking, though no doubt solemn, could hardly be described as binding. Labour's attempts to reform the unions had failed, but the Government survived intact.

LABOUR'S DOMESTIC REFORMS

The Government's rough ride on the economic and industrial front was also to some extent repeated with other parts of their domestic legislative programme. One such major problem arose over reform of the House of Lords. This provoked the opposition both of Conservative back-benchers who were determined to preserve the full powers of the Second Chamber and of left-wing Labour back-benchers who wanted to abolish the Lords altogether. Hence such unlikely bedfellows as Michael Foot and Enoch Powell joined a coalition opposed to the Bill. In the Commons Labour back-benchers employed highly effective filibustering tactics (a speech of over *two* hours by Robert Sheldon on 18 February was calculated to have been the longest speech made by a back-bencher for fifteen years). Faced with their parliamentary timetable in ruins, the Government decided to abandon the Bill.

The Government also found themselves in a difficult position over the highly charged question of immigration. The issue arose following reports from Kenya that there would be a mass exodus of Asians who had lost their livelihood through the Kenya government's Africanization policy. This resulted in increasing pressure, led from the Conservative side by Duncan Sandys and Enoch Powell, for restrictions on their entry. On 21 February 1968 the Conservative leader, Edward Heath, warned of 'serious social consequences' if they were to come to Britain 'at a rate which could not be satisfactorily absorbed'. Next day a Bill was promised. The Home Secretary, James Callaghan, told the House of Commons that 7,000 East African Asians had come in during the past three months – more than in the whole of 1966. The Government were 'extremely reluctant' to interfere with the entry of UK passport holders, but to let them in would put a severe strain on services in areas to which they went. The Bill, published on 23 February, was rushed through both Houses and enacted on 1 March. It placed controls on the entry of UK passport holders who had 'no substantial connection' with Britain, and set aside 1,500 vouchers a year, in addition to those already available for issue, for their use. The Bill was supported by the Conservative leadership, but at second reading (27 February) thirty-five Labour MPs, fifteen Conservatives and two Nationalists joined the Liberals in voting against it.

Labour argued that their strategy was to accompany tighter control of immigration by legislation to improve the lot of those already here. In pursuit of this policy, on 9 April the text of the Race Relations Bill was published. On 23 April it received a second reading in the Commons by 313 votes to 209. Three days earlier, at Birmingham, Enoch Powell, the Shadow Defence Minister, had made a lurid speech on race relations. The language was emotional, Powell declaring: 'As I look ahead I am filled with foreboding. Like the Roman, I seem to see the River Tiber foaming with much blood.' The effect of this inflammatory address was immediate, and Powell was dismissed from the Shadow Cabinet. Over 100,000 letters of support were received by him, a clear demonstration of the potential support he possessed at the grass-roots.

It was against this background that the Race Relations Bill was debated. The 1968 Act extended that of 1965 by banning discrimination in housing, employment, insurance and other services. Discriminatory advertisements were barred. As in the 1965 Act, the courts would be used only when all conciliation procedures failed. The Race Relations Board was given its own powers of investigation. A Community Relations Commission with Frank Cousins as Chairman was introduced to replace the National Committee for Commonwealth Immigrants.

A final piece of legislation in this field was enacted in 1969 with the Immigration Appeals Bill. Following the recommendations of a report by an official committee under Sir Roy Wilson, the Act set up an Immigration Appeal Tribunal with a full-time staff of adjudicators to hear appeals against decisions taken in the administration of immigration control under the Commonwealth Immigrants and Aliens Restrictions Acts. The Bill was given a second reading in the Commons on 22 January by 170 to twenty-four. The twenty-four were all Conservatives: most Conservatives abstained, and five Liberals voted with the Government. In the committee stage, the Government introduced an amendment requiring dependants to have entry certificates issued by British High Commissioners in their own countries. Appeals against refusal here would have to be dealt with by post to England, a procedure felt by Liberal critics to undermine the merits of the Act.

FOREIGN AFFAIRS

With the continuous economic crisis and with the drama of the confrontation over trade union reform, the equally far-reaching changes in Britain's position in the world which occurred during these years are all too easily minimized. Ironically, the most important single factor in seeing the end of Britain's 'world role' was not Labour's ideology but the harsh facts of economic life. Wilson's government were in office for three years before the overwhelming pressure of events forced them to revise their basic philosophy on defence and foreign affairs. It was the German mark more than any socialist belief that brought the end of Britain's 'East of Suez' role, that caused the abandonment of expensive defence weaponry and finally caused Wilson to turn to the Common Market.

A thorough re-examination of Britain's overseas defence commitments was anyway long overdue. One of the most blatant causes of the balance-of-payments crisis had been the rapid increase in government spending abroad, which had risen from just over £50 million in 1952 to more than £400 million in 1964. Defence items accounted for roughly two thirds of the bill. And yet Britain's economic power in relation to her chief trading competitors had been steadily waning until by the late sixties her Gross National Product was estimated at $109 billion – well behind West Germany ($150 billion), France ($140 billion) and Japan ($167 billion). However, Japan devoted less than 1 per cent of her GNP to expenditure on defence, while West Germany spent only 4·3 per cent. The figure for Britain was no less than 5·7 per cent, even though the size of Britain's armed forces had been slashed from a level of almost 700,000 in 1957, when Duncan Sandys announced the end of National Service, to less than 400,000 ten years later. But Britain's obligations to render military aid to her partners and allies overseas had not been cut back accordingly. British garrisons were still to be found in Malta, the Persian Gulf, the Far East and in such colonial territories as Belize. Britain was still attempting to be a world power, without world resources.

The case for cutting the defence budget had been prosecuted with enthusiasm on the left and with reluctance on the right. Yet the Labour government of 1964–70 moved much more slowly than their supporters wished to cut the cost of defence; indeed, it was only the continued economic crisis, and the need to cut overseas expenditure of every kind, rather than sober reappraisal of defence imperatives, which finally persuaded them to make the really significant cuts – principally on expenditure East of Suez – for which their supporters at Westminster and in the country had been clamouring. And the experience of government caused Wilson and his colleagues to think again about the condemnation in the party's 1964 manifesto of the Nassau agreement, under which their Conservative predecessors had agreed to buy Polaris missiles from the US.

The disarmers, however, enjoyed a regular diet of defence cancellations from the aircraft project cancellations of February 1965 (the P-1154 and VTOL), through the scrapping of the TSR 2 low-level bomber (April 1965) to the end of East of Suez and the rundown, announced in July 1968, of infantry battalions. At the same time, Denis Healey, who remained Defence Secretary throughout the Government's term of office, attempted to save money by rationalization, on the pattern set by the US Defence Secretary Robert McNamara at the Pentagon. Tighter controls were put on procurement, and an amalgamation of the service departments led to a saving on staff.

The most dramatic reversal in foreign affairs during this period concerned the Common Market. Historically Labour had never shown any marked fervour for the cause of joining the EEC. During the early 1960s most Labour leaders had shown consistent antipathy towards the European Community and little real appreciation of the benefits that might accrue for Britain. As has been seen, Labour's attitude during Heath's 1961–3 negotiations had been reflected in Gaitskell's hostile speech at the 1962 Labour Party conference. During the 1966 election, in a major speech at Bristol, Wilson differed little in tone from Gaitskell's earlier declaration. He reiterated the two main Gaitskellite conditions, namely full British independence in respect of foreign and defence policies, and freedom for Britain to continue to buy her food without hindrance in world markets. On the other hand, he confirmed that his own position remained as it always had been: a commitment to entry if the terms were right.

As time went on his conditions for entry became less exacting. Office had shown him the degree to which Britain's power and influence in the world had diminished. This view was reinforced by the fact that the Commonwealth was clearly not the instrument it had been in the early 1960s, while the problems of defending sterling as well as those arising from the French withdrawal from NATO all inclined Wilson towards Europe. Even so, he moved over only slowly towards full conversion. In May 1965, at an EFTA Conference in Vienna, the possibility of forming closer links between EFTA and the EEC had been discussed. When even this was seen to be unrealistic, Wilson toyed merely with *association* with the EEC under Article 238 of the Treaty of Rome. Yet gradually he saw that there was no alternative to EEC entry, although he knew he would face a tough battle with his cabinet and the party. Within the Cabinet the strongest supporters of entry were George Brown (although Crossman's diaries suggest Brown had some private doubts) and Roy Jenkins. Crosland also was enthusiastic, while Michael Stewart, the Foreign Secretary, was now in favour, too. In addition, Wilson may have been influenced by wider evidence of support – the recently formed Confederation of British Industry was enthusiastic for Europe and an opinion poll in July 1966 showed 75 per cent in favour of entry. Finally, in Europe itself, Italy and the Benelux countries were keen on British entry and would put their influence behind Britain.

A highly important Cabinet meeting on 22 October 1966 marked a landmark in the Government's path. The Cabinet had before it the report of the Committee, chaired by George Brown, on the social and economic implications of joining. This report greatly strengthened the case for entry and Wilson appears to have been strongly influenced by it. Although the Cabinet remained divided, it agreed that Wilson and Brown should tour the capitals of the EEC countries early in 1967. Hence Wilson was able to announce in the House of Commons on 10 November 1966 that the question of British entry into the European Community would be explored anew. Following an EFTA conference which took place on 5 December 1966, the tour of Continental capitals was duly undertaken during the early months of 1967. These soundings convinced Wilson to apply, even though there had been warnings from the Paris Embassy of the possibility of another veto by de Gaulle.

In due course, after the historic Cabinet meeting on 2 May 1967, Wilson announced the Labour government's intention to apply for full membership of the European Community. There were no resignations from the Cabinet when the decision was made, although seven of the twenty-one ministers were hostile, ten were in favour and the remainder, according to Crossman, were only 'possible' supporters. Although, earlier, some 107 Labour MPs had tabled a motion on 21 February recalling their party's stiff conditions for entry, Wilson's powerful support of the pro-Market case at a series of party meetings won a clear majority of the PLP into a pro-EEC position. In October both the NEC and Conference gave Wilson substantial backing. The Conservative Opposition, not surprisingly, welcomed these latest moves. Wilson's success could partly be explained by the fact that the natural leaders of the anti-EEC movement were in the Cabinet. The anti-Marketeers had to rely on such veterans as Shinwell to lead their cause. None the less, despite Wilson's powers of persuasion, there was a strong contingent of Labour MPs still hostile. Some seventy-four Labour MPs signed the Tribune anti-Market manifesto and on 10 May when the House of Commons supported the Government with an overwhelming majority – 488 votes to sixty-two – thirty-five Labour MPs voted against entry and some fifty abstained.

Yet Wilson's EEC initiative on Europe came to a sudden end. On 16 May de Gaulle vetoed the British application, announcing that Britain was not yet ready to join the Six. Like Macmillan, Wilson was baulked in his objective by French opposition and was unable to determine whether or not satisfactory conditions for entry could have been obtained. The

Labour government did not withdraw the British application, but left it on the table.

The atmosphere changed considerably following the resignation of General de Gaulle in April 1969. At the Hague summit conference of the Six in December 1969 the decision was taken to complete, strengthen and enlarge the Community. This opened the way for new negotiations with Britain, which the Labour government said they wanted to start as soon as possible.

In general, between 1966 and 1970, there was little open conflict between the main parties over the major issues of foreign policy. Divisions over Britain's part in the American alliance and NATO, or over British entry into Europe, existed within parties rather than between them. Both Conservative and Labour parties gave general support to the American presence in Vietnam, though there had been isolated critics (including Enoch Powell) on the Tory benches, and a strong and sustained opposition within the Labour Party. The Liberals alone came out firmly against the Vietnam war. British support for the Federal Government of Nigeria during the Biafra war split the Conservative and Labour parties. The Government's insistence that the flow of arms to Nigeria should continue had the general approval of the Conservative leadership, but was bitterly opposed by members on both sides of the House. A two-day foreign affairs debate in December 1969 exposed party differences on both these issues. In each case, attempts to adjourn the House were defeated. The great majority of the Conservative Party, including the entire Shadow Cabinet, abstained in both the divisions.

The issues which most sharply divided the Conservatives on one side from Labour and Liberals on the other arose in Southern Africa. In December 1967 the Cabinet decided (though only after an embarrassingly well-publicized split and various threats and counter-threats on both sides) not to supply arms which the government of South Africa wanted to buy. The decision, said Conservative leader Edward Heath, was 'damaging to our national interest in finance, in trade and in defence', and a Conservative government would reverse it.

It was over Rhodesia, however, that not only was party conflict most pronounced but also the Government found themselves in most difficulties. After 1966 Wilson made two major attempts to end the Rhodesian rebellion. The first occasion was in December 1966, in talks aboard HMS *Tiger*. These talks failed, and in 1968 a new initiative was attempted

In October 1968, in talks aboard HMS *Fearless* off Gibraltar, a new list of six principles was produced. This abandoned the original insistence that there should be no independence before majority rule, and laid down the following programme: unimpeded progress towards majority rule; guarantees against retrospective amendment of the constitution; immediate improvements in the status of Africans; progress towards ending racial discrimination; any basis of settlement to be shown to be acceptable to the people of Rhodesia as a whole; and no oppression of the majority by the minority, or of the minority by the majority. The talks seemed to have been partly successful. Further discussions followed, and a British cabinet minister visited Salisbury. But as the Smith régime embarked on a new constitution, the chances of a settlement grew steadily more remote.

As it was, on the left-wing Labour back-benches and amongst the Liberals the proposals had already met with strong opposition. The Liberal leader, Jeremy Thorpe, said they represented a further retreat from the stand taken in the earlier talks on HMS *Tiger*, which itself had been unsatisfactory. Then in a debate on the *Fearless* proposals on 22 October 1968, forty-nine Labour MPs voted against the Government. The Conservatives abstained, taking the view that there should be no judgement of the proposals until they reached their final form.

LABOUR AND THE ELECTORS

It was to be expected that the almost continuous economic crisis, with the swingeing increases in taxation which successive budgets introduced, would produce by-election reverses for Labour. The Conservatives had experienced this in 1957–8 and, far more pronouncedly, in 1962–3. Between 1964 and 1970, however, Labour's losses were so enormous as to be quite unparalleled in recent British history.

The Labour government of 1945–51 lost only one seat in a by-election. In the whole of their thirteen years in power, the Conservatives lost only ten – eight to Labour and two to the Liberals. Labour's current record, in comparison, was abysmal. From 1966 to 1970 Labour lost sixteen of the thirty-one seats they were defending – more than in the *whole* of the party's history from 1900 to 1964. Swings were so enormous that a Conservative swing of 10 per cent was greeted almost with relief. In England, the collapse of the Liberal vote after 1966, together with mass

Labour desertions, gave Conservatives victory in such unlikely 'safe' Labour territory as Walthamstow and Dudley.

Even more significant, however, were the dramatic changes in political support taking place in Wales and Scotland with the new phenomenon of Nationalism. The first victory was achieved by Plaid Cymru. A by-election in the Labour-held rural seat of Carmarthen occurred in July 1966. The result set Welsh Nationalism alight. The Plaid's candidate was Gwynfor Evans, president of the party since 1945 and easily its most commanding figure. In the 1966 general election he had achieved the party's second-best result in Wales – but he was still in third place, over 14,000 votes behind Lady Megan Lloyd George, who had held the seat for Labour. In the by-election, aided by such local factors as the closure of the Carmarthen–Aberystwyth railway line, Evans swept to a dramatic victory. For the first time in history, the Plaid had returned a representative to Westminster.

From its foundation in August 1925 until the Carmarthen by-election Plaid Cymru had never won a parliamentary election. Its record at general elections between 1945 and 1966 had been uninspiring. In 1964, when its twenty-three candidates had polled 69,507 votes, the party had saved its deposit in only two constituencies. These results emphasized the fact that its strength rested very much in rural, Welsh-speaking North Wales, with a small protest vote in some of the South Wales valleys. Very much the same pattern was to be seen in the 1966 election. With twenty candidates, its total poll had slipped to 61,071 votes.

There was little in either the 1964 or 1966 results to suggest that the Plaid was poised for a breakthrough; nor, indeed, had it previously ever polled particularly well in a by-election (between 1950 and 1966, it had saved its deposit only once). Yet after the euphoria of Carmarthen, a second by-election on 9 March 1967 provided the Plaid with a test of its revival. This time the constituency was Rhondda West, a normally rock-solid Labour seat; the Nationalists missed victory by only 2,306 votes. It was a sensational result. The increase in the Nationalist vote was far greater even than in Carmarthen; and whereas Carmarthen had been dismissed as rural, isolated and untypical, Rhondda was a bedrock of the Labour movement.

Alongside this dramatic revival in Welsh Nationalist sentiment came another blow for Labour – an equally clear revival of Nationalism in Scotland. The vehicle was the Scottish National Party. Originally formed in April 1928 as the National Party of Scotland, the party was renamed the Scottish National Party on being joined by the Scottish Party in April 1934. Its early electoral history hardly augured well. Although a Celtic cultural nationalism had long been in existence, the political wing of Nationalism was relatively insignificant. Nor did the situation change quickly. In each General Election from 1950 to 1959, the SNP polled less than 1 per cent of the votes cast in Scotland. From 1945 to 1959 it contested only five by-elections, on no occasion managing to save its deposit.

After 1959, however, the Scottish political climate began to change and in the 1964 general election, encouraged by support received in such by-elections as West Lothian, the Nationalists fought on a wider front than hitherto – fielding fifteen candidates. Although the party averaged only 10·9 per cent of the vote in the seats contested, in certain areas it made definite progress. Two years later, the general election of 31 March 1966 produced the first signs of a distinct Nationalist upsurge. The SNP fought twenty-three of the seventy-one Scottish seats, polling an average of 14·5 per cent in the seats contested. Compared to 1964, it had increased its vote from 64,044 (2·4 per cent) to 128,474 (5·0 per cent). The most noticeable feature of their progress was the increased support received in the industrial Labour-held seats of central Scotland. At the same time Scottish Conservatism was registering a marked decline in its electoral appeal.

The results of the 1966 election gave the SNP a new impetus and sense of purpose. On 9 March 1967, the same day as Rhondda West, polling took place in the Pollok division of Glasgow. The omens did not appear favourable for the Nationalists. They had not fought the seat before, and the constituency was a highly marginal one. The result, however, was a sensation. Although the Conservatives took the seat from Labour, the SNP came within 3,500 votes of victory, with over 28 per cent of the vote. It was a tonic whose effect was felt throughout Scotland.

Hamilton was a still greater sensation. In the second safest government seat in Scotland (the Labour party had obtained 71·2 per cent of the votes cast in 1966), Mrs Winifred Ewing was able to wrest the seat from Labour. The result was SNP 18,397 (46·0 per cent), Labour 16,598 (41·5 per cent), Conservatives 4,986 (12·5 per cent). Even though the result was very similar to the heavy anti-Labour swings in the by-elections in England, in Scotland the result was historic. Membership of the SNP rocketed upwards until by 1968 the party claimed 125,000 members. Pollok and Hamilton together had changed the political spectrum north of the border. There were parallels between government unpopularity in 1962 and the results of 1968, but the scale and dimensions heralded a new depth of disillusion with government not witnessed for many years.

The end of the Government's confrontation with the TUC in summer 1969 coincided with brighter news on the economic front. After June 1969, when Jenkins declared that he expected a balance-of-payments surplus for the year, the political tide began to turn. By September it was clear that sterling was once more back in the black. The long-awaited recovery was at last reflected in the trade figures. On 11 September the Treasury announced that Britain's balance of payments had moved into surplus during the first half of 1969, and that the overall surplus had been £100 million in the second quarter. Four days later the Board of Trade announced that exports for August had reached their highest ever level at £630 million and that there was a visible trade surplus for the month, the first since July 1967, of £48 million.

Thus the balance of payments was transformed in 1969, improving strongly throughout the year. One reason for the improvement, it must be said, was a statistical correction: it had been discovered that exports had been systematically under-recorded for some years and that this had reached a level of over £100 million by 1969. Another contributory factor may have been the import deposit scheme, introduced by the Government in November 1968, by which importers were required to deposit with HM Customs for a period of six months money equal to half the value of certain imports. The improvements in the balance of payments enabled the Government at the start of 1970 to abolish the restrictions on expenditure by British residents on travel outside the sterling area. The Government also benefited from Callaghan's firm but understanding handling of the situation in Ulster, where fighting had broken out in Londonderry in August (see pages 270–76). Meanwhile, the economic recovery was reflected in Labour's standing in the opinion polls. The Conservative lead, which had averaged over 19 per cent in July, was down to 12½ per cent in September. Against this background, even the Labour Party conference was in a brighter mood.

The conference discussed the new policy document prepared by the National Executive Committee, entitled *Agenda for a Generation*, proposing greater state ownership, a national investment board and new tax proposals including a wealth tax. In two sparkling speeches, Wilson brought the conference alive, and the trauma and the troubles of the last few years were set aside. Meanwhile, on the opening day, Barbara Castle announced that the Government would introduce legislation to provide for equal pay for women. By the end of 1975 it would be illegal to discriminate against women in rates of pay. Such was the turnabout in Labour's morale that when the Conservatives assembled at Brighton on 8 October they were confronted with an ORC poll showing the Conservatives' lead down to 4 per cent, and for the first time in two years there were serious doubts that Heath would bring the party back to power at the next election.

The news on the economic front continued to improve. The advent of Social Democrats to power in West Germany and the subsequent revaluation of the mark aided the pound. On 13 October, a £26 million trade surplus for September was announced. With continuing economic buoyancy, and with the decks cleared of controversial legislation, Labour ended 1969, despite the by-election loss of Wellingborough, in a mood of restrained optimism. In the closing days of December, sterling broke through its parity of $2·40.

Confirmation that Labour was improving its electoral position came in March 1970 with the Bridgwater by-election. The swing to the Conservatives, of 8·6 per cent, was less than in the 1969 by-elections. Much more heartening news for Labour came in the South Ayrshire by-election. In this Keir Hardie Socialist heartland, the Nationalist came third, and there was no swing from Labour to Conservative. The result provided a tonic for Labour morale, and speculation on a possible early election began to intensify. The first major test of the political climate after the economic improvement and the recovery in Labour morale came with the Greater London Council elections of Thursday 9 April. Labour fared moderately well, taking sixteen seats from the Conservatives and recapturing the Inner London Education Authority. However, it was clear that most of this recovery was in Labour's traditional working-class areas, not in the crucial suburban marginal districts.

On the economic front the position was still healthy. In January there had been a £39 million trade surplus. The pound reached its highest level for two years, while the balance of payments for 1969 showed a surplus of £387 million. An indication of these happy tidings had been the relaxation in bank rate to $7\frac{1}{2}$ per cent. Even so, it was vital that Jenkins's April 1970 budget strike the right note. In the event, he proved himself a subtle politician, avoiding charges of electioneering but none the less making a series of welcome concessions. The surtax threshold was raised by £500, the income tax personal allowance was increased, the earnings limit for pensioners was raised, and bank rate was cut from $7\frac{1}{2}$ to 7 per cent. The Chancellor claimed that his budget had benefited $18\frac{1}{2}$ million people, and relieved 2 million from paying any income tax at all. It was generally accepted as a fair budget; the public clearly liked the Chancellor's restraint; and by the May municipal elections Labour was again in the lead in the opinion polls.

The borough elections early in May confirmed that the electoral tide was flowing strongly towards Labour. In the Scottish burghs, morale soared as traditional Labour citadels were regained by the party, while the Nationalist vote slumped further. In the polling for the English and Welsh boroughs, Labour scored a net gain of over 400 seats on a swing of 11 per cent since the previous year.

The opinion polls, together with the borough results, transformed the political climate. Although it was doubtful if Labour could win an immediate election, the party rank and file now scented what had seemed impossible only a few months earlier – that Labour could be returned to power. Labour supporters, and the political pundits, were divided over the election date. Those favouring June or early July argued that, with public opinion so volatile, and with dangers of price rises and a deteriorating international situation, an early election was the wisest course. The October supporters believed that, in the vital marginal seats, Labour could not be certain of victory in an early election. Speculation was finally ended when on Monday 18 May polling day was fixed for exactly a month later.

THE 1970 ELECTION

The calling of the election found the opposition parties, the Conservatives and Liberals, in different degrees of preparedness.

In the wake of the 1966 election defeat the composition of the Conservative Party had changed with the departure of such right-wing figures as Julian Amery and the arrival of more progressive younger men. Although Heath had lost the 1966 election, there were no pressures on him to resign. Rather, he had set his target on victory in the next election. The massive swings to the Conservatives in municipal elections and in by-elections all helped to give a sense of impending victory – even though by early 1970 Labour was recovering fast in the opinion polls.

In January 1970 the Conservatives had set about detailed preparations for the general election. After fifteen hours' discussion at the Selsdon Park Hotel in Croydon, the Shadow Cabinet mapped out its main policy proposals. Among the items were the abolition of SET, a reduction in direct taxation and an increase in the size of the police force, together with an Industrial Relations Bill based on the Party's *Fair Deal at Work*. This conference clearly marked a shift to the right. It marked the beginning of the call to 'roll back the frontiers of government' and an end of liberal economics. It had been foreshadowed when Heath ridiculed Wilson's prices and incomes policy as threatening 'a totalitarian society'. Meanwhile Heath's replacement of the liberal Edward Boyle by Margaret Thatcher at the Shadow Education portfolio confirmed this shift to the right.

The coming of the election found a very different mood in the Liberal ranks. Jeremy Thorpe, who had succeeded Jo Grimond as Liberal leader, had inherited a difficult political legacy. Despite the growing unpopularity of the Wilson government the Liberals made almost no electoral impact and the early years of Thorpe's leadership thus proved an unhappy time for the party. Morale in the constituencies was low and there was a sharp decline in the number of really active associations. The performance of the party in by-elections was equally unencouraging. In twelve of the twenty-eight seats contested the party lost its deposit. Faced with a swing to the right at by-elections, and with Parliament preoccupied with the economic crisis, Liberals found it increasingly difficult to identify themselves on many issues or to present a clear image to the electorate – a problem compounded by the party's perennial financial problems. Ironically, the issues on which the party was most active (such as its vigorous opposition to the Immigration Bill) were hardly issues likely to win much popular appeal. A major development in the Liberal ranks during this time was the advocacy of community politics. This technique of intense local involvement was soon perfected by Liberals, and after 1966 they succeeded in building up local election successes in Liverpool, parts of Leeds and most of all Birmingham, where Wallace Lawler had proved himself a highly successful exponent of these tactics.

The calling of a by-election in the Ladywood division of Birmingham, almost at the heart of the Lawler empire, provided a critical test for the new 'community politics'. Ladywood hardly seemed likely Liberal territory. It was a Labour stronghold, with much slum housing; it was also the most depopulated constituency in Britain, in a city that had not sent a Liberal to Westminster since 1886. Yet the outcome was a triumph for Wallace Lawler. On 26 June 1969 he gained the seat from Labour with a comfortable majority. The publicity of this by-election victory, however, had faded a year later. In the run-up to the election, the omens were not very favourable. The last by-elections had been particularly discouraging; the 1970 municipal elections had produced the worsts results for a decade; nor was the party particularly well prepared, with only 282 prospective candidates when the dissolution was announced.

If the Liberals were hardly optimistic, the Conservatives fought the 1970 election (despite trailing in the opinion polls and despite doubts on Heath's popularity) by doggedly attacking the Government's record. Labour, in contrast, ran a campaign very much dominated by the personality of Harold Wilson, who ran perhaps the most 'presidential-style' campaign the country had yet witnessed.

1970 ELECTION ANALYSIS

Although the opinion polls remained almost united in forecasting a Labour victory, from the announcement of the very first results there was a significant swing to the Conservatives. As the *Annual Register* commented, 'one of the most dramatic and unexpected electoral turn-rounds of the century' had taken place. The final results are listed on page 246.

The Conservatives gained seventy-four seats, losing only six; Labour gained ten seats (recovering some of the seats lost in the previous by-election holocaust) for the loss of seventy. The Liberals suffered heavily, losing seven seats. Among Labour's highly unexpected personal defeats were the ousting in Belper of George Brown, the former Foreign Secretary and Deputy Leader of the Party, and Jennie Lee, Nye Bevan's widow and Minister for the Arts.

Party	Votes gained	Percentage of vote	Average vote per MP	Number of MPs
Conservative	13,145,123	46·4	39,834	330
Labour	12,179,341	43·0	42,437	287
Liberal	2,117,035	7·5	352,839	6
Plaid Cymru	175,016	0·6	—	—
SNP	306,802	1·1	306,802	1
Others	421,481	1·5		6
	28,344,798	100·1		630

Source: Derived from D. Butler and A. Sloman, *British Political Facts 1900–75.*

The results had shown a national swing of 4·7 per cent to the Conservatives. England had shown the largest swing (5·1 per cent), with Wales at 4·4 per cent and Scotland at 2·8 per cent. A significant feature of the election was the apparent failure of the Nationalists after their spectacular showing in previous by-elections. In Wales none of the thirty Plaid Cymru candidates were elected. In Scotland, Winifred Ewing went down to defeat at Hamilton, although the SNP did win its first-ever seat in a general election – the remote Western Isles constituency that had been held by Labour for thirty-five years.

The general election result came as a deep shock to Labour. And yet, because only a year previously Labour's electoral fortunes had been at rock bottom, the party could comfort itself on having come within thirty seats of victory. Wilson, certainly, rapidly recovered his natural self-confidence and there was none of the bitter recrimination inside the party that had marked the period after Attlee's defeat in 1951, although many Labour supporters believed Wilson's highly personalized campaign had been too relaxed and assured. There is still no entirely accepted reason for what appears to have been a last-minute change of voters' intentions, but the most common argument is that the publication of unfavourable trade figures three days before polling enabled the Conservatives to stir up anxiety over the cost of living and the economy. Perhaps it was almost fitting, after so much political drama during the previous four years, that the Wilson government should themselves have gone in a dramatic fashion.

THE 1964–70 WILSON GOVERNMENT: AN ASSESSMENT

In the immediate term, the Labour government of 1964–70 have not had a good press. Rejected by the electorate at the polls, bitterly attacked by their own back-benchers and party activists, the image of the Government seemed far removed from the happier days of 1964. This impression was heightened by the publication of the Crossman diaries, with their account of Cabinet intrigue, and the hostile memoirs of such people as Joe Haines, Wilson's press adviser.

A fair judgement on the Labour government, however, would be far from uniformly critical. Their cardinal and fundamental weakness lay in their management of the economy – or, more particularly, in Wilson's determination to uphold sterling and the value of the pound. In this sense, the failure of the Labour government lay in their conservatism rather than their radicalism. The strategic error in not devaluing sterling (until at the eleventh hour forced to do so by overwhelming circumstances) was compounded by a series of tactical mistakes – Wilson's own emphasis in the 1964 campaign on the balance-of-payments crisis, Callaghan's autumn mini-budget of 1964, the divisions between the Treasury and George Brown at the Department of Economic Affairs, and the impression Wilson gave that he was simply manoeuvring in order to win a larger majority. After 1966, when the economic dangers were obscured in the euphoria of electoral success, the results of Labour's own economic inadequacy were exacerbated by international financial movements. Thus devaluation – for all Wilson's talk of the 'pound in your pocket' – was a defeat. It was a symbol of the disillusion of the sixties in which the mistakes of the fifties had simply been repeated. A courageous early devaluation might have transformed the achievements of the Labour government. Instead, even the management of devaluation was not skilfully handled.

In terms of economic policy, therefore, the judgement on the Labour government must be one of overall failure. Yet in certain sections of industry and the economy Labour could list a string of useful accomplishments. The 1965 Redundancy Payments Act was a long-overdue measure, providing graduated redundancy payment according to the length of service of the worker concerned. A transformation of conditions in the docks was brought about by the 1966 Docks and Harbours

Act, which provided more regular employment and better conditions. Such measures of reform in industry can be multiplied, and to a limited extent they offset the overall economic failure of the Government. But equally, it is hard to accept that the high hopes the Government had to modernize British industry – a key to the economic problem – really amounted to very much in practice.

On paper, Labour could display a welter of legislative activity – the creation of the Ministry of Technology in 1964, the Industrial Reorganization Corporation two years later and new legislation which included the Science and Technology Act (1965), the Shipbuilding Industry Act (1967) and the Industrial Expansion Act (1968). However, many of the major industrial trends (for example, mergers and takeovers) owed as much to financial entrepreneurs such as Slater and Walker as to the Industrial Reorganization Corporation. In some specialized industries, such as computers or machine tools, the Government played a useful role – but overall it hardly amounted to the 'planning' that Labour claimed for its own.

Nor could Labour be said to have produced the fundamental constitutional changes in the structure (as opposed to the *style*) of government that many wanted. Such changes in political institutions as did occur were made necessary by the great increase in the *scope* of government – a process already beginning under the Conservatives but which accelerated under Labour. One of Labour's more important innovations, however, was the Ombudsman, or Parliamentary Commissioner for Administration, who took office on 1 April 1967. His function was to investigate complaints passed to him by MPs concerning the action of government departments – though there were such major exceptions as local government, the nationalized industries, the National Health Service and the police. Likewise, the mounting disquiet in the Commons over the increasing power of government found expression in the establishment of 'watchdog' Parliamentary Committees – but this experiment was largely a failure, as were Labour's attempts to reform the House of Lords. Still, Labour was aware of the need for constitutional change – as manifested, for example, in attempts to reduce the number of Cabinet meetings, leading in the spring of 1968 to the formation of an 'inner Cabinet' or Parliamentary Committee of the Cabinet. Yet probably the two most significant constitutional changes enacted during this period were the lowering of the age of majority (hence voting rights) to eighteen and the setting up of the Fulton Committee on the future of the Civil Service – the first comprehensive review since the Northcote–Trevelyan reforms of 1854.

To the ordinary family, Labour's most long-lasting achievement was perhaps in education. Under Labour the trends towards comprehensive schools continued apace: during the 1960s the number of comprehensives in the country increased ten-fold. By 1970 one third of the total secondary-school population was being educated in comprehensives – many taking the new Certificate of Secondary Education (CSE) introduced in 1965 for less able pupils. Thus the youth of the country were being educated (though some questioned the use of the word) in an egalitarian way unthinkable a generation earlier. Labour also furthered the cause of egalitarian eduation by establishing the Open University, which used the resources of radio and television to give large numbers of people an opportunity to receive a university education – an opportunity which they might otherwise never have had.

One aspect of the 1960s that was curiously reminiscent of the 1930s was the intense concern over pockets of poverty within the context of a more affluent society. Labour had particularly pledged itself, both in 1964 and 1966, to major improvements in the social services. Yet its record of achievement up to 1970 came in for very harsh criticism. Professor Victor George declared that 'the performance of the Labour government was certainly worse with regard to social reform than that of the Attlee government in the 1940s'. The influential academic Peter Townshend went further, arguing that Labour's reforms were little more than 'hot compresses on an ailing body politic'.

This criticism of Labour was perhaps exaggerated, but at heart it was correct. Not only Townshend but other academics such as Richard Titmuss and Brian Abel-Smith emphasized how wrong had been the complacent view of the 1950s that poverty was steadily being eroded. Labour's failure to do more constituted therefore a serious blot on its declared concern for the old, the sick and the poor, although it should not perhaps detract entirely from the achievements noted earlier.

The key criticism of Labour, however, was that this list of ministerial achievements, even when expanded with many more minor legislative achievements to the credit of the Labour government, did not really amount to a successful overall government strategy. Too many of the really big strategic decisions – decisions of the Chancellor of the

Exchequer, the Secretary of State for Economic Affairs, the Foreign Secretary and the Prime Minister himself – were misguided, and the political consequences were reflected in a variety of ways. At the highest level, there had been Cabinet resignations – Cousins, Brown, Longford and others. At the lowest level of the party, there was the silent testimony of the empty committee room and the tireless activist now quit from politics. Its most dramatic reflection was in by-election reverses. Although – as in previous protests against government – many returned to their former allegiance, certainly in Scotland and to a lesser extent Wales politics was never quite the same again. The seeds of Nationalism had been planted.

The predominant mood of the country after six years of Labour government was one of disillusion. It was hardly surprising. Back in 1964 the Conservatives had been voted out of office because they were not thought capable of delivering the goods; but the alternative government installed precisely for that purpose had proved no more adept. Normally sensible people now found themselves distinctly tempted by the calls for a coalition or government by businessmen which became very fashionable, as the pound, despite all the Government's attempts to protect it, slowly declined in value.

The disillusion with Labour – and from there, with party politics in general – was bitterest of all on the left. To the left, everything they stood for seemed to be in ruins. They had seen mounting unemployment, curbs on trade unions, and wage restraint – not even stopping short of the threat of prison. There had been support for the growing American involvement in Vietnam; limits on immigration, culminating in the panic moves to slam the door on the Kenya Asians; the maintenance of an independent deterrent; prescription charges, charges for school milk, and dearer school meals; and cutbacks in the rate of building new homes. All these and a host of other similar practices, which if carried out by a Conservative government would have been denounced by every member of the Labour movement, were being carried out by a supposedly Socialist government.

Too much had been sacrificed for many Labour supporters to stomach. Hence the by-election holocaust and the lapsed membership of the party. A consequence of disillusion not just with the Labour government but also the Labour Party was the drift of militant young radicals into the Young Liberal movement. By 1966 these new radicals were demanding the withdrawal of all American troops from Vietnam; workers' control of nationalized industries; non-alignment in the Cold War; Britain's withdrawal from NATO; opposition to the wage freeze; unconditional support for the 1965 seamen's strike; majority rule for Rhodesia; massive reductions in armaments; and entry into a Europe that would include the Communist bloc states of the East. These policies, adopted at the 1966 Young Liberal conference at Colwyn Bay, seemed to older Liberals more representative of the Young Socialists (or indeed Maoists) than of the party of the middle-class suburbs.

The militancy of such groups as the Young Liberals was seen elsewhere. In the factories these years witnessed a period of 'sit-ins' by employees. In the universities there were major confrontations in such institutions as the London School of Economics and Essex University. The middle classes were also part of this ferment of protest and disillusion, as seen in the vociferous and ultimately successful battle against the siting of London's third airport at Stansted. The environmentalist lobby was coming into its own.

Although left-wing extremist groups were active, they were never very large. The most effective expression of doubts about the adequacy of existing institutions came from the established politicians and financial commentators – in such publications as Christopher Mayhew's *Party Games*, Samuel Brittan's *Left or Right* and Tony Benn's Fabian pamphlet *The New Politics: A Socialist Reconnaissance*. Some of these proposals for popular – or indeed populist – involvement were no doubt the heirs of the radical movements of earlier days – the CND movement and Committee of 100. But they reflected also the more uncertain, unpredictable and excitable nature of British politics from 1966 to 1970.

There was, however, a curious paradox concerning this disillusion. In spite of all the economic failures, the successive sterling crises and devaluation, the ordinary person grew steadily richer and more affluent. To this extent, disillusion with government was not because living standards had *fallen*, but because they had not risen as *fast* as politicians had promised. As Roy Jenkins observed, the electorate had come to expect more than was actually delivered. The buoyancy in the growth of personal wealth could be seen in a variety of statistics: from 1964 to 1970 the proportion of all householders owning their houses rose from 46 per cent to 50 per cent, a key indicator of a nation's growing prosperity. The number of cars rose from 1 to 6·4 persons in 1964 to 1 to every 5 in 1968, an increase of over 3 million cars. The statistics for domestic consumer goods were equally buoyant. The proportion of all households owning washing machines rose from 54 per cent in 1964 to 64 per cent in 1969; the proportion for refrigerators rose from 39 per cent to 59 per cent. By 1970 over 90 per cent of all households possessed a television set. The 1960s thus present the paradox of a decade of disillusion in a second age of affluence.

No amount of statistics, however, can testify to the real quality of life led by an individual. A colour television in a prison in the Gulag Archipelago is an unreliable testimony to a person's happiness. Although not as official government policy, the period of Labour government from 1964 to 1970 saw the introduction of a series of changes in the law of inestimable benefit to minority groups (as their supporters claimed) – or moves towards a permissive and decadent society (as their opponents argued). They constituted a series of social reforms that changed the 'quality of life' for many millions of people.

Although these were ostensibly Private Members' Bills, the main initiative in many cases came from Roy Jenkins. The three main reforming bills, on all of which MPs had a free vote, were on homosexuality, abortion and divorce. Although in each case the Bills were sponsored by a private member, the Government gave the measures a helping hand. In the division lists, in general Labour and Liberals voted in favour of the reforms, the Conservatives against.

In addition to these social reforms, another important change was the abolition of the death penalty under the Murder Act of 1965. The Act was in fact passed only for a trial period but hanging was never to return.

Finally the Labour government introduced (following the recommendation of the Latey Committee) legislation enabling people of eighteen to have the right to vote, freedom to marry and freedom to enter into financial dealings such as hire purchase and mortgages. It may well be, therefore, that in the history of British society since 1945 the period from 1964 to 1970 may prove to have been more of a landmark than, for example, in the history of economic policy since the war.

10 | THE POLITICS OF CONFRONTATION: THE HEATH GOVERNMENT, 1970–74

Edward Heath became Prime Minister after an unusual apprenticeship. For five difficult years he had led the party in Opposition – in the face of considerable doubts not only about his personal popularity but about his overall ability. Then with his victory in 1970 he trounced his critics. He now dominated his own party as much as Wilson had his in the wake of 1964.

Heath's new Cabinet reflected his commanding position as leader. He had few debts that needed repaying. Sir Alec Douglas Home, as expected, became Foreign Secretary. The key post of Chancellor of the Exchequer went to Iain Macleod, the Home Office to Reginald Maudling and Defence to Lord Carrington. The appointments of James Prior to Agriculture and Anthony Barber to Employment were much more a reflection of their loyalty to Heath. Equally, the exclusion of Powell and du Cann revealed the depths of hostility with which Heath viewed them. Right from the start, the new Prime Minister made it clear that he intended his government to be substantially different from Wilson's both in style and policies. He determined to shun the publicity and personal initiatives which had characterized the previous tenure of 10 Downing Street. There was to be an end to the dramatic overnight rescue operations and the dashing new initiatives which had launched a thousand headlines but often little else.

Heath lost little time in putting his new policies into operation. The Government's programme had been outlined in the Conservative election manifesto and they used the parliamentary recess over the summer to prepare the details of their plans. In October 1970 they announced their three major domestic policy priorities. The new Government declared their intention to reorganize the machinery of government, to tackle the economy, partly by cuts in public expenditure, and to undertake a major reform of industrial relations. These were not new commitments; but they were undertaken against a background of inflation and the most dramatic confrontation in post-war Britain between Government and unions.

THE MACHINERY OF GOVERNMENT

The White Paper entitled *The Reorganisation of Central Government* was the first official publication on the machinery of government since the Report of the Haldane Committee in 1918. It proposed a number of changes in the division of functions between departments and the establishment of a new Central Policy Review Staff. Continuing the developments which had taken place under Labour towards the unification of functions within single departments (as seen, for instance, in the Ministry of Defence and the Department of Health and Social Security), the White Paper proposed the merging of the Ministry of Technology and the Board of Trade in a new Department of Trade and Industry and the creation of a new Department of the Environment by integrating the Ministry of Housing and Local Government, the Ministry of Transport and the Ministry of Public Building and Works. A number of other minor changes in ministerial responsibilities and departmental organizations were also proposed. By the end of 1970 all these changes had been effected.

Between 1970 and 1974 additional changes were made, apart from the transfer of the functions of the Northern Ireland Government and of the Northern Ireland Department of the Home Office to the new Secretary of State for Northern Ireland following the decision to suspend the Government of Ireland Act in 1972 (see page 274). During 1974 the Department of Trade and Industry was divided into four separate ministries. In January, as a result of the oil crisis, a new Department of Energy was created. In March the succeeding Labour government was to divide the rest of the Department of Trade and Industry into three, Industry, Trade, and Prices and Consumer Protection.

The other most important feature of the 1970 White Paper was the establishment of a small multi-disciplinary central policy review staff within the Cabinet Office. Under the supervision of the Prime Minister it worked for ministers collectively, outlining for the Cabinet as a whole the wider implications of government programmes, thus acting as a counter-balancing force for members of the Cabinet when considering the proposals of individual ministers who had the backing of their departmental staffs.

THE CONSERVATIVES AND THE ECONOMY

Even before beginning their efforts to tackle the economy the new Conservative administration suffered a severe loss on 20 July with the death of the Chancellor of the Exchequer, Iain Macleod. His death was a double blow. Next to Heath, he was one of the strongest and most purposeful members of the Cabinet as well as being a man of principle on the liberal wing of the Conservative Party. His successor was Anthony Barber, a Heath man with nothing like Macleod's stature in the party or, indeed, his experience.

In Opposition, and again during the election campaign, Heath and his Shadow Cabinet had insisted that the general economic strategy of the Conservatives would be in marked contrast to Labour. The Conservatives would reverse Labour's approach to an incomes policy, and the National Board for Prices and Incomes would be disbanded. The Conservative strategy to overcome inflation would be to maintain the economy in recession and squeeze company liquidity. 'Lame ducks' would go to the wall. In this way, it was hoped, wage pressures would be resisted strongly by the employers. The Government themselves would apply this policy in the public sector (as indeed they went on to do with some success against weaker groups of workers such as the postmen, although at the cost of embittered industrial relations).

The first moves on the economic front by the new Government had come on 27 October 1970, when Barber announced the main measures of what amounted to his 1971 budget. His proposals promised a 6d. reduction in income tax, reductions in corporation tax, the abolition of free milk for schoolchildren and an increase in the price charged for school meals. In addition, prescription charges and dental charges were to rise. These cuts in public expenditure and taxation were to take effect from April 1971. They were naturally attacked by Labour as essentially a shift of income away from the poor, a charge partly answered by the introduction of the Family Income Supplement (FIS) to provide a cash benefit for poorer families with children.

The economic strategy adopted by Barber held inherent dangers of creating a recession. During 1970 and 1971 these dangers became more apparent. With monetary restrictions, and with no obviously inflationary measures from the Chancellor, the economy began to stagnate. This stagnation was deepened by lower business profits and low liquidity, business confidence at a poor ebb and low private investment. By the time of the April 1971 budget Barber was aiming at a measure of reflation, offering tax reductions of £550 million for the financial year 1971–2. Other measures included a further cut in corporation tax to 40 per cent, a halving of SET, an increase in the tax allowances for children, a reduction in surtax, particularly for very high income earners, and a general increase in national insurance benefits and contributions. Overall Barber stated the budget's objective was a rise in output of 3 per cent. But however mildly reflationary Barber intended his budget, the economy failed to respond, and only minor further reflationary action was taken during the year. Just as, after devaluation in 1967, the expected benefits had not materialized, so during 1971 the economy obstinately refused to reflate. By January 1972 there was still very little sign of reflation and the unemployment total was approaching 1 million. The Chancellor had clearly underestimated both the depth of the recession in 1971 and also the time-lag before reflationary measures would work.

It was against this background that Barber introduced a highly reflationary budget in March 1972, aimed at achieving an annual growth rate of 5 per cent. Among the main features were the reduction of taxation by a massive £1,380 million, mainly in the form of increased personal allowances, but also purchase tax relaxations and certain industrial investment incentives. At the same time, old age pensions and other national insurance benefits were to be raised in the autumn.

As 1972 progressed it became an increasingly unhappy year for the Heath government. Apart from the bitter confrontation with the unions over the Industrial Relations Act (see page 261), a combination of circumstances forced the Government to make a fundamental about-turn over their economic policies. The problems centred around inflation, the balance of payments and a consequential sterling crisis.

The statistics of the rise in inflation were becoming ever more alarming. Whereas, between 1968 and 1970, retail prices rose by an average of 5·9 per cent per year, between 1970 and 1973 the average annual increase was 8·6 per cent. The basic trend had been increasingly upwards. One continuing factor throughout the sixties and early seventies had been the rise in labour costs. Between 1963 and 1975 the nationally negotiated weekly wage rates rose by 232 per cent, and weekly earnings – including overtime payments and payments negotiated on the factory floor – by 249 per cent. At the same time, the increase in productivity during this period was low. The result was that costs increased and were passed on to the public in the form of increased prices.

Apart from labour costs, inflation accelerated as a result partly of the increase in import prices following the devaluation of the pound in November 1967, partly of the increase in indirect taxes introduced after devaluation in order to free resources for exports, and partly of the spurt in money wages when the Government's incomes policy weakened. But in 1970 the root of the problem lay in the rapid deterioration in the balance of payments. One cause of this was the weakened competitive position caused by inflation more rapid than in competitors. It was a position aggravated by the devaluation of the dollar in 1971. During 1972, compared with 1971, exports were up in volume hardly at all and in value by only 4 per cent, despite an increase in the volume of world trade by 9 per cent. But imports rose by 11 per cent in volume and by no less than 15 per cent in value. There were sharp increases in demand for such consumer goods as cars and colour television sets – no doubt set off by the abolition of hire-purchase restrictions in 1971 – and the inability of domestic producers to expand their production correspondingly both constrained exports and accelerated imports. The trade balance deteriorated from a surplus of nearly £300 million in 1971 to a record deficit of almost £700 million in 1972; and the current account was just in balance.

This rapid deterioration during the first half of 1972 in the balance of payments was one factor behind a large outflow of short-term funds. The result was the sterling crisis of June 1972. On 16 June 1972, against a background of worsening industrial relations, sterling began to plunge. A week later the Chancellor took the decision to allow the pound to 'float'. The fixed parity which had been agreed upon at the Smithsonian Conference at Washington on 18 December 1971 was abandoned. Barber informed the EEC countries that he hoped to restore a fixed parity for sterling before Britain actually joined the EEC on 1 January 1973.

This was the first occasion that sterling had been allowed to 'float' since the 1930s and it clearly conflicted with the principles of the IMF system. During 1972-3 the pound floated from its level of $2·60 in June

1972 to a lower level of $2·40 during 1973. However, the falling value of the pound brought no immediate assistance to the balance of payments, while its impact on the domestic price of imports *was* immediate. Hence, one consequence of Barber's decision was to make the counter-inflation policy more difficult to implement at a time when it was vitally important that it should succeed.

Meanwhile, the weakness of the economy during 1973 was becoming all too obvious. The current account of the balance of payments deteriorated sharply in 1973, to reach the unprecedented deficit of £1·12 billion. Exports did reasonably well, rising by 25 per cent in terms of value and by 11 per cent in terms of volume. However, the import bill soared, increasing by no less than 41 per cent. Import volume increased by 14 per cent, reflecting the rapid upsurge of the economy during 1972 and the emergence of shortages and a need for stock-building during 1973; but more important was the higher *price* of imports: up by an average of 26 per cent between 1972 and 1973. This was due in part to a factor beyond Britain's control – the remarkable inflation in world commodity prices. Between 1 January 1972 and 31 December 1973, the price of copper rose by 115 per cent, cotton by 127 per cent, cocoa by 173 per cent and zinc by a massive 308 per cent. These rapid increases were set in motion by the expansion of the world's major industrial countries (such as West Germany, Japan and the USA) and fuelled by speculative buying as a hedge against inflation.

These economic problems forced the Government to abandon many of the initiatives they had started in 1970 and to adopt policies similar to those which they had attacked so vehemently when they had been in Opposition. This was particularly the case in the fields of regional policy, consumer protection and prices and incomes policy. Likewise on the industrial front the Government was driven into a massive reversal of their original intentions. The two most spectacular instances were the saving of Rolls Royce, which had run into trouble over a fixed-price contract for the delivery of RB 11 engines for the American Lockheed Tristar, and the rescue of Upper Clyde Shipbuilders.

From this point on there was a complete change of course. With unemployment staying stubbornly high and investment stubbornly low despite the available incentives, the Government began to make huge sums of money available to industry. In the spring of 1972 the Conservatives resurrected a form of the investment grant system which they had scrapped, in favour of investment allowances, on coming into office; and in March 1972 they produced an Industry Bill setting up an Industrial Development Executive under Christopher Chataway. Labour gleefully noted a resemblance between this and its own Industrial Development Corporation, also scrapped by the Conservatives. The initial spending programme of the new operation was £250 million a year.

More fundamentally still, after the failure of the Government's attempts to achieve a tripartite voluntary agreement with the CBI and the TUC to combat inflation, Heath was forced to do a major turn-around on economic policy. On 6 November 1972 the Conservative Government reversed their previous policy on inflation and introduced a Statutory Prices and Pay Standstill. In effect there was a 'freeze' on the prices of all goods and services other than imports and fresh foods, a standstill on rents, on dividends and on all negotiated wages and salaries including those previously negotiated but not yet in operation. The freeze was to last for ninety days, and possibly for a further sixty days thereafter. Offenders were liable to be fined.

The necessity for drastic action to control wages had rapidly grown during 1972 as wage demands became more difficult to contain because of the increase in the cost of living resulting from the effective devaluation of the pound in June and the rise in world food prices during the year. There was a marked increase in the number and seriousness of strikes, part of which also reflected the inflationary spiral. Meanwhile, during autumn 1972, the prospect of an imminent freeze had only served to encourage further wage and price increases.

The November freeze also coincided with the second important Cabinet re-shuffle of the year. Earlier, on 18 July, the Home Secretary, Reginald Maudling, had resigned following allegations that he had received money (when in Opposition) from John Poulson, the architect who was the centre of a major corruption investigation. Although it was not alleged that Maudling had done anything improper, nonetheless as Home Secretary he would have been responsible for police investigations into other aspects of the Poulson affair. For this reason Maudling felt he should resign. He was replaced by Robert Carr. The re-shuffle involved several Cabinet colleagues. Peter Walker moved from the Department of the Environment to Trade and Industry, John Davies from the DTI to Geoffrey Rippon's post as Britain's chief representative with the EEC, while Rippon completed the Cabinet musical chairs by moving to Environment.

As the first ninety-day period of wage control drew to an end, there was intense speculation at Westminster, in industry and in the unions as to the content of 'Stage Two' of the policy. On 17 January Heath spelled out the details: an Act of Parliament would establish two new agencies, a Price Commission and a Pay Board. Their function was to regulate prices, dividends and rent in accordance with the Price and Pay Code. From 31 March until the autumn there were to be no pay increases for any group of employees exceeding £1 a week, plus 4 per cent of their current pay bill excluding overtime. There was some flexibility for negotiation of increases within a group – with emphasis on the lower paid – and a maximum individual increase of £250 a year was fixed. The Pay Board had to be notified of all settlements involving less than 1,000 employees, and settlements involving more than 1,000 employees required its prior approval. It became an offence to strike or threaten to strike to force an employer to contravene an order of the Pay Board.

The unions were unenthusiastic. On 14 February Britain's gas workers began a campaign of strikes and overtime bans in support of their already-filed claim for wage increases which exceeded Stage Two limits. By 15 February nearly 4 million homes had experienced reductions in gas pressure and over 600 industrial plants had to close for lack of gas. On 27 February about 200,000 civil servants went on strike (for the first time in the history of the service) in support of their pay claim.

The Government experienced further trouble in February when panic selling of dollars produced an international monetary crisis. In spite of a meeting of finance ministers in Paris, the US dollar was devalued by 10 per cent on 13 February, with grave and continuing consequences for sterling. On 4 April, three days after his budget had substituted VAT for purchase tax and SET, Anthony Barber sought to ease the pressure on house owners by giving the building societies £15 million in return for an undertaking that they would increase mortgage rates to $9\frac{1}{2}$ per cent instead of 10 per cent for the next three months.

However, the international monetary situation continued to deteriorate and on 18 April the DTI announced a trade deficit for March of £197 million – more than two and a half times as much as the deficit for the previous two months. On 7 May, in an attempt to moderate the rise in the cost of living, the Government announced a subsidy of 2p a pound on the price of butter for everyone, and an additional 10p – to be claimed once a month – to about 5 million people receiving social security.

On 21 May Barber announced cuts in public spending of £100 million for 1973 and of £500 million for 1974–5.

In spite of these economies the Government went on to authorize a 5 per cent increase in rail fares on 8 June. The Bank of England's minimum lending rate was raised to 11½ per cent on 27 July (the highest rate since 1914), following the lowest-ever exchange rate for the pound caused by an ebbing away of confidence on 26 July. By 14 August, in spite of these measures, the building societies were obliged to raise mortgage interest rates to 10 per cent. All this activity took place against the political backcloth of the Heath government's determination to tackle the problem of the trade unions and industrial relations.

THE CONSERVATIVES AND THE TRADE UNIONS

Like the 1966–70 Labour government, the Conservatives were determined to legislate to reduce the damage done to the economy by strikes. In an attempt to reduce strikes the Government introduced an Industrial Relations Bill, which made collective industrial bargains enforceable at law and established the National Industrial Relations Court to enforce them. These measures, in particular, were obnoxious to the Opposition and the Bill was not enacted until 6 August after 450 hours of debate spread over sixty days. In the event, the successful passage of the Bill was followed by a period of industrial unrest which set new records for days lost from work.

The intensification of labour disputes and industrial strife was the product of a variety of factors. Trade union hostility to the Industrial Relations Act was the cause of numerous one-day stoppages and unofficial disputes. The fundamental cause, however, was the Government's policy of confrontation as a means of limiting wage disputes. Strikes by local authority manual workers, the dockers and in the electrical power industry were all due to this policy. All this was made worse, as we have seen, by the rapidly rising level of unemployment. Added to all these factors, after 1972, was industrial action in protest against the Government's prices and incomes policy.

The statistics of industrial disputes made grim reading. Figures for working days lost in the first quarter of 1971 showed a fourfold increase over the same quarter a year earlier. One of the most bitter industrial disputes began on 9 January 1972, when Britain's 280,000 coal miners came out on strike for more pay, having rejected an offer of up to £2 a week which conformed to the Government's wage policy at that time. As the strike dragged on into February the miners picketed power stations to prevent the movement of coal by road. There were violent incidents, in the biggest of which, at a Birmingham coke depot, 6,000 trade unionists successfully prevented supplies from being delivered. They were supported by the railwaymen who refused to move coal trains. Eventually, the miners were awarded pay increases about three times the size of the Coal Board's offer after these had been recommended by a Committee of Inquiry set up by the Government and chaired by Lord Wilberforce.

No sooner had this dispute been settled than the dockworkers' claim to container work produced a severe test for the Industrial Relations Act. In June three dockers who had been picketing a container depot refused to appear before the newly created National Industrial Relations Court and their arrest for contempt was ordered. By 16 June 30,000 dockers had stopped work in sympathy. The heat was taken out of the situation when the Official Solicitor successfully challenged the Industrial Relations Court's ruling and the order was quashed. These two disputes, by the miners and the dockers, effectively undermined the Government's whole industrial policy. They were important defeats for the Government, which neither Heath nor his Cabinet colleagues had forgotten by the time of the three-day-week crisis (see page 281).

Although during 1973 the strike figures showed a marked fall, the statistics were deceptive: the miners banned overtime and the railwaymen worked to a rule book which effectively disrupted the normal working of the railways. Not surprisingly, Labour interpreted all this as vindication of their stand against the Industrial Relations Act.

EUROPE AND FOREIGN AFFAIRS

The three main parties all went into the 1970 general election pledged to take Britain into Europe if the terms were right. All parties were thus now in line with the policies pursued by successive governments since the start of the sixties. In 1963 a Conservative government's attempt to take Britain into Europe had been approved by a substantial Commons majority; four years later, Labour's bid was approved by an even larger one (488 to 62), 'the biggest majority', Wilson noted later in his memoirs, 'on a contested vote on a matter of public policy for almost a century'. As we have seen, this Labour attempt was thwarted by the opposition of General de Gaulle. However, the resignation of de Gaulle on 25 April 1969 had removed the most obvious obstacle to entry and at a summit conference at the Hague on 1-2 December it was agreed that the Community should open negotiations with the UK, the Irish Republic, Norway and Denmark. A White Paper in February 1970 estimated that the cost to the balance of payments was likely to be somewhere around £1,100 million, but added that against the 'substantial' cost of joining must be set the substantial advantages which the dynamic effect of membership would have on the economy. The Labour application was, therefore 'picked up' by the incoming Conservatives and negotiations opened in Luxembourg on 30 June. Detailed discussions began in September and ran through to February.

These discussions – though eventually successful – had many hurdles to overcome. France, in particular, was difficult, insisting on an immediate British acceptance of the Common Agricultural Policy (CAP), raising doubts about the sterling balances and attacking the privileged position of the London capital market. By March 1971 there was dismay in the British negotiating team that yet another veto might be imminent – but the Heath–Pompidou summit of 20-21 May in Paris resolved many of the difficulties. Britain, this time, could also count on the friendly support of Willy Brandt in West Germany. In the end, the terms agreed for entry were not over-generous for Britain – although she did secure transitional periods of up to six years before the common external tariff, the CAP and contributions to the Community budget were applied fully. In addition, special transitional terms were agreed for New Zealand, anxious over her dairy products, and the Commonwealth sugar producers.

Negotiating the terms for entry, though crucial, was only the first step for Heath. He had now to carry the legislation through Parliament, with some redoubtable opponents of entry on his own back-benches and with Labour increasingly hostile. Between the de Gaulle veto of 1967 and the application by Heath, opposition to EEC entry had hardened in the country and most particularly in the Labour Party. The Common Market Safeguards Campaign had been launched at the end of 1969, its most prominent supporters being Barbara Castle, Ian Mikardo and Peter Shore. The two foremost union leaders, Hugh Scanlon and Jack Jones, were also members, reflecting growing TUC hostility to entry. Other anti-EEC supporters were grouped in the Anti-Common Market League and the Keep Britain Out organization. Indeed, within a year of their election defeat the Labour Party had swung sharply against Europe – although the leadership continued to emphasize that the terms, not the principle, were the source of their objection.

In a broadcast on 9 July 1971 – replying to one by Heath the previous night, commending the settlement to the nation – Wilson recalled that Labour had set four conditions for membership in 1967. The points on which satisfactory terms must be obtained, he stressed, were the balance of payments, the effect on sugar, the effect on New Zealand, and the scope for control of capital movements that would be left to Britain as an EEC member. It was on these tests that the Tory terms should be judged.

A special conference called by the Labour Party to debate the issue, which took place in London on 17 July, was largely hostile, although George Thomson, a prominent Marketeer who had been one of the ministerial negotiators, said he would have recommended a Labour cabinet to accept the terms the Conservative government had obtained. No vote was taken on the issue. Two days later the deputy leader, Roy Jenkins, told the Parliamentary Party he believed a Labour government would have accepted the terms. But on 28 July the party's National Executive passed a resolution condemning them. The Labour conference voted against entry by a substantial majority in October, while the Conservative and Liberal conferences produced substantial majorities in favour.

The Commons debated the application from 21 to 28 October 1971. There was a free vote on the Conservative side, a course which, the Conservative business managers correctly calculated, would encourage Labour's Marketeers to defy their own anti-Market whip and thus more than cancel out the expected defections on the Conservative side. The European Communities Bill, the Bill which effectively took Britain into Europe, turned out to be unexpectedly short: it had only twelve clauses and four schedules, of which the most crucial was Clause II, which allowed Westminster legislation to be over-ridden by legislation from Brussels. Labour and Conservative anti-Marketeers argued that this represented an unacceptable surrender of the sovereignty of Parliament. One Conservative, Enoch Powell, regarded this matter as of such supreme importance that he later counselled Conservatives to vote for the Labour Party in the 1974 general election, and did so himself. But Government spokesmen said this surrender of sovereignty was implicit in any move to join Europe and would certainly have been accepted by Labour had they got in in 1967.

The Bill took five months to complete its progress through the Commons. There were 104 divisions. The lowest majority, on a vote on the free movement of capital, was four. The crucial second reading, on 17 February, was approved by 309 votes to 301, a majority of eight. The most severe divisions in the Labour Party over the Bill occurred in April, when the Shadow Cabinet decided to support an amendment tabled by a prominent Conservative anti-Marketeer, Neil Marten, calling for a consultative referendum before a final decision on entry. Until then Labour had been opposed to a referendum and the Shadow Cabinet decision precipitated the resignation of the deputy leader of the party, Roy Jenkins. However, the referendum proposal was defeated by 284 votes to 235, a Government majority of forty-nine, with sixty-three Labour MPs abstaining. The Bill then went on to pass its third reading on 13 July by 301 to 284, a majority of seventeen, and Britain entered the Community on 1 January 1973.

The conflict both within and between the parties over Europe was by far the most serious foreign policy issue in British politics between 1970 and 1974. The parties might vary in degree in their attitudes to the American alliance, the Soviet Union and the United Nations, but their differences, between front benches at least, were rarely fundamental. The European question was the one which really roused passions.

On Rhodesia, the Foreign Secretary Sir Alec Douglas-Home resumed the search for a settlement that had taken Wilson to the HMS *Tiger* talks in December 1966 and the HMS *Fearless* talks in October 1968. On 9 November 1971 Douglas-Home announced in the House of Commons that he would be going to Rhodesia to see whether a settlement to the constitutional dispute could be reached. After ten days of difficult negotiations in Salisbury, the Foreign Secretary (who was accompanied by the Attorney General, Sir Peter Rawlinson, and Lord Goodman, who had done much to prepare the way for negotiations) came to an agreement with the Rhodesian government on proposals for a settlement to be put to the Rhodesian people as a whole. According to these proposals, a number of important changes would be introduced into the Rhodesian constitution, including a large African electoral roll, a strengthened Declaration of Rights to be enforceable in the Courts, and an effective mechanism preventing retrogressive amendment to the constitution. The proposed settlement terms conformed to five of the six principles originally laid down by the Conservatives themselves and later endorsed by Labour (see page 238 above).

To see whether they satisfied the principle of acceptance by the Rhodesian people as a whole, the Government appointed a Commission under the chairmanship of Lord Pearce, which visited Rhodesia for a period of two months from January 1972 in order to assess opinion towards the settlement. The Report of the Pearce Commission was published on 23 May 1972, and it concluded that the proposals were not acceptable to the African population. So the settlement failed, which meant that sanctions had to stay. Each November it was necessary for the House to vote for their renewal, and this was something some Conservatives were provoked to rebel over. There was a substantial Conservative revolt when the order for renewal was submitted to the Commons on 9 November 1972. Twenty-nine Conservatives voted against the Order and many more abstained. Of 266 votes for the Government, 159 were Conservatives (fifty-eight of them from members of the Government), 102 from Labour and five from the Liberals. There was a similar revolt when the Order again came up on 8 November 1973. Twenty-six Conservative members voted against it; there were 133 votes in favour – 108 Conservatives (fifty-six of them ministers), twenty-two Labour and three Liberals.

Party differences over Africa were also evident on another issue. The Labour government had banned the sale of arms to South Africa. The Conservatives consistently promised that sales would be resumed and the go-ahead was given by the new Foreign Secretary, Sir Alec Douglas-Home, within days of his arrival at the Foreign Office. Two law officers were sent on a fact-finding mission and reported that Britain was legally committed under the Simonstown Agreement to supply arms. This argument failed to convince a number of Commonwealth countries and the subsequent Commonwealth Conference of January 1971 was embittered by disputes between Britain and the African states, with Heath making no attempt to conceal his hostility to the way the African leaders were acting.

Important changes in British relations in the Far East also took place during this period. Having sunk to a low ebb in the years 1967–8, Sino-British relations showed a marked improvement during the period of Conservative government. On 13 March 1972 Sir Alec Douglas-Home announced that Britain and China had agreed to exchange ambassadors, thus ending twenty-two years during which the two countries were represented in each other's capitals by chargés d'affaires. Relations continued to improve thereafter. In June 1972 Antony Royle, Under-Secretary of State at the Foreign and Commonwealth Office, became the first Foreign Office Minister of any West European country to visit China since the setting up of the People's Republic, and at the end of October 1972 Sir Alec Douglas-Home paid a five-day official visit, which was reciprocated in June 1973 by Ch'i Peng-fei, the Chinese Foreign Minister.

At the same time, in the wake of the Labour government's decision made in January 1968 to withdraw all British troops from South-East Asia by the end of 1971, new developments took place in that arena. The Conservative Party had undertaken in its 1970 election manifesto to discuss with Britain's allies the possibility of a five-power defence force to help maintain peace and stability in South-East Asia. This undertaking was acted upon when the Conservative government came to power, and in April 1971, at a conference held in London, agreement was reached between Britain, Australia, New Zealand, Malaysia and Singapore on the setting up of a defence arrangement. The essence of the agreement, which came into effect on 1 November 1971, was an undertaking to consult together 'in the event of any form of armed attack, externally organised, or the threat of such attack, against Malaysia and Singapore'.

In other areas of foreign policy, sharp disagreements arose between the Government and the Opposition. The Conservative government's warmth towards Portugal affronted the Labour and Liberal parties, and there was a furious debate in the Commons on 17 July 1973 over the visit to London of the Portuguese Prime Minister, Dr Caetano. His arrival in London was signalled by reports alleging that Portuguese troops had massacred Africans in Mozambique. The Government was also under sustained pressure from the Opposition throughout 1973 to condemn French nuclear tests in the Pacific, against which the governments of Australia and New Zealand had protested. Heath and his ministers repeatedly assured the Commons that Britain's attitude to these tests was well known to the French government, but they declined to issue any public condemnation. That led to the charge – regularly made by Wilson against the Conservatives – that in this and other matters they were in President Pompidou's pocket.

In neither of these cases was there any great criticism of government policy from their own back-benchers. The Conservatives suffered none of the turmoil which was created in the Labour Party over British policy towards the Americans in Vietnam and the civil war in Biafra.

IMMIGRATION

One of the legacies of the Empire which impinged on domestic politics was the question of immigration. The Conservative manifesto of 1970 had taken a strong line on immigration, declaring that future immigration would be allowed only in strictly defined special cases and that there would be no further large-scale permanent immigration. The Conservatives followed up this pledge with the 1971 Immigration Bill. This obliterated the distinction which had formerly given Commonwealth immigrants a far more favourable claim to admission than aliens and supplanted it by a unified system. It created a new offence of illegal entry, doubled the maximum fine for harbouring illegal immigrants and extended the time over which offenders remained liable to prosecution. The Immigration Bill had been opposed by Labour and Liberals: for Labour, Roy Jenkins, the former Home Secretary, said the number of immigrants coming to Britain was not now of a size which made further control or restriction desirable. Liberals voted with Labour in opposing the Second Reading, which was carried by 295 votes to 265. Although Conservatives voted solidly for the Bill, there was criticism that it was not as strong as it might have been, a criticism most strongly voiced by Enoch Powell, who had by now taken over from Cyril Osborne as the party's chief proponent of a tough line on immigration.

Despite the passing of the 1971 Immigration Act, the political controversy over immigration refused to disappear. The impending admission of Britain to the European Community led to the introduction of revised regulations for the admission of entrants, the effect of which was to ease the admission of EEC nationals but to reduce the former preference given to Commonwealth immigrants. The proposed regulations were opposed by Labour and Liberals and they were joined by a large number of Conservative MPs. On 22 November 1972 the rules were rejected by the Commons by 275 votes to 240, an Opposition majority of thirty-five – the most substantial government defeat of the Parliament. The Government were therefore forced to redraft the rules. They were now split into two parts – one for Commonwealth immigrants, one for the rest. The effect of the changes was to give preference to Commonwealth citizens with 'grandpatrial' as well as 'patrial' connections with Britain, that is to say, the preference formerly extended to those immigrants who were British born was now extended to those with British-born grandparents.

In announcing these changes to the Commons on 25 January 1973 the Home Secretary, Robert Carr, also announced the results of the Government's consideration of the issues raised by the expulsion the previous summer of thousands of Asians from Uganda. The Uganda government's decision, announced without consultation by President Amin, led to predictions that 50,000 to 60,000 refugees might seek to come to Britain. Both Carr and the Foreign Secretary, Sir Alec Douglas Home, acknowledged a legal and moral duty for Britain to admit them, though this was challenged by Powell. Negotiations with the governments of India, Canada and other countries enabled Carr to say in the Commons on 18 October 1972 that only half the predicted number were now expected. (The final figure of Ugandan Asians coming to Britain was actually 28,000.)

THE REFORM OF LOCAL GOVERNMENT

For most people in Britain, these problems of foreign policy and the Commonwealth had little direct effect. Even the issue of immigration was largely confined to London, the West Midlands and cities such as Leicester and Bradford. Of far more relevance to people's daily lives was the fundamental reorganization of local government carried out during this period.

Since 1958 the structure of local government had been under almost continuous review. Following the report of the Herbert Commission in 1960, Greater London was reorganized under the terms of the London Government Act 1963. In 1966 the restricted Local Government Commission was replaced by two Royal Commissions with wider terms of reference, one for England, chaired by Lord Redcliffe-Maud, the other for Scotland, chaired by Lord Wheatley. Both Commissions reported during 1969. The Government did not accept the Redcliffe-Maud Commission's recommendations and instead proceeded with their own proposals for reform in England and Wales, which received the Royal Assent in October 1972 and came into operation on 1 April 1974. Legislation broadly conforming to the Wheatley Commission's recommendations for Scotland was enacted in 1973 and the new structure came into force in May 1975.

The new legislation removed the former dual framework of county councils (and their district councils) and all-purpose county borough councils. They were replaced by a two-tier system which, outside Greater London, was based upon forty-five counties. In six predominantly urban areas (Greater Manchester, Merseyside, South Yorkshire, Tyne and Wear, the West Midlands and West Yorkshire) new authorities called metropolitan counties were created; large metropolitan district authorities, whose boundaries were laid down in the Act and with a minimum size of about 200,000, formed the second tier of local government. In the rest of England many existing county boundaries were retained, although the number of counties was reduced. Former borough councils and district councils were rationalized to form second-tier, non-metropolitan district councils, with sufficient resources to carry out their responsibilities effectively, with a minimum population of about 40,000. The new legislation was not popular.

THE ULSTER QUESTION

Of all the problems inherited by recent British governments, none would more willingly and thankfully have been discarded than the bloody and seemingly interminable sectarian strife in Ulster.

The root of the conflict dated back to 1921, when the 'six counties' of Ulster had remained outside the Irish Republic (the Irish Free State, as it was then known). From 1921 until 1972 Northern Ireland was governed under the scheme of devolution embodied in the Government of Ireland Act, 1920. This created the Northern Ireland Parliament (generally known as Stormont, after its eventual location), consisting of a House of Commons of fifty-two members elected on the basis of single-member constituencies and a Senate of two *ex-officio* members and twenty-four others elected by the members of the Northern Ireland House of Commons. Executive powers were formally vested in the Governor of

Northern Ireland but were in effect performed by a prime minister and a small cabinet. The Act, while in the last resort preserving the sovereign authority of the UK Parliament in all matters, conferred upon Stormont extensive powers for regulating the affairs of Northern Ireland but excluded certain matters from its jurisdiction, such as foreign relations and defence, customs and excise and income tax, which remained the responsibility of the UK Parliament. Largely because of these reserved powers, twelve MPs continued to be returned to Westminster from Northern Ireland constituencies.

In the years after 1921 Ulster had been a forgotten province. In the 1930s its average unemployment rate had been one of the worst, yet least reported, in the United Kingdom. Fearful for their own security, the Protestant majority had traditionally maintained a policy of discrimination in housing, jobs and political rights. The Royal Ulster Constabulary (RUC) was the only armed police force in the United Kingdom and was supported by the Protestant-dominated paramilitary 'B'-Specials. Regarded by Loyalists as a pillar of the Protestant community and a guarantee of the settlement of 1920, the 'B'-Specials were hated by many sections of the Catholic population, who saw them as a symbol of Protestant domination.

At the opposite end of the spectrum was the large Roman Catholic minority, numbering over a third of the population, some of whom still favoured the complete unification of Ireland. On several occasions the Irish Republican Army (IRA) had engaged in terrorist operations against the North. A campaign after 1950 led to attacks upon customs posts and police barracks before it was finally abandoned in 1962.

It was against this long background of Protestant ascendancy and sectarian strife that, after 1963, the Prime Minister of Northern Ireland, Terence O'Neill, began a process of gradual reform in order to give greater equality of political rights to the Roman Catholic community. Encouraged by the election of the Labour government of Harold Wilson in October 1964, the Campaign for Democracy in Ulster, or CDU, was set up. In 1968, at a time of growing worldwide concern with 'civil rights', a moderate but Catholic-dominated organization, the Northern Irish Civil Rights Association, began to agitate for full equality for the minority community. In October serious rioting in Londonderry – a predominantly Roman Catholic city – was provoked by the questionable behaviour of the RUC. The breaking up of the People's Democracy civil rights march from Belfast to Londonderry early in January 1969 by the police was widely regarded as a blatant act of discriminatory policing. The resulting government inquiry into the disturbances urged the adoption of a reform programme in Ulster. By the summer of 1969, however, there was widespread violence in the province, including riots against the police and isolated acts of sabotage. In August there were again serious riots in Londonderry following a march by the Protestant Apprentice Boys, and the sectarian rift began to widen alarmingly. The Catholic population of Londonderry barricaded themselves into the Bogside district and set up 'Free Derry'. On 13 August 1969 the British Army was moved into Belfast and Londonderry in order to separate the warring factions and, implicitly, to protect the Roman Catholic population from a now largely discredited Ulster government.

From now on, Ulster's problems had become Britain's, and once again British politicians, like Gladstone a century earlier, found themselves involuntarily landed with a mission to pacify Ireland. In Ulster itself, however, the civil rights movement was increasingly overshadowed by the militant voices of Irish Nationalism: during 1969 the 'Provisional' IRA split off from the 'Official' movement and set up the Provisional Army Council. Consisting of about 600 activists, the 'Provos' began a campaign of urban terrorism. In February 1971 the first British soldier was killed in Ulster, and an intensification of street violence led to the introduction of internment without trial. This measure only provoked more violence, so that by the end of the year 175 people had died in bombings and shootings. The introduction of internment was significant also in marking a distinct change in the attitudes of the parties at Westminster.

For a long time after the riots of August 1969 had heralded the new wave of unrest in Northern Ireland, the parties at Westminster had maintained a united front. Both the general line of policy adopted by Labour Home Secretary, James Callaghan, which coupled firm action against violence with progressive measures to end discrimination against the minority community, and the individual initiatives he took were approved and applauded by all except a sceptical handful of MPs. Indeed, Callaghan was generally agreed to have managed a difficult task with skill and some success. But when he was succeeded at the Home Office by the Conservative Reginald Maudling, some significant cracks in bi-partisanship began to appear. For while his supporters praised him for his ability to keep calm, Labour – Callaghan included – began to accuse him of inaction; meanwhile the problems of the province grew steadily more serious – with the death toll now rising and a second Northern Ireland Premier – James Chichester-Clark – following Terence O'Neill into retirement in 1971.

Labour's restiveness was fully exposed for the first time in a debate in the Commons on 5 August. Its MPs opposed the adjournment of the House for the summer recess, saying this was the only way they could demonstrate the concern they felt about the way things in Northern Ireland were going. Their disquiet was compounded when Maudling spoke for only four minutes and announced nothing. In fact, the Cabinet was meeting that very day to discuss its plans for internment: the decision was announced on 9 August 1971, by which time 300 people had already been rounded up. As Shadow Home Secretary, Callaghan said on television (the House was not sitting) that this was only a short-term expedient, and he repeated the call he made in the earlier debate for the setting up of a Council of Ireland, North and South. For the Liberals, Thorpe said the policy would solve nothing and insisted that essential rights must be safeguarded.

The Commons was recalled to debate Northern Ireland on 22–3 September and Wilson, for Labour, repeated the case he had made outside the House on 8 September for a twelve-point programme for the province. This was to include a Minister for Northern Ireland with a seat in the Cabinet; elections by proportional representation in the province; an All-Ireland Council; and a ban on firearms. He did not condemn internment out of hand, but said it had created 'a new and grave situation'. Thorpe, for the Liberals, expressed astonishment that no Protestants had been interned. Though the Labour leadership did not divide the House, a group of their back-benchers did.

The party conflict was still more direct on 25 November when the House debated an Opposition motion regretting the failure of government policy in Northern Ireland, rejecting the continuation of internment and deploring 'the extraction of information from detainees by methods which must never be permitted in a civilised society'. (A commission under Sir Edmund Compton had reported that detainees had been ill-treated, though charges of cruelty and brutality were rejected.) Internment, said Callaghan, had marked the breaking point in Opposition support for the Government. The Opposition amendment was rejected on 29 November by 294 votes to 260.

In Ulster the horrors of urban terrorism continued. On 5 December a bomb estimated to contain at least 80 lb of gelignite exploded in McGurk's bar, near the centre of Belfast, killing fifteen people, all Catholics. On 30 January 1972 ('Bloody Sunday') a civil rights march staged in defiance of a government ban in Derry ended with thirteen people shot dead. Bernadette Devlin, who had won the mid-Ulster by-election on 17 April 1969, called it Ireland's Sharpeville, and on the following day she physically assaulted Maudling in the Commons. In an emergency debate on 1 February, on a motion for the adjournment, the Opposition divided the House. Voting was 304 to 266, with five Liberals voting with Labour.

The continuation of the troubles in the province, which had led to the presence of over 20,000 British soldiers there, and the withdrawal of the principal opposition parties from Stormont, forced the UK government, in March 1972, to the conclusion that responsibility for law and order should be removed from the Parliament and Government of Northern Ireland. A series of bomb outrages in Northern Ireland and another in England, at Aldershot, had increased the pressure on the London government to take control of the Northern Ireland situation into their own hands. In nine and a half hours' talks with Brian Faulkner, the Northern Irish Premier, and the Eire Premier, Jack Lynch, on 22 March, Heath called for three immediate measures: periodical plebiscites on the border issue; a start in phasing out internment; and the transfer of responsibility for law and order to Westminster. The Northern Ireland government accepted the first two, but refused to agree to the third. Hence, it was decided to suspend the Government of Ireland Act and to impose direct rule for a period of twelve months. The Northern Ireland (Temporary Provisions) Bill commanded Labour and Liberal support, but provoked the first real revolt on the Conservative benches: fifteen Conservative and Unionist members voted against it on the second reading. The Royal Assent was nevertheless given at the end of March. Stormont was prorogued and all legislative and executive functions were transferred to London. Direct rule had been imposed.

William Whitelaw, the Secretary of State for Northern Ireland, now had a doubly difficult task: he found himself with a dual responsibility of continuing the government of the province and of finding a solution to the troubles. The imposition of direct rule and Whitelaw's decision to release a number of internees was bitterly opposed by various Protestant groups, some of which resorted to violence. Nor did IRA violence subside, although there was a short-lived and fragile truce between the IRA and the security forces. Despite the continuing violence, a number of important developments occurred during 1972. Amidst growing evidence that politicians in Northern Ireland were more prepared to take part in formal and informal contacts, there was also an improvement in relations between North and South following the formation of a coalition government in the Republic, composed of Fine Gael and the Irish Labour Party and headed by Liam Cosgrave. In Ulster a plebiscite was held in March to determine whether the six counties wished to remain part of the United Kindom. The poll was boycotted by all the Catholic parties but 57·4 per cent of the total electorate voted in favour of union.

Most significant, however, was the publication of the Government's White Paper, *Northern Ireland: Constitutional Proposals.* Having reaffirmed that Northern Ireland would remain part of the United Kingdom for so long as this was wanted by a majority of its citizens, it proceeded to set out a new system of government for the province. The main proposals were that Stormont should be replaced by an assembly of about eighty members elected on the basis of the single transferable vote system, but that the Secretary of State for Northern Ireland should be retained. The White Paper also proposed the creation of an executive from members of the assembly, each member heading a Northern Ireland department. The executive would perform those functions previously performed by Stormont, except for law and order. Finally, the White Paper favoured the creation of a Council of Ireland, consisting of representatives of both North and South.

The constitutional proposals became law, and elections for the new assembly were held on 28 June 1973. The results showed that Brian Faulkner, leading the official Unionists, had won twenty-three of the seventy-eight seats in the new assembly but that the Loyalists led by William Craig (who opposed the White Paper) had won twenty-seven. The first meeting of the Assembly ended in uproar on 31 July and both the Assembly and the new Northern Ireland Executive began their careers uneasily. Earlier, the Northern Ireland (Emergency Provisions) Bill, implementing the recommendations of the Diplock Committee for a system of trials for alleged terrorists in Northern Ireland rather than straightforward internment, had been approved on second reading.

From this point on the rift which had opened up between the parties began to be healed – although the split between Conservatives and Ulster Unionists remained. When, during a brief truce in Northern Ireland, Whitelaw met IRA leaders, there was no condemnation from the Opposition (Wilson, in fact, had done the same), though some Conservatives and Unionists were bitter. The bombings continued unabated, accompanied now by indiscriminate murders, inexplicable except as the expression of sectarian hatred. On 21 July 1973 ('Bloody Friday') twenty large bombs killed eleven people in Belfast and injured 120. Ten days later, in 'Operation Motorman', troops successfully occupied the 'no go' areas of Belfast and Derry.

All-party talks on the future of Northern Ireland were held at Darlington, Co. Durham, on 25–7 September 1972. The Social Democratic and Labour party, which had emerged as the main anti-Unionist political force in Northern Ireland, boycotted the talks as a protest against the continued existence of internment – but it did submit its views, along with the Unionists, Alliance and Northern Ireland Labour Party, on a possible constitutional settlement for the province. Out of this came a consultative document (30 October) outlining a pattern of power-sharing. It foreshadowed an elected assembly, an executive made up of the chairman of assembly committees (the chairmanships would be shared between the parties), a Bill of Rights and new links with the South.

A year later, from 6 to 9 December 1973, further talks at Sunningdale, Berkshire, between representatives of the London and Dublin governments and the Northern Ireland Executive ended in agreement on the setting up of a Council of Ireland. The Dublin government solemnly accepted that there could be no change in the status of Northern Ireland until the majority of people in Northern Ireland desired a change in status. This opened the way for powers to be transferred to the new assembly and executive in Belfast. This did not, however, prevent the continuation of violence in the North or renewed outbreaks of letter-bombing and other outrages in England. By the time of the closing months of the Heath government, direct rule in the province was ended from 1 January 1974. Whether the new power-sharing executive would work had now to be tested.

THE LIBERAL AND NATIONALIST REVIVAL

The period from 1970 to February 1974 was most successful for both Liberals and Nationalists, while the Conservatives lost some of their safest and most traditional seats in the country. The Liberal revival was all the more remarkable considering their poor showing in the 1970 election. It can be ascribed to two factors: the development of a new style in British political life – 'community politics', as it was dubbed – and a Conservative government in increasing electoral difficulties.

The Liberal conference of 1970 accepted a radical Young Liberal resolution which proposed that the party should start campaigning and working on a community level – bringing politics to the people. The advocates of 'community politics' often had little time for Jeremy Thorpe or the other party leaders. Peter Hain, the former Young Liberal Chairman, declared that the party leadership did not understand what community politics was all about, and would not like it if they did. They constituted almost a separate entity within the party. The 'Radical Bulletin' group (as they called themselves) held their own seminars, published their own journal and helped secure election to key posts in the party. The group was to produce the famous Liberal names of the 1972–3 revival; thus David Austick, the by-election victor at Ripon, was a founder member, and Graham Tope, the victor of Sutton, was equally prominent.

In the 1971 local elections the first successes of the strategy became apparent. Significantly, the Scarborough assembly in 1971 was notable for the deep hostility between the mass of the party and the new radicals. But the radicals went on undismayed, making spectacular progress in local elections in Liverpool, a city in which in May 1968 Liberals had only one councillor, compared to seventy-nine Conservatives and thirty-four Labour. By 1973 the Liberals had become the largest single party, all this in a town where they had not won a parliamentary seat since the Free Trade election of December 1923. By autumn 1972 'community politics' had scored its second major victory. At the Margate assembly Trevor Jones, the new radicals' standard-bearer, was elected President of the Party, defeating the leadership's candidate. Meanwhile, the advocates of 'community politics' moved from purely municipal success to by-election triumphs as the discontent amongst Conservative voters became more apparent.

Their first parliamentary breakthrough came with a by-election in October 1972 in Rochdale (one of the very few constituencies in the country where the Liberals were the main challengers to Labour): Cyril Smith won a decisive (if no doubt partly personal) victory. Critics dismissed this result relatively easily, but the sensational Liberal victory in the Sutton and Cheam by-election of 7 December 1972 could not be treated so glibly. In a rock-solid true-blue Conservative commuter suburb, an able and youthful Liberal candidate, preaching (and indeed practising) the gospel of community politics, swept to a landslide victory. Naturally there was Liberal euphoria at overturning a Conservative majority of 7,417 on a bigger swing than even Orpington had witnessed. The winter of 1972–3 then began to produce much comment on the electoral triumphs of the Liberals and the failings of Labour, and on the possible desire of the voters for a 'Centre Party' and a realignment of British politics.

It was against this background that two English by-elections were held on 1 March 1973: at Lincoln and Chester-le-Street. The results were astonishing. At Lincoln the outcome was a victory for Labour rebel Dick Taverne with a majority of 13,191 – a result which was widely interpreted as confirmation of the 'Centre Party' thesis. Meanwhile the very strong Liberal poll in Chester-le-Street, part of the Labour stronghold of the industrial North-East and an area of virtual Labour one-party rule for a generation, also seemed to support this argument.

The 1973 round of municipal elections confirmed this Liberal upsurge. Then, on 26 July, polling took place in two of the safest Conservative strongholds in the country – Ripon and the Isle of Ely. At Ripon the Liberal candidate, David Austick, fought a campaign with a strong emphasis on community politics. He achieved a remarkable victory, taking the seat with 43 per cent of the vote. At the same time, an equally sensational victory was achieved by Clement Freud in the Isle of Ely. It was the first occasion in living memory that the Liberals had won two by-elections on the same day. In a further by-election Berwick-on-Tweed fell to the Liberal Alan Beith, confirming the power of their revival.

The events of 1972–3 were a significant comment on the disillusion of many Conservatives with the Heath government – just as Orpington had been witness to the failings of the Macmillan era. As before, Liberals did best in the safe Tory seats with a reservoir of protest votes. Significantly, they did worst in marginal seats – thus on the day Sutton and Cheam was won the party lost its deposit in marginal Uxbridge, a constituency not so very far away. As it had been with Orpington, the Liberal vote again proved to be largely a protest against the Government – though this time sufficient disgruntled Conservatives still voted Liberal in the February 1974 general election to see that Heath fell from office.

The Nationalist resurgence of 1972 and after bore close outward similarities with the Liberal revival. Thus in the immediate aftermath of the 1970 election little went right for the SNP. In the burgh elections of 1971 the sweeping gains of three years earlier were obliterated. In Glasgow every sitting SNP councillor went down to defeat. The climate changed, however, with a strong Nationalist vote in the Stirling and Falkirk by-election of 16 September 1971. In a safe Labour seat, a strong Nationalist challenge secured 34 per cent of the vote. This was followed, on 1 March 1973, by a remarkable campaign in Dundee East, in which the Nationalist challenge brought the party to within 1,141 votes of victory. It was a particularly significant by-election, for oil had been at the forefront of the Nationalist campaign. The Nationalist bandwagon received its final spurt with the capture of the Govan division of Glasgow in October 1973. Like the Liberals, the SNP thus went into the February 1974 election riding higher than they had ever been before.

In many ways, indeed, the party had a stronger base than the Liberals. In North Sea oil it had a powerful emotional rallying-cry. The Labour Party north of the border was demoralized and in many constituencies its organization was very weak. Scottish Conservatism was in decline. With very little serious Liberal challenge in many Scottish constituencies, the SNP stood a strong chance of polling well and, with its vote concentrated, of actually winning several seats.

THE OIL CRISIS AND THE MINERS' STRIKE

The Conservative government entered their last and most bitter period as 1973 ended. The battleground was the conflict with the trade unions over Stage Three of the counter-inflation policy. This conflict led to a historic confrontation between the miners and the Heath government – and, in the last resort, to the defeat of the government in the February 1974 election. It was a confrontation made all the more serious by the Arab–Israeli war and the subsequent oil embargo.

The details of Stage Three of the counter-inflation policy were announced on 8 October 1973. Price controls were similar to those under Stage Two. Wage increases negotiated for any groups of workers would be statutorily limited to an average of either £2·35 a week per head or, if preferred, 7 per cent per head, with a limit of £350 a year on the amount to be received by any one individual. In addition, certain further increases were permitted for such categories as efficiency and productivity schemes, work done in 'unsocial hours' and progress towards equal pay for women. A new feature of the pay policy was the proposal of a 'threshold agreement' to safeguard against possible increases in the cost of living (an experiment that had already been successfully used in Canada). This threshold, of up to 40p per week was to be payable if the Retail Price Index reached 7 per cent above its level at the start of Stage Three, with a further 40p per week for each additional percentage increase thereafter. In fact, under Stage Three, the threshold was triggered no less than eleven times, giving an extra £4·40 per week to the estimated 10 million workers in the scheme.

Stage Three came into force at a time of rapid changes in the economic situation. In the aftermath of the Arab–Israeli war of October 1973 problems arose in the supply of oil, on which Britain depended for 50 per cent of her energy. First, the Arab oil producers decided to boycott some countries and to restrict supplies to most others. British imports were cut by 15 per cent. Shortages of petrol produced panic among many motorists, leading to long queues and even violent scenes at some garages. The Government took the precaution of issuing ration coupons but managed to avoid introducing rationing, relying instead on voluntary restraint. At the same time as reducing supplies, all the oil exporting countries decided to increase the price of crude oil dramatically. The swift succession of price increases meant that Britain's oil import bill abruptly increased to something like four times its former level, with disastrous implications for an already grim balance-of-payments situation.

The crisis was all the more serious because in recent years the country's dependence on oil had been steadily and deliberately increased, while dependence on coal, a home-produced resource, had been diminished. The miners' union had all along condemned the pit-closure programme as dangerously short-sighted, but the Labour government, supported by other parties, favoured the continuation of the closure policy, and the miners' complaints were widely dismissed as so much special pleading.

In November 1973 the National Union of Mineworkers (NUM) decided to implement a ban on overtime and weekend working in support of a pay claim in excess of Stage Three. The rapidly deteriorating fuel situation was aggravated by an out-of-hours ban by electricity power engineers, which limited the ability of the Central Electricity Generating Board to cope with shortages at various power stations. Consequently on 13 November the Government declared a State of Emergency. Minimum lending rate (MLR), the successor to bank rate, was raised from $11\frac{1}{4}$ per cent to 13 per cent in a drastic move. Orders were issued restricting space heating by electricity, except in the home and certain other places, and prohibiting the use of electricity for advertising, displays or flood-lighting. The position worsened still further following the decision of the Amalgamated Society of Locomotive Engineers and Firemen (ASLEF) to ban Sunday, overtime and rest-day working. This had the effect of disrupting the delivery of coal to power stations as well as causing a considerable amount of inconvenience to passengers, especially in the South East.

The Government refused to make an offer to the miners outside the terms of Stage Three and were therefore compelled to introduce a package of tougher measures to deal with the crisis. Most important, as from 1 January electricity was only provided to industry on three specified days per week. In addition, a 50 m.p.h. speed limit was introduced on all roads, a maximum heating limit was imposed on all commercial premises and offices and television was required to close down at 10.30 p.m. each evening. The Chancellor of the Exchequer further announced large cuts in expenditure (amounting to £1,200 million) and tighter controls on consumer credit in an attempt to restore confidence in the Government.

A succession of attempts to settle the dispute, and so avert the enormous losses in industrial production and export trade which must inevitably follow, all came to nothing. Over Christmas there had been hope – encouraged by statements from the Employment Minister, William Whitelaw, in the Commons – that a way could be found by paying the miners for the time they spent changing before a shift and washing when the shift was over. That failed: the Pay Board ruled that this was not part of standard working hours by custom and practice, so to pay for it would breach Stage Three. There were also various attempts to construct a formula based on the special health and danger hazards of the job. The Government fully accepted that these should be recognized; but they wanted a Stage Three settlement first. Then on 9 January, at a meeting of the National Economic Development Council, the TUC made an unexpected offer. It said: 'The General Council accept that there is a distinctive and exceptional situation in the mining industry. If the Government are prepared to give the assurance that they will make possible a settlement between the miners and the National Coal Board, other unions will not use that as an argument in negotiations for their own settlements.' There was a two-hour discussion on this proposal in the NEDC meeting, and the Chancellor, Anthony Barber, appeared to rule it out completely. So, at first, did the Prime Minister, who was opening a debate in the Commons, which had been recalled to discuss the three-day week. But, as the exchanges continued, he seemed to soften. Next day, in a statement to the Commons, Heath said he had asked the TUC leaders to come to talk to him that evening.

There was still a wide gap between what Heath wanted and what the TUC had offered. After two and a half hours of wary discussion at No. 10 on the same night, the Government and the TUC agreed to resume on the following Monday. This time the TUC arrived armed with a promise of a special conference, to be held on the coming Wednesday, at which heads of individual unions would be asked to underwrite the pledge already made by the TUC. The meeting ran for five and a half hours without reaching agreement.

The TUC got the endorsement it wanted at its special conference at Congress House on Wednesday 16 January, when only two groups – the foundry workers and the journalists – failed to back the TUC offer. But there remained a deep scepticism on the government side, among the employers and among Conservative back-benchers as to how much the TUC offer was worth. By now the main theme of conversation at Westminster was not so much the credibility of the TUC's position as the likelihood of an immediate general election on the issue: 'Who governs Britain?'

Alarmed as they were by the menace of the miners, industrialists were if anything more alarmed by the likely consequences of a continued three-day week. The effect would be cumulative, as week by week firms were thrown more and more out of gear by the consequences of each other's problems. Both in the Cabinet and throughout the Conservative Party there was a school which saw a general election as the one way to break the deadlock. As early as 4 January Lord Carrington hinted that the Government might be forced to hold a snap election, even though he did not in any way indicate that he regarded this as desirable. At Westminster all eyes were fixed on 17 January, the day after the TUC's special conference. If Heath were to move then, he could fix polling day for 7 February – the date most hawks favoured, since to wait longer would run the risk that, as the three-day week bit deeper and deeper, the Government would become even more unpopular than the miners. Support for an election had risen in the Parliamentary Party over the week, and the 1922 Committee meeting on 17 January clearly indicated that many MPs were now impatient to go to the country.

But Heath hesitated. The day's Cabinet meeting came and went, with no sign of an election announcement. The balance of opinion in the Cabinet was clearly very even; but it was a Cabinet very much dominated by the Prime Minister, and he had thrown his weight on the side of those like the Employment Minister, William Whitelaw, who counselled holding back and giving negotiation a further chance. Then on Monday 21 January the TUC's self-denying formula was rejected by the Cabinet. The Government (in their own eyes) had done all they reasonably could to reach a settlement; the TUC, equally, felt that they had done all they could to limit the consequences of a special settlement for the miners. But the miners had not moved at all. They already had before them an offer which went to the limit of what the nation could afford, and which was coupled with the promise of discussion on the future of the industry, including a generous recognition of the special problems of its workforce. The Government could go no further to meet the miners' case: they should settle on what had been offered to them.

By now a new threat had appeared. On 8 January Lord Carrington had been moved from Defence to take charge of a new energy department. On 17 January he was predicting a major relaxation of power restrictions and a possible switch from a three- to a four-day week. The announcement was greeted on the Opposition side with incredulity, followed by black suspicion, but clearly the Government meant business. In the talks with the TUC on 21 January Heath laid before the union leaders the option of a four-day week or a five-day week on 80 per cent supplies. Perhaps the pit strike was not hitting the nation so hard, after all. Inevitably there was quick and tough response from the NUM. On 23 January the three top officials of the union – the president, Joe

Gormley, the general secretary, Lawrence Daly, and the Scottish miners' president, Mick MacGahey – agreed to ask their executive to ballot the membership on an all-out strike.

At the same time there was the publication on 24 January of a Pay Board report on relativities, the differences in the pay levels of various groups within industry. The Board had concluded that a procedure was needed within the counter-inflation policy for ensuring that some groups could resolve their relativity problems while ensuring that everyone else did not immediately follow suit. The Government's initial response, however, seemed peculiarly discouraging, especially since on 27 January the Board's deputy chairman, Derek Robinson, the man mainly responsible for compiling the report, stated that it could be implemented very quickly and could be used to settle the miners' dispute. But within a couple of days the Government suddenly began to look deeply interested after all. The Coal Board, too, was eager to start talking. On 28 January, and again the next day, Heath declared the Government's readiness to get discussions started on the report. He now seemed to see the relativities report as a way of creating exactly the situation which he had wanted in his earlier talks with the TUC.

For the left in the Parliamentary Labour Party and for the trade unions, this was confirmation of a fear they were already expressing: that the relativities solution was a trap. It would end with the unions agreeing to acquiesce in Stage Three except when the government-appointed Board said otherwise: a clear reversal of everything the unions had said until now. Thus by the time Heath came back to the House on Thursday 31 January the picture had changed completely. Now it was he who was emphasizing the urgency of getting talks moving and Wilson who was counselling caution.

On Friday 1 February the TUC agreed to meet the Prime Minister for talks on the relativities formula, though Len Murray spoke of 'serious doubts' about it, and Lawrence Daly said they would not entertain any meeting with the Prime Minister unless there was cash at the end of it. But the Government would go no further, and the talks duly foundered. The TUC wanted cash on the table for the miners; the Government said they had made all the concessions they could make; there could be no new offer to the NUM.

That looked like deadlock: and the election talk, which had never died down, now reached a crescendo. But still the Government – in their search for a settlement, according to their supporters, and in their campaign to win public opinion, according to the sceptics – had one more card to play. Against the advice of Len Murray, the miners' leaders were asked to come to Downing Street next morning.

Earlier in the day the results of the miners' ballot had been announced: they showed an 81 per cent vote to authorize the Executive to call a strike. The offer to come to Downing Street was not taken up – there was no assurance of cash on the table. The NUM Executive then declared that the miners would be out on strike from the following Saturday, 9 February.

THE GENERAL ELECTION OF FEBRUARY 1974

Clearly, Heath could now delay no longer: on 7 February it was announced that the nation would go to the polls on the 28th. In the extraordinary setting of the State of Emergency and a three-day week (though the television curfew was lifted so that viewers should not be denied their diet of concentrated politics), the campaign began, with universal predictions that it would be the hardest, cruellest, dirtiest contest on record.

Heath's strategy throughout remained exactly as he had outlined it in his opening broadcast. He defined the issue, and it was on that issue that the British people must cast their votes. He summarized it most succinctly on 12 February. The choice before the nation was

whether this country is now going to return a strong government with a firm mandate for the next five years to deal with the counter-inflation policy . . . a firm incomes policy, which Parliament will approve. The challenge is to the will of Parliament and a democratically elected government.

The same theme was vigorously pursued in the party manifesto, *Firm Action for a Fair Britain*. 'The choice before the nation today, as never before,' it proclaimed, 'is a choice between moderation and extremism.' The Conservatives offered firmness against the overwhelming demands of the unions. They would amend the social security system to see that the taxpayer no longer had to subsidize strikers and their families while union funds were left undisturbed. But the Conservatives offered fairness, too: they would introduce reviews of pensions twice yearly instead of once; they would introduce changes in the Industrial Relations Act to see there was conciliation before legal action; they would enhance the powers of the Price Commission. During the campaign, indeed, Heath represented the Conservative government as the union of all those groups who had no union to protect them, but suffered the results of the demands made by the unions on behalf of those who had. The Conservative campaign thus showed a peculiar blend of aggression and moderation.

The Labour strategy was to prevent Heath at all costs from choosing the ground for the contest. But the party had a difficult defensive action to fight. They needed to show the electorate that they were moderate and responsible people who could get the country out of the mess in which the Conservative administration and the harsh facts of world politics had jointly dumped it. Gradually they developed a persuasive theme: Labour had got the country out of its mess in 1964–70 and left it financially strong. Now Labour was ready to take on that thankless job again.

If the Conservatives looked to be the victors in the first week, there was hope on the Labour side that the tide could soon be turned. There were, Labour knew, some formidable natural obstacles between Heath and the winning post, just as there had been for Wilson in 1970. Adverse trade figures had helped turn Labour out then: perhaps the crop of economic indicators now due to be published could do the same to the Conservatives. The first of these indicators appeared on Friday 15th, when the index of retail prices showed a 20p in the pound rise in food prices over the previous twelve months. The unemployment figures, expected to be a dreadful testimony to the destructive effects of the three-day week, were not as bad as had been feared. But there was no escaping the trade figures which appeared on the final Monday of the campaign, 25 February. This was the biggest monthly deficit in history, and it would have been deeply serious even had there been no rise in the price of oil.

To add to Conservative problems came another bombshell. Right at the start of the campaign came the defection of Enoch Powell. Having declared the issue to be bogus and the election to be immoral, he wrote to his constituency chairman on the day of the dissolution saying he would not stand. Late in the campaign, however, Powell appeared twice on anti-Market platforms, at Birmingham and at Saltaire in Yorkshire. In a fine theatrical *coup* two days before the election Powell was able to show his supporters that he was as good as his word: he had arranged a postal vote in Wolverhampton, and now he was able to tell a television interviewer that he had already voted Labour.

Still more serious was the production of new figures by the Pay Board, now busy examining the miners' pay claim, which appeared to show that the earnings level of the miners, in relation to the national average earnings, had been overrated in the past. The impression immediately got about that the Board had discovered a long-standing error, and the miners' claim had been rejected on grounds now shown to have been wrong.

Also the same day came the startling statement by the CBI director-general, Campbell Adamson, that the Industrial Relations Act introduced by the Conservatives had 'sullied every relationship at every level between unions and employers and ought to be repealed rather than amended'. Even more damaging was his remark that a Conservative victory would not solve the country's problems. In retrospect it seems that the campaign turned in Labour's favour on the Thursday and Friday before the last weekend, that is, 21 and 22 February. In that case, the Adamson affair may not have been decisive, but the pit pay controversy probably was.

While Conservative and Labour politicians were embroiled in the fight, for the Liberal and Nationalist Parties the February election offered a unique opportunity. Never before had the Liberals faced an election when riding so high in the opinion polls. Never had the opportunity to transform a by-election revival into a general election breakthrough seemed so possible. An immediate consequence of this Liberal and Nationalist optimism was seen in the nominations. Of the 2,135 candidates nominated, no less than 517 were Liberals, the highest total the party had ever fielded (exceeding the 513 brought forward in 1929 and the 475 who contested the 1950 election). All thirty-six seats in Wales were contested by Plaid Cymru, whilst the SNP fought all but one of the seats in Scotland.

The main lines of the Liberal manifesto followed the resolutions adopted at the 1973 Annual Conference. The party laid much emphasis on a permanent prices and incomes policy backed by penalties on those whose actions caused inflation. Among other proposals were a statutory minimum earnings level; profit-sharing in industry; a credit income tax to replace the means test and existing allowances; pensions of two thirds average industrial earnings for married couples; a Bill of Rights; the replacement of the Housing Finance Act; and a permanent Royal Commission to advise Parliament on energy policy.

The election campaign was bitter. The stakes could not have been higher. And, in the event, the electors produced a result that had never been seen in post-war politics. For the first time since 1929 the election gave no party an overall majority.

The balance of power lay with the small parties: besides the Liberals, the Ulster Loyalists won eleven seats, the Scottish National Party seven, Plaid Cymru two, the Social Democratic and Labour Party one, and two Independent Labour MPs were elected – Dick Taverne at Lincoln and Eddie Milne at Blyth. Some 78·8 per cent of the electorate had voted, reversing the trend of declining turn-outs but still below the record polls of 84·5 per cent in 1950 and 82·6 per cent in 1951.

The results were a disaster for the Tories, who had lost 1·2 million votes despite the higher poll and forfeited thirty-six seats compared with 1970. The Labour Party polled 500,000 fewer votes than in 1970, losing less to the Liberals and Nationalists than did the Tories and thus regaining some of the seats lost in 1970. Although the Labour share of the vote dropped by 5·8 per cent, the Tory share fell by 8·3 per cent; altogether the Labour Party received its lowest share of votes since 1931 and the Tories received less support in 1974 than they had done for over fifty years. Perhaps the nearest parallel to the 1974 result was that of 1929. Then, Conservative and Labour between them polled 75·2 per cent of all votes cast and the outcome was also a minority Labour government.

Party	Votes gained	Percentage of vote	Average vote per MP	Number of MPs
Conservative	11,868,906	37·9	39,963	297
Labour	11,639,243	37·1	38,669	301
Liberal	6,063,470	19·3	433,105	14
Plaid Cymru	171,364	0·6	85,682	2
SNP	632,032	2·0	90,290	7
Others (GB)	240,665	0·8		2
Others (NI)*	717,986	2·3		12
	31,333,666	100·0		635

* For this election no candidates in Northern Ireland are included in the major party totals.
Source: Derived from D. Butler and A. Sloman, *British Political Facts, 1900–75.*

By far the chief beneficiaries of the decline in Conservative and Labour support were the Liberals and Nationalists. The performance of the Liberals was perhaps the single most outstanding feature of the February election. Having entered the contest with their highest hopes for a generation, they came out of the battle with a staggering 6 million votes. But in only a few seats was the Liberal total good enough to run the winners close – mostly in Conservative-held seats. In only fourteen Conservative-held seats were Liberals within 4,000 votes of victory, whilst the Labour citadels had hardly suffered at all from the Liberal advance. The only tangible Liberal gains were Cardiganshire and Colne Valley (from Labour), Bodmin and the Isle of Wight (from the Tories), and the new seat of Hazel Grove, won by the former Liberal MP for Cheadle, Michael Winstanley.

Unlike the Liberals, the Scottish National Party came out of the election with a dramatic increase in its parliamentary representation. The party had entered the election defending two seats (Western Isles and Glasgow Govan). Although Govan was lost to Labour, the SNP returned seven members to Parliament, a major success for a party that had never won a single seat in a general election until 1970. These gains were mainly at the expense of the Tories, who went down to defeat in Argyll, Moray and Nairn, Banff, and Aberdeenshire East, while Labour lost Stirlingshire East and Clackmannan and also Dundee East. Several of the SNP victories were little short of spectacular, although the SNP failed to make any real impression in Glasgow or Edinburgh. Overall, the SNP had every reason for satisfaction. Compared with 11·4 per cent of the Scottish vote in 1970, they obtained 21·9 per cent on this occasion. Only six deposits were lost (compared with forty-three in 1970) and, with its best results in exactly those areas most affected by the impact of the North Sea oil boom, the February 1974 election provided the SNP with a potential springboard for a further major parliamentary advance.

The stalemate results of the election provided Heath with an acute problem. Although the Conservatives had fared badly, no other party had an overall majority. Heath did not offer his resignation immediately, but entered into discussions with Jeremy Thorpe, the Liberal Leader, to see if the basis existed for a working arrangement. During the weekend of 1–4 March the nation awaited the outcome of these talks. After internal soundings of the party, Thorpe declined any arrangement. This was a very significant moment, since the failure of these talks weakened the Conservatives throughout 1974. For when Wilson came to form his administration he knew that a majority in the Commons for an anti-Labour government was unlikely.

Hence, after one of the most dramatic confrontations in British politics and an election result unheard of since 1929, Labour returned to power. For Heath, the politics of confrontation had ended in failure.

THE HEATH GOVERNMENT: AN ASSESSMENT

On 18 June 1970 Edward Heath had won a great personal victory. In less than four years he had lost office, with many of his most fundamental policies either reversed or abandoned and with the electorate divided and confused. The government that had seemed set to give Britain a new sense of purpose left a nation in the throes of a three-day week and amid a scene of industrial bitterness perhaps unparalleled since the General Strike of 1926.

What might appear to be a verdict of total failure is not, however, a fair assessment. Neither Heath nor his government could have foreseen the Yom Kippur War nor the oil crisis which followed in its wake. Nor could they be blamed for failing to see the enormous rise in commodity prices – the main worries on the international economy when Heath took office concerned the American balance-of-payments deficit. However, whilst these international factors could not be blamed on the Government, the question still remains whether Heath's overall strategy in 1973 was correct and whether his handling of individual issues – particularly labour relations – was wise.

Here the verdict on the Government must be critical. They lacked weight and experience – a legacy in part of Iain Macleod's untimely death. Secondly, they lacked patience. Such moves as the abolition of the Industrial Reorganization Corporation and the Prices and Incomes Board were over-hasty – the Government had to create new institutions at a later date. The 'lame-duck' policy, applied so rigidly, met immediate problems with the crisis in Rolls Royce and Upper Clyde Shipbuilders. In this sense, part of the criticism must not be in Heath's intentions, but in his methods, his timing and his style. The brisk and challenging image he projected helped alienate many potential supporters.

In the constitutional history of post-war Britain, the country's entry into the Common Market will, of course, be judged of supreme importance. Heath's premiership also witnessed important attempts to change the structure of government, which must be taken into consideration in any overall assessment. But even these successes are overshadowed by Heath's failure to come to terms with the trade unions.

During the period of the Heath administration it became very apparent that there had been a fundamental shift of power towards the unions. As the economic commentator of the *Financial Times* put it in a famous phrase, the unions were 'the robber barons of the system'. To many, they were the root cause of national decline – on the one hand pursuing inflation with excessive wage demands and at the same time resisting technological progress. Attitudes within the trade union movement towards their role in society had been changing, too, for some time: the succession of Hugh Scanlon, a noted left-winger, as General Secretary of the AEU in 1967, was an important landmark in this respect, as was the replacement of Frank Cousins by Jack Jones as General Secretary of the Transport and General Workers' Union. The new power and influence of the trade unions in society had been underlined before Heath came into office, when Wilson and Castle failed to put *In Place of Strife* on the statute book. The irony was that it was Heath's attempts to shackle this power which finally confirmed it beyond doubt: the events of 1970–74, from the mass picketing at Saltley to the last confrontation with the miners, established the position of the 'Fourth Estate'.

THE RETURN OF
HAROLD WILSON, 1974–6

Wilson became Prime Minister again on 4 March, at the head of the first minority Labour government since 1931. As in 1964, he acted swiftly and decisively, determined that Labour would govern as if they had a majority. There would be no retreat from the election manifesto and no alliances with other groups. There was no point in compromise, since any rebuff in the House of Commons could be met with an appeal to the country – and Wilson also knew that the other parties would be reluctant to force another election immediately.

The new Cabinet showed a mixture of old and new faces: Callaghan went to the Foreign Office, Jenkins was at the Home Office and Denis Healey was given the crucial job of Chancellor. Among the more surprising appointments, Michael Foot became Secretary of State for Employment and Wedgwood Benn became Secretary for Industry. For the first time in British history, the Cabinet contained two women members – Barbara Castle at Social Security and Shirley Williams in the new post of Secretary of State for Prices and Consumer Protection. The Cabinet was again a balanced mix of left- and right-wingers.

The whole of the 1974 parliament was dominated by the prospect of another general election, and it was indeed inevitable, once Wilson had ruled out a coalition with any other group, that another election would have to follow very soon. Wilson himself appears to have decided at a very early stage that it should be in the autumn.

Within a few days of the first Cabinet meeting of 5 March, the miners' strike was settled and the three-day week and the state of emergency came to an end. The Pay Board was abolished, and the policy of compulsory wage restraint finally ended in July 1974. The Price Code and the Price Commission were, however, retained. An immediate freeze was imposed on all rents, while a Queen's Speech was drafted that promised pension increases, stricter price controls, and food subsidies. Among other decisions was the ending of the much-criticized entry charge for museums (which the Conservatives had imposed) and the speedy abandonment of controversial plans for a third London airport at Maplin. Initial moves were also put in progress to end the Channel Tunnel project, but Concorde was allowed to go ahead.

In other areas, also, the Government seemed to be acting with purpose and determination. In deference to left-wing antagonism to the ruling military juntas in Greece and Chile, naval visits to these two countries were cancelled in March. In April Reg Prentice (the Secretary for Education) acted to speed the shift towards comprehensive education and Anthony Crosland as Secretary for the Environment took measures to discourage the sale of council houses. Labour had less success in its attempts to restore the £10 million in taxation and in pension funds to those unions who had refused to acknowledge the Industrial Relations Act – and in the end the Government suffered a parliamentary defeat on this question.

LABOUR, THE SOCIAL CONTRACT AND THE ECONOMY

This activity, though important, masked the crucial issue before the country: the state of the economy and in particular the vital problem of inflation. The indices for 1974 told their own story: during the six months of the 1974 parliament prices rose by 8 per cent and wages by 16 per cent. The Financial Times Share Index, which had stood at 313 on 1 March, had fallen to 202 by 20 September – a larger decline in the real value of shares since 1972 than had happened after the Great Crash of 1929. Nor were these phenomena confined to Britain. Throughout the world, stock markets were collapsing and prices soaring. It was this crisis, or rather Heath's handling of it, that had brought Wilson back to power, and now Wilson's handling of it would determine if Labour itself stayed in power. Wilson and the Government put their faith in the Social Contract.

During the election campaign an agreement between the Labour Party and the TUC had been announced – the Social Contract. The Labour Party hope was that, in return for such measures as the repeal of the 1972 Industrial Relations Act, food subsidies and a freeze on rent increases, the TUC would be able to persuade its members to cooperate in a programme of voluntary wage restraint. In this way it was hoped to avoid the strains caused by formal incomes policies, which had always appeared to trade unionists to leave them without any role to play. Under a voluntary system they could still do their job – that is, bargain about wage rates. The terms of the contract were that there should be a twelve-month interval between wage settlements, and that negotiated increases should be confined either to compensating for price increases since the last settlement, or for anticipated future price increases before the next settlement. An attempt by the TUC's General Secretary to tighten up the interpretation of the contract, so that nothing was generally allowed apart from compensation for past increases, was unsuccessful.

The Government's faith in the Social Contract underlay the budget tactics planned by Healey at the Exchequer. During this short parliament, the Chancellor introduced two budgets: on 24 March and 22 July. The first, presented only three weeks after returning to power, was only mildly deflationary in its intended effect on demand. Taxation was to be raised by about £1,500 million. The standard rate of income tax was raised by 3p to 33p in the pound, and the income at which higher rates were to be paid was lowered; but personal tax allowances and child allowances were increased, excise taxes on alcoholic drinks and cigarettes were raised, and VAT was introduced on petrol, sweets, soft drinks and ice cream. Corporation tax was raised to 52 per cent, and employers were to pay a higher flat-rate contribution to finance the higher National Insurance benefits announced in the budget. The main forms of additional planned expenditure were higher retirement pensions, £500 million additional subsidies on basic foodstuffs, and provision for an expanded local authority housing programme. The Chancellor announced very large increases in the prices of coal, electricity, steel, postage and rail fares, in order to reduce the growing need for State subsidy of these nationalized industries.

As it turned out, subsidies were not run down as intended. Healey's budget had in fact added seriously to the liquidity problems facing many companies. This, plus warnings from such key economic advisers as Harold Lever (created a Life Peer in 1979) that the danger of a serious recession was increasing, led to Healey's second budget, on 22 July. This time the package was mildly expansionary. VAT was reduced from 10 per cent to 8 per cent. Additional rate reliefs were introduced. The Regional

Employment Premium was doubled and dividend controls were eased. (In fact, yet another supplementary budget came in November, to bring tax relief to companies which were suffering heavy taxation on 'paper profits'.)

Given the political situation at the time, these budgets were tactical rather than strategic measures. After October 1974 the weaknesses of both the Social Contract and Healey's budgets became more obvious as the economic indices worsened. But in 1974 it must be admitted Healey had little enough room for manoeuvre. On the industrial front there was mounting anxiety at the prospect of serious union rebellion against the Government's economic policies. For despite the 'Social Contract' and the prospect that the new government would enjoy a period of industrial peace, there was a series of unofficial strikes. Thus although in April, the engineering union, led by Hugh Scanlon, refrained from pressing a £10 a week pay claim, there was almost constant industrial trouble in the motor industry. In May, widespread disruption occurred on the railways as a result of action by the locomen, led by Ray Buckton, and in July there was a prolonged strike by hospital workers. Like the Government, the unions also had their eye on an autumn election and to some extent militancy was restricted by this consideration. But these industrial troubles were portents of coming strains in the Social Contract.

THE OPPOSITION IN THE SHORT PARLIAMENT

Heath's defeat in the February election had meant a profound shift of power not only between the parties but within them. Inside the Tory Party criticism of Heath's leadership was mounting, and it was only the imminence of another general election which deferred serious moves to oust him. Meanwhile Labour as well as Conservatives were keeping an anxious eye on the Liberals and Nationalists, whose gains in February had been made at the expense of both major parties.

With the advent of a minority Labour government, and with it the probability of an early second general election, it was imperative for the Liberals and Nationalists to maintain their momentum. For the Scottish Nationalists this was a considerably easier task than for the Liberals. Oil and devolution continued to occupy much political attention, and both issues clearly aided the SNP. The party received a further boost when, after its success in February, it was joined by its most distinguished recruit so far, Sir Hugh Fraser, the Scottish millionaire.

Further evidence of increased support for the SNP came in the May local elections. Although Labour easily dominated the cities, and did especially well in Strathclyde, the SNP achieved some successes. At Cumbernauld it secured an overall majority. In East Kilbride it finished as the largest single party, whilst it took second place in many Glasgow seats. These were significant results, for they showed the party's growing appeal in the new towns and in areas such as Clydeside which had been Labour for a generation. Meanwhile they probably benefited also from the increasing discussion in the Tory ranks over devolution. At the Conservative Party Conference in Ayr during May, Edward Heath had launched a major five-point plan for Scotland which he pledged a future Conservative Government would introduce. Its proposals included the creation of a Scottish Development Fund to deal with the new environmental problems brought by oil and the establishment of a Scottish Assembly. Heath's proposals were immediately attacked by SNP chairman William Wolfe as 'half-baked'; he added: 'The people of Scotland are in no mood to be bought off by the broken leader of a discredited party.'

These were confident words; but the SNP had every reason for confidence, for the Nationalist tide was clearly flowing strongly in Scotland. In England, on the other hand, the Liberals were not finding the political course so easy. An invitation from Heath for Thorpe to support a Conservative administration (which met vociferous opposition from a majority of leading Liberals) had only served to emphasize how the party could indulge in fratricidal warfare if talk of coalition was not handled very carefully. Moreover, although Liberal support in the opinion polls held relatively steady during 1974, the absence of by-election contests prevented the Liberals from getting any renewed momentum going. As it turned out, the two most significant happenings for the Liberals during this short parliament were the launching of a 'coalition campaign' and the defection of Christopher Mayhew from Labour.

The Liberal coalition campaign was launched in a party political broadcast on 25 June by David Steel, the party's Chief Whip. The broadcast, with its appeal for a 'Government of National Unity', stated that Liberals would be 'ready and willing to participate in such a government if at the next election you give us the power to do so'. In an ITV interview the same evening Thorpe stated that such a Government of National Unity 'reflects the views of millions of people'.

Thorpe may have been right. But within the Liberal Party the coalition plan was not received with total approval. Ruth Addison, the Young Liberal chairman, attacked the scheme as ludicrous. Radical candidates, who needed Labour votes to win Tory-held county seats, were equally sceptical. The fact that a Government of National Unity would almost certainly not include any significant part of the Labour Party also tended to diminish the whole political realism of the scheme.

In July, however, Liberal attempts to foster a realignment in politics achieved a marked step forward with the defection of Christopher Mayhew, a former Labour minister and MP for Woolwich East, to the Liberal ranks. His defection increased the number of Liberal MPs from fourteen to fifteen and was accompanied by very wide press coverage. But those who expected further defections from sitting Labour members were to be disappointed. Meanwhile, the Liberals began frenetic activity to revitalize derelict constituency associations so that the party could fight virtually every constituency in the coming election. By the late summer of 1974, both Liberals and Nationalists were prepared for the largest-ever assault on the two-party system, whenever the election might be called.

THE OCTOBER 1974 ELECTION

Despite the Government's success in exploiting their weak parliamentary position, it had become clear during the summer that they would seek a new mandate from the electorate at the earliest opportunity. The summer was very noticeable for the large number of statements of policy to emanate from the Government. Meanwhile, the Labour Party remained ahead in the opinion polls. The signs were right for Wilson and in September 1974 he took the plunge. The Dissolution of Parliament announced on 20 September 1974 ended the shortest parliament since 1681. Parliament had been opened by the Queen on 11 March and had lasted a mere 184 days. For only the second time this century, two general elections had occurred within the same year.

A record number of candidates (2,252, compared to 2,135 in February) was nominated for the 10 October election. This figure, the highest ever, was partly explained by the 619 Liberals fielded in October – a rise of 102 on the February total, and an all-time record for the party. Every seat in England and Wales (except for Lincoln) was contested by a Liberal. Only Argyll, Glasgow Provan and Fife Central were not fought by Liberals in Scotland. Another party to greatly increase its tally of candidates was the National Front, who nominated ninety candidates compared to fifty-four in February, partly emboldened by municipal election successes in areas of high immigrant concentrations. Yet there was little new or unexpected in the campaign. Labour urged the electorate to give it a majority to finish the job on which it had embarked, while the Conservatives were still partly on the defensive after February.

Despite widespread predictions that Labour would win with a comfortable majority, the result proved to be yet another cliff-hanger. As more and more Conservative-held marginal seats stubbornly defied the swing to Labour, computer forecasts of Labour's eventual overall majority came lower and lower. The final result was as follows:

Party	Votes gained	Percentage of vote	Average vote per MP	Number of MPs
Conservative	10,464,817	35·9	37,779	277
Labour	11,457,079	39·2	35,916	319
Liberal	5,346,754	18·3	411,289	13
Plaid Cymru	166,321	0·6	55,440	3
SNP	839,617	2·9	76,329	11
Others (GB)	212,496	0·7	—	—
Others (NI)*	702,094	2·4	—	12
	29,189,178	100·0		635

* For this election no candidates in Northern Ireland are included in the major party totals.

Source: Derived from D. Butler and A. Sloman, *British Political Facts, 1900–75*.

Labour's majority, though even smaller than the photo-finish result of 1964, was in fact, in terms of practical politics, considerably more comfortable than it appeared. Over the Conservatives Labour's majority was a healthy forty-three, while Labour's majority over Conservatives and Liberals combined was still thirty. In all, Labour gained nineteen seats, for the loss of only one constituency (Carmarthen) to Plaid Cymru. The Conservatives suffered twenty-two losses with only two gains – Hazel Grove and Bodmin, both taken from the Liberals. The Scottish Nationalists gained four seats (all from the Conservatives). Over the whole country, Labour achieved a swing of 2·2 per cent from Conservative. If this swing had occurred uniformly in each constituency,

Labour would have achieved an overall majority of twenty-five, but in fact they could only achieve a small swing of 1·2 per cent in the key Conservative-held marginals that they needed to win.

The October election reinforced the division of England into two nations: the Tory shires and the Labour cities. The Conservatives had rarely returned fewer MPs for the big cities whilst Labour were further than ever from making inroads into the counties. In the fifty most agricultural seats, Labour achieved a swing of only 1·6 per cent. Labour's only loss at the election (Carmarthen) was its most agricultural seat, whilst the only Tory marginal seat actually to swing Conservative was Norfolk North West, one of the most agricultural seats in the country.

Particular interest in the results of October 1974 centred round the Liberal and Nationalist challenge. As we have seen, the 'third parties' entered the contest in a mood of optimism and at times euphoria. The Liberals, fortified by 6 million votes in February, and with a massive field of 619 candidates, were in buoyant mood. When, however, the results were announced, it was the Scottish Nationalists who had achieved the most substantial advance. Thus SNP representation increased from seven to eleven (and Plaid Cymru went up from two to three), but the Liberals fell back from fifteen (if Christopher Mayhew is included) to thirteen. Even so, Liberal and Nationalist representation combined was higher even than the twenty-one seats won by Liberals in 1935. The Liberals managed only a solitary gain in October 1974 (at Truro), for the loss of two seats to the Conservatives, and the reversion of Woolwich East (Mayhew's former constituency) to Labour.

Meanwhile, the Liberal vote had fallen from the 19·3 per cent won in February to 18·3 per cent in October. The relatively small apparent decrease tended to disguise the fact that, with 102 more candidates than in February, their vote in most constituencies had fallen quite considerably. In 93 per cent of constituencies contested by Liberals on both occasions, the Liberal share of the vote declined. The party had lost its momentum and faced the prospect of a difficult period under a new Labour government.

LABOUR, INFLATION AND THE ECONOMY

The extremely close Labour victory was not at all what Wilson had wanted – for it was likely to mean that in the near future by-election losses, to say nothing of defections, would produce a minority government. Wilson, however, went on as if all was well and the Government's legislative programme was outlined in the Queen's Speech on 19 November. Most of the proposals were expected. They included legislation for a development land tax, the phasing-out of private practice from the National Health Service, the extension of the dock labour scheme to inland depots and the abolition of selection in secondary education. Many of these proposals – particularly on 'pay beds' and comprehensive education – were bitterly attacked by the Conservative Opposition. But the most far-reaching proposal in the Queen's Speech was the promise of legislation – albeit on a very protracted timetable – to establish Scottish and Welsh assemblies.

All these proposals presupposed that the Government could win the battle of the economy, where inflation was the key factor. And whereas in 1972–3 the rate of inflation had been 9·2 per cent, between 1973 and 1974 it was 16 per cent and between 1974 and 1975 it was 24·1 per cent. By 1975 retail prices were 150 per cent higher than they had been in 1963. Apart from a temporary slowdown following the July budget, the rate of inflation had accelerated fairly steadily through 1974 as a whole; and whereas import prices had been the fastest-growing item of costs for the two years up to the middle of 1974, by then domestic wage and salary costs had taken over this role. Average earnings increased by no less than 25 per cent between the fourth quarters of 1973 and 1974, and since productivity growth was very slow, this meant a 23 per cent rise in labour costs. However, government policy had some effect in dampening down the rate of inflation, both through the operation of the Price Code and through increased subsidies.

Wilson faced a most difficult situation. The year had seen a simultaneous failure to meet all four main policy targets – of adequate economic growth, full employment, a stable balance of payments and stable prices. The volume of consumer spending fell for the first time in twenty years, and by January 1975 over 700,000 people were unemployed, over 140,000 more than at the beginning of the previous year. Despite this, the balance-of-payments deficit on current account was the largest ever recorded and retail prices in January 1975 had rocketed over the previous year. Moreover, the wages policy within the 'Social Contract' was increasingly seen not to be working.

By early 1975 it was evident that this policy had failed completely.

Some wage settlements were of the order of 30 per cent. Hence the budget introduced by Denis Healey on 15 April 1975 was, in his own words, 'rough and tough'. It was certainly stringent. The Chancellor announced that he planned to cut back the public deficit to 8 per cent of national output in 1975–6 and to 6 per cent in 1976–7. To do this he increased taxation in 1975, and aimed to reinforce this by cutting back public spending in the following year to the tune of £900 million. Defence spending was to be scaled down, as were food and housing subsidies. Subsidies on nationalized industry prices were to be reduced in 1975, and probably phased out altogether in 1976. Income tax rates were raised by 2p in the pound, so bringing the standard rate up to 35p, although this was partly offset by increasing the amount of income which could be earned before tax was levied. Though VAT remained 8 per cent at the standard rate, it was raised to 25 per cent on most 'luxury' items. The duty on tobacco, beer, spirits and wine was raised substantially. Excise duty on private cars was increased by 60 per cent, from £25 to £40. The company sector, already in difficulties, did not suffer as much as the personal sector. Corporation tax was unchanged, and no surcharge on advance payment was levied. There was to be some slight further relief from the Price Code provisions. More money was made available for retraining workers, and a temporary employment subsidy was planned to encourage the deferment of redundancies. Some capital gains tax relief was announced for farmers and small businessmen. Finally, a new scheme of family allowances was proposed for the future, which, amongst other things, would give an allowance for the first child. Overall, this was one of the harshest of recent budgets.

It was followed by what was effectively a compulsory wages policy. In July 1975 the Government announced that there would be a limit of £6 per week on pay increases, £6 representing 10 per cent of average earnings. There were to be no exceptions to this, and those earning more than £8,500 a year were to get nothing at all. The Government had the prior agreement of the TUC to such a policy, and the latter agreed to try to persuade its members to comply. The policy was voluntary to the extent that there were no legal sanctions against individual unions, but in a different sense there were very powerful sanctions operating through the Price Code. No firms could pass on in price rises any part of a pay settlement above the limit: this applied not only to the excess but to the whole of the increase. Up to April 1976 the limit was not apparently breached, and this was possibly due as much to these sanctions and to the recession in the economy as to the voluntary cooperation of the trade unions. Apart from avoiding the threat of penalties on trade unionists, this form of sanctions had the added advantage of covering all payments made at plant level. But the twin measures – budget and wages policy – taken to reduce the rate of inflation at a time of serious worldwide recession led to a sharp rise in unemployment.

As 1976 continued, an even more alarming feature was the behaviour of sterling. Yet again a Labour government was facing a crisis of confidence in the pound. On 1 January 1976 the pound had stood at $2·024; by 28 September it had collapsed to a lowly $1·637. This was a frightening performance. It could not simply be blamed (or explained) either on Britain's balance-of-payments deficit or on the high internal rate of inflation. The real explanation lay in a fear of the future course of the economy – and in particular of the Government's apparent inability to contain the Public Sector Borrowing Requirement, a fear which had been heightened by the publication of the White Paper *Public Expenditure 1979–80*. In time, as the oil factor aided Britain's economic recovery, the sterling crisis gradually faded, but it all made for an unhappy baptism for the Callaghan administration.

The problems on the economic front and the narrowness of Labour's electoral victory did not deter the party from beginning to implement significant changes in industry. Back in 1974 Labour had published its White Paper entitled *The Regeneration of British Industry*. Its main proposal, the creation of a new National Enterprise Board, was included in the Industry Bill introduced into Parliament in January 1975 and finally enacted in November. Labour had always believed that private enterprise on its own had not done enough to stimulate a high rate of growth. Hence the National Enterprise Board's functions were to assist the establishment and development of particular industries, extend public ownership into profitable areas of manufacturing and to promote industrial democracy. Since many of the Board's powers were discretionary, it was difficult to assess how significant it might become. The Conservatives bitterly attacked the Industry Bill as 'back-door' nationalization and doctrinaire socialism – arguing that it was by no means proven that state intervention would in fact be more successful than private enterprise. Moreover, even before the National Enterprise Board was in operation, state acquisitions in the private sector had rapidly mounted.

Thus by early 1976 the companies which were wholly or partly owned by the state included Ferranti, Alfred Herbert, British Leyland, Rolls Royce, Dunford and Elliot, Triang, and Harland and Wolff, and a further major extension of state ownership would come about as a result of the Aircraft and Shipbuilding Bill (see page 320).

Of very great importance, too, were the Government's moves to control the exploitation of North Sea oil. Labour was determined that the state should secure a substantial share of the returns of North Sea oil extraction and it was also particularly worried at the large amount of foreign-owned oil companies involved in these operations. Hence, in February 1975, a Bill was put forward proposing a petroleum revenue tax of 45 per cent and royalties of $12\frac{1}{2}$ per cent; the government calculated that this would still allow the oil companies a net return of 20 per cent, and they also made provisions so that firms were not discouraged from developing the more marginal fields. At the same time the Government pressed ahead for a 51 per cent stake in oil development. A new British National Oil Corporation was established as the vehicle for this state participation.

THE COMMON MARKET REFERENDUM

The Labour Party's manifesto for the October election had promised that within a year the people would decide 'through the ballot box' whether Britain should stay in the European Common Market on the terms to be renegotiated by the Labour government, or reject them and leave the Community. This formula left the option open between a referendum and yet another election in 1975. On 22 January the Government announced that they would bring in a Referendum Bill, and the White Paper published on 26 February established that there would be a national count. The decision was to be by simple majority on the question: 'Do you think the UK should stay in the European Community?' In the debate on the White Paper the principle of this direct consultation of the electors, a hitherto unknown British constitutional practice, was approved in the House of Commons by 312 votes to 262, five Conservatives voting with the Government and one Labour MP with the Opposition. The Government's original proposal of a single national declaration was lost during the debate: on a free vote on 23 April it was decided by 270 votes to 153, against strong government pressure, that the result should be declared regionally (a Liberal motion for declaration by constituency was lost by 264 votes to 131).

On 18 March Wilson informed the Commons that the Government had decided to recommend a 'Yes' vote. The Cabinet, however, was split sixteen to seven. The 'No' faction numbered Michael Foot (Secretary of State for Employment), Tony Benn (Industry), Peter Shore (Trade), Barbara Castle (Social Services), Eric Varley (Energy), William Ross (Scotland) and John Silkin (Planning and Local Government). It was an extraordinary state of affairs. Should the rebel ministers resign? Wilson neatly resolved the problem by stating that, while dissident ministers would otherwise be free to express themselves as they wished, all ministers speaking from the despatch box would reflect government policy. Apart from the dismissal of Eric Heffer, the Minister of State for Industry, this extraordinary Cabinet agreement to differ on a vital issue operated without resignation right through the referendum.

Though the Cabinet remained intact, the divisions within the Labour ranks remained as wide as ever. On 19 March a resolution signed by eighteen out of twenty-nine members of its National Executive recommended to a special party conference, successfully demanded by the left wing, that the party should campaign for withdrawal from the EEC. Later, in the Commons vote on the Government's pro-Market White Paper, 145 Labour MPs went into the No lobby, against 138 Ayes and thirty-two abstentions. The special conference on 26 April voted two to one for withdrawal.

Following the EEC summit meeting in Dublin on 10 and 11 March, when the assembled heads of government ratified certain decisions favourable to Britain which were regarded as part of the renegotiation, the Government's White Paper, *Membership of the EEC: Report on Renegotiation*, was published on 27 March. After describing the better terms which the Government claimed they had won, it concluded: 'Continued membership of the Community is in Britain's interest . . . In the Government's view the consequences of withdrawal would be adverse.' The White Paper went on to consider general questions like sovereignty, the European Parliament, Community legislation, the value of membership for Britain's world role, and the effects of withdrawal, which, it said, would threaten the political stability of Western Europe.

In the House of Commons on 9 April the White Paper was endorsed by a margin of 223 votes (393 to 170), almost double the majority of 112 recorded in October 1971 for the principle of entering the EEC. In many respects the claims and counter-claims of the debate had all been heard before. The 'Yes' side had a clear propaganda advantage in the support of most business firms, who did not hesitate to use their money, their advertising power and their communications with their workers, and of the great majority of the national and regional press. But the contest cut right across party lines, and politicians as far apart as Enoch Powell and Michael Foot united in the 'No' lobby. The 'Yes' lobby included such unusual allies as the Labour Cabinet majority, the bulk of the Tory and Liberal parties, the Confederation of British Industry, the National Farmers Union and the City of London.

Three pamphlets were duly delivered to every household in the kingdom. One was the Government's 'popular version of the White Paper'. The others, each half the size, were produced by the umbrella organizations 'Britain in Europe' and 'The National Referendum Campaign', and were straightforward exercises in public relations. The outcome fulfilled the best hopes of the pro-Marketeers. Turnout was high and the majority for 'Yes' was over two to one. The figures were: 'Yes' 17,378,000 (67·2 per cent), 'No' 8,470,000 (32·8 per cent). England voted 68·7 per cent 'Yes', Wales 65·5 per cent, Scotland 58·4 per cent and Ulster 52·1 per cent. Not only every one of the four national segments of the United Kingdom but also every English and Welsh region voted 'Yes'. The only 'No' majorities anywhere were recorded in two sparsely populated northern areas, the Shetlands and the Western Isles.

The outcome, though a triumph for the ardent champions of Britain in Europe – most particularly Edward Heath – was also a triumph for the astute political tactics of Harold Wilson. The left of his party had been appeased by the fact of the referendum, the right by its result, and the Wilson–Callaghan combination, having at last come down on the 'Yes' side and having been backed by the electorate, gained prestige as a national leadership. Other consequences also followed the 'Yes' vote. Labour belatedly sent a team to the European Parliament, and British trade unionists joined the appropriate bodies. Labour had survived the Common Market issue.

With almost as many divisions, the first steps were taken to put the Devolution Bill onto the statute book (see pages 315–18) and Labour pursued the search for a solution to the continuing troubles in Ulster (see page 319).

THE CONSERVATIVES AND LIBERALS

If Wilson faced a plethora of difficulties, the going was no less easy for the leaders of the two main opposition parties. Although many Conservatives had been deeply critical of Heath's leadership in the wake of the February election defeat, the proximity of another election had kept this discontent in check. The October election defeat opened the flood-gates. Long before October many Conservatives had disliked his personal style; now they possessed further grounds for attack. A commander who has lost two campaigns in quick succession, having himself chosen the battle-ground, the timing and tactics for a decisive conflict, is implicitly marked out for replacement. With the Conservative Party now in the wilderness, it seemed the right moment to rediscover a basic philosophy round which it could unite in regaining power. This task clearly needed a new leader. Despite the clamour for his replacement, Heath defiantly held his ground, waiting for the report of the Home Committee which had been set up to consider the future method of choosing the party leader. The Committee duly recommended that when the party was in Opposition there should be an annual election by all MPs. Heath accepted these proposals on 23 January 1975, and it was then announced that the date of the first round of the ballot would be 4 February.

In addition to Heath, two other candidates came forward: Margaret Thatcher, Heath's Secretary of State for Education, and Hugh Fraser, the MP for Stafford and Stone. This first ballot was clearly a vote of confidence or no-confidence in Heath. In this respect it was decisive. Margaret Thatcher received 130 votes, Edward Heath 119, Hugh Fraser 16, and there were 11 abstentions. Heath instantly stood down from the contest. Four additional former cabinet ministers, William Whitelaw, James Prior, John Peyton and Sir Geoffrey Howe, declared themselves candidates for the second ballot, while Hugh Fraser withdrew. Whitelaw was widely tipped to emerge as the heir of the Heath vote. The outcome, however, was somewhat unexpected. The result of the second ballot on 10 February made a third unnecessary. With 146 votes out of 271 cast, Margaret Thatcher had a clear overall majority. William Whitelaw received seventy-six votes, Sir Geoffrey Howe and James Prior nineteen each, and John Peyton eleven. For the first time a major British party had chosen for its leader a woman, who might one day become Prime Minister.

Thatcher's victory was widely interpreted as a swing to the right by the Conservatives. For the leadership vote had led not merely to defeat for Heath but also for such centre-moderates as Whitelaw and Howe. Thatcher's new team, however, was in most respects made up of a fair cross-section of the party, although the dropping of such 'liberals' as Robert Carr, Peter Walker and Nicholas Scott and the appointment of Sir Keith Joseph to take charge of policy and research rather obscured the fact. The key Shadow Cabinet appointments were announced on 18 February. William Whitelaw remained Deputy Leader, with special charge of devolution policy. Among the most important changes, Reginald Maudling took over Foreign and Commonwealth Affairs from Geoffrey Rippon, and Sir Geoffrey Howe replaced Robert Carr as Shadow Chancellor. An important change was also announced in the party organization with the appointment of Lord Thorneycroft, a former Chancellor of the Exchequer, as Chairman.

A rapid series of Conservative by-election victories under Margaret Thatcher's leadership diverted attention from the fact that Conservative policy on industrial and economic matters was somewhat sketchy. With the Conservatives seemingly taking almost every Labour stronghold that fell vacant (including the Stechford division of Birmingham, which became vacant when Roy Jenkins took up his post as President of the Commission), such policy gaps seemed immaterial. Margaret Thatcher was already, or so it seemed, set fair for No. 10 Downing Street.

The election of October 1974 had seen a distinct loss of momentum by the Liberals from their position in February. Historically, under every previous Labour administration, Liberals had always suffered a loss of support, partly as disaffected Tories who had voted Liberal went back to their old allegiance. After October 1974 this was repeated. In the eleven by-elections up to the Lib-Lab 'pact' of March 1977 (see page 313), the Liberal vote dropped by an average 5½ per cent.

This decline in the Liberal vote was partly cause and partly consequence of a most unedifying leadership battle which eventually led to the resignation of Jeremy Thorpe from the Liberal leadership. By 1976 Thorpe had been leader of the party for nine years. Some of his critics were suggesting the time was ripe for a change, to give a successor time to prepare for an election. Thorpe's luckless association with a collapsed secondary bank did nothing to mute this criticism, but it was the affair of Norman Scott which finally unseated him. Scott, a former male model, alleged that he had had a homosexual relationship with Thorpe, and despite Thorpe's denials the affair refused to die down. On 10 May, against a background of bad by-election results, Thorpe resigned.

Thorpe's resignation left the Liberals in a dilemma. The party had not yet finalized its new method of electing a party leader. As a stop-gap measure, on 12 May Jo Grimond agreed to resume the leadership on a temporary basis. Once the Liberals had agreed their new plan to elect a leader (a highly complex system involving the setting up of an electoral college based on constituency associations), Steel and Pardoe fought for the leadership. In the most democratic election for the leadership of a British political party, Steel won a comfortable victory.

THE RESIGNATION OF HAROLD WILSON

Unlike the bitter departure of Jeremy Thorpe, and unlike the ousting of Heath, which had been widely forecast, the resignation of Harold Wilson was as dramatic as it was totally unexpected. Wilson's decision was announced on 16 March 1976, but it was revealed that he had informed the Queen of his decision the previous December – a decision Wilson insisted he had secretly formed in March 1974. Wilson declared he had three main reasons: his long career in Parliament (on the front bench for thirty years and in the Cabinet for over eleven), including a period as Prime Minister spanning eight years; secondly, he argued that he should not remain so long that younger men were denied the chance to take his place (although, at sixty, Wilson seemed in his political prime and his eventual successor, Jim Callaghan, was older); thirdly – perhaps an important factor – Wilson argued that his successor would need time to impose his style and strategy for the rest of the parliament. These were sound reasons, although far from sufficient to prevent continued speculation on any secret reasons Wilson might have withheld. Certainly, Wilson's critics were ready to argue that the Prime Minister had quit with three major crises looming along the horizon – the economic crisis, including the steady slide of sterling on the foreign exchanges, a deep left–right split in the party and an ever-decreasing parliamentary majority which might force an election on the country.

Wilson's shock resignation opened the way for a highly significant contest for the Labour leadership. Six candidates stood in the first ballot – the left-wingers represented by Michael Foot and Tony Benn. Callaghan was widely regarded as the front-runner of the moderate camp, although Roy Jenkins's supporters were more optimistic than events were to justify. On the first ballot, Michael Foot polled ninety votes, Callaghan eighty-four, Jenkins an unexpectedly low fifty-six, Benn a creditably high thirty-seven, Healey a poor thirty and Crosland seventeen. Soon after the result was announced Jenkins stated that he was standing down from the contest. A similar announcement had come from Tony Benn, who said he would support Michael Foot. Crosland was automatically eliminated. In the ballot on the second round, both Callaghan and Foot consolidated their positions as the leading contenders. Callaghan topped the poll with 141, Foot polled 133 and Healey thirty-eight. In the third and final ballot, most of Healey's supporters duly switched to Callaghan, who won by 176 votes to Foot's 137.

Although Callaghan had eventually triumphed, the result was a striking demonstration of support for Michael Foot, who had not merely inherited the votes of Benn's supporters but had clearly picked up some support from the three losing right-wing candidates. No doubt Foot's style and personal charisma accounted for some of this appeal, but the result was also confirmation that a substantial leftward move had taken place in the Labour Party over the past decade.

WILSON: AN ASSESSMENT

Wilson did not accept a peerage, but on 22 April it was announced that he had received the Order of the Garter. Wilson's own resignation Honours List (a 'leak' of its contents was carried in the Sunday Times on 2 May) produced a furore, most particularly from the left of the Labour Party. Many of the names involved financiers or entertainment tycoons whose contributions to national politics were not always immediately apparent.

In a sense, the outcry over this list tended to make an impartial assessment of his contribution to British political life even more unenviable and invidious. The Annual Register declared that Wilson's memorial as party and national leader lay 'more in manoeuvre than in measures'. Wilson himself declared that the achievement he would most like to be remembered for by posterity was the creation of the Open University.

To assess Wilson's contribution already involves a long list of pros and cons. In Wilson's favour was the fact that he was a supreme politician, a manager of men, an election campaigner, rhetorician and debater. It is a tribute to his party skill that he is the only Labour premier to have won four elections and the only one to have seen the return of an outgoing Labour administration with an increased majority. Equally, he is the only Labour premier to have handed over office to a Labour successor. Perhaps even more of a tribute to his skill as a party manager was the way in which the 1975 referendum confirmed British membership of the EEC despite the opposition of the majority of his own party.

On the debit side, Wilson had promised the nation he would transform the 'stop-go' economic policies of the Conservatives; the reality was very different. The Wilson governments had been buffeted time and again by economic storms – some, at least, of which were partly of Wilson's own creation. The economic legacy which Wilson bequeathed to Callaghan was a most difficult one. Thus, with the sterling crisis of summer 1976, little seemed to have changed in a decade. In the Wilson era there seemed not only to have been more turning points than there were points to turn, but also each turning point seemed to make the circle ever more complete.

Wilson had also failed in a different way. If his aim had been to make Labour the natural party of government (and from 1964 to the end of 1976 it had been in office for $7\frac{1}{4}$ years to the $3\frac{1}{2}$ of the Heath government), within a year of his departure Labour was a minority government again, sustained in power by the votes of the Liberals, with some of the safest Labour strongholds in the country (such as Ashfield) lost in by-elections and with hardly a local authority in the land still under Labour control.

Wilson's image had also suffered over the decade. The homely pipe-smoking figure of 1963, the meritocrat with those high-sounding schemes of planning and technology, had disappeared a decade later. The prime minister whose government wanted reform of the House of Lords ended his political career by sending to the House of Lords an honours list which drew universal outcry from his own back-benchers and seemed reminiscent of eighteenth-century Whiggism. Back in 1964 Wilson had published a political opus entitled: *Purpose in Politics*. In 1976 that title seemed almost ironic. Yet, despite these shortcomings, Wilson put his own stamp on these years. He had introduced a new quasi-presidential style into British politics. And, whether intended or not, Wilson presided over major shifts in the balance of power in the body politic during his controversial years as premier. Like Lloyd George, Wilson will go down in history as an enigma whose mysteries only later historians can unravel, although this may well be the only respect in which they will compare him to Britain's premier in the First World War.

12 | THE CALLAGHAN ADMINISTRATION, 1976–9

Callaghan became Prime Minister on 5 April 1976. Few contrasts could have been more marked than between the new premier and his predecessor. Callaghan, a chapel-goer, teetotaller and non-smoker, was sixty-four. In contrast to Wilson's brilliant academic career at Oxford, he had had only an elementary and secondary-school education. He had made his career as a civil service tax officer, but growing involvement in trade union affairs had seen him rise to become Assistant Secretary of the Inland Revenue Staff Federation in 1936. Elected MP for Cardiff South in 1945, he held junior office under Attlee. Under Wilson he had been successively (even if not always successfully) Chancellor of the Exchequer, Home Secretary and Foreign and Commonwealth Secretary.

Although the leadership election had confirmed the growing power of the left in the Labour Party, Callaghan from the first adopted the tough 'above faction' line that was to dominate his premiership. Thus he told the Parliamentary Party he would not tolerate 'minority groups' trying to 'foist their views' on the party.

His Cabinet team, though relying on many of the stalwarts of the Wilson era, showed some important changes. Healey (whose budget was due the day after Callaghan became Prime Minister) was confirmed as Chancellor. Foot became Lord President and Leader of the House, replacing Edward Short and reflecting his strength in the party. Crosland became Foreign Secretary, Shore replaced Crosland as Environment Secretary, Dell became Secretary of State for Trade and Albert Booth took over from Foot at the Department of Employment. Among other significant changes, Shirley Williams became Paymaster General as well as Secretary for Prices and Consumer Affairs, while Barbara Castle was replaced as Social Services Secretary by David Ennals. Castle, a veteran left-wing campaigner (and, declared Crossman in his *Diaries*, of prime ministerial calibre but for the fact that she was a woman) had not enjoyed an easy time with the medical profession. Although Roy Jenkins remained as Home Secretary, he was to resign within a short while to become President of the European Commission. The untimely death of Anthony Crosland in May 1977 led to the promotion to the post of Foreign Secretary of David Owen, at thirty-nine the youngest person to hold the post since Eden.

THE LIB–LAB PACT

That the Callaghan administration could last for some three years before an election was called during 1979 was due to the working arrangement they came to with the Liberals, for within a short time of taking office the growing unpopularity of the Government had been witnessed in a series of humiliating by-election losses. Indeed, by the end of 1976 Labour had lost such strongholds as Walsall North and Workington to the Conservatives.

Excluding the Speaker and his three Deputies, the Government's overall majority had fallen to one by January 1977. Even this majority was dependent upon the two members of the breakaway Scottish Labour Party and the two non-Unionists from Northern Ireland supporting the Government. Weakened also by by-election losses, the Government were faced in March 1977 with almost certain defeat on a Conservative vote of 'no confidence', since the Nationalists had stated that they would vote against Labour. Callaghan ensured the survival of the Government by a pact with the Liberals. Unlike previous informal agreements, the pact was something of a constitutional departure, taking the form of a published agreement which allowed the Liberals to veto Cabinet legislative proposals prior to their introduction in the Commons.

In many ways, however, it represented a sensible assessment of the practical political situation. Neither Labour nor Liberals wanted an election. For Steel the pact represented a move towards possible future deals in a hung parliament – and hence electoral reform. But if this deal gave Liberals more influence than for many years at Westminster, in the country it did nothing to restore a disastrous slump in their fortunes. In the first nationwide test of Liberal support (the May 1977 local elections) they fared disastrously, and in by-elections their vote plummeted. For Callaghan – who certainly gained most from the pact – it bought time:

time for the economy to improve and time also to attempt to put the lengthy and controversial Devolution Bill onto the Statute Book.

THE ECONOMY

Of the difficulties inherited by James Callaghan, the most pressing still remained the management of the economy. The year 1975 had seen an even higher rate of inflation than 1974. Average weekly earnings had risen by 27 per cent. whilst productivity had fallen and prices had risen by 24 per cent. During 1975, however, there were the first signs that inflation was beginning to moderate, and by the end of the year there was some evidence that the bottom of the recession had been reached. But unemployment was still rising and in February 1976 stood at over 1·2 million. Inflation, though it had eased slightly, was still uncomfortably higher than in Europe or America. Hence the problem faced by the Government was to prevent any economic recovery leading to higher inflation and to further balance-of-payments difficulties. The obvious need was to have an export-led recovery, and to avoid stimulating home consumer demand. It was against this background, and with the £6 limit due to end in July 1976, that Healey introduced his next budget.

The intended effect of the April 1976 budget was broadly neutral. The higher VAT rate was halved and the duty on cigarettes, petrol and spirits was increased. Pensions were to be increased from November and Family Income Supplement was to be raised from July. The most important and novel aspect was the offer of tax cuts conditional on the unions agreeing to a limit of around 3 per cent on pay increases from July. If the Government secured such agreement, the single person's allowance would be increased by £60 to £735 and the married person's allowance by £130 to £1,085. In his Budget speech the Chancellor compared his suggested package with one where the pay limit was £3 per week higher but with no tax reliefs. Because of lower prices and the tax relief, married people would be better off under the 3 per cent limit; single people would be slightly worse off. This innovation was meant to give people an increase in take-home pay equivalent to a wage increase of $7\frac{1}{2}$ per cent.

Healey's new device met with mixed reaction. There were many doubts about the wisdom of the idea. Some people felt that the integrity of Parliament was threatened by making taxation decisions conditional on trade union agreement. Others felt that any new policy would have to allow some restoration of pay differentials, which had been previously squeezed, and that a 3 per cent limit did not leave sufficient scope for this.

A new agreement with the TUC was reached in May 1976, curbing average wage increases to $4\frac{1}{2}$ per cent in the year starting in August 1976. Price controls were also maintained, but there was some relaxation to encourage industrial investment. As important as restrictions on pay increases was a reduction in the soaring amount of government expenditure. Hence, during 1976 a vigorous campaign was mounted in favour of cuts in public expenditure. Concern that the Government was borrowing excessively to finance this spending also led to weakness of sterling on the foreign exchange markets. In July, to avert a further fall in the value of sterling, substantial cuts were announced in the Government's spending plans for 1977–8, and interest rates were raised to record levels. These measures were not sufficient, however, to prevent a dramatic slide in the pound during the autumn which forced the Government to seek a $3,900 million loan from the International Monetary Fund. To obtain this assistance increases in taxation and further cuts in public expenditure, amounting to £3,000 million over the next two years, were imposed in December.

The sterling crisis of 1976 marked the low point of the Government's struggle with the economy. During 1977 and 1978, definite signs of recovery appeared. Though the economy was still in recession – in February 1977 the enormous total of 1,420,000 people were unemployed and output was hardly rising – the benefits of North Sea oil were beginning to transform the balance of payments. For 1977 as a whole the balance of payments showed a surplus of £1 million. The pound was riding high – helped partly by the continuing weakness of the dollar. Even the rate of inflation – though uncomfortably high in comparison with Britain's major competitors – was at last reduced to single figures. The signs of economic recovery were reflected in the April 1978 budget, with its modest reductions in personal taxation and its mildly expansionary aims.

LABOUR AND DEVOLUTION

The most difficult – as well as the most significant – legislation which Callaghan inherited was the Devolution Bill. It provided another delicate issue which had already deeply divided the Labour Party.

The need for some degree of devolution had been given added urgency by the dramatic gains of the Scottish National Party in the October 1974 election. On top of the eleven seats it won in that election, the SNP was now the challenger in a further forty-two seats – no fewer than thirty-five of which were currently held by Labour. Devolution had thus become urgent politics for the Government. For if Labour lost its Scottish electoral base, its chances of once again forming a majority government at Westminister would be minimal. But what form should devolution take?

As early as April 1969 the Labour government had appointed a Royal Commission on the Constitution, under the chairmanship of Lord Crowther. Following the latter's death in February 1972, Lord Kilbrandon, a Lord of Appeal in Ordinary and a member of the Commission since its inception, was appointed chairman. The Commission's findings were published in October 1973. All the members of the Commission accepted that there was some dissatisfaction with the present system of government and that some change was desirable. They also unanimously rejected extreme solutions such as the division of Great Britain into three sovereign states or the creation of a federation. However, beyond this, they failed to reach agreement. Two of the Commission's members disagreed sufficiently fundamentally to produce a lengthy memorandum of dissent. The remaining eleven who signed the majority report in fact produced five different schemes, although some of these had elements in common. The most popular scheme, which was advocated by eight members when applied to Scotland and by six when applied to Wales, proposed the creation of regional assemblies elected on the basis of proportional representation. Out of these, governments would be formed, headed by a Scottish and a Welsh prime minister. The assemblies would be responsible for those matters at present handled by the Scottish and Welsh Offices. Other functions would remain firmly with the United Kingdom Parliament. In England no need was seen for elected regional assemblies, but eight regional councils were recommended, most of their members being nominated by local authorities. Their duties would be purely advisory. The authors of the memorandum of dissent recommended the creation of seven elected assemblies in Great Britain, one each for Scotland and Wales and five for English regions.

Initially the Kilbrandon Report was not received very favourably.

However, with the continuing successes of the Nationalist parties Labour gradually came over (despite the opposition of the Scottish Executive of the Labour Party) to supporting devolution with elected assemblies for Scotland and Wales, and in June 1974 the Government published a consultative document which set out seven possible schemes for greater devolution. In September 1974 a White Paper, *Democracy and Devolution: Proposals for Scotland and Wales*, was published, and following further discussions a second White Paper, *Our Changing Democracy: Devolution to Scotland and Wales*, was produced in November 1975. It proposed the creation of assemblies in Scotland and Wales, to be elected initially by simple majority on the basis of existing parliamentary constituencies. In Scotland the assembly was to have law-making powers on such matters as local government, health, social services, education, housing, physical planning, the environment and roads. Executive powers on these questions would be exercised by a Scottish Executive, a team drawn wholly or mainly from the assembly, headed by a Chief Executive, who would normally be the leader of the majority party in the assembly. In Wales the assembly would not have legislative powers but would have certain powers in relation to delegated legislation and would be given responsibility for many of the executive functions at present carried out by nominated bodies and by the Secretary of State for Wales. Executive powers would be vested in the assembly itself, operating through committees whose members would reflect the political balance in the assembly. Overriding responsibility would continue to lie with the UK Parliament and Government, and for this reason Scotland and Wales were to retain their existing number of MPs at Westminster and Secretaries of State for Scotland and Wales would continue to serve in the Cabinet at Westminster.

These were far-reaching proposals with very great constitutional significance. Within the Labour Party in Parliament there was likely to be strong opposition – not only from anti-devolutionists in Scotland such as Tam Dalyell, the Labour MP for West Lothian, but also from an English 'backlash' opposed to special treatment for Scotland. At the same time, the Conservatives were also hardening their position. Although they had in principle supported the creation of a Scottish Assembly since the late 1960s, in 1976 the party decided officially to oppose the Government's legislation – although a number of senior Conservatives resisted the change of attitude by the party.

These political difficulties were reflected in the fate of the Scotland and Wales Bill, which received its second reading on 13–14 December 1976 by a majority of forty-five. The Government had secured the votes of most Labour MPs by promising to hold referenda before bringing the assemblies into existence. The Conservatives attacked the Welsh proposals in the Bill as simply bureaucratic, costly and unwanted by the Welsh people. The proposed Scottish assembly was equally bitterly attacked, with the Conservatives arguing that the initial cost of its establishment would be £4 million and its annual running costs £12 million. The legislation was attacked on several sides for including both Scotland and Wales in one single Bill; and the future role of Scots and Welsh MPs in the House of Commons after the establishment of the assemblies produced equally large criticism. Since the Bill was becoming bogged down in the Commons, a timetable motion to limit debate at committee stage was introduced. On 22 February 1977 this crucial vote was lost by the Government and the Bill was effectively shipwrecked.

In November 1977 the Government started again. This time there were two Bills, one for Scotland and one for Wales, though, of the two, the Scotland Bill was far more important to the Government. On its second reading a reasoned amendment by the Conservatives calling for a Constitutional Conference was defeated by forty-eight votes and in November 1977 it was quickly guillotined by the Government, a move which secured approval in the Commons as a result of the Lib-Lab 'pact', even though the Bill had not yet gone into committee (with the Wales Bill, the guillotine was applied the day after second reading – the hastiest use of the guillotine in post-war legislation). Thus by spring 1978 the Scotland Bill had completed its committee stage in the Commons.

Even this second time, however, its passage had been badly mauled. The Government went down to several defeats: most particularly Clause 1, which declared that the unity of the United Kingdom was not affected, was removed; in addition a clause was added stating that a minimum of 40 per cent of the total electorate for a 'Yes' vote would be required for the referendum to be effective; and another clause required a separate referendum for Orkney and Shetland. These were damaging changes. But by the end of 1978 the Government had at last put devolution onto the statute book, with the referendum scheduled for 1 March 1979.

ULSTER

Labour also inherited the intractable question of the Ulster troubles. In the closing months of the Heath administration direct rule in the province had been ended on 1 January 1974 with the coming into operation of the main provisions of the Northern Ireland Constitution Act.

Right from the start, the political position of the newly established power-sharing Executive was weak. Its position was worsened by the result of the February general election in Northern Ireland, in which eleven out of the twelve seats were won by Loyalist candidates opposed to the Executive. None of the Unionist candidates supporting the Sunningdale agreement was elected and the anti-Sunningdale Unionists achieved a total of 367,000 votes (51·1 per cent of the Northern Ireland poll). The election thus sent back to Westminster a collection of MPs, all but one of whom were opposed to the power-sharing settlement.

The Chief Executive, Brian Faulkner, and his deputy, the SDLP leader, Gerry Fitt, soldiered on bravely until the Executive collapsed in May 1974. Following the ratification of the Sunningdale agreement in the Assembly, the Ulster Workers' Council initiated strike action, at first interfering with the supply of electricity and later affecting a large part of the economy. The UK Government's refusal to negotiate with the UWC led to the resignation of the Chief Executive, Brian Faulkner, and his Unionist colleagues. As a result the Assembly was prorogued and direct rule resumed.

In a new attempt to get a political initiative going in Ulster, it was announced in July 1974 that a constitutional convention was to be called so as to give the people of Northern Ireland, through elected representatives called together for this purpose, an opportunity to put forward recommendations as to how the province should be governed. Elections were held in May 1975 and the result was a massive Loyalist landslide, with the United Ulster Unionist Council taking 46 seats, the SDLP 17, the Alliance Party 8 and the Unionist Party of Northern Ireland a mere 5. From the start of the Convention's deliberations, the UUUC made it clear that it would not agree to the inclusion of Opposition members in a future cabinet. Thus the Convention failed to produce a unanimous report. However, its recommendations, which were submitted to the Government in November 1975, revealed that there was all-party agreement that direct rule should be ended and a Northern Ireland assembly and executive re-established, and the UUUC did propose that powerful all-party committees should be created in the assembly. The Convention was re-convened for one month at the beginning of February 1976 but was dissolved finally on 5 March and direct rule from Westminster continued.

Terrorism from both Protestants and Republicans continued throughout 1976. The collapse of a general strike call by Ian Paisley early in 1977 reinforced Mason's prestige as Northern Ireland Secretary, but any solution to the problems of the province seemed as remote as ever.

LABOUR'S DOMESTIC LEGISLATION

Callaghan had inherited from Wilson a large number of controversial Bills. Although some were severely mauled, important legislation had gone through despite strong opposition in the House of Commons, where the Government's small majority was frequently threatened, and in the House of Lords. The Lords attempted to make major changes in six Bills, but the conflicts eventually centred around two – the Dock Work Regulation Bill and the Aircraft and Shipbuilding Industries Bill. The former was returned to the Commons with its main provision (a five-mile zone reserved for dock labourers) transformed by the Lords, and the defection of two of their own back-benchers prevented the Government restoring their original proposal. Continuing difficulties over the Aircraft and Shipbuilding Industries Bill forced its re-introduction at the beginning of the 1976–7 session. It became law in March 1977, but only after the Government had made important concessions (notably dropping the nationalization of the ship-repairers).

Among other important legislative measures Callaghan could point to the Police Act, establishing a Police Complaints Board to take part, with the police, in investigating complaints against the police by the public. There was also the Health Services Act, providing for the progressive withdrawal of private medicine from National Health Service hospitals, the Education Act, requiring local education authorities to submit proposals to abolish selection in secondary education, and the Race Relations Act, which created a new Commission for Racial Equality.

THE BACKGROUND TO THE 1979 ELECTION

To the amazement of almost all political commentators, Callaghan announced at the Labour Party Conference in October 1978 that there would be no general election that year. The Government went on to survive the debate on the Queen's Speech relatively easily. However, on 13 December they were defeated in the Commons in two divisions over the application of sanctions to firms breaking the 5 per cent pay guidelines. The next day Callaghan won a vote of confidence by 300 votes to 290.

With the Government's decision to continue into 1979, the electors were guaranteed a veritable feast of elections for the coming year. Apart from the General Election (which had to be held by 15 November), there were the Scottish and Welsh referenda scheduled for 1 March, the local elections on 3 May and the first-ever direct elections for Europe on 7 June. The electors went into 1979 knowing that, if their verdict was cast decisively, it would determine the political balance for some time to come.

Callaghan must very soon have been bitterly regretting his decision to avoid an autumn election. He was able to continue in office, after the withdrawal of the Liberals from the Lib-Lab pact, only with the support of the Scottish Nationalists, who did not wish to see the devolution referendum prejudiced.

In the event all of Callaghan's judgements were to prove mistaken. The outcome of the referenda in Scotland and Wales could hardly have been politically more disastrous; the winter of 1978/79 proved a nightmare in terms of industrial conflict; and on 28 March 1979 the whole unhappy saga came to an abrupt and unseemly end when the Government was defeated by 1 vote in a vote of confidence in the Commons, the first such government defeat since 1924.

If Callaghan was preoccupied in these months with the precarious parliamentary position of the Government and with the fate of its devolution proposals the general public was far more concerned with the wave of strikes that swept the country. On 3 January, a nationwide strike of lorry drivers began in support of a 25 per cent wage claim. This already serious dispute was aggravated by a separate strike of tanker drivers. An average 14 per cent settlement soon ended the tanker drivers' dispute, but the damage done to the government's attempts to hold pay rises to 5 per cent was only too apparent. Meanwhile, not only was the transport dispute damaging the economy, but the extensive use of 'secondary' picketing, accompanied in several instances by appalling and much-publicized scenes of violence on the picket lines, and an injunction by the food firm United Biscuits to halt such picketing, all brought the issue of trade union power to the forefront of political debate. It was an ideal issue for the opposition. Increasingly, Margaret Thatcher's speeches centred on the need to restrict the power of the unions.

It was against this background that industrial disputes spread to the public services. On 22 January, 1½ million public service workers began a 24-hour strike. Other regional stoppages had already occurred. Water workers, ambulance drivers, sewerage staff and dustmen were among those whose industrial action was causing widespread misery in a winter that seemed unending. Under this barrage of industrial disputes, the pay policy of the government simply collapsed. When three of the public service unions accepted a '9 per cent plus £1' a week offer, it was obvious that the 5 per cent guideline had been broken forever. On 5 March Callaghan admitted the consequences of this, namely that the aim of single-figure inflation in 1979 was now unobtainable. Although a patched-up 'partnership' between the government and the TUC was announced on 14 February ('a boneless wonder' was Thatcher's derisory description), the memories of the 'winter of discontent' were to be a potent factor in the coming election. As the *Annual Register* commented, British trade unionism had shown the public its unacceptable face.

The electorate was to have an opportunity earlier than anyone had anticipated to deliver its verdict. On 16 January, although the government survived an emergency debate on the industrial crisis with a majority of 34, only three weeks later its majority fell to the low margin of 8. On 1 March, disaster struck. The devolution referendum held in Wales produced a 'Yes' vote of 243,048 (11·9 per cent) and a 'No' vote of 956,330 (46·9 per cent of the electorate). In Scotland, 1,230,937 voted 'Yes' (32·85 per cent), whilst 1,153,502 (30·78 per cent of the electorate) voted 'No'. Wales had overwhelmingly rejected devolution, Scotland had failed to bridge the 40 per cent level necessary for implementation of devolution to go ahead. On the same day, to add to the miseries of the government, there were swings of 9 per cent and 13 per cent respectively to the Conservatives in by-elections in Clitheroe and Knutsford.

The political strategy of the Callaghan government was in tatters. The Scottish Nationalists immediately gave notice that unless Labour went ahead with an Assembly for Scotland they would force an election. Labour's anti-devolution rebels were equally insistent that they would not abandon the 40 per cent requirement. In its dire straits, Labour urgently introduced a bill, calculated to secure the support of the three Welsh Nationalist members, to compensate quarrymen suffering from lung disease brought on by their work. It was perhaps the most cynically opportunist measure ever introduced in the post-war period. And, like so much of the opportunism of the Callaghan government, it too failed.

On 28 March, in one of the most dramatic votes ever seen at Westminster, the government was defeated by 311 votes to 310. Had two Irish Catholic MPs voted with the government, it would have won. Instead, they abstained. The long minority Labour government was over. Parliament was dissolved on 7 April and the election fixed for 3 May.

The ensuing election campaign centred around two very contrasting party leaders: the reassuring, avuncular figure of Jim Callaghan and the strident, aggressive style of a very confident Margaret Thatcher. Both leaders kept their supposed extremists – Benn and Joseph – very much on the sidelines. Callaghan succeeded in keeping Labour's manifesto conspicuously moderate. But, in a sense, the manifesto mattered little. The scenario for the election had already been set, with management of the economy and the role of the trade unions at the centre. Despite a by-election victory, on the eve of the general election, by the Liberals in the previously safe Labour Liverpool Edge Hill constituency on 29 March, that party too found it hard to make the headlines. There seemed also to be a feeling in the country that the time for real decision had come and that the electorate had had enough of minority government.

The result confirmed this, with a decisive and quite massive swing to the Conservatives.

It was a watershed election, with the most marked shift of opinion since 1945. The turnout in the election, at 76·2 per cent, was higher than in October 1974. Although all the country swung markedly to the right, the swing from Labour to Conservative varied very significantly. In northern England and Scotland, it was limited to 4·2 per cent whereas in the south of England it reached 7·7 per cent. There were also some individual groups of constituencies where particularly massive swings to the Conservatives occurred, notably East London, the Welsh-speaking

Party	Votes gained	Percentage of vote	Average vote per MP	Number of MPs
Conservative	13,697,000	43·9	40,404	339
Labour	11,509,000	36·9	42,944	268
Liberal	4,313,000	13·8	392,091	11
SNP	504,000	1·6	252,000	2
PC	132,000	0·4	66,000	2
Others	887,000	2·8	—	13

areas of North Wales (Anglesey and Montgomeryshire returned Conservatives, the latter having returned a Liberal at every election this century), some new towns such as Hertford and Stevenage (which unseated Shirley Williams) and the mining areas. Labour was relatively successful in immigrant areas outside London (it held all three seats it was defending in Leicester) and also did well in the large cities.

The British electorate had made its decision. Margaret Thatcher stood on the steps of Downing Street on 4 May 1979 not merely as Britain's first woman prime minister, but also backed by the largest swing at any post-war general election and with a majority of 43 over all other parties together.

LABOUR IN POWER IN THE 1970s: AN ASSESSMENT

If Wilson's record as prime minister was soon felt to have been one of failure, that sense of failure was powerfully reinforced by Callaghan's term as premier. Labour, it seemed, was incapable of positive achievements. It was unable to control inflation, unable to control the unions, unable to solve the Irish problem, unable to solve the Rhodesian question, unable to secure its proposals for Welsh and Scottish devolution, unable to reach a popular *modus vivendi* with the Common Market, unable even to maintain itself in power until it could go to the country at a date of its own choosing. It was little wonder, therefore, that Mrs Thatcher resoundingly defeated it in 1979. Unlike Callaghan she exuded determination to make a new start; few could believe that Callaghan was capable of one. Indeed, a strong case can be made out that he epitomized Labour's failings even more than Wilson had, for it could be argued that in every major policy-decision in which he had been involved since 1964 he had made the wrong decision – not to devalue the pound in 1964, to keep out the Kenyan Asians in 1968, to send troops to Ireland in 1969, to oppose *In Place of Strife* in 1969 and to continue in power until 1979 in the vain hope of sustaining a wages policy which by then was clearly unsupportable, by relying on a trade union movement to which his party with his blessing had already made too many concessions. To this must be added of course the fact that, unlike Wilson, he proved unable to win an election and that his plans for Welsh and Scottish devolution were rejected by the electorate.

It is interesting to inquire, for a moment, why, particularly in the case of Scotland, these plans had been rejected. For it looked at one point as if the 1970s would witness the 'break-up of Britain'. If this had been accompanied by Britain's withdrawal from the European Community, then it is conceivable that by 1979 Britain would indeed have reached a major turning-point in her historical development. It is quite easy to explain why she chose not to withdraw from the EEC – the media were in favour of membership, so too was the Government and, in any case, experience of membership was too limited for most people to be able to reach an independent judgement on the finely balanced economic arguments involved. Explaining the rejection by the Scots of devolution on the other hand is a more difficult task.

The rise of the SNP to a position in 1974, which seemed to presage 'home rule' if not independence for Scotland if the trend continued, cannot simply be attributed to 'protest voting'. The nationalist vote was not as temporary a phenomenon as a 'protest vote' implies. The reaction of the major political parties showed this also. In reality, the vitality of SNP organization demonstrated that it represented an alternative political system and one which might well have become the dominant one if the party had continued to tap the well of Scottish nationalism which evidently lay just beneath the political surface. Yet why had it had to wait until the 1970s to be in a position to mount its challenge? To some observers the answer lay in the discovery and exploitation of North Sea Oil – 'Scottish Oil' as the nationalists called it. This, it was claimed, enabled them to argue that an independent Scotland would be economically viable, whereas before the 1970s the fear of falling living standards had prevented them from gaining support. This interpretation of events, however, is difficult to accept. It neither explains the rise in the nationalist vote before the 1970s nor the lack of nationalism in Scottish politics for most of the period between 1750 and 1950. The discovery of North Sea oil in fact probably only made the SNP case more credible for those who already found it convincing. It has been argued that nationalism increased in the 1970s because the Scots were simply fed up with being treated as an English colony. But this too is difficult to accept. By the 1970s the Scots economy was beginning, albeit slowly, to catch up with the English one, while politically it was clear that the Scots were well represented at all levels of public life in Britain. Politically too, the Scottish vote had often been decisive in imposing Labour governments on Britain, while economically it is a strange 'colonial system' which subsidizes the alleged colony instead of the metropolis. Finally, the argument put forward by certain neo-Marxist thinkers that the break-up of Britain was the logical corollary of the break-up of empire was also historically unsound. The Union had never come about primarily to allow the Scots to build a British Empire in the first place. Nor had that Empire been of economic benefit to Britain. The Scots economy, like the British one, expanded more rapidly once the Empire had been dismantled. Its dismantling did not, therefore, create an argument for Scottish independence. On another level this explanation is inadequate for its failure to explain either Irish nationalism, which reached its peak at the height of empire, or the little-known fact that the British government conceded Scottish Home Rule in 1913. The most convincing explanation of the SNP success in the 1970s seems rather to be that, whereas in England the Liberals proved unable to capitalize on the failures of Conservative and Labour governments, the SNP was able to do so in Scotland on account of its younger and more efficient organization, its lack of class identification – nationalism transcended class barriers – its wide support in the Scottish media (where it was the main focus of attention politically) and its firm identity in terms of policies. As it was to turn out, however, the nationalists would suffer from the ambiguity of Scottish patriotism. For, given that the Union had left the Scots with their own system of law, their own church, their own system of education, given that they used their own currency, read their own newspapers and watched their own television programmes, it simply was not necessary for them to have a separate state to protect their sense of nationhood. Besides most Scots were proud to be British and many outside the Central Lowlands preferred London-dominated government to Glasgow- or Edinburgh-dominated government. As a result, the required approval of 40 per cent of the electorate for the Government's plans was not obtained in the 1979 referendum.

Still, if Britain survived that vote united, the vote itself and the consequent destruction of Labour's devolution proposals only heightened the sense of failure which clung to the Callaghan administration. This in itself was being made more prominent by a growing awareness among the public of Britain's relative decline. For it had by now become accepted wisdom that Britain was the 'sick man of Europe' on account of the so-called 'British disease'; and the fear was growing daily that the disease might prove to be fatal. The degree of illness was represented by one commentator in the following terms: 'A wide gap separates [Britain] from the rest of industrialized Europe. The difference as measured in national products per head between Britain and, say, Germany is now as wide as the difference between Britain and the continent of Africa.' More ominous was Peter Jenkins's article in the *Guardian* in September 1978 in which he warned:

No country has yet made the journey from developed to under-developed. Britain could be the first to embark upon that route. That is what it would mean to move away from a century of relative economic decline into a state of absolute decline. Here is how it could happen.

Productivity continues to increase more slowly than in other countries. Wages grow at the same rate or faster. Unit labour costs and consumer prices thereby grow much faster. Britain's share of world markets continues to diminish. So does the number of persons employed in manufacture. Export trade ceases to be sufficient to keep factories open while imports strike more deeply into the export market. The moment comes at which it is no longer possible to finance a growth in real incomes. Relative decline will have brought about absolute decline.

Against the background of this debate Mr Callaghan's failures made it extremely unlikely that he could win an election. For the future of British politics was profoundly affected by the nature of the debate on the 'British disease'. Of what did it consist? What had brought it about? In what ways could it be cured? A number of books appeared about this time which attempted to answer these questions: M. W. Kirby's *The Decline of British Economic Power since 1870*, Andrew Gamble's *Britain in Decline*, Martin J. Wiener's *English Culture and the Decline of the Industrial Spirit, 1850-1980* and Sidney Pollard's *The Wasting of the*

British Economy were just a few. Others had already made their case: for example, Roger Bacon and Walter Ellis with *Britain's Economic Problem: Too Few Producers* and Michael Stewart with *The Jekyll and Hyde Years.* The Institute of Economic Affairs was to make its case with *The Emerging Consensus.* The consensus which emerged from all of them was that radical change would certainly be needed if Britain's decline were to come to a halt. In terms of practical politics this came to mean, as far as the right was concerned, a much greater commitment to free-market economics, the reduction of public expenditure and control of the money supply. This was the programme, based on the economic thought of Professors Friedman and von Hayek which Mrs Thatcher adopted. On the left, on the other hand, the solution preferred was one of greater public ownership, withdrawal from the E E C, greater public expenditure, reform of institutional structures (education, the media, the House of Lords, the civil service, the police and the legal system) and a commitment to unilateral disarmament. This was the programme, based on the writings of Stuart Holland and others, which was best argued by Tony Benn. Logically, therefore, both Mrs Thatcher and Mr Benn had to repudiate the past records of both their parties. Politicians who refused to follow their example were left to occupy the diminishing middle ground of politics. Here the Liberals led by David Steel were to find themselves joined by SDP renegades from Labour and in practice by Mr Heath. Together they would continue to advocate the consensus politics of the 1950s and 1960s and in Ralf Dahrendorf's cutting phrase would offer 'a better yesterday' rather than a better tomorrow. It was Mrs Thatcher however who was to win the chance to shape Britain's future. And the policies which she adopted for this purpose were to make her the most controversial prime minister in post-war British history.

| # THE FIRST THATCHER GOVERNMENT, 1979-83

Mrs Thatcher came to office in 1979 determined to reverse the relative decline from which Britain was acknowledged to be suffering. To achieve this objective she promised to make a break with the past. There was indeed a consensus in the country that such a break was necessary. Within the Labour Party it was reflected by Mr Tony Benn and his allies who were to repudiate the 'Butskellite' past of the Wilson and Callaghan administrations. Like Mrs Thatcher herself, Mr Benn claimed to be a 'conviction politician' and in his case the convictions were well known – more nationalization, more public expenditure, more protectionism, more control over the police, the law, the civil service, the media; in short, more socialism.

PARTY POLITICS

In Mrs Thatcher's case it was less clear whether she stood for a new ideology or whether she represented merely a set of values or instincts. She was by 1979 certainly identified with several – thrift, patriotism, self-help, hard work and responsibility to the family. Her watchwords were initiative, duty, independence. John Nott spoke for many when he identified these values with those of nineteenth-century liberalism. 'I am a nineteenth-century Liberal,' he said, 'so is Mrs Thatcher. That's what this government is all about.' Professor Milton Friedman, the US economist and Nobel Prize winner agreed with Nott. He said: 'The thing that people do not recognize is that Margaret Thatcher is not in terms of belief a Tory. She is a nineteenth-century Liberal.'

Professor Friedman's view was an interesting one, because the ideology which Mrs Thatcher was often held to represent was that of monetarism. Indeed it was often referred to as 'Thatcherism' and in its academic form was the invention of Professor Friedman. Basically it held that the money supply was the central determinant of inflation and that governments could therefore by controlling it reduce the rate of inflation. This doctrine was certainly to be well reflected in Mrs Thatcher's policies. Mrs Thatcher, however, was also said to follow the beliefs of yet another Nobel laureate in economics, Professor Friedrich von Hayek. Hayek held that the function of government was not to redistribute wealth but simply to establish the conditions of order in which market forces could create it. Governments (in his view) were not to favour one group of citizens over another. This would lead merely to a growth of bureaucracy and social resentments. The role of the state should thus be kept to a minimum in economic affairs. Hayek, unlike Friedman, did little to popularize his views but others did, with the result that the Conservative Party, influenced by his and Friedman's views, became committed to market-oriented economic policies in the period 1974–9. And Mrs Thatcher, under the intellectual spell of Sir Keith Joseph, her political mentor as Leader of the Opposition, apparently accepted this political philosophy. For Sir Keith had established the Centre for Policy Studies while in opposition which, together with the Institute of Economic Affairs (IEA) run by Lord Harris and Arthur Seldon, had helped propagate 'monetarist' ideas throughout the Tory party, aided in particular by the Selsdon Group. The new Prime Minister, therefore, entered office apparently committed to a set of beliefs and values which stressed the primacy of market forces, individualism and sound money.

Others in the Conservative Party were less identified with such views. These were the ones who claimed the label 'Tory' and who stressed the primacy of community over individuality. Market forces, if not restrained, would undermine political solidarity and governmental authority. As Sir Ian Gilmour, the leading exponent of this viewpoint, wrote in his book *Inside Right*: '. . . if people are not to be seduced by other attractions they must at least feel loyalty to the State. This loyalty will not be deep unless they gain from the State protection and other benefits . . . Economic liberalism because of its starkness and its failure to create a sense of community is likely to repel people from the rest of liberalism.'

Tories of this kind therefore called for 'one nation' conservatism as preached by Benjamin Disraeli – himself the arch-enemy of the original nineteenth-century Liberals. They were aided in turn by Burkean conservatives who believed that it was the duty of conservatives to protect the public from experiments based on intellectual blueprints or general theories of any sort. The guide to action for conservatives of this mould was held to be tradition and scepticism. Hence they were very wary of the undoubted resurgence of ideology in both the Tory Party and in the country at large.

The debate inside the Conservative Party was soon reflected in political factionalism. Those who on the whole supported the views of Friedman, Hayek *et al.* became known as 'dries', their opponents known as 'wets'. The terminology derived from Mrs Thatcher's epithet of 'wet' to describe her cabinet opponents who resisted spending cuts. But there were several varieties of 'dries' and 'wets'. According to one political scientist there were 'three kinds of dry and two species of wet'. They were to be distinguished by their social origins and by their degrees of populism. Mrs Thatcher's great strength, it was to emerge, was her ability to win the support of several factions at any given time by recognizing where the balance of opinion lay. And this was important because on account of changes in the social background of Conservative MPs, the development of a new select committee system in the Commons under Norman St John Stevas, the Leader of the House between 1979 and 1981, and precedents established under Mr Heath's premiership, dissent in the House of Commons, fuelled by such factionalism, was always a potential threat to the Government's survival. In the event the massive unpopularity experienced by the Government between 1979 and 1981 followed by its equally large lead in the opinion polls after the Falklands War of April–June 1982, meant that factionalism was easily contained, at least as far as the division lobbies were concerned.

That is not to say, however, that there was party unity under Mrs Thatcher. In fact until September 1981 it seemed as if the Prime Minister still lacked control of her cabinet. It was not until a major reshuffle of that date – followed by the Falklands victory nine months later – that Mrs Thatcher's ascendancy was assured.

One reason why she failed to control her cabinet from the beginning was simply its initial composition. For having refused to shuffle her shadow cabinet between 1975 and 1979 she did not have much choice in selecting her real one. Nor did the fact that she allowed Mr William Whitelaw a great influence in selecting it for her give her much control over its eventual balance. This meant that when the Government was faced with a steep and unforeseen rise in unemployment the Cabinet soon split over the means by which to secure its objectives. These were, of course, to reduce public expenditure, to reform the trade unions, to begin privatizing nationalized industries and to reduce inflation and direct taxation. As increased unemployment led to greater public expenditure this led to further measures which in turn led to greater unemployment; a vicious circle was thus established, the political consequence of which was the exacerbation of factional strife. For the first half of her first term in office, therefore, the Prime Minister's relations with her cabinet were often strained.

It contained both wets and dries, for despite Mrs Thatcher's previous declaration to the *Observer* that she 'could not waste time having any internal arguments' all the factions had to be included. Lord Carrington was given the Foreign Office, Mr Francis Pym went to Defence, Mr Peter Walker went to Agriculture, Mr Mark Carlisle was given Education, Mr John St John Stevas became Leader of the House and Mr James Prior was given Employment. All these men were wets. They were joined in the Cabinet by Sir Ian Gilmour (Lord Privy Seal) and Lord Soames (Leader of the House of Lords) but their former leader Mr Heath was not offered a cabinet post. His relations with Mrs Thatcher, whose challenge to his leadership he still bitterly resented, were too frosty. Shrewdly she offered to make him British Ambassador to the United States but that offer, predictably, was spurned. Heath had never been an Atlanticist. The dries in the Cabinet were represented most of all in the economic field. The Chancellorship went to Sir Geoffrey Howe who became the Prime Minister's *alter ego*, while Sir Keith Joseph, her mentor, became Secretary of State for Industry. Mr John Nott was put in charge of Trade while Mr David Howell was made Secretary of State for Energy. Other dries to enter the Cabinet included Mr John Biffen as Chief Secretary to the Treasury (where he was to reveal occasional signs of rising damp), Mr Angus Maude as Postmaster General, who had the task of coordinating government information, and Mr Patrick Jenkin who became Secretary for Social Services. A 'loner' in between these groups was the Environment Secretary, Mr Michael Heseltine; like the Home Secretary, Mr William Whitelaw and the Lord Chancellor, Lord Hailsham, however, he was believed to be more wet than dry. Mr Whitelaw, however, turned out to be the key figure in resolving disputes. As Mrs Thatcher's deputy he attempted to remain as neutral as possible and always tried to encourage compromise. Significantly he usually chaired the cabinet committee (the so-called 'Star Chamber') which arbitrated disputes between the Treasury and spending departments.

ECONOMIC POLICY

The first problem facing the new government was how to set its course quickly on the economy, given that the budget was only about a month or so away. Clearly it would not be an easy task because the previous government had already both cut much of the fat out of the figures and left a number of spending commitments. In particular Professor Hugh Clegg's Pay Board had made a variety of substantial pay awards which Mrs Thatcher had promised to honour. Moreover, Sir Geoffrey Howe's version of monetarism, unlike that practised by Mr Healey between 1976 and 1978 did not pretend even in principle to ally monetary discipline with wage control. Thus although Mr Healey in his letter of intent to the IMF of December 1976 had pledged to reduce public spending and to set targets for the reduction of the public borrowing requirement, he had been motivated by his usual pragmatism. His successor, on the other hand, had to show his ideological mettle by spurning wage controls. Still the Government's beliefs had already been reflected in the Queen's Speech which contained proposals for legislation on picketing and the closed shop, for restructuring the National Enterprise Board, for allowing council tenants to buy their own houses – a measure which turned out to be a major vote-winner for the Government – for awarding the fourth television channel to the Independent Broadcasting Authority and for liberalizing regulations regarding long-distance coach-driving.

It was the Government's first budget, however, which nailed its colours firmly to the monetarist mast. For at the centre of its strategy was a cut in direct taxation and a firm commitment to reduce the money supply. In retrospect it appears to have been a very bold budget but in a sense it had to be since the underlying rate of inflation was calculated to be 15 per cent and rising. Indeed, public expenditure was in danger of climbing out of control given the large pay rises in the public sector and the increasing subsidies being paid to the nationalized industries. None the less, Sir Geoffrey's audacity was greater than expected. To begin with, he cut income tax at the top marginal rate from 83 per cent to 60 per cent and cut the basic rate from 33 per cent to 30 per cent. He also established a higher threshold for the investment income surcharge. To ensure that these measures did not increase the growth in money supply, however, he combined the split rate of VAT (8 per cent and 12·5 per cent) and raised it to 15 per cent. He also announced increases in other indirect taxation. Moreover, to emphasize the overall direction of his strategy he reduced public spending for the forthcoming year by an extra £1·5 billion, aimed to squeeze out yet another £1 billion by cash limits on government expenditure, and planned to raise yet another £1 billion from the sale of public-sector assets. Several measures were introduced to increase incentives in the economy – various capital taxes for example were significantly lightened – while controls on pay, prices and dividends were all abolished. A start was also made on abolishing exchange controls, a process which was completed at the end of October 1979. Significantly, the Chancellor made no announcements regarding wages policy. He avoided any mention of pay-norms, guidelines or even hopes. These instead were pinned on setting a target for the money supply which was defined as M3 (cash plus current and deposit accounts in banks). This was fixed within a range of 7 to 11 per cent (down from 8 to 12 in the previous year) and unions and management were expected to take their cue from it in negotiating wage settlements. In the public sector, of course, unions would find themselves bargaining within the constraints imposed by cash limits. The banks were also to take their cue from the M3 figure, but to give them guidance the Government raised the MLR (minimum lending rate) from 12 to 14 per cent.

As a result of this strategy, unfortunately, prices had to go up. The increase in indirect taxes alone raised the retail prices index by almost 4 per cent. But cuts in subsidies to the nationalized industries meant price increases there, too. Moreover, these price increases came on top of the inflationary pressures already in the economy. The Government tried to obscure the rise in prices by establishing a tax and prices index, but this was a move it would later regret. More immediately worrying was the fact that the increase in prices led to greater borrowing from the banks, while the cut in income tax reduced government revenue. Strikes in the public services reduced this further while rising unemployment increased the Government's spending commitments. All this meant an increase in the money supply as public borrowing grew. To emphasize the Government's determination to stick to its strategy, therefore, MLR was raised to a record 17 per cent in the early autumn of 1979. The Government also had to warn its supporters not to expect further cuts in income tax. Instead, a further cut of £680 million in public expenditure was announced in yet another attempt to reduce monetary growth.

The second budget of Mrs Thatcher's government in March 1980 attempted to make economic strategy crystal clear by introducing the so-called Medium Term Financial Strategy. This was designed to establish explicit targets for monetary growth over a number of years ahead. Targets were to be gradually reduced by a policy of cutting government spending and by raising taxation if necessary. As events were to prove, however, this was not an easy course to pursue, since for a number of technical reasons controlling the money supply was found to be rather tricky. Indeed, the very measurement of the money supply was to turn out to be immensely difficult. This led to a clash in the summer of 1980 between the Prime Minister and the Bank of England as well as to 'an inconclusive monetary review' carried out by it at her request.

The Government's position was being continuously undermined in 1980 by an increase in unemployment (of no less than 836,000), a rapid growth in labour costs and most of all by a sharp rise in the value of the pound. This had already risen by 9·25 per cent during the previous year and now increased by a further 12 per cent. All these factors led to greater public and private borrowing and hence to greater monetary growth. The result was that public expenditure programmes had to be cut once more in the autumn, a new tax was levied on North Sea oil and national insurance contributions increased for employers. The rise in the value of the pound, on the other hand, was now speciously employed to justify a cut in MLR to 14 per cent. Since monetary growth was still clearly in evidence this appeared to presage a change in Government strategy only a year and a half after its election. Yet, despite this possibility, no change occurred. Mrs Thatcher was determined not to emulate her predecessor in the Conservative leadership and execute a U-turn half way through her term of office. 'You turn if you like,' she said in a famous pun, 'the lady's not for turning.' Thus, despite the large increases in unemployment, the 1981 budget took no account of inflation and did not raise tax thresholds and allowances. On the other hand, the planned level of public-sector borrowing for 1981–2 was raised upwards to £10·5 billion from £7·5 billion, although this measure was in line with previous ministerial statements that the PSBR (public sector borrowing requirement) should only fall as a percentage of total national output if the economy was growing, and could remain unchanged in recession years. Overall, however, as the all-party Treasury and Civil Service Committee of the Commons noted, the 1981 Budget represented 'a tightening of the fiscal stance in 1981–2 compared with an unchanged policy position'. 'This tightening,' it added, came at a time when the economy was 'already in deep recession'. The rationale behind the budget, however, was to reduce MLR still further and this was now cut to 12 per cent. In fact, the Government began to take a more flexible line on monetary growth arguing that M3 alone was too rigid an indicator. It also interfered more with the exchange rate, cushioning the pound against a fall in oil prices, and began to make clear assumptions about the rate of wage increases when determining the cash limits it imposed on public expenditure. None the less the 1981 budget broadly confirmed the Government's strategy, and public-sector borrowing for 1981–2 was actually to undershoot its target by roughly £2 billion.

If there had been a temporary bulge in the PSBR in 1980–81, therefore, by 1982–3, in Peter Riddell's words, 'the level of borrowing was the lowest relative to GDP since the early 1970s and the deficit [had] been reduced more than in almost any other industrialized country'. One result of this – although how direct a result is a matter of great controversy – was that inflation began to fall. The twelvemonth rate of growth of retail prices had been 10·3 per cent in May 1979 and had risen to a peak of 21·9 per cent a year later. By April 1982 however it had fallen to single figures. If the Government claimed this was due to efficient monetary control and management, its critics, inside and out, attributed this more to the increase in unemployment. For during 1980 another 645,000 people had joined the dole queue pushing the total to 2·78 million. The official figure thereafter soon rose over the 3 million mark. It was the lack of purchasing power created by this rise in unemployment, according to the critics, which had really reduced inflation.

Behind all these figures however lay considerable political activity on a number of fronts. Strenuous attempts were made to cut out waste, cut government costs and improve its efficiency. The Government also embarked upon a programme of privatization and introduced new legislation to reduce the power of the trade unions. The nationalized industries which were unprofitable were instructed to plan for profit, while last but not least large-scale and expensive schemes were introduced to cushion the impact of unemployment, especially on the young. Still, in the period May 1979 to September 1981, the steep rise in unemployment and inflation overshadowed whatever progress was being made and was to lead to serious political strains within the Cabinet. Before these are discussed, however, more must be said about these other spheres of Government activity.

Regarding the need for improving productivity in Whitehall, a number of measures were introduced. Cash limits were one way of keeping a tight control over expenditure, although they could not of course be applied to social security spending. Another method was to control civil service manpower. This was partly achieved by a freeze on recruitment and by privatization, but even by 1980–81 the number of civil servants per 10,000 taxpayers had been reduced from the 1979 level of 24 to 21. The Government also claimed that the relative cost of administering social security benefits dropped by 6 per cent in the same period. In another move to boost the efficiency of the civil service Sir Derek Rayner was brought in from Marks and Spencers to review the whole field of government operations. He and the unit assigned to him undertook 135 scrutinies and six inter-departmental reviews which produced actual and potential annual savings of at least £300 million in addition to instant economies of £37 million. A further approach to efficiency was MINIS, a management information system launched in the Department of the Environment in 1980 by Michael Heseltine. This was aimed at developing a more clear-cut approach to policy objectives and manpower-allocation within government departments but it is still not clear how effectively it worked. The major field of Government activity was, naturally, its attempt to hold down public-sector pay increases. Cash limits were supposed to do the job here but the Clegg Commission awards of 1979–80 played havoc with these to begin with. Then in 1980–81 the Government decided to impose cash limits of 14 per cent on pay increases for non-industrial civil servants while the Civil Service Pay Research Unit recommended a rise of almost 19 per cent. The resulting compromise was a 'messy' one in the view of one distinguished commentator and led to criticism that the Government was not fully in control. The result was that after 1980 its style became more declaratory. Since it seemed inevitable that some kind of figure would have to be adopted as a guideline for public-sector pay increases the Government began to edge more and more towards a public-sector wages policy. This led to the suspension of the Civil Service Pay Research Unit and a head-on clash with the civil service unions in 1981 resulting in selective strikes. One of these affected the national computer centre and helped deny the Government access to much-needed revenue. This in turn had implications for government borrowing. Still the dispute was not finally settled until July 1982 when the unions reluctantly compromised. Not until the inflation rate began to fall, however was the Government able to negotiate pay settlements in the public services which were more or less within its total cash limits. Even then there was a lengthy dispute in the National Health Service over the pay of nurses and ancillary workers which once again arose partly over disputes concerning the status of review bodies. The result was that in July 1983, when a new body was established to review pay in the NHS, the Government reserved the right to exclude from it any group which 'resort[ed] to industrial action'. Thus if the Government eventually succeeded in containing public-sector wages within its financial targets, in Peter Riddell's words 'this was at the cost of considerable resentment and accusations of unfairness as traditional procedures were over-ridden'.

Two other areas of public expenditure were of course of vital importance to the Thatcher strategy. These were the nationalized industries and local government. Regarding the former, the ultimate solution foreseen by the Government was privatization (the positive synonym for 'denationalization'). This was a process which was indeed inaugurated in many cases but the most immediate problem facing the Government was how to finance their external deficits. These totalled around £1 billion in 1981–2 and £2·2 billion in 1982–3. In fact the latter was £0·5 billion less than was feared, for one of the major problems regarding these deficits was the frequent unreliability of the projected figures. None the less, the drain on government resources they represented was a constant thorn in the Government's flesh.

A privatization programme had been investigated while the Conservatives had been in opposition by a working party under Nicholas Ridley. However, the 1979 party manifesto had mentioned only the denationalization of the two industries nationalized under Labour (aerospace and shipbuilding) plus the National Freight Corporation. Now, under the influence of Sir Keith Joseph, a more ambitious approach was developed until in the end no nationalized industry was considered to be immune from eventual return to the private sector. The rationale was that this would make them more conducive to competition, enhance consumer choice, increase efficiency and reduce public-sector borrowing. In many cases, however, it was admitted that the industries concerned would either have to be made profitable before a return to the private sector could be envisaged or else only the profitable parts could be sold off.

At first the main priority in privatization was simply the need to hold down the PSBR. This accounted for the £1 billion sale of public assets in 1979–80 (sales in BP, advanced sales in oil). After 1981, however, the Government adopted a more radical approach. This began with an investigation of the nationalized industries by the Think Tank, followed by investigations by the Monopolies and Mergers Commission and the appointment of new chairmen to replace those left over from Labour's years in office. Most of the newcomers were deliberately brought in from outside the industries concerned, however, in order to promote 'a relationship on a strictly commercial basis'. Key figures included Mr Ian MacGregor at British Steel (and later at the National Coal Board), Sir John King at British Airways and of course, Sir Michael Edwardes at British Leyland. The latter, however, was to reveal in his memoirs, entitled *Back from the Brink*, that even his relations with the Government were far from smooth. Still since Sir John King and Sir Michael Edwardes were to bring their industries back into the black, and thus prepare them for privatization, the Government felt able to go ahead in other fields. It sold over half its shares in British Aerospace, nearly half its shares in Cable and Wireless, it sold the National Freight Corporation to consortia of managers and employees, sold its shares in the radio-chemical Amersham International, sold its shares in Associated British Ports, sold the British Leyland offshoots Alvis, Prestcold and Coventry Climax, sold its shares in Britoil, sold British Rail's hovercraft and hotels, and finally sold the National Enterprise Board's interests in companies such as Ferranti, ICL, Fairey and other groups. All this was completed by 1983. Yet on the cards for short-term future privatization were British Telecom, Sealink, British Shipbuilders' repair yards, British Airways, the Royal Ordnance Factories and various interests in British Gas. In the medium-term future it was hoped to privatize the warship yards of British Shipbuilders, the Jaguar, Land-Rover and Unipart sections of British Leyland, the National Bus Company and British Airports. In the long-term, finally, it was hoped to privatize British Steel, British Gas, the National Giro Bank, the National Coal Board, Rolls-Royce Aero-engines, the remainder of British Leyland, the Central Electricity Generating Board and perhaps even the Post Office. The principle behind the Government's policy had therefore become that outlined by Mr Nigel Lawson in September 1982. 'No industry,' he said, 'should remain under state ownership unless there is a positive and overwhelming case for it so doing. Inertia is not good enough. We simply cannot afford it.' On the other hand the Government's short- and medium-term programme offered it the opportunity of realizing some £12 billion and that was over and above the £1·7 billion it had already raised.

Inevitably, criticisms were made about the way in which the Government had disposed of its assets. It was claimed that these had been sold off to too few investors in the case of British Aerospace, Cable and Wireless and Amersham International. Likewise it was claimed that the price of sale had been too low. Yet, when another method was employed in the case of Britoil – sale by tender – the Government was criticized for the initial undersubscription of shares. Finally, in almost all cases – as in the sale of council houses to tenants – it was claimed that far too much was paid by the Government by way of fees to middle-men, agents, brokers and accountants. And overhanging the whole policy from beginning to end was the fear – most often expressed with relation to British Telecom, the privatization of which was debated in 1983 – that public monopolies would simply turn into private ones unless the Government paid greater attention to the claims of interested competitors. Still, it could hardly be denied that, with regard to nationalized industries, the Government's approach had become a vigorous one.

The Government had also been taking a robust approach to local government in its attempts to keep control of public expenditure. Here there were two major priorities: to contain local spending within overall targets for expenditure; and to keep down rate increases in accordance with the Government's anti-inflationary drive. Both priorities provoked a clash with local councillors, although, in the case of a limited number of Labour-controlled local authorities, local councillors went out of their way to invite a clash. It was very easy after all to present the issue as one of centralization versus local autonomy rather than a straightforward battle over expenditure control.

The Government's case was that since local government expenditure represented between a fifth and a quarter of all public expenditure, the Treasury simply could not ignore what local authorities spent. It also argued that in many cases local authorities were not democratically controlled: electoral boundaries often precluded any hope of change in political leadership in the localities; the turnout of voters was often extremely low; many voters in any case paid no rates, while those who did (e.g. local businessmen) had often long ago been disenfranchised. Under these circumstances, according to the Government, it was little wonder that in certain areas of the country – Ken Livingstone's London was most in mind – unrepresentative cliques of rabid left-wingers were able to dispense thousands of pounds of ratepayers' money to a variety of special interest groups including blacks, Irish, homosexuals and peace-campaigners, at the expense of the suffering majority, whose rates had to be increased to pay the necessary bills. The Government, however, stressed that it in no way wished to dictate the details of local government spending but merely the parameters in which it occurred. It thus hoped that such local authorities would be forced to choose between such actions and other less expensive and controversial ones.

The Government might also have argued that the powers held by local authorities had all, at one time or another, been delegated to them by central government. This was another indication of the Government's right to control how these powers were exercised. Yet it was really only the financial aspect of local authority activity in which the Government was interested because three-fifths of local spending was centrally financed by Rate Support Grants. In fact, it was its method of distributing this grant which was to cause many of the Government's problems.

In the 1970s central and local government had apparently cooperated reasonably smoothly. The Labour government in 1977 had called for greater control of local expenditure and this for the most part had been achieved. But the method of financing local government expenditure had always contained a potential difficulty. For the grant allocated to any local authority increased as local spending increased. Mrs Thatcher's government therefore, in coming into office, changed this method of allocating grants in an attempt to limit local spending. Under a new system of 'grant-related expenditure', local authority spending was to be brought into line with central government estimates of local needs. If local authorities exceeded these estimates they were liable to have their rate support grants reduced. The rub was, however, that they could compensate for any reduction by simply increasing their local rates. And this, in fact, was what happened in many inner city areas between 1979 and 1983. In the country as a whole for the same period, local authority expenditure exceeded government target levels by between 5·7 and 8 per cent. Conservative supporters, therefore, demanded a reform of local taxation in the hope of reducing rates, but a government Green Paper of 1981 showed just how difficult a task this was. As an alternative Mrs Thatcher was forced in 1983 to promise to abolish the metropolitan councils and the GLC, and to introduce reserve powers for the Government to enforce reductions in local authority spending if such a course of action should prove to be necessary.

Other measures taken by the Government to boost private enterprise and to reduce government spending included the abolition of various permits and controls; the establishment of enterprise zones and free ports (areas in which taxation was reduced and regulations lightened); lower contributions by employers to the national insurance surcharge; assistance for small businesses through the reduction of corporation tax, as well as by direct financial help through loan-guarantee and expansion schemes; and aid for high technology. After 1981 in particular the Department of Industry under Patrick Jenkin concentrated less on aiding lame ducks and more on aiding research. Thus between 1978/9 and 1983/4 support for innovation in science and technology increased five-fold to £250 million. One hundred and fifty Information Technology Centres were created for unemployed youths while microcomputers were introduced in all secondary schools and a third of all primary ones. The National Enterprise Board was forced to sell off its investments and to amalgamate with the National Research and Development Council to form the British Technology Group. This in turn was given the brief of coordinating industrial technology with university research. The lead in developing this policy was taken by the Minister for Information Technology, Kenneth Baker, but he was given the powerful support of Mrs Thatcher herself, who was proud to be the first science graduate to have become Prime Minister. She was criticized by some, however, for being more mercantilist than liberal in her attitudes in this field.

THE GOVERNMENT AND THE TRADE UNIONS

According to the 'Thatcherite' (and more particularly the Hayekian) view of Britain's past, of course, the main obstacle to British enterprise had been the privileged position and reactionary attitudes of British trade unions. These not only enforced overmanning and outdated restrictive working practices in industry but, on account of their dominant political influence in the Labour Party, had come to be able to intimidate British management. The latter, it was argued, on account of closed shops and the threat of strikes, were simply in no position to introduce new plant, investment or working practices into increasingly outdated British factories. Thus the question 'who rules Britain' or rather 'who rules British Industry' was seen as one which still had to be settled. The winter of discontent of 1979 had, after all, reintroduced it to the centre of politics. Mrs Thatcher thus had every reason to believe that she had been elected to put the unions in their place. And that place, she had made clear in her election campaign, would not be in the antechambers of 10 Downing Street. There would in future be 'no beer and sandwiches at number ten', in other words, there would be no attempt to buy industrial peace by buying off the union barons. And when she met them not long after the election at number ten she made this perfectly clear. On the other hand, memories of Mr Heath's 1974 débâcle were still in Mrs Thatcher's mind and so too was the awareness of public distaste for 'confrontation' in industry. The result was that she was prepared to accept that the unions would have to be constrained step by step. This was the case put forward by Jim Prior, her Secretary of State for Employment and arch-wet, whose Act of 1980 was to appear too moderate a measure for many of the drier members of the party faithful.

The specific areas of reform mentioned in the 1979 manifesto had included a review of existing legal immunities for trade unions with regard to secondary picketing, blacking and blockading; rights of appeal and compensation for those losing their jobs through the operation of the closed shop; and the offer of public money to finance postal ballots for union elections and other important union issues. In short, the manifesto had been a strictly minimalist one. Many in the Conservative Party, however, believed that a Thatcher government should go further, that it should outlaw secondary strikes, make trade unions liable to civil damages, cut off social security benefits to members of strikers' families (hence forcing the unions to risk bankruptcy by dispensing more of their own cash to strikers) and alter the PAYE system to prevent it giving immediate tax rebates to strikers. There was also a desire on the part of many Conservatives to end the system whereby members of any trade union affiliated to the Labour Party automatically paid a political levy ('contracted in') to Labour Party funds. Mrs Thatcher was felt – and probably rightly – to support moves in all these directions, for her rhetoric in 1979–80 on the trade union issue made clear her resolve to prevent 'a small minority's determination to impose its will upon the majority'.

The Employment Bill presented by Prior to Parliament in December 1979, none the less, was a very moderate one. Drawn up after almost daily consultation with Harry Unwin, the deputy general secretary of the TGWU representing the TUC, the Bill, in Hugh Stephenson's words 'proposed the minimum that was consistent with the manifesto, perhaps even less'. It thus offered some financial compensation for those who had run foul of the closed shop; promised financial support for union ballots; proposed the right of appeal to the High Court for those unfairly excluded from union membership; and contained provisions for employers to be able to obtain injunctions against secondary picketing by workers not directly involved in a dispute. Significantly, however, it said absolutely nothing about secondary or sympathy strikes, nothing about making unions liable to civil damages and nothing about social security benefits for strikers. The Minister might none the less have had a quieter life regarding his Bill if a legal dispute over trade union immunities (*MacShane* v. *Express Newspapers Ltd*) had not occurred at just this moment and had a strike not broken out in the steel industry which involved the violent mass (and secondary) picketing of private steel firms. Both of these caused Prior to alter his Bill, for the Tory press now cried out in apocalyptic terms for much stronger legislation and no less than 100 Conservative MPs put their names to an early day motion in February 1980 calling for a return of industrial equity. Then, with the premier's backing, the Chancellor, Sir Geoffrey Howe, spoke out on the need for stronger measures. In a speech at Taunton he declared: 'It would be fatal to Britain's chances, if this government lost its nerve and neglected its clear duty to take in hand the necessary reform of the law.' It was now an open secret that the Cabinet were divided over the issue and that Mrs Thatcher was moving her support behind the Cabinet dries. In fact she now raised the issue of social security benefits and tax rebates to strikers while, in his second budget speech in March 1980, Sir Geoffrey announced that £12 would be deducted per week from supplementary benefits to strikers' families. In the end, however, it was the wets who won the day and Prior introduced only cosmetic changes to his Bill in respect of secondary strikes (which were outlawed only if overtly political) and in respect of civil damages. Here anybody other than a direct customer or supplier of the firm involved in a strike was given protection through the courts against breach of commercial contracts, though still not against unions inducing their work force to break contracts of employment. Despite a number of backbench revolts, the Bill became law in April 1980. On the other hand, the Prime Minister, whose authority had been brought into question over trade union reform, made it clear in a television interview that the whole issue had not yet been finally settled. She told the broadcaster, Sir Robin Day, that she was still determined to go further to protect those who suffered commercially from secondary striking and promised further legislation in the future. She said: 'By the time the next election is here, we've got to have done it.' Predictably, therefore, another Act was passed in 1982. By then the extremely dry Mr Norman Tebbit, Mrs Thatcher's most prominent cabinet supporter, had replaced Mr Prior at the Department of Employment. His hostility to the unions was legendary and it was feared that his approach would be extreme. In fact, as in 1980, the legislation was more moderate than expected. It did, however, outlaw secondary strikes, strengthen the rights of individuals against closed shops, give employers greater freedom to dismiss employees, made it unlawful to exclude from lists of tender firms which did not recognize trade unions, and reinforced the liability to compensation of unions which took part in unlawful disputes. Lawful disputes were now restricted to those between employers and their own workers over conditions, pay and jobs.

Although these Acts certainly redressed the industrial balance in favour of employers, their effect was largely psychological. Managers' morale was raised supposedly on account of the restoration of the 'right to manage'. In practice, the psychological shift was due as much to the continuing rise in unemployment. For, faced with mass redundancies and closures and the consequent huge loss of membership and union dues, the trade unions were simply in no position to indulge in often suicidal strikes. Thus, time after time potentially (and often actually) bitter disputes were settled in the interests of management. British Leyland was brought under managerial control, the railway strike of 1982 was called off, the miners refused to come out at Mr Scargill's bidding and disputes in the civil and health services were resolved. For long the question whether the legislation would have to be used remained unsettled, and it was only at the end of 1983 that it was really put to the test. In the event, however, Mr Len Murray of the TUC ensured that any challenge to the courts would fail and that the unions would obey the law. He had already warned on another occasion, however, that in the event of an economic upswing, the trade unions would be far less willing to retreat.

THE WELFARE STATE

The most controversial aspect of the Government's policy of restricting the growth of public expenditure was its alleged hostility to the Welfare State. For while there was no overt attack on the post-Beveridge consensus – 'The National Health Service is safe with us' the Prime Minister was to repeat on several occasions – there was, none the less, a change in Government priorities and emphases. Its approach in fact was summarized by the Social Services Secretary, Norman Fowler, in January 1983 when he said that policy had been based on the following considerations: that the proper starting point was the economy; that better value should be had for money spent; and that it should not be assumed that everything could or indeed should be done by the State. Nevertheless, although the Government did introduce measures to encourage the private provision of hospital beds, assisted places in private schools, the growth of private insurance schemes and perhaps most spectacularly of all, the sale of council houses to tenants, it launched no general assault on the National Health Service or public education. Its main concern, predictably, was merely to keep a tight control of public expenditure, and to cut back (though not reduce in absolute terms) the planned increases of the Callaghan administration. In the case of the NHS, however, there was almost as much growth as had been planned. Critics often seemed to confuse the privatization of ancillary services – maintenance, catering and laundry, etc. – with a reduction of social services.

The 1979 manifesto in fact had been short on specific commitments on welfare. Generally, it had promised only to use available resources more prudently rather than redesign welfare provision as a whole. Any changes which occurred, therefore, came about in a piecemeal fashion and for reasons which were much more economic than doctrinaire.

The social security budget, of course, rose sharply in real terms as a result of the increase in unemployment. Clearly it was impossible for the government to reduce the claims for unemployment allowances, rent rebates and supplementary benefit. However, the real value in pensions actually rose – by 7 per cent between 1979 and 1982 – because of an overestimation of the inflation rate. Likewise there was a rise in real terms in one-parent benefit, family income supplement and attendance and mobility allowances. However, in other areas benefits lagged behind – child benefit by about 4 per cent behind prices – while changes in the method of calculating increases, the abolition of the earnings related supplement and the fixing of the rise in unemployment and other benefits 5 per cent below the increase in inflation, were all of them moves in the opposite direction. The savings gained by these changes amounted to £2 billion a year by 1982/3. Yet they represented no coherent assault on the welfare state and were absolutely in line with previous adjustments in benefits carried out in the 1970s by the Callaghan and Wilson administrations. The Government could also claim with justice that given the size of the social security budget, cuts simply had to be made to it if public expenditure was ever to come under control. It could also point out that the cuts which were taking place elsewhere in Europe were much more severe and that the change in method of calculating benefits brought in in 1983 failed even to compensate for the overestimation of the increase in benefits in 1982. In the meantime, the social security budget continued to rise.

It was over the National Health Service that the Government, however, was most fiercely attacked. Yet not only was expenditure increased on it in real terms – it rose on average by 3 per cent per year – but the number of nurses, midwives, doctors, dentists and administrators employed by it increased, although there was a minor drop in the number of ancillary workers. The number of in-patients treated also rose by 3 per cent per year, the only decline being in the number of the mentally ill and handicapped. Behind these figures, though, lay certain changes. Spending *per capita*, thanks to demographic change, was down as was that on real current expenditure. Thus, the real rise in standards and resources was perhaps only about 1·5 per cent per year. On the other hand, given the rising number of old people in the population and the escalating costs of medical technology, it was a genuine achievement for the Government to have secured even this much progress in a period of overall retrenchment. That it was achieved was due primarily to gains in productivity. Resources were redistributed around several regions, wage increases had to be found from existing budgets, and administrators had often to finance priority projects from savings from and postponements of others. The problem was that such productivity gains would not be available in the future. And given that increased prescription charges had made no significant contribution to costs and that private medicine was seen only to be able to operate on the margins, the Government knew that growth in the economy would be essential if standards were to continue to be maintained in the future.

On education the Government's record was determined by the following considerations: the falling number of schoolchildren; the need to reduce expenditure; and the desire to maintain and, if possible, raise standards. Yet there were limits on government action. Local rather than central government had control of school and further education budgets and was also responsible for student grants. The universities, of course, were centrally funded but only indirectly through the UGC (University Grants Committee). Under these circumstances it was extremely difficult for Education Ministers to exercise budgetary or policy control.

Given the projected fall in pupil numbers the Government planned to reduce expenditure in real terms by 6·9 per cent between 1979 and 1983. The actual figure, thanks to local government resistance, turned out to be 1·2 per cent. Still, the fall in pupil numbers, together with the reduction in resources did lead to certain changes in certain areas: the closure of schools, an increased number of classes of mixed ages and a lack of up-to-date textbooks. There were also regional differences in the availability of ancillary services.

The Government, meanwhile, tried its best to maintain or raise standards in schools. Sir Keith Joseph, as Secretary of State for Education, called in February 1981 for more attention to be paid to basic skills. His aim was to ensure that all children left primary school with the ability to read, write and count. He also called for a 'core curriculum' in secondary schools (where microcomputers were introduced) but this proved nigh impossible to bring about. One minor change within his power, on the other hand, was the establishment of 5,000 assisted places which were made available each year in independent schools to pupils whose parents could not afford to pay the fees.

With regard to the universities, of course, Sir Keith had greater scope. Here capital expenditure plans were curtailed, the fees of foreign students charged at twice the home rate and all fees raised. Home fees, of course, were paid mostly by local authorities. It was also planned to reduce the number of dons by one sixth by 1984–5 and the science-based universities of the North were selected by the UGC to bear the brunt of reductions. However, the Government ran into problems concerning the legal status of academics' tenure. It also very soon had to create 'new blooureships' to forestall a future shortage of academic staff once early retirement programmes began to cut into staff–student ratios. The number of students entering higher education, on the other hand, actually rose between 1979 and 1983. However, the supply of British graduate students was reduced to a trickle. The result was that morale in the universities sank considerably, especially since academic salary increases were kept extremely low. On the other hand, it should be pointed out with regard to the Government's record on education in general that, despite many fears and scares, there was no switch from student grants to loans; no education vouchers for schools were introduced; and the Robbins principle, allowing access to higher education for those qualified to benefit, was left undisturbed.

The main area for cuts in public expenditure turned out to be housing. Here public-sector completions fell from 104,000 in 1979 to 49,200 in 1982, the lowest figure since the 1920s. During the same period council house rents more than doubled (in cash terms) while subsidies from central government and rates were cut by more than 50 per cent (in real terms). The view taken by the Government was that the private sector should be the main supplier of housing and that the public sector should only provide a safety net. The balance was therefore tilted towards the private sector by maintaining existing levels of mortgage relief while raising council rents. On the other hand, by the Housing Act of 1980, sitting council tenants were given the right to buy their houses and flats at discounts of up to 50 per cent of the market price in certain cases, a right which was later extended to other classes of tenants. The results were dramatic and between 1979 and 1983 about half a million houses and flats were sold. Given other incentives for home buying, the percentage of owner-occupied households rose from 54 per cent to 59 per cent in England and Wales by 1983, the greatest change since 1945. The result was that by 1983 £1·87 billion had been raised from council house sales. The policy also made political sense. Almost 60 per cent of Labour voters who bought their houses voted Conservative in the general election of 1983 and of all the home-buyers concerned 56 per cent voted Tory and only 18 per cent Labour. It was little wonder then that the Government welcomed the new, mixed character of housing estates. In the new towns, like Basildon and Peterborough, Labour did particularly badly. Partly this was because local Labour authorities had often put obstacles in the way of home-buying. This was on the grounds that the sale of housing stock deprived councils of their best homes and created divisions on housing estates. It also, of course, meant a net reduction of the housing stock given the reduced number of houses which were being constructed. Moreover, the sale of council houses threatened to leave at the bottom of the social pyramid a minority of low-paid and disadvantaged working-class tenants. Finally, with regard to housing policy, the Government attempted to stimulate the market in privately rented accommodation but the measures adopted had little effect.

Overall, it can be argued that there was no concerted attack on the welfare state under Mrs Thatcher, but a continuation of the kind of policies pursued by Wilson and Callaghan. Under them too public expenditure had had to be constrained and, like Mrs Thatcher, they had occasionally indulged in some temporary de-indexation of benefits. Yet the squeeze after 1979 had become a harder one and without economic growth in the future it was a moot question by 1983 whether standards could still be maintained by productivity gains if public expenditure were not to be allowed to rise as a percentage of total output. There was also the suspicion that the poor were being allowed to suffer most since it was the squeeze on housing which was most severe. Finally, there were plenty of leaked documents and reports during this period which, predictably, were interpreted as indicating a future assault on the welfare state. One of these was a famous Think Tank Report (the dubious quality of which might well have speeded that body's demise) but others came from the Government's Family Policy Group which aimed at promoting family responsibility in fields of welfare. These aims were regarded with particular suspicion by many on the more doctrinaire Left. By 1983, however, there was at last some indication of renewed growth in the economy and an apparent acceptance by Mrs Thatcher that the welfare state was here to stay. Certainly opinion polls by 1983 were displaying a rise in the percentage of those who favoured increased taxes above welfare cuts. And the proportion of those who preferred tax cuts at the expense of social services provision fell from about one-third to one-fifth. In Peter Riddell's characteristically balanced assessment: 'Mrs Thatcher [had] yet to persuade the public of the need to challenge the post-Beveridge consensus on the social services.'

LAW AND ORDER

Yet, despite all the problems created by trade union reform and all the disputes over the need to fix and re-fix monetary targets and hold down public expenditure in the interests of an economy more attuned to private enterprise, the greatest challenge to the Government's authority came in a totally unexpected form. For perhaps the most ominous development in domestic affairs during the first half of Mrs Thatcher's premiership were the riots which erupted suddenly in the spring and summer of 1981, when police clashed violently with mainly coloured demonstrators in London, Liverpool, Manchester and several other English cities.

Only one of these clashes could accurately be described as a 'race riot', the one which took place in Southall (London) when members of the Asian community drove off white militants who had come to attack them. Elsewhere the riots were directed principally against the police by groups of people which included whites. As the *Economist* put it:

Nowhere else did an exclusively black crowd fight an exclusively white crowd, except in so far as many police forces have no black members. Violence was directed discriminatingly against property and the police, rather than against neighbours of other races. But the major disorders had a racial complexion, involving tension between local communities of mixed race and the police.

Behind the riots were a number of factors: the economic recession which hit young people with little education hardest; the decline of the inner cities; immigration; racial prejudice; crime, together with the fear which it inspired and the responses it occasioned. Each riot, however, had particular origins of its own.

There had been hints of rioting the previous year. In Bristol, for example, in April 1980, a police raid on the 'Black and White' café had sparked off disorders which prefigured in miniature the events of 1981. These events also began in April when in the aftermath of 'Operation Swamp' riots took place in Brixton in South London as a result of which 279 policemen and 45 members of the public were injured. 'Operation Swamp' was an exercise designed by the local police to prevent street crime, particularly mugging, by putting large numbers of plainclothes policemen on the street to stop and search suspects, mainly young blacks. It started on Monday 6 April 1981, and by the Friday of that week 943 people had been questioned – half of them black. Ninety-three were charged with minor offences, only one with robbery. This meant that 850 people in the view of the local community had been needlessly stopped. Then on 11 April two policemen tried to 'rescue' a black man with a stab wound in the neck whom they saw fleeing from some fellow blacks. He in turn, however, was 'rescued' from the police by a crowd of onlookers and sent to hospital by minicab. The extra police who by now had been summoned were subsequently abused by the crowd and pelted with bricks. Fighting then began which ended only when older blacks intervened. Yet on the following night violence again erupted and black and white youths used firebombs and missiles to attack the large police force which had been drafted into the area. Police and other cars were overturned and set alight, shop-windows were smashed throughout the shopping centre and a great deal of looting took place – often by whites. These scenes were repeated for the next three days until the riot petered out. The police blamed it on 'outside agitators' but presented no serious evidence to substantiate this claim. The Government, for its part, while very properly affirming its determination to maintain law and order, appointed Lord Scarman to report on events and to make recommendations. The public meanwhile feared their repetition and had their fears quickly vindicated in July, when riots erupted in London (Southall), Liverpool (Toxteth) and many other places.

These riots began when disturbances occurred by pure coincidence in Southall and Toxteth on the same day, 3 July. In Southall, in an atmosphere made tense by recent racial murders in South and East London, members of the local Asian community were threatened by skinhead followers of a band called the '4-skins'. Groups of Asians consequently gathered in self-defence, and in a gesture of retaliation burned down the pub in which the band had been performing. The police, who had been alerted to these events and who were forced to protect fleeing skinheads, then found themselves attacked by young Asians. Over 100 policemen were injured. On the same night police in Toxteth tried to arrest a young black who they believed had stolen a motor bike. The bike in fact was his own which led his friends to impede his arrest and to stone police vehicles. The following day, therefore, the police displayed themselves in force but were attacked with a variety of missiles. Worse still, many shops and buildings were set alight and looting took place. This provoked tough counter-measures and, for the first time ever in Britain, CS gas was fired at rioters. Since the police used cartridges, however, which were meant to penetrate doors many bystanders and rioters were injured. Yet over 200 policemen (many drafted in from outside) were also hurt before the violence simmered down.

After Southall and Toxteth there were 'copycat' riots, inspired by the media coverage of that weekend. On 8–9 July one of these occurred in Moss Side in Manchester but tough local policing and the cooperation of black community leaders soon contained the arson and looting. Likewise, in Handsworth in Birmingham, consultation with local community representatives brought a rapid return of order after another riot. Yet on the weekend of 10–12 July there was trouble once again in Birmingham, Blackburn, Bradford, Derby, Leeds, Leicester and Wolverhampton. Petrol bombs were even thrown in Welsh mining valleys and, according to the *Economist*, 'ordinary Saturday-night brawls outside the pubs won instant promotion to riot status'. There was trouble once again in Brixton where cars were burned and where as a result the police smashed up a row of houses owned by blacks. This was in the course of a bomb-search in which they found nothing. The last riot took place, in Toxteth again, on the night of 28–29 July, when even schoolchildren joined in the assault on the police. It was during this riot that a police van ran down a young, white cripple. Very surprisingly, he was the only fatal casualty of all the recent violence. The riots then simply stopped as suddenly as they had started and the press was left to concentrate its attention on the next great national event of the summer: the marriage on 29 July, of the Prince of Wales to Lady Diana Spencer.

The experience of almost American-style riots alarmed the British public, particularly since they raised awkward questions concerning the police. Traditionally the public had been proud of their policemen who still enjoyed enormous respect. They were also politically protected by a bipartisan approach by governments, although by 1981 the Labour Party was beginning to adopt a much more critical stance. Mrs Thatcher's government, on the other hand, had been a warm supporter of its law enforcers and had made its determination to uphold law and order a major part of its appeal. The threatened collapse of the rule of law was therefore keenly felt by it. So too was to be the fact that from 1981 onwards the police were to figure as prominently in the debate on crime as were the criminals. This process reached its culmination in 1983 when a report on the Metropolitan police by the Policy Studies Institute, a 400-page document which had been commissioned by the Metropolitan Police Commissioner himself, condemned them as bigoted, racist, sexist, bored, dishonest and often drunk. By then, however, expectations had greatly fallen. Londoners no longer expected their police to be wonderful though a surprisingly high 66 per cent still thought that they served the city well. By 1983 a series of events had undermined confidence in the police throughout the country – reports of corruption in London and elsewhere, the bungled hunt in Yorkshire for a notorious mass murderer, an intruder disturbing the Queen in her bedroom at Buckingham Palace, the aggressive questioning by police of a rape victim as shown on television, the almost fatal shooting and pistol-whipping of an innocent man in the centre of London amid the rush-hour traffic, not to mention numerous stories of racial and sexual prejudice. The system of investigating complaints against the police (operated by the police themselves) which had been established in 1977 was also considered a failure, while the rate of securing convictions for crimes – only 17 per cent in London – was clearly extremely low. Finally, there was the accusation that there was no democratic control over the police, nor even any means whereby locally elected representatives could influence police policy within their localities. All this meant that the Government came under increasing pressure to protect the public from the police as much as from criminals. It was a kind of pressure to which Mrs Thatcher had never dreamed of having to respond. For her thoughts regarding the police in 1979 had been restricted to raising their salaries to enhance recruitment, providing them with more resources to fight the rise in crime and, with luck, enhancing the criminal's fear of retribution by restoring the death-penalty.

Crime in Britain had certainly risen dramatically during the 1970s. In 1970 there were under 1·6 million 'serious crimes' known to the police in England and Wales; in 1981 there were 2·8 million. It was little wonder, therefore, that the British Crime Survey of 1982 showed that 60 per cent of elderly women living in the inner cities felt 'very unsafe' walking home at night or that 38 per cent of middle-aged ones should have felt the same. Indeed, Mrs Thatcher's reference in her last election broadcast to 'feeling safe in the streets' had already struck a responsive chord, with her party securing a 72 per cent lead over Labour on this issue in the opinion polls. Once in office moreover she had implemented her election pledges. Between 1978/9 and 1982/3 spending on the police in real terms had increased by almost 25 per cent. Between 1979 and 1983 the salary of a police constable was to rise in real terms by over 30 per cent with the result that the number of policemen employed in England and Wales rose by 9,500 to more than 120,000 during her first term of office. And of these an increasing proportion were put back on the beat. Other measures were also introduced: a wider range of penalties was made available to the courts; a 'short, sharp, shock regime' for young offenders was introduced in detention centres; more compensation was paid to the victims of crime; the largest prison building programme for decades was begun; and a free vote was held in the House of Commons on a motion which sought, albeit in vain, to restore the death penalty. Yet it was clear that reform of the police themselves had never been on the Conservative Party's legislative agenda and that despite tell-tale signs of the fall in public confidence – such as the increasing refusal of juries to convict on the evidence of policemen alone – it never would. Too many Conservative activists and voters believed that to do so would play into the hands of Marxists and criminals. Yet the demand for police reform was to remain central to the political debate thanks to both the Labour Party and Lord Scarman.

A number of developments within the Labour movement impinged on police affairs. In 1979, for example, the Labour MP, Jack Straw, had introduced a private member's bill which, if successful, would have made local police forces responsible to committees of local councillors. Then in May 1981 Labour won control of the Greater London Council (GLC) and established a police committee with a support staff in the capital. Meanwhile, after Roy Hattersley's appointment as Shadow Home Secretary in December 1980 the party became more officially outspoken in its criticism of the police. This change of emphasis was seen in its response to the January 1981 report of the Royal Commission on Criminal Procedure and in Hattersley's severe criticisms of the Government's handling of the 1981 riots. Its policy, he said, had been one of matching violence with violence by arming the police with tear-gas, water-cannons and armoured vehicles. Yet a greater problem for the Government than Hattersley's criticism was the publication of Lord Scarman's report which, while defending the measures adopted by the police to contain the riots, made a host of recommendations regarding police training and recruitment. These included the recruitment of more black officers, the screening of recruits for racial prejudice, better training in dealing with the public; greater disciplinary measures, including the dismissal of officers found guilty of discriminatory behaviour; greater consultation with local communities; greater guarantees against police abuse of authority; more on-the-beat policing; the banning of racist marches in mixed neighbourhoods; greater regulation of police powers of search; and safeguards for the use of water-cannon, tear-gas and other methods of riot control. Yet Scarman warned that the Government would have to deal not merely with police behaviour but with the wider social issues raised by the riots. 'Any attempt,' he wrote, 'to resolve the circumstances from which the disorders of this year sprang cannot be limited to recommendations about policing but must embrace the wider social context in which policing is carried out.' He therefore called upon the Government to help regenerate the inner cities and to ensure that blacks were not discriminated against in housing, jobs and education. Indeed, he called for a direct attack, coordinated by government, on racial disadvantage, arguing most controversially that this would 'inevitably [mean] that the ethnic minorities [would] enjoy for a time a positive discrimination in their favour'. His maxim was: 'Good policing will be of no avail, unless we also tackle and eliminate basic flaws in our society. And, if we succeed in eliminating racial prejudice from our society, it will not be difficult to achieve good policing.'

The Government welcomed the report but there was never any chance of it introducing 'positive discrimination', particularly at a time when many young whites were also unemployed. In any case, Mrs Thatcher did not accept that there was any simple or direct link between unemployment and crime. This, she pointed out, had risen rapidly even when unemployment had been low. Finally, on the narrow question of policing, her reaction was a cautious one. Thus, while the Police and Criminal Evidence Bill, introduced by her government in the autumn of 1982, provided for a statutory framework for consultation between the police and local authorities and introduced a more independent element into police complaints procedures, it, none the less, proposed to extend the powers of the police to stop and search suspects, to keep them in custody and to search their homes and work-places. It therefore gave rise to strong opposition and was not immediately reintroduced after the general election of 1983.

The police themselves, meanwhile, having examined the lessons of the 1981 riots and under pressure from Lord Scarman's report, attempted to establish consultative committees with local communities and authorities. In London, for example, the newly appointed Metropolitan Commissioner, Sir Kenneth Newman, a former chief of the Royal Ulster Constabulary (RUC) encouraged the establishment of such committees at borough level. This was not always easy – his middle-ranking officers were unenthusiastic and in Brixton the arrest previously of black race relations workers had led to ill-feeling on the part of local community leaders. Yet, before long, such committees were proving their worth. The Labour Party, on the other hand, still insisted that the police should be made formally responsible to committees of elected representatives.

The most spectacular result of the Scarman report, however, was the appointment as 'Minister for Merseyside' of Mr Michael Heseltine, the Environment Secretary, who was entrusted with the task of regenerating Toxteth and the poorer areas of Liverpool. His plan to tackle this was based on a partnership he hoped to establish between the government and private enterprise. With this objective in mind he organized a tour of the area for managers of pension funds, banks and other financial institutions and subsequently launched a number of projects designed to increase housing and job opportunities. This approach was in line with other Government policies to regenerate the inner cities, for example, the establishment of Local Enterprise Agencies and Urban Development Corporations. Yet, given cuts in government support grants to many inner-city authorities, as a result of the Government's efforts to control local government spending, the task of regeneration was clearly not going to be an easy one.

RACE RELATIONS

The other main policy area on which action had been called for by Scarman was race relations. The fact that so many rioters had been black was undoubtedly significant. Scarman himself had interpreted this significance in a particular way by drawing public attention to specific areas of racial discrimination. The Metropolitan Police the following year did so in another way by releasing statistics which showed that street crime was disproportionately committed by blacks. The figures were so poorly presented, however, that more discredit fell on the police. Yet the knowledge that much street crime and violence was committed by young blacks together with reports (such as the 1981 Rampton report) indicating an extremely poor level of achievement by West Indian children in schools, served to deprive the movement for 'positive discrimination' of support. Perhaps it was not discrimination after all which was to blame for the black predicament? Perhaps cultural factors were also at work? Certainly there was little sympathy among Mrs Thatcher's supporters for tackling racial problems by extending the machinery established by recent Race Relations acts. Many in fact still saw the basic problem in terms of immigration. This led the *Economist* in April 1982 to complain: 'Significant numbers of white people [still] go on pretending – encouraged by some elderly politicians – that one day the blacks can somehow be sent "home", as though home for most of them was anywhere else but in Britain.'

Ever since the 1960s, British governments had done their best to limit the number of immigrants entering the country. There had been Immigration Acts in 1962, 1968, 1969 and 1971 so that by the late 1970s only about 75,000 immigrants were being accepted each year – less people, in fact, than were emigrating. In 1979, however, Mrs Thatcher could still state that many people feared being 'swamped' by immigrants and her party promised to introduce further restrictions. In particular it proposed to pass a British Nationality Act which would define entitlement to British citizenship and residence in the United Kingdom; such an act was passed in 1981. This restricted British citizenship with full rights of residence to people already legally settled in Britain plus those who had one British parent and had been registered abroad at birth. Citizens of dependent territories were given no right to enter Britain. This provision was designed to exclude Hong Kong Chinese but in fact also excluded many Falkland Islanders. After the events of 1982, therefore, it was partly changed to remove this piece of irony. The Act also created a third category of British citizens – 'British overseas citizens'. These persons were people who lived abroad but who had no recent connection by family or residence with Great Britain. They too were given no right of entry, making it probable that few countries would recognize their passports. Following this, the Government in 1982 attempted to tighten up immigration rules with respect to marriages, suspecting that many marriages made by immigrants were often devices designed to enable young men (particularly from the Indian sub-continent) to evade immigration controls. These new regulations, however, ran into political trouble – from both left and right wings of the Tory party – as well as constitutional problems involving the European Convention on Human Rights. The result was that, contrary to the Government's original intentions, the regulations had to be changed in 1983 in such a way as to allow women holding British citizenship to bring in husbands or fiancés from abroad. The marriages involved however could still not be arranged ones. The result of all these measures was that by 1982 the number of immigrants entering Britain had dropped to under

54,000, of which only 30,300 came from the New Commonwealth and Pakistan.

By then there were already over 2 million non-whites in Britain, well over half of them of Indian, Pakistani or Bangladeshi origin, with most of the rest hailing from the West Indies. In 1951, there had been only about 75,000. The proportion of 'blacks' – as most non-white citizens increasingly preferred to call themselves – had therefore risen from 0·2 per cent of the population to 4 per cent of it. By the year 2000 it is expected to rise to about 6·7 per cent. The fears expressed by Mr Powell in the 1970s, therefore, do not seem likely to be realized. Nor does his policy of 'voluntary repatriation' appear to be a practical one since today the vast majority of 'immigrants' consists of citizens who have been born in Britain. Mrs Thatcher, therefore, has realized that immigration controls apart, her best policy with regard to Britain's blacks must be a mixture of retaining previous legislation on racial discrimination, encouraging consultation between black community leaders and the police but most of all ensuring that blacks benefit at least as much as whites from youth opportunity programmes and training schemes and can thus hope to be in a position to benefit from any economic recovery which may arrive. Indeed, by 1983, the Conservative Party – which had traditionally made the running with regard to immigration controls – had begun to realize that there were now black votes to be won. Perhaps not surprisingly, however, Britain's black voters in 1983 were overwhelmingly to support the Labour Party. This was an almost inevitable result of the Thatcher Government's refusal to introduce further safeguards against racial discrimination. The Government, of course, had its case, namely that such 'safeguards' would be difficult to enforce and, like 'positive discrimination', would almost certainly prove counter-productive, but black community leaders were unwilling to accept this. In any case, the government's record on immigration had left a legacy of mistrust.

NORTHERN IRELAND

Meanwhile, there were much more intractable problems to be dealt with in another part of the United Kingdom. For the 1981 riots were no more than momentary distractions compared to the daily experience of terror in Ulster. There the IRA in particular continued to terrorize its opponents, often bombing or shooting them in front of their very wives and children. Often it planted bombs which were designed to kill indiscriminately, occasionally choosing to do so in London as well as in Ulster. Its most original form of violence while Mrs Thatcher was in power, however, was to select members of its own organization and order them to starve themselves to death in prison. In this way it hoped both to win international sympathy and to blackmail the Government into making concessions.

Mrs Thatcher's first Northern Ireland Secretary was to have been the British Second World War hero, her close friend, Mr Airey Neave. He was tragically killed, however, in March 1979, when his car was blown up in the House of Commons car park by a bomb planted by the Irish National Liberation Army. His replacement as Conservative spokesman on Northern Ireland was Mr Humphrey Atkins who in May became Mrs Thatcher's first Secretary of State for the province. Like his predecessor, Labour's Roy Mason, he tried to bring local politicians together to agree on some kind of government for Northern Ireland, but in practice found that he had to concentrate on the security front, in particular, in an attempt to end the hunger strikes.

These were the culmination of a protest which had begun in 1976 when the then Northern Ireland Secretary, Merlyn Rees, had ordered the phasing out of 'special category status', in practice a set of prison privileges, which had been introduced by his predecessor, William Whitelaw, in 1972, to differentiate terrorists from ordinary criminals. This was a distinction which he later and rightly came to view as mistaken in principle. Yet in practice it had also been a mistake, for in the words of one authority: 'These privileges turned the prisons into schools of terrorism and distanced the paramilitaries from "ordinary" criminals, thus giving them a degree of respectability in the outside world.' There can be little doubt therefore that Rees's decision was the right one.

Convicted IRA and INLA terrorists, on the other hand, responded to it by refusing to wear prison clothing, a form of protest known as 'going on the blanket'. When this brought no concessions from the authorities it was escalated in 1978 into the so-called 'dirty protest' when prisoners smashed their cell furniture, refused to wash or use toilet facilities and smeared themselves and their cells with their excrement. When that, too, failed to win major concessions the republican terrorists decided to embark on a series of hunger strikes. The first series reached a climax in December 1980 but no one was allowed to die since the authorities were believed to be about to submit to IRA demands. This did not happen and in March 1981 a second round of strikes began when the Provisional IRA commander at the Maze prison, Bobby Sands, began a 'fast to the death'. He in turn was followed by other carefully selected prisoners. Their protest undoubtedly struck a responsive chord among the Catholic minority in the North – Sands even won the parliamentary seat of Fermanagh/South Tyrone in a by-election fought from his death bed – but the IRA's greatest propaganda success was in the USA where sympathizers poured funds into republican coffers. Mrs Thatcher, on the other hand, made it crystal clear that her government would never submit to violence or blackmail. Despite huge international pressure, therefore, no concessions were made. The result was that after ten deaths among the hunger strikers, the protest was called off when relatives of the IRA strikers intervened.

By this time, Atkins had been replaced by Mr James Prior, who, despite initial statements to the contrary, accepted the Northern Ireland Secretaryship in the government reshuffle of September 1981. He was now able to achieve a sort of compromise over prison conditions – 'special status', however, was not revived – but was more concerned to encourage the establishment of some kind of forum in the province in which politicians of all shades of opinion might work together. His efforts in this regard were to culminate in the creation in 1982 of the Northern Ireland Assembly.

Before then, however, progress appeared to be being made on another front, namely in relations between London and Dublin. This was unexpected given the hard-line republican views associated with the Taoiseach, Mr Charles Haughey, but his government, too, opposed the IRA. After increasing cooperation on security matters, therefore, summit meetings were held between him and Mrs Thatcher in May and December 1980. The second of these resulted in a communiqué which referred to 'the totality of relationships within these islands' and established joint studies by senior officials covering possible new institutional structures, citizenship rights, security matters, economic cooperation and measures to encourage mutual understanding. The rapprochement seemed to grow when in November 1981 a third summit took place between Mrs Thatcher and Haughey's successor, Dr Garret Fitzgerald. Indeed it was now given institutional form in an Anglo-Irish Council. This was to consist at first of an inter-governmental council which, it was hoped, would soon be followed by an inter-parliamentary one. The latter body, however, was never established, while the former met only seven times in 1982.

The cooling of relations between London and Dublin in 1982–3 can be traced to three sets of causes. The first was domestic political factors, particularly in the Irish Republic. In Paul Arthur's words:

Unprecedented economic and financial difficulties and constantly rising unemployment produced no less than three separate governments in under eighteen months in Dublin. In 1982 alone there had been two general elections, three budgets, a change of leadership in the Labour Party and two direct challenges to Haughey's leadership of the Fianna Fail party. To divert attention from the economy, Haughey tried to make more of his meetings with Thatcher than was warranted. Playing the nationalist card made little impact on the Republic's electorate, which was deeply concerned with immediate bread and butter issues, but it had a depressing and inevitable effect on Ulster loyalists. Thatcher had to draw back and reassure her Unionist allies.

The hunger strikes also played their part, since politicians in the South could not be seen to be too friendly with Mrs Thatcher at a time when republicans in the North were starving themselves to death. Finally, however, the rapprochement was killed when Mr Haughey, after the sinking of the Belgrano in the Falklands War (see below) attempted to persuade the European Community to remove its sanctions on Argentina. He used the traditional Irish policy of neutrality to justify this but Mrs Thatcher, predictably, saw no need thereafter to scratch his back while he was stabbing hers.

In any case, by 1982 Dublin was objecting to Mr Prior's plans for a Northern Ireland Assembly. According to Haughey these were 'unworkable'. They were, in fact, quite modest. Prior's aim, first of all, was merely to get representatives of the people of Northern Ireland elected; then, if and when they could find agreement on anything, Westminster would devolve power to them. This scheme was known as 'rolling devolution'. At the very least, according to Prior, it would allow himself and his officials to come under democratic local scrutiny and thus make direct rule more accountable to the people of Northern Ireland. In fact, given local conditions, it was a very sensible plan. It might encourage investment in the province, if agreement began to grow; perhaps the Assembly might even become 'a school of reconciliation'. But when elections were held on 20 October 1982 the Official and Democratic Unionists (Protestants) won 47 out of the 78 seats, the Alliance Party (bi-confessional) 10, the SDLP (Catholic) 14 and Sinn Fein (the 'civil' branch of the IRA) 5. The SDLP and Sinn Fein members immediately refused to take their seats while eventually the Unionists also boycotted the Assembly, after one of their members was shot in the head by the IRA at the end of 1983. Haughey, it turned out, had been correct. 'Prior,' in Paul Arthur's words, 'had gambled on the upsurge of the middle ground and failed.' There thus seemed no alternative to direct rule, which would not run the risk of open civil war.

FOREIGN POLICY

If the Government appeared to flounder for much of the period 1979–82 in domestic affairs, its handling of foreign and defence policy on the other hand displayed a greater sureness of touch. Here indeed there were undoubted successes and even in areas where final success remained elusive there was still a sense of direction, a feeling that the Government both had clear goals in sight and the ability to pursue these goals with energy. Thus by 1983, the Prime Minister, in the words of one commentator had 'become a figure to be reckoned with in international politics'. This was primarily but not solely the result of the Falklands War which both her friends and enemies in Great Britain, not to mention her Argentinian foes, regarded very much as 'Mrs Thatcher's War'. In the words of one of her colleagues: 'She took the risks on her shoulders and she won. She emerged as a remarkable war leader.' Indeed, it seemed to many people that her leadership in the Falklands War had once again demonstrated her by now instinctive articulation of the real feelings of the British people as opposed to the 'false internationalism of the Foreign Office'.

Yet at the start of her first administration there was little indication that Mrs Thatcher was much interested in foreign affairs or enjoyed any expertise in them. She promised no great initiatives and seemed content to let the experts run the show. Her inclinations however seemed to be those of a traditional Conservative – strong support for the Atlantic alliance, hostility towards the Soviet Union, a strong defence of the nuclear deterrent with only a rather mechanical deference towards the European Community or the new Commonwealth. In other words, in foreign as in domestic affairs, Mrs Thatcher's enthusiasms were different from those of Mr Heath. She also suspected that they were different from those of the Foreign Office, which she believed was too sympathetic towards the Third World, the Arabs, and the EEC. She would have no doubt agreed with David Owen's verdict, that it had 'a depressing tendency to split the difference in every negotiation' rather than, as she preferred, to fight à l'outrance to maintain British interests. Thus in the end she was to accept the resignation of her first Foreign Secretary and to demand the resignation of her second. She would also appoint a special adviser on foreign affairs at Downing Street and use independent advisers when she saw fit. The Foreign Office in short was to become one of those institutions on which, according to Julian Critchley MP, she could not refrain from using her handbag.

THE RHODESIAN QUESTION

As has already been indicated, however, this was not at all clear at first. For Mrs Thatcher until the Falklands War enjoyed in her first Foreign Secretary, Lord Carrington, an old hand in foreign affairs of internationally high reputation and undoubted charm. It seemed that his authority was respected by her and since, although 'wet', he refrained from interfering in the bitter debate over domestic policy, she allowed him to dominate the formulation of foreign policy. He did this by all accounts very effectively and soon became an internationally familiar figure. Moreover, as Foreign Secretary as early as 1979, he delivered the Government its first great and unqualified success by presiding over the negotiations which settled the Rhodesian Question. This was an achievement which had eluded the Callaghan Government and one which in the autumn of 1979 seemed destined to elude the new Conservative regime also. Yet by converting Mrs Thatcher to his views – indeed to the Foreign Office viewpoint – and with the invaluable aid of the Commonwealth, Lord Carrington was able to take advantage of the new configuration of circumstances in Rhodesia to bring about an internally and internationally recognized agreement.

By 1979 the political situation within Rhodesia had undergone enormous changes. These had begun in 1975 when, with the collapse of the Portuguese Empire in Africa, the South African government of Mr John Vorster had decided to force the rebel regime of Mr Ian Smith to concede black majority rule. Vorster's motives are explained by Martin Meredith as follows:

The *coup d'état* in Lisbon on 25 April 1974 forced Vorster to reconsider his entire strategy. In a single blow, the structure of white rule in southern Africa had changed irrevocably. The Portuguese army, once a firm ally in the confrontation against black liberation movements had become weary of incessant war and was intent on dismantling Portugal's African empire and handing over control of its territory to the guerillas. No longer were Mozambique and Angola part of Vorster's southern African buffer, the *cordon sanitaire* he hoped would insulate South Africa from external threat. No longer was Rhodesia important as a frontier defence. For the winds of change had reached South Africa's frontier. And Forster considered that in the long run Smith's position, without an open-ended South African military and economic commitment, was untenable. In his reassessment, white rule was ultimately doomed and Rhodesia's stubborn defiance of change only added an unwelcome element of uncertainty, likely to inspire communist involvement. Smith was no longer merely an embarrassment but a liability. An unstable white government in Rhodesia was less desirable than a stable black government, particularly a moderate one which, Vorster hoped, would have little alternative but to succumb to his designs for a southern African 'sphere of co-prosperity'. Discreetly he set about trying to achieve this aim.

Vorster's *realpolitik* involved the withdrawal of South African 'police-men' and planes from Rhodesia, financial and economic pressures on Rhodesia and the disruption of supplies by rail to Rhodesia. Moreover his efforts were assisted by those of another exponent of *realpolitik*, the US Secretary of State, Dr Kissinger. The latter, in April 1976, set out on a seven-nation tour of Africa to rescue American policy there from the consequences of his secret backing of South African intervention in 1975 in Angola. This intervention had seriously backfired when thousands of Cuban troops had been airlifted to aid the Angolans. One way to redeem America's reputation, therefore, was to make a clear-cut commitment to majority rule in Rhodesia, which Kissinger did in Lusaka. A couple of months later, therefore, he met Vorster in Bavaria to help bring this about. He also proposed to ease the transition to majority rule in Rhodesia by establishing a billion-dollar development fund which by guaranteeing white pension rights and offering other guarantees and compensations to whites, might encourage them to remain in the country once black rule had been established. Yet the main agreement was not over the fund but over a concerted US–South African diplomatic strategy to bring about majority rule. The two men met again to synchronize tactics in September 1976 in Zurich, and a week later Kissinger returned to Africa, where, in what was described as an exercise in 'meataxe' or 'nutcracker' diplomacy, he confronted Smith with a five-point plan. This he claimed had been agreed to by the presidents of the African 'front-line states' and the nationalist leaders in Rhodesia so that Smith felt compelled to accept it. In fact, as the wily white Rhodesian premier saw, it left him more scope for manoeuvre than Kissinger had foreseen. Basically the plan called for majority rule within two years, the establishment of a half-black, half-white Council of State to draft a new constitution and the creation of a Council of Ministers under a black premier with a majority of black members. It foresaw British legislation to legalize the agreement, an end to the war and the lifting of international sanctions once the interim government had been formed. Smith did get Kissinger to agree, however, that the Chairman of the Council of State might be white and that in the interim government the portfolios of Defence, Law and Order and Finance might remain in white hands. The trouble was that the black nationalist leaders and presidents had never agreed to these or indeed to any other terms in exchange for majority rule.

The latter had only been given the outlines of the Kissinger plan which they believed was based on a Callaghan formula of March 1975 which stipulated majority rule within eighteen months and no independence before majority rule. Kissinger's package deal with Smith was therefore rejected by them. But if the US Secretary of State had misled the Africans he also deliberately deceived Smith by informing him that the Africans had agreed to his amendments. This was in order to force Smith to broadcast publicly that he had at last accepted majority rule. Hence, when Smith did so he was unaware of his true position. Yet Kissinger hoped that by his use of 'tactical ambiguity' – the words of one of his assistants – the psychological blow which would be delivered to white morale would make a subsequent retreat from majority rule impossible. This in fact proved to be the case but by sticking to the details of the Kissinger proposals – details which the Africans rejected – Smith knew perfectly well that there would be no final settlement. Moreover, by having publicly accepted majority rule, Smith won renewed support from Vorster who had never supported the complete nationalist position in the first place and who now also clung to the terms of the Kissinger package. South Africa's financial squeeze on Rhodesia was therefore relaxed. Predictably, therefore, when in October 1976 a conference took place between Smith and the nationalist leaders in Geneva it soon broke up in disagreement. Meanwhile, the Rhodesian security forces killed more nationalist guerrillas during the seven weeks of the conference than in the whole of 1975.

The Callaghan government had been reluctant to become too involved in the Rhodesian negotiations, since it lacked the means of enforcing a settlement. Thus the Foreign Secretary in 1976, Tony Crosland, had declared that 'the main onus for reaching an agreement on an interim government will rest with the parties concerned'. None the less the British Ambassador to the UN, Ivor Richard, had presided over the conference at Geneva. When it broke up he still harboured hopes of achieving a settlement. He therefore drew up a new plan which envisaged a British Commissioner in Salisbury playing a major role in an interim administration. But he stressed that no British troops would be sent to Rhodesia. Instead, the Rhodesian security forces should take an oath to the Crown and Britain should run the country in the meantime through her Commissioner who would share power with an equally divided Council of Ministers and a National Security Council. Clearly Richard believed that since Smith had already conceded majority rule, the remaining details could be settled by some sort of compromise, no doubt under more intensive pressure from Vorster. Yet the white Rhodesians held Britain in contempt, saw it as having just reneged on the Kissinger package and believed that the 'details' were vital if a lasting, moderating influence for the whites was to be secured. And Vorster also believed that their presence was necessary to secure the emergence of a moderate black government. Predictably, therefore, the Richard proposals were rejected, especially since they were modified before they reached their final form in a direction much more approximating to nationalist demands. Smith said he stuck by the Kissinger proposals and on that basis alone would still negotiate with Rhodesia's blacks.

The nationalist leader he in fact had in mind was Bishop Muzorewa, head of the African National Council who had emerged in 1972 to rally the blacks against the 1971 proposals. Muzorewa, unlike Joshua Nkomo and Robert Mugabe, Rhodesia's best-known nationalist leaders, had no guerrilla following. Moreover, as a Christian moderate reputedly with little political sense, he presented a better bet as a front-man than the Marxist Mugabe or the common choice of the diplomatic world, Nkomo.

Still, before a deal could be patched up with Muzorewa, the new British Foreign Secretary, Dr David Owen, Crosland's young and ambitious successor, launched another diplomatic initiative, this time with help from the new US President, Carter.

Already in January 1977 Carter had asked Congress to ban the import of Rhodesian chrome. He also refused to aid Smith to combat the 'communist' guerrillas. Then in March 1977 he agreed with Callaghan to launch a new initiative, which was worked out by Owen and the US Secretary of State, Cyrus Vance. It envisaged a democratically elected government based on a wide franchise but not necessarily one-man, one-vote; it foresaw a justiciable Bill of Rights and an independent judiciary. It called for a development fund and a neutral interim administration to govern the country before elections. On a trip to Africa in April 1977 Owen found general support for his plan from Smith and Vorster and from the presidents of the front-line states. But Nkomo and Mugabe, now joint leaders of the Patriotic Front (PF) rejected it. They objected to US involvement and demanded that negotiations should proceed between Britain and the PF alone. Owen wisely realized that more attention would have to be paid to the PF demands and set up an Anglo-American consultative group to consider this. It was led by a Foreign Office official John Graham and the US Ambassador to Lusaka, Stephen Low, who toured Africa to narrow the areas of disagreement. Yet over the issue of the security forces in Rhodesia there could be no agreement. Smith demanded that they should remain under white (and certainly not British) control while the PF in turn demanded control for themselves. None the less in August 1977 Owen launched a new initiative and flew to Africa accompanied by the US Ambassador to the UN, the notoriously undiplomatic Andrew Young who in Lagos had just referred to Smith as 'a monster standing in the way of peace in Zimbabwe' (the African name for Rhodesia). The latest plan they had to present included a constitution guaranteeing fundamental rights and extra representation for Rhodesia's whites and a billion-dollar development fund. But they now also proposed to install a British Field Marshal, Lord Carver, as British Commissioner in the interim period with dictatorial powers to arrange a ceasefire and maintain law and order with the help of the Rhodesian police and some UN troops. He was also to disband the guerrilla armies and the government security forces and thereafter to integrate sections of these into a new independent Zimbabwe army.

Later Owen sensibly conceded that disbandment need not be a pre-condition to the establishment of a new army. Yet such proposals were hardly likely to be acceptable to the Rhodesian whites. Vorster in fact rejected them as did the P F. But Smith himself was careful not to do so outright. In any event Lord Carver effectively sabotaged the mission when, before flying out to Africa to take part in negotiations, he told a television interviewer: 'What I am totally committed to is that Rhodesia will become a basically black African country run primarily by black Africans for the benefit of black Africans.' Considering it was his job to persuade Smith to disband most of the white security forces, this state-ment was at the least insensitive. Predictably therefore the proposals were never accepted. Smith now abandoned all faith in the Anglo-American initiative which to his mind had made too many concessions to the P F. He turned for a number of reasons to the thought of an internal settlement instead.

There were a number of pressures on Smith. Defence expenditure for example rose by 44 per cent in 1977 taking 25 per cent of the budget. The war was now costing no less than £500,000 per day. Fuel costs too were four times higher than in 1973 and industrial output was stagnant. Chrome exports had slumped thanks to President Carter, inflation had reached 13 per cent, unemployment was rising and military service meant 190 days a year for all whites under 38, and 70 for those between 38 and 50. By mid 1977, 1,500 whites each month were leaving the country. On the other hand Smith was still the undisputed leader of those who remained and while he retained this popularity, he decided to make a final bid for majority rule on his own terms through an agreement with his moderate black opponents. The question was whether they would agree to bargain.

The two African leaders most concerned were Bishop Muzorewa and the Rev. Sithole. The former believed he had the support of a majority of Rhodesia's blacks and thus resented the attention paid by everyone to the P F guerrilla leaders. The latter had been Mugabe's predecessor as head of Z A N U, the chief political party, but had long ago lost power to his younger rival. He still claimed to be the party leader but in fact was without a political base. Neither man, despite occasional claims to the contrary, had much of a guerrilla following and thus could only take power through the ballot box. Hence they were both dependent on Smith. Smith in turn believed that a constitutional deal made with them and based on one man one vote would undercut the guerrillas and gradually end the war. It might also bring international recognition and an end to sanctions. Thus a deal known as the Salisbury Agreement was eventually reached in March 1978. There was to be one man one vote, but the whites would be protected by a Bill of Rights, an independent judiciary, dual citizenship and *de facto* white control of the police, security forces and the civil service. They were also to have 28 seats out of 100 set aside for them in Parliament and it was laid down that 78 votes would be necessary to change any of the 'entrenched' clauses of the constitution. Clearly, therefore, the Agreement was from Smith's point of view extremely good. Before elections were held he also retained the title of Prime Minister but shared membership of an Executive Council with Muzorewa, Sithole and another 'moderate' while a Ministerial Council of nine whites and nine blacks ran the routine affairs of government. The blacks for their part secured a clear majority in parliament, a promise from Smith not to play off black factions against each other by offering white support to any particular one in parliament and a pledge to allow any guerrillas who wanted to, to join the security forces. Clearly Smith had had the best of the bargain, yet he could credibly claim that the internal settlement closely resembled the Kissinger package. The question arose, therefore, whether the British and the Americans would accept the deal.

For his part, Owen was tempted to do so if the forthcoming elections demonstrated its popular acceptability. British public opinion favoured it and the Conservative Party was threatening to abandon bi-partisanship over the issue if he did not. The Americans on the other hand were hostile and Owen also had to weigh up the consequences for British trade in the rest of Africa if he accepted the settlement. Finally there was the risk of an East–West confrontation over Rhodesia if the PF sought Russian or Cuban backing. The result was that Owen still tried to bring the PF into the negotiations. He and Young had met Nkomo and Mugabe in Malta in January 1978 and Young met them again in Dar-es-Salaam in March. Since they appeared to be willing to make concessions over the security forces Carter once again called for a conference to be held and in mid-April Owen, Vance, Young and Lord Carver all flew to Africa, constituting in Meredith's words 'the most powerful diplomatic team ever assembled to tackle the Rhodesian issue'. But the Anglo-American initiative again miscarried. The PF insisted on controlling the security forces while Smith's only concession was his willingness to allow Nkomo into the Executive Council. This he knew would strengthen his hand enormously. Yet Nkomo, however tempted, would not agree. Owen's policy was soon reduced therefore to one of 'keeping people talking'.

In the meantime the actions of the security forces were alienating the blacks who often blamed guerrilla atrocities on army units in disguise. Moreover when one of Muzorewa's nominees in the government spoke out for more radical change, the Bishop was unable to prevent Smith dismissing him. This gave rise to a political crisis which undermined Muzorewa's appeal, and the lack of any real move towards desegregation had a similar effect. Meanwhile guerrilla atrocities continued unabated and the government seemed unable to defend farmers and missionaries in large areas of the country. Smith attempted to retrieve the situation by persuading Nkomo to return to Salisbury as Prime Minister. This manoeuvre almost succeeded but word of the secret negotiations (arranged through the Zambian President) leaked out to the natural fury of Mugabe, Muzorewa and nearly everyone else. In any case any hope of dealing with Nkomo came to an end when he boasted about the part played by his guerrillas in the shooting down of a civilian aircraft whose defenceless white survivors had subsequently been brutally massacred. Thereafter he was as loathed by Rhodesian whites as was Mugabe. Smith's only hope for survival therefore rested with international recognition. But first of all the regime had to demonstrate its public acceptability and produce a constitution.

The latter was finally published in January 1979. Apart from the provisions mentioned above it contained more safeguards for whites. They were to have five cabinet seats for five years after the first elections and one-third of those in a new Senate which had never been discussed before. This would also give them a larger say in the election of the first black President who would be head of state. Most astonishing of all, however, the state itself was to be called not 'Zimbabwe' but 'Zimbabwe-Rhodesia'. Given these concessions by Muzorewa and Sithole and given the lack of any alternative, it was not surprising that the whites voted overwhelmingly to accept the new constitution. Seventy-one per cent of the white electorate voted in a referendum on 30 January 1979 and 85 per cent of the voters said 'yes'. The real test of the new constitution, however, would be the general election which was to be held in mid-

April. There were fears that this would be disrupted by the guerrillas but in the event, according to government figures, 64 per cent of the black electorate turned out. This was probably an over-estimation (the refugee factor and security problems made it difficult to estimate the total number of eligible voters) but it was probably not wildly inaccurate. The real dispute arose about whether the elections had been free and fair. Certainly blacks had not been asked whether or not they approved the constitution and many had been falsely told by black candidates who did that the election would end the war. Nor had the case against the constitution been made in the government-controlled media. Thus independent observers like Lord Chitnis and Professor Claire Palley denounced the whole exercise as a sham. Several reservations were also made by the former Colonial Secretary, Lord Boyd, who had gone to Rhodesia at the head of a five-man team to assess the election on behalf of the Conservative Party. He reported that neither the censorship nor the martial law nor the refusal of the PF to participate had invalidated the results. Nor had there been undue pressure from employers and the security forces. The elections therefore, he concluded, were as free and fair as possible given wartime conditions and could be taken as 'a kind of referendum' on the constitution. His report appeared to be almost as important as the election results – which gave Muzorewa 67 per cent of the vote and 51 of the 72 black seats in Parliament – since a couple of weeks later Margaret Thatcher became Prime Minister of Great Britain and she was known to favour both the recognition of Muzorewa's government and the lifting of sanctions. The Boyd report thus provided her with a justification for doing so and the right wing of the Tory party demanded immediate action. In America, too, there was pressure for recognition. In 1978 Congress had passed a law which required the lifting of sanctions if Smith proved willing to negotiate with the PF and held free and fair elections. Thus when on 15 May the US Senate passed a resolution declaring that the Rhodesian elections had been free, it looked as if Smith might yet retrieve his position.

Carter, however, although admitting that the elections had been 'free' declared that the constitution under which they had been held was in no way 'fair'. He also argued that on several issues Ian Smith had been unwilling to negotiate with the PF. Thus on 7 June he announced that US sanctions would remain in force. He was clearly wary of the reaction of Nigeria (which supplied 15 per cent of US oil imports) and other black African countries if sanctions were lifted and feared lest isolation should push the PF completely into the hands of the Russians and Cubans. Given Carter's reactions there was yet another reason for the Thatcher government to think twice before it recognized the Muzorewa government. Lord Carrington as a result, while claiming not to disregard the Rhodesian election, declared his intention of consulting the US, the Commonwealth and various African and European states. In other words, he would play for time.

Mrs Thatcher, on the other hand, seemed to be more in a hurry. On her way back from her first western economic summit in Tokyo at the end of June 1979 she stopped off at Canberra, where despite having failed to convince the Australians to recognize Muzorewa, she hinted at a press conference that sanctions would be lifted and the Muzorewa government recognized by Great Britain. This was to be just one of many examples of her habit of pronouncing policy as she went along. Yet when she returned to London on 3 July she found a memorandum from Carrington on her desk stating that recognition as a policy would be wrong. It would split the Commonwealth and the Atlantic Alliance, lead to greater Russian influence in Africa and result in economic losses in Africa for Great Britain. In any case, it argued, the Rhodesian constitution was unfair and could only lead to greater violence. Under these circumstances a change in policy should be ruled out. Mrs Thatcher apparently accepted these arguments – she had already heard them from the right-wing Australian leader Malcolm Fraser – but this was not known until the beginning of August when she flew to Lusaka in Zambia for the Commonwealth Conference.

This latest get-together was expected to be a complete disaster for her. There was a violent press campaign in Zambia against her policy and the Nigerians on 31 July nationalized the Nigerian assets of British Petroleum to indicate their mood. Yet the Lusaka Conference became a triumph for her, for having accepted Carrington's arguments she then pushed harder than he for a negotiated settlement with the PF. And with the help of Malcolm Fraser of Australia, Michael Manley of Jamaica and the Secretary General of the Commonwealth, Sir Sonny Ramphal, she was able to get the framework of a settlement hammered out. It was also useful that she accepted the risk – which Callaghan and Owen had never done – of sending British troops to Rhodesia to monitor the ceasefire. The result was that the Commonwealth leaders agreed to a conference being held at Lancaster House before the end of the year to settle the problem. And this time, given that British and Commonwealth troops under a British Commissioner would monitor the ceasefire, the front-line presidents agreed to pressure the PF leaders into attending. Smith had little choice but to go along: Muzorewa was clearly seen by the majority of Africans as his stooge; the guerrillas were proving ever more difficult to contain; almost a quarter of the white population had emigrated; and he still lacked international recognition. None the less, Carrington was pessimistic about the chances of a successful outcome to the London talks right up until the end. But on 21 December Mrs Thatcher who had allowed him to take all the limelight at Lancaster House was able to attend the final session at which an agreement was signed. This provided for the guerrilla armies to assemble at 'collection points' after a ceasefire and for an interim period of government under a British Commissioner who turned out to be Lord Soames. The constitution which was agreed on established a separate voting roll for a minority of white seats but the London constitution unlike the Salisbury Agreement gave the whites no blocking mechanism in parliament. Instead they were given an independent judiciary and all signatories agreed that there should be no constitutional amendments for at least ten years. The blacks on the other hand got one man one vote and the clear prospect of instant desegregation under a black government. This was something which Smith could simply no longer postpone. Thus after fifteen years of UDI the Rhodesian problem was settled. Lord Soames carried out his task as Commissioner with great distinction and firmness and won the trust of black and white leaders alike. The result was that the ceasefire held and in 1981 Rhodesia, now called Zimbabwe, experienced her first and perhaps last free elections. For they were won by Robert Mugabe who openly proclaimed his intention of creating a one-party state as soon as the initial period of multi-party democracy envisaged by the Lancaster House constitution was over.

Lord Carrington received most of the credit for the Lancaster House Agreement and indeed had deserved much. Yet it is obvious that it had come about as a result mostly of changed circumstances inside Rhodesia itself. These in turn had been the direct result of guerrilla activities and international pressures exerted by South Africa, the black African states, the Commonwealth and the USA. Moreover, the final agreement had been partly presaged in the Anglo-American initiatives and in the Salisbury Agreement. It was to the credit of Mrs Thatcher and Lord Carrington, however, that they had discerned the direction in which events were moving and had been able to manipulate them in such a way as to obtain a final settlement. The clear losers were Smith and Muzorewa. But this had always been probable. Smith at least could content himself that he had staved off the inevitable for a surprisingly long time and even in the end had salvaged something. Just how much remains to be seen. The other loser was Nkomo whose tribal origins and dealings with Smith deprived him of much black support with the result that Mugabe's victory was an absolute one.

THE COMMON MARKET

The settlement of the Rhodesian problem won Mrs Thatcher the admiration of President Carter who had had little hope of a successful outcome. In this way it consolidated his gratitude for her 'robust' – a favourite Thatcher word – support of US policy on Afghanistan, the boycott of the Moscow Olympics and the bitter issue of the US hostages in Iran. But if her reputation grew in Washington it sank just as quickly in Europe. For here Mrs Thatcher's natural 'instincts' to maintain British interests could not be restrained or converted. The result was that her Common Market partners soon grew exasperated with her. They had as yet no idea just how tenacious the 'Iron Lady', as the Russians (on account of her anti-Soviet rhetoric) had christened her to her delight, could prove to be.

Neither President Giscard of France nor Chancellor Schmidt of Germany, the European leaders whose 'Paris–Bonn axis' seemed to dictate European political developments, were prepared for the force of Mrs Thatcher's attack on the Common Market budgetary mechanisms, particularly the financial arrangements of the CAP (Common Agricultural Policy). They believed that the 1975 referendum had settled the issue of British membership and although they knew the European Community was relatively unpopular in the United Kingdom they were not prepared to negotiate the issue of British payments once again. Britain had joined the 'Club of Ten' and as far as they were concerned should abide by the rules and pay the accepted costs as foreseen by the White Paper of 1970, including the costs involved in the CAP. Probably they were glad to see Mrs Thatcher elected in 1979. The Labour Party had been tediously 'anti-EEC' and Wilson and Callaghan's tactics over 'renegotiation' had bored and frustrated them, especially as they had produced only cosmetic changes in Britain's relationship with the Community and only then for reasons of purely domestic politics. Mrs Thatcher might prove to be a refreshing change. Giscard, for one, characteristically admired her admiration of his French nuclear power programme and on 4 July 1979 Schmidt had declared to the West German parliament that he was 'particularly impressed by the knowledge, authority and sense of responsibility' displayed by her at recent summit meetings. Yet within a few months' time both were utterly disillusioned. Mrs Thatcher for a start supported President Carter's strong anti-Soviet reaction to the Russian invasion of Afghanistan and displayed much more interest in coordinating her foreign policy with that of the USA rather than with 'Europe'. Schmidt, who believed that Carter's handling of US–Soviet relations had been incompetent, was consequently not impressed. Yet it was to be Mrs Thatcher's attitude to the EEC as expressed in Dublin in November 1979 that brought relations to a nadir. For there she announced that she wanted 'Britain's own money back' and precipitated a full-scale Community crisis – the first of many – over the Community budget.

The root of the trouble was the £1 billion which the Treasury estimated Great Britain would have to pay to the EEC as her net contribution in 1980. Within a week of becoming Prime Minister Mrs Thatcher had given notice that on this matter her government would not be a 'soft touch' and would be 'resolute' in defending 'British interests'. At the Conservative Party Conference in October 1979 she promised 'very real progress at the next European Council' in Dublin. Then, later in November in a speech at Strasbourg entitled 'The Obligations of Liberty' she stated: 'I must be absolutely clear about this. Britain cannot accept the present situation on the budget. It is demonstrably unjust. It is politically indefensible: I cannot play Sister Bountiful to the Community while my own electorate are being asked to forgo improvements in the fields of health, education, welfare and the rest.' Hence when she arrived in Dublin Mrs Thatcher astonished the Community by demanding 'a broad balance' or a 'juste retour', in short, 'Britain's own money back'. In the words of the Irish premier she was 'adamant, persistent and, may I say, repetitive'. The result was a complete deadlock. Schmidt 'ostentatiously' fell asleep at one moment and the summit broke up with a compromise agreement to reconvene the following year in special session as a fig-leaf to cover its failure. In fact this never happened. Mrs Thatcher meanwhile was attacked by her critics in Britain and elsewhere of lacking 'community spirit'. Her chief British detractor, Mr Heath, accused her of ignorance both of the working of the EEC and of the art of negotiating, while the French Foreign Minister declared that the notion of a *juste retour* 'was not a Community idea'. He added: 'The British and we are not speaking of the same Community.'

Perhaps he was right. From the point of view of her critics, Mrs Thatcher's case was weak. They pointed out that in joining the EEC Great Britain had estimated that the cost to her would be about £175–250 million per year and that the cost of the CAP per year would be about £300–400 million. At 1981 prices this was the equivalent of £1,000 million per annum. Hence in their eyes Britain had nothing to complain about. Moreover, if, unlike the Germans, the British had failed to take advantage of the increased export market which the Community represented, this was their own fault – and certainly not that of the French who gained relatively little from the CAP but who rightly regarded it as the essential part of the bargain they had made in return for giving West Germany's industrialists access to their markets. It was, from the French point of view, simply unfortunate that whereas the benefits to Germany or Britain of increased trade were largely uncountable, those deriving from the CAP could be calculated quite accurately. By 1980 in fact *per capita* net receipts were +£9 for France, +£49 for Belgium and Luxembourg, +£86 for Denmark, +£154 for Ireland. For West Germany the figure was –£24, for Italy –£1 and for Britain –£24. Yet the French argued that the sums involved were relatively small. Even if Britain's deficit with the EEC in 1981 reached the feared £1,300 million – this was only the equivalent of 3·5 per cent of the British annual budget. The EEC budget after all was only equivalent to 1 per cent of the total GNP of the member states. Moreover Britain wasn't really 'poor' in any way. She after all had North Sea oil in an era of oil crises. She should therefore either agree to a 'Community compromise' – exchanging concessions on the CAP budget, for example, by making offers over fishing or energy policy – or else she might adopt a *positive* Community viewpoint by developing new Community policies from which all might benefit. On the other hand a strictly profit and loss approach based on straightforward national contributions was deemed *uncommunitaire*. This then was the 'European' answer to Mrs Thatcher.

The British premier would have none of this. She did promise to 'learn' to be patient but patience was never one of her virtues. In her clearheadedness she had many counter-arguments, the main one being that if the Community was ever to make further progress, the overweening role ascribed to its farmers would simply have to be regulated. It couldn't remain for ever primarily an agricultural cartel. In terms of practical politics moreover Mrs Thatcher knew that the British had entered 'Europe' for short-term financial gains and still expected to receive them, especially at a time when cuts in public expenditure made relief from any source welcome. Nor had British politicians ever promised to view the Treaty of Rome as Holy Writ. On the contrary it was an open secret in 1973 that once in, the British would attempt to 'reform' the EEC. And, now that Europe was overflowing with wine lakes and overshadowed by a variety of edible mountains, the case for change seemed imperative. Worse still, the prospective entry of Spain and Portugal into the Community threatened to establish olive oil lakes and citrus mountains also. By the end of 1983, however, no solution to the problem had presented itself and another spectacular Community deadlock occurred at the Athens summit of December 1983.

Yet by then Mrs Thatcher had achieved a great deal more in temporary relief than anyone had imagined possible and her shock tactics in November 1979 were seen to have paid off. The Community in 1980 and 1981 agreed to rebates for Britain which eventually totalled £1·8 billion. This in turn meant that Britain's net contributions for these years amounted to less than £200 million. This was less than had been expected and seemed to promise a reconciliation. Yet a new crisis developed in 1982 over the annual farm price package, a crisis which saw the Community override a British veto. Mrs Thatcher was too involved with the Falklands War at the time to deal with this personally. Instead she wrote it off as a Foreign Office blunder and defused it more or less happily by negotiating a rebate for 1982. However this proved more difficult to secure than in previous years and the release of the funds involved was in fact held up by the European Parliament. The 1983 refund of £440 million once again ran into trouble – it was slightly cut by Budget Ministers in July 1983 and once again was frozen (December 1983) by the European Parliament. By now Mrs Thatcher was demanding a permanent solution to Britain's grievances and threatening to allow the

Community to go bankrupt if one were not found. And given the fact that Community resources no longer covered Community expenditures and could not be increased without her consent, she seemed to be in a strong position to get her way even if President Mitterrand of France at the December 1983 summit in Athens had unexpectedly, in the view of the Foreign Office, refused to contemplate any long-term changes. Mrs Thatcher's achievements regarding rebates in the meantime had been assessed by Peter Riddell as follows:

> Overall the 1980 deal has ensured that the UK's net contributions have been substantially lower than they would otherwise have been. Assuming that the £440 million rebate will be paid for 1983, the total refunds since 1980 will have amounted to over £2·5 billion, equivalent to a rebate of 65·4 per cent of the unadjusted net contributions before rebates.

This was one reason why the Labour Party was totally unable to use the EEC as a weapon against Mrs Thatcher in the 1983 election. On this, as on most other issues, she had outmanoeuvred them.

Was Mrs Thatcher really 'anti-European', however, in the Eurospeak sense of the term? Common Market traditionalists would believe that she was. Yet from another point of view the answer is a different one. It can easily be argued after all that the budgetary mechanisms of the CAP reflected less a principle of federalism than a defence of French and other national interests. Certainly the 100,000 French farmers who demonstrated against Mrs Thatcher's stand in Paris in March 1980 – constituting the biggest demonstration seen there since May 1968 – were not defending a political philosophy of international brotherhood. Thus Mrs Thatcher's defence of national interests within the Community may be seen as having precedents. And her hostility to majority voting was directly in the tradition of General de Gaulle. She herself would argue that she merely wanted to update the Community's procedures to reflect the realities of its enlarged membership. Thus she quoted Burke to the European Council when it met in London in November 1981 to the effect that 'a state without the means of change is without the means of its conservation'. This might infuriate the French but partly this was on account of being beaten at their own game. In one other sphere, moreover, Great Britain did contribute to European solidarity. For while in possession of the European Presidency, Lord Carrington drafted the London Report which was designed to strengthen European 'political cooperation'.* It advocated the establishment of a small secretariat to assist each presidency on matters of political cooperation; greater co-operation between successive presidencies; a new crisis mechanism whereby a meeting between ministers or representatives of member states would be obligatory within forty-eight hours at the request of any three member states; and increased association of the European Commission in political cooperation as well as greater consultation with the European Parliament. The member states agreed to institute the crisis mechanism and the Secretariat, but the latter has still to emerge. As far as Carrington was concerned the London Report was a genuine attempt to promote a more innovatory role for Europe in international affairs – a role which he had already supported the previous year through the albeit fruitless European proposals for the neutralization of Afghanistan and the relatively pro-Palestinian Venice Declaration on the Middle East. On the other hand, 'political cooperation' – with French approval – remained outside the scope of the Commission so that when moves were made by the West German and Italian Foreign Ministers in 1982 to rectify this and to promote greater use of majority voting in the Council of Ministers by means of a plan for 'European Union' (the so-called Genscher–Colombo Plan), both Britain and France allowed the Danes and Greeks to water down the scheme significantly. Thus, when in June 1983 the heads of state eventually signed a 'Solemn Declaration on European Union' it contained merely a general reference to the provisions of the Paris and Rome Treaties with regard to voting in the Council, together with a suggestion that on those occasions where unanimity was required by the Treaty any member state with a non-vital objection should resort to abstention to facilitate decision-making. The Declaration however also called for more 'political cooperation', for more cooperation on terrorism, high technology, security and the European Monetary System (EMS) and for greater consultation with both the Commission and the European Parliament. Britain's own attitude towards 'European Union' had meanwhile been more specifically outlined in Parliament on 17 June by the Minister of State at the Foreign Office, Mr Douglas Hurd, who said: 'In our view, a union amounts to the development of an ever-closer framework of cooperation between the sovereign states of the Com-

---

* The term associated with moves towards the formulation of a common European foreign policy.

munity in all areas where this cooperation can be shown to be useful . . . It does not entail the creation of any new institution or increases in the formal powers of existing ones.' It was, he said, 'not a commitment to a federal system or to the progressive erosion of national sovereignty'. Given that the Genscher–Colombo proposals had tried to bring security matters within the aegis of political cooperation, the British reaction was not surprising. NATO, after all, remained the proper sphere for that and one of the Ten, Ireland, was not an allied but a neutral state. Moreover, the whole issue of security might well have forced several members to choose between cooperating with their European partners or with the Americans on certain issues. This was a problem which nearly all members of the Ten recognized. On the whole, therefore, it can be argued that Britain under Mrs Thatcher's first administration was neither fundamentally more 'pro' or 'anti' the European Community than most of its other members. Like them, it defended its national interests within an increasingly confederal framework. This may not have been the intention of the founders of the Common Market but then life goes on and democratic institutions alter to reflect the needs and wishes of changing electorates.

DEFENCE

One reason why member states among the Ten had been reluctant to bring security matters within the aegis of 'political cooperation' was the fact that in the late seventies and early eighties the Western Alliance seemed under considerable strain. Differences emerged between America and her European partners over a variety of issues, differences which indeed divided politicians within Western Europe itself. At the root of these differences lay divergent perceptions of the nature of the Soviet challenge and how to respond to it, the result being that many European politicians found themselves reluctant to support US policy on a wide range of issues.

There was, for a start, a fundamental difference in views over the very nature of the Soviet state. The alleged manipulation of *détente* by the USSR in the early and mid-seventies in order to bring about Soviet parity with, if not superiority over, the USA in conventional and nuclear forces confirmed the so-called 'essentialist' view of many American politicians that the Soviet Union was an inherently expansionist power with which no deals could be made. President Carter appeared to believe this after 1979 and President Reagan's main security adviser on Russian affairs after 1981, Professor Richard Pipes, certainly did so. In his view the USSR was not only ideologically driven towards expansion but was also impelled in this direction by the need to divert attention from its incompetently managed economy. The USA, therefore, had no choice but to re-arm against it. The Western European allies, on the other hand, although they did not deny a need to re-arm (France after 1976 began to modernize her deterrent and all the NATO countries after 1977 agreed to spend 3 per cent more per year on defence; moreover in 1977 it was Chancellor Schmidt of West Germany who raised the issue of stationing theatre nuclear weapons in Europe to counter Soviet SS-20s) tended to see the USSR as a more traditional power. Thus, while they recognized the importance of Marxist-Leninism to Soviet policy-makers, they argued that the latter also acknowledged the constraints of the so-called 'correlation of forces'. In short, the USSR could act pragmatically and agreements could be negotiated with her. The Europeans, in any case, had already learned to live with a Soviet Union which was their military superior even if the Americans had no wish to share this experience. Finally, US political culture was inherently hostile to Marxism, while that of Western Europe was not. It might not approve of it 1917-style, but Marxism was none the less intellectually respectable. All this meant that European views of the Soviet challenge rested on different intellectual bases from American ones. Yet in practical terms there were differences too. The West Germans in particular, but the West Europeans in general, still derived benefits from *détente*. It eased strains in world politics, strengthened human contacts across the divide and led to inter-bloc discussion of many topics – particularly disarmament – in which both sides shared an interest. It also led to greater trade and more prosperity. Thus European statesmen could point to the 300,000 ethnic Germans who had returned to the West since the early 1970s and to the growth of trade between Western Europe and Comecon. By 1980, for example, Western Europe accounted for 91 per cent of all OECD imports from and 77 per cent of all exports to Comecon countries. Significantly the figures for the USA were only 3 per cent and 9 per cent respectively. Finally Western Europe always suspected US policy of being over-influenced by US electoral politics. The Salt II treaty, for example, was pushed aside by US electoral considerations in 1979–80 and the hardening

US attitude towards Russia was often blamed on President Carter's need to repudiate the claims of his Republican opponents.

These differences surfaced openly when in 1979, after the invasion of Afghanistan, Mr Carter called for trade sanctions against the Soviet Union and a boycott of the Olympic games which were to be held in Moscow. His European allies openly doubted the effectiveness of either measure – although Mrs Thatcher supported the boycott – and several of them even doubted whether the invasion marked the turning point in Soviet policy which a newly proclaimed 'Carter Doctrine' was designed to meet. Thus, while the US President warned the world against a Soviet bid to seize the oil resources of the Middle East and promised to intervene with a Rapid Deployment Force if one materialized, the view of several Western European chancelleries seemed to be that the invasion had been a defensive act undertaken by the USSR to protect her southern frontier from Iranian-type Islamic revivalism.

The imposition of martial law at the end of 1981 in Poland provoked another inter-allied quarrel. President Reagan blamed Moscow for Poland's sufferings and imposed sanctions on both Moscow and Poland which went beyond those previously agreed to by his European allies. They included in particular a ban on the export by US firms of technology for the pipeline being built between Siberia and Western Europe at a cost of between five and six billion dollars, despite the fact that the main contractors for this project as well as its co-beneficiaries were West Europeans. Reagan's plans in fact threatened to damage not merely West German, French and Belgian fuel supplies but the economic prospects of West German, British, French and Italian engineering companies. Reagan, for his part, objected to the deal for two reasons: it provided the USSR with hard currency; and it made his allies partly dependent on his enemies. The Europeans, on the other hand, Mrs Thatcher included, saw the US President's policy as hypocritical. The US at this time was selling billions of dollars worth of grain to the USSR and had not placed an embargo on that (Reagan indeed had ended Carter's embargo of 1979). The Americans argued that the grain trade in fact deprived the USSR of much-needed foreign currency but it could equally be argued that if the Russians were forced to spend more on agriculture, they must spend less on defence. The political influence of the mid-western farm lobby was therefore held in Europe to be dictating Reagan's embargo policy. Finally, several European statesmen believed that the USSR was actually exercising restraint in Poland. The Russians, after all, had not actually invaded the country as had been widely expected.

In June 1982 an attempt was made to patch up the quarrel over the pipeline at the Versailles economic summit, with the West Europeans agreeing to levy higher interest rates on loans to the Soviet bloc. But after the President of France rejected this compromise, his US counterpart announced that it would be illegal for European subsidiaries of US firms to sell technology to the USSR. This once again threatened the pipeline contract and Mrs Thatcher denounced Mr Reagan's disregard for international law. Both Britain and France defiantly ordered the subsidiaries concerned to complete their contracts with the Soviet Union and five months later the US President agreed to drop the restrictions he had imposed. The European allies for their part agreed to coordinate policy on strategic aspects of East–West trade.

Both these episodes gave rise to complaints from Americans that their Western European allies neglected Western strategic interests in favour of short-term economic gain. Moreover, the West Europeans were accused of ignoring the Soviet challenge outside Europe. For example, their refusal to help the US defend the Middle East on whose oil they were dependent led to charges of pusillanimity, while their criticisms of US policy in Latin America and the Third World caused much aggravation. The European view, on the other hand, was that large-scale armed Western intervention in the Middle East would be counter-productive and that in any case US policy there was too uncritically pro-Israeli. This latter view was implicit in the Venice Declaration in June 1980 which called for a Palestinian Homeland as well as for Palestinian participation in peace negotiations. None the less, America's European allies did contribute to the policing of the Camp David Agreements between Israel and Egypt and later to the peace-keeping force in Lebanon. As far as Latin America was concerned, France and Denmark proved particularly critical of the Reagan administration's anti-Communist crusade there and of the murderous sort of regimes ('autocratic' rather than 'totalitarian' to give credit to Mrs Kirkpatrick's famous distinction) which the President supported in that region. Mrs Thatcher, however, passed the litmus test of loyalty by retaining British troops in Belize and selling arms to Chile and Argentina. Later on, on the other hand, her reaction to the invasion, firstly of the Falkland Islands and then of

Grenada, would complicate her special relationship with Reagan. As far as the Third World in general was concerned, almost all the European allies deplored what they regarded as the American obsession with Soviet interventionism, viewing it as a distraction in many cases from the complexities of regional conflicts. For their own part they preferred to keep out of local controversies and concentrate on what they believed to be the real Western interest of preserving steady markets and raw material supplies by encouraging regional stability and a generally sympathetic attitude towards the industrialized countries. They therefore disagreed with Reagan's policy of replying in kind to Soviet military involvements in the Third World.

The US reaction to such criticism was to question its allies' commitment to mutual defence; Senator Stevens of Alaska, for example, the Chairman of the US Senate's Defense Appropriation Sub-Committee, in 1982 linked the pipeline dispute with the maintenance of US forces in Europe. Meanwhile, Deputy Secretary of State for Defense, Carlucci, in 1981 had already declared that Congress would want 'to demonstrate that our allies and friends in Europe [were] contributing their fair share of the common burden', a viewpoint which was widely echoed in the American press. After all, the average West European defence budget amounted to only 3·5 per cent of GNP in 1981 compared to America's 5·6 per cent and whereas in 1979 President Carter had increased US defence spending by 5 per cent (to be followed by President Reagan's massive increases) a number of the European allies were having difficulties implementing the 3 per cent p.a. increases to defence spending agreed on in 1977. There was also widespread resentment that the USA was still bearing over 50 per cent of NATO's overall costs. This led the West German Defence Minister in 1981 to correct 'the impression that the major part of the Alliance's defence effort' was 'made by the United States'. He argued that 'the European allies make available about 91 per cent of the allied ground forces and 75 per cent of the allied forces in Europe ... 75 per cent of the tanks of the allied nations and more than 90 per cent of their armoured and mechanized divisions come from European countries ... the European nations of NATO maintain about three million soldiers in time of peace [a figure which could] be doubled by the mobilization of reservists'. That compared with a figure of about 250,000 US troops in Europe.

Ironically, America's European allies were at this very time beginning to doubt America's commitment to the common cause. For given the huge increase in Soviet nuclear force which occurred in the 1970s and increased Soviet adventurism abroad there was a growing fear that the US nuclear guarantee to Western Europe would no longer hold. Combined with this was a fear that the Superpowers would negotiate some sort of private military agreement over the heads of their respective allies. After all, they had already signed two SALT treaties on arms limitations and Dr Kissinger in a speech in Brussels in September 1979 had pointed out that in the event of a nuclear war they would share a common interest in limiting both the weapons used and the geographical scope of the conflict. Common sense, moreover, seemed to indicate that it would be extremely unwise to expect a US President to risk American nuclear destruction for the sake of Western Europe. Part of NATO's concern therefore between 1977 and 1979 to balance the USSR's SS-20 missiles aimed at Western Europe with US Pershing and Cruise ones *sited in Europe* was the need to ensure that, if a nuclear war ever did start there, it would immediately involve the Americans. In short, in the event of a Russian nuclear attack, US missiles would be fired from Europe by US troops. There could therefore be no question of the US guarantee ever failing to work.

It was a double irony therefore that once the Americans agreed to station their missiles in Europe, European public opinion, concerned by American rhetoric and re-armament, came to fear that President Reagan might use them to start a nuclear war in Europe, without risk to the United States. The decision to install the Cruise and Pershing missiles, however, had been only one part of a 'dual track' strategy decided in December 1979 by the NATO allies. In other words, it had at the same time been decided to use the threat of installing them to force the Soviet Union into disarmament talks. President Reagan would thus offer to install not a single missile in Europe if the USSR would remove all of its SS-4s, SS-5s and SS-20s. This 'zero option' was rejected by the Russians but in December 1981, IRT talks opened in Geneva which went on until the end of 1983. These led to no agreement but the Soviets used the negotiations there to stimulate the European peace movement to which the NATO decision had given life. This acquired great strength in most of Europe (with the notable exception of France) and in Britain it revived the fortunes of the Campaign for Nuclear Disarmament. Yet CND had already been given new life by the evolution of British defence policy and the role within it played by the independent nuclear deterrent.

Despite the Labour Party's electoral wins in 1964, 1966 and twice in 1974, the British deterrent had remained in being. Politically this had been justified by Wilson on account of its lack of independence. So tied was it to the USA, Wilson argued, that his Labour governments had agreed to assign it totally to NATO and in public he mocked any possibility of Britain 'going it alone' in a nuclear war or of attempting 'a nuclear Suez'. He even offered to make Britain's submarines part of an Atlantic Nuclear Force (ANF), his alternative to the MLF proposals of President Johnson. Yet within the framework of this suggestion Wilson had also made it clear that there would 'not be any system of locks which interferes with our right of communication with a submarine or our right to withdraw the submarine' – which sounded very much like a restatement of the 'supreme national interests' clause which Macmillan had originally negotiated at Nassau in 1962. And in practice Labour and Conservative governments throughout the 1960s and 1970s agreed that a degree of independence remained, although there was a gentleman's agreement not to argue over how much. The real reason, however, why the nuclear deterrent had never been scrapped was simply that the deal made by Macmillan turned out to be an extremely good one. It was cheap, it gave Britain a nuclear force which would last a generation and, given that it also had the capacity to destroy fifteen to twenty-four Soviet cities or up to 25 millions of the Soviet population, it was one which had to be taken seriously by the Russians. Its financial advantages have been stressed by Professor Freedman:

The capital costs for purchasing the missiles had been estimated originally to be £92·9 million. Allowing for inflation, it came out at 42 per cent less, at £53 million. Even the submarines were comparatively inexpensive and didn't stray too far from the original estimate of £140·3 million coming out at 6 per cent higher in real terms at £162 million. In consequence the whole programme cost 13 per cent less than anticipated ... as well as arriving on schedule, a most unusual phenomenon.

This cost-effectiveness, therefore, together with Denis Healey's argument that two centres of decision-making would make the NATO deterrent more effective had persuaded the 1964 Labour Cabinet (against the advice of George Wigg and Lord Chalfont) to retain the programme.

They did however agree to build only four nuclear submarines instead of five, a decision which was later regretted, although the decision to buy A-3 Polaris missiles (instead of A-1s or A-2s) was to turn out to be justified. (The A-3 missile divided into 3 parts before hitting its target.)

For most of the 1960s and 1970s (the last submarine came into service in June 1968) the Polaris force met Britain's needs. However, there were two developments which undermined its usefulness. The development of an anti-ballistic missile (ABM) system around Moscow was one of these; the need for continual refits which meant that only one boat would be operational for about six months of any year was yet another. This meant that by the mid-1970s thought had to be given to updating or replacing the programme. In 1967, however, Wilson had ruled out the possibility of purchasing the US Poseidon missile – it would have meant added expense, revived the debate inside the Labour Party on nuclear weapons and upset the French at a time when Britain was still trying to enter the Common Market. Instead, and partly to boost the reputation of UK technology, Wilson gave the go-ahead to the Government's research establishment at Aldermaston to devise a new warhead for Polaris which would be more capable of penetrating Moscow's ABM defences and would also possess greater accuracy. The resulting programme was to become known as Chevaline.

The Heath government of 1970–74 made no fundamental changes in nuclear policy. In 1973, Lord Carrington as Defence Minister decided not to build a fifth Polaris submarine, not so much on grounds of cost (although they seemed significant) but on account of doubts over the long-term future of the missiles. Apart from those factors which have been mentioned above, various clauses in the first SALT treaty had given rise to doubts over US cooperation in future, doubts which were apparently significant enough to rule out any new approach to the US over Poseidon. It was now feared, and Kissinger hinted as much to Heath, that the US Congress would not approve the sale of the missile to Britain. Fortunately, the Aldermaston scientists by 1973 had almost completed the Chevaline programme to improve our Polaris missiles. In the words of Francis Pym as Defence Minister in 1980 it involved: 'a very major and complex development of the missile front end, involving also changes to the fire control system. The result will not be a MIRV-ed system. But it includes advanced penetration aids and the ability to manoeuvre the payload in space.' In 1973, therefore, this seemed the only way forward. The costs were likely to be on the high side (well over £250 million) but once again the programme appeared to be politically attractive. The French once again would have no cause for complaint – especially at a time when the UK was finally set to join the Common Market – and the Labour Party could not oppose a decision which was so in line with its own past practice; moreover public opinion would not be disturbed by the purchase of a MIRV-ed missile (such as Poseidon) at a time when the SALT talks between the USSR and the USA had turned to the problem of controlling MIRVs (Multiple Independently-targeted Re-entry Vehicles). Still, although the Chevaline programme was given government encouragement in 1973 it was not finally approved until after the return to power of the Labour Party in 1974.

Wilson's cabinet in 1974 was almost immediately faced with the need to make a decision on the Chevaline programme. An underground nuclear test – the first for nine years – was planned for May and needed to be approved. This was done by a Cabinet committee while the full Cabinet was informed that a Polaris improvement programme was under way at the cost of £250 million. There was in fact little objection, the costs involved being more controversial than the programme itself. However, it was agreed that defence costs in general should be subject to a major review. The trouble was that by the end of the following year, by which time the review had been completed, the cost of Chevaline had risen to £450 million. By mid-1977 it would be costing £800 million and by 1980, £1 billion. However, the defence review of 1975 left the programme intact. Savings were found by cuts elsewhere including the withdrawal of the fleet from the Mediterranean. By 1977 on the other hand the Treasury was actively questioning the need for Chevaline. Fred Mulley, the new Defence Minister, and David Owen, the new Foreign Secretary, were both less convinced than their predecessors of the strategic necessity to go ahead with it. However, to have scrapped the programme altogether would have represented a tremendous waste of money. Moreover it would have faced the Labour Party with a very fundamental decision – either to find a replacement for Polaris or to scrap Britain's nuclear deterrent once and for all. Since such a decision would inevitably have led to a major controversy both within the party and the country, the Chevaline programme was continued. In this way, it was hoped, the biggest decision looming over Britain's defences could be left until after the 1979 election.

Nor could there be any escaping the fact that a major decision would soon be necessary. Not merely was Soviet ABM technology eroding the effectiveness of the British deterrent, but after 1982 the USA itself would no longer have Polaris submarines in service. Lockheed, therefore, as sole manufacturers of the Polaris missiles, would have no need to keep its production lines open, and even if this problem could be (and in fact was) met by special arrangements with the company, more worrying was the problem of the submarines themselves. Their active life was expected to come to an end in the 1980s – at the latest they could probably remain operational until the mid-1990s – so that the question arose of whether to replace them. If they were to be replaced by about 1990, then a decision would be needed by around 1980. In the words of a report of the Royal Institute of International Affairs published in 1977 'Any delay beyond that time [would] entail increasing constraints, increasing costs and increasing risks.' Between 1977 and 1979, therefore, Whitehall began to examine the choices available. The Deputy Under Secretary at the Foreign Office, Sir Anthony Duff, chaired one working party on the military and international repercussions of a successor to Polaris while another, on delivery systems, was chaired by Professor Ronald Mason, the Chief Scientific Adviser to the Ministry of Defence. A group of senior Whitehall mandarins monitored the progress of both bodies while the Ministers involved laid it down that they wished only to see the final reports which were to review all options, without prior commitment to any. It was not until the end of 1978 that both reports became available. From these it seemed clear that a final decision would indeed be necessary around 1980 and that probably a submarine-based system would be best. The Government, however, still wanted to avoid a decision before the election so that Mulley, in a defence debate which took place immediately beforehand, took care to sound absolutely noncommital. He said:

I could not say today that in no circumstances would I be in favour of moving towards a new generation [of missiles]. I accept that the arguments for and against are finely balanced. The answer depends a great deal on what happens in the next year or two.

His party also attempted to ignore the issue and in its statement on defence in its election manifesto merely stated:

In 1974 we renounced any intention of moving towards the production of a new generation of nuclear weapons or a successor to the Polaris nuclear force; we reiterate our belief that this is the best course for Britain. But many great issues affecting our allies and the world are involved and a new round of Strategic Arms Limitation negotiations will soon begin. We think it is essential that there must be a full and informed debate about these issues in the country before any decision is taken.

The decision on a successor to Polaris was therefore left to Mrs Thatcher's government. On coming into office it received the reports of Duff and Mason and in October 1979 it announced that, while it would prolong the life of the Polaris force into the 1990s, it was giving consideration to Britain's 'strategic deterrent capability' thereafter. This meant in practice purchasing either an improved British Polaris-type missile, the submarine-launched Trident missile from the USA or fitting cruise missiles to submarines. There was, it is true, the option of an Anglo-French missile in line with several overtures which had come from Paris, but the *force de frappe* by this time was rather out of date and Congress had so limited Britain's ability to share nuclear technology of American origin that cooperation with the French would have been fairly pointless. The Americans, for a number of reasons however, did not object to continuing to cooperate on nuclear defence with Great Britain. Their base at Holy Loch was valuable; it was useful to be able to discuss nuclear technology with an informed and friendly power; two centres of decision-taking helped boost the deterrent force of NATO; while the deterrent itself helped to sustain the flagging prestige of a reliable ally. The Pentagon in January 1980 therefore declared that nuclear cooperation with Great Britain contributed 'to our mutual defense interests'. Meanwhile, President Carter in December 1979 had already agreed to help Mrs Thatcher maintain 'a credible British strategic deterrent'. The result was that on 24 January 1980, in the first parliamentary debate on the British deterrent to be held for fifteen years, the new Defence Minister, Francis Pym, said that between four and five billion pounds would be assigned to developing or purchasing a post-Polaris generation of missiles. Which kind was to be purchased, however, was not as yet announced. On the other hand, improving Polaris itself seemed an increasingly expensive option; fitting cruise missiles to submarines seemed even more expensive (save perhaps if they were to be fitted to hunter–killer submarines, in which case new problems of tactics and strategy would arise) whereas the US Trident missile had many advantages. It was both proven and modern; it had a range of 4,000 as opposed to Polaris's 2,500 nautical miles (which meant that it could be fired either from base or from more remote new stations at sea); and each missile was MIRV-ed and could carry eight warheads of 100 kilotons each. By the end of the year, therefore, Pym announced that the successor to Polaris would be Trident. It was a decision which by then was widely expected.

In 1983 the annual statement on the defence estimates gave the total cost of the Trident programme as £7·5 billion. This of course was to be spread over some fifteen years, although costs will peak in the late 1980s. This means that, by then, the programme will be absorbing about 6 per cent of the total defence budget compared to the 1·5 per cent taken up by Polaris in the 1960s and 1970s. Polaris itself will by then be absorbing another 2 per cent of that budget. The probability is therefore that, unlike the Polaris programme in the mid-1960s and 1970s, the Trident budget may not escape defence cuts in the future. Yet the costs of nuclear defence to Great Britain as part of defence costs overall will still remain relatively small.

The defence budget itself on the other hand is undoubtedly high by the standards of our European allies. By 1982–3 indeed defence expenditure was 16·7 per cent higher in real terms than it had been in 1978–9 and was accounting for more than 5 per cent of GNP. Moreover, this was only partly as a result of the Falklands War. The 3 per cent increase each year as part of the 1977 NATO commitment was, of course, one factor but more important were the large pay rises awarded to the armed forces by the Thatcher government. Yet, given that there was no growth in the economy in the period 1979–83 and given Mrs Thatcher's resolve to reduce government spending, these increases had to be balanced by cuts in other areas of defence expenditure. The result was yet another defence review in 1981 carried out not by Francis Pym, who had resisted cuts to the defence budget, but by his successor John Nott who replaced him in January of that year. Nott was given a clear mandate by Mrs Thatcher to place limits on defence expenditure and chose to do so principally by cutting the navy budget.

Given his government's decision on Trident, Nott's room for manoeuvre in making cuts was somewhat limited. In practice he had to choose between cutting Britain's forces in Germany or cutting her naval commitments. In fact, Nott chose to cut the surface fleet by reducing the number of destroyers and frigates from fifty-five to fifty and the number of *Invincible*-class aircraft carriers from three to two. The emphasis in naval defence was shifted instead to submarines – the number of nuclear-powered attack submarines was to be increased from twelve to seventeen – and Nimrod patrol aircraft. One result of all this was that the naval dockyards at Chatham and Gibraltar were to close. Another was that the ice-patrol ship *Endurance* was to be withdrawn from the South Atlantic. A further result was that Britain's admirals were provoked into conducting a semi-public campaign against the Defence Minister. In this, moreover, they were joined by the Navy Minister, Mr Keith Speed, who was finally sacked by Mrs Thatcher in May 1981 before the White Paper was published in July. Speed, a former navy officer who believed that the size of the Royal Navy should have been expanded rather than cut, wrote in a book published at the end of 1982 that Nott might have passed O-level economics but had failed A-level history. 'We have a highly developed island economy, world-wide interests and major national resources lying under the seas around us,' he wrote, 'and depredations in the strength of the Royal Navy must cease now if we are to continue to be adequately protected.' To many people Speed, in retrospect, had appeared to have a point. For had the cuts which had been ordered by Nott taken place immediately it might well have proved impossible a few months later for Mrs Thatcher to lead Britain to victory over Argentina in the Falklands War. That campaign, after all, fought at a distance of 8,000 miles from Great Britain, was first and foremost a demonstration of British naval prowess, particularly that of the surface fleet. Speed's book, when it appeared therefore, was an exercise in 'I told you so'.

THE FALKLANDS WAR

The Falklands War broke out on Friday 2 April 1982 when an Argentinian task force occupied the Falkland Islands and forced the surrender of the eighty or so Royal Marines there. In the following weeks no less than 12,500 Argentine troops were landed which meant that the 1,800 inhabitants of the islands were many times outnumbered by their occupiers. The success of the Argentines in taking over the colony was seen as such a humiliation for Mrs Thatcher's government that it almost fell from power. After a few nervous days, however, and the resignation of Lord Carrington, Mrs Thatcher was able to organize a military, diplomatic and political response which brought about not only the humiliating defeat of the Argentines, but the destruction of the regime which had begun the war and the liberation of the islands. At the same time she established that complete ascendancy in British domestic politics which would enable her to win the general election of 1983. The Falklands conflict on the other hand took almost everyone by surprise. Indeed, it was a totally unforeseen development which may well have completely altered the history of British politics.

The Argentinians had invaded the Falklands in order to exercise their claim to sovereignty over them, a claim which had never been recognized by the British. It had, after all, been an Englishman who had first discovered the islands (John Davis in 1592), an Englishman who had first landed on them (John Strong in 1690) and it had been British settlers who had occupied them continuously since 1833. True, the French had colonized the islands in the eighteenth century, calling them the Isles Malouines after their Breton sailors from St Malo; it was true also that the French had later sold their settlement to the Spanish who had called the islands the Malvinas and who in 1768 ejected British colonists who had established themselves there in 1764. Yet in the aftermath of this incident, which brought Britain close to war with France and Spain, the latter had restored the British colony. The British evacuated it on their own initiative in 1774 but left behind a plaque at Port Egmont declaring that the islands were still the property of the British crown. The Spanish eventually lost interest in the islands during the Napoleonic Wars and the Argentinian war of independence but Argentinian historiography notwithstanding, they never formally transferred their claim to the Falklands to Buenos Aires. The Argentinians in fact never really established a colony on the islands at all. While it is true that Louis Vernet, a Hamburg merchant of French descent established a settlement there between 1826 and 1831 and managed in 1829 to obtain the title of governor from the Argentines, he was expelled in 1833 by the Americans for seizing three US schooners. An interim governor, Juan Mestivier, was appointed to replace him, but he was murdered almost on his arrival on the islands by Argentinian mutineers and on the day his body was being returned to Buenos Aires a British sloop, the *Clio*, arrived to reassert British rights. The Union Jack was raised without a shot being fired and from 1833 the islands became a British colony of some strategic importance, off which famous sea battles were fought in both world wars. One reason for the timing of the 1983 invasion was that the military junta which was now in command in Argentina wished to put an end to British rule in the Falklands before the celebrations marking the 150th anniversary of the establishment of the colony could take place there.

There were, of course, a number of other reasons behind the 1983 invasion. Domestically, the junta was in trouble: Argentina was almost bankrupt; inflation was running at 130 per cent per annum; and there was fierce controversy over the fate of perhaps up to 30,000 citizens who had 'disappeared' under military rule. On 30 March the Perónist labour unions had been able as a result to mobilize a huge demonstration in the capital against the 'military assassins'. Yet it was perhaps the diplomatic scene which most of all convinced the junta that an invasion of the Falklands might succeed. For the United States was seeking Argentinian aid to combat the spread of communism in Latin America and General Galtieri, the Argentinian President, seemed convinced that in return for such aid, President Reagan would stop the British resisting an invasion of the Falklands by force. Moreover, according to the Argentinian Foreign Minister, the allegedly Anglophile Costa Mendez, the British were so weary of running the Falklands that they would almost welcome the opportunity to be rid of them. He had thus assured the junta that the islands could be seized without a war. Nor can it be denied that, in the words of one book on the subject, 'Successive [British] administrations had done little to discourage the belief in Buenos Aires that at some point they would be allowed to become masters of the Malvinas.'

The Argentine claim to the Falklands was revived after 1945 by the country's fascist dictator, General Perón. Thereafter there were intermittent threats to invade the islands – one of which led to a warning from Churchill in 1952 – but in 1965 the government of Argentina registered at the United Nations its desire to negotiate a transfer of sovereignty and the UN instructed both sides to begin talks. These continued right up until 1982, with each round occurring almost annually. Each however was usually 'preceded by fierce sabre-rattling in Buenos Aires, including threats of invasion'. These, in turn, were generally forestalled by the promise of future negotiations and the British rarely took them seriously. Certainly they never stationed more than a tiny force of marines on the islands as a symbol of their will to defend them. These marines were meant to act as a trip-wire. If the islands were invaded they were to resist and cause a state of war to ensue between Britain and Argentina. Britain would then come to the rescue of the islands by dispatching a naval task force. The Argentinians, it was hoped, understood this position, but by 1983 this was no longer true. The British Foreign Office now appeared to want to transfer sovereignty to them and seemed only to be blocked in this desire by the opposition of the islanders themselves in alliance with a number of backbench MPs in the House of Commons. In reality the situation was very different but the Argentinians were unaware of this.

From the Argentinian point of view the situation appeared to have developed in the following way. Between 1971 and 1973 the British had concluded agreements with them on the islands regarding communications, postal services, travel, medical facilities, education and customs. Argentinian workmen and technicians had built an airstrip at Port Stanley, where Argentine airline officials later opened an office and Argentine ships and tourists called. Young Falklanders began to win scholarships to Argentine schools and in 1974 a new agreement was signed on sea transport links and fuel supplies. There was, as will be seen, a serious dispute with Britain between 1976 and 1977 but by the end of 1977 the transfer of sovereignty was already being discussed for the first time in the joint talks. Then in 1979, after the election of Mrs Thatcher's government the Foreign Office Minister with responsibility for the Falklands, Mr Nicholas Ridley, appeared to believe that the solution to the dispute might be found in a 'leaseback' arrangement, whereby Britain would cede sovereignty to Argentina who would in turn lease the islands back to Britain to administer for a long period. In this way, it was hoped the Argentines could satisfy their national pride while Britain could safeguard the way of life of the islanders. The problem was that, when Mr Ridley tried to explain this proposal to the islanders themselves in 1980, he was given a very rough ride; he was also attacked savagely on 2 December that year in the Commons by a cross-section of MPs who for various reasons disliked the Argentinians. Indeed, the attitude of most members of the House was summed up by the former Labour minister Mr Douglas Jay who asked bluntly: 'Why can't the Foreign Office leave the matter alone?' That was also the point of view of the Falklanders who, when asked by Mr Ridley to choose between a

British–Argentinian condominium, leaseback or a freeze on negotiations, predictably chose the latter. Thus, when the Argentinians rejected Britain's proposals to freeze the dispute, the British government was left without a policy. More talks were held in New York in February 1982 between Ridley's successor, Mr Richard Luce (accompanied by two representatives of the islanders), and the Argentinians. But although the atmosphere was extremely cordial by all accounts, the talks got nowhere. Meanwhile the British Defence White Paper of July 1981 had announced that the *Endurance* was being withdrawn from the South Atlantic, a development which appeared significant to the Argentines. By January 1982, therefore, the Buenos Aires newspaper *La Prensa* was predicting an invasion of the islands before the 150th anniversary of British rule there. All Mr Luce could do in reply was to get the Foreign Office to postpone the withdrawal of *Endurance*. This required considerable pressure (and the backing of Lord Carrington) but only really came about after some Argentinian scrap merchants landed illegally on the Falklands dependency of South Georgia on 19 March and raised their national flag, an incident which preceded the outbreak of hostilities between the two countries.

Britain's willingness to discuss a transfer of sovereignty along with the announced withdrawal from patrol of the *Endurance* may well have convinced the Argentinians that the former colonial power was no longer really interested in retaining the Falklands. It was their misfortune that counter-signals remained invisible. For example, they seemed unaware after 1979 of the opposition to Ridley's proposals which had been mounted inside the cabinet by Mrs Thatcher – one reason why Lord Carrington had refused to push them very hard. Indeed, they appeared totally unaware of Mrs Thatcher's general political determination to reverse the nation's decline and to stand up for British interests. They were also unaware that in 1977 the Labour government of Mr Callaghan had in fact made military preparations to resist an invasion of the islands.

The 1977 episode was a rather curious one. In 1976, relations with Argentina had deteriorated rapidly when Lord Shackleton was sent to the Falklands to report on their economic prospects. The Argentines had seen his visit as a provocation and had even fired on a research vessel which bore his name in the mistaken belief that he was on board. The Falklands' dependency of Southern Thule – uninhabited like South

Georgia – was seized by the Argentinians in another manifestation of their hostility to British plans, while finally in October 1976, fuel supplies to the Falkland Islands themselves were cut off. Since there seemed to be trouble brewing at the same time in Belize (a British colony in Central America which was threatened by invasion by Guatemala) the defence and overseas policy committee of the British cabinet, consisting of Callaghan, Owen, Mulley and Benn, arranged for a hunter-killer submarine and two frigates to be stationed off the Falklands for a month to forestall any attempt at invasion. The frigates in fact remained 400 miles away in order to avoid detection while the Government neglected to inform the Argentines of the presence of the submarine, lest this itself should provoke hostilities. The result was that the Argentinians had no knowledge of this now famous piece of contingency planning. Thus they can hardly be said to have been deterred by it as Owen and Callaghan were later to argue. Nor indeed could one submarine and two frigates have prevented an invasion of the islands by air. At the most they could merely have constituted a larger trip-wire, albeit one whose lethal potential might well have caused the Argentines to reconsider. A more significant result of the incident in the words of the *Economist* 'was that the Foreign Office, having apparently cried "wolf" once, had weakened its case for a trip-wire force next time'.

By March 1982, of course, 'next time' had already occurred. The Foreign Office responded to the South Georgia incident by sending marines there on the *Endurance*. Meanwhile in Buenos Aires protests were made by the British Ambassador to Costa Mendez. Since the latter reassured the ambassador that the scrap merchants would be safely removed by ship, the *Endurance* was instructed merely to stand offshore at South Georgia. It looked, therefore, as if the incident might quickly blow over, despite the reports of an impending invasion which were now filling the British press. In fact, after a week or so Costa Mendez sent not one but three ships – warships – to give protection to the scrap merchants so that the *Endurance* was forced to retreat. By then, however, more serious Argentine fleet movements were worrying the British cabinet.

President Galtieri at some stage agreed to take advantage of the South Georgia dispute to enable him if he so desired to execute an invasion plan of the Falklands which had been drawn up by his Junta colleague, Admiral Jorge Anaya. This involved a sham exercise with the Uruguayan navy and the necessary naval preparations began to take place during the weekend of 26–28 March. Part of these involved the only Argentine aircraft carrier, the *Veinticinco de Mayo*, but since it put to sea carrying paratroopers and marine commandos, British Intelligence refused to believe that it was merely participating in 'exercises'. British Intelligence was later accused however of having arrived at this conclusion too late. There had been other, earlier indications of hostile Argentinian intentions, it was claimed, which British Intelligence sources had missed – leaks in newspapers, charts of the islands purchased in London, a reconnaissance visit paid to Stanley by an Argentine air-force officer in a helicopter. Yet it is not clear even today at what precise stage the invasion was actually decided on.* Was it before or after the Perónist demonstrations in the Argentine capital on 30 March? We do not know.

In any case by the Monday of invasion week Downing Street had begun to feel alarmed. The Uruguayans were reported to have asked whether there were any Falklanders who wished to be airlifted from the islands 'before the invasion'. Diplomatic leave was, therefore, cancelled and a submarine and support ships dispatched from the Mediterranean to the South Atlantic. Mrs Thatcher now also began to look at the contingency plans which she had requested shortly beforehand. Yet in public nothing was done which might provoke the Argentinians, for it was not until 1 April that British Intelligence concluded that an invasion was inevitable. By then, of course, nothing could be done to stop one – in fact short of keeping a fleet in the South Atlantic this had always been the case – so that the Prime Minister was forced to launch a diplomatic offensive. In short she telephoned President Reagan to ask him to intervene with Galtieri. This he did at 20.20 hours Washington time on 1 April, but despite fifty minutes' pleading with the Argentine dictator there was no agreement. President Galtieri simply refused to call the invasion off. On the following day, 2 April, Mr Rex Hunt, the Governor of the Falklands, after a vain display of resistance on the part of the marines was therefore forced to surrender the islands to the Argentinians.

News of the success of the invasion was reported in the British press

* The multi-party Franks Report into the origins of the war later cleared British Intelligence of negligence.

and radio on the afternoon of 2 April. The Government, however, was made to look foolish by being unable to confirm it officially until 6 p.m. that evening. However, at 3 p.m., Francis Pym, now Leader of the Commons, had announced that the House would be recalled 'if the situation in the Falklands deteriorated'. It did, of course, and the next day, Saturday 3 April witnessed the spectacle of one of Parliament's rare weekend debates. It was also 'the first great parliamentary occasion in a major international crisis directly concerning Britain since the BBC had been authorized to place its microphones in the Chamber itself'. The result was that the public were able to listen carefully to what MPs and ministers had to say. Nor did the latter fail to understand that there was 'a speak for England' atmosphere about. The popular press had cried 'shame' and Parliament was expected to take steps to retrieve the nation's honour. In such an atmosphere it was to prove impossible to divide the House along party lines.

Two points emerged from the debate: firstly, that the aggression should be resisted – that was practically the unanimous view of the House; secondly, that party points would not be tolerated. On the first score, the Government had already announced that a task force was being assembled to sail to the Falklands, an action which was justified by Lord Carrington under article 51 of the UN Charter. This gave the victim of aggression the right to self-defence. It was a course of action which Michael Foot, the Labour leader firmly supported: 'The Government,' he said, 'must now prove by deeds – they will never be able to do it by words – that they are not responsible for the betrayal and cannot be faced with that charge . . .' There was no point in negotiating with the Argentine: 'Any guarantee from this invading force,' he declared, was 'as worthless as any of the guarantees that are given by this same Argentine junta to its own people.' Mr Enoch Powell summed up in a similar spirit: 'There is only one reaction,' he said, 'which is fit to meet unprovoked aggression upon one's sovereign territory: that is direct and unqualified and immediate willingness – not merely willingness, but willingness expressed by action – to use force.' He added that although the Prime Minister had been called the Iron Lady, the nation would soon learn of what metal she was really made. At this point Mrs Thatcher was seen to nod her agreement. Her opening speech had in any case concluded:

The people of the Falklands Islands, like the people of the United Kingdom are an island race. They are few in number, but they have the right to live in peace, to choose their own way of life and to determine that their own allegiance is to the Crown. It is the wish of the British people and the duty of Her Majesty's government to do everything that we can to uphold that right. That will be our hope and our endeavour and I believe, the resolve of every Member of this House.

Almost the whole House agreed. Argentinian aggression was denounced and Galtieri condemned as 'a bargain basement Mussolini' by Labour's defence spokesman, Mr John Silkin. The only member to counsel understanding of the Argentinian position was a former diplomat, the Tory MP Ray Whitney, who called for careful consideration of the implications of any military action which might be taken. 'The easy way would be to respond thoughtlessly,' he said. He was interrupted, however, by two of his colleagues who were to become notable spokesmen for a severe response: Mr Alan Clark and Sir Bernard Braine. Clark accused Whitney of 'talking as though this were a head-on confrontation with a world power' instead of a 'bankrupt totalitarian country . . . with no capacity for replacing ammunition' while Sir Bernard denounced the 'weasel words' of 'successive Foreign Office Ministers' in a manner that made it clear that he referred to all former diplomats as well. Memories of 1939 were in the air and this time too it was clearly felt that there had already been sufficient appeasement of Argentina's 'tin-pot fascists'.

Given the atmosphere of the occasion party points were out of place. Thus when two were made, one in the opening speech by the Prime Minister, another by John Nott, the Defence Minister, in the closing speech of the debate, they were greeted with cries of 'resign'. Indeed, inter-party unity was all too evident in this respect with Conservative MPs such as Mr Patrick Cormack and Mr Edward du Cann condemning the Government's 'astounding' lack of preparedness. Cormack did not go quite so far as Mr Silkin for Labour in naming Mrs Thatcher, Mr Nott and Lord Carrington as the 'three most guilty people' of the crisis but he did come close to this. 'Someone has blundered,' he declared, 'I do not know whom and I do not know how, but I have my suspicions, and they are directed inevitably – and regretfully – at both the Secretary of State for Defence and the Foreign Secretary.' The public, in fact, agreed with Mr Silkin's assessment, for a NOP opinion poll published in the *Daily Mail* on 6 April showed that 60 per cent of those questioned blamed Mrs Thatcher for what had happened. Between 2 and 6 April indeed her position as premier was clearly in the balance. And even if she survived the immediate crisis, her political future would still depend on the fortunes of the task force. Yet, not for the first time, her political luck, which was considerable, was to hold.

The Minister who defused the immediate crisis was Lord Carrington who insisted on resigning on 5 April. He denied that the Foreign Office had in any way blundered or that his trips to Brussels and Israel on the eve of the invasion had rendered him out of touch with events; nevertheless, in his letter of resignation he conceded 'that the invasion of the Falkland Islands has been a humiliating affront to this country' and he felt obliged as a result to resign. The Prime Minister prevailed on Mr Nott to remain at his post – his resignation would almost certainly have necessitated her own – and replaced Lord Carrington with Francis Pym. The latter under normal circumstances would never have been her own choice for the post, but given that he had opposed the cuts made in the 1981 defence review it had become the general feeling of the House of Commons that he should now be given the Foreign Office. Mrs Thatcher in any case was in no position to resist and, having resolved the immediate political crisis, could now concentrate her energies on winning the diplomatic and military battle with the Argentines.

She had already received good news on the diplomatic front. On 3 April the UN Security Council had passed Resolution 502 which ordered a cessation of hostilities between the two countries, the withdrawal of all Argentine forces from the Falklands, and called upon Britain and Argentina to respect the principles of the UN Charter and to seek a diplomatic solution to their dispute. Only one state – Panama – voted against the resolution whereas ten voted for and four abstained. This constituted a significant diplomatic victory and Resolution 502 soon became the bedrock of British diplomacy. The reference to the UN Charter was particularly helpful in the light of Article 51, but best of all was the implication that the Argentines must first of all withdraw their forces from the islands before negotiations could ensue. The resolution also enabled the Government to request support from the Commonwealth, the EEC and the United States.

That same weekend also witnessed a miracle of military improvisation which recalled the British effort at Dunkirk in 1940. In the course of a few days thousands of servicemen were called back from leave – including HRH Prince Andrew – and 'stores, weapons, aircraft, sailors and soldiers appeared on quaysides as if by magic'. A British task force in fact was ready to sail out of Portsmouth harbour as early as 5 April – and it did so past crowds of enthusiastic well-wishers all waving their Union Jacks. The flagship of this fleet was HMS *Hermes*, a 23-year-old aircraft carrier of 28,700 tons. She was joined by the two-year-old *Invincible*, also a light-aircraft carrier, and these two ships between them formed the nerve-centre of the task force. The rest was made up from the amphibious assault ship HMS *Fearless* and a complement of destroyers, frigates and supply vessels of the Royal Fleet Auxiliary. At sea they would later be joined by a larger group of frigates and destroyers which had been taking part in the annual exercise, 'Spring Train', at Gibraltar. Nuclear-powered submarines would also join the fleet although the story that the submarine *Superb* was already en route for the Falklands was a piece of misinformation put about to worry the Argentines. She was in fact on course for her home base in Scotland. The task of organizing this fleet has been well summarized by Brian Bond: 'the emergency,' he writes, 'prompted admirable cooperation between the Services, the Merchant Navy, the Royal Dockyards and the commercial ports. The task force had to be improvised virtually over a weekend and provisioned for at least three months at sea. Eventually over one hundred ships were deployed, including 44 warships, 22 from the Royal Fleet Auxiliary and 45 merchant ships whose civilian crews were all volunteers.' It was supported, one must add, by the unstinting efforts of thousands of British workmen who laboured around the clock in subsequent weeks in factories and dockyards to ensure that equipment and munitions were continuously supplied and that merchant and container ships were converted for military use. Those commentators who had spoken of parallels with the Suez expedition in 1956 were rapidly proved wrong – all the obvious parallels were with 1939 and 1940.

The commander of the fleet was named as Rear-Admiral John or 'Sandy' Woodward, a submariner who declared himself 'astonished' at his nomination. 'I am,' he said, 'an ordinary person who lives in South West London in suburbia.' He added: 'I have been a virtual civil servant for the past three years, commuting into London every day.' He now had to forsake his office for the South Atlantic. Above him, in overall command of the enterprise was to be Admiral Sir John Fieldhouse, Commander in Chief, Fleet, who from the underground headquarters of the navy at Northwood could communicate with Woodward by satellite. The army commander was Brigadier Julian Thompson, who was to oversee some 5,000 fighting men including commandos, parachutists, Scots and Welsh guardsmen, engineers and Gurkhas. The first wave of these – some 2,000 men – was carried on the assault ships *Fearless* and *Intrepid*, various warships, the ferry *Norland* and the luxury liner *Canberra*. The second wave – some 3,000 men – were transported by the *Queen Elizabeth II*. The Government had clearly requisitioned the best ships available in order to get the fleet sailing quickly. Once again therefore there was no parallel with Suez.

The immediate destination of the task force was Ascension Island, a barren rock in the middle of the Atlantic which housed a US military base. Without use of the facilities there, there could be no question of Great Britain establishing supply lines between England and the Falklands. In normal circumstances the Americans cooperated happily with respect to the base – the island itself was British – but given their interests in Latin America, would they now support Great Britain? Memories of Suez were in this respect uncomfortable.

The British were only too aware that there was a strong 'Latino lobby' in Washington. Galtieri himself was aware of this and in August 1981, even before becoming President of Argentina, he had visited Washington where he had mentioned the possibility of establishing a South Atlantic Treaty Organization to further hemispheric cooperation. Once he had become President himself, after December 1981, he had offered military assistance to President Reagan in El Salvador and had cultivated the friendship of General Vernon Walters, former Deputy Director of the CIA and one of Washington's trouble-shooters in Latin America. He had also acquired influence with Ambassador Thomas Enders, the Under-Secretary in the US State Department who dealt with South America and who had visited Buenos Aires in March 1982, and with the ineffable Mrs Jeane Kirkpatrick, the US Ambassador to the UN, a specialist in Argentine affairs, who held both cabinet rank and President Reagan's ear. Mrs Kirkpatrick saw fit to attend a dinner in her honour at the Argentine embassy in Washington a few hours after the invasion, a decision she later defended by saying 'Now, if the Argentines own the islands, then moving troops into them is not armed aggression.'

President Reagan's immediate reaction was one of bemusement. He couldn't really understand how such a Gilbert and Sullivan affair had arisen in the first place over 'that little ice-cold bunch of land down there'. On the other hand he did appreciate the dilemma for US policy if he was forced to choose between his staunchest European ally on the one hand, and a potentially useful partner in Latin America on the other. 'It's a very difficult situation for the United States,' he said on 6 April, 'because we're friends with both of the countries engaged in this dispute.' It seemed that his policy would be one of 'even-handedness'. But clearly his priority would be to attempt to settle the quarrel before the task force reached the Falklands. The result was that General Haig, the former NATO commander-in-chief, who was now US Secretary of State, began talks with the UK and Argentine Ambassadors in Washington. Haig had been described by his former boss and predecessor, Dr Henry Kissinger, as 'strong in crises, decisive in judgement, skilful in bureaucratic infighting, indefatigable in his labours'. This last qualification would turn out to be a welcome one, for, as negotiations developed, he would become involved in shuttle diplomacy which would clock up some 26,000 air miles within nine days. US public opinion on the other hand was never 'even-handed'. Press and public, as well as Congress, became enthusiastically pro-British and in the words of the British Ambassador, 'the intensity of United States diplomacy over the Falklands can only be understood if it is realized how closely the American public followed what was going on. From the Argentine invasion to the surrender of Port Stanley, the Falklands crisis was front page news and the lead story for television in America every day.' The influence of the Latin lobby proved worthless. Even those politicians in the United States who were Britain's greatest critics over Northern Ireland – Senators Kennedy and Moynihan and Speaker O'Neill – were to back Britain openly during the Falklands crisis.

If Reagan's 'even-handedness' was at first disappointing, it did mean two things. First, of course, it was better than opposition, for that might well have led to the fall of the Thatcher government and even Britain's withdrawal from NATO. Secondly, it meant that the US was in a position to act as an intermediary and her mediation was soon personified in the 'Haig mission'. Between 9 and 19 April, the US Secretary of State flew continually between Washington, London and Buenos Aires to try to achieve a settlement. Yet it was all in vain. The British insisted on a solution based on UN Resolution 502, the Argentinians on one which would have left them with a comparative military advantage, the promise of sovereignty and the right to populate the islands with Argentinian settlers. In the words of Sir Nicholas Henderson, our Ambassador to the US:

The Argentines were not prepared to accept any settlement that did not provide either for negotiations on sovereignty, to be concluded in their favour within a specific time limit or for an interim régime for the islands, after the withdrawal of forces by both sides that would promote the acquisition of sovereignty by administrative means, including population and economic transfers. The British government insisted that Argentine troops must withdraw, that sovereignty was theirs, that the traditional administration of the islands must be restored and that there must be no infringement of the right of the islanders to decide their own future.

It is possible that the Argentinians believed that time was on their side, that the longer they remained in occupation of the Falklands, the readier international opinion would become to accept a *fait accompli*. There was also the fact that as winter advanced it would become ever more difficult for the task force to mount a military operation in the mountainous seas of the South Atlantic. The British, for their part, realized that time was not on their side. However, it was still hoped that there would be a diplomatic solution and Rear-Admiral Woodward in particular was in favour of this. He told reporters that the two to three week voyage provided 'an invaluable period of military preparation and time for politics to try to resolve the issue without resorting to force'. Admiral Fieldhouse shared this view, aware as he was of the risks involved in a military encounter. 'I hope that people realize,' he said on a visit to Ascension Island in April, 'that this is the most difficult thing that we have attempted since the Second World War.'

If the US began the war as 'even-handed' the same could not be said of the Commonwealth and the European Community. Both backed Britain's imposition of economic sanctions on Argentina with dramatic speed. The British, as expected, had immediately blocked all trade and credit with the enemy and had frozen $1·4 billion of Argentine's reserves. Within a week of the invasion, however, France, Belgium, West Germany and the Netherlands agreed to embargo arms sales – a policy which, on the part of the Germans at least, represented a major sacrifice. This embargo was then followed on 10 April by a total ban on

Argentinian imports by all members of the European Community, a step which was also taken by Norway. This meant that about 30 per cent of all Argentine exports were now blocked – a severe blow to a country which was desperately short of foreign currency. The Commonwealth, too, rallied round. Australia and Hong Kong stopped all Argentine imports while Canada halted the export of military spares. New Zealand not only halted imports but broke off diplomatic relations with Buenos Aires. There was, of course, the danger that the Japanese might intervene to fill the huge trading gap created by all these steps, but Japan, although refusing to impose sanctions herself, promised not to take advantage of the sacrifice of others. Britain had to wait until the failure of the Haig mission before the US imposed economic sanctions, but when they were eventually announced they included the suspension of all military exports to Argentina, the withholding of certification of Argentine eligibility for military sales and the suspension of new export–import bank credits and of commodity credit corporation guarantees. No embargo was placed on trade with Argentina, however, or on private American bank loans. This was because of the great fear then prevalent in the banking world that if Argentina was forced to default on its $32 billion international debt, the whole world banking system might collapse as a result. On the other hand, Mr Haig when announcing his restrictions on 30 April added that his government would 'respond positively' to UK requests for military aid, although he ruled out any possibility of direct US involvement. To the British Foreign Secretary, moreover, he sent a message of support, reassuring him that the United States would veto any resolution in the UN Security Council or the Organization of American States which in its judgement departed from UN Resolution 502.

The US turnabout had been caused not merely by growing evidence of popular support for the British case within the United States or even by the failure of the Haig shuttle. It had been brought about by the Argentines' rejection of a compromise proposal drawn up by Haig on 27 April, which the British had been prepared to consider. It involved a staggered withdrawal of the Argentine troops and of the British task force, the declaration of a demilitarized zone around the Falklands, a five year tripartite administration, dual nationality for the islanders and a compensation scheme for anyone who wished to leave. With the rejection of this plan, events now entered a more decidedly military phase, although only the first round of negotiations, as it turned out, had actually been completed.

Military affairs had already taken a turn for the better from the British point of view, for on 25 April some frigates of the task force – which had taken three weeks and two days to reach its zone of operation – had sailed ahead of the main fleet and had quickly recaptured South Georgia which, despite some inspired British resistance, had been occupied on 3 April. Its recapture had involved putting an Argentinian submarine, the *Santa Fe* out of action and landing marines on the island by helicopter in a blizzard. Its Argentinian defenders, however, had surrendered without a shot. The recapture of South Georgia proved significant in two respects: firstly, it provided a safe anchorage for British ships and somewhere for shipbound soldiers to have some exercise ashore; more importantly, it did wonders for morale back home, which the negotiating process had slightly cooled. Now, however, came the navy's telegram to the Admiralty which ran: 'Be pleased to inform Her Majesty that the White Ensign flies alongside the Union Jack on South Georgia. God Save the Queen.' Mrs Thatcher herself broke the news of it to reporters in Downing Street and parried their further inquiries with a stalwart 'Rejoice ... just rejoice.' These words were to enter the Falklands lexicon along with others she had used in an earlier interview when she had been questioned about the possibility of defeat. She had then retorted with, 'Do you remember what Queen Victoria said? "Failure – the possibility does not exist." ' The Iron Lady was beginning to show her mettle. Indeed, during the next few weeks the sight of her in full armour was to alarm many of her opponents at home as well as abroad.

During most of April the Falklands War had remained one of words. On 7 April, for example, Britain had declared a 200-mile 'exclusion zone' around the islands. This in itself was in no way meant to limit Britain's right to self-defence elsewhere but on 23 April, in any case, the Government announced that British forces would attack any Argentine ship or aircraft, wherever it might be found, if it was felt to pose a threat to British forces in the South Atlantic. It was not until 1 May that military realities intervened. Then a solitary Vulcan bomber from Ascension Island attempted to destroy the runway at Stanley airport. It failed – as indeed all British attempts to put the runway out of action failed – but this raid, which was followed up by raids on Argentine positions by British Sea Harrier jets, served notice that the real war had begun. The Argentine counter-attack with Dagger jets the same day led not only to the first loss of aircraft of the war but to the establishment of propaganda machines in London and Buenos Aires to inform the public of events. The British Defence Ministry spokesman, Mr Ian McDonald, thereafter became as familiar a figure on television screens each night as any BBC newscaster and to his slow, measured tones, the British listened impatiently for news of the latest events.

They were not to wait long. For on 2 May, the Argentine cruiser, *Belgrano* was sunk by the British submarine *Conqueror* on direct orders from the British war cabinet, which had been meeting at Chequers. The latter consisted of Mrs Thatcher, with Mr Pym (Foreign Secretary), Mr Nott (Defence Secretary), Mr Whitelaw (Home Secretary) and Mr Cecil Parkinson (Chancellor of the Duchy of Lancaster and Chairman of the Conservative Party). It was advised by Sir Terence Lewin, the Chief of the Defence Staff, and the man who sought its permission that day to order the sinking of the *Belgrano*. That permission was granted and the cruiser was torpedoed with the loss of 370 lives. If it was the news of this event which really, for the first time, brought home to people the very serious nature of the contest which was now being fought, it also carried with it the possibility that world opinion would transfer its sympathy to Argentina. Another tragedy, however, prevented this, for on 4 May, only two days later, the British destroyer *Sheffield* was hit by an Exocet missile, fired by an Argentine pilot twelve miles away, which struck it at the speed of sound. Only 20 out of the crew of 250 died but it seemed as if the 'Argies', as the British popular press condescendingly called them, had found a secret weapon. Thereafter, there was great anxiety lest the task force might prove incapable of completing its mission.

It certainly suffered from several disadvantages. For a start, it lacked air cover since it had only about 40 Harrier jets with which to oppose the 160 or so planes of the enemy. This made it extremely vulnerable to air attack. It also lacked radar cover, since the Harrier has a very limited range of operation. This meant that frigates had to be constantly deployed as 'radar pickets' for the fleet. Yet only two of these, *Broadsword* and *Brilliant*, both type 22s, were equipped with the Sea Wolf anti-missile system which alone was capable of dealing with Exocets. The

Sea-Dart system, employed on other ships, was effective only against missiles launched above 1,000 feet. The Exocet, on the other hand, travelled practically at wave level. Finally, there was the danger from two German T209-type submarines which still remained unaccounted for. It was possible that either of these might attack a British carrier and if either carrier were hit, the task force would be put out of action. With the destruction of the *Sheffield*, therefore, the vulnerability of the fleet became a much more acknowledged fact of life. Still, between 2 and 21 May no ship was lost. Instead the Argentine spy vessel, the *Narwal*, was captured on 9 May and during the night of 11 May the frigate *Alacrity* sailed up the narrow channel between East and West Falkland and destroyed an enemy supply ship. The following day, an attempt at revenge on the part of the Argentines was frustrated when the Sea Wolf system was used to down two of their Skyhawk fighter jets. Then on 14 May the first British land attack was made on the Falklands when forty-eight members of the 22nd Regiment of the SAS (Special Air Services) destroyed a radar station and several aircraft – including Pucara ground attackers – at Pebble Island, off the northern coast of West Falkland. The task force itself meanwhile was gaining strength. The destroyer *Exeter* replaced the *Sheffield* and another frigate, the *Battleaxe*, arrived equipped with Sea Wolf. More merchant ships were requisitioned but, most significant of all, was the news that the *Canberra*, laden with marines, paratroopers and the cavalrymen of the Blues and Royals, along with their Scorpion light tanks, was approaching the war zone together with her support ships. Since the *Queen Elizabeth II*, with her cargo of Guards and Gurkhas was also on her way, all this meant that the fleet would soon be in a position to attempt a landing on the Falklands if diplomacy had not by then achieved a settlement.

Diplomatic initiatives, on the other hand, were fast getting nowhere. For example, a peace plan drafted by Peruvian diplomats in consultation with Washington, a plan which very closely resembled the one which General Haig had drawn up on 27 April and which the junta had already rejected, was rejected in turn by them on 2 May, ostensibly as a reaction to the torpedoing of the *Belgrano*. It might very well have been rejected anyway. In any case, negotiations directed at a settlement continued. The British not only told Haig that they would accept the Peruvian plan subject to certain amendments, but accepted a new set of proposals worked out by Haig on 5 May which, in Sir Nicholas Henderson's words, 'presented considerable difficulties for London'. The Argentine junta, however, rejected these proposals also, choosing now to invest their hopes of a diplomatic victory in the UN, where the Secretary-General, the 62-year-old Peruvian diplomat, Mr Javier Perez de Cuellar, had reluctantly agreed to attempt a mediation.

The UN Secretary-General was a diplomat of great experience. He had served as the UN special representative in Cyprus, negotiated with the USSR in the aftermath of its Afghanistan invasion, and had been UN observer at the 1980 elections in Zimbabwe. All his skills would now be needed if he were to bring the two sides together. The Peruvian plan had involved a ceasefire, a withdrawal of military forces supervised by the US, Peru and two other countries, and the start of Anglo-Argentine talks which were to be held without preconditions, but which were to end early in 1983. The junta, however, had not favoured withdrawing its troops or surrendering its claim to sovereignty. Perez de Cuellar hoped, however, that by changing the terms of the Peruvian proposals slightly and by getting both sides to agree on less contentious matters first, he might still be able to produce an agreement. He had one advantage: neither side could afford to turn down his mediation for fear of alienating world opinion, although the British suspected – and probably rightly – that the Argentinians were playing for time. They also disliked the manner in which Mr Costa Mendez would agree to proposals only to find himself subsequently overruled by his junta superiors. The negotiations therefore continued, conducted by Sir Anthony Parsons, the British representative to the UN, and Mr Enrique Ross for Argentina. Indeed, by 14 May, some progress had been made, with the British conceding that a ceasefire could be established prior to any Argentinian troop withdrawals. There was also British flexibility concerning the nature of an interim administration for the islands. The Argentinians however still disliked the idea of withdrawing their troops without prior agreement on the issue of sovereignty, and over this the British refused to compromise. Parsons and Henderson were therefore (14 May) recalled to London for consultations, but even after their return no further progress was made. Thus, replying on 19 May to Mr Perez de Cuellar's remark that his 'patient' was 'in intensive care', Sir Anthony Parsons stated candidly that 'The patient [had] died.'

Details of Britain's role in the negotiations were presented the following day to the Commons by Mrs Thatcher. Britain, she said, had presented seven sets of peace proposals to the Argentinians since the invasion, all of which had been turned down flat. A final nine-point plan – 'the farthest Britain could go' – had not only been rejected but had led to tougher Argentinian demands. She therefore accused the Argentinians of 'obduracy and delay, deception and bad faith'. The British, she revealed, had offered to withdraw the task force 150 miles from the Falkland Islands; the Argentinians on the other hand had insisted that both sides should pull back to their home territories and that South Georgia should be evacuated of British troops. They had also insisted that Argentinian citizens should be given free access to the Falklands and had refused to enter discussions on an interim administration unless sovereignty had been previously conceded to them. The UN negotiations as a result had come to an end.

The Commons debate of 20 May had witnessed yet another development. It became the first occasion on which the House was divided on the issue of the war, a division organized by Mr Tony Benn and Dame Judith Hart, who mustered 33 Labour votes against the Government's record. Mr Foot reacted to this 'declaration of civil war in the Labour Party' by accusing Mr Benn of stabbing in the back 'those who are being sent into battle'. Yet Mr Benn's views on the war had always been consistent. Supported by Dame Judith, whose speeches were often less coherent than his own, he had argued that the task force should never have been assembled, should now be recalled and that the dispute should be settled by the United Nations. Moreover, in expressing these views he claimed that he represented 'a majority of people who don't want to see any killing'. His position was supported by Ken Livingstone and Ted Knight, leaders of London's left-wing socialists and editors of the *Labour Herald* which referred to the Falklands as the Malvinas and condemned British 'colonialism' and 'imperialism' there. It was supported, too, by a mixture of groups including CND supporters, the Socialist Workers Party, Iranian students, Methodists and Quakers, 1,200 of whom demonstrated against the war in April in Hyde Park. There, banners exclaimed support for Argentina, and the CND Vice-Chairman, Professor Prentz, warned that if the life of Prince Andrew were to be threatened by the Argentinians the Government might even resort to using nuclear weapons. Finally, a position similar to Mr Benn's was adopted by the maverick Scottish MP, Tam Dalyell, who consistently prophesied naval disasters and who too, referred to the Falklands as the Malvinas. Mr Dalyell also put forward the theory that the *Belgrano* had been sunk not for military reasons but deliberately, on Mrs Thatcher's orders, to sabotage the Peruvian peace plan. In fact, he was later to ask literally hundreds of parliamentary questions on the subject and to write two books on the matter, one of them entitled *Thatcher's Torpedo*. Yet, there seems little doubt that he was wrong on both counts, for Sir Nicholas Henderson's account of the diplomacy of the war proves that the British government on 2 May had no expectation that the junta would accept the Peruvian plan. Moreover, the military evidence suggests that the *Belgrano* was indeed a threat to the fleet. She had the largest guns in the South Atlantic and was believed to be involved in a pincer attack on the task force. Had she been allowed to press home this attack and destroy even the radar of some British ships, the damage inflicted could have been fatal. As it was, her sinking meant that the Argentine navy remained in port for the rest of the war. It did not mean, as Dalyell later asserted, that negotiations ended or that the fighting only then started in earnest. That had already begun the day before when Argentine Mirages had attempted to sink the *Glamorgan* and Harriers had raided the Falklands.

The majority of Labour MPs never subscribed to Dalyell's conspiracy theory. Michael Foot for one told the television interviewer Sir Robin Day that Mrs Thatcher, in his opinion, had had no option but to agree to sink the *Belgrano*. Similarly, his shadow cabinet colleague, Mr Peter Shore, denounced with passion the viewpoint that British imperialism had caused the conflict. He argued instead that it was the Argentinians who were acting as imperialists since it was they who wanted to colonize islands, the overwhelming majority of whose small population wished to retain their democratic way of life and allegiance to the British crown. The major spokesman for the Opposition, however, was Denis Healey, who in mid-April called for UN mediation and who, although he basically agreed with the Government's conduct of the war was none the less careful to criticize it whenever necessary, and not merely in the interests of party unity. He too was critical of the sinking of the *Belgrano* but, like Foot, he believed that without the task force, the Argentinians would never negotiate.

If Healey emerged as one of the two most authoritative spokesmen on the Opposition benches, the other was the SDP spokesman, David Owen, the former Labour Foreign Secretary and Navy Minister who also represented Plymouth. He too managed to be 'firm and sensible' and followed the line 'prepare for war but be ready for negotiation'. He completely over-shadowed both his party leader, Mr Jenkins – who, like his colleague, Mrs Williams, remained strangely silent during the conflict – and the Liberal party leader, Mr Steel, who also failed to make much of an impact.

The Government for its part presented an almost united front. The 'war cabinet', in spite of rumours that Mr Parkinson had been included specifically to neutralize the caution of Mr Pym, was never seen to be divided, although opposition to the Government's line was expressed by two ex-diplomats on its backbenches, Mr Ray Whitney and Sir Anthony Meyer. Both were opposed to the use of force. Their views, however, were more than counterbalanced by several of their colleagues who felt that, if anything, insufficient force was being employed. The leaders of this group of MPs were Mr Alan Clark, Sir Bernard Braine and Mr Winston Churchill. They pressed for bombing raids on the Argentine mainland to prevent air attacks on the British fleet. They also kept their eyes open for any signs of a 'sell out'. Generally speaking, however, the Government had wide support in Parliament, including that of former premiers Home, Wilson and Callaghan, and even sometimes of Mr Heath. It also had the support of Mr Enoch Powell who, for the first time in many years, was happy to praise a Conservative leader.

Mrs Thatcher, indeed, had been very careful to keep both parliament and public behind her. The debate of 20 May, for example, had been the sixth to be held on the Falklands dispute, and she arranged for David Owen and David Steel to be given access to privileged information on 'Privy Council terms'. Mr Foot was offered similar access but surprisingly chose to decline. Finally, she never had much reason to doubt that public opinion was behind her government. True, the *Guardian*, *Observer* and *Financial Times* maintained a reserve respecting its conduct, but the popular press on the whole proved rabidly 'anti-Argy', with the *Sun* running headlines such as 'Stick it up your Junta' above a story about peace proposals, and another above a photograph of the sinking *Belgrano* which ran simply 'Gotcha!' By 20 May, according to opinion polls, 55 per cent of the public favoured an assault on the islands if negotiations broke down, a figure which the following day rose to no less than 76 per cent. No less than 53 per cent, moreover, considered that a successful operation would justify heavy casualties, a finding which in itself seemed to indicate a hardening of the public mood. For two weeks beforehand politicians like Denis Healey had been stressing the need for a 'proportionate response'; some indeed had even speculated on the maximum number of casualties which might be tolerated. This had led to the charge that they considered war 'an extension of accountancy by other means', yet under different circumstances their insistence on 'proportionality' could well have restricted the war cabinet's options. As it turned out, Mrs Thatcher's diplomacy retained for her the support of both public and parliament. And, mercifully, after the invasion had been launched, the inevitable casualty lists proved relatively short.

The Falkland islanders themselves by this time were growing impatient for an assault. For seven weeks they had endured the rule of the Argentines whom they manifestly detested. Their occupiers had brought police files on 500 of them, had arrested their most outspoken leaders, had told them to drive on the right hand side of the road and had made Spanish the official language. They may not have terrorized them, but neither had they lived up to their previous claim of not wishing to disturb the traditional Falkland way of life. The islanders consequently had been much cheered by news of the recapture of South Georgia and of the raid on Pebble Island. Some may even have been aware of the presence on the islands of the SAS and SBS before the British invasion. That itself began on the night of 20/21 May, immediately after the collapse of the negotiations in New York, negotiations which, given the altered circumstances, the British felt in no way compelled to resume.

The plan to liberate the islands by landing 5,000 British troops there would in any circumstances have constituted an extraordinarily risky enterprise. Conventional military wisdom held that an attacker ought to have no less than three times the number of men behind him as were available to the defender. The British, however, were outnumbered by more than two to one by their foe. Moreover, their initial assault would have to be made without the benefit of adequate air cover so that the ships of the assault force would remain incredibly vulnerable to attack. This was especially true of the liner *Canberra*, which would depend on other ships for her defence. There was also the probability that military resistance by the Argentines would prevent the establishment of a British bridgehead. Indeed, if the troops were held down on the beaches for any length of time, the Argentine air force would have a field day, destroying both them and the ships which had landed them. Rear-Admiral Woodward's only hope of avoiding such an eventuality therefore was to choose a propitious landing place. The spot chosen was Port San Carlos on East Falkland, on the other side of the island from Port Stanley. It had a good anchorage, was sheltered by hills from wind and low-flying planes and had seen little of the enemy's army. Between 21 and 27 May it witnessed the major battle of the campaign, a battle which saw the destruction of the British frigates *Antelope* and *Ardent*, the destroyer *Coventry* and the container ship, *Atlantic Conveyor*, the latter packed with vital supplies. Yet by the end of that week the bridgehead had been fully established and large numbers of enemy planes destroyed. In a crucial move, the Argentine military commander on the Falklands, General Menendez, chose not to commit his army to the battle. Moreover, the bravery of many Argentinian air force pilots, all of whom were flying at the very limit of their range, was offset by their failure to concentrate on bombing British landing craft rather than ships, not to mention the failure of their bombs to explode when, as often happened, they were dropped from too low a height.

With the establishment of the bridgehead, the assault fleet could withdraw and the British army push forward towards Port Stanley, the Falklands capital. This, again, should have been no easy task but, in fact, only one major encounter ensued between the opposing forces. This was the battle fought at Goose Green on 28 May which became 'one of the most skilful and courageous in the history of the British Army'. There the 600 men of the 2nd Battalion of the Parachute Regiment overcame entrenched Argentine resistance to capture 1,400 prisoners. Two VCs were subsequently awarded posthumously to the battalion commander, Lt Colonel 'H' Jones, and Sergeant Ian MacKay. Thereafter military measures were concentrated on the build-up towards the final assault on Stanley. This involved transporting vehicles and ammunition by helicopter, although the troops were forced to 'yomp', that is, to march rapidly to their positions with 220 lbs of equipment on their backs. The advance on Stanley however encountered relatively little opposition. The Argentine air force, it is true, launched a surprise attack on British forces at Fitzroy and Bluff Cove, an attack which led to serious casualties and the loss of the *Sir Galahad*, but there was still no sign of the Argentine military. Their commanding General, Menendez, was apparently keeping them in Stanley to resist the final British assault. He was reported as calling on them 'to inflict a crushing defeat' and had apparently told them, 'The eyes of the nation are on you and you must not let the people down.' By this time, however, the fighting spirit of his men was being questioned. The vast majority of them were pathetic conscripts, ill-fed and ill-clad, freezing in the Falklands weather and neglected by their officers. Many were still teenagers. They were not expected by the British professionals to put up much of a fight. Nor did they as it turned out.

Towards the end of the campaign, therefore, Mrs Thatcher came under pressure to be 'magnanimous in victory' – a Churchillian phrase this – and to spare the Argentines the humiliation of utter defeat. President Reagan, attending an economic summit meeting at Versailles, attempted to persuade the Prime Minister to order a delay in the British advance and at the United Nations, Spain and Panama attempted to introduce a resolution which would have enforced a ceasefire. Predictably, Mrs Thatcher resisted all such pressure. Mr Churchill, she declared, had spoken of magnanimity only *after* victory, while the withdrawal of enemy forces, she said, would constitute not a humiliation but 'liberty, justice and democracy'. The UN ceasefire resolution was therefore vetoed by Sir Anthony Parsons, with the support of the United States, although its ambassador, Mrs Kirkpatrick, later announced that she had subsequently received instructions to abstain. This announcement was almost certainly made with the intention of embarrassing General Haig whose 'boys' club vision of gang loyalty' to Great Britain, she had reportedly much resented. She apparently regarded him as an 'amateur' who was 'insensitive to Latin culture', while he, for his part, condemned her 'emotional' incapacity to disassociate herself from the Latin mentality. Their different viewpoints in the final analysis merely reflected the opposing pressures on US policy. In spite of all these pressures, however, US assistance proved invaluable to Britain, diplomatically, politically and militarily in terms of communications and intelligence assistance. The fall of Stanley, when it came on 14 June – and once again without a fight – was therefore greeted with enthusiasm by the American as well as by the British public.

The news of the Argentine surrender was given to the Commons by Mrs Thatcher. It was received with resounding cheers and she was at last acknowledged as a national leader. In the words of one book on the subject she 'tower[ed] over the Falklands drama from its inception to the euphoria of the final triumph. Her personality matched its often eccentric sense of proportion. Her single-mindedness, her belief in the futility of negotiation, even her arch phraseology at moments of crisis, all seemed to armour her against the suspicion that this might be a dangerous, even absurd adventure ... In a world that was accustomed to brand war as an ugly obscenity, the Prime Minister was determined that the Falklands conflict should be seen as a noble and principled crusade. Her longing undoubtedly matched the mood of the nation and captivated those working around her.'

The war, of course, had meant losses. In all, 225 task-force lives were lost in the operation and a further 777 people were injured. Under the circumstances, however, according to a leading military historian, these figures should not be considered 'excessive'. The Government and the Chiefs of Staff had certainly been fearing worse. And of the 777 injured servicemen 700 were to resume their careers. The costs in financial terms were also significant and they were increased, of course, by the refusal of the Argentines to agree to end hostilities. This obliged the Government to institute a 'Fortress Falklands' policy and to maintain considerable forces there. The result in Peter Riddell's words was:

The Falklands war and subsequent garrison duties cost between £700 and £900 million in 1982-3, while to meet the island's defence costs the Government's expenditure plans provided for £624 million in 1983-4, £684 million in 1984-5 and £552 million in 1985-6. These figures include the cost of replacing all the equipment lost in the Falklands – roughly a third of the total from 1983-4 onwards – as well as the expense of maintaining a garrison to protect the islands, but there will also be the £215 million cost of constructing a new airfield and the sums spent on rebuilding the local infrastructure. The total cost of the Falklands war up to 1985-6 may be at least £2·75 billion and probably over £3 billion, though some of the re-equipment spending will help to meet the NATO commitment. Critics have questioned not only this expense but also the diversion of a sizeable part of the Navy's ships to the South Atlantic – committing over a fifth of available frigates and destroyers according to one unofficial estimate. The possible implications for NATO worried members of the Defence Committee of the Commons during an inquiry into the subject in early 1983.

This means in fact that the expense of the campaign in its widest definition has cost Britain since 1983 about the same amount of money as the Common Market. The British seem to have been prepared to accept this. The defence of the islands apparently involves principles and, as Mrs Thatcher has said, principles often have to be paid for. Certainly when her Labour opponents were unwise enough to raise the

Falklands issue during the General Election campaign of 1983 it redounded spectacularly upon them. If it had been 'Mrs Thatcher's War' it seemed that the British people were proud that she had won it.

The critics of Mrs Thatcher's Falklands strategy had come in two varieties. Apart from those who believed that the islands were not worth the expense of maintaining – in blood or money – there were those, like Mr Speed, whose criticisms of John Nott's cuts of 1981 appeared in retrospect to have been fully justified. The Government itself partly acknowledged the case of such critics in its White Paper of December 1982 entitled *The Falklands Campaign: The Lessons*. From this it became clear that 'at least a half-turn on the intended naval reductions' would occur. It announced that two carriers would henceforth be available for deployment at short notice, creating the need to keep a third one in reserve. *Invincible* was not (as foreseen in 1981) to be sold to the Australians after all. Also, contrary to previous plans, an increase was to be made in the number of front-line frigates and destroyers. According to the White Paper, 'Front-line numbers [would] be about 55 at 1 April 1983 and 1984'. These steps, however, amounted to an adjustment to rather than a complete change in policy.

CRUISE

The main issue relating to defence and foreign policy which caused some concern for Mrs Thatcher and her colleagues in 1982–3 was the decision to install Cruise missiles in Britain. This had been agreed to as part of a NATO decision of 12 December 1979 to modernize its theatre nuclear weapons. That decision in itself had arisen partly out of fears about the US nuclear guarantee to Europe, partly because the Germans were worried about the asymmetry of the nuclear balance in Europe (see p. 386 above). The NATO ministers had therefore agreed that US Pershing and Cruise missiles should be stationed in Europe to counter the USSR's SS-4, SS-5 and SS-20 missiles. The Pershings, because of their limited range, were to be mainly situated in West Germany. However, to prevent the Germans from being placed in a special position, their NATO partners also agreed to house Cruise missiles and Britain's share was settled at 160.

The British government was pleased to accept these, for although steps had already been taken to modernize British intermediate theatre weapons, by replacing Britain's Vulcan bombers with the Tornado, a multi-role combat aircraft (the costs of which had contributed to the dilemma over defence expenditure in the 1980s), the Tornado lacked 'deep-strike capacity' and, being a collaborative project, was unlikely to acquire this given German sensibilities regarding nuclear defence. The result was that the Defence Ministry was still looking for an intermediate theatre weapon which would be available before resort might have to be made to the Polaris force. Moreover, since Aldermaston had enough to cope with working on a warhead for Trident, it was convenient for the Government to forgo the chance of developing new weaponry and to agree on Cruise. As Professor Freedman has written: 'If extra missiles were to be bought the country could replace Vulcan while benefiting once again from an American production line and logistics support ... [even] without a more direct involvement, the cost of the NATO programme to Britain [would be] remarkably cheap – a £10 million contribution to infrastructure costs. The United States, which would produce and own the missiles [would] bear the brunt of the estimated costs of £2·5 billion.' Hence, Cruise it was.

The first missiles, however, were not due to arrive in Britain until the end of 1983. There was a possibility that they would never do so, if the IRT (Intermediate Range Talks) at Geneva proved successful, but this was always a slim hope, given the USSR's belief that Cruise and Pershing were strategic missiles and its consequent insistence that any deal on Europe should also relate to the British and French 'deterrent' forces. Thus, as 1983 approached, Britain's peace movement mobilized itself increasingly in its campaign to prevent the missiles' arrival.

The revival of the peace movement in Britain had been a response partly to revived international tension after the Soviet invasion of Afghanistan, partly to the news of the Trident programme, partly to the 1979 NATO decision on Cruise and Pershing but also to fears which arose as a result of developments in the United States. There, the alarm raised by (mainly Republican) right-wingers at the alleged nuclear superiority of the USSR had not only led to the failure to ratify the SALT II Treaty of 1979 but had given publicity to new trends in strategic thinking in the USA. These included not only a perceived need to establish nuclear symmetry at all levels but also the need to find a strategy based on increasingly accurate weapon technology which would avoid placing the USA in the position, in the event of war, of choosing between suicide or surrender. Such a strategy, it was hoped, might lead to the possibility of limiting nuclear wars, if they ever in fact took place. However, a strategy of limiting nuclear war, it soon became clear, implied the possibility of 'winning' a nuclear war and the development of highly accurate weapon technology might enable this to be done by the use of 'first-strike' weapons. Such possibilities, not surprisingly, greatly alarmed the European peace movements as it was all too clear that if any 'limited' nuclear war were ever to be fought it would most likely be limited to Europe. Speeches by President Reagan and his Defence Secretary, Caspar Weinberger, reflecting these new trends in nuclear thinking did nothing to reassure most Europeans.

Mrs Thatcher and her European colleagues, on the other hand, knew perfectly well that Cruise and Pershing were not being brought over to Europe by the Americans as 'first-strike' weapons. They were being brought instead at NATO's request to cement the US guarantee. This in fact – apart from cost – was the main reason why no demand had been made for a 'dual key' system to be attached to them. Predictably this was yet another factor which terrified the peace movement, but it was one which was difficult to neutralize since explaining it in any other terms than cost or 'traditional arrangements' would have meant expressing doubts in American good faith. Nor was the Government's position made any easier by former Ministers like David Owen giving public support to the demand for a dual key. The result was that in Britain protests grew and CND's membership rose from a mere 4,000 in the early 1970s to over 40,000 by 1982. Its general secretary, Mgr Bruce Kent, estimated that there were over 200,000 people affiliated to it through local peace groups. Mgr Kent also declared that it was his intention to steer the movement clear of 'cranks and partisan extremists on the left' though, in spite of this, he was later to find himself immersed in controversy by publicly thanking the Communist Party for its support.

Large numbers of women became the focus of public attention when they established a 'peace camp' in 1982 at Greenham Common, the air base at which the first Cruise missiles were to arrive in December 1983, and indulged in daily protests against government policy. Indeed, it was almost as a direct result of their activities that after Mr Nott's retirement from politics in 1983, his successor as Defence Minister was Michael Heseltine, the star performer at Tory party conferences, whose powers of persuasion, it was hoped, could be relied upon to undermine public support for CND. His charge that the organization merely gave unwitting aid to Moscow, on the other hand, offended many who were genuinely worried by what they regarded as a major escalation of the arms race. Thus, although opinion polls consistently demonstrated strong support for the maintenance of Britain's nuclear deterrent, public opinion proved much more evenly divided on the issue of Cruise missiles. They none the less arrived on time at Greenham Common at the end of 1983 after an election in which public support for the deterrent was affirmed.

THE FIRST TERM

In Simon Jenkins's words, 'the nadir of the Government was reached in the period of July to November 1981'. The Prime Minister had had to attend a summit in Ottawa 'carrying the humiliation of the Toxteth riots', and with the party trailing in the polls. She had then returned to find 'a cabinet in silent revolt'. Only the Treasury Ministers and Sir Keith Joseph were prepared to give their backing to the Medium Term Strategy. Planned spending for the following year was already running £7 billion over target and the wets seemed totally unwilling to salvage the Government's policies. Indeed, having won a majority in the cabinet they were preparing to assault them at the party conference at Blackpool. Opposition was being conducted meanwhile in ministerial speeches in the usual coded phrases of 'Disraeli', 'one nation', and 'Macmillan'. In Jenkins's words again, 'Political observers were offering odds on Mrs Thatcher not leading the party into the next election.' At this critical juncture, however, the premier displayed her strength. Having already removed Mr St John Stevas from the cabinet in January 1981, she now dispatched Lord Soames, Sir Ian Gilmour and Mr Carlisle as well. Mr Prior was exiled from Employment to Northern Ireland while Sir Keith – never a heavyweight as a minister – was transferred from Industry to Education. Finally, Lord Thorneycroft was dismissed as Chairman of the Conservative Party. Mrs Thatcher now promoted her trusted worthies into the cabinet. Mr Tebbit was given Employment and Mr Lawson went to Energy. Yet another, Mr Cecil Parkinson, was made Conservative Party Chairman.

From then on Mrs Thatcher finally began to take control of the

Government. Yet even at this point in its history it did not begin to lurch to the right. Mr Tebbit proved more moderate than feared – he had been described as the 'bovver boy' of the Tory Right; spending targets were once again upwardly revised; and the various youth unemployment programmes (which took hundreds of thousands of teenagers out of the dole queues) were expanded at a cost of between £2 and £3 billion. In January 1982 the premier's poll rating was the worst of any prime minister since the war with only 25 per cent of the electorate expressing themselves satisfied with her performance in office. Unemployment was still rising and it was only a divided opposition which enabled her to give an impression of being politically on top. But 'then came the Falklands'. The war allowed Mrs Thatcher to display all her best qualities to the people. The rebellions stopped, the wets were stilled if certainly not dried, and the premier was spared the agonies of daily economic wrangling. Victory then transformed Mrs Thatcher from an electoral liability into an indispensable asset. Pre-Falklands the Tories had been in humiliating third place in the polls for almost a year. Post-Falklands, their lead was a stunning 20 per cent. As Simon Jenkins put it, it remained 'impregnable' ever after. Domestically, of course, it was helped by the continuous and eventually dramatic fall in inflation. In November 1982 there was also a further cut in the employers' surcharge, and in his last budget in March 1983 Sir Geoffrey Howe again dispensed some modest tax relief. Tax thresholds and allowances were raised well above the level of inflation and the employers' surcharge was again reduced. It was certainly no give-away budget but against the falling rate of inflation it once again provided signs of hope. In the run-up to the election, therefore, it was the Opposition which had most to fear. For if the Government had spent the first half of its term of office as close as possible to political despair, the second half of its lifetime had brought about a totally unexpected reversal of roles.

LABOUR IN OPPOSITION: 1979–83

Labour's defeat in the 1979 election had been a severe rebuff. At 36·9 per cent, the party's share of the national vote was at its lowest at any election since 1931. Not only had its national vote slipped alarmingly, but in terms of geographical support Labour was increasingly falling back on its strongholds in northern England, industrial Scotland and

South Wales. The scale of the 1979 reversal was repeated even more decisively when the first direct elections took place for the European Parliament on 7 June 1979. The outcome in Great Britain was:

Party	Seats won	Votes	% Votes
Conservative	60	6,509,000	51
Labour	17	4,253,000	33
Liberal	–	1,691,000	13
SNP	1	219,000	2
Plaid Cymru	–	83,000	1
Others	–	88,000	1

With only 33 per cent of the vote, Labour had won only seventeen seats, compared to the Conservatives' sixty, though the hapless Liberals had failed to secure any seats at all.

Against this background it was vital that Labour united to recover its lost support. Instead, as after previous election defeats, Labour entered a period of bitter internal wrangling. On this occasion, the controversy arose over those parts of the party's constitution dealing with the power of the party rank and file to control their leaders. In October 1979 the party conference endorsed two important changes in the constitution favoured by the left. These required sitting MPs to be re-selected during the life of each parliament and instructed the NEC to put before the next party conference proposals to give the final decision on the election manifesto to the NEC. A Committee of Inquiry into the party's organization was also instituted, although disagreement over its composition delayed the start of its work until January 1980. The Committee finally emerged as a joint committee of the NEC and the TUC – thereby ensuring the left a 2:1 majority. Although James Callaghan was re-elected leader shortly after the election defeat, a notable absentee from the Shadow Cabinet was Tony Benn, who had chosen, amidst much publicity, to return to the backbenches in order to be able to speak more freely. Meanwhile the activities of such left-wing pressure groups as the Labour Coordinating Committee infuriated the right of the party. Constitutional questions continued to dominate the Labour Party throughout the coming months. On 15 June 1980, the commission of inquiry into the party's organization recommended after a meeting at Bishop's Stortford that an electoral college should be established for electing future leaders. The 1980 Blackpool Conference (from 29 September to 3 October) was dominated by constitutional resolutions. Conference very narrowly rejected by 3,625,000 votes to 3,508,000 an amendment proposed by the NEC which would have provided that the NEC 'after consultation with the leader of the party and the parliamentary committee of the PLP' should decide which items from the party's programme should be included in the manifesto to be issued by the NEC prior to every general election. Although conference decided (by 3,609,000 votes to 3,511,000) that the procedure for electing a new party leader should be broadened, no acceptable formula for an 'electoral college' could be agreed. It was then decided to hold a special conference on this issue at Wembley in January 1981. On 15 October 1980, less than two weeks after the party conference, Callaghan informed the Shadow Cabinet of his decision to retire from the leadership of the party. This decision came at a sensitive time for Labour, whose method of electing a new leader had not yet been agreed. Hence the leadership contest took place under the existing rules, namely by the 268 members of the Parliamentary Labour Party (a call by the NEC on 22 October to defer the election until after the Wembley Conference was rejected by the parliamentary party by 119 votes to 66). The contest was between four people: Michael Foot, the deputy leader since 1976; Denis Healey, the Chancellor of the Exchequer from 1974 to 1979 and the standard-bearer of the right of the party; Peter Shore, the Shadow Foreign Secretary; and John Silkin, Shadow Industry spokesman, who portrayed himself as a candidate who could be acceptable to both right and left.

FOOT'S ELECTION

It was a crucial contest. On the first ballot, Healey emerged in front, with Foot polling unexpectedly strongly. Shore and Silkin came nowhere. On the second ballot, Michael Foot beat Healey by a margin of ten votes (Healey was subsequently elected deputy leader). The contrast between Foot and Callaghan could hardly have been greater. A man of the left, a passionate orator, the biographer of Nye Bevan whom he so greatly admired (Foot had even succeeded to Bevan's Ebbw Vale constituency), Foot had perhaps more experience of rebellion within the party than he had of high office. His first ministerial experience had come only in 1974, when he was appointed Secretary of State for Employment. Then, on Wilson's resignation in 1976, he was runner-up to Callaghan in the leadership contest and was appointed Lord President of the Council and Leader of the House of Commons. Shortly after he became leader, the special rules revision conference was held at Wembley on 24 January 1981. A multitude of amendments and variations on the electoral college theme were debated. In the end, an agreed formula was adopted which gave the trade unions and other affiliated organizations (such as socialist and cooperative bodies) 40 per cent of the votes, the Parliamentary Labour Party 30 per cent and the constituency parties 30 per cent. This motion was passed by 5,252,000 votes to 1,868,000.

For many on the right of the Labour Party, the decision of the Wembley Conference marked the end of the road. It seemed to demonstrate that the party had irrevocably fallen to the left. The revolt of the Labour right had been growing for some time. The successive gains of the left over constitutional issues such as re-selection and the electoral college, the election of Michael Foot, the activities of Benn, Heffer and the Labour Coordinating Committee, to say nothing of policy defeats over the Common Market and unilateralism as well as infiltration from the Trotskyist Militant Tendency, had all produced warning shots from the right wing. Within the Shadow Cabinet, the outspoken opponents of the left were David Owen and William Rodgers, respectively opposition spokesmen on Energy and Defence. On the NEC, Shirley Williams (who had lost her seat in the General Election) made up the so-called 'Gang of Three'. They were joined by Roy Jenkins, whose term of office as President of the European Commission was shortly to expire. On 1 August 1980, Owen, Rodgers and Williams issued an open letter effectively arguing that Labour would only return to power if it upheld the ideals of parliamentary social democracy. Earlier, in his Dimbleby lecture back in November 1979, Roy Jenkins had called for a realignment in British politics – a call that had received the enthusiastic endorsement of Liberal leader David Steel. The first steps towards the formation of the Social Democratic Party had been taken. The antecedents of this movement stretched back many years. Thus, back in March 1973, Dick Taverne had forced a by-election (and been successfully returned) in his Lincoln constituency as a Democratic Labour supporter in protest at the growing activities of the left in the party. The Liberals had welcomed Christopher Mayhew, the Labour MP for Woolwich East, as a defector to their ranks in July 1974. In 1975, a few opponents of the left in the party had organized themselves into the Social Democratic Alliance. These, however, had been relatively isolated examples.

Following the Wembley Conference, the four leaders of the new movement (Shirley Williams, David Owen, William Rodgers and Jenkins himself – now popularly known as the 'Gang of Four') moved swiftly. A week after Wembley the Gang of Four published the Limehouse Declaration, announcing the establishment of a Council for Social Democracy. Initially, this was not a separate party, simply a pressure group round which potential support would gather. On 2 March, however, twelve Labour MPs (including David Owen and William Rodgers) resigned the party whip and announced that they would not seek re-election as Labour MPs. On 26 March 1981 the new Social Democratic Party was formally launched, consisting initially of fourteen MPs (thirteen Labour and a lone Conservative, Brocklebank-Fowler, MP for Norfolk North-West). A new party had been launched in British politics. One of the SDP's first decisions was to start to negotiate an electoral arrangement with the Liberals. A new alliance had been born, the product of the lengthy series of negotiations between David Steel and Roy Jenkins.

From the outset, the SDP made rapid progress in the opinion polls. The timing of the launch had been carefully chosen. But the fledgeling party had yet to fight its first real electoral battle. This came on 16 July 1981 with the Warrington by-election. Warrington was a safe industrial Labour seat in Cheshire, but Roy Jenkins decided to take on the challenge. In a seat in which the Liberals had polled less than 3,000 votes in 1979, Jenkins achieved a major moral victory. The outcome was Labour 14,280, SDP 12,521 and Conservative 2,102. Although it was the first election battle Jenkins had ever lost, he described it as 'by far the greatest victory in which I have participated'. Prior to the autumn party assemblies, the SDP continued to strengthen its organization. The Llandudno Liberal Conference marked an important stage forward. The previously unratified alliance with the SDP was overwhelmingly supported at the conference. The following month, the SDP held its first ever conference, beginning on 10 October in Perth before moving on to Bradford and London. The alliance with the Liberals was endorsed by enthusiastic acclamation. By now the SDP ranks had swollen to twenty-one, further aided by defecting Labour MPs. A further opportunity for the Alliance came with the by-election vacancy in Croydon North-West. Since the Alliance involved Liberals and Social Democrats alternating in fighting by-elections, the Liberals fought Croydon. On 22 October, William Pitt, the Liberal candidate swept to a remarkable victory, with 13,800 votes compared to 10,546 for the Conservatives and 8,967 for Labour. Although the seat was near to Sutton (won in a famous 1973 by-election), it was the first time ever in modern times that Liberals had won a Tory–Labour marginal. If Croydon North-West was a remarkable victory, the Crosby by-election produced a political sensation. Crosby, a middle-class Merseyside constituency, had been a rock-safe seat for the Conservatives since its creation. In May 1979, the Conservative majority had exceeded 18,000. It was a daunting majority which, when the local Liberals withdrew in her favour, Shirley Williams decided to tackle. The result was a dramatic triumph for her, for she captured the seat with 28,118 votes compared to the 22,829 of the Conservative. A left-wing Labour candidate lost his deposit. Thus Shirley Williams became the first elected SDP MP, having captured one of the safest Conservative seats anywhere in the country. This batch of Liberal–SDP by-election gains was mirrored in local authority by-elections. Of 214 contests from July to December 1981, the Alliance made 100 gains. Meanwhile, on 13 October, the Alliance leaders announced their electoral pact for the next general election. Each party would field candidates in half the constituencies. The arrangements concerning the allocation of individual seats would be worked out at regional level. With Shirley Williams returned to Westminster, only Roy Jenkins of the 'Gang of Four' was without a seat. The by-election at Glasgow Hillhead provided the opportunity. On 25 March 1982, Jenkins won a remarkable victory, taking the seat with 10,106 votes to 8,068 Conservative and 7,846 Labour.

The capture of Hillhead, however, was the prelude to a dramatic change in the political mood of Britain. The British public responded with a wave of patriotic enthusiasm to the Falklands War. A month after the recapture of Port Stanley, the opinion polls gave the Conservatives the support of 46 per cent of the country, while the Alliance came third with 24 per cent; in March, by contrast, the Alliance and Labour had shared first place with 33 per cent. The 'Falklands factor' had arrived.

Its effect was to be seen in the first *national* test of public support for the Alliance which came with the May 1982 local elections. In the wake of the victorious Falklands task force, the results showed a 9 per cent swing from Labour to Conservative since the previous year, with the Alliance failing to make any sort of breakthrough. The parliamentary by-elections after the May elections repeated this pattern. The Alliance lost Mitcham and Morden on 3 June 1982, came a deposit-losing fourth in Coatbridge and, even with Dick Taverne as candidate, came nowhere near to winning Peckham. The only further by-election victory of the Alliance came in the exceptional circumstances of the Bermondsey contest.

Meanwhile, the birth of the Social Democratic Party did nothing to halt Labour's internal wrangling. In April 1981 Tony Benn announced his intention of standing against Denis Healey for the Deputy Leadership of the Labour Party, thereby bringing into play for the first time the new procedures which had been agreed at the Wembley conference. In a bitter six months of campaigning, Benn and Healey were joined by a third candidate, John Silkin, who again offered himself as a conciliator between the Party's left and right wings. At the electoral college, held the day before the annual conference in Brighton in October, Silkin was eliminated in the first ballot and, in a photofinish, in which the abstention of a number of M Ps who had supported Silkin was decisive, Healey defeated Benn by the narrowest of margins. After the deputy leadership contest, however, there was growing pressure from within the Party for a truce, symbolized by a meeting of the N E C and trade union leaders at Bishop's Stortford in January 1982. But as 1982 progressed, the problems facing Michael Foot were compounded by the popularity gained by the Government over its use of military force to retake the Falklands. This popularity was reflected in a steady decline in Foot's own standing and a commanding Conservative lead in the opinion polls.

This decline in Labour's fortunes was exacerbated by the bitter row within the party over the report into the activities of the Militant Tendency; after much legal wrangling, the leaders of Militant were eventually expelled from the party. On the electoral front, the main by-election sensations had been achieved by the Alliance. In October 1982, however, Labour made its solitary by-election gain of the parliament, narrowly capturing the marginal Birmingham Northfield constituency from the Conservatives. This victory was soon overshadowed by the crushing blow of the loss of Bermondsey – one of the safest Labour seats in the land – to the Liberals. Although Labour held Darlington (a key 'marginal' seat) in February 1983, the Conservative lead in the opinion polls remained both massive and consistent. It was against this background that, on 9 May 1983, Margaret Thatcher signified the end of her first administration by seeking an early dissolution of Parliament. Parliament was duly dissolved on 13 May with polling day fixed for 9 June 1983. The long weeks of election speculation had finally been replaced by a short sharp campaign.

THE 1983 GENERAL ELECTION

Despite such problems as the record level of unemployment, Mrs Thatcher entered the election from a commanding position. The public support engendered by the Falklands War had not substantially diminished. No Prime Minister had approached an election with such a sustained and convincing lead over so long a period. It was not only in the opinion polls that the Conservatives were riding high. They also knew that Labour, weakened by defections to the SDP, would need a swing of 5·4 per cent to secure an overall majority – a larger swing than at any election since 1945. Meanwhile, the local elections on 5 May had done little to dispel the view that the Conservatives remained well ahead of Labour.

The 1983 election was fought on new constituencies, their boundaries redrawn to take account of recent shifts in population. Overall, there were now 650 seats, compared to 635 at the 1979 election. England returned 523 members (516 previously), Scotland 72 (71) and Wales 38 (36). The representation of Northern Ireland, which had previously been relatively under-represented, increased from 12 to 17. When nominations closed, a record 2,579 candidates had been fielded. In every constituency outside Ulster, the electors faced a choice of Conservative, Labour or Alliance. Never before had this happened. Meanwhile, all 72 seats in Scotland were fought by the SNP, all 38 seats in Wales by Plaid Cymru. With 107 candidates in the field, the Ecology Party provided the fourth largest total of candidates.

The Conservative election manifesto centred around three challenges for Britain: defence, employment and economic prosperity. Most of its proposals were not new. The party remained committed to membership of the European Community, the maintenance of an independent nuclear deterrent, reform of the trade unions, a further large bout of privatization, a long-term aim to reduce taxation and a continued war on inflation. Among other specific manifesto proposals were pledges to abolish the Greater London Council, the Inner London Education Authority and all the Metropolitan Councils. The Labour manifesto, entitled *New Hope for Britain*, offered a radically different way forward for the voters. Its central proposal was a 12-point plan to bring about a complete change of direction for Britain. Among its firm pledges were withdrawal from the Common Market, early action to abolish the House of Lords, the creation of a National Investment Bank, major increases in public investment in transport and housing, re-nationalization of the shipbuilding and aerospace industries and greater spending on the social services. On defence, the party pledged itself to cancel the Trident programme and prevent the deployment of Cruise or Pershing missiles in Britain. The Alliance manifesto (the first to be published) offered a firm commitment to a programme of economic expansion aimed at reducing unemployment by 1 million within two years. Among other proposals were the imposition of compulsory secret ballots for union elections, reform of the social security system, an incomes policy, continued membership of the Common Market and multilateral disarmament. The Alliance also called for proportional representation and for devolution of power to Scotland, Wales and the regions. The SNP manifesto called for an independent Scotland with control over North Sea oil revenue, while Plaid Cymru called for Home Rule and a £2 billion investment programme for Wales. The campaign itself soon centred round such issues as unemployment and defence (particularly when a speech by former Labour leader Jim Callaghan seemed to expose a major rift on Labour's defence policy).

Many observers noted that the general election had a presidential-style element to it, with the voters asked to decide on Thatcher versus Foot rather than on policy issues. Mrs Thatcher made a brief visit to the Williamsburg economic summit halfway through the campaign. At about this time (the weekend of 28–30 May), the Alliance began to move forward in the opinion polls. The Conservatives remained comfortably in the lead with Labour apparently trailing far behind, only just ahead of the Alliance. Increasingly the Alliance appealed to disenchanted Labour voters to vote tactically (i.e. to vote Liberal to unseat sitting Conservatives). From the first result (declared at Torbay) the outcome of the election was clear. With the Labour vote in retreat everywhere, and with the Alliance polling strongly but failing to secure a real breakthrough, the Conservatives were heading for a decisive electoral victory. In the event, the Conservatives finished with an overall majority of 144, only two short of the massive majority achieved by Attlee for Labour in 1945. The result was as follows:

Party	Votes gained	Percentage of vote	Average vote per MP	Number of MPs
Conservative	13,010,782	42·4	32,772·75	397
Labour	8,456,504	27·6	40,461·74	209
Alliance	7,781,764	25·4	338,337·56	23
Nationalist	457,284	1·5	114,321	4
Others	962,940	3·1	—	17

In terms of votes, as the table above shows, the Conservative share had fallen since 1979. Indeed, no Conservative victory had been achieved with such a small proportion of the vote (42·4 per cent) since Bonar Law back in 1922. This paradox was easily explained. The Conservatives had won their commanding victory due to the divisions of the opposition, with the Alliance eating everywhere into the Labour vote. The final strength of the parties was as follows: Conservatives 397, Labour 209, Alliance 23 (made up of 17 Liberals and 6 Social Democrats), 2 Plaid Cymru, 2 Scottish Nationalists and 17 from Ulster (11 of these Official Unionists, 3 Democratic Unionists, 1 Popular Unionist, 1 SDLP and 1 Sinn Fein). In terms of votes, the Conservatives had won 42 per cent, Labour 28 per cent and the Alliance 26 per cent. This was Labour's worst share of the vote since the early 1920s. Nationally, there had been a swing since 1979 of 3·8 per cent from Labour to Conservative. This swing had been most pronounced in southern England (and also in Wales), with distinctly weaker swings to the Conservatives in the Midlands, the North and Scotland. These figures of Conservative–Labour swing, however, cast little light on the major phenomenon of the election – the dramatic upsurge in popular support for the Liberal–SDP Alliance. With a total vote of 7·78 million (26 per cent of all votes cast) the Alliance achieved a quite resounding success. Although winning only 23 seats, the Alliance came second in no less than 313 seats. No party other than Conservative or Labour had done so well since the 1920s. Parts of the new political map of Britain revealed how Labour had almost ceased to have representation. Thus in southern England (excluding London) Labour won only two seats out of 110 (in Bristol South and Thurrock). The Alliance had become the alternative to the Conservatives. But for the Liberals the election was a frustrating one. The party had gained only five seats, all but Leeds West being rural seats won from the Conservatives. For the SDP, despite a large poll for them, the night was a major disappointment. Only five of their sitting MPs were returned and only one gain was made (in the remote Ross, Cromarty and Skye constituency). Apart from Roy Jenkins and David Owen, the SDP big names went down to defeat. The severe Labour reverse produced a long list of well-known names failing to secure re-election; this included Tony Benn (defeated in the marginal Bristol East constituency) and two members of the Shadow Cabinet (Albert Booth at Barrow and Joan Lestor at Slough). Other Labour losers included Shirley Summerskill, David Ennals, Alex Lyons and Stan Newens. For Margaret Thatcher, the result was a personal triumph. Not since Lord Salisbury, back in 1900, had a Conservative Prime Minister been re-elected after winning the previous general election. The Conservative majority was not only the largest since 1935, but the increase in Conservative seats won (from 339 to 397) was the largest ever achieved by an outgoing administration. And yet, as we have seen, the Conservative share of the vote had *fallen* since 1979. In this sense, the significance of the election was not so much in its overwhelming endorsement of the new Conservatism as in its rejection of a left-wing Labour programme.

The Prime Minister's commanding position was reflected in the composition of the cabinet. Francis Pym was summarily removed from the Foreign Office, which was entrusted to Sir Geoffrey Howe. Nigel Lawson, a somewhat abrasive figure, became Chancellor of the Exchequer. Cecil Parkinson, who had been Chairman of the Party (and who was shortly to resign over the scandal that arose because of his affair with his former secretary), became Secretary of State for Trade and Industry. Other appointments included Michael Heseltine (Defence), Norman Tebbit (Employment) and Leon Brittan (Home Office, replacing William Whitelaw who received the first hereditary peerage since 1961). The Conservative election victory had its aftermath for the Opposition too. Almost before the dust of the battle had settled, Roy

Jenkins announced that he was stepping down as leader of the SDP. The obvious successor (indeed, almost the only possible contender of the six surviving SDP MPs) was David Owen. His forceful campaigning style had earned him a personal triumph in his Plymouth Devonport constituency. He was duly elected unopposed as leader. For the Liberals, David Steel's own commanding position in his party was reaffirmed at the 1983 Harrogate Conference when a proposal that the party should have a Deputy Leader was heavily defeated. For Labour, as we have seen, the election had been a nightmare. With 27·6 per cent of the vote, it was the lowest share ever won in British history by the principal opposition party. Never, since the foundation of the party in February 1900, had the average vote for Labour candidates been so low. It was inevitable, in these circumstances, that Labour would look for a new leader. On 12 June, Michael Foot's decision not to seek re-election as leader was prematurely released. A long and bitter leadership battle began. From the start, the feeling that Labour needed a young leader was pronounced. With the Deputy Leadership also at stake (Denis Healey had earlier indicated he did not wish to seek re-election), there was also a strong feeling that a balanced leadership of left and right would best keep the party together. The leadership contest (fought under the terms of the electoral college) produced a decisive victory for the left-wing Neil Kinnock over his right-wing challenger, Roy Hattersley. Kinnock polled 71·3 per cent, Hattersley 19·3 per cent with the other contenders (Peter Shore and Eric Heffer) coming nowhere in sight. Hattersley, however, became Deputy Leader with a convincing victory over his nearest rival, the left-wing Michael Meacher. Thus Labour achieved its so-called 'dream ticket'. With Labour thus equipped with a new leadership, with the Alliance now firmly established under Owen and Steel, and with the Conservatives armed with their largest majority for fifty years, the new battle-lines of British politics had been drawn.

THATCHERISM: AN INTERIM ASSESSMENT

If Mrs Thatcher had come into power with the ambition of reversing Britain's relative decline, she had signally failed to do so by 1983. Indeed, relative decline in many ways had become absolute decline. Thus, between the second quarter of 1979 and the fourth quarter of 1982, the gross domestic product had fallen by 4·2 per cent. Between May 1979 and February 1983 industrial production had fallen by 10·2 per cent and manufacturing production by 17·3 per cent. Unemployment meanwhile had increased from 1,253,000 to 3,021,000 (calculated on the new basis of measurement), an increase of 141 per cent, while an additional 134,000 school-leavers had still to find work. Taxation overall had also increased by 7 per cent while public spending had risen from 41 per cent of total output to 44 per cent. Within this last figure, defence expenditure had risen by 23 per cent, social security by 21 per cent, health and social services by 14 per cent, while spending on education had fallen by 6 per cent and housing by 55 per cent. Allowing for higher prices, pensions had risen by 7·5 per cent, child benefits fallen by 6 per cent. There were 6,500 more doctors, 45,000 more nurses and 100,000 more students (13,000 of them university students). There were 9,453 more policemen but an increase in crime of 28·6 per cent. Average earnings were up from £94.20 per week to £172.30, which, allowing for higher prices and taxes, meant that those in work were only about 5 per cent better off.

These statistics were not at all the sort that Mrs Thatcher had looked forward to in 1979. They meant that the frontiers of the state had not been rolled back in any significant way, that taxes and public expenditure had not been reduced and that the course of Britain's post-war history – its relative decline, in short – had not been altered. Indeed, by 1983, for the first time since the industrial revolution, Britain had become a net importer of manufactured goods. Part of the problem, of course, had been the international recession. Yet, despite claims by Mr Whitelaw that Britain had 'weathered the recession a great deal better than most of our competitors', this was demonstrably untrue. For if Britain's 11 per cent fall in industrial output between the second quarter of 1979 and the fourth quarter of 1982 (according to OECD figures) was matched by that of the USA, the figure for the developed countries as a whole was only 4 per cent. Thus German production fell by only 7 per cent, French by only 4 per cent, while the Japanese managed to increase theirs by no less than 13 per cent. Also, despite the gains made in the fight against inflation, the British rate in March 1983 of 4·6 per cent compared with 3·3 per cent in Germany, 3·6 per cent in the USA and only 2·4 per cent in Japan. Had Thatcherism therefore achieved anything at all? Given statistics like these plus the cautious approach adopted by Mrs Thatcher's government to trade union reform, people began to wonder by 1983 whether the Prime Minister herself was a 'Thatcherite'.

There was, however, another side to the coin. First and foremost, it has to be remembered that the Government had spent four years resisting calls – from 'wets' among others – to reflate the economy by many billions of pounds. A Labour government, for example, would have added at least another £6 billion to its expenditure plans of 1979, a figure which only *might* have been offset by added revenue from increases in employment. In short, under a Labour government led by Michael Foot, government expenditure as a proportion of total output would have risen to between 50 and 55 per cent. Thus in the light of the alternative programme at hand, Mrs Thatcher had resisted a significant growth in public expenditure. Again, even despite her cautious approach, she had more or less emasculated the trade union movement. This was partly due, of course, to the increase in unemployment but it was also due to a change in public attitudes. This change was signally acknowledged in 1983 when the General Secretary of the TUC, Len Murray, refused to give official backing to the NGA – the printers' union – in its challenge to the courts over the new trade union laws. Well before then, however, Mr Murray and his colleagues had already conceded that their ability to intimidate governments had been well and truly lost. This was initially demonstrated by the failure of the militant president of the National Union of Mineworkers, Mr Arthur Scargill, to persuade his members to come out on strike over pay or pit closures. On no less than three occasions in two years before the national strike of 1984, they repudiated his advice, and his humiliation was increased both by Mrs Thatcher's bestowal of a peerage on his rival and predecessor Mr Gormley, and by her appointment of the tough, Scots-American, Mr Ian Mac-Gregor to head the National Coal Board. The public respect for Mr MacGregor like that for Sir Michael Edwardes at British Leyland and Sir John King at British Airways – not to mention the affection still held by many for that fallen angel among entrepreneurs, Sir Freddie Laker – seemed at first yet another symptom of the change of mood which Mrs Thatcher had brought about. It was a change of mood moreover which affected not merely trade unions, but all sorts of other areas of public life.

It was best demonstrated perhaps by the survey of public opinion expensively conducted at the start of 1983 by the local government trade union NALGO and reported in the *Guardian* on 27 March. The results proved especially 'devastating' for the union concerned. Local government was seen to be 'wasteful and politically motivated'; privatization was generally welcomed, immigrants were blamed for rising crime and higher taxes, social workers 'were poorly regarded and not taken particularly seriously' while 'at no point was central government blamed for the current state of affairs'. Not only were government cuts not resented, but many saw them as involving positive aspects. Many nationalized industries and social services were held to be overmanned and mismanaged while 'cutting school budgets meant that many parents were becoming more involved through PTA fund-raising activities in their children's education'. Parks, libraries, and transport were found to be 'marginal concerns' while in general, 'the state of the nation [was] accepted with resignation and seen as an inevitability about which little [should] or could have been done'.

This mood of resignation regarding cuts and unemployment had undoubtedly been encouraged by the Thatcher government. The public seemed to accept its case that these were the result of past failures. Likewise, there was plenty of evidence from opinion polls to indicate that Mrs Thatcher remained the best hope for long-term change. Whereas *in the short term*, Labour policies might relieve the growth in unemployment, the public seemed to be convinced that *in the long term* it was Thatcherite policies which made sense. Indeed it was in the field of economics that the premier's populism was most effective. Her stress on the need to be competitive, to adopt the latest techniques, to seek out new markets, and to acquire the latest skills seemed to make more sense than the policy, attributed often and no doubt wrongly to Labour, of subsidizing outdated industries and increasing the bureaucracy. Mrs Thatcher, by contrast, had cut the number of civil servants in Britain by 14 per cent and planned to increase those cuts to 20 per cent by 1988. This too seemed to be publicly appreciated in a country which, according to an IMF report of 1983, had twice as many civil servants as might be expected from the size of its population and its living standards.

Changing public attitudes, cutting the size of the bureaucracy, resisting great pressures for massive increases in public spending, not to mention the control of inflation were parts of the Government's record which the Prime Minister took credit for. In the industrial field, apart from taming the trade unions, she claimed responsibility for an increase in productivity and the start which had been made on privatization. The trouble was that it was too early to tell whether the increase in productivity was a once-and-for-all increase gained as a result of the huge increase in unemployment, and whether the change in mood regarding the need to be competitive would ensure a continuing rise in competitiveness. Likewise, it was too early to tell whether the privatization of large public companies would do more than turn public monopolies into private ones. That too, if it happened, might pose problems for future governments concerned with industrial efficiency.

Certainly the Government had made mistakes. Allowing the pound to rise so steeply in the early years of its term of office and using record interest rates to control the money supply had led to the sacrifice of many firms which under better national economic management might well have survived the recession. As a result, the manufacturing base of British industry experienced a further decline. This not only meant that the cost paid for Government policies in terms of unemployment was appallingly high but that the acute danger remained of any recovery bringing with it an immediate balance of payments deficit.

The voters in 1983 however were prepared to give Mrs Thatcher and her colleagues the benefit of the doubt. Her victory in the Falklands War had reinforced their respect for her undoubted determination and patriotism. It therefore seemed that if anyone would see them through whatever difficulties lay ahead she would. Perhaps despite the obvious setbacks she had suffered, despite the awful price which they had paid, she had indeed laid the foundations for a new beginning. Certainly no one else seemed more prepared than she to face up to realities in a way which sounded convincing. In this sense the public seemed to accept the Prime Minister's claim that there was no alternative to her programme. Indeed she came absolutely to dominate the political scene. Yet if she was to be given the benefit of the doubt in 1983, one thing was clear: by the end of her second administration she would no longer be in a position to claim that she still required more time. By then results would be in order, unambiguous results of economic competitiveness and recovery. By 1988 the British people would know for certain whether 'Thatcherism' had worked. If not she would discover, like nurse Edith Cavell, that 'patriotism is not enough'.

To the degree of her success must inevitably be linked the question of whether she in fact broke with the political consensus. After all, it might well be argued that she had merely redressed the political and economic balance. That is to say, that by controlling trade union power, reducing inflation, and privatizing a number of companies, she had merely corrected the excesses of previous (especially Labour) administrations. It is difficult to deny that public opinion was much more averse to the 'convictions' of the Labour left, which seemed to have permeated the Labour party in opposition, than it was to Mrs Thatcher's. Thus there is a case, indeed a strong case, to be made out that support for her represented support for traditional values. After all she proposed no institutional changes, she represented the defence of national interests, her foreign policy was a completely traditional one and she had launched no attack on the welfare state. Even her attempts to control local government expenditure were designed to protect citizens from local left-wing excesses. It was too early to tell in 1983 therefore whether Mrs Thatcher represented political continuity or discontinuity.

14 | THE SECOND THATCHER GOVERNMENT, 1983-7

Mrs Thatcher's second term in office was rather less dynamic than her first. However, the need for renewed momentum was recognized and exploited by her party in time for it to win its third general election in a row in 1987. In the meantime her government witnessed many dramatic episodes – the Brighton bombing, the miners' strike, the Westland affair – and claimed credit for several pieces of controversial legislation. By 1987, too, Nigel Lawson was being acclaimed the country's most successful post-war Chancellor, and although his reputation was to suffer a rather rapid reappraisal, there was no gainsaying the remarkable economic recovery that was by then under way and which was already giving rise to claims of a Tory 'economic miracle'.

The parliament that reassembled on 15 June 1983 contained 157 new members and soon acquired a new Speaker in Bernard Weatherill. His predecessor, the remarkably popular George Thomas, had been given a hereditary viscountcy and was thus elevated to the House of Lords. William Whitelaw was similarly honoured. Since Thomas was a bachelor and Whitelaw had no male heirs, this means of elevation was regarded as an experiment by Mrs Thatcher, designed to discover the reaction of British public opinion to the possible reintroduction of hereditary peerages. In the event it proved negative, and no more were awarded.

The Cabinet also had a new look. Francis Pym, who had long been regarded as a leading wet and who, during the election campaign, had been publicly corrected by the Prime Minister for suggesting that a small majority would be more manageable than a large one, was replaced as Foreign Secretary by the faithful Sir Geoffrey Howe. He, in turn, was replaced as Chancellor by Nigel Lawson, reputedly the toughest of monetarists. Whitelaw became Leader of the House of Lords and deputy premier and was replaced as Home Secretary by Leon Brittan.

He remained a powerful figure in the Government, however, as chairman of the 'Star Chamber' (cabinet committee MISC 62, which finalized departmental spending targets) and the colleague on whom the Prime Minister most relied to smooth over factional differences. Cecil Parkinson became Secretary of State for Trade and Industry, while the arch-wet Peter Walker was moved to the Department of Energy, replacing David Howell. Finally, a former speechwriter of the Prime Minister, John Gummer, a 'baby-faced' forty-three-year-old, replaced Parkinson as Chairman of the Conservative Party. As a result of these and other ministerial changes the Prime Minister was held to have strengthened her grip on the Government; her influence was also supposed to have been furthered by the appointment of sympathetic nominees as Governor of the Bank of England (Robert Leigh-Pemberton), permanent secretaries of the Treasury and the Ministry of Defence (Peter Middleton and Sir Clive Whitmore respectively), not to mention Sir Anthony Parsons as her personal adviser on foreign affairs. All in all, therefore, the prospect was for an even more robust Thatcherite administration.

The actual programme foreseen by Mrs Thatcher was outlined in the Queen's Speech of 22 June 1983, which included plans for further privatization (British Telecom, British Airways, British Gas, the Royal Ordinance factories); the bringing into profitability of the remaining nationalized industries; the reform of the rating system; tougher measures on law and order; and a third Trade Union Reform Bill. The pace of change therefore was set to continue. In reality, the Government was soon wrong-footed. A series of embarrassing 'banana-skins', the initial popularity of the new Labour leader, the campaign to save the Greater London Council and other metropolitan councils from abolition, continuing fears about unemployment and the future of the National Health Service, not to mention the US invasion of Grenada, all quickly served seriously to undermine its popularity.

Post-election euphoria was soon dissipated by the news, revealed during the Conservative Party Conference of October 1983, that Cecil Parkinson had been having an affair with his secretary, Sarah Keays, who had become pregnant. The Prime Minister persuaded Parkinson to stick by his wife and family (to the great annoyance of Miss Keays, who claimed that Parkinson had promised to marry her) but could not dissuade him from resigning. The result was a government reshuffle that made Norman Tebbit Secretary of State for Trade and Industry;

Tom King Employment Secretary; Nicholas Ridley Transport Secretary; and John Gummer Employment Secretary. The latter, however, retained the Chairmanship of the Conservative Party.

The following year witnessed two more 'banana-skins' on which the Government was held to have slipped. Both concerned security matters. In the first case, the Government, allegedly acting under American pressure, banned the operation of trade unions at GCHQ, the secret government communications headquarters at Cheltenham. Each trade union member was offered £1,000 in compensation, but many observers believed that the rights of ordinary people had been infringed and failed to see any positive advantage in the move; they wondered also why the Government was being so deferential to the Americans, who in October 1983 had invaded the island of Grenada, a Commonwealth member-state, without first consulting or indeed even informing the British Government or Buckingham Palace. This incident had caused Mrs Thatcher to telephone President Reagan, who, in the words of one expert, 'received one of the less pleasant telephone conversations of his life in consequence'. Still, the damage had been done and the 'special relationship' looked rather limp. Why then had the Government bothered to enforce a ban on trade unions at GCHQ? Its own answer was that the civil service unions had exploited the sensitivity of Chelten-ham as a security centre in order to further their pay claims. They had thus acted irresponsibly. A trade union ban there was consequently the logical response.

Security interests also underlay the prosecution in March 1984 – two months after the trade union ban at GCHQ – of Miss Sarah Tisdall, a junior clerk at the Ministry of Defence, for having supplied the *Guardian* newspaper with a copy of an embarrassing government minute relating to the arrival of Cruise missiles at Greenham Common. Miss Tisdall was sentenced to six months' imprisonment for breaking the Official Secrets Act, an outcome which was felt by some to infringe on civil liberties. In the eponymous year of Orwell's novel, these were seen to be peculiarly at risk, a viewpoint which did not lose currency the following year when another, this time more senior, civil servant, Clive Ponting, was prosecuted for providing Tam Dalyell MP with information relating to the sinking of the *Belgrano*. Despite the summing up by the judge in the case, who argued that the national interest could be defined only by the Government, the jury chose to acquit Mr Ponting, whose defence had been that he owed a higher obligation to parliament and the country. By 1987, indeed, several cases had arisen in which the Government's concern for security had clashed with the public's desire to know more. These included the Home Secretary's (Leon Brittan's) request to the BBC to withdraw a *Real Lives* programme that neither he nor anyone else outside the BBC had seen; a further dispute over a television programme concerning the Zircon satellite project, which led to a police raid on the BBC studios in Glasgow; the revelation by the *Observer* newspaper that BBC employees were being vetted by MI5; and last, but hardly least, the *Spycatcher* affair, in which the Government began a long and ultimately unsuccessful struggle in courts around the world to prevent the former British secret agent Peter Wright from publishing his memoirs. Long after the book had been published in Ireland and the USA and excerpts had been published in the British press, the Government still persevered in its attempts to prevent publication in the United Kingdom, Australia and New Zealand. The highlight of its efforts was to be the court case in Australia in which the Cabinet Secretary, Sir Robert Armstrong, admitted to having been 'economical with the truth'. In Britain itself, the Government was finally to lose its battle only in October 1988, when the House of Lords ruled that newspapers might publish extracts; however, it also upheld the lifelong duty of confidentiality imposed on MI5 agents.

The result of all these incidents was to convince nearly everybody that a review of the 1911 Official Secrets Act was long overdue. The Government itself was to propose changes after the 1987 election. In the meantime, although everyone recognized the difficulties involved in protecting national security without undermining basic freedoms, the popular view seemed to be that Mrs Thatcher's government was inclined to act rather too hastily where security interests were involved and appeared too high-handed in its determination to protect them. If Thatcherism was a classically liberal doctrine regarding economics, it was a classically conservative one regarding state security. And its popular reputation in this regard did nothing to improve its poll ratings in the period 1983–6.

The role of the central government was in fact to become the dominating theme of the second Thatcher administration. This was certainly not the intention of the Government or of the Prime Minister herself. None of the above incidents could have been foreseen and she would no doubt have wished to avoid the next test of her authority and that of her government. Nevertheless, the determination of Arthur Scargill to manipulate a miners' strike which he could exploit to bring down the government as in 1974, was now to provide the most dramatic episode of her premiership since the Falklands War of 1982.

THE MINERS' STRIKE, 1984–5

The miners' strike lasted from 12 March 1984 to 5 March 1985. In the words of the editor of the *Sunday Times* it was 'one of the most significant events in Britain's post-war history'. His description of it is dramatic but not misleading:

... it matched a Marxist revolutionary, Arthur Scargill, against the apostle of market forces, Margaret Thatcher. Never before had the battle lines been so starkly drawn. Scargill believed his mass pickets were in the vanguard of the socialist revolution. Thatcher believed she had a parliamentary majority for the market economy. Scargill thought that the coal industry should be run largely for the benefit of his members, Thatcher that it should conform to the dictates of the market-place. Scargill saw union power as the key to building a society fit for the working man. Thatcher saw union power as the single most important reason for Britain's post-war economic decline. Above all, Scargill thought that, although the government had just won a famous victory, it could still be defeated by direct action. Thatcher, although she had gone out of her way to avoid a head-on clash with the unions in her first term, knew that the recent history of the country made some sort of confrontation inevitable.

The 'recent history of the country' had, of course, included a number of famous victories by the unions over government. In 1969, Harold Wilson had been forced to drop his plans for trade union reform; in 1972 and 1974 the miners had challenged the industrial strategy of the Heath government and had brought it down; in 1979 the trade unions had undermined James Callaghan's government through the 'winter of discontent'; Scargill himself had already called for a miners' strike three times during the course of the first Thatcher government; and the Prime Minister had ducked a challenge in February 1981, when she backed down over proposals to close twenty-three pits. Now in March 1984 Scargill was determined to get his way, and the proposal to close the Yorkshire pit at Cortonwood, made at the beginning of March 1984, provided him with the opportunity. Cortonwood had lost £10 million between 1977 and 1983 and was already losing £4 million in the current year. Its coal cost £64 a tonne to bring to the surface and could not be sold for more than £47. Its closure, therefore, should have been predictable. The local miners, none the less, had not been prepared for the bad news, and Scargill told them that their union would not accept the 'closure of uneconomic pits' in principle. He held – extremely tendentiously – that the 1974 *Plan for Coal* did not propose this, although nobody else believed that the Coal Board disavowed the principle.

The truth was that mining as an industry was in decline in Britain. It had reached its peak in 1923 when there had been 1,250,000 men employed in the industry. In 1947, when 958 of the largest pits were nationalized, it still accounted for 90 per cent of the nation's energy requirements but employed only 700,000 men. In 1950 a *Plan for Coal* was drawn up which looked forward to 240 million tonnes of coal a year being produced, but this target was never met. The plan was revised, however, and a new target of 250 million tonnes by 1970 inserted. But by then, the prospects for the coal industry had changed very much for the worse. Cheap oil supplies from the Middle East, smokeless zones, nuclear-generated electricity and the introduction of natural gas from the North Sea all meant that the traditional customers for coal disappeared. The 1967 White Paper on fuel policy thus cut back the 1970 target to 152 million tonnes. However, the decline was irreversible and by 1974 coal was accounting for barely one third of the British fuel market.

Technological developments were also defeating the miners. The powered hydraulic roof support, the rotary cutter and the armoured conveyer belt meant that whereas only 9·2 per cent of production had been power-loaded in 1955, the figure by the end of the 1960s had already reached 92.2 per cent. Together with declining demand for coal, these technological developments meant that more and more mines had to be closed down. By 1970 less than 300 were active, representing a shrinkage of two thirds in less than twenty-five years. It was little wonder that as a result 346,000 miners voluntarily quit the industry between 1960 and 1968. The oil crisis of 1973 plus the advent of a Labour government, however, seemed to offer one last hope of salvation. For Labour not only settled the miners' strike of that year on extremely generous terms (see Chapter Ten; the dispute largely concerned wages policy) but also published, with the support of the NCB (National Coal

Board) and the NUM (National Union of Mineworkers), a new and ambitious *Plan for Coal*, which was to become Arthur Scargill's bible. (It was in fact the fourth such plan since 1950.) Unfortunately for everyone concerned, it 'turned out, in almost every economic, industrial and political respect, an unattainable dream', with the result that a decade later the Coal Board was looking at a very different strategy. Its plan now was to reduce production from the levels foreseen in 1974, concentrate output around massive, new 'supermines', close down smaller, uneconomic pits and retire older workers on remarkably generous redundancy terms. The announcement made on 6 March 1984 envisaged production falling by four million tonnes in 1984–5, the closure of twenty pits and the loss of 20,000 jobs. It was a plan which Arthur Scargill refused to accept or even consider.

The Government, for its part, had always accepted that at some stage or other there would probably have to be a miners' strike. Scargill's political ambitions were no secret, nor was the general belief in the country that a miners' strike was irresistible. The Conservative Party had been told as much by Lord Carrington himself, who, in a confidential report at the end of 1977, had delivered his specially commissioned post-mortem on the 1974 debacle. (He had been Energy Secretary under Heath.) This had concluded that strong unions with command over sophisticated technologies could no longer be defeated by the old expedient of sending in the troops. Instead, groups of workers like the miners or the power workers could virtually hold the country to ransom. It was fortunate for the Tory Party, however, that Carrington's report, 'with its undertones of appeasement and compromise', was not the only analysis that was made of the events of 1974.

A report on the nationalized industries drawn up by the right-wing Tory MP Nicholas Ridley covered much of the same ground as Carrington's. Its conclusions, on the other hand, were markedly different. Those in particular which referred to government contingency planning to defeat any challenge from 'communist disrupters' were distinctly more robust. Ridley suggested the following strategy: that the Government should try if possible to choose the field of battle; that if this were to be the coal industry, it should build up maximum coal stocks at the power-stations; it should make contingency plans to import coal; it should encourage the recruitment of non-union drivers by road-haulage companies; it should introduce dual coal–oil firing in all power-stations;

it should 'cut off the money supply to the strikers and make the union finance them'; and there should be a large, mobile squad of police equipped and prepared to uphold the law against violent picketing. Amazingly, these recommendations were published in the *Economist* on 27 May 1978, so that Arthur Scargill had almost six years' notice of what Government tactics were likely to be. But, although many pickets during the strike were found in possession of copies of the relevant article, Scargill himself was to give no sign of having taken Ridley's proposals seriously. This was to turn out to have been an egregious mistake. Worse still, he chose to let battle commence in the coalfields at a time when the Government was best able to retaliate. Such an overwhelming display of hubris was soon to be consummated by nemesis.

The decision to strike at Cortonwood was followed by an appeal to all the regions of the NUM to come out in support. The prospects looked good: a national overtime ban had already been in operation since October 1983 and the industry had a reputation for solidarity. By 12 March, therefore, a national strike had commenced on a 'rolling basis', that is to say, with one region joining in after another. One week later, no less than ninety of the 174 NCB collieries were on strike. Yet this situation was a peculiar one. Scargill had organized what amounted to a national miners' strike, although there had been no national ballot. When a ballot *was* held in Nottinghamshire, an area noted for its productive, low-cost pits, the vote went against the strike by a margin of three to one. Worse still from Scargill's point of view, a ballot held by NACODS, the pit supervisors' union, also failed to achieve the (two-thirds) majority necessary to support the strike. This was an important set-back, since the pit supervisors were responsible for pit safety, and it would have been impossible to have kept the pits open legally without their cooperation. Scargill could have recovered from both these set-backs, on the other hand, if he had been able to demonstrate that a national majority of his members were in favour of the strike. However, afraid that yet another national ballot would go against him, he preferred to rely on appeals to solidarity and intimidation instead. Despite pleas by Neil Kinnock and other leaders of the Labour movement, an appeal to the ballot box was ruled out. Hubris took charge once again.

During the year that the strike lasted the principal opponent of Arthur Scargill – certainly as far as the media were concerned – was not so much Mrs Thatcher, who remained as far as she could in the background, but the new Chairman of the NCB, Mr Ian MacGregor, a canny ex-patriot Scot, who had become one of the most sought-after international business brains of his time. The Bishop of Durham was to refer to MacGregor as an 'elderly imported American', yet this condescending description hardly did justice to the doughty seventy-two-year-old tycoon, who had built up such a formidable reputation. Born in Kinlochleven, Argyllshire, MacGregor had taken a first-class degree in metallurgy at Glasgow University, had become part of Beaverbrook's wartime team that had cajoled essential supplies from the Americans, and had remained in the US after the war. There he had become chairman of the billion-dollar Amax Corporation and a self-made multi-millionaire. British governments had continually sought his services during the 1970s, but it was not until 1980 that he agreed to accept a three-year contract as head of British Steel. He did not come cheap, for parliament had to agree to a fee of £1·8 million – on top of his salary – to be paid to the New York investment house of Lazard Freres, which he had joined after reaching Amax's statutory retiring age. In 1983, when he joined British Coal, the fee was set at £1·5 million, in Nigel Lawson's words 'only the amount that the NCB is losing every day'. Indeed, 1984 was a financial year in which the NCB would record a loss of £410 million, before paying interest charges of £467 million; it would thus require an £875 million deficit grant from the British government in order to remain in the black. MacGregor's task was to put an end to this situation, and given his record in America and at British Steel, the NUM could be under no illusion but that he would set about that task with gusto. In the USA, for example, he had defeated the United Mineworkers in a dispute that had lasted two years, while at British Steel, he had turned the industry's abysmal productivity record into nearly the best in Europe. Profitability had almost been restored there too before he left – it was to be established under his successor – but at the cost of cutting the payroll from 166,000 to 85,000 men. On MacGregor's appointment to British Coal, therefore, Scargill warned: '. . . this man's mission is to savagely butcher the British coal industry.' MacGregor replied that he was no hatchet man but 'a plastic surgeon, trying to redeem the features of aged properties that need some kind of face-lift'.

The scene was thus set for Britain's most bitter industrial dispute since 1926. It was one on which the future of the Government depended and on which, in many people's eyes, the future of the country depended also. Caught up in the human tragedy of it were the miners' families, bitterly divided in many areas, subjected to intimidation and violence by militants in some parts of the country, and in others facing a desperate struggle to make ends meet while the dispute continued.

The Government's tactics were to sit back and pretend that the dispute was an ordinary one to which the normal procedures applied. Or, in other words, that the NCB was the body in charge. MacGregor was happy enough to live with this, but resented Government interference behind the scenes. Peter Walker, the Energy Minister, for his part, was not alone in deploring MacGregor's limited skills in the sphere of public relations. The dispute, however, was by and large conducted in the way in which Nicholas Ridley had foreseen. Scargill banked on intimidating the miners into supporting him and on winning the strike through the massive and violent use of 'flying pickets'. He also hoped that a violent police reaction would stimulate wider working-class or trade union support. Perhaps he actually believed his own rhetoric – that there were no such things as uneconomic pits, that coal stocks would run out, that there would soon be power cuts. His energy was certainly demonic and proved to have a mesmerizing affect on thousands of miners. Yet, in the final analysis, in Peter Jenkins's words, he was merely the 'exponent of the big lie'. He was leading the past in a fight against the present and was relying less on a realistic strategy than on pious hopes. Jimmy Reid, a former Scottish trade union hero, summed up the situation when he said that militants had their place, but ignorant ones had not. Scargill, in fact, had begun a strike when winter was turning into spring, when coal stocks were at an all-time high, and when power stations could be switched to oil. Worse still, his refusal to risk a national ballot meant that the miners were split. To quote Peter Jenkins again: '[He] had placed their banner on the top of a slag heap. His fatal blunder was to try to "picket out" the Nottinghamshire miners against their will. With the rich, modernized Nottingham coalfield continuing to mine coal and Nottingham railwaymen continuing to move it, the strike was lost before it had begun.' In the end, the Nottinghamshire miners, far from being cowered, demonstrated their independence by establishing a breakaway union, the UDM or Union of Democratic Mineworkers, under the leadership of Roy Link.

If the miners themselves were split, so too was the trade union movement as a whole. There was some patchy support from railwaymen, dockers and seamen, but coal continued to come in through the ports and to reach the power stations and other customers by road. The steel workers, road-hauliers and power-workers were not prepared to be used for Scargill's purposes. Thus in the first week of November 1984 when winter was setting in, one million tons of coal could be delivered to customers throughout the land.

Nor could violence retrieve the NUM position. The lessons of the previous miners' strike had been absorbed by the police who also had experience of Northern Ireland and the urban riots of 1981. By 1984 there were some 140,000 police in Britain trained in 'tactical operations' and supplied with riot gear who could be employed to neutralize Scargill's mobile army. The police also set up a National Reporting Centre at Scotland Yard, which operated to all intents and purposes as a national command centre for the force. Hence the defeat of the flying pickets. Their impotence was demonstrated at the Orgreave coking plant near Sheffield, where ten thousand of them were prevented by the police from shutting down the plant.

Scargill's position was further undermined by a series of factors. For a start a number of incidents of militant violence against individuals received widespread media coverage. There was for example the manslaughter of a South Wales taxi driver, crushed to death in his cab when a couple of striking miners dropped a huge concrete block on his vehicle while he was taking another miner to work. (Mining families actually demonstrated in support of the killers.) Then there was the curious incident of the Libyan connection. Scargill, it was discovered, had flown under a false name to Paris on 11 October 1984 in order to meet a terrorist paymaster known to the French security services as 'Gadaffi's bagman'.* He was later to deny the episode, but the whole story was exposed by John Swain of the *Sunday Times*. The tortured history of the union's finances during the strike provided not only a motive for the Paris meeting, but also a third factor which helped undermine public support for the miners. It was the Libyan connection, however, that was undoubtedly to represent Scargill's greatest public relations disaster.

---

* Scargill's linkman with the Libyans, Roger Windsor, alleged in 1990 that Scargill had used Libyan money to pay off his mortgage and had also asked Gadaffi for guns. Colonel Gadaffi himself confirmed that £163,000 had been paid to the NUM.

For if his efforts to secure financial aid from the Soviet Union had failed to provoke controversy (social security benefits had been made extremely difficult to obtain by the Government), aid from Colonel Gadaffi's regime was another matter altogether. Earlier in the year a member of the Libyan People's Bureau had shot and killed Woman Police Constable Yvonne Fletcher from the window of his London office and diplomatic links with Libya had been broken off. The thought of establishing a connection with the regime was therefore one which even members of the NUM executive were prepared to condemn. The Labour leader, Neil Kinnock, said: 'By any measure of political, civil, trade union or human rights, the Gadaffi regime is vile. Any offers from them would be an insult to everything the British labour movement stands for.'

The strike lasted until 5 March 1985. Only when there was a walk-out by NACODS members in September–October 1984 did it look as if the strikers might stand a chance of winning. This episode was ended, however, by the NCB agreeing to a new pit-closure review procedure. Thereafter it became clear that the Government would remain firm; there were also no power cuts. Instead, a special offer of seasonal bonuses led to a small trickle of miners returning to work before Christmas. This in turn divided mining communities even more bitterly. But after the turn of the year the trickle became a flood and on 5 March an organized return to work by the 50 per cent who were still on strike meant that the year-long dispute was at an end. It had left a legacy of great bitterness and had cost the Government some £3 billion. Yet the significance of the miners' defeat could not be overestimated. It had removed a sword of Damocles which had been hanging over the Government's head since the day it had entered office. It therefore convinced everyone that the 'Thatcher revolution' was at last secure. Scargill's defeat in fact was as significant in terms of domestic policy as that of Galtieri had been in terms of foreign policy. It was no surprise or coincidence therefore that Mrs Thatcher, in a speech at the Carlton Club, had referred to the miners as 'the enemy within'.

The Tory Party reacted in a subdued manner to the victory which had been won. There was a great deal of sympathy in the country for the miners, who had suffered many privations and whose industry was being run down. The Conservatives were all too aware therefore that gloating would be out of place. Besides, it had been Ian MacGregor who had borne the main burden of the dispute, and, in any case, the significance of the victory was obvious to all. On the other hand, Scargill and his colleagues learned nothing from their defeat. 'All our future struggles will be stronger as a result,' they declared, adding that the strike had inspired 'hope, effort and solidarity not only in Britain, but around the world'. Tony Benn said much the same: 'The miners' strike was the greatest piece of radicalization I've seen; there have never been as many socialists in the country in my lifetime. We're only half way between Dunkirk and D-Day.' Within just a few years Scargill was calling for yet another strike.

The Labour Party leadership meanwhile knew all too well that the strike had set back any hopes of a political recovery. Both the Labour Party conference and that of the TUC in 1985 had lent vociferous support to the miners. Neil Kinnock himself, the Labour Party leader, had been compromised by failing to condemn the picket-line violence soon enough or in sufficiently unequivocal terms. His view of Scargill was clear enough: 'He's destroying the coal industry single-handed. He's the Labour Movement's nearest equivalent to a First World War general.' Yet he was under enormous pressure in the party to support the strike, while under outside pressure to condemn the violence. His response was an impossible compromise. He distanced himself from the strike as much as he could, first visiting a picket line only in January 1985 and sharing a platform with Scargill only at the end of November 1984. On the other hand, his speech to the party conference in the autumn of 1984 included a condemnation of picket-line violence merely as part of a blanket condemnation of violence in all its forms. It therefore lacked force. The conference itself passed a motion condemning 'police violence against the miners' and Tony Benn attributed violence '100 per cent to the Government'. When the electricians' leader, Eric Hammond, warned 'The cult of violence will harm this Movement for many years to come', he was roundly booed.

The miners' strike, finally, helped convince Tory as well as many Alliance MPs that the Trade Union Reform Bill piloted through the Commons in 1984 by Norman Tebbit, the Employment Secretary, was a measure deserving support. This made unions liable for damages incurred during a strike unless majorities for strike action had been secured by secret ballots of members beforehand. Secret ballots were now also required both for the election of trade union leaders and (every five years) for the affiliation of trade unions to political parties. On the other hand, Conservative hopes to deprive the Labour Party of financial support in this way, or even to win over trade unions to the Tory Party, were doomed to disappointment.

LOCAL GOVERNMENT

If an admittedly ready concern to protect national security interests plus victory in the miners' strike had led to accusations that government power was too great, the determination shown by central government during Mrs Thatcher's second term in office to control local government spending was to bring howls of protest, not merely from the left, but from many sections of the Conservative Party as well. Geoffrey Rippon, a former Tory minister, for example, was to condemn rate-capping proposals as 'wide, sweeping, general powers of a kind that have not hitherto been regarded in this country as being in accordance with the rule of law'. He declared: 'We stand for the Town Hall, not Whitehall.'

The Government, however, felt obliged to take action regarding local authorities for a number of reasons. In the first place, Mrs Thatcher had promised as far back as 1974 to abolish rates (local property taxes), and the 1983 manifesto had renewed this pledge. Secondly, the monetarists in her government believed that local as well as national government spending had to be brought under control. Thirdly, the antics of left-wing local authorities, particularly in London and Liverpool, presented the Government with a challenge it could hardly ignore.

Local government, however, was not to prove easy to control. As one Environment Secretary put it:

Complaints by ratepayers and government exhortations have largely been ineffective in persuading local authorities to pull in the reins. There is a strong culture in local government which is driven by municipal socialism and continues to be expansionist, interventionist, and monopolistic in its approach, when we are successfully pursuing a national priority of *reducing* the burden of the state in how much it spends, how much it borrows and taxes; indeed, in how much it intrudes into people's lives.

He continued, however:

These problems persist because of the inherent weaknesses of the rating system. We have a system in which there are no direct controls on local authority spending; in which in many areas a small minority of those eligible to vote for councils actually pay directly towards local services: representation without taxation. We have a system of Exchequer grants to local authorities of Byzantine complexity which not only compensates authorities for their needs to spend, but also rewards authorities with a low rateable value base and penalizes those with a high rateable value base, despite the fact that rateable values bear little relation to people's disposable incomes. Crudely put, a poor family in south Buckinghamshire, already coping with high costs of living there, is subsidizing richer families in areas of lower rateable values.

Local authorities in Britain accounted for about a quarter of all public spending. Central government provided for more than half of their income, but had no control over their expenditures. Moreover, as the minister quoted above said, only a minority of voters actually paid rates, with the result that most voters had an incentive to retain high-spending councils. In fact, out of an electorate of 35 million, only 18 million paid up and of these some 6 million received full or partial rebates. It was perhaps not surprising then that between 1979 and 1983 rates had increased on average by 91 per cent while prices in general had gone up by only 55 per cent. The logic of this situation was eventually to produce the poll tax, but before it was introduced the Government spent a whole term of office struggling to contain local government spending.

Between 1979 and 1983 the Government had made strenuous efforts to do so. In general, three approaches were pursued. In the first place, 'block grants', the central government funds allocated to local authorities, were reduced, falling from 61 per cent to 49 per cent of local government expenditure between 1979 and 1985. Secondly, a highly complex formula based on demographic, social and other indices, known as the 'grant-related expenditure assessment' (GREA) was developed by the Department of the Environment to determine the appropriate level of spending for any given local authority. Councils which exceeded the level deemed appropriate for them were penalized by the loss of government grants. Local authorities, finally, were encouraged to be more efficient in their use of revenue by employing new management and accounting techniques, in particular by putting out ancillary services such as cleaning, catering and refuse disposal to private tender.

The result was that local authorities were faced with the choice of either submitting to Government policy or risking the loss of funds by defying Government wishes. Predictably, the reaction of many Labour-controlled councils was to ignore Government advice and to make up for lost grants by simply raising their rates. The risk of any political penalty was small since, as has already been pointed out, only a minority of voters actually paid rates. Conservative-controlled councils, on the other hand, attempted to keep within Government guidelines, but often discovered to their chagrin that their GREA was reduced the following year as a result. Finally, a considerable number of councils (particularly Labour ones) resorted to 'creative accounting', as a means of forestalling spending cuts. This took many weird and wonderful forms, including the mortgaging of town halls, libraries, schools and art galleries, not to mention street lights, bath fittings and abattoirs. On 12 April 1987 the *Sunday Times* revealed: 'Councils using creative accountancy have built up financial burdens totalling as much as £5 billion ... debt raised in this way totals more than the national debts of many Third World countries; much of the money is owed to Japanese banks.' These claims were confirmed by the new Audit Commission, which had been established in 1983 to scrutinize local government spending. It was little wonder then that the Government felt compelled to act. Already between 1979 and 1983, twenty local authorities had overspent to the tune of £750 million.

Yet what was it to do? Unable to find an acceptable alternative means of raising local taxes, an immediate solution was discovered in the Rates Act of 1984, which came into effect in the spring of 1985. This allowed the Environment Minister (Patrick Jenkin) to draw up a blacklist of overspending councils and to fix their rates for the coming year, a procedure known as 'rate-capping'. The councils involved could negotiate regarding the rate imposed, but only if they allowed the Department of the Environment to closely examine their accounts. Councillors who voted to defy the Government became personally liable for the overspending involved and could be discharged from office. The rate they set would become illegal. The Act, finally, invested the Secretary of State for the Environment with certain reserve powers.

Traditional Conservatives viewed these measures with anxiety and expressed concern for the independence of local government. However, the knowledge that controls would apply largely to high-spending Labour councils meant that most Conservative MPs supported the Government. Only thirteen, including the former prime minister Edward

Heath, voted against the Bill in January 1984, although another twenty abstained.

Much greater passions were aroused by the 1984 Bill to abolish the Greater London Council (GLC) and the Metropolitan Counties. This was less because of the intention to transfer services such as fire, police, transport and planning from these authorities to new, non-elected 'joint boards' created from other councils and boroughs, than on account of the Government's plan to abolish the elections for the metropolitan counties and the GLC that were due to be held in May 1985, and to transfer their powers to 'transitional authorities' for the last eleven months of their existence. In London this would have led to the GLC coming under Conservative control without any local ballot. Hence the outrage felt by many politicians, including Conservative ones. According to Heath it laid the party 'open to the charge of the greatest gerrymandering in the last 150 years of British history'. He was once again to lead a backbench revolt on the issue, this time securing nineteen followers, yet it was the opposition of the House of Lords that was to force the Government to compromise. As a result, the existing councillors of the metropolitan counties and the GLC were allowed to remain in office until their authorities were finally abolished on 1 April 1986.

The politics of abolishing these local authorities made the Government highly unpopular. In London, for example, the GLC waged a highly successful and very expensive campaign to persuade the public that the policy was wrong. Opinion polls as a result showed consistent majorities against the Government. Why then did it persist in its aim? The answer was that the antics of the left (New, Hard, or Militant) hardly gave it any choice.

The original reaction of the left to the Government's rate-capping policy had been one of 'non-compliance'. The Labour Party's local government conference at Sheffield in 1984 supported this line (i.e. setting no rates at all), which was subsequently approved by the party's National Executive Committee. In February 1985, however, Kinnock had warned Labour councillors in Birmingham: 'We don't want to weaken the broad coalition by wrangles over legality or public dramas or exciting excursions. Our basic concern is – and must remain – jobs, services and democracy.' It was after this that many of the rate-capped local authorities stepped back from the brink of defying the law and began to experiment with 'creative accounting'.

Not all councils, however, were prepared to take Kinnock's advice. In many areas, particularly run-down inner-city ones where local Labour parties had grown moribund, new far-left middle-class elements had taken control. Disillusioned by the records of the Wilson and Callaghan governments (whose leaders soon became non-persons inside the party as a whole), these new members made their constituencies arenas for a new type of politics attuned to all sorts of interest groups – women, blacks, lesbians, gays, tenants, peace groups, etc. They also opened up local government to one another, with activists from one area being hired as council employees by another. In Peter Jenkins' words: 'A jobs-for-the-boys system grew up: people who were in reality professional politicians obtained for themselves well-paid part-time positions, or sinecures, with neighbouring authorities. In the London borough of Camden, 48 per cent of Labour councillors were dependent directly or indirectly on other councils for their livings, in Lewisham 55 per cent. Others were employed by unions representing council workers or council-funded voluntary groups.' They were to be found particularly in the council chambers of Islington, Haringey, Brent, Lambeth, the Greater London Council and Sheffield. And they were not at all keen to take Kinnock's advice. On the contrary, in the words of David Blunkett, the Labour leader in Sheffield, they wanted to see 'the local state used as an example of what we could do as a socialist government at national level'. That they might succeed in this respect was to become Neil Kinnock's greatest nightmare. For thanks largely to Ken Livingstone and his London allies, municipal socialism was soon to be identified with the 'Loony Left'.

Livingstone had come to national prominence in May 1981, when, almost immediately after Labour's take-over of the GLC, he had ousted Andrew McIntosh, the moderate party leader there, in a left-wing coup. He had joined the Labour Party in 1968, become a Lambeth councillor in 1971 and from 1973 had also sat on the GLC. A known left-wing organizer (with a reputation as an opportunist), he had helped build up a London-wide caucus around the far-left newspaper *London Labour Briefing* after 1979. Hence the power base from which he could organize his coup. Two factors now boosted his career. The first was that the GLC had very little to do apart from providing public transport. On the other hand it had plenty of rate revenue and a fairly free hand with which to spend it. Livingstone as a result could turn the GLC into a propaganda centre for all the policies of the New Left. The second factor was the press. It made Livingstone into a national figure by reporting everything he said and did. All his remarks disparaging the royal family, supporting blacks and gays, apologizing for the IRA, were grist to its mill. And all publicity as far as he was concerned was good publicity. If the funny little man with the nasal whine who collected newts was at first dubbed 'the most odious man in Britain', he soon became the darling of the tabloids. They grew to need him as much as he needed them.

Politically, once the House of Lords frustrated his transport policy ('Fares Fair'), he found that he had nothing much to do save give away money and lend vocal support to causes such as CND and the IRA. Spending money became his personal contribution to the defeat of monetarism, and while he was in power in County Hall almost £9 billion were spent. This amounted to an increase of 170 per cent in GLC spending at a time when inflation had increased by only 29 per cent. The recipients of a small part of this were a 'rainbow coalition' of blacks, feminists, gays, Irish, homeless, one-parent families, peace campaigners and others who made up the 'ersatz proletariat' of the 'Loony Left'. Altogether, however, £42 million was handed out in 1983–4, £47 million in 1984–5. Then, during the last two years of its existence, £10 million alone was spent by the GLC on propaganda to save its own skin. It even spent £250,000 on its farewell party, which included the most expensive firework display ever seen in London. Yet, astonishingly enough, by the end of a slick propaganda campaign, 'Red Ken' had become something of a folk hero. In the words of one of Britain's leading political commentators, he had actually 'conned Londoners that he and the GLC had been "running" London'.

Livingstone's erstwhile personal popularity, on the other hand, did not extend to the other Labour councillors who formed part of the 'Loony Left' and who were reinforced by Labour's victory in the London borough elections of May 1986, which took place just after the GLC had expired. They continued to generate the sort of headlines which had established their reputation in the first place. Haringey for example would purchase only Nicaraguan coffee; Hackney ended town-twinning arrangements with France, West Germany and Israel and replaced them with ties to the Soviet Union, East Germany and Nicaragua; Hackney staged an Open Day for gays and lesbians; Lambeth banned the use of the word 'family' from council literature as 'discriminatory';

Haringey introduced courses on homosexuality into primary and even nursery schools; the Inner London Education Authority (ILEA) allowed one school to introduce 'non-competitive sports' and put together a teaching package called 'Auschwitz: Yesterday's Racism' that compared Hitler's policies with Mrs Thatcher's trade union reforms; Brent employed ninety new officers to eradicate racism from schools; Lambeth barred the police from all council facilities; Lewisham voted £64,000 for complaints against the police; while in Hackney a pistol was fired as representatives of Sinn Fein (the political wing of the IRA) addressed the local council. All this may have amused rather than alarmed some commentators, but to quote Peter Jenkins once again: '. . . the word "loony" did not do justice to the sinister nature of some of them. Parents were appalled at the idea of their children being instructed in homosexuality. They were outraged by some of the political propaganda that passed for teaching. Workers employed by some of the councils were reported by informers for making "racist" jokes or remarks and were disciplined or sacked. In some cases their unions refused to represent them. Life-long supporters of the Labour Party were alienated and lost in these ways.'

If the 'London effect' were not bad enough, Labour also had to suffer the headlines generated in Liverpool, where the local Labour Party had been taken over by the Militant Tendency. This was the cover name for the Revolutionary Socialist League, which was itself a Trotskyite splinter group from the internationalist communist movement. It was run on strict Leninist lines and employed more full-time organizers than Labour. By the 1970s it had adopted a strategy of 'entryism' into Labour, a strategy that had become so effective by the middle of the decade that it had been investigated by the Labour Party's national agent, Reg Underhill. His 1975 report, however, which concluded that Militant was operating as a party within the party in defiance of Labour's rules, was not acted on by Labour's left-controlled National Executive Committee (NEC). Not until 1983 was action taken, when, after a new investigation, Michael Foot managed to get the NEC to expel the five members of *Militant*'s editorial board – in fact the key members of its central committee – from the Labour Party. But this was merely a gesture. Militant Tendency now had more than 8,000 members, two of whom, Terry Fields and Dave Nellist, actually became Labour MPs in June 1983. Even before then, with Labour's victory in the May

1983 local elections in Liverpool (its first there for a decade), Militant had been able to establish control of a city council.

Only sixteen out of Labour's sixty-one councillors in Liverpool were actually Militant members, but their efficient organization placed them in a dominant position. The Labour council leader was John Hamilton, but real direction came from his flashy, flamboyant deputy, Derek Hatton, an ex-fireman who had become a community worker and was employed by a neighbouring Labour council on £10,000 a year for a 17-hour week. In his own account of his experiences in the Labour Party, appropriately entitled *Inside Left*, Hatton described Hamilton as a 'nowhere man' and wrote that 'He often reminded me of Mr Magoo, the cartoon character, bumbling his way through life like a genial uncle.' There was nothing genial about Hatton, on the other hand. He now admitted that he had been a member of Militant all along: 'From the moment I joined in, it was a total commitment. I lived and breathed Militant.' And Militant, he explained, controlled the council: '. . . it controlled the machine . . . what the Labour group said didn't make a blind bit of difference.' He added: 'People have accused me of handing out jobs to the boys. Of course we did. We wanted people around us who understood the plan, who were committed to it.' Opponents of Militant inside the local party or administration were therefore ruthlessly removed: 'like any organization worth its salt who finds opponents in its ranks, we soon sorted them out. We shunted them sideways.'

Like the GLC, Liverpool demonstrated its opposition to Government policy by increasing its budget. On taking office, it increased its Liberal predecessor's planned expenditure of £218 million by £34 million, cancelled 1,200 projected redundancies and created a further 1,000 posts. Sympathetic unions were allowed to nominate candidates for half the new jobs. A five-year urban regeneration strategy was set in motion to remedy the city's chronic housing problem. These policies had broad support from Labour councillors, but it was clear that Militant intended to use Liverpool as a testing ground for revolutionary politics through open defiance of the Government.

A clash over spending seemed inevitable in the run-up to the 1984–5 budget. Militant set about mobilizing Liverpool and preparing the workforce for a general strike to strengthen the council's bargaining position. In March 1984 the council threatened 5,000 redundancies, a 17 per cent rate rise or a deficit budget, if the Government failed to provide adequate finance. Opinion polls showed the council to have considerable local sympathy, and in the May 1984 local elections Labour gained a further seven seats. The council now entered into protracted negotiations with an alarmed Environment Secretary, Patrick Jenkin, amidst threats of bankruptcy if finance were not forthcoming. In the end Hatton claimed to have wrested over £50 million from the Government and, though the figures were disputed, Militant gained an undeniable propaganda victory. *The Times* reported: 'Today in Liverpool municipal militancy is vindicated.' Not only the Government was embarrassed (Jenkin's political career was ruined), but so too was Neil Kinnock, who had persistently argued against confrontational tactics in local government. At the 1984 Labour Party Conference, Militant, despite its shaky constitutional position, was triumphant. Encouraged by Liverpool's apparent achievement, delegates voted to support councils illegally defying the Government's ratecapping legislation.

In Liverpool itself, however, Militant's political style was beginning to alienate crucial sections of the community, whose support the council would depend upon in further clashes with the Government. In October 1984 the white collar union NALGO entered into a long-running dispute over the appointment of a Militant member as Principal Race Relations Officer. This had a wider impact on council relations with black leaders. Militant's centralized politics also led to conflict with Liverpool voluntary organizations and housing associations. It was accused of staffing the council's Static Security Force with its own supporters and using it to intimidate opponents at Labour Party meetings. Then, in June 1985, Liverpool Council set a 9 per cent rate, effectively making its budget for the year illegal. However, with the loss of two Labour seats in council by-elections, Militant's position weakened, despite the Tendency's hopes of creating a 'revolutionary situation'. Finally, council leaders blundered into a tactical mistake in September 1985 that undermined trade union support and gave Kinnock the opportunity he had been waiting for to denounce Militant's politics. Council officers advised that Liverpool would be unable to pay its workforce at the end of the year, so Militant decided to issue 31,000 90-day redundancy notices and use the ensuing period to mobilize the city for resistance. When NALGO and the teachers' union refused to accept the notices, council shop stewards toured the city in thirty taxis to deliver them.

Kinnock now condemned Militant's rigidly confrontational tactics at the Labour Party Conference on 1 October, attacking what he called 'the grotesque chaos of a Labour council hiring taxis to scuttle round the city handing round redundancy notices to its own workers'. Hatton, sitting in the hall, interrupted him with shouts of 'liar', while Merseyside MP Eric Heffer stormed off the platform. The dividend came for Kinnock, however, in improved opinion-poll ratings after his speech.

Militant's moment of triumph was over. On 22 November Liverpool council was forced to turn to Swiss banks for a £30 million credit to balance its books and was forced to make cuts in education and social services. This provoked a backlash among non-Militant members of the Labour group, and Labour's National Executive suspended the District Labour Party on 27 November, Kinnock having described Militant as 'a maggot in the body of the party'. Then, at the end of a legal battle lasting a year, Liverpool's Labour councillors were surcharged and disqualified from holding public office for their delay in setting a rate. By the 1986 Labour Party conference Hatton and a number of his Militant colleagues in Liverpool had been expelled from the party. Paradoxically, however, Labour's two Militant MPs survived to be returned with increased majorities in Liverpool Broadgreen (Terry Fields) and Coventry South East (Dave Nellist) at the 1987 general election. They were to be joined in Parliament by two more members of the Tendency within the party, Pat Wall (Bradford North) and Ronnie Campbell (Blyth Valley). Finally, Militant was able to retain considerable influence in certain trade unions.

As far as local government was concerned, however, the tide had been turned. 'Loony Left' authorities had already retreated from extreme positions despite Liverpool's challenge to Conservative policies. Thus although sixteen rate-capped Labour councils – led by Margaret Hodge of Islington, David Blunkett of Sheffield and Ken Livingstone of the GLC – had at first illegally refused to set a rate, hoping to provoke a crisis from which the Government would retreat, most backed away from a final confrontation and adopted a legal budget. On 10 March 1985 the GLC led the way and most of the others followed suit. Livingstone thus revived his reputation for opportunism, leaving only the far-left leader of Lambeth council, Ted Knight, and his colleagues to join Hatton and the Liverpool councillors before the courts. They were all duly surcharged and disqualified from holding political office for five years.

The 'Loony Left' succeeded in squandering for Labour a good deal of the sympathy which was originally felt for areas whose genuine social problems – high unemployment, inadequate housing, the social pressures created by large numbers of the elderly, single-parent families and blacks – required high levels of public spending. Jobs-for-the-boys networks, well-founded accusations of inefficiency from the Audit Commission, 'loony' decisions, real or alleged – and the tabloid press was ever fertile in inventing 'loony' stories – all these factors served regularly to divert attention from the truly serious problems facing inner-city areas and populations.

The story of the Government's clash with the local authorities, however, was still far from over. In 1985 a rating revaluation took place in Scotland, with the inevitable result that householders and businessmen who found themselves paying more protested by voting against the Government. The Prime Minister, reacting under pressure, promised to abolish domestic rates in Scotland. She had been promising to abolish these throughout the United Kingdom since 1974, but the 1981 Green Paper on the subject, 'Alternatives to Domestic Rates', had, in spite of its title, been quite unable to point to any better method of raising local government finance. Now, government ministers were forced to think again. The usual alternatives were re-examined, albeit without any enthusiasm. Local income tax was unacceptable because, in the words of one expert, 'the Government . . . did not want to hand such a buoyant tax to local authorities at just the time that the rate of tax was being reduced . . .' The Treasury in any case wished to keep full control of income tax as part of its general management of the economy. The Prime Minister herself was supposed to be in favour of a local sales tax. Yet two objections ruled it out: in the first place, it would be too easy for people in high-tax authorities to cross local boundaries in order to shop in low-tax ones; secondly, there was the danger that such a tax might infringe European Community regulations. Thus, with rates, local income tax and local sales tax all ruled out, and with no other obvious alternative under consideration, a group of ministers (including, crucially, Kenneth Baker at Environment) opted, in the Spring of 1985, for the poll tax. This had always been rejected previously, but now it was made to fit the bill.

The system was outlined in a Green Paper in January 1986. It was to be introduced into Scotland in 1988–9 and into the rest of the United

Kingdom the following year. From then on domestic rates would be abolished; the 'community charge', as the poll tax was officially designated, would be paid by all adults over the age of 18; and everyone under the same local authority would pay the same amount. The aim was to provide an incentive for citizens to vote against high-spending local councils. Most money for local finance would continue to come from the government in the form of central grants, which would vary according to the needs of individual authorities, while businesses would be taxed by a uniform national business rate on newly revalued properties. Local authorities would collect this money for the government, which would recycle the national total to councils as a flat-rate amount.

The poll tax would, according to the Government, enhance individual responsibility, encourage local accountability and provide a fairer system of financing local government. The Opposition damned it as regressive, complaining that rich and poor would pay the same. The counter-argument employed here was that since those most in need would receive rebates (up to 80 per cent as it turned out), and since most of the money for local finance would continue to come from the Exchequer, the rich would in fact be paying up to sixteen times more than the poor. However, since there were bound to be more losers than winners, this argument failed to carry much weight. The prospect, therefore, of larger numbers of rich and poor alike paying the same (and in most cases, higher) tax to the same local authority was not to prove popular. On the contrary, its introduction in England and Wales in 1990 was to shake Mrs Thatcher's third government to its very foundations.

THATCHER UNDER CHALLENGE

By her second administration, Mrs Thatcher had largely overcome the challenge from her party's 'wets', most of whose leading representatives had been removed from government by 1983. Francis Pym joined these, as has been seen, immediately following her second election victory, while James Prior, who had surprisingly but reluctantly accepted the post of Northern Ireland Secretary in 1983, decided in September 1984 to renounce not merely his political exile in Belfast, but any further active part in politics. He chose instead to become chairman of the electrical giant GEC. His resignation allowed the Prime Minister to reshuffle her cabinet once more and to bring in a fervent supporter of her free-market approach to economics, David Young, since 1982 the Chairman of the Manpower Services Commission. The latter was given a peerage and as Lord Young became an unpaid minister without portfolio in charge of small businesses, deregulation and job creation, replacing Lord Cockfield, who had left to become one of Britain's two members of the European Commission in Brussels.

The Government, at this time, seemed to be retaining its popularity. The miners' strike was being firmly dealt with, while public opinion was outraged by the attempt of the IRA to murder Mrs Thatcher and her colleagues at the Conservative Party's annual conference at Brighton in October 1984. A bomb, timed to explode when guests were asleep, had been planted weeks before in the Grand Hotel by a member of the Provisional IRA, Patrick Magee, and now claimed the lives of five Conservatives, including the wife of the party's Chief Whip, John Wakeham. It severely paralysed the wife of Norman Tebbit, Secretary of State for Trade and Industry, and left the latter severely injured. Mrs Thatcher herself narrowly escaped death, but on the day after the tragedy none the less delivered her annual speech to the party faithful, vowing that there would be no surrender to terrorism. Her defiance was magnificent and was echoed by public opinion.

By the following spring, however, the Government's popularity had declined as a result of more 'banana skin' episodes. The Ponting affair came in January 1985, but even before then, Sir Keith Joseph, the Education Secretary, had had to beat an undignified retreat when ninety-three Tory MPs denounced his proposals to make better-off parents contribute more towards the costs of their children's education. This was a vested interest that Thatcherism did not yet have the courage to challenge. Still more discontent was engendered in 1985 concerning the review of social services to be carried out by Norman Fowler, the Secretary of State concerned. This, in fact, would not amount to very much (it would propose spending cuts of only £750 million out of a social welfare budget of £36 billion) and would offer no support for radical reforms; yet its inauguration, with hints of the abolition of SERPS (the state earnings related pension scheme) and greater selectivity in welfare benefits, helped reanimate the Tory wets and encouraged them to organize.

Mrs Thatcher's leading critic on the Tory back benches, of course, remained Edward Heath. He attacked on nearly all fronts and led parliamentary revolts over local government legislation. His rebellions, however, were predictable and counter-productive. According to one Tory whip: 'more backbenchers were inclined to support the Government if Heath was rebelling.' Heath, in fact, was considered not only a bad loser but a hypocrite. In Patrick Jenkin's words: 'I do not deny that Mr Heath felt strongly about rate-capping and GLC abolition. What stuck in my gullet was his accusing us of taking powers that had only ever been taken in wartime. William Waldegrave pointed out that it was Mr Heath who had sought to control by law every wage and price in the country.'

In April 1985, Heath, together with other Tory wets, including Sir Ian Gilmour and Francis Pym, joined the all-party 'Employment Institute' set up by LSE professor Richard Layard to encourage state action on employment. A Keynesian think-tank financed by the Rowntree Memorial Trust and designed to produce alternative economic strategies to the Government's, the Institute issued a 'Charter for Jobs', which drew attention to the still rising unemployment in the country. Then, after disappointing local election results in May 1985, Pym himself established an all-party pressure-group entitled 'Centre Forward', which he launched with a strong speech in Oxford attacking Mrs Thatcher's style of government. In his memoirs, he claimed to have been pursuing 'the politics of consent', advocating 'more public investment in the public sector ... and the development of an effective regional policy'. He claimed to be a loyal Tory, but his group failed to make any impact after its launch, precisely because it was felt to be acting disloyally. One backbench wet declared: 'It failed to have any attraction for me once it was suggested it would act together as if whipped in concert.' Six members actually left the group after Pym's initial speech; in any case it failed to publish its membership list of MPs and thus lacked credibility. Mrs Thatcher, for her part, made fun of her 'fair-weather friends' and confirmed that she would not be diverted from her own priorities. Pym himself soon seemed to lose interest in the group and retired from parliament at the 1987 election. None the less, many Tory MPs were genuinely anxious about the apparent lack of success of the Government's economic policy. Pym's group was only one testimony to this, as was the establishment of yet another body, CARE (Conservative Action for Revival of Employment), set up at almost the same time by another ex-minister, Jim Lestor. This called for a £2–3 billion reflationary package to be spent on education, training and the national infrastructure. Nor did the result of the Brecon and Radnor by-election in July 1985 stiffen Conservative resolve on the backbenches. The Liberals took the seat after a 20 per cent slump in the Tory vote.

Mrs Thatcher's response to growing Tory jitters was a cabinet reshuffle in September 1985. Out went Peter Rees as Chief Secretary to the Treasury; out went John Gummer; and out went the unfortunate Patrick Jenkin. In came John MacGregor, Norman Tebbit and Kenneth Baker to replace them. Baker and MacGregor were once close colleagues of Edward Heath (the former had been his parliamentary private secretary, the latter, head of his private office), but both had made a reputation for themselves during the Thatcher years. Baker in particular had been an enthusiastic Minister for New Technology and, as Jenkin's deputy at Environment, had displayed a flair for media management that his chief had sorely lacked. Joining him now at Environment was William Waldegrave, whose task was to look after 'green' issues. Other changes included Leon Brittan's move to Trade and Industry, Douglas Hurd's promotion to Home Secretary, Tom King's relegation to Northern Ireland and Lord Young's appointment as Secretary of State for Employment, assisted in the Commons by the Postmaster-General, Kenneth Clarke. Clearly, the Prime Minister was now concentrating her forces to be able to win the next general election. Lord Young had the task of ensuring that the unemployment figures came down; Baker had the job of presenting a more acceptable television image; while Tebbit, whose instinct for the political jugular was legendary, had the job, as Party Chairman, of preparing the Conservative Party for battle. He was given as deputy, however, the former MP turned best-selling author Jeffrey Archer, a somewhat strange choice considering his limited political skills. Finally, the monetarist expert Professor Brian Griffiths replaced the young John Redwood as head of the Prime Minister's Policy Unit.

The political dividends expected from these changes did not occur immediately. Ministerial talk of increased expenditure on projects such as the Channel Tunnel, new hospitals and railway electrification also failed to produce returns. Instead, September and October 1985 witnessed urban riots in Handsworth, Brixton and Tottenham, where an unfortunate policeman suffered death by near-decapitation. His horrific murder plus the involvement of criminal elements in the riots meant that these were analysed less sympathetically by commentators than those of 1981. Once again, however, the issue of race was not confronted. Yet it was not the recurrence of urban violence – however serious – but a different, if equally unexpected, series of events that was to bring Mrs Thatcher's reputation to its lowest ebb so far – the so-called 'Westland Affair' of January 1986.

The Westland Affair was the most serious domestic political crisis faced by Mrs Thatcher during her premiership. It led to the resignation of two of her cabinet ministers and the threatened resignation of her Law Officers; it undermined her personal reputation for integrity; and it threatened her leadership of the Conservative Party. One MP recalled: 'Westland was very shaky for the Government. I felt the PM could have fallen. On the big occasion Kinnock blew the debate with a poor speech and from that moment support began to rally for the PM. Westland was a hothouse issue and the sincerity of the PM was at stake. There has always been a feeling that she was honest and straight and this was put at issue.' Mrs Thatcher herself confessed: 'It was a kind of period we hope never to go through again.'

The crisis revolved, at least superficially, around the fortunes of a financially troubled helicopter manufacturing company, Westland, which was badly in need of new funds if it were to escape bankruptcy. The Government preferred a private-sector rescue to investing in the company itself. The most likely private source of funds was an American company, Sikorsky, with whom Westland had done business in the past, and negotiations were conducted between the two firms during 1985. The Defence Secretary, Michael Heseltine, on the other hand, wished to find a 'European' solution to the problem and attempted to create a European helicopter consortium in which Westland could take part. His initial efforts won cabinet approval, but by December 1985 both the Prime Minister and the Trade and Industry Secretary, Leon Brittan, were having doubts about the nature of the rescue package. They feared it would be too vague, too protectionist, and too anti-American. It might even frighten off Sikorsky without producing the necessary funds in time to save Westland. Heseltine believed that the Sikorsky bid would reduce Westland's future to producing frames for a helicopter that no one in Europe, save a partisan British Government, would want to buy.

The crunch came during a meeting of the Economic Strategy Committee of the Cabinet on 9 December 1985, which was chaired by Mrs Thatcher. The Westland chairman, Sir John Cuckney, was present along with his financial adviser, both of whom were firmly in favour of the Sikorsky bid. The committee was split, and Mrs Thatcher at one point said that it would be necessary to meet the following Friday to discuss the matter further. She did not, however, repeat this statement in her summing up, and Brittan assumed that no meeting was planned. Heseltine assumed the opposite and was furious to discover on 11 December that Mrs Thatcher's view accorded with Brittan's. He consequently raised the issue at the regular cabinet meeting the following day but was ruled out of order by the Prime Minister, since the question was not on the cabinet's agenda. His intervention on the matter was not even recorded in the cabinet minutes. Altogether it was a bad week for the Defence Secretary, for on 14 December, the Westland board came out in favour of the Sikorsky offer.

Heseltine, however, was not to accept the prospect of defeat with equanimity. Instead, he inaugurated a public campaign in favour of the 'European' bid, winning the support of both the Tory backbench defence committee and the Commons' all-party Defence Select Committee. The Prime Minister and Brittan responded by doing everything possible behind the scenes to influence the Westland shareholders to accept the Sikorsky bid. In retrospect, there is little doubt that the Prime Minister should simply have sacked Heseltine. He was, after all, going public on an issue which was bound to embarrass the Government. Yet in her own words afterwards, she chose not to do so because everyone would have accused her of acting like a 'bossy-boots', that is, of acting too autocratically. Instead, she and Brittan put pressure on Heseltine's allies to desert him – Sir Raymond Lygo, the chairman of British Aerospace, for example, was warned by Brittan that he was endangering the national interest – while, almost fatally as it was to turn out, the Solicitor General, Sir Patrick Mayhew, was prompted by Mrs Thatcher to write to Heseltine informing him that he had got certain issues wrong. It was this letter, parts of which were leaked to the press, that almost brought about the downfall of the Prime Minister.

The political crisis blew up on 9 January 1986, when at a meeting of the full cabinet, Heseltine was asked to agree that all future statements on Westland should first be cleared with the Cabinet Office. His response was dramatic. Collecting his papers, he swept out of the room, protesting that he refused to submit to such 'gagging'. He told Mrs Thatcher: 'If you are insisting, then I can no longer remain a member of your Cabinet.' Not all his colleagues appear to have been aware of what was happening. Some thought he had just gone to the toilet. No one seems to have imagined that he had actually resigned. One cabinet colleague recalled:

There was no vote in Cabinet over Westland. Heseltine said that he could not accept that statements had to be submitted for approval on government policy. She [Mrs Thatcher] said, 'I am very sorry, let's order some coffee, complete the item and have a break.' Heseltine walked out and when I left the meeting, was giving his press conference.

It was at that press conference that Heseltine complained that he had not been able to raise the Westland case in full cabinet. He concluded that there had been 'a breakdown of constitutional government' and said of the Prime Minister's conduct that it was 'not a proper way to carry on government and ultimately not an approach for which I can share responsibility'.

Following Heseltine's resignation, all the wets indulged in their usual complaints about Mrs Thatcher's allegedly autocratic style of government. The press was also full of leaks about the Westland affair, and emergency debates were held in the House of Commons. The result was that the Government was forced to concede an internal inquiry into the leaking of Sir Patrick Mayhew's letter and to agree that the matter should be investigated by the Defence and Trade and Industry Select Committees of the House of Commons. On 24 January, after much criticism of his role in the affair – especially with regard to the leaking of the letter for which he chose to carry the responsibility – Leon Brittan resigned. His resignation exposed Mrs Thatcher herself to serious attack when she faced the Commons for the crucial debate only three days later. She told the House, however, that she had been unaware of the decision to leak the letter, which had been done by civil servants in Brittan's department, on the false assumption that they had obtained the permission of 10 Downing Street. Her speech was a strong one, although not everyone believed it. In any case she was helped both by the failure of the Labour leader, Neil Kinnock, to impress the House (Tory MPs barracked him thoughout his speech) and by a statement from Heseltine that actually offered her support. The Conservative Chief Whip, John Wakeham, had clearly been working overtime.

Officially, the House of Commons debate was not the end of the affair. Both Select Committees continued their investigations, but the Prime Minister's Office blocked their efforts to call key civil servants as witnesses. The Defence Select Committee issued a highly critical report but its verdict on the Prime Minister's conduct, inevitably, had to be an open one. Despite that, however, Mrs Thatcher's reputation had suffered a body blow. Her honesty had been impugned and her reputation as an autocrat, despite her reluctance to sack Heseltine, had been enhanced. Not everybody, on the other hand, believed that the leak should have been treated so seriously in the first place. There was, it must be confessed, a great deal of pomposity and hypocrisy invested in it. According to one commentator, the affair, 'taken in a broader perspective, raised immediate questions about the Government's *laissez-faire* approach to industrial matters and its readiness to allow the transfer of ownership to foreign buyers'. In fact, almost the opposite was true. In Charles Moore's assessment:

Westland was used in tawdry arguments about patriotism and as a means of countering anti-Americanism. Heseltine made it the occasion for his agreement with the armaments directors of Britain, France, West Germany and Italy on a new European helicopter policy. Prestige, diplomacy, votes – everything mattered except, it seems, whether Westland could be a well-run, profitable enterprise.

Mrs Thatcher, according to Moore, was just as bad. Her government lost £40 million on a loan to the company to build a certain type of helicopter, on which she then invested a huge diplomatic effort persuading the Indians to buy. The helicopter in fact was inappropriate for India, but the Prime Minister believed that she was 'batting for Britain' in lending the company her support. Moore sadly concluded: 'Westland provides a classic Thatcherite critique of interventionist policies, but here it was the Thatcher government that did the intervening.' The true issues that Westland raised, therefore, concerned less the autocracy of the Prime Minister or her allegedly *laissez-faire* policies, but relations between politicians and civil servants and the powers of select committees to investigate government actions. US congressional committees, for example, could simply not have been blocked in the way in which those of the House of Commons were by executive action over Westland.

The loss of both Brittan and Heseltine meant that the Prime Minister had to reshuffle her cabinet once again. The result was that the Scottish Secretary, George Younger, was promoted to Defence, with Malcolm Rifkind, formerly a minister at the Foreign Office, being promoted to the cabinet to take charge at St Andrew's House. Paul Channon, Brittan's deputy at Trade and Industry, replaced his former boss as Secretary of State. All of these men were regarded as Tory moderates, and their promotion was taken to mean that Mrs Thatcher would from now on have to watch her step. Inside the cabinet, it was said, a more collective regime would be the order of the day. Whether this was true still remained to be seen. On the other hand, it was certainly the case that from now on the Prime Minister would have to keep a close eye on the backbenches. For to be found there was now the dashing figure of Michael Heseltine, the only Tory to have had the courage (or more likely the impulse) to quit her cabinet, and a man who was both a first-rate public speaker and television performer. He was also a darling of the Tory Party conferences and someone, therefore, who had the potential to replace her as party leader. No doubt he would make a bid to do so one day. The only question that remained was when.

ECONOMIC POLICY

The economic policy priorities of the second Thatcher government were in theory fairly predictable: monetary rectitude, reduced public borrowing, reduced taxes, more privatization, and a fall in unemployment. Whether these aims were practicable, however, remained to be seen. The Government, for its part, could begin its new term of office on a high note. In Sarah Hogg's words:

[Sir Geoffrey Howe] departed at a rare peaceful moment. The slump was over, if growth was still slow. The 'miracle' was under way: manufacturing productivity had jumped $12\frac{1}{2}$ per cent in the past year. There was a £4 billion current account surplus on the balance of payments that year. Inflation was a mere 3 per cent. The money numbers had come in on target in 1982–3 – so remarkable an event that a graphical record of it was presented to the Foreign Office-bound Chancellor as a keepsake.

Sir Geoffrey's successor as Chancellor was Nigel Lawson, who was to retain that post until 1989. By 1988 he had managed to build up his reputation to the point where many commentators considered him the greatest Chancellor since the War. He was also said to be arrogant, brilliant and lucky, and certainly it was not until 1988 that his luck ran out. He returned to the Treasury in 1983 with the formidable reputation of having been the main architect of the Medium Term Financial Strategy – devised when he had been Financial Secretary – and obviously liked to be thought of as an innovator. In his 1984 Mais Lecture, for example, he assigned 'microeconomic (or supply side)' policies the job of promoting conditions favourable to growth and employment and 'macroeconomic policy' (what others would call demand management) the task of suppressing inflation. In Samuel Brittan's words: 'This reversal was old hat, if still controversial, to those who had been following the international debate, but the British economic establishment seems to have an endless economic capacity for astonishment, as its reaction to the Mais Lecture showed.' Lawson, in fact, liked to shock, especially the orthodox. It was an essential part of his character. Yet this abrasive, arrogant side of his nature was unlikely to appeal to others. In the words of yet another financial journalist: 'His party colleagues admired his talents and his command of finance and economics, but they found it difficult to like him. Lawson was a man of ideas with a short attention span. He was, if anything, too clever for his own good.'

His first act as Chancellor was to introduce a £500 million emergency package of 'cuts' in July 1983. These affected defence, employment, health, education and transport but were in fact only limits on the rate of growth of public spending. They had to be made to assure the City that the Government's commitment to a tight monetary policy, as outlined in the Queen's speech, would be adhered to. Moreover, there was little hope of implementing any tax cuts unless public spending remained under control. The November 1983 Public Expenditure statement therefore announced the intention of holding public spending at the 1983 White Paper level of £126·4 billion. The prospect of actually cutting it was implicitly abandoned. The February 1984 White Paper announced that spending would remain broadly unchanged until 1986–7, thus allowing for tax cuts provided that economic growth was sustained. In fact, spending was expected to rise to £136·7 billion by 1987, but this would represent a fall from 43 to 40 per cent of GDP, just below the level the Government had inherited in 1979. Lawson, therefore, gave the impression he meant business.

His 1984 budget turned out to be much more radical than anyone had expected. Any reduction in income tax was postponed until the following year, but within the confines of a broadly neutral budget, the tax burden was re-distributed by increasing the basic income-tax threshold by 12·5 per cent, 7 per cent more than the rate of inflation. 850,000 of the lowest paid were removed from the tax net by this step, which was financed by extending VAT to building alterations and hot take-away food and by raising excise duties on drink, tobacco, petrol and vehicle licences. The surcharge on substantial investment incomes was abolished and the stamp duty on share deals and home sales was reduced.

The budget also set out to cut the PSBR (public sector borrowing requirement) substantially from the outcome of £9·7 billion in 1983–4 to £7 billion or an expected 2·25 per cent of GDP for 1984–5. The Treasury, in fact, wanted to contain the PSBR at that level for the next four years and to reduce the ratio to GDP from 3·25 per cent in 1983–4 to 1·75 per cent in 1988–9. But given the costs incurred by the miners' strike, the totals for the next two years increased, the figure for 1984–5 exceeding £10 billion or just over 3 per cent of GDP.

The most significant aspect of the 1984 budget, however, was the reform of corporation tax, the original aim of which had been to produce faster investment and higher growth. By 1984 it was open to criticism on a number of grounds. In particular it encouraged wasteful investment with a low rate of return, while, together with the high taxes imposed on labour through the National Insurance contribution and the National Insurance surcharge, it contributed to rising unemployment by substituting capital for labour. Lawson therefore reduced the first-year allowances on plant and machinery from the existing 100 per cent to 25 per cent by 1986 (Enterprise Zones were excluded) and reduced the corporate tax rate from 50 per cent in 1983 to 35 per cent in 1986. The National Insurance surcharge was also reduced.

The move from direct to indirect taxation and the reduction of corporation tax meant, in Martin Holmes's words, that the 1984 budget was 'the most Thatcherite hitherto'. Yet, to quote Holmes again, 'it was still the case after the budget that 9p off the standard rate of income tax would have been required to reduce the tax burden for a couple on average earnings to its 1978–9 level. Tax cuts, therefore, continued to be a high priority for the Chancellor.'

Between 1984 and 1985, as has been seen, not only did the PSBR have to rise but Lawson faced a mini sterling crisis when, in January 1985, the pound fell to almost parity level with the dollar. On 29 January, however, interest rates were increased by 2 per cent, with the result that by budget day the pound was appreciating rapidly. The 1985 budget itself was conspicuous for its emphasis on job promotion. At the fiscal level employers' and employees' National Insurance contributions for lowest-paid workers were cut from 9 per cent to a range of 5–7 per cent, whilst the upper earnings limit on employers' contribution was abolished (i.e., after a certain level the implicit payroll tax became a proportional one). It was expected that as a result of these changes firms would save £900 million on the 8·5 million people employed at less than £130 per week. Basic income-tax thresholds were likewise raised by 10 per cent, or twice the rate of inflation, thus substantially reducing average tax rates on low pay. Other measures included the expansion of Youth Training Schemes and community programmes, the review of Wages Councils and unfair dismissal laws (both of which were held to discourage employment), the inflation indexing of capital gains, 100 per cent first-year allowances for scientific research, the abolition of fifteen stamp duties, and the raising of taxes on alcohol, tobacco and motoring. At the level of macroeconomics, the PSBR target was set at £7 billion, as compared with a £10·2 billion outcome for the previous year, implying a very sharp fall in the ratio to GDP. The Government, therefore, appeared determined to put the Medium Term Financial Strategy back on course. Yet in Geoffrey Maynard's words: 'Even so, there were signs that the Government's attitude towards macroeconomic policy was shifting, in the sense that it seemed to be becoming more agnostic on the question whether monetary or fiscal policy was the key. Also in his budget statement, the Chancellor indicated that the exchange rate would assume greater significance in policy making.'

This shift in emphasis was even more apparent in 1986. For example, the Financial Statement and Budget Report stated that 'economic policy is set in a nominal framework in which public expenditure is controlled in cash terms and money GDP growth is gradually reduced by fiscal and monetary policy.' Still the PSBR outcome for 1985–6 (£5·9 billion) was well short of the 1985 target (£7 billion), which was reaffirmed for the next four years. A decline in the ratio to GDP from 2 per cent in 1985–6 to 1·5 per cent in 1989–90 was thus envisaged, something that enabled the Government to retain the credibility of its anti-inflationary stance. The budget itself was overshadowed by the rapid fall in the price of oil from roughly $30 to $10 a barrel from the beginning of the year. Since each dollar fall in price represented a loss of about £500 million in revenue to the Treasury, significant cuts in tax had once again to be postponed. Instead, Lawson contented himself with cutting the standard rate of income tax by one pence in the pound (from 30p to 29p) and by spending relatively small amounts of money on job-promotion schemes. Income tax thresholds were raised by no more than the rate of inflation and there were no more cuts in National Insurance contributions. One surprise was the introduction of Personal Equity Plans (PEPs) to encourage the purchase of shares in industry; more predictable was the expansion of the Enterprise Allowance Scheme to help people set up small businesses.

If this appeared to be rather small beer, Lawson's luck was about to turn. By the summer of 1986 economic growth was the highest in Europe at 3 per cent; Treasury revenues were buoyant, aided by higher consumer spending and thus greater VAT receipts; oil prices had begun to creep upwards; and corporation tax revenue had increased thanks to corporate profit growth and previous tax reforms. In the words of one commentator

Lawson found that the economy had entered a virtuous circle. Low inflation and low interest rates boosted economic growth. Strong growth boosted strong tax revenues, giving scope both for tax cuts and a more relaxed approach to public expenditure. Strong growth also brought with it the winning combination of rapid productivity growth *and* falling unemployment. In the first half of the 1980s it was thought that there was a trade-off between the two.

As a result of all these factors, Lawson could announce to the Commons in the autumn of 1986 an increase in public spending in the politically vulnerable areas of health and education 'without adding a penny piece to the borrowing requirement'. Most of the money was to be spent in the year 1987–8 but the extra cash amounted to £7·5 billion, with an extra £5·5 billion earmarked for 1988–9.

In the 1987 budget, income tax was cut from 29 per cent to 27 per cent and the PSBR reduced from £7 billion to £4 billion. Lawson could boast as result that he had achieved a 'hat-trick' of reduced taxes, falling public borrowing and increased social spending. The budget could also be presented as a responsible one, with income tax cuts limited to only 2 per cent in order to allow for lower borrowing and interest rates. If this was meant to pre-empt Opposition claims of government 'bribing the electors' in an election year, the tactic failed. Mr Kinnock, quite predictably, accused the Government of precisely that.

It was at this point that Nigel Lawson began to be hailed as a truly great Chancellor. Some even saw him as the man who had made monetarism work. In this respect, however, three things must be borne in mind. First, he never managed to reduce government spending or even to hold it steady; what he achieved was to reduce government spending as a proportion of a growing GDP. Second, he soon gave up all attempts to manage government policy by reference to monetary aggregates (Mo or M3), choosing to pay more attention to exchange rates and fiscal policy. Finally, however, it has to be conceded that even if fiscal and monetary policy in the later years of the Medium Term Financial Strategy was looser than the Government initially intended, it nevertheless, to quote Geoffrey Maynard, 'contained the growth of nominal (money) GDP to less than 10 per cent per annum after 1981 (average 8 per cent per annum 1982–6) as compared with almost 15 per cent per annum throughout most of the 1970s'. This was perhaps the real test. Moreover, given that the PSBR now equalled only 1 per cent of GDP, the Government could legitimately claim that it had implemented the fiscal side of its Medium Term Financial Strategy.

In overall terms, therefore, to quote Martin Holmes,

the 1983–7 economic strategy was consistent with Thatcherite ideology and, given the existing economic circumstances outside the Government's control, was as radical as could be expected. Low inflation, sustained recovery, a high growth rate, falling taxes, drastically reduced borrowing and a balance of payments surplus was an impressive record.

The failure actually to cut public spending or get rid of such anomalies, from a Thatcherite viewpoint, as mortgage interest tax relief or the over-generous tax status of the pensions industry, not to mention the inability to do anything about demand-led welfare benefits or EC subsidies for agriculture, could be defended in terms of electoral necessity. Yet if all this meant that by 1987 the economic situation was looking rather rosy for the Government, Nigel Lawson was not the only one responsible. Lord Young's assault on the unemployment figures plus the continuing success of the privatization programme had both considerably aided the Chancellor in his work.

Lord Young was one of Mrs Thatcher's most valued and trusted colleagues. In a famous phrase, he 'brought her solutions, not problems'. A fervent believer in a free-market economy, he had already played a prominent part in setting up the Enterprise Allowance Scheme for small businesses, a number of inner-city development corporations on the lines of the 1981 East London Docklands and Merseyside models, as well as a number of youth training schemes for 16–18-year-olds. Having become Employment Secretary in September 1985, he first concentrated on removing planning restrictions to enable businesses to be established more easily and to facilitate the creation of planning zones in inner cities. Then in May 1986 a White Paper entitled *Building Business not Barriers* put forward eighty proposals to help cut dole queues and encourage enterprise. Lord Young told the House of Lords: '. . . only by removing barriers to business will enterprise flourish and the essential creation of wealth and jobs follow.' The encouragement of self-employment became a hall-mark of his strategy. In the 1970s self-employment had fallen by a catastrophic 100,000. However, by 1987 it had increased by 750,000. None the less, unemployment took a long time to fall and was still above three million at the time of the 1987 general election. New ways of calculating the figures (over twenty of them eventually) helped a little, as did the demographic trend of a disappearing 1960s baby-boom, but new job-creation schemes for 18–25-year-olds ('New Workers' and 'Job Training'), a programme for the long-term unemployed ('Restart'), plus the expansion of existing Enterprise Allowance and Community Programme schemes, were also needed before the upward trend in the unemployment figures was eventually checked. October 1985 witnessed the biggest single fall for fourteen years, and from July 1986 unemployment fell each month until the election, the fall of 71,427 in March 1987, for example, being the largest monthly one recorded since 1973. In Lord Young's view, 'The unemployment figures were phoney. We had allowed our society through thirty years of welfare state principles to become distorted. Too much tax was taken from the low paid. None of my colleagues believed in the black economy. They did not think it existed. I went in for Restart and 10–15 per cent went off the register just by being asked to fill out a form.' His discovery, it must be confessed, was very useful to the Government so soon before the election.

The privatization programme, begun under Mrs Thatcher's first government, was much accelerated during her second. In the words of one MP, 'It did not lend itself to dispute between wets and dries and everyone jumped on the bandwagon.' The pattern was the same as before. Loss-making companies were given break-even targets followed by profit targets prior to flotation, the simulated private-sector atmosphere being regarded as a necessary preparation for the free market. The system worked well with Rolls-Royce and British Airways, but has been less successful with companies such as British Rail or British Coal. The Treasury attempted to speed up the process by suggesting an all-embracing nationalized industries act, which would grant ministers powers to hire and fire chairmen and board-members of government-owned firms and allow them to sell off viable sectors of loss-making companies. By November 1985, however, this plan had been abandoned. The traditional programme, therefore, continued, with Sealink and Jaguar being privatized in 1984, followed by the really popular sell-offs of British Telecom, British Gas and British Airways between then and the election. The advertising campaigns promoting these sales were much criticized. Yet there is no doubt that they caught the public mood, besides enabling millions of small, often first-time, investors to make a quick profit. Michael Heseltine proclaimed that they inaugurated an era of 'popular capitalism', boasting that 'the three million new share owners and the 400,000 who now hold shares in the former state businesses which employ them are enjoying the fruits of a profound and wholly benign revolution in which there are no losers.' After the privatization of British Gas, Peter Walker recalled: 'When NALGO organized rallies against it, only six people or so turned up and 99 per cent of gas workers bought shares.' The old criticisms, of course, were still made. The timing was wrong, the price was wrong; public monopolies in any case would only turn into private ones. With regard to the latter charge, Martin Holmes has written: 'The obvious reply is that the change of ownership has in many cases liberated the taxpayer from perpetually subsidizing industries which had precious little incentive to run themselves even moderately efficiently.' Or in the words of the Financial Secretary to the Treasury, John Moore: '. . . if the Government stands behind nationalized industries . . . with a bottomless purse, it is no wonder that inefficiencies flourish and market responsiveness does not stand very high in an industry's scale of priorities.'

Two final points deserve to be made with regard to privatization. First, it was widely perceived throughout the rest of the world to be both innovative and successful. Hence the fact that it was taken up not merely by conservative regimes abroad, but also by socialist ones in Spain, Portugal, Australia and New Zealand. Secondly, evidence has emerged of impressive gains in efficiency induced by the drive to sell off state industries. In Leslie Hannah's words: 'The somewhat paradoxical experience of the 1980s has been that Mrs Thatcher has been the most successful manager the nationalized industries have ever had.' Thus Bishop and Kay have demonstrated that total factor productivity in percentage terms per annum increased between 1979–83 and 1983–8 in the following firms as follows:

Company	1979–83	1983–8
British Airports Authority	0.0	2·8
British Gas	− 0·2	6·2
British Steel	8·4	12·4
British Telecom	2·0	2·5
Electricity Supply	− 1·6	4·0

Curiously, these results, to quote Samuel Brittan, were 'grudgingly reported on the grounds that "these are changes in management culture associated with clearer commercial objectives" – as if these objectives had nothing to do with privatization.' Mrs Thatcher, on the other hand, had no need to begrudge such results. Not only could she point to productivity gains, but the privatization programme, by bringing in almost £5 billion per annum during 1986 and 1987, enabled her government not only to cut income tax and to meet its targets under the MTFS, but to make its 1986 autumn statement on increases in public expenditure.

THE WELFARE STATE

Nearly all the major reforms of the Thatcher period regarding the welfare state were to come during her third government. During her second, the main issue concerned funding. The debate over the National Health Service, for example, rarely left the headlines, and the Government's major industrial dispute, after the miners' strike, turned out to be one with the nurses and health-service workers. The key question regarding the NHS was whether the Government was spending enough on it. The Government, for its part, claimed to be spending record amounts. The Opposition and the NHS, on the other hand, condemned government 'cuts'. What then was the truth? Was the NHS safe in Mrs Thatcher's hands or not?

From figures taken from the relevant all-party House of Commons committee, it can be established that in the period 1980–81 to 1986–7, the cash available to the NHS in England increased by 58·6 per cent, from £9,971 million to £15,811 million. For the family practitioner service it rose by 79·8 per cent; for the hospital and community health services it rose by 48·7 per cent. There could thus on the face of things be hardly any talk of 'cuts'. Likewise, in terms of efficiency, the record seemed to hold good. Taking 1980 as 100, the same committee produced the following figures for 1986 in terms of staff and output:

HCHS (Hospital and Community Health Services)	101·0
HCHS doctors	107·6
Nurses (not adjusted for reduction in contractual hours in 1981)	108·8
Professions allied to medicine	121·3
FPS (Family Practitioner Service) GPs	113·0
In-patients	111·9
Day cases	157·0
Out-patients	109·1
Cases treated in acute sector (1980–85)	110·4
Acute conditions seen by consultants (1980–85)	111·2
All operations (1980–85)	109·7

Figures for health promotion were also up. Taken in thousands, the following table compares those from 1978 with those from 1986:

	1978	1986
Sight tests	9,000	12,100
Dental treatments	30,800	36,800 (1987)
Cervical smear tests	2,840	4,270
Percentage of children vaccinated against polio, diphtheria and tetanus	78	85

Finally, clear efficiency gains were registered within the NHS, with cost improvements averaging 1·2 to 1·5 per cent of the budget per year. For example, the average cost per case was reduced by shortening the average length of stay per patient from 9·4 to 7·3 days.

As a result of all this statistical evidence a commentator as distinguished as Peter Riddell could write that 'Britain's health record (was) in many ways ... impressive during the Thatcher years.' In fact, he might have argued that the NHS had become about the best value for money in the world in terms of health systems. In 1987, after all, health care in Britain took up only 6 per cent of GNP compared with 11 per cent in the USA, 9 per cent in West Germany, France and the Netherlands, and 7·7 per cent in the western world as a whole. Yet in terms of life expectancy and infant mortality, the usual indices of international comparison, the NHS put Britain on a par with Europe and America; in terms of insurance cover – unlike the USA – it covered every citizen in the country; while in terms of nursing, it provided 85 nurses for every 100,000 citizens, compared with 50 in the USA, 45 in France, and 35 in West Germany. Moreover, British in-patients stayed in bed about twice as long as their American counterparts. Part of its cost-effectiveness was due to the fact that British doctors were paid only two-and-a-half times the national average wage compared with five times in the USA and over seven times in France. Yet contrary to popular belief, administrative costs were also low. An OECD study found them to be about half those of other countries as a proportion of total health spending. Finally, research done by Professor Julian Le Grand and published by the LSE on health inequalities *within* thirty-two countries found 'that England and Wales were among the countries with the *least* differences, with Scotland and Northern Ireland not far behind'.

Why then were there so many scares and newspaper headlines about 'cuts'? The answer is that there was indeed another side to the story. It was that despite the increases in expenditure under Mrs Thatcher, these increases had not always been sufficient to satisfy increased demand for services. In practice, the demands of inflation, demographic trends (the increasing number of elderly), advances in medical technology, new medical techniques and discoveries, new illnesses (AIDS) and other factors had all meant that much of the extra money had been rapidly eaten away. Real increases in purchasing power in hospitals as a result had been restricted to only about 1 per cent per year. Even with efficiency gains, therefore, hospitals could not always cope with the increased pressure on their staffs and budgets. The result was all sorts of expedients, including ward closures, cancelled operations and extended waiting lists, all of which attracted easy headlines. The critics said that only more money would solve the problem; the Government, that that had already been provided and that better management was now required in order to put it to more efficient use. The argument became an almost permanent one during Mrs Thatcher's years in office.

As with the Health Service, so too with other aspects of the welfare state. If morale sank in the NHS it also sank among teachers, social workers and others dependent upon government largesse. Greater efficiency was demanded in schools and universities, while pay rises were held back and not always funded. Again there were cries of 'cuts', while official figures showed that the Government was spending more money than ever before. Thus between 1979 and 1986 spending rose in real terms by 6 per cent on education (at a time when the number of school children was falling, it should be pointed out), 25 per cent on health, and 40 per cent on social security, within a budget that rose by 14 per cent overall. This was not a record of 'cuts', as Nigel Lawson knew only too well. Yet the public was always prepared to believe, given Government monetarist rhetoric, that cuts were what the Government really wanted.

FOREIGN AND DEFENCE POLICY

The second Thatcher government witnessed a number of important developments in foreign and defence policy. These included an agreement with China over the future of Hong Kong; an agreement with Ireland over the future of Northern Ireland; disagreements with both the Commonwealth and the European Community over sanctions against South Africa; negotiations over nuclear disarmament; and the signing and ratification of the Single European Act. All of these developments meant that Mrs Thatcher continued to enjoy a high international profile and that she became almost as important and controversial a personality on the world stage as she was at home.

The agreement with China was necessary because the lease on parts of Hong Kong ran out in 1997. Hong Kong Island itself had been leased to Britain in perpetuity under the terms of the 1842 Treaty of Nanking.

The 1860 Convention of Peking had added Southern Kowloon and Stonecutters Island, again in perpetuity. But the 1898 Convention of Peking which had added the New Territories, a mainland area adjoining Kowloon, plus 235 adjacent islands, had leased these territories for only 99 years. This meant that they would have to be returned in 1997. This, in turn, meant that the whole colony would have to be returned in 1997, since without the New Territories the rest of Hong Kong was not viable:

Without the leased areas, Hong Kong would have virtually no agriculture and no industry. It would lose its container port at Kwai Chung and thus its shipping industry, the third largest in the world, and it would probably lose its airport ... incoming and outgoing aircraft have to overfly Chinese territory to the north.

The matter was a very serious one, since under British rule Hong Kong had prospered mightily:

The colony was Asia's most important financial centre and the world's third largest after New York and London. It was also a major manufacturer, being a leading exporter of garments, electronic products, plastic goods, toys and watches. Hong Kong also had the world's largest concentration of Rolls-Royces, consumed more cognac per capita than the French, and real estate prices were higher than those in Manhattan.

The question became an urgent one by the early 1980s. Not only were all land leases in the New Territories due to expire in 1997, but in 1982 the Communist rulers of China made it clear that they wanted the matter settled by 1984. They also made it clear that they did not recognize the validity of the nineteenth-century treaties under which Britain governed the colony. The sovereignty of Hong Kong, they let it be known publicly, had always belonged to China.

This made it very difficult for Mrs Thatcher, on a visit to Peking in September 1982, to negotiate with the Chinese. She believed in both the validity of the treaties and in British sovereignty. 'We stick to our treaties,' she declared. Yet she was in no real position to bargain, given the significance of the New Territories and Chinese control of water and power supplies. There could certainly be no question of the use of force against China, such as had been used against Argentina in 1982. The only hope was that China would be reasonable, something which premier Zhao had hinted at before Mrs Thatcher's arrival, when he told reporters: 'Of course China will recover sovereignty over Hong Kong. But I think the question of sovereignty will not influence Hong Kong's prosperity and stability.' Mrs Thatcher, however, insisted on British sovereignty, an important question in that it determined whether the governor of the island would be British or Chinese after 1997. The 1982 talks were therefore deadlocked, but an incident occurred at the end of them which for Hong Kong reporters was portentous. In Frank Ching's words:

Descending the steps of the Great Hall of the People in Tiananmen Square after the two and a half hour meeting with Premier Zhao, Mrs Thatcher slipped and fell on her hands and knees, making what appeared to be a crude kowtow in the direction of Mao's mausoleum.

At the next day's meeting with the Communist leader Deng Xiaoping, she was told that if he extended the lease to Britain, he would go down in history as another Li Hung-chang, the diplomat who had signed the 1898 convention and whose name had become a by-word for treason in China as a result.

Deadlock was broken only when, in the summer of 1983, Mrs Thatcher sent a private message to Mr Zhao, informing him that if a deal could be struck which ensured the stability and prosperity of Hong Kong, she would recommend that the British parliament should accept Chinese sovereignty. From then on serious negotiations got under way. But Mrs Thatcher had once again to reassure Mr Zhao that Britain would cut all ties with the colony after 1997 before agreement could be reached. The people of Hong Kong were not informed of this until Sir Geoffrey Howe gave them the news at a press conference held there on 20 April 1984. It was not well received and, along with statements from Mr Deng soon afterwards announcing both that the Chinese People's Liberation Army would be stationed in Hong Kong after 1997 and that a Sino–British monitoring committee would be set up in the colony before then, helped to induce a mood of near panic among the local population, who were not directly involved in any way in the negotiations. (Their views were taken into account by consultations with their appointed representatives on the Governor's council.)

What Sir Geoffrey had neglected to tell the people of Hong Kong was that the Chinese had already made a number of concessions. These included a commitment by China to underwrite any agreement for fifty years (not fifteen as had previously been mooted); a willingness to refer to any document as an 'agreement'; recognition that Britain alone would rule the colony before 1997; and an agreement to treat the annexes to the document under negotiation as just as binding as that document itself. Given these concessions, negotiations could concentrate on the four main issues of substance: special status, passports, airlines and land leases. Progress, came quickly, and on 26 September 1984, four days before the deadline set by the Chinese for the completion of negotiations, a Joint Declaration was initialled by both delegations. This was presented to the people of Hong Kong on a take-it-or-leave-it basis. They could make known their views but could not alter it.

Under the terms of the agreement, China was to take over the colony in 1997; until then it was to be run by Britain. China agreed, however, to make Hong Kong a Special Administrative Region of the People's Republic, with a high degree of autonomy, save in foreign affairs and defence. An impressive list of rights and freedoms were guaranteed and were to be set out in a Basic Law. Reference was even made to a Hong Kong legislature which was 'to be constituted by elections'. Hong Kong's status as an international financial centre and a free port was to be maintained. The Basic Law indeed, would stipulate that 'the socialist system and socialist policies (would) not be practised . . . and that Hong Kong's previous capitalist system and lifestyle (would) remain unchanged for fifty years.' The previous legal system, including the right of foreigners to participate, was to be upheld, as was the educational one; civil servants were to remain employed and to secure pension rights; and all revenues raised in Hong Kong were to be used there exclusively. The currency was to remain fully convertible. All foreign countries could maintain consulates after 1997, with only South Korea, Israel and South Africa being unwelcome.

On the issues of passports, airlines and land leases, suitable compromises were reached. Thus, after 1997, all Hong Kong residents holding British Dependent Territories passports would in practice have dual citizenship outside of China. This privilege, however, would not be extended to those born in Hong Kong after that date. Nor would holders of such passports be eligible for residence in the United Kingdom. As far as air travel was concerned, Cathay Pacific was allowed to continue to operate as an independent airline outside the Chinese mainland. Finally, as far as land leases, a major source of revenue in Hong Kong, were concerned, the British authorities could extend these up to fifty years after 1997. Half the revenues obtained until then, however, would have to be placed in a special fund for the post-1997 regime to use in Hong Kong.

The Joint Agreement was formally signed by Mrs Thatcher and premier Zhao on 19 December 1984 and came into effect with the exchange of instruments of ratification in Peking on 27 May 1985. Nearly everyone – including the inhabitants of Hong Kong – regarded it as a 'good first step' and, considering the basic weakness of the British bargaining position, it was probably as good a deal as it was possible to get. Certain issues, however, still gave cause for concern: the reference to the stationing of Chinese troops in Hong Kong; the absence of any reference concerning the conscription of Hong Kong youths into the Chinese army; worries about how the chief executive was to be chosen after 1997 and how the legislature was to be elected; and the question of whether the Chinese government itself would assert the right to interpret the Basic Law it was to draw up, however liberal that law might appear on paper. In practice, the future of Hong Kong would depend on the degree of confidence the Chinese government could inspire in the people of the colony before 1997. That in turn would depend upon how these outstanding issues would be settled. In the meantime, the people of Hong Kong would watch developments in China very carefully.

In the negotiations leading up to the Anglo-Irish Agreement of 15 November 1985, signed at Hillsborough Castle outside Belfast, the British government commanded a very much more powerful position. Yet the Agreement, in its own way, was almost as extraordinary as the one that had already been signed with Peking. For if the Sino-British Agreement on Hong Kong meant that China recognized Britain's right to rule for twelve years over territory over which China claimed sovereignty, Britain, likewise, was granting Eire extensive influence over a sovereign part of British soil.

The background to the Anglo-Irish Agreement was the continued frustration of all attempts to reach a peaceful, political settlement between the representatives of the Protestant and Catholic communities within Northern Ireland itself. In particular, once Jim Prior's scheme of 'rolling devolution' (see previous chapter) had been undermined by the

SDLP (Social Democratic and Labour Party) boycott of the Assembly that had been set up, new methods had to be tried to normalize the political situation.

The SDLP itself, and especially its leader John Hume, had for some years been emphasizing the point that any settlement would have to have an international dimension. Indeed, in an article written in the journal *Foreign Affairs* in 1979, Hume had argued that London and Dublin would have to act together 'in a positive and decisive initiative' to remove any 'unconditional guarantees for any section of the northern community'. Then in 1983 he was instrumental in setting up the New Irish Forum, a body composed of representatives of the SDLP and the major parties of the Republic of Ireland (Fianna Fail, Fine Gael and Labour), whose task it was to redefine Irish nationalism in the light of contemporary problems. This met for almost a year and produced a report on 2 May 1984 that expressed support for Irish unity, albeit to be achieved through 'agreement'. However, it also examined alternative solutions, including both a federal/confederal model and an Anglo-Irish condominium. The report was important in a number of ways. First, it was issued by the representatives of political parties that taken together represented the vast majority of Irish people. Second, by appearing more open-minded than had been expected, it necessitated a reasoned response. Third, it helped divert attention from the Northern Ireland Assembly, while, fourth, it helped isolate the Northern Ireland unionists. In short, it was a brilliant public-relations success – and not merely on this side of the Atlantic.

As it happened, the report also fitted in with other developments, namely the evolution of relations between London and Dublin. In May 1980, Mrs Thatcher and the Irish Prime Minister, Charles Haughey, had reached agreement on 'new and close political cooperation'. The commanders of the police forces in north and south had then met for the first time ever to discuss cross-border security. Thatcher and Haughey met again at the end of the year and agreed to establish joint Anglo-Irish political studies. They even stated that the aim of these studies would be to examine 'the totality of relationships within these islands'. The joint studies then reported in November 1981 that an 'Intergovernmental Council' should be set up on a ministerial level to review the policy of both governments towards Northern Ireland. This impressive degree of progress came to an end in 1981–2, however, with disputes between the two governments over London's handling of the hunger strikes in the Maze prison and Dublin's neutrality in the Falkland's War. Mrs Thatcher, as a result, encouraged Jim Prior to concentrate on the search for an internal settlement. Good relations with Dublin were re-established in November 1983, when Mrs Thatcher met Haughey's successor as Taoiseach, Garret Fitzgerald, and both agreed that the Intergovernmental Council should go ahead. This met thirty times between then and March 1985 and, in the words of Paul Arthur and Keith Jeffery, 'paved the way for the Anglo-Irish Agreement'.

The Anglo-Irish Agreement provided clear, indeed startling, proof that both governments regarded the Northern Ireland problem as a joint one. It was bound therefore to be acutely controversial and to anger extreme unionists and nationalists. Its foundation was a simple bargain: in return for conceding that Irish unity could come about only 'with the consent of a majority of the people of Northern Ireland', the Dublin government, 'within the framework of the Anglo-Irish Intergovern-mental Council', obtained the right to discuss almost all aspects of Northern Ireland with its British counterpart on an institutional basis. To be exact, an intergovernmental conference was to be convened that would regularly examine '(i) political matters; (ii) security and related matters; (iii) legal matters, including administration and justice; (iv) the promotion of cross-border cooperation.' It was to be serviced by a secretariat composed of senior officials from London and Dublin and was to be based at Maryfield outside Belfast. It was to act simply as a conduit between governments, however, not as a decision-making body. The Agreement also laid down that the two governments would look for international support to aid the economic regeneration of those parts of Ireland which had 'suffered most severely from the consequences of the instability of recent years'. The USA, Canada and New Zealand all in fact agreed to contribute money to an International Fund as expressions of their good will. Indeed, the Agreement was very well received in Britain, Ireland and internationally, the House of Commons approving it with a majority of 426, the Irish Parliament (or Dáil) with a smaller one of 88 to 75.

In Northern Ireland itself there was bitter opposition from the Ulster Unionists. James Molyneaux, the leader of the UUP (Ulster Unionist Party), told a special meeting of the Northern Ireland Assembly (event-ually abolished in June 1986): 'We are going to be delivered, bound and trussed like a turkey ready for the oven, from one nation to another.' Ten per cent of the entire Protestant population of Northern Ireland displayed its hostility at a mass rally in Belfast on 23 November. Only 14 per cent of Protestants, according to opinion-poll evidence, favoured the Agreement. It was not surprising therefore that Molyneaux and Ian Paisley, leader of the DUP (Democratic Unionist Party), should have organized a campaign of street demonstrations, political boycotts (Westminster and local government) and civil disobedience against it. Violence occurred outside Maryfield on 11 December 1985 and 4 January 1986, during a 'day of action' on 3 March 1986, and at Portadown in March and July of that year. Two people died and seventy were wounded on the first anniversary of the Agreement, and there were even attacks by Protestants on the RUC. Predictably, the DUP was more militant in its opposition than the UUP. In the year 1986 fatalities rose by 21 per cent in the province, and by August 1987 the total number of deaths for 1986 had already been surpassed. By the end of 1986, too, over 1,100 families, including those of Catholics and RUC members, had been driven from their homes by Protestant paramilitary terror. By the summer of 1987, on the other hand, a certain degree of calm had been restored, with Protestants hoping that they would hold the balance of power at Westminster after a hung election. That indeed was their only hope of influencing events, for the Agreement had been specifically designed to be immune to their opposition. They could not boycott it or bring it down with a general strike. Yet it also held out the hope of future cooperation. To quote Arthur and Jeffery again: 'In the first instance local politicians were not to be involved in its workings. Yet Articles 4(b), 5(c) and 10(b) were designed to act as catalysts towards achieving powersharing devolution within the province in place of an *enhanced* role for the conference.' It should also be pointed out that, despite the institutionalized role assigned to the conference, Article 2(b) had included the statement: 'There is no derogation from the sovereignty of either the United Kingdom Government or the Irish Government, and each retains responsibility for the decisions and administration of government within its own jurisdiction.' None the less, the result of the Agreement was to alienate the Protestant population of Northern Ireland, some of whom began to play around with alternative futures for the province, not excluding independence. The British and Irish governments, on the other hand, hoped that time would reconcile these opponents and persuade them that compromise was inevitable.

Mrs Thatcher could thus boast of two international agreements signed during her second period in office, which were extremely important for British subjects. A third agreement signed during this same period will be discussed presently. In one area, however, far from forming agreements, she became diplomatically the 'odd man out'. Her policy of resisting as far as possible the implementation of economic sanctions against South Africa brought her into conflict not merely with her Commonwealth partners but with those in the European Community as well. Thanks to the importance of British trade with South Africa, however, efforts to impose sanctions were largely blocked.

For those in favour of resorting to sanctions, the arguments in support seemed clear-cut and moral. Apartheid was evil; the regime which practised it had to be overthrown as quickly as possible; and the best means of achieving that was to impose, preferably total, economic sanctions against it. This would force the South African government to come to terms with its disenfranchised and disaffected black majority. Mrs Thatcher also opposed apartheid, denounced racial segregation and called for the release of Nelson Mandela and other jailed black leaders. But she did not believe that sanctions would aid her in her attempts to persuade Pretoria to change its course.

Her reasons for opposing sanctions were based on both moral and practical grounds. As far as morality was concerned, there were a number of factors to be considered. What right, for example, did one country have to dictate the domestic policy of another? Was not this a recipe for conflict? Again, if the consequences of such interference might include bloodshed, war, mass unemployment and administrative chaos, was it moral to proceed along such a path without the certain knowledge that such consequences could be avoided? Finally, there was the question of black opinion. Was there unequivocal evidence that the majority of South Africa's blacks actually favoured economic sanctions? For her part, Mrs Thatcher believed that the consequences of imposing sanctions were unpredictable and fraught with danger, that the majority of blacks were opposed to them, and that they would almost certainly provoke violence and economic chaos. It would be immoral, therefore, to support them. Some African critics, it should be added, went further, regarding white support for sanctions as hypocritical. White liberals, they pointed out, never suggested imposing sanctions on the twenty-eight black African regimes which had worse civil rights records than

South Africa; nor had they made such suggestions in previous years when black dictators were known to be slaughtering their subjects in their thousands. Why then were they so concerned about South Africa? White guilt? Or white racism – did they simply expect higher standards from white governments?

For the most part, the debate centred on the practicalities of sanctions. Mrs Thatcher argued that historically they had never worked and mentioned League of Nations sanctions against Italy in 1935–6 as an example. (She might usefully have alluded to the 1940 American oil sanctions against Japan which helped provoke the bombing of Pearl Harbor.) The dependency of the economies of the 'front-line' African states on the South African one was also mentioned. (She reputedly told President Robert Mugabe of Zimbabwe, who threatened at one point to impose sanctions unilaterally, that if he insisted on cutting his own throat, she would not provide a bandage.) So, too, was the impossibility of policing sanctions. Yet at the heart of the debate was Britain's relationship with South Africa itself. And in this context Mrs Thatcher's opponents consistently accused her not merely of protecting British economic and security interests (which it was her duty to protect in any case), but of doing so in a way that merely protected them in the short term (a future black government would have a long memory) and at the expense of South African blacks. Several were not prepared to believe that she opposed apartheid at all.

Britain certainly had a vested interest in keeping the South African economy strong. For a start, there were two million people of British origin there, with perhaps more than 800,000 entitled to British passports. Britain had dominated white emigration to South Africa since the war. Thus, there would certainly be major problems for the British government if all these people suddenly decided to return. There were also strong economic ties between Britain and South Africa. Most of the country's strategic minerals came from there – 54 per cent of its manganese, 70 per cent of its chromium ore, 65 per cent of its platinum and 60 per cent of its gold. British companies were also heavily involved in extracting, processing and trading these minerals. If sanctions were imposed, then the only alternative source of supply would be the Soviet Union. Mrs Thatcher told the *Guardian* columnist Hugo Young: 'It is absolutely absurd that people should be prepared to put increasing power in the hands of the Soviet Union on the grounds that they disapprove of apartheid in South Africa.' She was aware that the Cape route was vital to the West and that the majority of the executive of the African National Congress were Communists or pro-Communists. Finally, there was the large trade that Britain conducted with South Africa. She was the largest foreign investor there, and although according to IMF figures she was only South Africa's fourth largest trading partner by 1986, taking a mere 4.2 per cent of her exports, she still imported $1,218 million worth of South African goods and exported $1,247 million in return. 500,000 British jobs, it was estimated, would be at stake if sanctions brought this trade to an end.

Pressure for sanctions, however, was building up internationally. For example, the European Community (EC) in 1977 drew up a code of conduct for EC companies situated there. Two broad aims were involved: better treatment for South African blacks and an attempt to counter criticism that the West was pro-apartheid. This code was actually drawn up by the British Foreign Office and until 1984 was Europe's only direct instrument for promoting change in South Africa. The declaration of a state of emergency in that country on 22 July 1985, however, led to a critical reappraisal of European foreign policies. The foreign ministers of the EC denounced the development and urged dialogue between whites and blacks instead. The French government went further and called for economic sanctions.

Britain opposed the call for sanctions on all the grounds that would soon become the usual ones: they would make South African whites more resistant to change; they would be difficult to apply; they would impose a heavy burden on the UK economy; and in any case they would hurt South African blacks, who did not support them. Instead, she preferred the US policy of 'constructive engagement' – increased aid and investment in the 'front-line' states and scholarships and other forms of aid for black South Africans.

In 1985, however, a European mission visited South Africa and issued a call for the withdrawal of military attachés and a ban on all cooperation regarding nuclear and other technology. West Germany now swung behind the French in support of these measures, and Britain, in order to avoid isolation, agreed in September 1985 to enact them. Since she already avoided cooperation with South Africa over nuclear and other sensitive technology, this only involved withdrawing her military attaché. Sir Geoffrey Howe, however, still opposed 'mandatory sanctions' and justified the current, largely cosmetic step as sending 'a legitimate and necessary political signal' to Pretoria. The new measures, in fact, were not implemented by the Community until February 1986.

The Commonwealth, too, began to take up the South African issue. The heads of government, meeting at Nassau in October 1985, also pressed for mandatory economic sanctions. Once again, Mrs Thatcher opposed. Instead, a compromise was reached, whereby a group of 'eminent persons' was sent to visit South Africa. The British even made use of their trip as a means of delaying European moves on the issue. Their report in favour of sanctions, plus a second declaration of emergency in South Africa in June 1986, however, made the British position more difficult.

This second declaration of emergency occurred ironically at a time when Britain was in the chair at the European Council meeting at the Hague. However, she managed to avoid isolation by agreeing to seek talks with other countries on a possible ban on new investments and imports of coal, steel, iron and gold coins. Mrs Thatcher, with West German and Portuguese support, meanwhile declared that such sanctions would not be mandatory and repeated her opposition to punitive measures. She also announced that Sir Geoffrey Howe would visit South Africa as president of the Council of Ministers (i.e. not merely as British foreign secretary) in order to encourage dialogue there, press for Mandela's release, and help end apartheid. The trip turned out to be a disaster. Sir Geoffrey was snubbed by South Africa and berated and insulted by President Kaunda of Zambia. 'If it was intended to show that sanctions were not needed, it backfired.'

In September 1986 the South African issue was raised once again at the Council of Ministers; given the failure of the Howe mission, the UK realized that it would have to compromise on sanctions. Thatcher in any case had foreseen this and had already promised the Commonwealth that she would implement EC measures. The final agreement, however, was merely to impose a ban on new investments and imports of iron, steel and gold coins. Coal was missing from the list, despite the fact that it represented twice the value of all the other items. Britain had had to compromise, therefore, but not very much. She had been supported by both West Germany and Portugal and had got Europe to agree to a period of evaluation to examine whether sanctions actually worked or not. In 1987, therefore, Europe concentrated more on aiding the 'front-line' states, and moves to ban imports of coal and issue a Declaration of Principles were blocked by the UK and Portugal. At the Commonwealth Conference at Vancouver in October 1987, Mrs Thatcher once again blocked sanctions and stressed the need for aid and dialogue instead. Other heads of government, in particular the Canadian prime minister, Brian Mulroney, were left in no doubt that she did not share their views. She was again in a minority of one at the 1989 conference at Kuala Lumpur.

Her international isolation, however, served merely to obscure the fact that she was successfully blocking sanctions and winning time for her policy of dialogue to bear fruit. Her European partners in the end adopted policies which were not very different from her own. Thus Martin Holland's assessment of the South African issue in the context of European Political Cooperation (EC foreign policy coordination) concludes: 'The South African policy was not an amalgam of member states' bilateral positions; rather the existing British policy was adopted, marginally adapted and applied to an EC context.'

Britain was to expend a considerable part of her diplomatic energy during the second Thatcher government on regulating her relationship with the European Community. The budget dispute remained to be settled, while pressures for a more federalist or centralized institutional framework had continually to be resisted. In the end, however, compromise solutions were reached on both sets of issues that, temporarily at least, suited British interests.

As far as the budget was concerned, the low point of Britain's relationship with her European partners was reached at the Brussels summit of March 1984. The main bone of contention was the size of the British rebate. The French had accepted that a permanent formula would have to be found and that a ceiling should be placed on agricultural spending (milk quotas). They were also aware that if a deal could be struck on the budget issue, Britain would agree to increase the Community's 'own resources' from 1 per cent to 1.4 per cent of VAT. There was fundamental disagreement, however, over the size of Britain's rebate. Mrs Thatcher demanded 1.25 billion ecus, while the French reckoned that the most they could concede was 1 billion. Mitterrand eventually raised his offer to 1.1 billion, but Mrs Thatcher still held firm. This exasperated Chancellor Kohl of West Germany, who walked out of the summit, declaring that Britain should get no more than 1 billion. In the aftermath of the dispute there was talk in Paris of excluding Britain from Europe, while in London there were threats of non-payment of Community dues. Mitterrand lowered the temperature finally by implying that British membership continued to be indispensable.

At the next summit meeting, Mrs Thatcher was more conciliatory. She turned up with a document entitled 'Europe: the Future', which set out positive ideas on developing the internal market, and finally accepted the previous best offer of 1.1 billion ecus. Her European partners agreed to a permanent formula in future (66 per cent of Britain's VAT contribution was to be rebated), while Mrs Thatcher agreed to raising the VAT rate from 1 per cent to 1.4 per cent. The Fontainebleau summit therefore successfully concluded Mrs Thatcher's struggle to 'win her money back'. It also meant that Europe began to get a better press in Britain.

This did not mean, however, that Mrs Thatcher's differences with the Community were over. On the contrary, they were only beginning. It did mean, though, that she had once again acquired the experience of standing up for what she believed in and of winning against enormous odds. She had also acquired first-hand experience of how the Community worked.

Her next struggle was to prevent Europe's growing number of federalists from turning the Community into some kind of federal state. That this was a possibility was highlighted by the European Parliament, which on 14 February 1984 adopted by 321 votes to 31, with 43 abstentions, a Draft Treaty on European Union. This was to come into force if ratified by two thirds of member states. Inspired by the Italian statesman Altiero Spinelli, the Treaty enhanced the powers of the European Parliament, gave the Council of Ministers responsibility for economic and foreign policy and abolished national vetos. It was ratified by the Belgian House of Representatives, the German Bundestag and the Italian Parliament. President Mitterrand in May 1984 also told the European Parliament that he was in favour of a new treaty, whilst the Dooge Committee, which had been set up by the Fontainebleau summit to look into European union, took up the idea as well. (The British representative on the Committee, Malcolm Rifkind, naturally opposed it.) By December 1985, however, British and other opposition had killed off the idea. Instead, the Single European Act (SEA) was agreed, which amended previous treaties. The Act itself fell far short of federalist hopes and was described by Spinelli as a 'mouse'.

Spinelli's comment reflected the fact that the SEA had nothing to say about a common security, energy, education or development, policy; that it did not mention a common currency or a European central bank; that it merely codified, rather than extended, European Political Coopera- tion (EPC or coordinated foreign policies); finally, that it left many areas of decision-making subject to the unanimity rule. What it did was to prepare Europe for the completion of the internal market by the end of 1992. 'The Community,' it stated, 'shall adopt measures with the aim of progressively establishing the internal market over a period expiring on 31 December 1992 ... the internal market shall comprise an area without internal frontiers in which the free movement of goods, persons, services and capital is ensured.' In order to expedite the measures concerned, the SEA laid down that in all relevant areas, decisions would be taken by qualified majority vote (i.e. not all member states would have the same number of votes). The SEA did not stop there, however. It also enhanced the powers of the European Parliament *vis-à- vis* the Commission and the Council and introduced what has become known as the 'cooperation procedure' between them. This, in practice, encouraged the Parliament and the Commission to 'cooperate' against the Council. Other steps were also taken: a new court of first instance was set up to assist the European Court of Justice; new competencies were given to Community institutions in areas such as research and development, the environment, and health and safety at work (the 'social dimension'); EPC acquired its own secretariat; the economic and techni- cal aspects of security policy were brought within the framework of the treaties; while there were hints about further monetary union. All this may well have fallen short of Spinelli's hopes, but how can one explain Mrs Thatcher's agreement to such a document?

Clearly, the whole concept of the SEA was unwelcome to the British government. On the other hand, there was the fear that if Britain did not agree to something, then the other member states would sign a new treaty without her. By agreeing to the SEA, therefore, an even greater degree of integration could be avoided. In any case, Britain sought, and with a great measure of success, to turn the negotiations to her own advantage. For having secured 'her money back', Mrs Thatcher's next priority was to complete the internal market and break down all (or nearly all) barriers to the free movement of people, goods, services and capital in Europe. To her this signified the extension of Thatcherism to the Continent. Indeed, the whole 1992 programme had been mapped out by the British Commissioner, Lord Cockfield, a former member of her cabinet whom she had sent to Brussels, and whose 1985 paper, *Completing the Internal Market*, had envisaged the adoption of 300 relevant directives by the start of 1993. It was no coincidence, therefore, that weighted majority voting was restricted to precisely this area of Community activity. There were thus four reasons why she agreed to sign the Act: it would block a more radically federalist initiative; it would encourage the completion of the internal market; it would otherwise change nothing in her view; and it still left the Luxemburg Compromise of 1966 intact.

As usual, Mrs Thatcher was robust in explaining her policy when she justified the SEA to the House of Commons and the nation. Among her explanations were the following: 'It does not change anything. If it did, I would not have signed it'; 'There is no erosion of essential national sovereignty ... on a question where a government considers that vital national interests are involved, it is established that the decision should be unanimous'; 'We wished to have many of the directives under majority voting because things we wanted were being stopped by others using a single vote'; 'The whole time, part of our task has been to diminish their expectations and to bring them down from the clouds to practical matters.' In Mrs Thatcher's view, therefore, she had saved Europe from utopian folly and had directed its vision towards the more practical goal of completing the internal market. This view was shared by Sir Geoffrey Howe, who in April 1986 explained developments in Europe as follows. The EC, he said, 'was not talking about the declaration or proclamation of a United States of Europe or about vague political goals ... but about practical steps towards the unity that is essential if Europe is to maintain and enhance its economic and political position in a harshly competitive world.'

The British press agreed on the whole. One newspaper wrote of 'moderate reforms', another of 'minimal changes'; a third commented that the SEA was 'a charter to safeguard and preserve national interests in the face of pressures for greater EC action in new and old areas'. A report of the House of Lords in June 1986, however, expressed the view that 'in the long term the position of the UK Parliament will become weaker.' The SEA in any case was ratified by parliament as the European Communities Amendment Act of 1986 and, after ratification by the other member states, came into effect on 1 July 1987. That the European Commission, revived from 1985 under its new French president, Jacques Delors, saw this as a much more significant development than the British government, became apparent very soon, precipitating new clashes with Mrs Thatcher in 1989, first over a proposed European Social Charter and then over European Monetary Union.

In the wider sphere of foreign affairs, Mrs Thatcher's greatest concern was the negotiations with the Soviet Union concerning nuclear weapons. Western policy in this area had been determined by the 'dual track' decision of 1979, namely the agreement to bring American Cruise and Pershing missiles to Europe and to negotiate a disarmament deal with the Soviets at the same time. European policy, however, had been motivated as much by the need to cement the US link as the need to counter the threat from Soviet SS-20s. There were about 420 of these in existence by 1984, with two thirds targeted on Western Europe. They were both mobile and out of the range of NATO's new INF systems. In the words of Peter J. Byrd:

The SS-20 threatened NATO's ability to mobilize and fight, and removal of the weapons became a goal in itself. However, removing all the SS-20s at the expense of the entire Western deployment undermined NATO's concern with coupling. Hence, there was a conflict of objectives and uncertainty about whether NATO's primary objectives were the SS-20 and the INF armaments imbalance or the renewal of the American guarantee, even if achieving this meant at least some of the SS-20s remaining.

A further complication was President Reagan's Strategic Defence Initiative (SDI), or 'Star Wars' project as it was popularly known, which was announced in March 1983 with no prior warning to America's allies or even to large parts of the US administration. This had the long-term objective of constructing a defensive shield in space against Soviet ballistic missile attack. By 1984, however, for several reasons the European members of NATO saw it as potentially destabilizing. First, it appeared to reduce the chances of concluding arms-control agreements, since President Reagan clearly regarded it as non-negotiable. Second, if it worked, it would make all offensive nuclear forces at least much more expensive and perhaps entirely obsolete; the relevance of the British nuclear deterrent would therefore come into question. Third, it might accelerate the arms race and extend it to space, while fourth, it might encourage a belief in 'Fortress America', a reliance on defence rather than deterrence, and hence promote US isolationism. Finally, there was a question mark over its extension to Europe and doubts whether European companies would be allowed to participate in its research and development. The Russians, for their part, were adamantly opposed to the scheme, claiming that even laboratory testing would violate not only the 1972 treaty limiting defence against ballistic missiles, but also the unratified, though generally observed, Salt II agreement.

British fears were expressed in March 1985 in a speech by the Foreign Secretary to the Royal United Services Institution in London, in which he claimed United States policy reflected a 'Maginot mentality'; he called instead for the inclusion of SDI in disarmament negotiations. According to Michael Smith, 'American reactions were sharp, and it was apparent that both in making the speech and in more generally supporting the growth of a "European" voice in defence matters the Foreign Secretary was pursuing a rather different line from that advocated elsewhere in Downing Street.' The signing of an SDI 'framework agreement' for research in December 1985, which held out the prospect of contracts for British firms, helped, on the other hand, to reconcile the US and UK positions.

With the resumption of disarmament negotiations by the Soviets in 1985 (they had been broken off with the arrival of Cruise and Pershing missiles in Europe), the Europeans were again worried that their interests might be ignored. This indeed seemed possible after the Reagan–Gorbachev summit meetings in Geneva and Reykjavik in 1985 and 1986. At the first, the idea of a zero option was discussed (no INF missiles to be held by either side), whilst at Reykjavik there was a rather woolly commitment to the concept of a nuclear-free world. Only President Reagan's personal commitment to SDI appeared to have prevented an agreement on short-term total nuclear disarmament. The Europeans were alarmed that such agreements could arise bilaterally, and their fears were echoed by the NATO supreme commander, US general Bernard Rogers, who was sacked shortly afterwards. Almost immediately after the Reykjavik summit, Mrs Thatcher flew to Camp David to explain the European viewpoint to President Reagan, namely that the withdrawal of all INF forces there would threaten to uncouple US and European defence. The same point was pursued in discussions in NATO the following year. Mrs Thatcher's efforts appear to have been successful, since she later readily gave her blessing to US–Soviet agreement on a 'double zero' option. Indeed, she was often used (for example, over SDI) to express Europe's position on defence matters to the President, with whom she had established an extremely close working and personal relationship. In Washington in March 1985, she explained: 'We see so many things in the same way and you can speak of a real meeting of minds. I feel no inhibitions about describing the relationship as very, very special.'

Following Reykjavik, Mr Gorbachev took the diplomatic initiative, and after a veritable *tour de force* succeeded in negotiating an INF Treaty with the USA in December 1987. To achieve this, he had to make a number of concessions, including agreement to exclude from the Treaty previous Soviet demands regarding the modernization of the British and French nuclear deterrents. The Treaty also left in place in Europe all nuclear weapons with a range of under 500 kilometres. It did not really end European fears of decoupling, but at least it was an agreement that Europe's NATO members were willing to live with.

The existence of a 'very, very special' relationship between Mrs Thatcher and President Reagan led to charges that she was much too ready to agree with him. Evidence of her supposed subservience included the banning of trade unions at GCHQ, Britain's withdrawal from UNESCO, British entanglement in the Gulf War in 1986-7 (the Armilla patrol and minehunting fleet) and, most of all, British involvement in the US bombing of Libya in April 1986. In all of these cases, on the other hand, there were independent motives for British action, which is not to say that the American relationship was totally irrelevant. In the case of GCHQ, the unions had already called out their members there on strike action; the scandalous maladministration of UNESCO was well known; the Armilla patrol (inaugurated in 1980, long before the Gulf War) served British interests in helping to preserve the freedom of the seas; and allowing the Americans to use British bases from which to bomb Tripoli both emphasized the Government's determination to oppose terrorism and paid back a debt for US assistance during the Falklands War. The Libya raid was certainly a most dramatic display of the special relationship at work. No other country in Europe allowed the US to use its bases or even to overfly its airspace in the course of it. But the bombing proved unpopular with British public opinion once it became clear that civilians had been killed and that British hostages in the Middle East had been murdered in revenge. America was accused of fighting terrorism by terrorism, in short, of violating international law. This was a policy which the Thatcher government had hitherto always condemned, and the Prime Minister soon let it be known that a repeat performance of the operation would not be countenanced. Her debt to America over the Falklands War was now repaid. Accusations of subservience were partisan. She was always prepared to speak her mind to the President, but was careful to cultivate a sympathetic hearing.

If Mrs Thatcher's cultivation of the special relationship with the US was no surprise, the emergence of a special relationship with Mikhail Gorbachev and a revised policy towards the Soviet bloc were the most unexpected aspects of British diplomacy during her second term as Prime Minister. In the summer of 1983 British policy towards Eastern Europe was reassessed. The Soviet Union was judged capable of change, while a policy of differentiating between the states of Eastern Europe appeared promising. The origins of this reappraisal are disputed. It may have been a natural development of British policy or of Mrs Thatcher's growing interest in international affairs. It may have been a reaction to US policy on INF and SDI. It may even have come about as a result of West German Christian Democratic urgings. In any case, both the Prime Minister and the Foreign Secretary began to visit Eastern Europe and to send other ministers there as well. Mrs Thatcher made her first prime ministerial visit there to Hungary in February 1984, where she was warmly received, while Sir Geoffrey by 1986 had visited Hungary, East Germany, Czechoslovakia, Poland and Yugoslavia. Both visited Moscow in 1984 for Andropov's funeral, but as yet nothing much had changed in relations with the USSR. The visit of Mikhail Gorbachev to London in December 1984, on the other hand, brought hopes of improved relations. Gorbachev was being groomed as Soviet leader, and his meeting with Mrs Thatcher proved that she was seen by Moscow as a figure of influence, in particular someone who might influence Reagan. Gorbachev also expressed hopes of improvements in Anglo-Soviet trade. Thatcher was much impressed by her visitor and declared enthusiastically to the press that he was 'a man I can do business with'. A rapport had been established, which was to become obvious later on.

Relations with Moscow were not to improve dramatically overnight, however. The expulsion of thirty-one Soviet agents from Britain in 1985 was matched by the reciprocal expulsion of Britons from Russia. The Soviets also threatened to suspend all fuel supplies to Britain during the miners' strike, but soon backed down when London protested. Mrs Thatcher's visit to Moscow in 1985 for Chernenko's funeral appears to have been routine. With Gorbachev's assumption of power in the USSR, however, things did begin to change. Indeed, by April 1986, the Soviet leader was getting greater approval ratings in British opinion polls than Reagan. The latter, in any case, was also changing his mind about Soviet policy and was impressed by the Gorbachev he met at Geneva and Reykjavik. Gorbachev, in fact, had become the man of the hour. Mrs Thatcher, who had already detected the possibility of change, now undertook to encourage *détente* with characteristic energy, although she never, it has to be admitted, underestimated the forces of conservatism among the Soviet elite.

There was a flurry of diplomatic activity between London and Moscow in 1986–7. The Soviet Foreign Minister, Edward Shevardnadze, visited Britain in July 1986. Three Anglo-Soviet agreements were concluded in the same year: on trade, the prevention of incidents at sea, and the waiving of all outstanding claims from the period 1917–24. The latter made possible future Soviet operations in the London capital markets. The following year brought more visits and agreements: the Soviet jamming of BBC Russian-language broadcasts came to an end after six years; a finance and credit agreement was signed that was to run till 1990; and there were – significantly – exploratory talks on the prevention of terrorism. Capping all these developments, however, was Mrs Thatcher's own immensely successful visit to the Soviet Union from 28 March to 2 April. In Moscow she had thirteen hours of talks with Mr Gorbachev, and in an unprecedented and unedited fifty-minute interview on Soviet television was extremely frank and very critical of communism. The viewers loved it and by the time of her departure she was being referred to by ordinary Russians as 'our Maggie'. More importantly, she appeared to have struck up an excellent relationship with the Soviet leader, with whom she argued in a free but friendly manner, and raised a number of cases of human rights. Her trip also saw the signing of many agreements – on diplomatic exchanges, cooperation in space, and cultural and educational information – but was significant most of all for the huge boost it gave to her international standing in the run-up to a general election. (It was boosted again in December 1987, when Gorbachev stopped off for a two-hour meeting with her *en route* to Washington to sign the INF treaty.) Mrs Thatcher herself was clearly overjoyed by her trip. It was, she said, 'the most fascinating and invigorating visit I have ever made abroad as Prime Minister'.

Altogether, therefore, Mrs Thatcher's foreign-policy record in her second term, as in her first, was hugely successful. Her government had negotiated two international agreements (over Hong Kong and Northern Ireland) that had commanded international respect; prevented the imposition of economic sanctions against South Africa, which, in its opinion, would have undermined change there; and so managed developments in the European Community that a permanent deal on rebates was secured and federalism confined within the limits of the Single European Act. Meanwhile, the special relationship with America was intensified and a new one established with the USSR, which contributed to disarmament and peace.

THE OPPOSITION

By choosing a leader aged only 41, Labour had perhaps recognized that its road back to power would be a long one. Certainly, Kinnock was a relative newcomer to the political scene. Elected MP for Islwyn in South Wales in 1970, he had been a member of the party's National Executive Committee (NEC) since 1978. Yet he had no experience of government office and was widely regarded as an intellectual lightweight. His previous record within the party was one of expansive, easy rhetoric, opposition to the European Community and Welsh devolution and support for CND (his wife Glenys was another prominent member). However, he typified the youth and vigour that the party clearly needed on its road to electoral recovery.

The direction in which Neil Kinnock sought to take the Labour Party had become clear in the course of his campaign for the leadership. On Britain's membership of the European Community – a litmus test of left-wing credentials – he stepped back from advocating immediate withdrawal. On nuclear defence he stuck more to his previous position, declaring that Britain's nuclear weapons should be a lever to negotiate reductions 'culminating in a non-nuclear defence strategy within the lifetime of a parliament'. On economic and social policy he suggested Labour had lost votes to the Alliance in the general election through an overemphasis on the poor, the unemployed and minority interests. If Labour was to be of 'real use to the deprived and insecure,' we must have the support of those in more secure social circumstances'.

In September 1983 the TUC acknowledged the need for a reappraisal of its own policies by 5·8 million to 4 million votes. When TUC General Secretary Len Murray warned, 'We cannot just say that our policies are fine and that it is our members who are all wrong', he could equally have been expressing the new leadership's own view of its relationship with the electorate. The lesson of the general election appeared plain. The Alliance had eaten into Labour's vote from the centre. The more closely Labour was identified with left-wing policies, the larger future bites might be.

In the aftermath of Labour's disastrous election performance, Tony Benn's optimistic claim that 8·5 million people had voted for 'socialism' offered little comfort. Benn, now out of parliament, would find his position as tribune of the Labour left weakening. Much of the trade union and constituency party support that had bolstered him in his 1981 deputy leadership campaign shifted to Kinnock. The Labour Co-ordinating Committee, formerly Benn's most enthusiastic supporter, moved in the same direction, severing its links from the hard left.

From 1983 on, Labour's left lost the dominance it had achieved in the early 1980s, buffeted by events – the failure of the 1984–5 miners' strike and the collapse of local authority resistance to Government pressure to reduce spending – and by the party leadership's determination to rebuild electoral credibility. In the ensuing realignment a soft left emerged, epitomized by Ken Livingstone, David Blunkett and Michael Meacher. Their view appeared to be that left interests could be better protected by standing with Kinnock rather than by openly confronting him. The hard left – which saw extra-parliamentary campaigning and adherence to socialist fundamentalism as at least as important as wooing the electorate – was represented by Tony Benn, Eric Heffer, Dennis Skinner, Arthur Scargill and, beyond them, the Trotskyite entrists of the Militant Tendency and the Socialist Action and Socialist Organiser factions.

Perhaps ironically, the very success of the left-inspired constitutional changes of the early 1980s strengthened Kinnock's authority. Their object had been to make Labour leaders more answerable to party activists. But, having been placed in office by the party as a whole through the electoral college, rather than – as in the past – the Parliamentary Labour Party (PLP) alone, Kinnock and Hattersley could deliver their arguments from a distinctly firmer base. For two years Kinnock sought to consolidate his position. It was not until the 1985 Labour Party conference that he felt secure enough to turn decisively against the hard left.

The immediate impact of Labour's new leadership had been to improve the party's standing in opinion polls. But by the 1984 conference the continuing miners' strike was damaging Labour's image and threatening longer-term hopes of electoral revival. Kinnock was unwilling to give complete political backing to a disastrously mistimed and ill-led conflict. Equally, trade union and left-wing sensitivities made it impossible to condemn the strike out of hand. Clearly uncomfortable, Kinnock, as has already been noted, limited himself to calling for a ballot and expressing concern at violence – from both miners and police – on picket lines.

If Kinnock's object was to curb his own left wing, he was twice disappointed at the 1984 Labour Party conference. He could be satisfied by a shift away from wholesale nationalization and by a four-to-one rejection of a demand for the return of privatized industries without compensation. As pleasing was a modification of the previous commitment to withdraw from the EEC. In addition, the conference increased the centre right–soft left majority on the NEC against the hard left. In the PLP's shadow cabinet elections the leading hard-left candidates were rejected, with Eric Heffer voted out and Tony Benn – who had returned to the Commons at a by-election – failing to gain a place. But delegates rejected a proposal – one the NEC had agreed by 15 votes to 12 – to extend voting for the reselection of MPs from constituency management committees to all members. Kinnock's fear, mistaken in the event, was that wholesale ousting of moderate labour MPs by tiny groups of left-wing constituency activists would further tarnish the party's image. The conference went on to support local authorities contemplating illegal resistance to government-enforced spending cuts.

Defence continued to be a divisive issue. Unilateral nuclear disarmament – anathema to the Labour right and unattractive to the electorate – remained party policy, a position from which Kinnock showed no sign of retreating. But an effort to paper over divisions by reasserting

Labour's commitment to NATO and going on to advocate increased conventional arms spending in a non-nuclear Britain angered the left.

1985 proved to be crucial for Kinnock, the year in which he stamped his personality on the Labour Party. It opened in January with the appointment of Larry Whitty as party General Secretary in succession to Jim Mortimer. Whitty took office on 10 June. There was an increasing emphasis on style and efficiency in Labour's organization and presentation. The red rose replaced the red flag as the party's emblem and party spokesmen were more carefully groomed, with shorter hair and smarter suits the order of the day for television appearances. But, more fundamentally, Kinnock took decisive steps to further himself from the left.

In March 1985 the miners acknowledged defeat. Kinnock had tried to limit the strike's damaging effect on himself and the Labour Party, though both had suffered in the opinion polls. He now moved against what had become known as the 'Scargill factor', an identification of Labour in the public mind with conflict and radical rhetoric. When Scargill demanded in July that a future Labour Government should free miners convicted in the strike and place the coal industry under workers' control, Kinnock dismissed his ideas as 'fantasy'.

At the party conference in Bournemouth in October, Kinnock worked his way through a series of targets on the left. He condemned (and delegates rejected) proposals for black sections (i.e. separate organizations within the party for black members; thirty-five constituency parties had already set these up, a policy which violated Labour's traditional 'colour-blindness'). An NUM demand for reimbursement by a Labour government of funds confiscated during the strike he dismissed on the grounds that 'people would be confused about our attitude to the rule of law'. It was rejected by 55 per cent to 45 per cent on a card vote. Most dramatic of all was his scathing denunciation of the activities of Militant councillors in Liverpool. A writer on Labour affairs noted: 'For a potential Labour Prime Minister needing to establish his leadership credentials, and needing to show he could be just as tough and firm as Mrs Thatcher, the speech did the trick.' There was an immediate improvement in Kinnock's personal position in the opinion polls.

Kinnock may have partially succeeded in shifting his party away from the wilder policies he had inherited in 1983 and in effectively isolating the hard left. But the defence issue, and with it Kinnock's personal commitment to unilateralism, remained Labour's vulnerable point. In a television interview on the eve of the Labour Party conference in September 1986, he pledged a future Labour government to scrapping nuclear weapons, closing American nuclear bases in Britain and refusing American nuclear protection in the event of war. There was an immediate declaration from US Defence Secretary Caspar Weinberger that such a policy would destabilize NATO. An otherwise successful conference in Blackpool was dominated by the issue and by Weinberger's response.

In his speech on 30 September Kinnock attempted to set at rest American fears about Labour's commitment to NATO. He was determined that the Labour Party should not appear to be a pacifist party. In a remarkable peroration, he declared: 'I tell you in no casual spirit, with no bravado, that like most of my fellow citizens I would, if necessary, fight and die, give my life for my country. But I could never let my country die for me.' At the Conservative Party conference in Bournemouth the following month Mrs Thatcher attacked what was manifestly Labour's weak spot in the approach to an election year. 'A Labour Britain would be a neutralist Britain,' she said. 'It would be the greatest gain for the Soviet Union in forty years. And they would have got it without firing a shot.'

Nor was Mrs Thatcher the only enemy Kinnock had to worry about. Britain in the period 1983–7 had a three-party system, and the Alliance hoped to overtake Labour as the main challenger to the Tories. It had after all come out of the 1983 election with 25·4 per cent of the vote, only 2·2 per cent less than Labour. And in the period from July 1983 to March 1987, it actually captured more votes in by-elections (39 per cent) than either Labour (29 per cent) or the Conservatives (30 per cent).

The figure who dominated Alliance politics during this period was Dr David Owen, who had become leader of the SDP in 1983 on the resignation of Roy Jenkins. The liberal leader, David Steel, had retired exhausted to his Scottish home after the election and kept a low profile for the next two years. Owen, therefore, had the opportunity to shape the Alliance in his image.

The image he chose was one of a 'tough but tender' party coalition, aware of the need to take a strong line on defence and trade union reform, but sufficiently sensitive to the needs of the unfortunate in society to condemn the government's 'cuts' in welfare spending. He spoke often of the need to copy the West German 'social market economy', i.e. to establish a free market system, but one that left room for state intervention in favour of the poor and sick. Aware that the Alliance had already made inroads into the Labour vote, he was determined to attack the Tory one, looking particularly for gains among the skilled working-class voters who had recently crossed from Labour to the Conservatives. His strategy involved three tactics: steadfastly supporting the nuclear deterrent; talking up the Alliance vote by referring constantly to a 'hung' parliament after the next election (he modestly conceded that the Alliance was more likely to hold the balance of power in such an event, rather than form a government); and making skilful use of the many media opportunities that came his way as a former Foreign Secretary. Moreover, unlike Kinnock, he was able to exude an air of gravitas which was of immense benefit to his cause. The real test of his leadership, however, was the electoral record which the Alliance could maintain between general elections. Traditionally, this was crucial to third-party fortunes, and here Dr Owen's leadership more than passed the test.

Between the 1983 general election and the second direct elections to the European parliament in June 1984, only five by-elections occurred. In March 1984, Tony Benn was safely returned to Westminster by the voters of Chesterfield. Labour also held Cynon Valley. In the three Conservative seats which fell vacant, however, the Alliance came within a whisker of victory. It missed taking Penrith and the Borders (Whitelaw's former constituency) by only 552 votes and in South West Surrey was only 2,500 votes short of victory. These were exciting and encouraging results, which were partly repeated at the 1984 local elections. But in the major nationwide test in June for the direct elections to the European parliament, the Alliance received a drastic rebuff. The outcome was as follows:

Party	Seats won*	Votes	% Votes
Conservative	45	5,426,866	40·8
Labour	32	4,865,224	36·5
Alliance	0	2,591,659	19·5
Others	1	429,149	3·2
	78	13,312,898	100·0

* Excluding Northern Ireland.

Since the general election, Labour had clearly staged a modest recovery, with its share up to 36·5 per cent compared to a lowly 27·6 per cent in 1983. Labour had won thirty-two seats compared to seventeen in the 1979 European elections. The Alliance, which had once again failed to win a single seat, was bitterly disappointed. Apart from two seats (North Wales and Plymouth and Cornwall), it had not come remotely close to victory. In only twelve constituencies had it polled more than 25 per cent of the vote.

Ironically, whereas the Alliance had failed in this national test, in individual by-elections its success continued, often in dramatic fashion. Thus on 14 June, the same day as the European elections, it gained a narrow victory in the suburban middle-class constituency of Portsmouth South, hitherto a Conservative seat since 1918. The following year brought only two by-elections. One of these, held in the rural mid-Welsh constituency of Brecon and Radnor, saw a second Alliance victory. Labour's chance to create headlines had to wait till June 1986, when Fulham, a traditional Labour seat which had gone Tory in 1983, was recaptured for the party by an impeccably moderate candidate. The Alliance, meanwhile, was looking to more promising by-elections in West Derbyshire and Rydale, a vast rural Yorkshire constituency.

The outcome of these two by-elections was dramatic. In West Derbyshire, the Alliance came within 100 votes of victory. In Ryedale, a seat the Conservatives had never believed at risk and which had a 16,000 majority, the Alliance raced to victory with a 5,000 majority. It was a by-election sensation on the scale of Orpington or Crosby. The Alliance could look forward to a leap in the opinion polls, perhaps to the stage where, as in September 1985, it was actually in the lead with 35 per cent, compared to Labour's 33 per cent and the Tories' 31 per cent.

Certainly, everything appeared to be going well. The two parties (Liberal and SDP) had managed to share out the 633 mainland parliamentary constituencies, a joint election campaign strategy team had been established, and joint 'commissions' had been set up to ensure unity over policy. In June 1986, however, the defence commission's report, entitled *Defence and Disarmament*, was criticized by Dr Owen. It had tried to work out a compromise policy between the two parties, by stating that the alliance would keep Polaris in operation until the mid

1990s, but would cancel Trident and make no decision on a successor to Polaris until the outcome of disarmament talks was known. This policy was condemned by Dr Owen as a 'fudge', and a new one, formulated around an as yet non-existent Franco-British nuclear missile programme, was hastily put together by Owen and Steel. However, at the Liberal Party conference at Eastbourne in September, this policy was rejected. Instead, delegates voted by the narrowest of margins – 652 votes to 625 – for an amendment, opposed by most of the parliamentary Liberal Party, which stated that any closer cooperation between Britain and her West European partners should *not* include a nuclear defence capacity. It was not the result the leadership wanted, and it had disastrous consequences. In the opinion-poll ratings, the non-nuclear vote and the protracted wrangling which ensued saw Alliance support slump to its lowest level for two years. Both opposition parties, therefore, ended the 1986 conference season in trouble over their defence policies.

THE GENERAL ELECTION OF JUNE 1987

The Westland Affair had seen the Government reach its lowest ebb in public esteem. Opinion-poll ratings barely registered 30 per cent support. On 27 January 1986, before the crucial House of Commons debate, Mrs Thatcher had even hinted to her staff that she might no longer be Prime Minister by 6 p.m. that evening. She indeed survived, but her authority was temporarily impaired and for about a year or so afterwards the press was full of assurances that cabinet or 'collective' government had been 'restored'. Certainly, Mrs Thatcher's critics within the party felt it safer to speak out, with the Leader of the House, John Biffen, for example, calling in the aftermath of poor local and by-election results in May 1986 for the party to enter the next election with a 'balanced ticket'. Then in the autumn of 1986, during the annual battles over the 'spending round', a rather public split became evident between 'wets' and 'dries' once again, over whether priority should be accorded to tax cuts or increased public spending. Nigel Lawson, as has been seen, was to manage both. Before budget day, however, the cabinet chose to relinquish Thatcherite plans to sell off the Austin-Rover car company to Ford, and Land Rover and Leyland Trucks and Buses to General Motors. Yet this was due, arguably, less to the reassertion of cabinet authority over the Prime Minister, than to the extent of the revolt organized by Tory West Midland MPs. Fearful of job losses if the sales went ahead, and quick to play the patriotic card, they forced the party whips to conclude that the relevant legislation would never get through the House of Commons. In the words of one rather weary commentator: 'To listen to some Conservative MPs from the Midlands was to get the impression that BL was a world-respected market leader rather than an unsuccessful, loss-making nationalized concern.'

From the autumn of 1986, however, the Government's fortunes markedly improved. Partly this was due to a change in presentation. Kenneth Baker, for example, who succeeded Sir Keith Joseph in May 1986 as Education Secretary, began a strong attack on alleged left-wing political indoctrination in schools. He also announced the establishment of twenty new city technology colleges, which were to be partly supported by industry. Social service ministers began to talk less of benefit-threatening 'reforms' and more about the money they had spent and the hospitals that had been built. Water privatization was delayed and a management buy-out of the Tyneside shipbuilding firm, Swan Hunter, accepted in preference to a private-sector deal. This greater concern for presentation was most dramatically demonstrated at the party conference at Bournemouth in October 1986, which not only capitalized on Labour and Liberal mistakes, but was marvellously orchestrated by Harvey Thomas, the party's communications director, to reveal a new agenda of legislative priorities for the next parliament. Minister after minister talked of future plans and programmes in a manner specifically designed to recapture the political initiative. And this political offensive continued right up until the next election. It was aided by a number of factors: Nigel Lawson's autumn spending programme; the continuing fall in unemployment; the 1987 budget success; and Mrs Thatcher's spectacular visit to Moscow.

For Labour, meanwhile, a number of setbacks occurred. First, the MP for Knowsley North, Robert Kilroy-Silk, resigned, complaining of hard-left manipulation of his constituency party. Then Neil Kinnock's two visits to America (November 1986, March 1987) turned out to be unmitigated disasters, with the Reagan administration condemning his unilateralist policies as a danger to NATO and world peace. His second one, of course, stood in stark contrast to Mrs Thatcher's success in Moscow. Worst of all for the party, a by-election arose in Greenwich in

February 1987 for which the constituency party chose as candidate a local 'loony/hard left' councillor, Deirdre Wood. The seat was a traditionally Labour one which had gone Tory in 1983. Yet the result was a sensation: the Alliance won with a majority of 6,611. Labour's opinion-poll ratings began to slump.

The Alliance had appeared, until Greenwich, to be also losing support. The wrangle over the nuclear issue had severely dented its credibility, and the loss in a car accident in December 1986 of the able liberal MP David Penhaligon meant that the year had closed in gloom. A 'relaunch' took place in January 1987, however, with a rally at the Barbican and the publication of a new policy report, entitled *Partnership for Progress*. Yet the Greenwich result was unexpected, with the SDP candidate, Rosie Barnes, coming from behind to take a massive 52 per cent of the vote. The Alliance opinion-poll ratings now began to move up and were consolidated in March by the predicted Liberal win at Truro in the by-election to fill Penhaligon's seat. Soon the polls were showing the Alliance level-pegging with Labour. In a way, this was good news for the Government (the opposition was split down the middle), so when the May 1987 local election results were deemed favourable to the Conservatives, an early general election was called for 11 June.

The campaign, on the whole, was uneventful. No one issue predominated, and no incident seriously disrupted the stage-management of the party campaign experts, although Neil Kinnock's answer to David Frost in a television interview on 24 May, concerning a Labour government's response to the threat of a Soviet invasion, was seized on by the Tories to demonstrate his unfitness for office. Kinnock said: 'the choice is exterminating everything you stand for . . . or using the resources that you have got to make any *occupation* untenable.' Tory Central Office rushed out a poster showing a British soldier with his hands up, with the caption underneath reading 'Labour's Defence Policy'. Until then Labour's campaign had been going remarkably well, with its initial party election broadcast on the Kinnocks, done in soft focus with inspiring music, held to be a model for political advertisers. The Labour rallies with the red rose theme, featuring Kinnock and Hattersley as the 'dream ticket', were also well managed, although one cynical *Guardian* correspondent, weary of the sight of the two of them together holding bunches of roses, wrote that it was beginning to remind him of a gay wedding. All the money spent on the campaign, however, did not appear to have much impact on public opinion. Labour's position in the opinion polls improved a few points, but it was entirely at the expense of the Alliance. The Tory lead was hardly dented, although one opinion poll indicating a closer race was enough to send jitters through the party. 'Nervous Thursday' (3 June) caused Mrs Thatcher to change its advertising strategy and clash with the party chairman, Norman Tebbit. The professionalism of Labour's advertising campaign had thus at least succeeded in worrying the Government. The Alliance leaders became increasingly dispirited. Their rating in the polls, which had fallen below its 1983 level, did not respond to their campaigning efforts and they were left simply with the hope that a last-minute surge in support might convert votes into seats. By the eve of poll, the only real uncertainty concerned the size of the Conservative majority and the impact that tactical voting might have in some of the marginal constituencies. At no stage did the Conservatives really look like losing and at no stage did Labour look like potential winners. Nor did the two-headed leadership of the Alliance ever look either comfortable or really convincing.

From the first result declared, in the safe Conservative seaside resort of Torbay, it was clear that the Conservatives were heading for a major election victory. Although early results from Scotland, Wales and parts of northern England showed substantial swings to Labour, elsewhere Conservative marginals obstinately refused to succumb to the Labour challenge. Even such seats as Hyndburn and Darlington stayed Conservative. Meanwhile, the Conservatives actually gained a seat in Wolverhampton in the West Midlands. Most astonishing of all was London: here, in a devastating night for Labour, the Conservatives gained Battersea, Walthamstow and Fulham. Also, in the South-East, two of Labour's last remaining bastions (Ipswich and Thurrock) also fell. As the results came in, it became clear that British politics was becoming polarized as never before. Nearly all the Labour gains were north of the line from the Wash to the Severn. Not since 1945 had Labour done so well in Scotland. Along the Tyne, the Mersey and the Clyde massive Labour majorities were piled up. Yet in the prosperous South, Labour had done worse in London and the Home Counties than in living memory. The final outcome, with the Conservatives taking 375 seats, compared to 229 for Labour, was a bitter disappointment for Labour after a campaign that was more professional and effective than in 1983. The full results were as follows:

Party	Votes gained	Percentage of vote	Average vote per MP	Number of MPs
Conservative	13,763,747	42·2	36,703	375
Labour	10,029,270	30·8	43,796	229
Alliance	7,341,275	22·6	333,694	22
SNP	416,873	1·4	138,957	3
PC	123,587	0·3	41,196	3
Others *	881,669	2·7	48,982	18

* Including Northern Ireland and the Speaker.

It was not only Labour who had suffered a night of bitter disappointment. The Alliance, with its overall vote in retreat, suffered some grievous blows. With a final tally of only 22 seats, it lost such leading figures as Roy Jenkins (victim of the Labour landslide in Glasgow Hillhead) and Clement Freud (in Cambridgeshire). Worse still, all the hoped-for gains failed to materialize. Shirley Williams failed to take Cambridge, Bill Rodgers made little impact on Milton Keynes. The Alliance had hoped to take such Conservative marginals as Richmond, Chelmsford and Cheltenham. All stayed very firmly Conservative. Instead of gains, the Alliance lost such seats as Ryedale, Colne Valley, the Isle of Wight and Portsmouth South (although it gained Southport, Argyll and Bute, and Fife North-East). None the less, despite its inability to make a breakthrough in terms of seats, its vote had held up remarkably well. In fact, Kinnock's main achievement in retrospect was to have ensured that the Alliance had not overtaken Labour. That, at the start of the election campaign, had still been a distinct possibility.

Nationally, the Conservatives had gained 12 seats for the loss of 29. Labour gained 27 for the loss of 6 (5 of them in London and the South-East). The Liberals gained 3 seats, but lost 5; the SDP lost 3 seats and failed to register a single gain. In Wales Plaid Cymru gained the Isle of Anglesey (Ynys Mon), while the Scottish Nationalists gained 3 seats but lost 2. The most spectacular result in Ulster was the defeat of Enoch Powell by 731 votes in Down South by the SDLP. The Greens, fielding 133 candidates, polled 89,354 votes but lost their deposit everywhere.

THATCHERISM AFTER TWO TERMS: AN ASSESSMENT

Even after two terms in office it was difficult to make an objective judgement about the scale of Mrs Thatcher's achievement as Prime Minister. Some things were crystal clear. First, she had utterly transformed Britain's standing and reputation in the world. She had become the leading political figure in Europe and had established excellent working relations with the leaders of both super-powers. She had been able to negotiate international agreements over Northern Ireland and Hong Kong which judged by any standard of diplomacy were positive achievements. The Rhodesian problem had been solved and the Falklands War had been won despite enormous odds. In all parts of the world she cut a high profile and commanded respect if not always warmth or sympathy. Domestically, she had become the most successful British politician of the century, winning three elections in a row with substantial majorities. She had also been responsible for changing the whole climate of British politics by emasculating the political power of the trade unions and returning vast sectors of the economy to private ownership. Corporatism was dead and the sword of Damocles held for so long over the head of elected governments by Arthur Scargill and his like had finally been removed. Indeed, she had set a new agenda in economics, with a new emphasis on competition, monetary rectitude, lower taxes, private ownership, fewer state subsidies and a balanced budget. All this was a world away from prices and incomes policies, lame ducks, closed shops and endless strikes. And it had come about not only without the dismantling of the welfare state but with larger sums spent than ever before on health and education (in real terms). From 1982 also, she could boast that the British growth rate was the highest in Europe and that the increase in productivity was the highest too.

There was, of course, another side to the story. It had less to do with her international reputation, which was unimpeachable, despite accusations of subservience to the USA, anti-Europeanism and warmongering. The doubts centred more on the durability of her domestic record. Had so much really changed? Had Britain's relative economic decline really been halted or reversed? Critics pointed to the fact that trade unions could still manage to negotiate wage increases higher than the rate of inflation, often without conceding real productivity gains. Indeed, the steep rise in productivity was often ascribed to the one-off effects of the steep rise in unemployment during 1979-83. Had management really learned to manage? Had the attitudes of the workplace really altered? What had certainly not seemed to have altered was the poor qualification's and training of both management and men. There were also doubts about the reversal of decline. The growth rates looked excellent only if the years 1979-81 were excluded; otherwise they appeared pedestrian. The international comparison was helped by the fact that European rivals were doing unusually badly. In 1986, after all, for the first time since the industrial revolution, Britain had become a net importer of industrial goods. By 1987, Italy had overtaken her in terms of GNP per capita and had proclaimed this event *il surpasso*. Many suspected that without oil or with full employment there would quickly be a balance of payments crisis. Had there been an economic miracle therefore or simply a mirage? Public attitudes afforded no easy answer either. Most people preferred more spending to lower taxes, lower unemployment to lower inflation. Spending on the health service was never sufficient and every increase seemed to highlight 'cuts'. The government therefore proved unable to cut the overall tax-take. Thatcherism at home seemed only skin-deep.

In truth, it was still too early to tell how lasting or significant 'the Thatcher effect' would be on British society or the British economy. After so many decades of relative decline, probably decades of change would be required to alter fundamentally both attitudes and working practices. All sorts of vested interests would have to be challenged and the work ethic would have to spread from the Prime Minister herself – who indubitably personified it – to a population still inclined to take too much for granted. Mrs Thatcher seemed aware of this. She said modestly that she would be prepared to 'stay on and on and on' to finish the tasks which she had set herself as premier.

If the 1987 Conservative Party general election triumph seemed to herald a new dawn for Thatcherites, it soon turned out to be a false one. Radicalism continued for a couple of years, but boom soon turned to bust and Lawson's burgeoning reputation as an historic Chancellor vanished amidst claims that he had wrecked the whole Thatcherite experiment. The Prime Minister herself became increasingly unpopular and an ungrateful party, deeply divided over the poll tax and Europe, replaced her in November 1990 with John Major, who reversed many of her key policies.

The key Cabinet posts remained unchanged. Howe remained Foreign Secretary; Hurd, Home Secretary; Lawson, Chancellor of the Exchequer and Younger, Defence Secretary. Ridley remained at Environment and Baker at the Department of Education and Science. Norman Tebbit, on the other hand, retired from the Cabinet in order to spend more time with his wife (permanently injured as a result of the IRA Brighton bombing), although he retained the Tory Party Chairmanship. Altogether, the signs were for a more radically Thatcherite Government. As before, the key economic ministries were in the hands of Thatcherite 'dries', while Thatcherites now also dominated several of the spending ministries. Given that most new Tory MPs were also held to be 'dries' and that they had been elected on an unambiguously Thatcherite programme, there seemed little to stop the Prime Minister from spending yet four or five more years attempting to shift the country irreversibly away from its collectivist past.

THATCHERISM AT ITS PEAK

The new parliament assembled on 17 June 1987. It contained a record number of female MPs (41), the first British Asian MP since 1929 (Keith Vaz, Labour member for Leicester West) and Britain's first black MPs (Diane Abbott, Bernie Grant and Paul Boeteng – all Labour). Newcomers also included former CND Chairwoman Joan Ruddock, and former local-government luminaries David Blunkett and Ken Livingstone (again, all Labour). In fact, almost 30 per cent of Labour members (as opposed to 14 per cent of Conservatives) were new to the House of Commons, which, of course, also saw the disappearance of familiar faces, including Enoch Powell, Roy Jenkins, Sir Keith Joseph, James Callaghan, James Prior and Francis Pym.

On 13 June the Prime Minister had reshuffled her Cabinet. Predictably, in the light of her victory, she had got rid of John Biffin (regarded as something of a maverick), and had demoted Peter Walker, albeit to the Welsh Office. (This was a great surprise, although Walker was allowed a free hand there in return for moderating his criticism of the Prime Minister. He was subsequently rated a great success in the job.) A rehabilitated Cecil Parkinson returned as Energy Secretary, while Lord Young and Kenneth Clarke were moved from Employment to Trade and Industry in the hope of boosting the enterprise spirit. John Moore was promoted from Transport Secretary to Social Services Secretary in what many saw as a key appointment. Still under fifty, good-looking and a self-made man, Moore was widely, if wrongly, tipped to be Thatcher's successor. He had worked in the USA and was a firm exponent of private enterprise. Thatcher's real successor, John Major, now joined the Cabinet for the first time as Chief Secretary to the Treasury. His rise to power was to be meteoric.

The Queen's Speech on 25 June set out the Government's priorities. There was to be an overhaul of the education system, new initiatives to encourage private enterprise in inner-city areas and the replacement of the rating system by the new 'community charge', or 'poll tax' as it was commonly known. More privatization measures were announced, including the British Airports Authority (BAA) in July 1987, the Government's remaining share in BP in October 1987, the British Steel Corporation (BSC) in November 1988, the electricity industry, and regional water and sewerage authorities between 1989 and 1991. Income tax was to be reduced to 25 per cent and among other free enterprise initiatives promised were a further trade union reform bill, and deregulation of rented housing, local government, licensing hours, radio and television.

Most of these proposals were highly controversial, if none more so than the poll tax. Nearly all of them seemed designed to abolish local initiative and accountability. The educational reforms included the right of schools and colleges to opt out of local-government control and the imposition of a 'national curriculum'. The regeneration of inner cities was to come about by direct links between central government and local employers and developers.

The educational reforms were part of the so-called Great Educational Reform Bill (or 'Gerbil') of 1987–8. (A counterpart was introduced for Scotland in 1989.) Its main aim was to reduce the allegedly baleful effect of left-wing educational theory, by forcing teachers to follow a centrally imposed national curriculum and by excluding local authorities (often Labour-dominated) from controlling the budgets and personnel of local schools and colleges. Parents, headteachers and school governors were to be given a more powerful role. The national curriculum was to be introduced into all primary and secondary schools and was to centre around three 'core' subjects (English, maths and science) and seven 'foundation' ones, to which 70 per cent of time was to be devoted. Pupils were to be tested and graded regularly at the ages of seven, eleven, fourteen and sixteen to ensure that schools were meeting standards and to enable Government inspectors to compare one school against another. Results were to be made available to parents, school governors and to the Government. These results would also enable parents to select the school of their choice for their children, which school would be under an obligation to accept them so long as space was available. In this way, an element of market discipline would be brought into education. In order to aid this process further, all state schools with more than 200 pupils were to be given full control of their budgets. Schools (larger primary as well as secondary) with more than 300 pupils were given the right to ballot parents and governors with a view to opting out of local-authority control altogether and becoming 'grant-maintained' schools. These would be directly funded by the Government and could be selective in admission. They could not, however, charge fees.

Other provisions of Gerbil included the abolition of ILEA, the democratically elected Inner London Education Authority, whose powers were transferred to the London boroughs. This part of the Bill came about after Norman Tebbit and Michael Heseltine, both now on the back benches, tacked on an amendment to the Government's Bill on 4 February 1988. Their argument was that not only was I L E A an anomaly after the abolition of the G L C, but one which was particularly susceptible to left-wing influence.

Gerbil also provided for the establishment of new, Government-funded City Technology Colleges, run by independent bodies linked to local industry and commerce. They were to provide an education with a strong scientific base. The Government hoped that industry would volunteer to provide part of the (substantial) cost of these foundations, but, perhaps predictably, there was little response.

Finally, Gerbil abolished tenure for new university staff or for those who were henceforth promoted.

The Bill emerged from parliamentary scrutiny more or less unchanged. Opposition came from Edward Heath and Labour's education spokesman, Jack Straw, who feared that the real intention behind the Bill was to set the clock back to the age of maintained grammar schools and secondary moderns. The educational professional bodies also expressed their opposition, as did the House of Lords, although the Upper House could effect only minor concessions. In the end, this greatest educational reform measure since Butler's Act of 1944 entered the statute book practically unaltered. It was not to come into effect until 1992 (to give teachers and others time to prepare the national curriculum), by which date, it was hoped, a national consensus on education could finally be established.

The other controversial measure enacted in the 1987-8 parliamentary session was the poll tax, which has already been discussed (see pp. 463-4). This was eventually passed by both Houses with large majorities, although Tory rebels in the Commons included Heath, Heseltine, Biffen, Sir Ian Gilmour and Sir George Young. The House of Lords majority was attained by imposing a three-line whip and 'chauffeuring in' scores of peers who were rarely seen there, many of them hereditary, and many of them standing to gain personally from the legislation. Originally the new tax was to be phased in gradually between 1990 and 1994, but after a grassroots revolt at the 1987 Conservative Party Conference, led by ex-MP Gerry Malone, the Government chose to introduce it in one fell swoop on 1 April 1990. Clearly it was never going to be popular, since opinion polls showed up to 70 per cent of the public opposed to it, especially those lower-middle-class and working-class converts to the Conservative Party whom Thatcherism was supposed to have won over. Nor did the fact that Nicholas Ridley was the Environment Secretary responsible for the tax help in selling it to the public. His style was abrasive and unsympathetic and in July 1989 he was replaced by the wet, compassionate and 'cuddly' Chris Patten, whose task it was to make the tax more acceptable. He attempted to do this by bringing in a 'safety net' for individuals and businesses that faced excessively steep rises in their local taxes. For the first year of its existence, therefore, low-tax authorities were to subsidize high-tax ones, this subsidy to be assumed thereafter by central government. As things were to turn out, the Government would have to spend many billions of pounds on subsidies in an ultimately vain attempt to make the poll tax workable.

Other controversial measures enacted in 1987–8 included Norman Fowler's Employment Act which embodied further trade union reform. Henceforth all strikes had to be preceded by union ballots, which ballots (as well as those for union leaders who now also had to be elected regularly) had to be carried out by post under independent scrutiny; nor could workers who refused to strike even after such ballots (or join closed shops after similar ones) be any longer disciplined or expelled. The resulting Act of May 1988 became known therefore to the Labour movement as 'the scabs' charter'. (Even some employers believed the Government had gone too far.) But the Government insisted that it had only returned union power to union members.

If its educational and trade union reforms had been designed to protect individuals against the powers of local and national institutions (and the same case was made for the poll tax), the Government also decided to aid individuals regarding housing. Its 1988 Housing Act allowed tenants of council houses to opt for new landlords, particularly 'housing associations' from a list approved by central government. It also provided for the decontrol of new rents and relets and allowed for the creation of Housing Action Trusts (HATs) to help renovate derelict urban areas. The Local Government Act of the same year, meanwhile, required local councils to open various services to competitive public tender from August 1989. These included road and vehicle maintenance, catering services, street cleaning and refuse collection. It also banned 'propaganda on the rates' as well as the promotion of homosexual activities by local authorities (by means of the notorious, but as it turned out more or less redundant, Clause 28, which had come about owing to back-bench pressure). Other controversial measures of the 1987–8 session included the abolition of state benefits to those aged between sixteen and eighteen who refused places on youth training programmes, and the decision taken by John Moore in 1988 (and again in 1989) not to raise the level of child benefit in line with inflation. The Government now also began to charge for dental check-ups and eye tests. Such measures led to back-bench revolts, but on the whole were seen by Conservative supporters as part and parcel of the Government's policy to encourage individual responsibility.

Succeeding parliamentary sessions witnessed the introduction of yet more Thatcherite measures. These included the sanctioning of new radio stations and television channels; 'top-up' loans for students rather than an overdue large increase in grants; the abolition of the 'dock labour scheme' which dated from 1946; not to mention changes in the law relating to working hours and mergers. The high point of Thatcher-ism, however, came with the extension of privatization to sensitive areas such as electricity (thus raising the issue of the future of nuclear power stations) and water (raising equally sensitive issues such as public health standards and environmental protection), not forgetting longer-term plans which were announced for the privatization of both British Coal and British Rail. Other indications that Thatcherism was reaching a peak were the decisions to reform the legal profession and the National Health Service. The latter in particular was the 'holy cow' or even the 'holy of holies' of British politics and it spoke volumes for Mrs Thatcher's prudence that she had refrained from tackling it until her third term as Premier. If the public became convinced that she meant to 'privatize' the NHS, her days in Downing Street would be over.

Public opinion as measured by opinion polls was consistently and heavily against the privatization of water. To most people, water and sewerage seemed to be a natural Government monopoly. Private companies were not reckoned to be capable of running such public assets in the public interest. Nicholas Ridley had in fact been forced to abandon privatization plans for the industry in 1986. However, having attempted to appease the environment lobby by establishing a National Rivers Authority in 1987 to look after river management and regulate water pollution, the Environment Secretary introduced a new Water Bill in 1988 which became law in 1989. Its parliamentary progress was dogged by battles in the House of Lords, not to mention struggles over EC directives on the standards of water quality which involved billions of pounds of extra spending, and criticism of the Government's advertising programme for the final sale of the ten new water authorities for England and Wales. These were floated for £5·2 billion, a rather modest price in the view of commentators who pointed out that 30 per cent of shares changed hands at a large profit on the first day of trading. The Government, on the other hand, had been concerned to ensure the success of the flotation, given the poor market reception in 1987 for the remaining state-held shares in BP.

The privatization of the electricity industry for a projected £20 billion – the biggest privatization measure ever – was to prove no more popular with the public. As with water privatization, all that was expected were higher prices and lower standards. Still, the new Energy Secretary, Cecil Parkinson, was determined to press ahead. He was also determined to meet right-wing critics who warned against creating a private monopoly out of a public one (just as Ridley had been with regard to the water industry). In the event a rather complicated scheme was decided on involving the creation of twelve independent electricity supply companies out of the existing English and Welsh area boards; the division of the Central Electricity Generating Board (CEGB) into two competing generating companies (National Power and Power Gen); and the establishment of a National Grid Company (NGC), which was to be jointly owned by the twelve new supply companies, with customers and generating companies having equal right of access to it. A different model was used in Scotland, where two integrated companies, based on the North of Scotland Hydroelectric Board (NSHEB) and the South of Scotland Electricity Board (SSEB), were established. If complicated, therefore, the scheme was not unduly radical. And what radical qualities it did possess were further diluted when the Government withdrew the country's nuclear power stations, of all types, from privatization. This brought about a temporary postponement of the flotation as well as the resignation of the chairman-designate of National Power, Lord Marshall. Yet the sale of the electricity industry in 1990 was to be another success.

Decisions, meanwhile, had been taken to reform the legal profession and the NHS. In both cases, Thatcherism demanded greater competition as the key to better performance. However, it faced entrenched opposition, in the first case from barristers and judges, in the second case from the medical profession backed by a fearful public.

The reform of the legal profession was the task of Lord Mackay of Clashfern, a former Lord Advocate of Scotland with few links with the English legal establishment, who became Lord Chancellor in October 1987. The outlines of his reforms were made public in a series of Green Papers published in January 1989. The main points were that solicitors, if properly 'certified', should be allowed to act as barristers; that they should be eligible to be judges; and that they should be able to combine their legal practices with those of other professions such as accountants and estate agents. Conveyancing, on the other hand, was to become open to banks and building societies. The Lord Chancellor allowed three months for comment, during which period his proposals were condemned by the General Council of the Bar, the Judges' Council, the Master of the Rolls, the Lords of Appeal, and three former Lord Chancellors, Lords Elwyn-Jones, Hailsham and Havers. Lord Lane, the Lord Chief Justice, condemned the planned reform as 'one of the most sinister documents ever to emanate from Government'. Predictably, only the Law Society, the body which represented the nation's solicitors, spoke up in defence of reform. Yet a White Paper entitled *Legal Services: A Framework for the Future* was presented by Lord Mackay to the House of Lords in July 1989, indicating that he was determined to press ahead in the following session with his proposals more or less unaltered. The end result was the Courts and Legal Services Act of 1990, which allowed the Bar Council and the Law Society to work out many of the details.

Throughout her period in office, Mrs Thatcher had taken care to repeat regularly that 'the National Health Service is safe in our hands'. And from the figures, discussed in the previous chapter, her claim held good. None the less, the Prime Minister was prone to treat the NHS as just another state industry whose efficiency and cost-effectiveness had to be improved as part of Government good housekeeping. Perhaps, ideally, she would have liked to privatize the NHS – certainly most members of the public credited her with this personal belief – yet she was all too well aware that such a policy would spell political death. Instead, the NHS was to be treated rather like the EC: lip service was to be paid to the ideal, whereas in practice it was to be made as market-oriented as possible. The crunch came at the end of 1987, when an additional

£100 million had to be found for the NHS after a number of ward closures had produced both public and medical protest. The Prime Minister announced the establishment of an 'internal review' which would be conducted by a Cabinet committee chaired by herself. Its other members would include John Moore, the Secretary of State for Health and Social Security; David Mellor, the Health Minister; the Scottish and Welsh Secretaries; and John Major, the Chief Secretary to the Treasury. It would hear evidence presented by interested parties and formulate reforms with a view to increasing efficiency and restructuring finance. Moore himself made the running in 1988 as an exponent of 'New Right' ideas on private health finance, but, ironically perhaps, had to be hospitalized with pneumonia and lost the opportunity to influence the debate. Thanks to back-bench revolts on social security issues, his star was beginning to fade politically in any case, so that in July 1988 his department was split in two, with Kenneth Clarke coming in from the Department of Trade and Industry to take command of health matters, leaving Moore to concentrate on social security. From this point on, no one was under the illusion that he might succeed Mrs Thatcher as Prime Minister.

Clarke, for his part, stressed that the NHS would remain free at the point of use, but backed schemes for the establishment of an 'internal market' within it. This meant that hospitals would be encouraged to become 'self-governing trusts' and general practitioners (GPs) to take charge of their own budgets, reducing the role of local health authorities. Meanwhile, these local health authorities would be able to buy and sell services to and from each other, in an attempt to force down prices for operations and services through competition, while hospital trusts could also sell and buy services to and from the private sector. (In fact, it was reckoned that only now would most NHS hospitals be forced to work out exactly what each operation and hospital service cost.) The parallels with Thatcherite housing and education policies were not difficult to find. But the Government was at pains to stress that privatization of the NHS was not envisaged. It would continue to be financed through taxation and patients would pay nothing to see their doctor or to enter hospitals, although private health insurance was to be encouraged and from April 1990 those over sixty were to be entitled to tax relief for private medical insurance premiums.

Predictably, these proposals, contained in a White Paper of January 1989 entitled *Working for Patients*, met furious opposition. Labour insisted that the real aim of the Government *was* to privatize the NHS. But among the medical profession, too, opposition was intense. The British Medical Association (BMA), representing GPs and junior doctors, denounced the plan as designed to turn doctors into bureaucrats and accountants and wondered where they were supposed to find the time, still less the skills, to run their own businesses. The Royal Colleges of Surgeons and Nurses were equally opposed. Many professionals wondered how sick patients could be transferred around the country to 'cheaper' beds for 'cheaper' operations perhaps hundreds of miles away. Would not GPs refer patients to their local hospitals as usual since that was what their patients would prefer? Many doctors saw the reforms as a political exercise designed to substitute ideology for hard cash, which would simply involve them in more time-wasting bureaucracy and deprive them of the opportunity to look after patients. Yet the Government insisted that the reforms were a genuine attempt to produce the best health care possible at the most effective price. Despite the appearance of hostile BMA advertisements, not to mention the appearance of a GP 'Protect the NHS' candidate at the Vale of Glamorgan by-election (a previously safe seat which the Government lost in May 1989 to Labour), Kenneth Clarke announced that the reforms – certainly the most radical since the NHS was founded – would come into effect in April 1991.

THE ECONOMY

If before the 1987 election Nigel Lawson was being hailed as a truly great Chancellor ('the most brilliant and innovative since the war' in the words of the *Sun* newspaper), his reputation was not to last. Very soon, the 'Lawson boom' was to turn into the 'Lawson bust'. The Chancellor himself would have done best to retire after the election, as he had often hinted, but given that the 'right job in the City' did not turn up, he remained at his post, hinting at retirement or expressing a wish to take over at the Foreign Office. Resignation, as it turned out, was to be his means of leaving the Government.

The quarrel which was to cause his resignation centred on the nature of exchange rate policy and Britain's relationship with the Exchange Rate Mechanism (ERM) of the European Monetary System. This tied the currencies of the Common Market countries to the Deutschmark. Lawson had become a convert to the ERM in 1985 and no longer believed in running the economy primarily by setting domestic monetary targets (see previous chapter) and leaving the exchange rate more or less to the market. Shifts in the value of the pound, he believed, threatened to set off inflationary spirals and, besides, his cooperation with his G5 colleagues in the September 1985 Plaza Agreement to reduce the value of the dollar was to boost his faith in international currency management. The similar Louvre Agreement of the G7 countries (the G5 plus Italy and Canada) in February 1987 was to bolster further his confidence in such management. Mrs Thatcher, on the other hand, believed that you could not 'buck the market' and that such currency manipulation would ultimately fail. She thus refused in 1985 to back Lawson's suggestion that Britain join the ERM. British inflation rates outside that body were better than those of France or Italy within it, and besides, given that the pound was now a petro-currency, its entry would merely subject the ERM to intolerable strains. Both Europe and Britain would be better off if it remained outside. By the end of 1986, however, Lawson was no longer prepared to take no for an answer and, very much on his own authority (the Bank of England does not seem to have been involved), pursued a policy – later disguised as having been necessary to implement the Louvre Agreement – of having the pound shadow the Deutschmark at an exchange rate between DM 2·8 and DM 3.

Until the 1987 election such a policy was sustainable. Money was flowing into London in anticipation of a third Thatcher election victory, so that both electoral and monetary considerations allowed interest rates to be reduced in accordance with Lawson's plans. In the aftermath of the election, however, matters would be rather different, given the need to rein in demand (house prices rising by up to 20 per cent, consumer spending up 6 per cent, incipient balance-of-payments difficulties). Even Lawson recognized this at first, raising interest rates from 9 to 10 per cent in August 1987. In New York in September, on the other hand, he advocated a 'more permanent regime' of internationally managed exchange rates based on the Plaza–Louvre framework, apparently with the support of his US and French counterparts. Thatcher's support, however, did not materialize.

More important, 19 October 1987 witnessed 'Black Monday', when stock markets plunged around the world. London alone saw £90 billion wiped off share values in two days. Since the previous Friday had witnessed a freak hurricane in South-East England which had pulled up centuries-old trees throughout the London commuter belt, there was talk of cosmic forces at work meting retribution to British yuppies. The truth of the matter was that the US market had decided that the Louvre agreement was unsustainable given the size of the US trade and budget deficits, and that world markets had followed Wall Street's fall.

Lawson condemned these events as an absurd over-reaction and ridiculed the 'excitable young men in striped shirts' in the City who had been responsible for the panic. The sell-off of BP shares already announced by the Government thus went ahead, albeit with a special buy-back scheme to reassure investors. Much more questionable, however, was Lawson's decision to cut interest rates – from 10 per cent to 8·5 per cent by the beginning of December – apparently to compensate for the crash and avoid a repetition of 1929. The US Federal Reserve, on the other hand, actually tightened monetary policy, which, as Lawson's critics were soon to point out, should have been the UK response also. The root of the crash, after all, had been fears about the US trade and budget deficits and worries that the managed exchange rate of the dollar could not be supported. The British economy was now also under inflationary pressures, as had been recognized in August. The trouble was that any tightening of British monetary policy (i.e. interest rate rises) would have sent the pound above the DM 3 ceiling to which Lawson was committed. Hence the real reason for the interest rate cuts, which Black Monday had disguised. In David Smith's words, 'The idea that Lawson carried on cutting interest rates solely in response to what he had viewed as an absurd market over-reaction, defies logic. Sterling, according to officials, was the dominant factor.' Ironically, Lawson's very success as Chancellor had so encouraged foreign invest-ment (£30 billion in 1987 and 1988 combined) that confidence had survived the crash intact. There was now huge upward market pressure on the pound. Lawson, therefore, had a dilemma: domestic monetary pressure required higher interest rates, which would only serve to increase the value of an already much sought-after pound. Any currency link with the DM within a band of 2·8–3 could only be achieved therefore by severely reducing interest rates and thereby considerably increasing inflationary pressures within the domestic economy. Yet as the Chancellor told the Treasury and Civil Service Committee of the House of Commons at the end of the year, 'When I think interest rates should go up, they go up. And when I think they should come down, they come down.' He clearly thought they should come down.

From now on, Lawson's policy was wrong. His 1988 budget, for a start, 'a budget to end all budgets', was designed in the words of one Downing Street critic to be 'a showcase for all his talents' before he retired to the City. It was certainly memorable. All higher rates of income tax were reduced to 40 per cent, while the standard rate was reduced to 25 per cent. A new target of 20 per cent was proclaimed for future Tory Chancellors. Politically, it was his apotheosis and undoing. For, to quote Smith again, 'the total size of the Budget "giveaway", including the higher-rate reductions, was £4 billion in the first year and £6 billion in the first full year. By the standards of post-war demand management, it was a huge fiscal boost to the economy, and this at a time of boom, not slump.' The tax cuts were thus soon to be seen 'as the most ill-timed tax change in the post-war period'.

Lawson's supporters argued that the sums involved were small compared to the £40 billion expansion of credit in the economy in 1988. But this missed the point, which was that the Chancellor's policies merely stoked the fires and suggested that the good times could last for ever. Lawson, in his statements to the Commons, dismissed all worries about the growth of credit: Government revenue was now in surplus rather than in deficit (and by no less than £14·4 billion). Indeed, even the balance-of-payments deficit served merely to reflect the strength of the economy. He argued, therefore, that tax cuts, a stable exchange rate and a balanced budget would sustain Britain's 'economic miracle' and set the course for long-term growth. The trouble was that the tax cuts had come too soon, the exchange rate could only remain stable by accepting inflation, and the suppression of that inflation would put an end to long-term growth.

One other aspect of the budget was also disastrous. In an attempt to limit the cost to the Treasury of tax relief on mortgage payments (£8 billion per year by the early 1990s), Lawson announced that henceforth relief would be limited to one person per household – the same situation which already applied to married couples. The change was to take effect from 1 August in order to give the Inland Revenue time to cope. The problem was that the South-East of England was full of people who could only afford to buy homes together, given the already huge increase in house prices. They therefore had four months during which to find properties which would allow them multiple tax relief. In these four months, therefore, thanks to the ingenuity of estate agents, house prices in the South-East rose by 15 per cent. For the year as a whole, prices rose by 30 per cent, in some areas by 50 per cent. This mistake was soon admitted by the Government. Yet if this one small change was responsible for so much inflation, the Government was reluctant to admit that its tax cuts were bound to generate a great deal more. The rest of the world did not seem to care much either – at least not yet. The financial press of almost every continent hailed Lawson's 1988 budget as further testimony to Mrs Thatcher's transformation of Britain.

The result of foreign confidence in the budget, of course, was further upward pressure on the pound. This was probably inevitable since in March, even before the budget, Mrs Thatcher, alerted by her personal economic adviser Sir Alan Walters, had ordered Lawson to abandon any policy of shadowing the Deutschmark. In the Commons she had made her famous statement that 'there is no way in which one can buck the market'. She saw a strong pound as confirmation of foreign confidence in her policies; besides, it also kept down inflation. Yet Lawson was determined to have his way and, in the weeks after his 15 March budget, once again began cutting interest rates. Sterling had already risen to DM 3·08. It was not to fall below DM 3 again until the autumn of 1989, thanks to the market's faith in Thatcher. By 18 May, however, interest rates were down to 7·5 per cent, and this in the wake of an unprecedented giveaway budget, at the time of a booming housing market (a converted cupboard in Knightsbridge sold as a flat at this time for £36,500), a credit boom and balance-of-payments difficulties. Clearly Lawson had learnt nothing from the experience of the previous autumn. One commentator was to paraphrase Oscar Wilde in this context: for Lawson to go down this route once was unfortunate; to do so twice was unforgivable. Yet down it he went until Sir Alan Walters, Thatcher's bluntly monetarist personal economics adviser, now also adviser to the World Bank in Washington and Professor at Johns Hopkins University in Maryland, intervened. During the summer and autumn of 1988 he denounced the policy of shadowing the Deutschmark as 'half-baked'. Lawson's policies were like a Greek tragedy, he said, the denouement of which was already clear. Yet still the pound kept on rising, and even Thatcher praised her Chancellor publicly. Only when the pound began to fall in early June were the brakes first applied. By the end of June 1988 interest rates were up to 9·5 per cent, having been increased by 0·5 per cent at a time. Lawson was not unduly concerned: the change did not seem to repudiate his policy (Walters was advocating interest rates of 12 per cent); the exchange rate was still above DM 3 (his target rate for the pound *vis-à-vis* the Deutschmark was now DM 3–3·10); and he still denied that there were significant inflationary pressures in the economy. Finally, if the economy had to be cooled down, he believed this should happen gently (the 'soft landing' strategy). And there was every reason to try to achieve this. Personal credit liabilities amounted to £328 billion in 1988 – in Christopher Huhne's words, 'Never [had] so many borrowed so much so quickly.' Companies were equally over-extended, their net borrowing requirement amounting to £45 billion in 1988. But a soft landing really did depend on a stable currency and no steep rise in interest rates. Unfortunately past policies were to make this impossible.

Inflation at the start of 1988 had been 3·3 per cent; by the year's end it was 6·8 per cent. As inflationary pressures became clear, interest rates had to rise steeply. Sir Alan Walters was proved right. By mid-July they were up to 10·5 per cent, and by the end of August to 12 per cent. The balance of payments also began to deteriorate rapidly. In his Autumn Statement of 1 November 1988 Lawson forecast a current-account deficit of £13 billion for 1988 (the budget forecast had been just £4 billion) and £11 billion for 1989. The real figures were to turn out to be £15·2 billion and £19·1 billion respectively. This was to put quite a different complexion on the relationship between interest rates and exchange rates. High interest rates were now essential to attract short-term capital to balance the current-account gap. The seriousness of the situation was underlined by November's record £2·4 billion trade gap published on 25 November. Sterling fell and interest rates went up to 13 per cent. Heath now ridiculed Lawson as a 'one-club golfer' with no policy at all for the economy save interest-rate rises. And in a sense he was right, since the Chancellor spurned credit controls or other alternatives.

Yet interest-rate increases worked rather slowly. Inflation increased throughout the first half of 1989 and had barely abated by the end of the year (8·3 per cent in May; 7·7 per cent in December). House prices rose by 12 per cent in 1989, consumer spending by 3·9 per cent. The current-account deficit reached more than £19 billion. Manufacturing output rose by 4·2 per cent, manufacturing investment by 5 per cent. The economy was still growing strongly therefore in 1989. Perhaps a soft landing would still prove possible, despite the steep rise in interest rates.

However, with the return to Downing Street of Sir Alan Walters in May 1989 as part-time adviser to the Prime Minister, this possibility disappeared. His differences with Lawson were well known and the fear of Mrs Thatcher undermining her Chancellor caused a loss of confidence in the foreign exchange markets. Sir Alan's views against Lawson moreover were regularly quoted. The pound began to slip below DM 3 with the result that by 24 May interest rates had increased to 14 per cent. The final rise to 15 per cent came just before the Conservative Party Conference on 5 October 1989, following a rise in German rates. So important had exchange rates become that Lawson felt he had no choice but to follow suit. Thatcher and Walters were incensed. Neither of them had ever believed in shadowing the Deutschmark and this was the last straw. A second recession was without doubt on the way after a decade of Thatcherism. There was no excuse for it. The Confederation of British Industry (CBI) agreed: it condemned the latest interest-rate rise as 'a spectacular own goal', pointing out that house prices were now falling by £2,000 per month. The staunchly Tory *Daily Mail* headlined its front page, 'This Bankrupt Chancellor'. Lawson still managed a standing ovation at the party conference, but his time was up. An article by Walters, reprinted in an American newspaper, caused him to demand the latter's resignation. Three times on 26 October Mrs Thatcher refused. So Lawson himself resigned and Walters followed his example. Mrs Thatcher, who claimed not to understand why Lawson had left (given her own views, she should have sacked him months before – in the event he was too popular within his party and in the City), replaced him with John Major, who had only recently replaced Howe at the Foreign Office (see below).

At first it seemed as if Lawson's resignation would steady market nerves. Government unity, it was argued, had been preserved. By the end of the year, however, the pound was on the slide again, down to DM 2·70. Major resisted pressure to raise interest rates again, perhaps to 17 per cent, informing the Treasury Committee on 4 December, 'I do not in fact anticipate a recession.' The truth was that with an election looming in the not-too-distant future, the Chancellor was still vainly hoping for a soft landing. But it was already too late and he should have raised interest rates in order to limit the damage of the hard landing which was now bound to come. By the spring of 1990 the pound had fallen another 20 per cent against the Deutschmark. Unemployment started to rise again in April. Major's March 1990 budget was relatively soft too. Excise duties were raised by 10 per cent (Lawson had chosen not to raise them in line with inflation the previous year in order to massage the figure, leaving his successor the task of catching up and thus adding 0·5 per cent to the current inflation rate of 8·1). But tax allowances were raised in line with inflation also. The centrepiece of the budget was the introduction of Tax Exempt Special Savings Accounts or 'Tessas' (exempt from tax if money was held there for at least five years). It was not a memorable budget and in any case was soon overshadowed by the very serious riots (especially in London where Downing Street was attacked and the South African Embassy set alight) which accompanied the introduction of the poll tax in April. The poll tax itself added yet another 1 per cent to the inflation rate, which rose to 9·4 per cent in April, making Thatcherite financial management look decidedly shabby.

Major's rise to power within the Government (as indeed his future premiership) was intimately connected with the ERM of the European Monetary System (EMS). The latter had been established in 1979 after an earlier experiment in European Monetary Union (EMU), the Werner Plan, had come to grief in 1974. It involved fixing European currencies to the Deutschmark, within broad (6 per cent above or below a certain rate) or narrow (2·25 per cent) bands. Great Britain had supported part of the scheme – the European Monetary Cooperation Fund – allowing for a common pool of reserves, but had refused to join the ERM. Denis Healey, still Chancellor in 1979, believed, after discussions with Manfred Lahnstein, Permanent Secretary at the West German Finance Ministry in Bonn, that West Germany's real intention was to use the scheme to force the rest of Europe to hold down the value of the Deutschmark. He recalled, 'The Bank of England was mildly in favour, since they thought it would exert a useful discipline on British governments. The Foreign Office was strongly in favour; it is in favour of anything which includes the word "European". I was fairly agnostic until I realized, from long discussions with Lahnstein and others, how it was likely to work in practice.'

Mrs Thatcher's Government had had little interest in the ERM to begin with. It was more interested in free markets and the abolition of exchange controls, and was involved in acerbic discussions with the EC regarding the British contribution to the EC budget. Yet, by 1985, Lawson's attitude had changed. The steep rise of the pound in the early 1980s and its sharp fall in early 1985 (both phenomena connected to its new status as a petro-currency) convinced him that a more stable exchange rate was necessary. By now, in any case, he was looking to the exchange rate rather than monetary targets to control inflation. A falling pound, he feared, would serve as a transmission belt for inflation through dearer imports and would trigger off an inflationary spiral. The ERM, on the other hand, could force internal discipline on the economy by fixing the exchange rate. He was supported in this argument by Sir Peter Middleton, the Permanent Under-Secretary to the Treasury; Sir Terence Burns, the Chief Economic Adviser to the Treasury; Robin Leigh-Pemberton, the Governor of the Bank of England; not to mention his Cabinet colleagues, Sir Geoffrey Howe and Leon Brittan. Their support, in the words of Professor Charles Goodhart of the London School of Economics, represented 'a staggering intellectual somersault'. Yet the key question was whether Mrs Thatcher could be converted. Sir Alan Walters, for one, was adamantly opposed to Britain's entering the ERM.

Walters argued that exchange rates were not a very sophisticated guide to monetary conditions and that foreign exchange markets relied too much on fashions and rumours. Besides, if there were no expectation of currency realignments, markets would pour money into weak currencies with the highest interest rates. Low-inflation countries would then have to put up interest rates, and high-inflation countries eventually would have to pull theirs down. The result would be a monetary squeeze in sound economies and inflation in unsound ones. In other words, the ERM would serve not to encourage convergence in Europe but to drive currencies further apart. In so far as currency realignments were actually quite common at this stage of the ERM's development, Walters merely took this to be further proof of the system's inherent instability.

Thatcher finally killed off any bid to enter the ERM at a crucial meeting at the Treasury in November 1985. Also present were Whitelaw, Lawson, Brittan, Howe, and senior Bank and Treasury officials. All were in favour of Britain entering the ERM. According to William Keegan's account, Thatcher responded to their pressure by echoing Abraham Lincoln: 'Ayes seven, noes one, the noes have it.' Lawson and Howe were later to argue that it was this 'missed opportunity' rather than Lawson's subsequent mismanagement of monetary policy which caused the future recession. Yet, as will be seen, Britain's entry into the ERM in 1990 brought no obvious respite from that recession, serving instead to lend credence to Sir Alan Walters' predictions.

The official line was that Britain would only enter the ERM 'when the time was ripe'. On 25 June 1989, with the economy entering a recession, Lawson and Howe decided that the time was indeed ripe. As Howe revealed later, they confronted Mrs Thatcher in her study in 10 Downing Street and forced the issue: 'The then Chancellor and I, as Foreign Secretary, made it clear we could not continue in office unless a specific commitment to join the ERM was made.' In the light of this double resignation threat, a cornered Prime Minister that very same day explained to a surprised European Council (heads of government) meeting in Madrid that Britain would enter the ERM, albeit when the right conditions had been met. These so-called 'Madrid conditions' included British inflation falling to the European average, a strong British economy and the liberalization of capital movements by other European countries, especially France and Italy. Sir Alan Walters was later to claim credit for them, but Lawson dismissed the claim, calling the conditions 'irrelevant', as indeed they turned out to be. Mrs Thatcher, on the other hand, was to have her revenge, for within three months she had sacked Howe as Foreign Secretary and had accepted Lawson's resignation. Major, seen as an efficient and personable, if relatively mindless *apparatchik*, replaced first Howe and then the Chancellor. The Prime Minister seemed under the impression that he was 'one of us'.

Major, in fact, had spoken up in favour of joining the ERM as far back as 1981. In 1989 he was still keen for Britain to do so. By 1 July 1990, moreover, he was aware that France and Italy would remove their impediments to capital movements. The key was now to reduce the level of British inflation, in order to argue that the Madrid conditions had been met. And from his point of view, this was all the more pressing since at Strasbourg in December 1989 the European Council had agreed to establish an inter-governmental conference (IGC) on European

Monetary Union. Major apparently convinced himself that it was necessary to join the ERM in order to influence this discussion.

Yet he faced severe problems. There was no sign of inflation falling to the average EC level and little sign of any coherent monetary policy. Medium-term monetary targets had gone, any hope of shadowing the Deutschmark had disappeared, and according to the Treasury there was no alternative to high interest rates. Worse still, the poll tax riots, the Tory slide in the opinion polls and Thatcher's own plummeting popularity were all factors which might undermine confidence in the currency on the foreign exchange markets. In David Smith's words, 'the prospects looked grim'. Major thus stepped up the pressure for ERM entry, arguing, with the support of his successor as Foreign Secretary, Douglas Hurd, that this alone could provide the necessary market reassurance. Other EC member states were informed therefore of Britain's serious intent to join in the near future, making any Thatcher veto extremely risky for the pound. Major and Hurd were well aware, in any case, how difficult it would be for the Prime Minister to rid herself of a Chancellor and Foreign Secretary again, so soon after the removal of Howe and Lawson.

Ideally, Major would have liked Britain to enter the ERM on 1 July 1990, to coincide with the abolition of capital controls in France and Italy and with the first meetings of the IGC. Instead, he planned to take Britain in during the weekend before the Conservative Party Conference in October, arguing that the Madrid conditions would be met so long as inflation was falling towards the EC average. He did not really have much choice, for having informed the world that entry was a matter of 'when' not 'if' (his formulation in the budget in March), he risked losing market confidence if he delayed any longer. Surprisingly, Mrs Thatcher agreed to Britain entering, so long as the announcement was accompanied by a 1 per cent cut in interest rates. Since inflation in the wake of Iraq's invasion of Kuwait had now risen to over 10 per cent, this was not a wise decision and must have been born of desperation. Britain, in other words, would ignore the Madrid conditions and enter the ERM with an inflation rate above 10 per cent, in the middle of a recession, and with the pound fixed to the Deutschmark at DM 2·95 within a 6 per cent band either side (i.e. at a relatively high exchange rate). Given that inflationary pressures were still strong and that the economy was already in recession, and therefore that there could be no quick reduction in interest rates or any fall (now) in the value of the currency, the recession was bound to be a long one. It is little wonder therefore that Mrs Thatcher, who by now had no more control of economic policy than she had of her Cabinet, was later to admit that UK entry into the ERM was her worst mistake. A few months later, having made a final attempt to resist a European take-over of her country, she was to lose control of her parliamentary party altogether.

FOREIGN AND DEFENCE POLICY.

Mrs Thatcher's last Government coincided with one of the most remarkable periods in world history. The Soviet Empire fell apart and the Soviet Union itself disappeared. Communism was repudiated throughout the world, except in the Republic of China and Cuba. Even Albania overthrew its communist dictatorship. In South Africa, President de Klerk announced the end of apartheid and began negotiations on Black rule with Nelson Mandela, whom he had freed from jail. Iraq was forced out of Kuwait by an alliance of first, second and third-world nations. Germany was unified in 1990, the Berlin Wall came down – in short, the political map of the world was permanently altered for the better. Or so it seemed. The American intellectual Francis Fukayama argued in an essay entitled 'The end of history', that, with the conquest of fascism and communism, liberal democracy had triumphed as the ultimate political system of mankind. Future wars or political unrest would merely signify that other parts of the world were falling into place.

Mrs Thatcher was to argue that Thatcherism had played its part in all these developments. Her 'special relationship' with Ronald Reagan had persuaded the Soviets that they could not win the arms race, so they had given up. Her economic policies had helped revive capitalism throughout the world. Her victory in the Falklands had shown that dictators could be outfaced – and indeed she had been partly instrumental, as will be seen, in forcing that logic on President Bush when he decided to fight the Gulf War against Saddam Hussein of Iraq. She had often also been the only Western leader to defend the South African President's policy of peaceful change in that country, a policy which had patently paid off. There was clearly something in all her claims, although she tended to exaggerate them. On the other hand, most of the energy she expended on foreign affairs during her last period in office had to be spent defending British national sovereignty against the growing power of Brussels. And her most formidable diplomatic opponent in this context was the President of the European Commission, the Frenchman Jacques Delors.

Under his leadership the Commission interpreted the Single European Act in a manner regarded as arbitrary by the British Government. The end results were the Delors Report on European Economic and Monetary Union of April 1989 and the Community Charter of Basic Social Rights for Workers of the following month. The first outlined a three-stage process towards European monetary union, which would culminate in the establishment of a single European currency issued by an independent European Central Bank (more accurately, a European System of Central Banks or ESCB, but soon everybody spoke of a Eurofed or European Central Bank). The Commission recognized that a new treaty amending the Treaty of Rome would be necessary in order to implement this report. The second document listed a number of rights which the Commission believed all Community citizens should possess, including the right to worker information, consultation and participation. The Charter had no force in law, as Social Affairs Commissioner Vasso Papandreou conceded, but the Commission produced action programmes of directives through which it hoped to enforce it using Article 100A of the Rome Treaty as amended by the Single European Act. These directives could be passed in the Council of Ministers by majority vote, thereby nullifying any British veto. Both schemes were anathema to Mrs Thatcher, who prophesied (correctly as it turned out) that they would be implemented only over her dead body. Yet the meeting of the Council of Ministers at Strasbourg in December 1989 gave the green light to both. Even worse, in the spring of the following year political union was added to the agenda. How then had this come about?

As has already been seen, Thatcher had agreed to the Single European Act and the completion of the Single Market by the end of 1992. At the Brussels meeting of the European Council in June 1987 she had also managed to get some reform of the EC budget agreed: the phasing out of green currencies and monetary compensation amounts (MCAs) by 1989; agreement that new levels of resources must take into account 'the proportionality of contributions in accordance with the relative prosperity of member states'; finally, the Common Agricultural Policy (CAP) was to be so amended, in the words of Derek Urwin, 'that spending on it would be based upon a more realistic market balance between supply and demand, with any increase in . . . expenditure on guarantees to be pinned, at a maximum, to the rate of growth of the EC's own resources'. Mrs Thatcher could therefore work in harmony with her partners.

The 1989 initiatives, on the other hand, in her opinion directly threatened Britain's national interests. The Delors Report would deprive the country of the ability to manage its own economy, while the Social Charter threatened to undermine the Thatcher revolution itself. Its defenders might describe it as anodyne – what, after all, was wrong with better working conditions, better health and safety provisions at work, greater sexual equality in the workplace, better training, more opportunity and greater freedom of movement? Yet Delors had made clear that the implementation of such rights would mean that within ten years '80 per cent of [all] social legislation' would be made in Brussels. He had hinted to the British TUC conference in September 1988 that social policy might even be used to reverse Thatcher's trade union reforms in Great Britain. Little wonder then that the Prime Minister was to condemn the Charter as 'socialism by the back Delors' or that she should consider the right to workers' participation and consultation as 'Marxist'. She also believed that the Charter was meant to saddle the poorer economies of the Community with social overheads designed to prevent them from competing with their richer neighbours. Finally, she dismissed it as bureaucratic and uneconomic. It would cost British industry £5 billion per year to implement and would merely increase unemployment and red tape. Besides, if Britain needed more laws of this type, she could invent her own. The Prime Minister, in fact, had already made her position crystal clear in her famous speech to the College of Europe in Bruges on 20 September 1988: 'We have not successfully rolled back the frontiers of the state in Britain,' she declared, 'only to see them reimposed at a European level, with a European super-state exercising a new dominance from Brussels.' (This speech also inspired the creation in February 1989 of the Bruges Group, founded by Oxford undergraduate Patrick Robertson, and chaired by Lord Harris of High Cross, who brought many IEA economists with him. It operated as a supposedly all-party, but in practice Conservative, intellectual pressure group, with a council composed of academic Eurosceptics such as Patrick Minford, Martin Holmes, Tim Congdon,

Norman Stone and Alan Sked. The latter became its most controversial pamphleteer but was later expelled, having in November 1991 founded the Anti-Federalist League to run candidates against Conservative MPs among others at the 1992 election.)

The Delors Report was a much greater challenge to Mrs Thatcher than the Social Charter. She found herself able to support stage one, which called for all Community currencies to join the ERM and for the liberalization of financial markets. But stage two, which called for the establishment of new institutional structures including the ESCB or Eurofed, a common monetary policy, the pooling of reserves and central supervision of national budget deficits and their financing was rejected along with stage three, which looked forward to a single currency, tightened central supervision and stronger structural and regional policies. Acceptance would mean the end of Britain's ability to run its own economy.

Proponents of European Monetary Union argued that a single currency would bring major advantages: the abolition of transaction costs, price stability and greater growth. Their opponents pointed out that transaction costs were marginal (less than 0·5 per cent of GNP), that imposing an untried currency on the whole of Europe would create unprecedented instability, that weaker economies would suffer from huge increases in unemployment and deindustrialization, not growth, as indeed the experience of East Germany after its monetary union with West Germany in 1989 seemed to prove, while, finally, a single market did not require a single currency. The USA, Canada and Mexico were establishing one with separate currencies which were not even fixed. Critics, therefore, concluded that the real impetus behind monetary union was political: Europe could only become a single state if it had a single currency. Hence the political objection to the Delors Report by Mrs Thatcher: it was really designed to put an end to British national sovereignty.

The Prime Minister promised her Community colleagues at Strasbourg, however, that her opposition would be constructive. Thus, in the first half of 1990, much thought was given to a British alternative to the Delors Report, which centred round a 'hard ecu' (European Currency Unit). John Major and Norman Lamont at the Treasury took up this scheme with great enthusiasm. It involved a parallel or thirteenth currency for the Community which could be used by anyone who wanted it (although the idea seems to have been that it would only be used for large international transactions, as there were no plans to introduce new cash registers). There would thus be no plan to impose it on Europe. It was to be managed by a European Monetary Fund and if found more attractive by market forces than national currencies, might eventually replace the latter by a natural process. As Brian Tew describes it, 'its initial central value in terms of national currencies would have to be negotiated, but thereafter its central value would never be devalued in relation to the national currency of any Community member. The instrument of policy by which the EMF would keep the hard ecu sufficiently hard would be the level of the interest rate it would pay on its hard-ecu-denominated deposit liabilities.' Major, who proposed this scheme as a free-market alternative to stage two of the Delors Plan throughout 1990, told the House of Commons Treasury Committee, 'my fundamental objection to the Delors approach ... is that its prescription for economic and monetary union centralizes power. It relies on administrative fiat and institutional change. It skates over vital issues of political accountability. Changes in economic and monetary arrangements must reflect real changes in economic behaviour in the market place and they must work with the grain of the market and not against it. In my view, the Delors route is quite the wrong way for the future development of Europe.' Yet the hard-ecu plan was never likely to be accepted. It was complicated and would have added yet another currency to the Community's twelve; there was an ambiguity as to whether it was ever meant to become the single currency of Europe (what then of the constitutional objections?); and it was technically difficult to see why it should have been more effective in eliminating inflation than an ERM containing all member states and operating within narrow bands. By 1992 Europe had rejected the scheme and had settled for the Delors version. So, too, in fact, had Major and Lamont, who would soon eat their words.

By 1990, a debate was also raging inside the Community over the relative merits of broadening it to include the EFTA countries, not to mention those East European ones which had by now liberated themselves from communism. Turkey, too, wanted to become a full member. Mrs Thatcher, who in her Bruges speech had stated, 'we shall always look on Warsaw, Prague and Budapest as great European cities', was a powerful voice for widening the Community in order to stabilize democracy in the Continent. But many saw her enthusiasm as merely a ploy with which to hold up political and monetary union. For his part, Jacques Delors wanted to deepen the Community as soon as possible, although he understood that East Germany would soon have to be integrated into it as part of a united German state. As early as January 1990, therefore, in a speech to the European Parliament in Strasbourg, he called for institutional reform of the Community to supplement his demands for EMU and the Social Charter. The Commission, he argued, should be given greater powers and become a 'real executive', although one which would be balanced by and answerable to 'the democratic institutions of the future Federation', especially a reformed and more powerful European Parliament. The latter then began its own campaign for greater powers. Once the leaders of France and Germany had lent their support in April, the two Dublin summits which followed agreed that a parallel IGC should convene in December to consider European Political Union (EPU) as well as EMU. The British, who had politely condemned Delors's January speech as 'premature' and whose policy, stated in Thatcher's Bruges speech and repeated at Aspen, Colorado on 5 August, was based on 'willing and active co-operation between nation states', found it no more possible to prevent this development than those of December 1989. Clearly, Mrs Thatcher would have to fight a rearguard battle of huge proportions, although she could console herself with the thought that any changes to the Treaty of Rome would require the unanimous ratification of all member states. In other words, she had a veto, which she was fully prepared to exercise.

In the meantime, there were other problems of European diplomacy to worry her. One of these – which did not help to make Community diplomacy any easier – was the re-emergence of the German Question. Developments in East Germany, leading to the opening of the Berlin Wall on 9 November 1989, had taken all European statesmen by surprise. After all, as recently as 1987 Erich Honecker, the East German communist leader, had been welcomed to West Germany as a distinguished foreign guest from a state whose existence seemed as secure as any other in Europe. Now it was on the verge of collapse. Then on 28 November 1989 Helmut Kohl had presented an immediate ten-point plan for German unity to the Bundestag. Mutual co-operation between East and West Germany was to lead first to a confederation of the two states and thence to reunification on a federal basis. The international context was mentioned, but this was a clear bid by the West German Chancellor to take exclusive control of events in Central Europe. At a special EC summit in Paris on 18 November, morever, he offered his EC counterparts no opportunity to discuss the matter. Mrs Thatcher, therefore, appeared distinctly cool. In an interview published in January 1990 in the *Wall Street Journal* she warned the Germans to make due allowance for the Soviet position and to consider the ramifications for the Community also. None the less, she declared in favour of German unity.

Charles Powell, Thatcher's personal adviser on foreign policy, telephoned his opposite number in Bonn, Horst Teltschik, on 9 February to explain the Prime Minister's position. In a three-hour conversation, he explained that Mrs Thatcher was of a different generation and felt 'uneasy' about a large and powerful Germany. She wanted the Soviets drawn into negotiations (conscious of her good relationship with Gorbachev) and was worried about the ramifications of German unity for NATO and the EC. Her solution was negotiations within a 'Two plus Four' context, i.e. negotiations between the German states should be paralleled by negotiations with the Four Powers who still held rights in Germany: Britain, France, the USA and the USSR. These, in fact, took place, beginning on 5 May and ending on 12 September. In all discussions Mrs Thatcher was adamant that Germany should remain a member of NATO, a position with which Kohl was only too happy to agree. He did not, however, wish to station German NATO troops on former East German soil, or introduce NATO short-range nuclear weapons there. Finally, he realized the need for transition arrangements regarding Soviet troops.

Mrs Thatcher was also concerned at West Germany's reluctance to recognize the legitimacy of the post-war Polish–German border. Yet once this was agreed by West Germany at the beginning of March, she congratulated Kohl on 'a most statesmanlike step'.

From now on, as for example in Oxford at the end of March, she reassured Kohl that she was as much in favour of German unity as anyone else, emphasizing, however, the need to retain NATO nuclear weapons in Germany, and making no apologies for earlier doubts. Teltschik described her as 'impressive and exciting to talk to as always, if also difficult. Margaret Thatcher knows what she wants, represents her position fearlessly, and pays little regard to the possible sensibilities of her negotiating partners. She has a tremendous command of detail, is mostly well prepared, asks precise questions, listens carefully to those negotiating with her and tackles them directly. She adheres to the famous maxim, that Britain acknowledges no friends or enemies, but merely interests.' He and Kohl expressed their relief when on 13 April in a joint press conference in Bermuda with the new US President, George Bush, she declared unambiguously for the first time that a united Germany 'must have unlimited control over its own territory, without any sort of limitations on its sovereignty'. This was much more reassuring than stories of her Chequers seminar with academic experts on the Germans, which had patronizingly analysed the chips on German shoulders and their need to be loved, albeit concluding that the best policy was to be nice to them.

In fact, in June 1990 in Moscow, Mrs Thatcher had encouraged President Gorbachev to allow a united Germany to remain in NATO, and at a special NATO summit conference in London at the beginning of July she repeated her support, adding that US nuclear and conventional forces should remain in Germany, which she described as 'the navel of NATO'. Any force reductions were to be coordinated and NATO was to retain its technological lead, including the Strategic Defence Initiative (SDI). Gorbachev, who badly needed German financial support, at last agreed to Kohl's negotiating position when the latter visited the Soviet Union in mid-July. Germany, once united, could join NATO. Her sovereignty would be absolute. NATO troops might not enter the territory of the former GDR, but non-integrated West German units could. There would be transitional arrangements for Soviet troops, Germany would renounce nuclear, biological and chemical weapons (as it had since 1955) and would remain committed to the nuclear non-proliferation treaty. The total troop strength of a united Germany would be reduced within four years to a maximum of 370,000. With this deal secured, the main obstacle to unification was removed and on 3 October 1990 Germany once again became a united, sovereign state. Despite her detractors, Mrs Thatcher had not ruined Anglo-German relations by her attitude or in any way impeded the process of reunification.

All these developments, as has already been pointed out, took place within the context of a rapidly changing international order. The collapse of the Soviet empire and the growing trend towards European unity naturally had repercussions for defence policy. One of these was the revival of West European Union (WEU) as a possible focus for European defence efforts. The French and Germans tended to see it as the basis for a future, separate European army within NATO, while the British and US governments viewed its role with caution, not to say suspicion. It had proved useful for the coordination of warships deployed in the Persian Gulf during the Iran–Iraq War of 1980–88, but even then most staff-work had been done by NATO. Given that there had been no breakthrough in the Conventional Forces in Europe (CFE) talks in Vienna, Britain was reluctant to contemplate any change in command structures. On the other hand, with the breach in the Berlin Wall and the collapse of Soviet power in Eastern Europe, the Government was tempted to look for a 'peace dividend'.

In 1990 the Ministry of Defence embarked on a study known as 'Options for Change'. Despite Mrs Thatcher, the July NATO summit held in London had ended with a communiqué stating, 'As Europe changes, we must profoundly alter the way we think about defence.' Hence the new Defence Secretary, Tom King, proposed significant reductions in all three Services. Trident was not affected, but the RAF's airfields in Germany were reduced from four to two and the RAF would no longer contribute to the air defence of that country. All seven air-defence Tornado squadrons would be based in Britain. The Phantoms would go, as would the anti-shipping role of the Buccaneers. The navy's three carriers and amphibious capacity would remain. The destroyer/frigate force would be reduced to about forty, the non-Trident submarine fleet to about sixteen, three-quarters of it nuclear-powered. The army in Germany would be reduced by about half; its four divisions reduced to one, which in an emergency could be reinforced from Britain by another. Troops would remain in Berlin, however, until Soviet forces withdrew from East Germany. By the mid-1990s, therefore, the regular army would be about 120,000 strong, the navy (including the Royal Marines) about 60,000, and the RAF about 75,000. All this amounted to a reduction in manpower of 18 per cent. Civilian manpower was to fall by the same amount, while the choice of a replacement tank was deferred.

Only a week afterwards, however, on 2 August 1990, Saddam Hussein of Iraq invaded Kuwait. On 8 August he announced its annexation. That same day President Bush announced that US forces would assist in the defence of Saudi Arabia, seen as Saddam's next victim. If Saudi Arabia fell, the Iraqi dictator would control a quarter of the world's oil supplies. Worse still, the independence of sovereign states would count for nought. Meanwhile the UN Security Council passed two resolutions, the first condemning the invasion and calling for Iraq's unconditional withdrawal, the second imposing mandatory sanctions.

Britain reacted quickly. Mrs Thatcher was in Colorado when the crisis erupted and used the opportunity to impress on President Bush, who flew to consult her, that a firm stand was needed. He later recalled her saying, 'George, this is no time to wobble.' One of the President's aides described her as having exercised 'a big influence'. Bush later remarked, 'Thank God for allies and friends like Margaret Thatcher when the going gets tough.' According to another aide, 'Bush was really impressed with her, perhaps for the first time.' It was just as well. Bush seemed to have a dislike of strong personalities and the rapport which had existed between Reagan and Thatcher had not been reproduced between her and Bush. Indeed, the fear existed in London, after his first trip to Europe as President at the end of 1989, that he might prefer a 'special relationship' with the Germans. In C. J. Bartlett's words, 'British officials in Washington were privately acknowledging the influence of a small group of advisers in the State Department (with supporters in the White House), who wanted the United States to establish a special relationship with the EC as a whole, and with West Germany in particular. Closer integration was imperative to bind West Germany to the West, especially in anticipation of German reunification. The British would most please by becoming fully committed and wholehearted Europeans.' The Gulf War, on the other hand, would soon demonstrate who was really America's best ally in Europe.

Meanwhile, the Cold War came to a symbolic end with the signing in Paris on 18 November of the Conventional Forces in Europe Treaty, which agreed equal limits on major items of equipment between Eastern and Western Europe and the maximum individual holding of any individual state. In practice this maximum would only apply to the Soviet Union, since no other nation, in Michael Carver's words, 'was likely to come anywhere near it'. Britain's declared totals – 1,198 tanks, 636 artillery pieces, 3,193 armoured combat vehicles, 842 combat aircraft and 368 attack helicopters – were all to be reduced in the near future under the 'Options for Change' scheme. Once the Treaty was signed, negotiations could begin for the reduction of short-range nuclear forces, including a mutual withdrawal of all nuclear artillery shells.

The signing of the Treaty proved to be significant in one other respect: it was the last international appearance of Mrs Thatcher as British Prime Minister.

THATCHER'S FALL FROM POWER

The strains inside the Tory party leadership were first dramatically revealed when Mrs Thatcher, revenging herself for the Madrid conditions imposed by Howe and Lawson, sacked her Foreign Secretary in July 1988. He was offered the post of either Leader of the House of Commons or Home Secretary, and chose the former after several hours contemplating resignation. Even then, he demanded the title of Deputy Prime Minister, the chairmanship of several Cabinet committees (including the so-called Star Chamber which settled departmental budgets), not to mention the use of Dorneywood, the Chancellor's official residence. But the demotion was not obscured, the press office at Number 10 describing the deputy premiership as a courtesy title only. Lawson's resignation in October served merely to reinforce the impression that the Government was split from top to bottom. Indeed, the only Conservative who gained from these events was John Major.

The European issue returned to haunt the party with the 1989 elections to the European Parliament. As usual, the vast majority of the electorate (almost two-thirds) stayed at home, but the Tory campaign, based on ridiculous advertising (including the slogan, apparently personally approved by the Prime Minister, 'Stay at home on June 15th, and you'll live on a diet of Brussels') was an expensive disaster. The party received only 35 per cent of the vote and lost 13 seats to Labour. In Scotland it came third behind the SNP, while the Greens picked up a protest vote of about 15 per cent. Coming as they did on the tenth anniversary of Mrs Thatcher's advent to power, these results were seen as a rejection of her policies. The deteriorating economy meant in any case that by the end of 1989 she was registering only 25 per cent support in opinion polls. Indeed, so strife-ridden had the party now become that Sir Anthony Meyer MP, a former diplomat, noted federalist on European matters and Heseltine supporter actually ran against her for the party leadership on 5 December, gaining 33 votes to her 314. (There were 24 spoiled ballot papers and three abstentions, including that of Heseltine.) Many observers, however, thought that this had only been a dry run for Heseltine himself. And they were to be proved right when he challenged her less than a year later.

Meanwhile, the party attempted to present a new face to the electorate, with the disappearance from the Cabinet by the end of January 1990 of Lord Young, John Moore, Norman Fowler and Paul Channon. Kenneth Baker, who became Tory Party Chairman after the Euro-election disaster, got the job of ensuring the party was in fighting condition by the next election. Chris Patten, a notorious 'wet', got the job of introducing the poll tax as well as the more congenial task of framing a new Green Bill on environmental protection (Mrs Thatcher had taken up the issue the previous year, going so far as to convene an international conference in London in March 1989 on the protection of the ozone layer). Yet the outlook was fairly bleak. The introduction of the poll tax led to riots as well as resignations from Tory councillors, not to mention a political war of attrition by non-payment campaigners. The Tory party was in fact as split over the poll tax as it was over Europe, making it extremely difficult for the leadership to contain unrest. The steadily worsening economic situation meant that back-bench nerves were becoming frayed. Even Norman Tebbit began a campaign against the Government's decision to accept 50,000 families, if need be, from Hong Kong, where confidence in China's intent to keep its promises after 1997 had been badly impaired by the Tiananmen Square massacre.

In the end, however, Europe was the issue which was to precipitate disaster for the Prime Minister. The outcry for blood after Nicholas Ridley's interview in the *Spectator* was one sign that it would not go away. Ridley had described the ERM as a 'German racket to take over Europe' and had expressed the opinion that Britain might just as well have given in to Hitler. Despite Ridley's record of unstinting loyalty to her, Mrs Thatcher felt compelled to accept his resignation in order to appease the press and the European wing of her party.

In October, of course, she acquiesced in British entry into the ERM in a rather desperate attempt to secure a 'quick fix' on interest rates and recoup some lost popularity on the eve of the party conference. Yet the issues of European monetary and political union still had to be addressed and at a special EC summit in Rome at the end of October she found herself 'ambushed' by her European partners. She once more defied them, her report to the House of Commons including her 'No! No! No!' to European unity, which proved too much for Sir Geoffrey Howe. He resigned as Leader of the House. Sir Geoffrey had in 1972 and 1986 given explicit and absolute assurances, first as Solicitor General and then as Foreign Secretary, that British national sovereignty would never be impugned. Recently, however, he had been giving lectures explaining that he no longer knew what national sovereignty meant. Instead, he spoke of the need to avoid missing buses and trains, which had led Mrs Thatcher to comment that people who got on buses and trains without knowing their destination were often taken for a ride. Worse still, their vehicle could 'go over a ravine or plunge into the abyss'.

There was little indication that Mrs Thatcher saw Howe's resignation as an immediate threat to her tenure of office. Speaking at the Lord Mayor's banquet at the Mansion House, she declared, 'I am still at the crease though the bowling has been pretty hostile of late . . . And in case anyone doubted it, can I assure you that there will be no ducking the bouncers, no stonewalling, no playing around for time. The bowling's going to get hit all round the ground. That's my style.' Yet that was partly the problem; her style was beginning to wear a little thin by now. Too many, even among her own back-benchers, thought that with the end of the Cold War, the retirement of Reagan, the poll tax, the failing economy after more than a decade of Thatcherism, the 20-point Labour lead in the opinion polls and the endless rows over Europe, the style was out of date. Thus in his resignation speech the next day, Sir Geoffrey could convincingly turn her cricketing metaphor against her, speaking of being sent out to play with a broken bat, and hinting that Heseltine should challenge her: 'The time has come for others to consider their own response to the tragic conflict of loyalties with which I myself have wrestled for perhaps too long.'

Heseltine needed little encouragement to throw his hat into the ring. He had been waiting for this moment ever since his resignation over Westland. He challenged the Prime Minister on Europe and the poll tax, although he claimed not to repudiate her record entirely: 'Wherever you look, you find that I have been at the leading edge of Thatcherism . . . Anyone who knows anything about me will know that I am nothing if not radical. Every department I have ever had will testify to that.'

The first ballot was held while the Prime Minister was in Paris attending the ceremonies connected with the signing of the CFE

Treaty. Her campaign team in London, however, on whom her political future depended, proved woefully inadequate. Thus, although she secured 204 votes to Heseltine's 152, she failed to win the 208 votes necessary to avoid a second ballot. In Paris, where the news was conveyed to her, she announced her immediate intention to fight on. Yet on her return to London she soon realized that her chances of victory were small. She consulted her Cabinet colleagues individually and they advised her to retire. She herself felt that even if she were to win by a small majority, her authority as Prime Minister would soon be destroyed by the press. Early in the morning of 22 November, therefore, she informed the Cabinet of her decision to resign. A second leadership ballot was held on 27 November. By now she was actively backing Major against Heseltine, whom she loathed. Douglas Hurd was also a candidate. The results were: Major 185, Heseltine 131, Hurd 56. Heseltine and Hurd then withdrew, leaving Mrs Thatcher to console herself with the thought that she had still received more votes than anyone else. More distressing, however, must have been the realization that, after three election triumphs, she had been the victim of the most ruthless act of political ingratitude in the history of modern Britain. Worse still, within just a couple of years her 'chosen successor', John Major, had repudiated nearly all her major policies.

THE MAJOR GOVERNMENT, 1990-92

Not a great deal was known about the new Prime Minister except that everybody seemed to like him. He was frequently referred to as 'nice', although 'grey' was an adjective used almost as often – the satirical television puppet programme *Spitting Image* had him painted grey from head to foot. To many voters, however, his relaxed, natural style was a welcome relief after Mrs Thatcher. He came from relatively humble origins, the son of a former trapeze artist who had subsequently become an, albeit none-too-successful, small-businessman. The original family name seems to have been Major–Ball, a name which the Prime Minister's family still kept.

Unlike many of his colleagues, the new Prime Minister had not enjoyed a brilliant academic career. At school he had acquired only six O-levels (grades unknown) before leaving at the age of sixteen. His early career is unclear, although it included a spell as a navvy and an unsuccessful attempt to become a bus conductor. By the age of twenty-two, however, he had found employment in banking, managed to pass professional exams and thereafter rose through the public relations side of the industry to become a troubleshooter for Lord Barber, Heath's undistinguished Chancellor of the Exchequer, who now worked in the City as head of Standard Chartered Bank.

Given this background, the joke quickly gained currency that Major was the only boy in history to run away from the circus to become an accountant. His political career, on the other hand, first in local government where he became a highly successful Chairman of Housing in Lambeth, then at Westminster, was dramatically to belie any impression that he lacked ability. Still, he remained touchy about his academic background and in one of his first interviews as Prime Minister declared that he found university professors for the most part out of touch with reality.

Most people were only too glad to give him the benefit of the doubt and it was noticeable that he had the ability to charm those he had to deal with. At the Rome meeting of the European Council in December, for example, he made a good impression on his colleagues, who were content to leave him more time to deal with his political problems over EMU and EPU – although Jacques Delors commented acidly that he had arranged one crisis (for Mrs Thatcher the previous month, thereby taking some credit for her political demise) and could always arrange another. He was to get on extremely well with Helmut Kohl and George Bush (another grey personality and suspected by his right-wing critics, just as Major would be, of being a 'wimp'). How much weight he carried in foreign affairs as a result of these good personal relations was difficult to determine. Certainly, he was never to get much change out of Kohl in spite of the latter's apparently avuncular fondness for the new Prime Minister.

As far as domestic policy was concerned, Major claimed to follow naturally in Thatcher's footsteps, although he clearly resented being known as her 'chosen successor'. He particularly resented an interview she gave in 1992 in which she declared that he was not his 'own man' and that there could be no such thing as 'Majorism'. When asked to list his most admired prime ministers he chose Baldwin and Chamberlain, failing to mention either Churchill or Thatcher. Very soon, in little ways, he had distanced himself from her record. For example, child benefit was once again raised in line with inflation and compensation was paid to haemophiliac AIDS victims. True, he remained faithful to Thatcher's privatization programme and continued her reforms in health, law and education, but on the most controversial aspects of her third term in office he chose a different path. The poll tax was abolished and, on Europe, he ended up signing a treaty establishing economic and political union, which Thatcher was to denounce. By the time she entered the House of Lords in the summer of 1992, having kept her counsel during the previous election, Lady Thatcher had emerged as his main opponent within the Conservative Party. She had no liking for his economic policy either, which saw her budget surplus turned into deficit, and now regretted the consequences of entry into the ERM, which in private she admitted had been a mistake. Major's men tried, in turn, to write her off as yesterday's news, but, given the warm support she still enjoyed among Conservative constituency party activists, not to mention Young Conservatives and Conservative students, they had to be wary of her. For example, she enjoyed a rapturous reception at the party conference in October 1991 and Major felt it necessary to accompany her on stage lest he be overshadowed. The new Party Chairman, Chris Patten, on the other hand, had taken care to deny her the opportunity to speak. Still, she had managed to make her presence felt and would continue to do so regularly, despite unfitting comparisons with Edward Heath.

DOMESTIC AND ECONOMIC POLICY

John Major made no spectacular changes to the Cabinet when he became Prime Minister. Hurd remained at the Foreign Office and he promoted Norman Lamont, previously Chief Secretary to the Treasury, to replace him as Chancellor. The key change was Michael Heseltine's re-entry to the Cabinet as Environment Secretary, with the job of killing off the poll tax. This was politically a poisoned chalice, but Heseltine managed to survive by inventing a 'council tax' which was to be introduced in 1993. In practice it sounded more like the old rates than anything else: all houses were to be valued and assessed for taxation depending on which band they fell into. The Government was forced to agree to an extra (eighth) band, but its real problems would only arrive in 1993 by which time house values had collapsed. Meanwhile, many people seemed to get the impression that they need not pay the poll tax at all. This led to higher bills for the majority who did and even greater pressure on the Government to authorize billions of pounds of expenditure to keep poll tax bills down. Since there was no alternative if the Government wanted to win the general election that was looming, the poll tax became the most expensive tax in history to administer.

Economic policy was determined now by the exigencies of ERM membership. In practice this meant that the recession, which began in the third quarter of 1990, continued until it became by mid-1992 the longest recession in post-war history. The economy shrank by 2·5 per cent in 1991 and looked like shrinking again in 1992. By then, unemployment had risen to 2·7 million and was still rising; interest rates had come down, but only to 10 per cent. The rate of inflation, meanwhile, had fallen to 4·3 per cent, which meant that real interest rates had in fact gone up. The trade deficit was forecast in 1992 to be at least £7 billion, despite the lack of growth and despite the fact that the figures depended on the 'transplanted economies' of Japanese and multinational companies contributing to 'British' exports. The Public Sector Borrowing Requirement (PSBR) was forecast to be £28 billion and unofficially reckoned to be heading for nearer £40 billion. In 1991, 48,000 businesses failed, and more were forecast to do so in 1992. In the same year 75,500 homes were repossessed, with the prospects for 1992 looking even worse: more than a quarter of a million people were already at least six months behind with mortgage payments. Social security spending was at a record high, as was Government expenditure. Government revenues, meanwhile, had fallen from £252 billion in 1988 to £230 billion in 1992.

The outlook was grim, with forecasts of slump, but both Major and Lamont insisted throughout the whole period that the picture was not as bleak as their critics painted. At first neither admitted to a recession; then it was supposed to be world-wide; finally 'recovery' was always just around the corner, or as Lamont told the 1991 Tory party conference, 'the green shoots' were already showing. A Tory election victory would dispel uncertainty and lack of confidence, but even after Major's win in 1992 the situation failed to improve. Forecasters seemed to agree that, at the earliest, recovery would be delayed until 1994. The Government, meanwhile, stressed that there was no alternative policy. Devaluation would not enable interest rates to come down; it would merely force them up to stop the pound from entering free-fall. Eventually, low inflation would lead to renewed and 'stable' growth. The Prime Minister let it be known that he even envisaged the pound replacing the Deutschmark as Europe's strongest currency and spoke of zero inflation. Only the right wing of his own party seemed to challenge these assumptions, with the so-called 'Liverpool Six' economists (Patrick Minford, Tim Congdon, Bill Martin, Gordon Pepper, Peter Warburton and Sir Alan Walters) writing to *The Times* as early as 13 February 1991, predicting 'real disaster' unless the Government left the ERM or else devalued within it and lowered interest rates. Tory MPs such as Nicholas Budgen, Sir Richard Body, Richard Shepherd and Sir Teddy Taylor took the same line. Labour and Liberal opponents differed from the Government only in their desire to raise taxes or spend more.

The ERM was indeed at the centre of the Government's dilemma. Given that the pound remained the weakest currency in it, interest rates had to remain high in order to maintain its value in relation to the Deutschmark. Yet so long as interest rates remained high the domestic economy would remain depressed. Nor was there any other way to revive it: rising unemployment and the collapse of the housing market meant that people refused to spend. Many were paying off mortgages which were now higher than the value of their homes. Small businesses had been devastated and would probably never recover. Worse still, given Germany's own economic problems in the wake of reunification, the Government had tied itself to an economy whose interest rates were going up. There was every possibility, therefore, that British interest rates would have to follow, perhaps just before the 1992 Tory party conference in a repeat of events two years before.

Lamont's own desire to be a tax-reforming Chancellor did not help matters either. In 1991, in order to provide funds for an across-the-board reduction in poll tax charges of £140, he increased VAT to 17·5 per cent. This did nothing to aid recovery and hit the poorest-paid and unemployed. He also managed to hit the car industry by announcing that industry would have to pay National Insurance on company cars. The net effect was to add £350 a year to the cost of a company car. The Society of Motor Car Manufacturers and Traders condemned the move as 'indefensible'. Finally, he announced that tax relief for mortgages would be abolished for those on the higher income-tax rate of 40 per cent. This effectively increased mortgage payments for 860,000 people.

Lamont's 1991 budget was mildly deflationary; his 1992 one roughly neutral. Hemmed in by the exigencies of the ERM once again, he had little room for manoeuvre. His main task was to produce a political budget which would contrast with Labour's tax-raising policies. Unable actually to cut taxes, he again displayed himself as a reformer, this time by introducing a new tax band of 20 per cent income tax on the first £2,000 of taxable income. He said Tory policy in the long term would be to expand this band upwards until it represented the standard rate. Also announced were some VAT-related changes to help small businesses. Meanwhile, excise duties were raised above the rate of inflation, the uniform business rate was reduced by 3·75 per cent, the basic tax threshold was raised in line with inflation, while the basic rate limit was frozen at £23,700. Two announcements which made the news were that the PSBR had mushroomed to a forecast £28 billion and that henceforth the annual budget and autumn statements would be combined in a December statement. Altogether, it was a budget of gimmicks which very soon was seen to be a 'damp squib' both as an economic booster and as a potential election winner.

DEFENCE AND FOREIGN POLICY

Major's first challenge in the sphere of defence and foreign policy was the Gulf War. Here the Thatcher Government's first reaction had been to provide air forces, but it soon became clear that ground troops would be needed and by mid-September the 7th Armoured Brigade, or 'Desert Rats' had been mobilized from Germany. British forces were put under the 'control' of the United States, but were under the command of Lieutenant-General Peter de la Billière, who had previous experience of working with US and Arab troops. In November Thatcher's Government committed the 1st Armoured Division from Germany as well, stripping the British Army of the Rhine (BAOR) of most of its Challenger tanks and their spares. The British army in the Gulf now numbered 33,000 men (more than half of BAOR), the service strength (air and naval support included) totalling about 45,000.

The hope that sanctions might work with Iraq faded throughout January 1991 and everyone knew that action, if it came, would have to start before Ramadan in February. The United Nations gave Saddam Hussein until 15 January to comply with its resolutions and authorized military force if he did not. Just before then Major visited France, but

President Mitterrand gave him no hint of the French peace plan which was presented to the UN a mere hour after Major left Paris.

The aims of military action (Operation Desert Storm) as laid down in UN resolutions were: to secure a complete and unconditional Iraqi withdrawal from Kuwait; to restore Kuwait's legitimate government; to re-establish international peace and security in the area; and to uphold the authority of the United Nations. After war broke out on 24 January, the US commander, General Schwarzkopf, planned to use his 2,400 aircraft and sophisticated electronic weapons systems first to destroy the Iraqi airforce and then its army. Only then would he move his coalition army of US, Arab, British, French and other troops forward. His general plan was to feign an attack near the Saudi coast, while actually attacking 200 miles inland round the edge of Iraq's defences.

Despite all sorts of rumours, Iraqi defence proved feeble. The 1st US Infantry took only one hour and twenty minutes to break through Iraqi defences and clear sixteen lanes for the advance of armoured divisions. The British 1st Armoured Division advanced 180 miles in the 100-hour campaign, destroying almost three Iraqi divisions and capturing 7,000 prisoners, and itself losing only nineteen men, nine to US 'friendly fire'. In the air war, meanwhile, the RAF lost six GR1 Strike Tornados and only five crew, a remarkably low casualty rate given its 4,000 sorties. On 28 February the war ended with Schwarzkopf's forces close to Basra and actually on the Euphrates near Nasiriyah. By this time thousands of Iraqi troops were being slaughtered as they desperately retreated towards Baghdad. Douglas Hurd later made this an excuse for the allied failure to oust Saddam Hussein. Yet it was an unconvincing one. An extra twenty-four hours would have been all that was necessary to capture Baghdad, so weak was Iraqi resistance. Hurd's other excuse was that the allies did not wish to become involved in the messy job of determining a successor regime in Iraq. Yet they did so by default, by leaving Saddam Hussein in clear control. In doing so they left both the Kurds in Northern Iraq and the Shiah in the South to the mercy of the cruel dictator, having encouraged both to resist.

Given that Mrs Thatcher had stated that Saddam Hussein would have to be brought to trial, the failure to finish the job seemed almost incomprehensible. When on 8 April, therefore, John Major used a European Council meeting in Luxembourg to call for 'safe havens' for the Kurds, without detailing any preparations for such a scheme, he came under attack politically for the first time. A Bruges Group press statement asked, 'was the overthrow of Mrs Thatcher paid for with the blood of thousands of innocent Iraqis?' Safe havens were indeed established during the following months by allied troops for the tens of thousands of Kurds who had fled to the mountains on the Turkish border, but by July their allied protectors had withdrawn. Nothing was done to aid the Shiah who had risen in the South. Meanwhile, the British Government banned all contact between Conservative MPs and the Bruges Group, of which, since January, Mrs Thatcher had become President. (She, however, dissociated herself from the press statement.)

By 1992, Saddam's defiance of the UN made further US action in the Gulf appear likely, but the reasons why he had not been overthrown by the allies the previous year were still unknown. Nor was it clear whether the Major Government had been in agreement with US policy in refusing to enter Baghdad at that point.

The other factor which was to emerge from the war was the total disarray of the European Community when faced with the question of military action. Only Britain had provided a sizeable military contribution to the war. The French also contributed a few thousand troops, but only after their Defence Minister had resigned and after a French aircraft carrier had left for the Gulf carrying only helicopters. Most EC countries did not want to become involved, with the Germans and Belgians at first actually impairing the war effort by refusing to supply the allies with spare parts. The West German Government then interpreted its constitution to mean that it was illegal to send troops outside the NATO area, although it had been written six years before West Germany had actually joined NATO and the majority of German constitutional experts disagreed with their interpretation. After the war was over, the German Government conceded as much; its real problem lay with a public reluctant to send conscripted troops abroad; a reaction to the Second World War. Still, when all this was pointed out in a Bruges Group pamphlet entitled 'Cheap Excuses', an official protest was made to the Foreign Office by the West German Embassy. The West German Government, meanwhile, announced that it would contribute to the war financially by compensating the allies generously for their costs. (Mrs Thatcher remarked at this time on the paradox that 'it is those who have oil who are doing the fighting, while those who have not, are not'.) The Americans received $10·5 billion, the British $560 million. Jacques Delors, for his part, admitted that the war had been a disaster as far as Europe was concerned: 'the European Community has been ineffectual. Its inadequate response has cast doubt over the whole process of European Union.' But these doubts were not to last. Instead, he used the fiasco of the European performance to call for a European defence and security policy.

NATO's European members were in fact split on this issue, which in the short term at least focused on the role of Western European Union (WEU). The British, Dutch and Portuguese were much less keen on creating a European pillar for NATO than were the Germans, Italians, Spanish, Belgians or, more particularly, the French. As a compromise, the 1991 Defence White Paper revealed the establishment of an Allied Command Europe Rapid Reaction Corps, under British command but with a multinational staff. It was to have four divisions, two British, two multinational. The 1st and 3rd Armoured Divisions, stationed in Germany and the UK respectively, were to be the backbone of the British contribution, but at least one British brigade was to take part in the multinational divisions. France had wanted a separate European Reaction Force outside NATO command, to which she would contribute. Thus the Allied Command Europe Rapid Reaction Corps was described as 'autonomous from NATO', given the authority to operate outside the NATO area, and allowed to draw on 'forces allocated to the Alliance, along with national forces of countries not part of the integrated structure'. The Reaction Corps was to be associated with WEU which 'could serve as a bridge between the transatlantic security and defence structure of NATO and the developing common political and security policies of the Twelve ... but would be subordinate to neither'. The White Paper stated, 'neither we nor any other country could contemplate or would wish to retain separate forces for NATO and WEU'. It condemned totally distinct Western European defence entities, involving the eventual absorption of WEU by the Twelve, as 'disruptive of NATO' and 'inviting confusion and a less reliable defence than we have enjoyed over the last forty years'. The impression given, however, was that confusion reigned within the Government, which seemed, once again, to be moving reluctantly and imperceptibly towards the 'European' viewpoint, without wishing to admit this even to itself.

The White Paper, finally, not merely confirmed the reductions announced the previous year under 'Options For Change' but added to them. By 1997, the army was to be reduced to 104,000 men. Its strength in Germany was to be reduced to 23,000. By then there were to be only sixteen artillery regiments (down six), ten of engineers (down four) and twelve armoured ones (down seven). Infantry regiments were to be amalgamated, reducing the number of battalions from fifty-five to thirty-six. The army's 'tail' was also to be completely reorganized with the formation of a new all-encompassing 'Adjutant-General's Corps'. The navy also suffered further reductions. How large the ultimate peace dividend was supposed to be remained difficult to predict. (Defence spending in 1990 was estimated as 4 per cent of GDP.) Critics, however, regretted not merely the demise of old regiments but insisted that cuts would only make sense in the context of a new defence review. Given an uncertain international environment, there was a case against cutting too soon.

The most contentious foreign policy problem facing the new Government was its attitude to 'Europe' (the word long having been hijacked by the integrationists). Here Major was advised that a difference in tone would be helpful (Mrs Thatcher's strident tone having somehow undermined Britain's interests). The Foreign Office also believed that the 'Franco-German axis' could be broken by a 'charm offensive' towards Bonn. This began in earnest on 11 March 1991 when John Major visited the German capital and declared, 'I want us to be where we belong. At the very heart of Europe, working with our partners in building the future.' He even addressed his audience as '*Meine Damen und Herren*'. The speech reached the headlines in the British press, but, ominously, was ignored in Germany. At home, alarm bells began to ring among *Brugistes* and Mrs Thatcher was urged to remain in the Commons in order to fight against Brussels and its new ally, Major. Enoch Powell suggested that the Prime Minister should consult a map, pointing out that Germany, not Britain, was at the heart of Europe. However, the new Tory Party Chairman, Chris Patten, added to the concern of the party's right wing by declaring himself as a Christian Democrat and soon thereafter approving an application by Conservative MEPs to join the European People's Party in the Strasbourg parliament, on a platform which included 'the institutional development of the Community into a European union of a federal type'. In his speech in Bonn, Major had also advocated closer ties between Tory and Christian Democrat MEPs.

It soon became clear that the new relationship with Bonn was producing little other than photo-opportunities and statements of mutual admiration. It certainly did not undermine Bonn's 'special relationship' with Paris or bring Major concrete advantages. For example, the Common Agricultural Policy (CAP) still eluded reform, although according to the Institute for Fiscal Studies it cost the average British family of four some £850 per year. Britain still remained the second largest net contributor to the EC budget, despite the continuance of the rebates negotiated by Mrs Thatcher. More worryingly, German and French resistance to CAP reform jeopardized the success of the Uruguay Round of the GATT (General Agreement on Tariffs and Trade) negotiations. Yet, according to Rosemary Righter of *The Times*, 'European businesses and consumers have billions to gain from this mammoth negotiation between 101 countries. If successful, it would open up new markets for trade in services such as banking and software, lay down fair international rules governing foreign investment and provide protection for patents, industrial designs and other "intellectual property". The gains from trade in services alone are worth some £600 billion a year. Agreement on the whole package could increase global economic activity by $4,000 billion within a decade.' The more likely alternative, thanks to German and French intransigence over CAP subsidies, was a world divided into hostile trading blocs, conducting a trade war throughout the 1990s. German policy during the Gulf War was equally unreassuring, while inside the ERM it raised its interest rates with little regard to the consequences for its partners. In 1992 Germany was to withdraw from the European Fighter Aircraft programme, thereby threatening the jobs of 40,000 British workers, while in the field of foreign policy it forced Britain and the rest of the Twelve in December 1991 to recognize the independence of various former provinces of Yugoslavia, thereby at worst precipitating a series of bloody wars and at best undermining the peace process in the Balkans.

The charm offensive had the paradoxical result that, in order to prove his credentials, Major had to agree to greater European integration. He had to endorse everything Mrs Thatcher had said no to, including EMU and EPU. This process culminated in the Maastricht Treaty, agreed in December 1991 and signed in February 1992. President Mitterrand of France was to describe it as even more fundamental and far-reaching than the original Treaty of Rome – which indeed it was –

despite the efforts of Douglas Hurd to downgrade it. Yet even Hurd was to admit in an interview in *Le Monde* (2 July 1992) that it 'went beyond' what the British Government had sought. Major, as will be seen, was allowed some concessions thanks to Kohl. Yet they constituted a very meagre dividend indeed for the new pro-German policy, considering that the Germans had been given monetary and political union and that Major's own scheme for a hard ecu had been dropped to make way for what was essentially the Delors Plan and the Social Charter combined, plus a variety of measures which amounted in all but name to a blueprint for a federal Europe.

As the IGCs on EMU and EPU deliberated under the guidance of the Luxembourg and then the Dutch Governments (who held the Presidency of the Council during 1991), it was clear that Major would face problems more from within his own party than from the official Opposition. In particular, Mrs Thatcher insisted on speaking her mind on Europe, while all the time praising the Prime Minister: 'I did my level best for John. I supported John and am desperately anxious for him to be successful.' In January 1991 she accepted the honorary presidency of the Bruges Group, but from March she began to voice her fears publicly. In an American television interview on 10 March, for example, she not only opposed the Government's European policy, but also its new pro-German basis: 'The Germans would dominate Europe because they are the biggest country. I think that many of us would not necessarily like that. So long as we are separate nations then each of us can control that and stop its (Germany's) domination.' Speaking in Chicago and New York on 17 and 18 June, she called plans for a European defence identity 'half-baked' and those for a single currency 'unnecessary'. She added, 'What a single European currency would mean is that the control of the economy would leave your own country and go to non-elected people in the European Community. That would take the heart out of the purpose of our Parliament.' In London an enraged Edward Heath commented that her speeches 'were full of falsehoods, in ordinary English, lies'. Describing her as 'ignorant', having a 'minute' mind, and being 'entirely out of touch', he exclaimed, 'She does not realize that in Europe she is regarded not only as irresponsible but entirely not to be considered at all.'

Tension built up with the approach of the Luxembourg summit at the end of July. The Luxembourg draft treaty on European Union (which now combined political and economic union) was known to be a federalist document. This hardly worried the Commission, whose own comment on it was that union should be built 'on a unitary base' and 'must absorb the Community and all it has achieved'. Nor were most member states very bothered. The draft after all was the end product of long deliberations with them at a time when Horst Teltschik, for example, was calling for the proposed European Union to become a superpower rival to the USA. Chancellor Kohl, meanwhile, was boasting that having unified Germany he would now unify Europe. The draft treaty thus provided among other things for the creation of a single European citizenship, a 'federal vocation', and provided the new European Union with whatever means it found necessary to reach that destination. And all this was in addition to political and monetary union and the social charter, all of which it incorporated.

Major managed at the Luxembourg summit, in what was described as a personal triumph, to get all explicit references to federalism removed from the draft treaty. (Later on he would manage to kill off an even more radically federalist Dutch draft and revive the Luxembourg one as the basis for the Maastricht agreement.) There was little European opposition to this as the substance of the treaty remained unaltered. Mrs Thatcher paid the Prime Minister a dutiful tribute, but speaking in the House of Commons for the first time since she lost the premiership, in a speech described by *The Times* as a 'performance of primal force that had Tory MPs applauding even as they squirmed', she returned to the attack. Those who supported a federal Europe, she declared, were not more European than the rest. They were 'just more federal'. The Community had no right to talk about devolving powers *to* member states, since power could only be devolved *from* member states. But once given away, she warned, it would never be returned. Nor were vague declarations useful; the Commission merely interpreted them to its own advantage. Finally, Britain should not look only to Europe, but should reach out to the wider world. The core of her argument was the defence of parliamentary sovereignty: 'What is now being considered is a massive extension of the Community's powers and competence into almost every area of our national life and that of other member states. It will be the greatest abdication of national and parliamentary sovereignty in our history.' The next day she announced her retirement from parliament at the forthcoming election. In a television interview with

ITN, she revealed the bitterness she still felt about her defeat, saying, 'They chose to do *that thing* to me at a time when I was actually abroad negotiating and signing a treaty for my country with everyone else.' She then returned to Europe and the German question: 'Mitterrand thinks that France will be able to influence the Germans more than can any other country. He thinks he might have more freedom than he has now within the monetary system . . . that is a great misjudgment . . . The stronger Germany becomes . . . the less she will heed others.' Since Major's policy was the same as Mitterrand's, it was clear that Mrs Thatcher was absolutely opposed to it. Major's own repeated response was that Britain had no choice but to remain 'at the heart of Europe'.

Public opinion by now was clearly swinging in an anti-federalist direction. Polls showed that 55 per cent were against monetary union, 53 per cent against political union with a common foreign policy and 52 per cent against giving more powers to the European Parliament, with 39 per cent, 35 per cent and 39 per cent respectively in favour. Later polls would show 75 per cent of Conservative, 66 per cent of Liberal Democrat and 55 per cent of Labour supporters against giving more powers to Brussels. By July 1992, the European Commission had received the results of a poll which showed that only 48 per cent of the British had a 'positive' attitude towards the Community. 'Seventy per cent of Britons never thought of themselves as anything but British and 60 per cent would not care if the EC were scrapped tomorrow.' Little wonder that the Government always ruled out a referendum on Europe.

Part of the anti-federalist swing was due to reports of apparently silly directives emanating from the Commission, or to more serious threats to parliamentary sovereignty such as the decision by the European Court of Justice on 25 July to overturn parts of the 1988 Merchant Shipping Act designed to prevent Spanish fishing vessels plundering the British North Sea fish quota. This Act, specifically designed to enforce the European fisheries quota policy, was now rendered ineffective by the European Court which allowed the Spanish to fish two quotas. Not unnaturally this decision caused considerable resentment in Britain.

The final treaty on European Union was agreed in Maastricht in December. It was based on the Luxembourg draft with the amendments made in July plus certain concessions to a variety of countries. The British press declared it a victory for Major, and Downing Street proclaimed that he had won 'game, set and match', saying that Major had secured three major concessions: an opt-out on the Social Charter; the removal of all references to the word 'federal'; and an opt-in regarding a single currency. The treaty was formally signed in Maastricht in February 1992, when Douglas Hurd was overheard declaring that he had not actually read every page of it. In October 1992 the Home Secretary, Kenneth Clarke, admitted that he had not read it, and suggested that Major had not read it either. Curiously, it was not published until after the general election and remained extremely difficult to obtain even after it was submitted for a Second Reading to the House of Commons immediately after the general election. It was clear from the start, however, that the concessions made to the Prime Minister were merely cosmetic. The removal of the word 'federal' made no difference to the substance of the treaty; the opt-out from the Social Charter was fairly meaningless since all its provisions would go through in any case via Article 100A of the Single European Act; finally, given that the country had agreed to hand over control of its monetary and exchange policy to Europe, it did not really matter all that much whether its currency was called an ecu or a pound. Besides, the treaty's other provisions laid down a blueprint for a European army and police force, and established European citizenship of a new state called the European Union. It also set up a new independent Regional Council (with implications for Scotland and Northern Ireland), practically abolished the use of the veto in security and foreign policy, and extended majority voting to almost every other area of policy. Finally, it retained the blanket clause of the Luxembourg draft empowering the new Union to take whatever powers necessary to achieve its objectives. This came in the first section of the treaty; section two contained a somewhat incomprehensible definition of subsidiarity – the principle of deciding at a higher level only that which cannot be decided at a lower.

According to Article 236 of the Treaty of Rome, the Maastricht Treaty had to be ratified by all Community member states. John Major was determined that Britain would ratify it as soon as possible in order to clear the decks for her assumption of the EC presidency in June 1992. Since a general election had to be held by then also, the Government relied on party solidarity to prevent any split. Besides, the Bill would not receive its Second Reading till after the election. Thus there were only a handful of Tory rebels after its First Reading, including Norman Tebbit. Mrs Thatcher herself abstained, and decided (as did

Nicholas Ridley and other prominent Eurosceptics) not even to mention the subject during the election in the interests of party unity. In a letter to Dr Alan Sked, who had founded the Anti-Federalist League in order to run candidates on an anti-Maastricht platform (all the major parties officially endorsed the treaty), she wrote, 'I cannot do anything which would split the Party at this critical time. The most important thing now is to secure the return of a Conservative Government. The alternative would reverse everything we have tried to do in the last few years. Differences over Europe can be fought out *after* the election *before* the question of ratifying the Treaty.' Others, normally Conservative voters, believed that a Labour victory would push a future Conservative Opposition into repudiating the treaty, especially if it were recommended by a Kinnock government. But could Labour win?

THE OPPOSITION: LABOUR

Whilst the Conservative Government embarked with undiminished energy on a third radical term of office, for the Labour Opposition the future seemed difficult. Labour's problems after the 1987 general election were compounded by several factors: a protracted and distracting contest for both the leadership and deputy leadership in 1988; and a far from happy party conference at Blackpool in the autumn of 1988. In the background (and occasionally in the foreground) lay continuing questions about Labour's relationship with the trade unions.

Since 1979 trade union membership among voters had fallen from 30 per cent to 23 per cent, despite a rise in the number of jobs. Industrial change had seen the core manual working class, the source of the unions' former strength, decline from 33 per cent to 27 per cent as a proportion of the working population. As Labour attempted to adjust itself to a transformed social and electoral profile, the unions struggled with fundamental questions about their own role. John Edmonds, the increasingly influential leader of the General, Municipal and Allied Trades Union (GMB), warned at the 1987 TUC conference that 'unless we change, we will cease to be a mass movement which can claim to speak for all the working people of Britain'. In the aftermath of the 1987 general election Ron Todd, General Secretary of the Transport and General Workers' Union (TGWU), reminded the unions 'that they have got to live with another Tory Government for the next four or five years'.

Todd would not, at this stage, go as far as the Electrical, Electronic, Telecommunication and Plumbing Union (EETPU) in acknowledging the tilting balance of industrial relations by negotiating single-union no-strike deals with employers. The TUC conference in September 1987 deferred an inevitably bloody clash by referring the issue to a review body. Eric Hammond, the EETPU leader already unpopular for his union's role in the Wapping events back in 1986, threatened to withdraw from the TUC if other unions interfered in what he saw as his members' own affairs. This foreshadowed longer-term bewilderment about the precise purpose of an increasingly fragmented and marginalized TUC.

An inter-union dispute in March 1988 between the TGWU and the Amalgamated Engineering Union (AEU), over a single-union agreement the latter had negotiated with Ford, revealed the stress that industrial change imposed on the unions and invited pointed Conservative frontbench attacks on the Labour Opposition. As the argument raged, Ford withdrew its proposal to create 1,000 jobs, leaving the unions (and Labour) charged with being a cause of unemployment. In June the TUC general council suspended the EEPTU for its refusal to compromise over its pioneer single-union no-strike deals. The autumn TUC conference in Bournemouth voted overwhelmingly to expel the 330,000-strong EEPTU from the TUC, despite vocal opposition from Bill Jordan, the AEU leader and articulate 'new realist'.

Europe, however, seemed to offer a glimpse of a brighter future. The TUC conference in September 1988 warmly welcomed Jacques Delors, who promised that '1992' meant more than the creation of a single market and offered the prospect of European legislation to guarantee workers' rights, encourage collective bargaining and extend social reform. Mrs Thatcher's response to this 'back-door' socialism was predictable. For the unions it offered a lifeline. By the 1991 TUC conference John Edmonds was presenting the choice facing the unions as Europe or death in the wilderness.

TUC conferences, and the role the unions played in party policy-making, continued to embarrass Kinnock in his modernization project. In 1988 delegates voted for unilateral nuclear disarmament and rejected Labour's commitment to increase conventional arms spending. A hard-left TGWU executive was initially reluctant even to support the Kinnock–Hattersley leadership ticket at the Labour Party Conference.

When they were returned Todd warned them not to think they had uncritical support and attacked what he called 'sharp-suited, cordless telephone socialism'. However, by the September 1990 TUC conference at Blackpool the unions and Labour were closer in step. A NALGO motion demanding the repeal by a future Labour government of all Conservative trade union legislation and the restoration of the right to secondary picketing was defeated, a rejection repeated even more decisively the following year. Kinnock was given a standing ovation after declaring that although the unions' interests were best served by the election of a Labour government, an administration under his leadership would pursue a policy of justice for all rather than favours for particular friends.

The question of Labour's future electability, however, went beyond its relationship with the unions. There was no doubt in Kinnock's mind that Labour had to broaden its appeal to what a Fabian pamphlet called the 'home-owning, credit-card-carrying majority'. As a prerequisite he needed to continue refashioning the party. Elections to the Shadow Cabinet in July 1987, and to the party's National Executive Committee (NEC) in September provided a comfortable soft-left–centre-right base. This he would retain and improve upon in successive years. He failed to achieve one-member, one-vote in the selection and reselection of parliamentary candidates, but a compromise electoral college system agreed upon at the September party conference removed much union influence. More fundamental was the agreement to review Labour's policies. Kinnock insisted there was no longer a natural Labour vote to depend upon and policy should reflect this. But the delegates resolved on unilateral nuclear disarmament within the lifetime of a future Labour government, and a motion to renationalize all privatized industries went to a card vote before eventual defeat.

The hard left, beleaguered but still angry, challenged Labour's 'new realism' in the 1988 party leadership elections. The contest, which dominated the start of the 1988 conference, gave overwhelming victory to Kinnock against the perennial standard-bearer of the left, Tony Benn. Some 89 per cent of Labour's electoral college went to Kinnock. In the contest for the deputy leadership, in which most of the unions lined up behind Roy Hattersley, the dual challenge from John Prescott and Eric Heffer was easily defeated. The battle, divisive as it initially seemed, in practice helped rather than hindered Kinnock. It demonstrated how far out of touch the left had become with party feeling in the wake of the 1987 general election. Kinnock was now in his strongest position yet to push for the compromises that electoral respectability demanded.

That summer the initial policy review reports – in broad-brush rather than detail – had been approved by the NEC, despite charges from Benn and his supporters that they were merely a programme for a Social Democrat Party mark two. In June Kinnock dropped undisguised hints that Labour, whatever the conference might say, would abandon unilateral nuclear disarmament. But at the October conference the unilateralist position retained a majority, albeit by only a little over a million votes. The keynote document 'Aims and Values', the fruit of the policy review, won five to one support while left-inspired demands for renationalization and for extra-parliamentary (i.e. illegal) action against the poll tax were defeated.

In 1989 the new model Labour Party had the opportunity to mount a challenge to ten years of Thatcherism. In February Kinnock cleared the ground by unequivocally abandoning unilateralism, giving as justification the Soviet Union's apparently genuine willingness to negotiate an end to the nuclear terror. The coming elections to the European Parliament, he said at a Birmingham rally in April (with Labour's red rose much in evidence), would be a referendum on Thatcher's decade. In May the final working-out of the policy review was presented to the public in 'Meet the Challenge, Make the Change'. The timing was fortunate. The Thatcherite economic miracle had lost its bloom while the Conservative Party itself was riven by divisions over Europe. The new programme abandoned much of the sacred symbolism of the early 1980s. There was to be no unilateralism, no penal redistributive taxation, no restoration of trade union legal immunities, no renationalization, and an end to hostility towards the EEC as a 'rich man's club'. Opinion polls immediately showed a public awareness that the party had cast off what the overwhelmingly anti-Labour press called 'extremism'. It was clear now what the Labour Party did not stand for. But the polls also revealed that the public had no real idea what the party did stand for. Nevertheless, the June Euro-elections (see pp. 579–80) proved a triumph, an astute and effective campaign bringing Labour 40·2 per cent of the vote to the Conservatives 34·2 per cent.

Riding an anti-government (though not necessarily pro-Labour) wave, the party's lead in the opinion polls remained solid throughout 1990. In March Thatcher reached an historically unique low in prime-ministerial popularity. But worries persisted about Labour's competence as a party of government in general and about Kinnock in particular. He was consistently less popular in the polls than his party. He therefore concentrated, against the background of the Gulf crisis (see pp. 556–7), on placing himself firmly in the public mind as the leader of a future Labour government. When, in October, six Shadow Cabinet members supported a party conference resolution demanding a reduction in defence spending to the West European average, he insisted that such disloyalty would not be tolerated in government.

Meanwhile, Shadow Chancellor John Smith attempted to counter the interconnected fears about Labour's competence and the party's links with the unions. He warned the party conference that wage increases not backed by productivity improvements led inevitably to unemployment. As a token of the changing relationship, the trade union block vote at party conferences was reduced from 90 per cent to 70 per cent, with a less prominent place for the unions promised as individual party membership increased. On 2 October Kinnock warned union leaders that there would be a clear choice under Labour between wage increases and improved public services.

Labour had now moved into a commanding position in the opinion polls. Unprecedented leads persisted throughout 1990. The Conservatives might denounce Kinnock for lacking principles, for opportunism, for being merely the creature of his image-makers, but he was beginning to look a far more likely election victor than the fading and deeply unpopular Thatcher. When in November Mrs Thatcher was replaced as Conservative leader and Prime Minister by John Major (see pp. 548–51), Labour lost one of its greatest electoral assets. Despite the continuing failure of the economy to recover, Labour began to lose its lead in the opinion polls in 1991.

A final mopping-up operation against the remnants of Militant infiltration continued as the election approached. In May 1991 – following open opposition to official Labour candidates by the 'Broad Left' in local government elections – twenty-five Liverpool councillors were expelled from the party. These followed expulsions in London and Birkenhead. The eight-year campaign against Militant reached its culmination at the party conference. Two MPs, Dave Nellist and Terry

Fields, were suspended from the party for their alleged Militant connections. They were formally expelled in December. The conference itself was more akin to those mounted by the Conservatives, with a smooth corporate image replacing a genuine clash of views. None the less, Kinnock made an effective speech on 1 October, stressing that Labour represented not the 'politics of envy but the ethics of community'. He promised an expansion in the NHS, constitutional reform and an attack on poverty.

Kinnock would be facing his second general election as the challenger. Whatever the result, it would be his last as Leader of the Opposition. On becoming leader in 1983 he had inherited a Labour Party which, it appeared, might cease to be the main opposition to the Conservatives, let alone have any hopes of forming a government. On the eve of the 1992 general election he led a party which even some Conservatives believed might have power within its grasp. The irony for Kinnock was that, whatever reserves of courage and will had enabled him to take the party to this position, doubts remained about the plausibility of his own aspiration to be Prime Minister. His verbosity and the sense that he had a weak grasp of the larger issues grated. Politically, the charge persisted that a man who could apparently so easily abandon his most basic political beliefs – unilateral nuclear disarmament above all – might prove to have no beliefs at all, simply an urge for higher office. From this came the fear that the party he had so assiduously worked to reconstruct was now similarly bereft of principle.

THE OPPOSITION: FROM ALLIANCE TO LIBERAL DEMOCRATS

Whilst Labour had its problems in the aftermath of the 1987 general election, these were as nothing compared to the disastrous events within the Liberal/SDP Alliance. The Alliance in general, but most of all David Steel, had reason to feel bitter disillusion at the results of the 1987 election. The two-headed Alliance leadership had not helped, and Steel was determined to end the situation of two parties, each with a separate leader. Hence the electoral disappointments of June 1987 were rapidly followed by moves initiated by David Steel on behalf of the Liberals to secure an early and full Liberal/SDP merger. His call, almost before the dust of the election battle had settled, was for 'democratic fusion'. If Steel's timing was somewhat precipitate, his call undoubtedly reflected the views of many Liberals and SDP members at constituency level. Indeed, a variety of local 'grassroots mergers' had already occurred. However, within the hierarchy of the SDP a major split occurred between the pro-merger and the anti-merger faction. The leading supporters of a merger from the SDP ranks were three of the original 'Gang of Four' – Roy Jenkins, Bill Rodgers and Shirley Williams. None of these, however, was now in the Commons. So, whilst in the SDP at large the great weight of senior figures supported a merger, within the five-strong SDP parliamentary party only Charles Kennedy initially supported such a move, to be later joined by Robert Maclennan.

From the outset, David Owen and his supporters prepared to fight a strong and often bitter campaign within the ranks of the Social Democrats to prevent a merger with the Liberals. Owen immediately made it clear, that, whatever actions might be taken by the other members of the SDP's founding 'Gang of Four', he would not be influenced by them. His allies on the SDP National Committee also made it clear that they were determined to preserve the separate identity of their party. They made the point that on numerous issues, such as defence, terrorism, the miners' strike and the market economy, they regarded the Liberals as weak, wet and woolly-minded. Owen's closest supporters included two SDP MPs, John Cartwright in Woolwich and Rosie Barnes in Greenwich.

The SDP National Executive called a ballot for August to gauge the grassroots feeling of the party. The result of the ballot of the SDP's 58,509 members was announced on 6 August: a comfortable, rather than a runaway, victory for merger. The pro-merger vote totalled 25,897 (57·4 per cent), the anti-merger vote 19,228 (42·6 per cent). On a turnout of 77·7 per cent the majority for merger was 6,669. None the less, the 42 per cent preferring the alternative option of a constitutional framework for the Alliance 'short of merger', which would preserve the identity of the SDP, was substantial. Thus the majority for merger was just enough for David Steel and the pro-merger faction of the SDP.

The satisfaction that the pro-mergerites might have enjoyed from this result was overshadowed by the dramatic resignation of Owen as SDP leader. His resignation on 6 August not only reflected his personal bitterness with events since the election, but also indicated that, like such figures before him as Lord Randolph Churchill and Oswald Mosley, he was prepared to go into political exile.

More immediately, however, Owen's resignation left the party leaderless only weeks away from the annual SDP Party Conference at Portsmouth. When the SDP MPs met to nominate leadership contestants on 27 August, Robert Maclennan was elected unopposed. A former Labour MP (he had represented Caithness and Sutherland since 1966) and one of the earliest supporters in January 1981 of the Council for Social Democracy, he was an uncharismatic, retiring figure but a tough negotiator. He was largely unknown to the general public.

His first task was to preside over the Portsmouth Conference. Here, the SDP took the road to merger and the split in the party became irrevocable when David Owen rejected an impassioned appeal by Shirley Williams, the SDP President, not to lead a breakaway faction into the political wilderness. The Portsmouth Conference was followed on 14 September by the start of the Liberal Party Conference at Harrogate. On 17 September the historic resolution to open merger talks was overwhelmingly carried by 998 votes to 21, a majority of 977 with just 9 abstentions. The successful motion declared its resolve 'to set its hand, together with the SDP, to the creation of a new political party as the successor to the Liberal Party and the SDP'. A negotiating team was to be established and, after its work was complete, a special Liberal Party Assembly would meet and a final ballot of all members would be held.

On 29 September, the Liberal and SDP negotiating teams set to work. So far, although there had been confusion and bitterness in the SDP, the Liberals had been reasonably happy. The merger negotiations transformed this complacence. As the Liberal–SDP negotiations wore on, it became clear that progress would be neither swift nor easy. Eventually, on 18 December, the draft constitution for the party was published jointly by David Steel and Robert Maclennan. The constitution began with a preamble which included a commitment that Britain should play a full and constructive role in NATO, an item of controversy for the many Liberals who believed that this should be regarded as a current policy rather than an enduring statement of values. The constitutional proposals themselves, though in many respects extremely democratic, provided far too rich a diet of centralization for Liberals accustomed to the traditions of old Liberal Assemblies. And the proposed new short name of the party ('The Alliance') was also a source of controversy to many Liberals.

Whatever the merits of the proposed constitution, opposition mounted amongst many Liberals. This grassroots opposition found its strongest outlet at the Liberal Party Council's December meeting in Northampton. This meeting delivered a severe rebuff both to Steel himself and to the merger proposals. It became clear, in the wake of Northampton, that a marked split was developing within the party. Steel made it clear that he was not willing to renegotiate the merger terms with the SDP. Against this background, Steel's behaviour in agreeing the policy proposals of the new party with Maclennan in January 1988 was quite astonishing.

The merger deal agreed by Steel and Maclennan was eventually concluded in the early hours of 13 January. During the long night of negotiations, the fury of the Liberal negotiating team erupted: by the end of the negotiations, half the eight-man team had walked out. This was as nothing to the fury that followed when the extraordinary details of the Steel–Maclennan 'mini-manifesto' emerged. It proposed, amongst other things, to extend VAT to food, children's clothes, fuel and newspapers, to phase out tax relief on mortgages, to end universal child benefit, and to pledge continued firm support for the Trident nuclear missile. Such policy declarations produced surprise and incredulity.

More important, they produced massive and open rebellion. The Liberal MPs were united in revolt, Steel's leadership of the party was in jeopardy and the merger hopes seemed wrecked. Isolated, weary and dejected Steel had no alternative but to retreat. At an emergency meeting of the Liberal National Executive called that evening, Steel accepted that the policy document which he had signed earlier that day was not acceptable to the party and would not be part of any merger package put to rank-and-file Liberals at the Blackpool Assembly. The Liberal National Executive then agreed, by nineteen votes to eleven, that the merger negotiations should continue so long as the controversial policy declaration was abandoned. A new negotiating team was hastily put together with the most urgent brief to rescue the merger.

This, somewhat unbelievably, it achieved. The 'Mark 2' policy document rejected the controversial innovations of only a week earlier. These latest proposals involved a climbdown by Maclennan, but the pro-merger SDP welcomed the deal as the best that could be salvaged. Maclennan gave his approval, and appealed to Owen to reconsider his position. On the Liberal side, opponents of the merger hinted that a hidden agenda lay behind the new agreement. A battle royal was promised for the Blackpool Conference on 23 January. In fact, it proved to be a rout for the anti-merger faction and the key vote was won by 2,099 votes to 385 with 23 abstentions.

On 30 January, a week after the Liberal Conference at Blackpool, the SDP met in Sheffield to decide on merger. The debate was bitter and emotional, but the outcome was decisive. The Council for Social Democracy voted 273 for union to 28 against, with 49 abstentions. In fact, the result had never been in doubt, for Owen's supporters were determined to show their strength by abstaining or not participating rather than by blocking the merger. As a result of the Blackpool and Sheffield Conferences, a new party in British politics, the Social and Liberal Democrats, was to be established in March, subject only to ratification by the final ballots of party members still to be held. Thus, by February, the realignment of the centre-left in British politics was taking shape. After the ferment and near disasters of the previous weeks, the birth of the Social and Liberal Democratic Party was at hand.

On 2 March 1988, the final stage of the Liberal/SDP merger was reached. On a turnout of 52 per cent, the Liberal membership voted 87·9 per cent to 12·1 per cent in favour of merger. On such a poor turnout, this was at best a half-hearted vote. Even worse for the pro-merger camp was the SDP ballot. On a 55 per cent turnout, 65·3 per cent voted for merger, 34·7 per cent against. These were inauspicious indications of enthusiasm, but they were enough. On 3 March, the new Social and Liberal Democratic Party (SLDP) was formally inaugurated with David Steel and Robert Maclennan as joint interim leaders.

The first months of the new party were overshadowed by the contest for the leadership. Once Steel declared that he would not be a contestant (and few had expected Maclennan to put in for the post), the election became a two-horse race between Alan Beith, the Deputy Leader of the old Liberal Party, and the more youthful and dynamic, if inexperienced, Paddy Ashdown. At 47, and Liberal MP for Yeovil only since 1983, Ashdown remained the favourite to win throughout the eight-week campaign. On 28 July, Ashdown was comfortably elected the first leader of the Social and Liberal Democrats. In the contest for the Presidency, the former SDP MP Ian Wrigglesworth convincingly beat off his challengers. Thus, after so many months of bitter wrangling, the centre-left stage of British politics had a new leader.

A daunting array of tasks awaited Ashdown after the divisions and débâcles of the preceding months. He faced major problems of party morale, low membership and financial problems, as well as the continuing existence of the Social Democratic Party under Owen. This SDP had been relaunched in March 1988 under the leadership of David Owen and the presidency of John Cartwright.

Paddy Ashdown's first challenge – and his first opportunity to shape the SLDP in his own image – came with the initial annual party conference in September 1988. Ashdown announced his allocation of the key portfolios, including foreign affairs to David Steel and the important treasury and economy post to Alan Beith. Home affairs went to Robert Maclennan. The conference formally adopted the short title Democrats (although it was to reverse this decision a year later, settling on Liberal Democrats after much debate and wrangling). Paddy Ashdown's first major conference speech set out the policy priorities he was to develop over the coming years, with emphasis on fair voting, Scottish and Welsh parliaments, industrial democracy, freedom of information, high-quality education, proper housing and an effective health service.

During 1989 the problems of the SLDP failed to go away. On the electoral front, the party's position in the opinion polls plummeted, the second party conference, held in Bournemouth in March, was overshadowed by the question of rival SDP candidates contesting by-elections, and the direct elections to Europe in June were an unmitigated disaster (see p. 579). These problems were reflected in a continuing membership and financial crisis. By September, membership was around 82,000 – down 10,000 over twelve months. There were doubts that the party could retain its Cowley Street headquarters in Westminster for much longer. And the continued wrangling over the party's short name resurfaced. The one small comfort for Paddy Ashdown was that the continuing SDP was visibly disintegrating.

The tide at last turned for the Liberal Democrats during 1990. Both in opinion polls and by-elections, the upsurge in Green support receded as quickly as it had arisen. By September 1990, the Greens were registering 4 per cent in the polls, compared to the Liberal Democrats' 10 per cent. Liberal Democrat morale was further boosted by the final demise of the SDP. The 'independent fourth force' that Owen had relaunched on 9 March 1988 had rapidly become a political laughing stock. The municipal elections of May 1989 had been disastrous. On 25 September 1989, Rosie Barnes (one of Owen's closest supporters) had conceded that the party would concentrate on only 10 targeted seats at the next election. But the crowning humiliation came with the Bootle by-election of 24 May 1990 when Jack Holmes polled 155 votes for the SDP, making the 418 secured by Screaming Lord Sutch seem positively respectable.

After Bootle, Owen and his two fellow MPs called an emergency meeting of the SDP's 25-strong National Committee. With support in the opinion polls at a derisory 1 per cent, with membership down to 6,000 and financial reserves exhausted, it was agreed that the game was over. Owen defiantly stated that he would never rejoin the Labour Party, but the SDP which had begun amid a blaze of publicity and high hopes back in 1981 was now finally dead. The epitaph was written in the April 1992 general election: Owen did not stand in Plymouth, while Rosie Barnes and John Cartwright were defeated by Labour in Greenwich and Woolwich (despite being given a clear run by the Liberal Democrats).

Meanwhile, the Liberal Democrats, buoyed by a by-election revival (see pp. 578–81), approached the 1990 party conference in a happier mood. The September 1990 Blackpool conference marked an important step in the evolution of party policy. Ashdown made clear his desire not to lose the opportunity of getting rid of Thatcher at the next election if the opportunity arose. His vision of the Liberal Democrat future was one of a radical, reforming party. Ashdown's keynote speech repeated the party commitment in four key areas: investment in education; protection for the environment; a full, enthusiastic role in a new 'Europe of the Regions'; and democratic constitutional reforms including proportional representation, home rule for Scotland and Wales, and the transformation of the House of Lords into a Senate. The Liberal Democrats would thus be a party which supported both social justice and the enterprise culture, wholeheartedly committed to Europe and ready to innovate with such ideas as the pollution added tax (PAT) and ready to risk electoral unpopularity by raising basic-rate tax to fund education.

In a sense, the new emblem the party had adopted, the bird of freedom, was apt. The party had at last broken free of the events of the merger era. The by-elections were coming good. Local-election support was consistent at 18 per cent. Membership was reported to have passed 85,000 while even the party's accumulated debts had fallen to £200,000 from £500,000 a year earlier. A further indication of the new Young

Turks' rising to prominence in the party was the election of Charles Kennedy as party President in succession to Ian Wrigglesworth (defeating Tim Clement-Jones by 24,648 to 4,818).

Between September 1990 and the general election of April 1992, the Liberal Democrats continued to build on these foundations. They enjoyed spectacular by-election victories during 1991 in Ribble Valley and at Kincardine and Deeside. Even broader electoral success came with the municipal elections of May 1991. The Liberal Democrats, defending seats gained by the Alliance in 1987, expected losses. Instead, they enjoyed a night that was little short of triumph, gaining 750 seats for the loss of 230 – a net gain of 520. The Liberal Democrats were now in good heart for the following general election.

THE ELECTORAL RECORD

The fortunes of the Government and the Opposition between 1987 and 1992 can be divided into three episodes: the by-elections from 1987 to 4 May 1989 (when the Vale of Glamorgan result saw Labour's first by-election victory); the third direct elections to Europe on 15 June 1989, which provided the first nationwide parliamentary test of electoral support; and the often sensational by-elections of 1989–92, a particularly unhappy period for the Conservatives.

The relatively quiescent period after July 1988 (when Kensington heralded the first by-election of the parliament) produced two noticeable phenomena: on the Conservative side, sharply reduced Conservative votes in their safe seats such as Epping Forest and Richmond, but with rival SDP and Liberal Democrat candidates enabling the Conservatives to retain each seat. On the Labour side, the party was hit by a Nationalist upsurge in Glasgow Govan, where it lost the seat to Jim Sillars (and a later strong Plaid Cymru showing in Pontypridd). For Labour, the loss of one of the safest of the party's seats was calamitous. Scottish Labour MPs rounded on the party's leadership in general and Kinnock in particular. Labour had won 50 of the 72 Scottish seats in 1987 (the 'feeble fifty' as the Scottish National Party derisorily termed them) and an SNP upsurge would clearly decimate Labour's ranks. Govan, however, had a wider significance than merely heaping yet more misfortune on Labour. It reopened the whole question of devolution or independence for Scotland – an issue which had lain largely dormant since the late 1970s. Sillars made much of his call for an independent Scotland within the EEC. With the third direct elections for Europe due in June 1989, this issue would clearly be kept before the public eye.

Labour's best result was on 4 May 1989 when, on a swing of 12·4 per cent, it swept to victory in the Vale of Glamorgan.

The Vale of Glamorgan result marked something of a watershed. It heralded the electoral rehabilitation of Labour which was seen most markedly in the direct elections to Europe. In the previous European elections (five years earlier in June 1984), Labour had won 32 seats on 36·5 per cent of the vote while the Conservatives had taken 45 with 40·8 per cent of the vote. This time, the result was almost exactly the reverse.

Party	Seats won	Votes	Percentage of Vote
Labour	45	6,153,604	40·2
Conservative	32	5,224,037	34·2
Liberal/SDP	0	986,292	6·4
Greens	0	2,292,705	15·0
Others	1 (SNP)	521,748	3·5

Labour had good cause for satisfaction, recovering much lost ground especially in the Midlands and North. Although turnout was again low (only 35·9 per cent), Labour had both won more seats and polled more votes than the Conservatives. A swing of 5·2 per cent to Labour was enough to wipe out all Conservative representation in the European Parliament from Wales and Scotland. Coming on top of the Vale of Glamorgan victory, as well as a good showing in the municipal elections, Labour was riding high. As the table on p. 580, showing the percentage of votes cast in national elections from 1979 to 1989, indicates, it was the first time for fifteen years that Labour had polled more than the Conservatives in a national contest.

The Liberal Democrats, by contrast, had rarely been in a worse situation. Not only had they again failed to elect a single MEP, but even more alarmingly, the Greens had come from nowhere to sweep into third place nationally. Moreover, the Greens had done best in the South of England and in precisely those middle-class constituencies in which the Liberals had formerly prospered.

	Conservative	Labour	Liberal/SDP Alliance	SNP/Plaid Cymru
1979 general election	43·9	36·9	13·8	2·0
1979 European election	50·6	33·0	13·1	2·5
1983 general election	42·4	27·6	25·4	1·5
1984 European election	40·8	36·5	19·5	2·5
1987 general election	42·2	30·8	22·6	1·7
1989 European election	34·2	40·2	6·4	3·5

In retrospect, these European elections can be seen as something of an aberration. Whilst Labour had regained its position as the natural alternative to the Conservatives, the Green success was clearly due to temporary disillusion with the divisions and difficulties of the birth of the Liberal Democrats. The Greens faded as swiftly as they had arisen.

Against a background of growing difficulties for the Government, not least over the poll tax and the economy, the by-elections of 1989–92 reverted to a more familiar pattern: Labour successes in the more obvious two-way marginals, Liberal Democrat gains in safe Conservative seats on a protest vote.

Labour's second by-election victory of this period occurred in Mid-Staffordshire on 22 March 1990. Here they achieved a massive swing of 21·4 per cent to take the seat with a 9,499 majority. This startling victory was matched by an equally spectacular Liberal Democrat gain at Eastbourne on 18 October. The by-election was caused by the assassination of the sitting Conservative M P, Ian Gow, by the I R A. Gow was a close confidant of Mrs Thatcher and it was widely assumed that a sympathy vote would keep the seat safely Conservative – even though the Liberals had a strong local base in the constituency. However, the Liberal Democrat David Bellotti swept to victory by 4,550 votes on a swing from the Conservatives of 20·1 per cent. After the Liberal Democrat humiliation in the European elections, it was a result which galvanized the party. At last it seemed that Paddy Ashdown had exorcized the ghost of the disastrous merger, and that the Liberal bandwagon was rolling again. During 1991, both Labour and Liberal Democrats repeated these successes. For the Liberal Democrats, the most spectacular result was the capture of Ribble Valley.

The by-election, caused by the elevation of Home Secretary David Waddington to the Lords, took place in one of the Conservatives' safest seats (they had taken over 60 per cent of the vote in 1987, a majority of 39 per cent over the Liberal challenger). It was, however, a by-election dominated by the issue of the poll tax – a particularly emotive issue in this part of Lancashire. The Liberal Democrats captured the seat with a majority of 4,601, on one of the highest swings (24·8 per cent) recorded in a modern by-election. By comparison, Labour's victory in the marginal north-eastern constituency of Langbaugh in November 1991, on a swing of 3·6 per cent, seemed positively modest. It was also overshadowed by a second Liberal Democrat victory. On the same day as Langbaugh, the Liberals took the Scottish Conservative seat of Kincardine and Deeside on a swing of 11·4 per cent, briefly reducing the Conservatives to the third largest party, in terms of representation from Scotland, at Westminster. The very obvious tactical voting in Kincardine (i.e. voting to unseat a sitting Conservative) led to much speculation that such tactical voting at the coming general election might well virtually eliminate the Conservatives in Scotland.

THE GENERAL ELECTION OF APRIL 1992

The calling of a general election for 9 April 1992 came against a background of considerable excitement. For the first time since the Conservative victory of 1979, there was some real belief among Labour supporters that victory was obtainable. More cautious observers thought that the possibility of a 'hung parliament', particularly if the Liberal Democrats and Scottish Nationalists made inroads into Conservative seats, was a more likely result.

When nominations closed, the electorate had a choice of 2,948 candidates (compared to 2,335 in 1987 and 2,600 in 1983). There were no straight fights between two candidates. Labour fought 634 seats, the Conservatives 645 (a higher total than Labour because they contested 11 of the 17 seats in Northern Ireland) whilst the Liberal Democrats contested 632 (all the seats on mainland Britain except for Greenwich and Woolwich, where Rosie Barnes and John Cartwright were not opposed). The Greens fielded 254 candidates, nearly twice the 1987 figure.

All parties had grounds for optimism. The Conservatives, with a new leader and with some of the most unpopular features of Thatcherism discarded (most notably the poll tax), were quietly confident. They wanted a fairly low-key campaign, concentrating on Labour's taxation proposals and also presenting Major in a 'presidential situation' in a highly personalized capacity.

Thus the Conservative campaign began with an onslaught on Labour's tax plans, claiming Labour's campaign pledges would require an extra £37·9 billion expenditure (a somewhat wild exaggeration). The Conservatives, although portraying their experience in foreign policy, kept the issue of Europe well in the background. In all, it was a fairly negative campaign. Labour emphasized their 'fair taxation' policies and also concentrated on the future of the NHS and the question of unequal access to health-care by some who could afford to pay for immediate treatment and others who had to suffer long waiting lists. The Liberals fought on the policies that had evolved under Ashdown's leadership, with much emphasis on education and their pledge to increase the standard rate of tax by one penny to pay for extra education spending.

As the campaign progressed and the polls seemed to indicate the prospect of a hung parliament, the Liberal Democrats were increasingly questioned on their role in such a situation. Paddy Ashdown reiterated that only a formal pact with a commitment to electoral reform would satisfy his party. Whether this prospect of a 'hung parliament' helped persuade would-be Liberals to return to the Conservative fold was much discussed in the wake of the election. Likewise, in the final week of the campaign, growing Scottish sentiment in favour of a substantial measure of devolution forced its way on to the agenda. With the Conservatives resisting any change in the constitutional relationship, many commentators believed they faced electoral disaster.

From the result of the first key marginal constituency, the Essex seat of Basildon which the Conservatives retained, it was clear that Labour was not going to achieve an overall majority. As the results came in (in particular as Liberal Democrats also failed to take Conservative-held marginals) it became equally clear that even a hung parliament would not occur. On a national swing of only 2·2 per cent from Conservative to Labour, John Major was returned to power with an overall majority of 21. The full result is set out on p. 583.

Labour made a net gain of 39 seats from the Conservatives. The swing to Labour varied greatly from region to region. Its vote rose most (7·4

Party	Seats won	Votes
Conservative	336	14,092,891
Labour	271	11,559,735
Liberal Democrats	20	5,999,384
Nationalists	7	783,991
Others (UK)	—	436,207
Others (NI)	17	740,485

per cent) in the East Midlands (a region where the aftermath of the miners' strike had damaged its prospects in 1987), East Anglia (6·3 per cent), where the Liberals had slipped badly, and London (5·6 per cent), where the effect of left-wing Labour councils seemed now to have less impact. The Conservatives' best results were in Scotland, where there was actually a swing of 2·5 per cent from Labour to Conservative. Instead of being annihilated North of the Border, the party actually retained such seats as Ayr and Stirling and made a net gain of one from Labour.

For the Liberal Democrats, the results were also a bitter disappointment. Nationally, they had polled nearly 6 million votes, taking 17·8 per cent of the vote (down 4·8 per cent from the 22·6 per cent achieved by the Alliance in 1987). Considering the dark days of 1988 and 1989, this was a reasonable achievement. Nationally, the swing from Liberal Democrat to Conservative was 2·1 per cent, from Liberal Democrat to Labour a rather more marked 4·2 per cent (reflecting, no doubt, the collapse of the old SDP vote in constituencies such as Stevenage or Norfolk North-West which had no Liberal tradition). The greatest disappointment, however, was in terms of seats gained and lost. The final tally of 20 reflected 4 gains and 6 losses. The gains, all in England and largely in the South-West, included Bath (the sensation of the election, where Tory Party Chairman Chris Patten was defeated) and Cheltenham (where the local Conservatives had not been totally united over the selection of a black candidate). The remaining two gains were in that most traditional of Liberal areas, Devon and Cornwall, where Liberal Democrats won North Devon (once Jeremy Thorpe's seat) and North Cornwall (regained by Paul Tyler). The losses however, included all three seats won in the by-elections of 1987–92 (Eastbourne, Ribble Valley and Kincardine) together with Southport, Brecon and Radnor and Ceredigion.

One small feature of the results provided the Liberals with some grounds for consolation. All 254 Green candidates lost their deposit (their best single result in percentage terms was 3·75 per cent in Islington North). Their overall share of the vote – 1·3 per cent – was but a shadow of the 15 per cent achieved in the 1989 European elections.

Although the Scottish Nationalists substantially increased their vote, they achieved no parliamentary breakthrough. Instead, Labour easily recaptured the Govan seat lost in the 1988 by-election. But, once again, Scotland could feel aggrieved. Scotland had voted overwhelmingly for Labour. Once again, the outcome of the election nationally was a Conservative Government at Westminster.

The election had thus delivered John Major a mandate to form the next Government. It was a comfortable majority, but not a convincing one. At 41·9 per cent, it was the smallest vote share on which the Conservatives had won an election since 1922. Labour had made strides forward, but still suffered its fourth successive election defeat and it marked the end of Neil Kinnock's leadership. If the Thatcher era was over, the electorate was treading somewhat cautiously to find a political way forward after her.

A FINAL JUDGEMENT ON THE THATCHER YEARS

For a short period between 1985 and 1988, it seemed just possible that Thatcher's governments had succeeded in reversing Britain's relative decline. By 1990, certainly by 1992, that claim was no longer credible. Instead, her period in office would be remembered as one which both began and ended with recessions, the first the deepest, the second the longest in post-war British history. When asked what her greatest achievement as Prime Minister had been, she replied unhesitatingly, 'changing attitudes'. The enterprise culture was begun and people were taught to take more responsibility for their own lives and rely less on the state at national or local levels. Yet by 1990, many of those who had followed Thatcherite principles were feeling deceived. Small businesses were devastated by the second recession, and many new home-owners were to have their homes repossessed. Inflation had not been conquered and unemployment once again rose to desperate heights. Compared with foreign competitors, Britain seemed to be doing very badly: less investment, less growth (a 1·6 per cent per annum rise on average over the Thatcher period), less industry, worse inflation, huge balance-of-payments deficits and higher unemployment. After more than a decade of Mrs Thatcher, this seemed a poor reward indeed. Even granted that productivity had risen, there was still a long way to go before Britain could rival its main industrial competitors, as the following OECD figures for 1989 showed:

Manufacturing Net Output per Worker (UK = 100)

UK	100
Germany	127
Japan	139
Italy	149
France	159
USA	204

Exports per capita

Country	Exports $m/capita
Japan	2,225
UK	2,672
France	3,190
Denmark	5,460
West Germany	5,578
Ireland	5,880
Holland	7,257
Belgium	10,075

Under Major's government, the figures got even worse.

Mrs Thatcher placed the blame for all this not on herself but on Nigel Lawson and his obsession with Europe, which had wrecked her hopes and dreams. Yet she herself had been Prime Minister and could not escape the responsibility for retaining him as Chancellor. This leads to the inevitable conclusion that either she did not know what was happening at the time, or else she could not prevent it. The latter is almost certainly the correct explanation, but one which highlights the greatest paradox of the Thatcher years – that she was a weak Prime Minister who was not in control of her Cabinet. Hence her inability to sack Heseltine before he resigned or to sack Lawson. Hence, too, her inability to prevent herself being railroaded into the ERM by Major and Hurd. All this was partly her own fault. For reasons which are still unclear, but which probably have to do with her personality, she did not care to discover the views of her Cabinet colleagues when she first appointed them. As a result, she was often surrounded by men who fundamentally were not in agreement with her. For example, she seems to have been unaware of Major's views on the ERM. And why did she not appoint Ridley as Chancellor as Sir Alan Walters advised? If in the end she lacked Cabinet support it was partly on account of the very men she had put there herself. She too readily assumed that they would follow her lead, and was slow to get rid of them when they did not.

Her greatest triumphs were in foreign policy, where, quite unexpectedly, she left a permanent mark. Indeed, she would always be more valued abroad than at home. In the end, however, here too she was to fail, falling at the last fence in her race to prevent European monetary and political union. The price of that failure was very high indeed, given that her successor, her 'chosen successor' no less, was persuaded by the Foreign Office to sign the Maastricht Treaty and thereby virtually sign away Britain's independence. By this time it seemed that the Foreign Office had given up any attempt to pursue an independent policy. In fact, under Douglas Hurd it appeared to have lost all sense of initiative. It had shifted towards the 'European' position on defence, was notably reluctant to recognize the Baltic republics, was clearly ready to accept the 1991 coup against Gorbachev, had been pusillanimous with China over Hong Kong, and was content to leave Saddam Hussein in Iraq after the Gulf War. Over Europe, it claimed to be anti-federalist, but recommended acceptance of the Maastricht Treaty which all our European partners agreed was a federalist document, despite its few cosmetic concessions to the UK. British diplomats now brought to mind the girl in Dorothy Parker's story who was fluent in fourteen languages but did not know the word for 'no' in any of them. And if Mrs Thatcher resembled one of those British lions in Trafalgar Square, Hurd was more reminiscent of one of its pigeons, occasionally stopping to puff himself up, but for the most part contentedly nodding his head, walking round in circles and feeding off whatever crumbs of comfort were offered by benevolent, if ill-comprehending foreigners. His motto was the old Foreign Office one: 'All decisions have consequences, all consequences are unpredictable, therefore take no decisions.'

After twenty years of Common Market membership, during which British net manufacturing output actually fell, during which Britain paid over £25 billion in net contributions, and during which an enormous trade deficit with Europe was accumulated, John Major and Douglas Hurd concluded that there was no alternative to even greater links with the EC. Yet if unanimously ratified, the Maastricht Treaty threatened to end Britain's independence as a nation. Great Britain had not merely declined. She had now given up.

BIBLIOGRAPHICAL NOTE

There is – surprisingly, perhaps, in the view of the fact that the archives are still largely unopened – quite an extensive literature available on post-war developments in Britain. This bibliographical note, however, seeks only to inform the reader of the works that were found most useful. Those who require a more comprehensive list of titles are advised to consult the bibliographies of A. F. Havighurst, *Modern England, 1901–70* (Cambridge University Press, 1976), and C. J. Bartlett, *A History of Postwar Britain, 1945–74* (Longman, 1977). For the research student the indispensible new work will be Chris Cook *et al, Longman Guide to Sources in Contemporary British History* (2 vols., Longman, 1993–4).

The most useful general studies of the period are W. N. Medlicott, *Contemporary England* (Longman, 1976); Arthur Marwick, *Britain in the Century of Total War* (The Bodley Head, 1968); and Bartlett, op. cit. Medlicott is strong on foreign policy, Marwick outstanding on social history and Bartlett unexciting but reliable on both. To these one should add, perhaps, M. Proudfoot, *British Politics and Government, 1951–70* (Faber, 1974), an extremely curious handbook which for no obvious reason begins in 1951 and which forsakes normal prose for enumerated paragraph notes. The important themes in post-war politics are pursued in Chris Cook and John Ramsden (eds.), *Trends in British Politics* (Macmillan, 1978).

The period 1945–51 is best served by the following works. On political history, apart from those already noted, the reader is recommended Michael Sissons (ed.), *The Age of Austerity* (Hodder & Stoughton, 1963), an invaluable collection of essays on the post-war Labour government; Paul Addison's excellent *The Road to 1945: British Politics and the Second World War* (Cape, 1975); and Henry Pelling's *Britain and the Second World War* (Collins, 1970), which contains interesting insights on the period after 1945. The Nuffield study of the 1945 General Election is R. B. McCallum and A. Readman, *The British General Election of 1945* (Oxford University Press, 1947). Two interesting essays, one by Marwick, the other by Addison, are to be found in Alan Sked and Chris Cook (eds.), *Crisis and Controversy: Essays in Honour of A. J. P. Taylor* (Macmillan, 1976). For the reader who prefers the biographical approach there is Michael Foot's absorbing, if wordy and over-committed, *Aneurin Bevan, 1945–60* (Davis-Poynter, 1973); the excellent study by Bernard Donoghue and George Jones, *Herbert Morrison: Portrait of a Politician* (Weidenfeld & Nicolson, 1973); and F. Williams, *Ernest Bevin* (Hutchinson, 1952).

Attention should perhaps be drawn also to Henry Pelling's *Winston Churchill* (Macmillan, 1974). Memoirs of the period include Hugh Dalton's *High Tide and After* (Muller, 1962), and F. Williams's *A Prime Minister Remembers* (Heinemann, 1961). Finally, there are two outline sketches by Henry Pelling: *A Short History of the Labour Party*, and *A History of British Trade Unionism* (both Macmillan, 1976).

For diplomatic history in this period one should consult Elizabeth Barker's outstanding *Britain and a Divided Europe, 1945–70* (Weidenfeld & Nicolson, 1971); R. B. Manderson-Jones, *The Special Relationship: Anglo-American Relations and Western European Unity, 1947–56* (Weidenfeld & Nicolson, 1972); P. Darby, *British Defence Policy East of Suez, 1947–68* (Oxford University Press, 1973); P. S. Gupta, *Imperialism and the British Labour Movement, 1914–64* (Macmillan, 1975); D. Goldsworthy, *Colonial Issues in British Politics, 1945–61* (Clarendon Press, 1971); Elizabeth Monroe, *Britain's Moment in the Middle East, 1914–56* (Chatto & Windus, 1963); D. C. Watt, *Personalities and Policies* (Longman, 1965); and M. A. Fitzsimmons, *The Foreign Policy of the British Labour Government, 1945–51* (Notre Dame, 1953). A survey of the Labour government's foreign policy in German by Alan Sked, 'Die weltpolitische Lage Grossbrittaniens nach dem Zweiten Weltkrieg' is to be found in Oswald Hauser (ed.), *Weltpolitik III, 1945–53* (Musterschmidt-Gottingen, 1978), along with an essay by R. A. C. Parker on 'Das Ende des Empire'. One essential article is Geoffrey Warner's 'The Reconstruction and Defence of Western Europe after 1945' in N. Waites (ed.), *Troubled Neighbours: Franco-British Relations in the Twentieth Century* (Weidenfeld & Nicolson, 1971).

More general coverage of the period can be found in W. N. Medlicott's

British Foreign Policy since Versailles, 1919–63 (Methuen, 1968), and F. S. Northedge, *Descent from Power: British Foreign Policy, 1945–73* (Allen & Unwin, 1974).

Back on the home front, social policy is best covered by Marwick, op. cit., but one should also consult his article 'The Labour Party and the Welfare State in Britain 1900–1948' in the *American Historical Review*, December 1967. Economic policy is covered very technically by J. C. R. Dow, *The Management of the British Economy 1945–60* (Cambridge University Press, 1968), while the man who seems to make most sense of it is N. Davenport in a neglected, unacademic and no doubt unfair extended essay entitled *The Split Society* (Gollancz, 1964). More specific aspects are studied in S. Strange, *Sterling and British Policy* (Oxford University Press, 1971), and A. A. Rogow, *The Labour Government and British Industry, 1945–51* (Blackwell, 1955). Finally, a work which must become definitive is Sir Norman Chester, *The Nationalization of British Industry, 1945–51* (HMSO, 1977).

The period 1951–64 is, naturally, partly served by some of the works already mentioned. To these, however, one should add for political history the outstanding collection of essays edited by V. Bogdanor and R. Skidelsky, *The Age of Affluence, 1951–64* (Macmillan, 1970), as well as a no less useful collection edited by David McKie and Chris Cook, *The Decade of Disillusion: British Politics in the 1960s* (Macmillan, 1972). For the Liberals, see Chris Cook, *A Short History of the Liberal Party 1900–1984* (Macmillan, 1984). Useful on the Labour Right is S. Haseler, *The Gaitskellites* (Macmillan, 1969). General elections are covered in a series of studies authored or co-authored by D. E. Butler on behalf of the Nuffield Foundation and published by Macmillan. These are entitled *The British General Election of 1951, 1955, 1959* and *1964* respectively. Economic policy should be supplemented by S. Brittan, *The Treasury under the Tories* (Secker & Warburg, 1964); biography by N. Fisher, *Iain Macleod* (Deutsch, 1973); memoirs by R. A. Butler's *The Art of the Possible* (Hamish Hamilton, 1971); Lord Avon's *The Memoirs of Sir Anthony Eden, Full Circle* (Cassell, 1960); and Harold Macmillan's *Memoirs 1914–63* (6 vols., Macmillan, 1966–73). The key book on diplomatic history for this period is H. Thomas, *The Suez Affair* (Weidenfeld & Nicolson, 1966), which, however, should be read in conjunction with A. Nutting, *No End of a Lesson* (Constable, 1967), and S. Lloyd, *Suez 1956: A Personal Account* (Cape, 1978). An excellent general work on social change during this period is T. Noble, *Modern Britain, Structure and Change* (Batsford, 1975).

For the period since 1964, the literature is less extensive. In addition to the general works already cited, a useful survey can be found in Robert Rhodes James, *Ambitions and Realities: British Politics 1964–70* (Weidenfeld & Nicolson, 1973). Several important essays on the period can be found in david McKie and Chris Cook (eds.), *The decade of Disillusion: British Politics in the 1960s* (Macmillan, 1972). The Labour government is well covered in Brian Lapping, *The Labour Government* (Penguin, 1971). Far more detailed, if naturally sympathetic, is Harold Wilson's own account, *The Labour Government 1964–1970: A Personal Record* (Michael Joseph, 1971; Penguin, 1974). On the workings of government, see Frank Stacey, *British Government 1966–75: Years of Reform* (Oxford University Press, 1975), and Patrick Gordon Walker, *The Cabinet* (Cape, 1970). On the electoral traumas of the Wilson government see Chris Cook and John Ramsden (eds.), *By-elections in British Politics* (Macmillan, 1973). Two entertaining accounts of the years 1966–70 are William Davis, *Three Years' Hard Labour* (Deutsch, 1968), and Patrick Jenkins, *The Battle of Downing Street* (Knight, 1970). For the rise of nationalism and devolution, see the respective essays in Chris Cook and John Ramsden, *Trends in British Politics* (Macmillan, 1978). On Welsh nationalism, see Alan Butt Phillips, *The Welsh Question: Nationalism in Welsh Politics 1945–70* (Cardiff, University of Wales Press, 1975).

Very few of the published memoirs of the period are of importance. The major exception is Richard Crossman, *The Diaries of a Cabinet Minister* (2 vols., Hamish Hamilton and Cape, 1975–6). Some material can also be found in Cecil King, *The Cecil King Diaries 1965–70* (Cape, 1972). See also Lord George-Brown, *In My Way* (Gollancz, 1971), and Nigel Fisher, *Iain Macleod* (Deutsch, 1973).

For the party politics of the period, the Nuffield election studies for 1970, February and October 1974, 1979 and 1983, co-authored by David Butler, are indispensable. The referendum is dealt with in *The 1975 Referendum*, edited by David Butler and Denis Kavanagh (Macmillan, 1976).

On Europe, see M. Camps, *European Unification in the Sixties* (Oxford University Press, 1967), and the two important studies by Uwe Kitzinger, *The Second Try: Labour and the E.E.C.* and *Diplomacy and Persuasion: How Britain Joined the Common Market* (Thames & Hudson, 1973).

On particular issues, see Janet Morgan, *The House of Lords and the Labour Government* (Oxford University Press, 1975); B. Pimlott and C. Cook, *Trade Unions in British Politics* (Longman, 1982); Paul Foot, *Immigration and Race in British Politics* (Penguin, 1965); and C. Cook and I. Taylor, *The Labour Party: An Introduction to its History, Structure and Politics* (Longman, 1980).

For the recent social history, there is material in Christopher Booker, *The Neophiliacs* (Collins, 1969); Christie Davies, *Permissive Britain* (Pitman, 1975); and Pauline Gregg, *The Welfare State from 1945 to the Present Day* (Harrap, 1967).

For the Lib-Lab pact, which sustained the Callaghan government, see the article by Alan Sked, 'The Liberal Tradition and the Lib-Lab Pact', in *West European Politics*, No. 2, May 1978. For the early part of the Labour government 1974-9, see David McKie, Chris Cook and Melanie Phillips, *The Guardian/Quartet Election Guide* (Quartet, 1978). The background to the first direct elections is given in Chris Cook and Mary Francis, *The First European Elections: A Handbook and Guide* (Macmillan, 1979).

For the period 1979-83, the best book by far is Peter Riddell, *The Thatcher Government* (Martin Robertson, 1983) but it should be supplemented by Hugh Stephenson, *Mrs Thatcher's First Year* (Jill Norman, 1980) and Henry Drucker *et al.* (eds.), *Developments in British Politics* (Macmillan, 1983). Also very useful is Simon Jenkins' article on 'The Thatcher Style' in the *Economist* (21-27 May 1983). One crucial aspect of domestic politics is best covered by Keith Webb, *The Growth of Nationalism in Scotland* (Pelican, 1978). For the contemporary Liberal Party and the birth of the Social Democratic Party see V. Bogdanor, *Liberal Party Politics* (Oxford University Press, 1983) and also C. Cook, *A Short History of the Liberal Party, 1900-1992* (4th edn, Macmillan, 1993). For foreign policy key books include Martin Meredith, *The Past Is Another Country, Rhodesia 1890-1979* (Deutsch, 1979) and Lawrence Freedman, *Britain and Nuclear Weapons* (Macmillan, 1980). A key article is Paul Taylor, 'The EEC Crisis over Budget and Agricultural Policy' in *Government and Opposition*, Vol. 17, No. 4, Autumn 1982. The general background to this crisis is best illuminated by Juliet Lodge (ed.), *Institutions and Policies of the European Community* (Francis Pinter, 1983). On the Falklands War the best researched book is Max Hastings and Simon Jenkins, *The Battle for the Falklands* (Michael,

Joseph, 1983) although the clearest account is to be found in Christopher Dobson, John Miller and Ronald Page, *The Falklands Conflict* (Coronet, 1982). Unfortunately this does not quite cover the final stage of the war. An indispensable source is the memoir by Sir Nicholas Henderson on 'America and the Falklands' published in the *Economist* (12–18 November 1983).

There is now a substantial bibliography on the Thatcher era. The memoirs which have appeared so far are of little value, but among the secondary works there are many which deserve to be read. These include: Martin Holmes, *Thatcherism, Scope and Limits, 1983–87* (Macmillan, 1989); D. Kavanagh and A. Seldon (eds.), *The Thatcher Effect: A Decade of Change* (Oxford University Press, 1989); Peter Jenkins, *Mrs Thatcher's Revolution: The Ending of the Socialist Era* (Jonathan Cape, 1987); Geoffrey Maynard, *The Economy under Mrs Thatcher* (Basil Blackwell, 1988); K. Minogue and M. Biddiss (eds.), *Thatcherism: Personality and Politics* (Macmillan, 1987); Peter Riddell, *The Thatcher Decade* (Basil Blackwell, 1989); Robert Skidelsky (ed.), *Thatcherism* (Chatto and Windus, 1988); and Hugo Young, *One of Us* (Macmillan, 1989). Foreign policy is best covered in Peter Byrd (ed.), *British Foreign Policy under Thatcher* (Philip Allen, 1988), and M. Smith, B. Smith and B. White (eds.), *British Foreign Policy: Tradition, Change and Transformation* (Unwin Hyman, 1988). Northern Ireland is best covered in Paul Arthur and Keith Jeffrey, *Northern Ireland since 1968* (Basil Blackwell, 1988), while the question of Hong Kong is admirably explained by Frank Ching, *Hong Kong and China: For Better or for Worse* (The China Council of the Asia Society and the Foreign Policy Association, 1985). On South Africa, see Martin Holland, *The European Community and South Africa: European Political Cooperation under Strain* (Pinter, 1988).

For the period 1987–92, the following works are very useful: David Smith, *From Boom to Bust: Trial and Error in British Economic Policy* (Penguin, 1992); Michael Carver, *Tightrope Walking: British Defence Policy since 1945* (Hutchinson, 1992); J. Denis and Ian Derbyshire, *Politics in Britain from Callaghan to Thatcher* (Chambers, 1992); Dennis Swann (ed.), *The Single European Market and Beyond: A Study of the Wilder Implications of the Single European Act* (Routledge, 1992); and Horst Teltschik, *329 tage, Innenansichten der Einigung* (Siedler Verlag, 1992).

INDEX

Discover more about our forthcoming books through Penguin's FREE newspaper...

Penguin
Quarterly

It's packed with:

- exciting features
- author interviews
- previews & reviews
- books from your favourite films & TV series
- exclusive competitions & much, much more...

Write off for your free copy today to:
Dept JC
Penguin Books Ltd
FREEPOST
West Drayton
Middlesex
UB7 0BR
NO STAMP REQUIRED

READ MORE IN PENGUIN

READ MORE IN PENGUIN

HISTORY

The World Since 1945   T. E. Vadney
New edition

From the origins of the post-war world to the collapse of the Soviet Bloc
in the late 1980s, this masterly book offers an authoritative yet highly
readable one-volume account.

Ecstasies   Carlo Ginzburg

This dazzling work of historical detection excavates the essential truth
about the witches' Sabbath. 'Ginzburg's learning is prodigious and his
journey through two thousand years of Eurasian folklore a *tour de force*'
– *Observer*

The Nuremberg Raid   Martin Middlebrook

'The best book, whether documentary or fictional, yet written about
Bomber Command' – *Economist*. 'Martin Middlebrook's skill at description and reporting lift this book above the many memories that were
written shortly after the war' – *The Times*

A History of Christianity   Paul Johnson

'Masterly ... It is a huge and crowded canvas – a tremendous theme
running through twenty centuries of history – a cosmic soap opera
involving kings and beggars, philosophers and crackpots, scholars and
illiterate exaltés, popes and pilgrims and wild anchorites in the
wilderness'– Malcolm Muggeridge

The Penguin History of Greece   A. R. Burn

Readable, erudite, enthusiastic and balanced, this one-volume history of
Hellas sweeps the reader along from the days of Mycenae and the
splendours of Athens to the conquests of Alexander and the final dark
decades.

Modern Ireland 1600–1972   R. F. Foster

'Takes its place with the finest historical writing of the twentieth century,
whether about Ireland or anywhere else' – Conor Cruise O'Brien in the
Sunday Times

READ MORE IN PENGUIN

HISTORY

The Guillotine and the Terror Daniel Arasse

'A brilliant and imaginative account of the punitive mentality of the revolution that restores to its cultural history its most forbidding and powerful symbol' – Simon Schama.

The Second World War A J P Taylor

A brilliant and detailed illustrated history, enlivened by all Professor Taylor's customary iconoclasm and wit.

Daily Life in Ancient Rome Jerome Carcopino

This classic study, which includes a bibliography and notes by Professor Rowell, describes the streets, houses and multi-storeyed apartments of the city of over a million inhabitants, the social classes from senators to slaves, and the Roman family and the position of women, causing *The Times Literary Supplement* to hail it as a 'thorough, lively and readable book'.

The Anglo-Saxons Edited by James Campbell

'For anyone who wishes to understand the broad sweep of English history, Anglo-Saxon society is an important and fascinating subject. And Campbell's is an important and fascinating book. It is also a finely produced and, at times, a very beautiful book' – *London Review of Books*

The Making of the English Working Class E. P. Thompson

Probably the most imaginative – and the most famous – post-war work of English social history. 'A magnificent, lucid, angry historian ... E. P. Thompson has performed a revolution of historical perspective' – *The Times*

The Habsburg Monarchy 1809–1918 A J P Taylor

Dissolved in 1918, the Habsburg Empire 'had a unique character, out of time and out of place'. Scholarly and vividly accessible, this 'very good book indeed' (*Spectator*) elucidates the problems always inherent in the attempt to give peace, stability and a common loyalty to a heterogeneous population.

READ MORE IN PENGUIN

HISTORY

Citizens Simon Schama

The award-winning chronicle of the French Revolution. 'The most marvellous book I have read about the French Revolution in the last fifty years' – Richard Cobb in *The Times*

To the Finland Station Edmund Wilson

In this authoritative work Edmund Wilson, considered by many to be America's greatest twentieth-century critic, turns his attention to Europe's revolutionary traditions, tracing the roots of nationalism, socialism and Marxism as these movements spread across the Continent creating unrest, revolt and widespread social change.

Jasmin's Witch Emmanuel Le Roy Ladurie

An investigation into witchcraft and magic in south-west France during the seventeenth century – a masterpiece of historical detective work by the bestselling author of Montaillou.

Stalin Isaac Deutscher

'The Greatest Genius in History' and the 'Life-Giving Force of socialism'? Or a despot more ruthless than Ivan the Terrrible and a revolutionary whose policies facilitated the rise of Nazism? An outstanding biographical study of a revolutionary despot by a great historian.

Aspects of Antiquity M. I. Finley

Profesor M. I. Finley was one of the century's greatest ancient historians; he was also a master of the brief, provocative essay on classical themes. 'He writes with the unmistakable enthusiasm of a man who genuinely wants to communicate his own excitement' – Philip Toynbee in the *Observer*

British Society 1914–1945 John Stevenson

'A major contribution to the *Penguin Social History of Britain*, which will undoubtedly be the standard work for students of modern Britain for many years to come' – *The Times Educational Supplement*

READ MORE IN PENGUIN

POLITICS AND SOCIAL SCIENCES

National Identity   Anthony D. Smith

In this stimulating new book, Anthony D. Smith asks why the first modern nation states developed in the West. He considers how ethnic origins, religion, language and shared symbols can provide a sense of nation and illuminates his argument with a wealth of detailed examples.

The Feminine Mystique   Betty Friedan

'A brilliantly researched, passionately argued book – a time-bomb flung into the Mom-and-Apple-Pie image ... Out of the debris of that shattered ideal, the Women's Liberation Movement was born' – Ann Leslie

Peacemaking Among Primates   Frans de Waal

'A vitally fresh analysis of the biology of aggression which deserves the serious attention of all those concerned with the nature of conflict, whether in humans or non-human animals ... De Waal delivers forcibly and clearly his interpretation of the significance of his findings ... Lucidly written' – *The Times Higher Educational Supplement*

Political Ideas   David Thomson (ed.)

From Machiavelli to Marx – a stimulating and informative introduction to the last 500 years of European political thinkers and political thought.

The Raw and the Cooked   Claude Lévi-Strauss

Deliberately, brilliantly and inimitably challenging, Lévi-Strauss's seminal work of structural anthropology cuts wide and deep into the mind of mankind, as he finds in the myths of the South American Indians a comprehensible psychological pattern.

The Social Construction of Reality
Peter Berger and Thomas Luckmann

The Social Construction of Reality is concerned with the sociology of 'everything that passes for knowledge in society', and particularly with that 'common-sense knowledge' that constitutes the reality of everyday life for the ordinary member of society.

READ MORE IN PENGUIN

A CHOICE OF NON-FICTION

Ginsberg: A Biography Barry Miles

The definitive life of one of this century's most colourful poets. 'A life so dramatic, so dangerous, so committed to hard-volume truth, that his survival is a miracle, his kindness, wisdom and modesty a blessing' – *The Times*. 'Read it to the end' – Michael Horovitz

Coleridge: Early Visions Richard Holmes

'Dazzling ... Holmes has not merely reinterpreted Coleridge; he has re-created him, and his biography has the aura of fiction, the shimmer of an authentic portrait ... a biography like few I have ever read' –*Guardian*. 'Coleridge lives, and talks and loves ... in these pages as never before' – *Independent*

The Speeches of Winston Churchill David Cannadine (ed.)

The most eloquent statesman of his time, Winston Churchill used language as his most powerful weapon. These orations, spanning fifty years, show him gradually honing his rhetoric until, with spectacular effect, 'he mobilized the English language, and sent it into battle'.

Higher than Hope Fatima Meer

A dramatic, personal and intimate biography drawing on letters and reminiscences from Nelson Mandela himself and his close family, *Higher Than Hope* is an important tribute to one of the greatest living figures of our time. It is also a perceptive commentary on the situation in South Africa. No one concerned with politics or humanity can afford to miss it.

Among the Russians Colin Thubron

'The Thubron approach to travelling has an integrity that belongs to another age. And this author's way with words gives his books a value far transcending their topical interest; it is safe to predict that they will be read a century hence' – Dervla Murphy in the *Irish Times*

READ MORE IN PENGUIN

A CHOICE OF NON-FICTION

When Shrimps Learn to Whistle Denis Healey

Taking up the most powerful political themes that emerged from his hugely successful *The Time of My Life,* Denis Healey now gives us this stimulating companion volume. 'Forty-three years of ruminations ... by the greatest foreign secretary (as the author quietly and reasonably implies) we never had' – Ben Pimlott in the *New Statesman & Society*

Eastern Approaches Fitzroy Maclean

'The author's record of personal achievement is remarkable. The canvas which he covers is immense. The graphic writing reveals the ruthless man of action ... He emerges from [his book] as an extrovert Lawrence' – *The Times Literary Supplement*

This Time Next Week Leslie Thomas

'Mr Thomas's book is all humanity, to which is added a Welshman's mastery of words ... Some of his episodes are hilarious, some unbearably touching, but everyone, staff and children, is looked upon with compassion' – *Observer*. 'Admirably written, with clarity, realism, poignancy and humour' – *Daily Telegraph*

Reports from the Holocaust Larry Kramer

'A powerful book ... more than a political autobiography, *Reports* is an indictment of a world that allows AIDS to continue ... he is eloquent and convincing when he swings from the general to the specific. His recommendations on the release of drugs to AIDS patients are practical and humane' – *New York Newsday*

City on the Rocks Kevin Rafferty

'Rafferty has filled a glaring gap on the Asian bookshelf, offering the only comprehensive picture of Hong Kong right up to the impact of the Tiananmen Square massacre' – *Business Week*. 'A story of astonishing achievement, but its purpose is warning rather than celebration' – *Sunday Times*

READ MORE IN PENGUIN

A CHOICE OF NON-FICTION

Bernard Shaw Michael Holroyd
Volume 2 1898–1918 The Pursuit of Power

'A man whose art rested so much upon the exercise of intelligence could not have chosen a more intelligent biographer ... The pursuit of Bernard Shaw has grown, and turned into a pursuit of the whole twentieth century' – Peter Ackroyd in *The Times*

Shots from the Hip Charles Shaar Murray

His classic encapsulation of the moment when rock stars turned junkies as the sixties died; his dissection of rock 'n' roll violence as citizens assaulted the Sex Pistols; superstar encounters from the decline of Paul McCartney to Mick Jagger's request that the author should leave – Charles Shaar Murray's *Shots From the Hip* is also rock history in the making.

Managing on the Edge Richard Pascale

The co-author of the bestselling *The Art of Japanese Management* has once again turned conventional thinking upside down. Conflict and contention in organizations are not just unavoidable – they are positively to be welcomed. The successes and failures of large corporations can help us understand the need to maintain a creative tension between fitting companies together and splitting them apart.

Just Looking John Updike

'Mr Updike can be a very good art critic, and some of these essays are marvellous examples of critical explanation ... a deep understanding of the art emerges ... His reviews of some recent and widely attended shows ... quite surpass the modest disclaimer of the title' – *The New York Times Book Review*

Shelley: The Pursuit Richard Holmes

'Surely the best biography of Shelley ever written ... He makes Shelley's character entirely convincing by showing us the poet at every stage of his development acting upon, and reacting to, people and events' – Stephen Spender